WORLD'S GREAT MEN OF COLOR

VOLUME II

J. A. ROGERS

*Edited with an introduction, commentary,
and bibliographical notes by*

JOHN HENRIK CLARKE

A TOUCHSTONE BOOK
Published by Simon & Schuster
New York   London   Toronto
Sydney   Tokyo   Singapore

TOUCHSTONE
Rockefeller Center
1230 Avenue of the Americas
New York, NY 10020

First Touchstone Edition 1996

TOUCHSTONE and colophon are registered trademarks
of Simon & Schuster Inc.

Manufactured in the United States of America

5   7   9   10   8   6   4

ISBN 0-684-81582-6

World's Great Men of Color *was originally published in*
hardcover by J. A. Rogers and is reprinted in this revised
edition by arrangement.

Contents

SOUTH AND CENTRAL AMERICA

THE WEST INDIES

THE UNITED STATES

ADDITIONAL GREAT MEN OF COLOR

Illustrations

Introduction

THIS VOLUME CONTINUES J. A. Rogers' lifelong research into the role that personalities of African descent have played in the development of world history. In this field of biographical research he journeyed further and accomplished more than any other writer before him. He was particularly astute in researching the neglected aspects of history. In this volume his main areas of concentration are Europe, South and Central America, the West Indies, and the United States. Except for Europe, of course, the personalities whose lives are described here had an impact on the geographical area that is referred to as the "New World."

In the section that deals with the great black personalities who influenced Europe, Mr. Rogers calls attention to the fact that Europe did not emerge in the years before and after the establishment of Christianity independent unto itself. A large number of persons whose ethnic origin was not European made major contributions to European history and culture. Some of the most illustrious of these were black or of mixed African and European ancestry.

The continuity of this influence is shown in the section on South and Central America. In the short time since the death of J. A. Rogers in 1966 there has been a revolution in research and scholarship relating to this still developing area of our hemisphere. Some of the old research, long ignored, has been reconsidered.

New scholars, black and white, have emerged with a broader view of the interplay of peoples and cultures in the making of the so-called New World before and after the appearance of the Europeans. This new scholarship has found recurring evidence of a fact that Western academies have been ignoring, or denying, for years—the presence of African people in pre-Columbian South and Central America, and in the United States. The best presentation of this new evidence can be found in the following books and articles:

The Art of Terracotta Pottery in Pre-Columbian Central and South America, by Alexander von Wuthenau. New York, Crown Publishers, 1969. This book details the best physical evidence for the pre-Columbian appearance of Africans in the New World.

Introduction to African Civilization, by John G. Jackson. New Hyde Park, N.Y., University Books, 1970. In Chapter 6 of this book Mr. Jackson interprets the evidence, new and old, and adds new materials from his own files.

In a two-part article published in *A Current Bibliography on African Affairs*, Vol. II, Nos. 11 and 12, Washington, D.C. (1969), a young writer, Legrand H. Clegg, II, opens up new areas of this subject for consideration and puts the evidence in a more readable order. His article is entitled "The Beginning of the African Diaspora: The Black Man in Ancient and Medieval America."

The formal investigation into this subject was started in 1920 with the publication of Professor Leo Wiener's massive three-volume work *Africa and the Discovery of America*. In the first volume of this work Professor Wiener shows that American archaeological studies on both the Africans and the Indians are built on sand and suppositions, and that the accepted chronology of cultural development for both of these peoples is totally out of order. He also shows that the Africans have had a far greater influence on American civilization than has heretofore been suspected.

The second volume is a study of African religions and their influence on the cultures of this hemisphere. His documentation proves to an extraordinary extent that the Indian medicine man evolved from the African medicine man.

In explaining the diaries of Christopher Columbus, Professor Wiener calls attention to the fact that this European explorer admits that he found a dark-skinned people trading with the Indians in the Caribbean Islands. Who were these dark-skinned people? Columbus infers that they were people from the coast of Guinea (West Africa).

In 1936 Carter G. Woodson published his book, *The African Background Outlined*. This book had additional information on the pre-Columbian presence of the Africans in the New World. Dr. Woodson's observations are that several authorities believed that Africans discovered America long before the Europeans had any such dreams, for the Occident was all but in a state of savagery until awakened by contact with the more enlightened Orient during the Crusades. The early European explorers on the Isthmus of Darien found in caves there skulls which were identified as African. Students of ethnology observed also that the religion of the North and South American Indians is very much like that of the Africans. Professor Leo Wiener had previously made the same observation. In Indian languages, moreover, certain words were discovered which appeared originally in an African language, such as "canoe," "tobacco," and "buckra." (These, however, should not be confused with African words like "goober," "yam," "banjo," and "voodoo," which were later brought from Africa to America.)

The cultural and philological evidence to support the claim that Africans on the west coast attained a high level of culture and maritime skill is more apparent with each new book on the subject. The matter is out of the realm of pure speculation. It can now be said with a high degree of certainty that Africans braved the roaring waters of the high seas and established relationships with the Indians of the Americas well over a thousand years ago.

In the article "African Explorers of the New World" by Harold G. Lawrence (1962), this statement is made:

We can now positively state that the Mandingoes of Mali and Songhay Empires, and possibly other Africans, crossed the Atlantic to carry on trade with the Western Hemisphere Indians, and further succeeded in establishing colonies throughout the Americas. During the thirteenth century, Mali, the earliest of these two great empires, building on the ruins of Ancient Ghana, rose to become one of the leading nations of the world. . . .

Professor Lawrence elaborates on these early African voyages to the West in the following statement:

It is more important to note here that voyages across the Atlantic were resumed, or continued, during the reign of Askia. Proof of this is evidenced by the fact that Columbus was informed by some men, when he stopped at one of the Cape Verde Islands off the coast of Africa, that Negroes had been known to set out into the Atlantic from the Guinea coast in canoes loaded with merchandise and steering towards the west. The same Christopher Columbus was further informed by the Indians of Hispaniola when he arrived in the West Indies that they had been able to obtain gold from black men who had come from across the sea from the south and southeast. The dates of these accounts coincide precisely with the time that Askia the Great held sway over Songhay. It must also be added that Amerigo Vespucci on his voyage to the Americas witnessed these same black men out in the Atlantic returning to Africa.

Fifteenth and sixteenth century Spanish explorers and early American art, legends, and burials provide the principal sources of information on what happened to these African seamen after their arrival in the Americas. In effect, the Spanish conquistadores found dispersed all over the New World small tribes who were from the very first considered Negroes. The largest African colony appears to have been a permanent settlement at Darien where Balboa saw them in 1513.

American Indian legends abound with accounts of black men who came to them from far off lands. Aside from the report that Columbus obtained at Hispaniola, a notable tale is recorded in the Peruvian traditions. They inform us of how black men coming from the east had been able to penetrate the Andes Mountains. Furthermore, Indian traditions of Mexico and Central America indicate that Africans were among the first occupants of that territory. Some Indians there yet claim descent from these same Blacks.

In the magazine *West Africa*, for Saturday, June 7, 1969, there is an article by Basil Davidson with the title "Africans Before Columbus?" In this article we are told that:

Columbus and other early Europeans' arrivals in the Americas came back with quite a bit of evidence, suggestive but inconclusive, that black peoples from Africa had already reached these shores. Various writers have pointed, from time to time, over the past twenty years and more, to the likely West African origins of the black explorers, notable of that "tribe of Almamys" who were said to have settled in Honduras.

This obviously was the first African impact on the Americas.

In order to understand the magnitude of the second African impact of the Americas, and the West Indies, it is necessary that we look two ways, both at Europe and at Africa. The origin of Africa's troubled years is in both places.

Early in the fifteenth century Europe began to recover from the wounds of the Middle Ages and the Crusades. European skill in shipbuilding had improved and, in search of a food supply for their hungry population and for new worlds to conquer, Europeans began to venture beyond their shores. There are many reasons why the Europeans had not embarked upon worldwide exploration before this time: their ships were small and unsafe for long sea journeys; oars were sometimes used to propel these ships and the outcome of all voyages depended largely on the wind; there were no good maps or instruments to guide sailors through unknown waters.

At that time most Europeans were ignorant about the shape of the world, and some of them thought it was flat. The Portuguese set out to disprove this, and about the middle of the fifteenth century they began trading with the people along the west coast of Africa, to which they gave the name "Guinea" after the Sudanic Empire of Ghana. At first they traded mainly for gold, but before long they began to take slaves also.

Social and political unrest began to develop among some of the nations of West Africa at the time Europe was regaining its strength and a degree of unity. The first Europeans to visit the west coast of Africa did not have to fight their way in—they came as guests and were treated as guests. Later, they decided to stay as conquerors and slave traders. In order to gain a position strong enough to attain these ambitions, they began to take sides in African family disputes, very often supplying the family or tribe they favored with arms and using their favorites as slave catchers. A number of African nations went into the slave trade in order to buy guns and other European-manufactured items. Others were forced to capture slaves or become slaves.

The Europeans did not come to Africa initially to find slaves. For years they had been hearing stories about the great riches of Africa. At the Battle of Ceuta against the Moslems in 1416, Prince Henry the Navigator, as he later became known, who was Prince Henry of Portugal, heard about the prosperity of Timbuctoo and the wealth of the great states along the west coast of Africa. He also heard stories about a great African Christian king named Prester John.

Before the end of the fifteenth century the Portuguese sailors had come to know the general shape of the continent of Africa. They traded regularly with African countries from 1471 on. Forts were built along the west coast of West Africa. The most famous of these forts, still in existence, is Elmina Castle in what is now Ghana. This fort was started in 1482 by a Portuguese captain, Don Diego d'Azambuja. Because of the large profits gained by the Portuguese in their trading in this country, they called it the Gold Coast.

During the latter half of the fifteenth century European nationalism was reflected in the expansion of trade in both slaves and manufactured goods. The marriage of Queen Isabella and King Ferdinand of Spain gave Europe the unity to drive out the Moors. Both Spain and Portugal were becoming powerful Mediterranean nations.

In 1488 Bartholomew Diaz had sailed around the southern tip of Africa. About ten years later another Portuguese sailor, Vasco da Gama, sailed past the point reached by Diaz. With the help of an Arab pilot, Vasco da Gama reached India in 1498. For Europe, the door to the vast world of Asia was open.

The story of the African slave trade is essentially the story of the consequences of the second rise of Europe. In the years between the passing of the Roman Empire in the eighth century and the partial unification of Europe through the framework of the Catholic Church in the fifteenth century, Europeans were engaged mainly in internal matters. With the opening of the New World and the expulsion of the Moors from Spain during the latter part of the fifteenth century, the Europeans started to expand beyond their homeland into the broader world. They were searching for new markets, new materials, new manpower, and new land to exploit. The African slave trade was created to accommodate this expansion.

In this book Mr. Rogers shows that Africans were far from being passive about their plight in the West Indies and in the colonies that became the United States. The slave systems and the attitude to support them were slow in getting under way. In the meantime, the Africans were a part of other developments.

The first Africans who came to the New World were not in bondage, contrary to popular belief. Africans participated in some of the early expeditions, mainly with Spanish explorers. The best-known of these African explorers was Estevanico, sometimes known as Little Steven, who accompanied the de Vaca expedition during six years of wandering from Florida to Mexico. The remarkable thing about Estevanico, who came into America in 1527, is that he was an astute linguist. He learned the language of the Indians in a matter of weeks. Because of his knowledge of herbs and medicines, he was accepted as a deity by some Indian tribes.

In 1539 Estevanico set out from Mexico in a party with Fray Marcos de Niza in search of the fabulous Seven Cities of Cíbola. When most of the expedition, including Fray Marcos, became ill, Estevanico went on alone and opened up what is now known as New Mexico and Arizona.

A number of historians have stated that Pedro Niño, one of the pilots of the command ship of Christopher Columbus, was an African. In the discovery of the Pacific in 1513, Balboa carried thirty Africans, who helped to clear the road across the isthmus between the two oceans. In the conquest of Mexico, Cortez was accompanied by a number of Africans. Incidentally, one was a pioneer of wheat farming in the New World.

In the exploration of Guatemala, Chile, Peru, and Venezuela, Africans arrived nearly a hundred years before they reappeared as slaves in Jamestown, Virginia, in 1619.

Thus, Africans were major contributors to the making of the New World, and they did not come culturally empty-handed. Many of the Africans brought to the New World such skills as ironworking, leatherworking, and carpentry.

Before the breaking up of the social structure of the West

African states such as Ghana and Songhay, and the internal strife that made the slave trade possible, many Africans, especially West Africans, lived in a society in which university life was fairly common and scholars were held in reverence.

In that period in Western African history, the university of Sankore at Timbuctoo was flourishing, and its great chancellor, the last of the monumental scholars of West Africa, Ahmed Baba, reigned over the university. A great African scholar, he wrote forty-seven books, each on a separate subject. He received all of his education within West Africa; in fact, he did not leave the Western Sudan until he was exiled in 1594 to Morocco (following the invasion of 1591).

The African slave in the Americas, in addition to assisting in the freedom and the economy of these countries, made a major contribution to his own freedom.

In the story of the rise and fall of great African states, and subsequently the slave trade, we are trying to deal with something much bigger than history itself. We are trying to deal with an old situation and a new situation and trying to address ourselves to the current cry for Black History and Black Power.

Our major point is this: The African people who became slaves in the United States have been many things in history, good and bad. They have ruled great nations and they have destroyed great nations. They are profoundly human. And they have played every role in the human drama, from saint to buffoon. Slavery does not represent the sum total of their history.

Nearly all of the personalities in this book were involved in a struggle against some of the many forms of racism. There is no way to completely understand the impact of the African personality on the Western world without understanding this fact. There is also a need to understand racism itself as an evolving issue in Western social thought.

Early in this century the elder scholar among Afro-Americans, Dr. W. E. B. Du Bois, said, "The problem of the twentieth century is the problem of the color line." Unfortunately, his prophecy was correct. In spite of all the talk and the sociology—good and bad— we have not made much progress in resolving this issue. We have talked about it extensively without really dealing with it. To deal with it we will have to identify and explain its genesis. To explain its genesis, we will have to ask ourselves some hard questions and we will have to be boldly honest with our answers. Some of the hard questions are: How did racism start in the first place and for whose benefit was it created? Who benefits from it now? Why do we lack the strength, or the nerve, to destroy it?

I maintain that the racism that haunts the world of our day was created for a specific reason, and that reason was to justify the expansion of Europe, starting in the fifteenth and sixteenth centuries. This forces us to deal with both the genesis and the present application of racism.

The great human drama now being called "The Black Revolution in the U.S.A." has deep historical roots, and it cannot be fully understood until it has been seen in this context. In his book *Capitalism and Slavery*, Eric Williams places the origin of this revolution in historical perspective and calls attention to its early development:

When, in 1492, Columbus, representing the Spanish monarchy, discovered the New World, he set in train the long and bitter international rivalry over colonial possessions for which, after four and a half centuries, no solution has yet been found. Portugal, which had initiated the movement of international expansion, claimed the new territories on the ground that they fell within the scope of a papal bull of 1455 authorizing her to reduce to servitude all infidel people. The two powers (Spain and Portugal), to avoid controversy, sought arbitration and, as Catholics, turned to the Pope—a natural and logical step in an age when the universal claims of the Papacy were still unchallenged by individuals and governments. After carefully sifting the rival claims, the Pope issued, in 1493, a series of papal bulls which established a line of demarcation between the colonial possessions of the states: The East went to Portugal and the West went to Spain.

Though the announcement of the fact came much later, the European "scramble for Africa," and subsequently Asia and North America, started with this act. The labor and raw materials of Africa, Asia, South America, and the West Indies financed the European Industrial Revolution.

In the year 1457 the Council of Cardinals met in Holland and sanctioned, as a righteous and progressive idea, the enslavement of black Africans for the purpose of their conversion to Christianity, and to be exploited in the labor market as chattel property.

This devilish scheme speedily gained the sanctimonious blessing of the Pope and became a standard policy of the Roman Catholic Church, and later of the Protestant churches, enduring for three centuries: thus the ghastly traffic in human misery was given the cloak of respectability and anointed with the oil of pontifical righteousness in Jesus' name. And so, the slave trade began, inaugurating an era that stands out as the most gruesome and macabre example of man's disregard for the humanity of man.

The discovery of the New World opened up more than new territory. It opened a new era in human relations, mostly bad. The Europeans, being "Christians," had to find a way to live with their consciences after the formal starting of the slave trade. The Africans made the original mistake of asking the Europeans to settle some of their family disputes. Unfortunately, the Europeans many times conquered both branches of the family in question.

The Europeans were no strangers to Africa, and this really wasn't their first meeting. But in order to justify the slave trade, they had to forget, or pretend to forget, all that they had previously known about Africa. They had to forget that a lot of the early culture of Europe has an African base. They also had to forget that there were periods when Africans and Europeans lived in comparative harmony and Europeans married into African royalty. The Europeans had to forget that the Africans had a history and a heritage that could command respect.

In the opening up of the territory called the New World, two competitive slave systems were set in motion, and each of these systems served as some form of racism. The dehumanization of the African had started in European textbooks, geographies, and travel books. In South America and the Caribbean area the plantation owners generally bought slaves in large lots and kept the lots together principally because they thought they could work them better that way—and they were right. In the United States, however, where the most vicious form of racism was manifested, the slavery system operated more like a brokerage system. A plantation owner would very often buy ten slaves and resell five of them before the end of the week. This meant the immediate breaking up of the cultural continuity, linguistic continuity, and all things that held the African together within Africa, therefore creating a family dislocation from which the black American has not recovered to this day. This dislocation was a form of racism.

The mentality, the rationales, and the various ways of justifying the slave trade had already started in Europe with Europeans attempting to justify the enslavement of other Europeans. This is a neglected aspect of history that is rarely taken into consideration. There was at first a concerted effort to obtain European labor to open up the vast regions of the New World. It is often forgotten that in what became the United States white enslavement started before black enslavement.

In an article, "White Servitude in the United States," in *Ebony*, November, 1969, the Afro-American historian Lerone Bennett, Jr., gives the following information about this period:

When someone removes the cataracts of whiteness from our eyes, and when we look with unclouded vision on the bloody shadows of the American past, we will recognize for the first time that the Afro-American, who was so often second in freedom, was also second in slavery.

Indeed, it will be revealed that the Afro-American was third in slavery. For he inherited his chains, in a manner of speaking, from the pioneer bondsmen, who were red and white.

The story of this succession, of how the red bondsmen and of how white men created a system of white servitude which lasted in America for more than two hundred years, the story of how this system was created and why, of how white men and white women and white children were bought and sold like cattle and transported across the seas in foul "slave" ships, the story of how all this happened, of how the white planter reduced white people to temporary and lifetime servitude before stretching out his hands to Ethiopia, has never been told before in all its dimensions. As a matter of fact, the traditional embalmers of American experience seem to find servitude enormously embarrassing, and prefer to dwell at length on black bondage in America. But this maneuver distorts both black bondage and the American experience. For white bondage and red bondage are the missing legs on the triangle of American servitude. And this triangle defines the initial American experience as an experiment in compulsion.

Both red and white bondage were integral parts of this experiment, but white bondage was particularly important. In the first place, white bondage lasted for more than two centuries and involved a majority of the white immigrants to the American colonies. It has been estimated that at least two out of every three white colonists worked for a term of years in the fields or kitchens as semi-slaves. A second point of immense importance in this whole equation is the fact that white servitude was the historic foundation upon which the system of black slavery was constructed.

In other words, white servitude was the historic proving ground for the mechanisms of control and subordination used in Afro-American slavery. The plantation pass system, the fugitive slave law, the use of the overseer and the house servant and the Uncle Tom, the forced separation of parents and children on the auction block and the sexual exploitation of servant women, the whipping post, the slave chains, the branding iron; all these mechanisms were tried out and perfected first on white men and white women. Masters also developed a theory of internal white racism and used the traditional Sambo and minstrel stereotypes to characterize white servants who were said to be good natured and faithful but biologically inferior and subject to laziness, immorality, and crime. And all of this would seem to suggest that nothing substantial can be said about the mechanisms of black bondage in America except against the background and within the perspective of the system of white bondage in America.

How did the system develop? And why?

Mr. Bennett's statement is indicative of the new insight into the slave system. African slave labor and the raw material taken from their countries were important features in the development of the European Industrial Revolution.

American abolitionists, black and white, were fighting against a form of racism that had begun to crystallize itself in the embryo of the colonies' educational systems, filtering down from the attitude prevailing in the churches. During the period of the founding fathers, the black Americans heard promises about democracy and liberty and justice and thought that these promises were meant for them. Once more they were beguiled by illusions. The blacks weren't brought to this country to be given democracy, and the American promise wasn't made to them. That was the basis of the black American's dilemma during the formative period of this country, and it is the basis of his dilemma right now. This country was born in racism and it has evolved in racism.

Finally, in the early years of the nineteenth century, the system of chattel slavery gave way to the colonial system, after the British abolished slavery—at least on paper—in 1807. This was not the end of racism as it affected Africans and other nonwhite people throughout the world; it was only a radical change in how it would be manifested. The Europeans would now change the system of capturing Africans and other nonwhite people and enslaving them thousands of miles from their homes. They would now enslave them on the spot, within their own countries, and use them as markets for the new goods coming out of the developing European Industrial Revolution and out of their countries, and their labors to produce grist for new European mills. So the industrial rise of the West has as its base a form of racism. Racism helped to lay the base of the present economic system we now call capitalism.

Theoretical racism, in the main, is of nineteenth-century origin in America and in Europe. And yet, the nineteenth century was a century of the greatest resistance against racism. It was during that century when Africans the world over began to search for a definition of themselves. The concept of African redemption is of nineteenth-century origin. The theoretical basis of the Black Power concept started in 1829, with the publication of David Walker's appeal. The great black ministers of the nineteenth century, such as Henry Highland Garnet, Samuel Ringgold Ward, and Prince Hall, who founded the black Masons, were all using Christianity in a struggle against racism. Near the end of the nineteenth century the great intellectual giant, W. E. B. Du Bois, took up this fight and ably carried it to the middle of the twentieth century. He is the father of the present struggle against racism and for African redemption. Men like Marcus Garvey, though they differed with W. E. B. Du Bois, would draw in part on his intellectual conclusions on this subject.

There is now an international struggle on the part of people of African descent against racism and for a more honest look at their history. On university campuses and in international conferences they are demanding that their history be looked at from a black perspective or from an Afro-centric point of view. This has taken the struggle against racism to the world's intellectual centers, where the theortical basis of racism started. This has helped to create new battle lines and a lot of fear and frustration on the part of white scholars. They still do not recognize that removing the racism they created is the healthiest thing that present-day black scholarship can contribute to the world; that in the cry for Black Power and Black History, black people are saying a very powerful, complex, yet simple thing: "I am a man." The struggle against racism all along has been a struggle to regain the essential manhood lost after the European expansion into the broader world and the attempt to justify the slave trade. This struggle has brought us to where we are now, standing on the "black and beautiful" plateau. From this position black people will go into another stage, much higher and more meaningful for mankind. After reclaiming their own humanity, I think they will make a contribution toward the reclamation of the humanity of man.

In many ways this is what this book is about, and this is what the life and researches of J. A. Rogers were about. In more than forty-five years of travel and research (two generations) he, more than any other writer of his time, attempted to affirm the humanity of the African personality, and to show the role that African people have played in the development of human history. This was singularly the major mission of his life; it was also the legacy that he left to his people and the world.

JOHN HENRIK CLARKE
1972

EUROPE

Commentary and Notes
on References

THE STORY OF Benedict the Moor represents an African contribution to the later development of Christianity. It can best be understood in context with the early African contribution that helped to make Christianity one of the world's major religions. Many aspects of the present-day Christian Church were developed in Africa during the formative years of this religion, when the heavy hand of imperial Roman rule held sway over North Africa and large parts of the Middle East.

In spite of the many difficulties it had to face, there was a spectacular expansion of Christianity after the conversion of thousands by St. Peter on the first Pentecost. Among the first to hear and embrace the Christian religion were those living in parts of North Africa. Jesus Christ had spent some of his early years in Egypt to escape the murderous designs of Herod, the Roman governor. This event was well remembered and later helped to gain acceptance for the church in Africa.

There is some evidence to support the belief that Carthage, in North Africa, was the first African center of the Christian Church. The first known bishop of Carthage was Agrippinus. As early as A.D. 180 we learn of the martyrdom of twelve Carthaginians during the reign of Commodus, the son and successor to Marcus Aurelius. They are known as the Scillitan Martyrs.

Pontaenus became the founder of the world-famous Catechetical School of Alexandria and made it a great center for Christian scholarship. It was an Egyptian by the name of Anthony who became the father of the eremitic life.

Other African saints were Perpetua, a noblewoman, and her servant Felicitas, who were martyred at Carthage in A.D. 205. That Africa was a flourishing center of Christianity is proved by the fact that more Christians suffered martyrdom in the ampitheatre of Carthage than in the Coliseum of Rome.

Many aspects of the present-day Christian Church were developed in Africa during the formative years of Christianity. One of the more notable of African contributions to the early Church was monasticism. Christian monasticism probably began with the hermits of Egypt and Palestine about the time when Christianity was accepted as a legal religion.

From the north the church continued to spread southward and eastward. Ethiopia received Christianity at an especially early date. Tradition infers that St. Matthew, who wrote one of the gospels, preached in Ethiopia.

When an Ethiopian emperor was converted to Christianity in the middle of the fourth century, it marked a turning point in the history of the country. Eventually, the national church that emerged became the strongest supporter of Ethiopian independence.

It is said that about A.D. 316 a ship bearing a number of Christian missionaries was wrecked off the coast of Ethiopia. On contact with the Ethiopians, some of the men started preaching Christianity. About A.D. 328 the Christian Church in Alexandria was extended to include Ethiopia. The Egyptian Christians were known as Copts, and their church was referred to as Coptic. Much later, the Ethiopians freed themselves from the influence of the church in Egypt and reorganized their own church to reflect nationalist feelings. The liturgy became distinctly Ethiopian.

The Ethiopian "Orthodox" church today is a self-governing body. Its ruling principle is the belief that the Ethiopian people have formed their own church, and that this national unit enjoys complete equality and freedom within the great family of the "Orthodox."

The most famous, and to most students of Church history, the greatest single personality that Africa gave to the church is St. Augustine. The rich story of his life is only briefly told here.

Augustine was born at Thagaste in Numidia in A.D. 354 and showed early signs of genius. Unfortunately he led a dissipated life for some time. His mother, St. Monica, prayed for twenty years for his conversion.

Meanwhile, Augustine had become a scholar at Carthage, then a city of more than a half million inhabitants. When he had finished his studies, he opened a school at Thagaste, but later moved back to Carthage. He became professor of rhetoric at Milan in A.D. 385.

Augustine became friends with Ambrose, the saintly, learned Bishop of Milan, and within two years became a changed man. He grew in holiness with the years and lived a life of such sanctity that the people of Hippo (now called Bone) begged him to become a priest (A.D. 391). Four years later Augustine was consecrated Bishop of Hippo.

He wrote many books, but his two most famous are the *City of God* and *Confessions*. These rank among the world's classics and are widely read. Although Augustine was reputed to possess the highest possible degree of intelligence, his love of God, his contrition, and his humility were no less extraordinary. For him, humility was the greatest of all virtues.

Augustine, one of the Fathers of the Church and perhaps its greatest, died in A.D. 430.

The story of Africa and the rise of Christianity can in no way be completed without some reference being made to the three North African Popes. They, like St. Augustine, were the builders of the early Christian Church. The three referred to are Victor I (A.D. 189–199), Melchiades, also known as Miltiades (A.D. 311–314), and Gelasius (A.D. 492–496). All are honored in the church as saints. At least one of them, Victor, was a martyr for the faith.

In the years when Benedict the Moor was growing up in Sicily, Europe was emerging from the Middle Ages. The African slave trade had started, but had not developed to the tragic proportions that would unfold in the next two centuries. The best new work on the life of this remarkable Christian is *The Black Saint* by Brother Ernest (1949).

Alessandro de' Medici was another kind of Moor. He became an outstanding man of affairs in Europe before color became an important factor in the European's relationship with the broader world of Africa and Asia. The story of Alessandro de' Medici and his family is woven through all of the literature on the Medici Popes. The book *A Cardinal of the Medici* by Mrs. Hicks Beach (1937) is most revealing.

The best-known invader of Europe is the Hannibal who came from North Africa. The life of Abraham Hannibal is in contrast to this; he was brought to Europe from Africa against his will. His is a story of struggle and triumph in eighteenth-century Russia. Detailed accounts of his life can be found in the books *Introduction to the Economic History of Ethiopia* by Richard Pankhurst (1961) and *Distinguished Negroes Abroad* by Beatrice Jackson Fleming and Marion Jackson Pryde (1946).

Antonio Vieira is an example of a Christian of part African descent who took the church and its teaching more seriously than most Europeans, and who played an important part in helping the Europeans, through the church, expand to the New World. He was one of the many blacks who believed that the europeans would keep their promises about bringing justice and order to the indigenous people of South America and the West Indies. In his lifetime he called on the church to keep its Christian promises only to see these promises shamefully betrayed. Today he is honored as one of the great figures in the Christian Church of the seventeenth century.

John VI, King of Portugal, Algarve, and Brazil, earned his place in history when he dared to impose himself in the disputes between France and England during the era of Napoleon. His leadership of Portugal at this time in history is no small diplomatic miracle. Most of his last years were spent in Brazil, where his contributions make him one of that country's founding fathers. In the histories of Portugal and Brazil during the late eighteenth and early nineteenth centuries, the story of John VI is told again and again, and most of the time with great respect.

No personality contributed more to the romantic history of

eighteenth-century Europe than the black nobleman Chevalier de St. Georges. His life has been the basis for a novel, a film, and several books. He was practically unknown in the United States until J. A. Rogers in one of his early pamphlets called attention to his life and adventures. In recent years there has been a renewed interest in this remarkable black nobleman, who stirred the social and cultural circles of France and other parts of Europe for more than twenty-five years. The basic details of his life and career can be found in the following publications: *Negro History Bulletin,* December, 1937, and March, 1946; *Black Heroes in World History* (Bantam Books, 1969), and *Distinguished Negroes Abroad* (1946).

Jean-Louis, who became one of the greatest swordsmen in France, is one of many black patriots who distinguished themselves in the service of the country that had colonized the place of their birth. When he came to France, a boy of eleven years old, the Haitian Revolution was only in its rumor stages. When he died in France at the age of eighty the Civil War in the United States was over and the period called the Reconstruction had started. His name and career are still highly regarded in the literature on the art of fencing.

Aleksander Sergeevich Pushkin is referred to as the Father of Russian Literature, and the Shakespeare of Russia. The Russians to this day consider him to be one of their great cultural heroes. His books, and the books about his life, are extensive. Some of the descendants of Aleksander Pushkin are still living in present-day Russia.

A number of officers of mixed European and African ancestry, and some pure Africans, rose to distinction in the armies of Napolean. Joachim Murat was one of them. Many of these officers and soldiers who served in the French and other European armies were descendants of the Moors who had once controlled Spain and parts of southern Europe. J. A. Rogers was the first writer to call attention to this breed of soldier, who was a major factor in the armies of European nations until the beginning of the twentieth century.

So much that is generally thought of as European cultural contributions can be, with honesty, attributed to a large number of people who were, at least in part, African. The career of George A. P. Bridgetower proves this point. His father was known as "The African Prince." This remarkable musician, who was a friend of Beethoven, astounded the Europeans of his day and left his mark on the early nineteenth-century musical heritage of Europe. The writer Philip St. Laurent brought his life to the attention of present-day readers in an article in *Tuesday* magazine, August, 1968.

It is not generally known, but there were three black Frenchmen named Alexandre Dumas. The first of the three illustrious men to bear this name was an officer in the armies of Napoleon Bonaparte. He served with distinction in the Egyptian campaign.

Alexandre Dumas, père, the second of the three, was born in 1803, when Napoleon was still involved in the attempt to reconqueror the once highly prized colony of Haiti. As a writer, he laid the basis for the adventure and romantic literature of Europe. Of his many books the best known are *The Three Musketeers* and *The Count of Monte Cristo*.

Alexandre Dumas, fils, the younger, was the third of the eminent men to immortalize the name Dumas. During his lifetime he was regarded as the foremost dramatist of France. As such, he was awarded membership in the famous French Academy of Arts and Sciences, an honor that was denied his father, Alexandre Dumas, pére. Short biographies of the two literary Dumases can be found in the books *Distinguished Negroes Abroad* (1946) and *Five French Negro Authors* by Mercer Cook (1943).

Ira Aldridge was one of a number of black actors who distinguished themselves abroad before getting any appreciable recognition in this country. He reached the zenith of his fame in Europe while the last debates over slavery were being heard in the United States. When he died in Poland in 1867 the Reconstruction had already started. The best single book about his life and career is *Ira Aldridge: The Negro Tragedian* by Herbert Marshall and Mildred Stock (1958).

José T. de Sousa Martin was born in Portugal, of mixed African and Portuguese parentage. His life is indicative of the contributions that a number of highly trained black professionals were making to the development and well-being of Europe at a time when the system of slavery was gradually being transformed into the colonial system. In his day he was Portugal's most honored physician. His medical writings, mostly on public health, are still being studied in some of the universities of present-day Europe.

After George A. P. Bridgetower, Claudio J. D. Brindis de Sala was the greatest black instrumentalist to appear in Europe. Some of the music critics of Europe referred to him as "King of the Octaves." In his lifetime this black Cuban received some of the highest honors that are bestowed on artists. In 1930 his body was returned to Cuba from Buenos Aires, where he had died in 1911. He is now considered to be one of the cultural heroes of his country.

Samuel Coleridge-Taylor, another black musician, achieved fame as a composer working against great odds. During this period in England (1900 to 1912) it was difficult for a black composer to get conductors to perform his work and take it seriously. When he was finally accepted, he became the musical sensation of England and his fame soon spread to other parts of Europe.

Today Blaise Diagne is a national hero in Senegal, West Africa. There is an impressive statue honoring him on the island of Goree, off the city of Dakar. Blaise Diagne was born on the island of Goree in 1873. He was a major influence in the political evolvement of colonial French West Africa. He assisted Dr. W. E. B. Du Bois in convening the Pan-African Congress of 1919. Among the many books that deal, at least in part, with the life of Blaise Diagne, I call your attention to the following: *Pan-Africanism or Communism* by George Padmore (1957), pp. 119–197; *Dusk of Dawn*, by W. E. B. Du Bois (1940), reprinted 1968, pp. 261–276; and *History of the Pan-African Congress*, edited by George Padmore (1947), reprinted 1963, pp. 13–23.

J. H. C.

St. Maurice of Aganaum

St. Maurice of Aganaum

🌿

ROMAN GENERAL AND SAINT OF THE CATHOLIC CHURCH
(c.a.d. 287)

OF THE DETAILS of the life of St. Maurice, few are known. Even his real name is lost. His surname has survived because he was black. (Maurice is derived from Latin and means "like a Moor." "Moor" was the popular term for Negroes all over Europe and its use persisted long after Shakespeare.) The little that is known of St. Maurice, however, rings through the ages.

St. Maurice was a general of Rome at the time that the capital of the world was ruled jointly by Diocletian and Maximian Herculius. He was in command of a legion believed to have been composed of black men in the Roman province of Mauretania, or probably even in Upper Egypt, and was ordered from there to Rome in A.D. 287, a critical time in Roman history. Despite the lash, the red-hot irons, the gladiators, and all the tortures they were being subjected to, the Christians would not yield. The new gospel was spreading like wildfire, the believers were emerging from the catacombs, until like a tiny plant in a crevice which finally splits a rock asunder, the Christians threatened the very throne of the Caesars. To cope with them, Maximian and Diocletian made a hasty peace with the tribes on the outskirts of the vast empire and called as many soldiers as possible to Rome.

The influence of the Christians had spread to Gaul and there the slaves were in revolt. When St. Maurice and his legion arrived at Rome, they were dispatched to suppress this uprising. Upon reaching Aganaum, a desolate region in what is now Switzerland, he learned that the people he was sent to suppress were Christians. Stunned by this knowledge because he and his men were also Christians, he assembled his men and told them that he intended to go no further. The soldiers hailed the decision. With touching honesty, St. Maurice reminded them of the certain fate that awaited them. But they did not flinch, on which St. Maurice sent a message to the emperors informing them of his decision.

Maximian was resting at Octodorum when the news reached him. In high rage he assembled an army and set out for Aganaum. When he arrived he found the African legion calmly waiting for him. His first order was to command St. Maurice and his men to sacrifice to the pagan gods. They refused. Addressing the emperor, St. Maurice said:

"Sire, we are soldiers but we are also servitors of Christ, a fact that we proudly confess. To you we owe military service; to Him, the homage of a pure and innocent life. From you we receive our pay; from Him, we hold the benefit of life.

"That is why, sire, we cannot obey you without denying God, the Creator of all things, our Master as well as yours, whether you acknowledge it or not."

The emperor, in a rage, ordered the usual punishment—decimation. Every tenth man was to be killed. The men were ordered to number and every tenth one was made to step out. Six hundred came forward. The emperor now called on these to submit, promising them promotion and wealth. Despite all inducements and entreaties they would not yield, whereupon they were killed.

Confident that the others had been taught a lesson, the emperor again gave the order for sacrifice; but there was no response, the survivors instead bidding one another to be courageous in the name of Christ. Again every tenth man was called forward, and again each fell under the sword.

For the third time the emperor ordered obedience; for the third time he failed.

"We have seen our companions fall under the sword," replied St. Maurice. "We have been spattered with their blood. We do not grieve for them. We rather envy them the privilege of dying for the One who died on the cross for us. Do what you will. No terror or torture can frighten us. We are ready to die. We boldly confess that we are Christians and that we cannot attack fellow Christians."

Finding the men inflexible the emperor ordered the remainder put to death. Only a few of the original 6000 escaped to Germany and Italy. Among the dead was St. Maurice.

This singular example of devotion gave great impetus to the faith. It heartened the Europeans by proving to them that the church in Africa was as firm as in Rome, that the glowing accounts of African heroism and martyrdom reaching them were true. They recalled that it was an African, Simon of Cyrene, who had helped Christ with his Cross, that the eunuch of Candace of Ethiopia had been won to Christianity by the Apostle Philip, and that Candace herself had embraced the faith. They remembered, also, that the great standard-bearers of Christianity such as St. Augustine, St. Cyprian, Tertullian, Origen, Clement, and St. Athanasius were all Africans.

In the troubled era that followed, St. Maurice and his men were for a time forgotten. In the next century, however, St. Eucherius, Bishop of Lyons, gathered up the threads of the story of their martyrdom from survivors and from their descendants, and told it from the pulpit. His recital thrilled Christendom, and a church was built on the spot where the devoted black men had fallen. Later Sigismund, King of Burgundy, in gratitude for the inspiration he had received from St. Maurice, founded a monastery that ultimately became one of the richest and most noted of its kind in Christendom.

During the Mohammedan invasion of Europe it was destroyed by the Moors, but it was rebuilt by St. Louis, King and patron saint of France, in 1264. This edifice still stands in the town of St. Maurice-en-Valais, Switzerland, with the towering peaks of the Alps as its background.

A chapel not far away from the monastery is said to contain the relics of St. Maurice and his brave men. The abbey is still rich in treasures, reputed to be among the finest in Western civilization. Exquisite masterpieces of the jeweler's art—the gifts of many kings—are in its collection.

The fame of St. Maurice stood firm for twelve centuries. During the Reformation, however, he, like other Catholic saints, was the subject of great controversy, till today, like Christ, Homer, and Shakespeare, his very existence is doubted.

Nevertheless, one fact stands in favor of his mortality. Unlike so many of the other saints, no supernatural event is connected with him. He walked and talked like other men and gave an example of Christian steadfastness and courage such as could be seen in England during the reign of Mary, a thousand years later. Allard, an authority on the subject of Christian martyrs, says, "The martyrdom of the legion, attested as it is by ancient and reliable evidence, cannot be called into question by any honest mind."

In any case, the supreme heroism and faith attributed to him had a profound influence on millions of human beings for more than a thousand years.

In Germany his fame reached still greater heights. In A.D. 962 Otto I selected him as the title patron of the Archbishop of Magdeburg and the great cathedral there, one of the finest of all the Gothic edifices situated in Saxony, the most German part of Germany, was named after him.

W. S. Seiferth says:

The Magdeburg Mauritius is not only a realistic and noble portrayal of the Negro by a mediaeval anonymous master, it is just as much the realization of Christian properties in the Negro, the appreciation of human dignity and value. The Negro was accepted in the illustrious company of saints, the chosen patron of feudal knighthood and of princely families."

St. Maurice is now the principal saint of central and southern Germany, and parts of France, Switzerland, Spain, and Italy. He is also the title patron of Cracow, Coburg, Lauenberg, and Savoy. He is on the coat-of-arms of each of these princely houses. September 22 is his saint's day and he is the celestial saint of millions of Christians. He is the patron of dyers, clothmakers, and swordsmiths. Sufferers from the gout plead for his intercession. The Sardinian Order of St. Maurice, one of Italy's most prized decorations, is named in commemoration of him.

REFERENCES

There was more than one St. Maurice, and he of Aganaum is often confused with St. Maurice of Apamea, a Roman, who might have been white. This is probably the St. Maurice portrayed by El Greco. In any case, St. Maurice of Aganaum is always represented in northern Europe as an unmixed Negro. He is so shown by Peter Vischer the Elder on the tomb of Archbishop Ernst at Magdeburg and by Walter Greischel in the same cathedral; by Hans Baldung with the Prussian eagle on his head; by Peter Vischer the Elder on a fountain at Naumburg; and by Grünewald. The picture by this artist hangs in the Alte Pinakothek, Munich, and portrays a "typical" Negro, hair and all. The figure shows extraordinary dignity and poise. Its armor is represented as jewel-studded and so is its collar. The wreath on its head is of gold finely wrought. The picture once hung before the altar of the Cathedral of Halle.

The original portrait of St. Maurice, like that of so many other Christian saints, may be apocryphal. It was executed by an unknown artist probably soon after his memory was revived by St. Eucherius in the fourth century.

Among other portraits of St. Maurice as a Negro are one in the Cathedral of Lucerne, near the big organ; in the coat-of-arms of the city of Coburg; in the houses of the Schwarzkopf in Riga and Reval; and in the Abbey of St. Maurice at St. Maurice-en-Valais, Switzerland. For a reproduction of this last see *The 100 Amazing Facts about the Negro*, p. 3.

Allard, *Le Martyre de la Légion Thebéene* in *Histoire des Persécutions*, pp. 335–364. Paris, 1890.

Leclercq, H., *Dict. arch. Chrètien et de lit*, Vol. I, pp. 850–871. 1903.

Stolle: *Das Martyrium der Thebasischen Legion*. Breslau, 1890.

Guerin, P., *Vies des Saints*, Vol. IX, pp. 452–458.

Seiferth, W. S., *St. Mauritius, African*, pp. 370–376. Phylon, 1941.

Atlantis (Berlin), July–Dec., 1932, p. 665.

ADDITIONAL REFERENCES

Walsh, Martin De Porres, O.P., *The Ancient Black Christians*. San Francisco, Julian Richardson Associates, Publishers, 1969.

St. Benedict the Moor

Benedict the Moor

SAINT OF THE CATHOLIC CHURCH
(1524–1589)

BENEDICT THE MOOR was born in Sicily. In an age when devout Christians took pride in seeing how humble and self-denying they could be, he excelled. In the matter of chastity, it is said that beautiful women, some of them of high nobility, tempted him in vain.

He was born on the estate of the Chevalier de Lanza at San Fratello, where his father Christopher and his mother Diana, both African blacks, were slaves. Knowing that children born to them would be slaves, they had decided to have none; but, Christopher, who had won the high esteem of his master, received a promise from him that their firstborn should be free. This child was Benedict.

Benedict was piously trained but his education was neglected and he could neither read nor write. Among his neighbors was Father Jerome Lanza, who saw him for the first time one day when he was crossing a wheat field and heard the harvesters twitting Benedict about his color. He stopped to talk with Benedict, and discovering that he was intelligent, said to the reapers, "You are laughing at him now, but someday he is going to astonish you all." This remark, coming from one so respected greatly impressed everyone, Benedict most of all.

Years later, when Benedict was twenty-one, Father Lanza again saw him at work near the same spot with an ox team that Benedict had bought with his hard-earned savings. "Benedict," he said, "sell your oxen, give the money to the poor, and follow me."

Benedict obeyed. Placing himself under the guidance of Father Lanza, he became one of his monks, pledging himself to a perpetual Lenten vow. The monks at Lanza's monastery lived in small, wretched cells and ate only the coarsest food. When not engaged in hard manual labor they knelt in prayer on stone floors. No diversions of any kind were permitted.

Benedict showed such zeal that although he was the last to enter the monastery he was the first to attain perfection in the mortification of the flesh. Seeking still greater purification, he made a pilgrimage into the deserts of Syria and Egypt, where he hoped to learn of even harder penance. Discovering that St. Paul, the first hermit, had reduced his clothing only to a tunic of palm leaves, which garment had been inherited by St. Anthony, Benedict made a similar garment for himself, adding only a coarse woolen shirt in winter. His ambition was to reach the heights of patience, gentleness, and Christian love. Even as others fought for wealth and power, Benedict strove for poverty and self-denial. On the streets he welcomed the taunts of those who regarded the voluntary poor as vagabonds.

Later, deciding that even his hermitage was too comfortable, he undertook a rougher one at Cattolica, where he lived for eight years. Then, wishing to attain to even greater privation, he removed to the caves in the mountains near Palermo.

Soon it came to be said that Benedict was so holy that even the wolves would not touch him. If that were so, it was more probably because of his leanness. People from all parts of the island, and even from the mainland, came to seek his blessing and his prayers. One woman with a cancer of the breast, declared that Benedict had cured her. The fame of the "miracle" spread, and superstitious folk flocked to him in such numbers that he was forced to retire into the interior.

Still later he went to live on Mount Pellegrino, overlooking Palermo, having a hole in the rocks as his cell. Here the Duke of Medina-Coeli, ruler of the island, visited him and was so impressed that he built him a chapel at his own expense.

When Father Lanza died, Benedict was unanimously elected head of the Order, but true to his ideals, he refused all honor and authority. At about this time Pope Pius IV, hoping to discourage these monks, and especially Benedict, from their excessive privations, told them that they might accomplish their vows in any monastery they chose. The suggestion was equivalent to a command. Benedict thereupon thought of becoming a Capuchin because the rites of this order were in closest accord with his mode of living. But while at prayer in the Cathedral of Palermo, asking for "light," it occurred to him that a newly reformed order known as Minor Observations suited him better. Seeking out the father superior of this order, he pleaded for admittance.

The latter, on learning Benedict's identity, accepted him joyfully, seeing in his coming a proof of God's blessing on his order. Benedict spent the next three years there, chiefly in prayer and meditation.

His next and last retreat was the Convent of St. Mary, where he strove to attain even greater self-denial. Discarding his sandals, he went barefooted even in the snow. His wretched cell, with its coarse coverlet and a board for a bed; its few pictures of saints; and its cross drawn on the wall with charcoal, he called his palace. And he was humility incarnate. Once, when he gently chided some novices for throwing scraps of food in the gutter and they laughed at him, to make them ashamed he seized a coarse wire brush and closed his hand so tightly over it that the blood streamed down. A picture was painted of the incident and distributed. One copy was hung in a Negro church in Portugal.

To preserve complete chastity, Benedict never looked at a woman's face. None of the many women, high or low, who sought his guidance could boast that she had ever seen his eyes. Among those who came most often was the Duchess of Montalvo. When anyone wished to touch his hand he would offer the tip of his garment, out of humility.

When food and choice fruit were brought to him, Benedict, to show his gratitude to the givers, would eat a little of it, and send the rest to the poor.

His fame became so great that the Order decided to make him the father superior. Benedict refused, pleading his imperfections, his incapacity, and his illiteracy. But when everyone insisted, he yielded.

More than ever now, he practiced self-denial. He led all in waiting on the sick; in washing the feet of others of strange religions; in prayers for the community; in mortifications; and public penances.

He "employed himself in all the labors of the house and in the lowest employments. His rest and recreation consisted of helping in the kitchen, washing the dishes, drawing water, carrying wood, sweeping the floor, digging in the garden, and begging in the city. The principal lesson which his subjects drew from these beautiful examples was a continual encouragement to the exact practice of their vigorous reform and particularly of holy humility."

To the priests under him he showed a sovereign respect. He was full of charity to the lay brothers, discreet in guiding the novices, and in his dealings with the subordinates in the house he was Christ-like. When he found it necessary to correct anyone he did so only by advice, ingeniously given, or by loving example. His model was St. Chrysostom, who said, "The master's principal function is to share from the bottom of his heart the pains and sorrows of his subordinates."

Though unable to read or write, he knew whole chapters of the Bible by memory. His sermons, coming straight from his heart, embodied the principles he lived.

Learned men came to hear him and were amazed. Three leading Franciscans—Father Joseph of Syracuse, professor of Holy Scripture; Father Paul of Messara, distinguished theologian; and Father Vincent of Messina, theologian of the Council—all affirmed upon oath that Benedict had enlightened them on difficult passages of Scripture.

When a convention was held in the ancient city of Girgenti, Benedict, in his quality of guardian, assisted. Allibert says:

As soon as his arrival became known, the whole city was in a tumult of joy. Nothing was spoken of but Benedict and his sanctity, and at the news of his approach the clergy of the cathedral accompanied by many of the inhabitants went to meet him. What a beautiful spectacle it was to see the humble Benedict surrounded by the most respectable ecclesiastics, the most distinguished inhabitants and the crowds of people who disputed for the happiness of kissing his habit, or at least touching it. The more confused and mortified the Saint became, the more he vainly sought to fly the applause, the more did they cry aloud: "Behold the Saint." Some recommended themselves to his prayers; others wept for joy; they never grew weary of contemplating his modesty and humility amidst so peaceful and glorious a triumph. The like happened at Bivona, where the people's joy was so excessive and the crowd so great that he hid himself and fled to escape such honors.

When Benedict traveled, he was forced to choose the most unfrequented paths to avoid demonstrations.

People came from distant countries to throw themselves at his feet and returned to boast of it. But as his power grew, so grew his charity and his humility.

Legends sprang up about him while he was still alive. Many are the "miracles" and prophecies credited to him. He was said to have predicted the death of Princess Bianca; to have cured the diseased eyes of a noble lady by merely laying his hands on them; to have restored the sight of a blind man before a large gathering merely by making the sign of the cross on the eyes. To escape the joy of the astonished mob he was once forced to hide in a thicket.

Nobles of Palermo and the rich came to the door of his kitchen to entreat his prayers. It was even said that the light of his countenance at times illuminated the darkness of the chapel. Sister Frances Locitraro declared that she once saw Benedict standing in the air before the altar of the Virgin, unsupported.

Allibert gives a list of the miracles credited to him, and the names of some of those who were reported to have been healed. Among those named as having been "raised from the dead" by Benedict was one George Russo, who had been accidentally killed.

These were delusions, of course, but they serve to show the extraordinary esteem and veneration in which this unassuming black man was held by the greatest in the land.

In spite of the severe hardships he imposed on himself, Benedict lived to the age of sixty-five. During his illness, rich and poor, nobles and peasants, came in numbers to the convent gates for news of him. He died April 4, 1589. His last words were, "Into thy hands, O Lord, I commend my spirit."

Around his neck was found a cord he had placed there with his dying hands as a penance for "all my faults" and for all those "whom I have wronged."

The mob fought frantically for bits of his tattered raiment, and for anything that he had touched. Those who saw him even said that a halo shone around his corpse and that a faint sweet odor came from it.

Death increased his fame. Philip III of Spain gave a silver coffin for his body; but it was finally decided to enshrine it in crystal so that all could see it. The sick and the afflicted went for a long time to pray before it, blocking the long road that led from the city to the church. Many declared themselves healed.

In 1652 the city of Palermo honored him with the title of "Blessed" and the senate went in a body to his shrine and offered fourteen torches of white wax each weighing six pounds.

His fame speedily passed from Spain to Portugal, where he was designated "The Holy Black." The Christian Negroes of Lisbon established a confraternity in his name and celebrated his feast every year with great devotion. Thirty years after his death the Catholic King, Philip III, assisted at their procession, being then at Lisbon in quality of the heir of Philip II, his father.

From Europe his renown spread to the two Americas. In South America he became the most honored saint of the Negroes, and also of the Christian Indians of Brazil and Peru. Many churches were erected in his honor, among them one in New York City. In 1807 he was canonized by Pope Pius VII.

REFERENCES

Baring-Gould, S., *Lives of the Saints*, Vol. X, pp. 329–337. Edinburgh, 1914.

ADDITIONAL REFERENCES

Carletti, Benvenuto, *Life of St. Benedict Surnamed "The Moor,"* trans. from M. Allibert's *St. Benedict of San Fratello*. Philadelphia, Peter F. Cunningham & Son, 1875.

Ernest, Brother, *The Black Saint*. Notre Dame, Ind. Dujarie Press, 1949.

Hardy, M. L'Abbé J., *La Morale en Action des Noir*. Jacques LeCoffre et Cie, Libraires, Paris, 1846.

Alessandro de' Medici

FIRST REIGNING DUKE OF FLORENCE
(1510–1537)

To STUDENTS of color discrimination European history offers no more astonishing figure than Alessandro de' Medici, "The Moor," first reigning Duke of Florence. His mother Anna was a fine and robust black peasant of Colle Vecchio, Italy, in the employ of Alfonsina Orsini, a near relative of Pope Clement VII, while his father is very generally said to be the Pope himself, who was then Cardinal de' Medici.

As Duke of Florence, Alessandro, after the death of Pope Clement, became the head of one of the most illustrious families in European history—a family that furnished a long roll of statesmen and patrons of art, as well as three popes, three kings of France, three queens, and a mother of one of England's kings.

Allesandro's nominal father, Lorenzo II, died while he was still young and left the dukedom to his brother Pope Clement VII, the same who had a dispute with Henry VIII over the divorce of Catherine of Aragon. Living in the Medici Palace with Alessandro were his cousin Ippolito and his supposed sister Catherine—the Catherine of the Massacre of St. Bartholomew's Day. They, with the Pope, were the last of the elder branch of the family. Of the four, all were illegitimate, except Catherine, and perhaps Clement.

But being born out of wedlock in those days, especially in the homes of the great, was not a serious handicap. As in the Orient, many of the noblest names were carried on by a capable bastard who had proved himself superior to the legitimate offspring.

Alessandro made his debut into politics at a time critical for the fortunes of his family. The Pope, its head, was having considerable difficulty trying to preserve the orthodox faith, and with it his hold on European politics. Not only was he at odds with the Florentines, but also with Charles V, the Napoleon of his time, the ruler of Spain and part of Italy and France, all of Austria, Germany, and the Netherlands.

The quarrel between the Pope and the Florentines broke into open revolt. An attack was made on the palace and Cardinal Cortina, the guardian of the three children, fled, taking Alessandro and Ippolito. The people held Catherine as a hostage.

To make matters worse, Charles V defeated the Pope's ally, Francis I of France, and marching on Rome, sacked it. The Pope fled and locked himself up in the fortress of San Angelo.

The Pope, seeing that his only hope was to make peace with Charles V, promised him his entire support. If Charles dominated the bodies of men, the Pope would dominate their souls. Accordingly, a treaty was made between them, one of whose provisions was that the emperor should restore the Pope's family to power in Florence. To bind the agreement a match was arranged between Alessandro and the emperor's daughter Margaret. She was nine, Alessandro, twenty.

In fulfillment of his promise, the emperor sent an army under the Prince of Orange against Florence. The Florentines, among them Michelangelo, fought desperately for a year, but finally surrendered. They were heavily fined and had to yield to the government that the Pope and the emperor imposed upon them. This was a heavy blow to the Florentines who had always prided themselves on their independence. Their city, now made into practically an absolute monarchy, was given to Alessandro to rule with the title of duke.

The young duke began his reign well. Ceccghereghi, Italian historian, credits him with wit and wisdom, a fine sense of justice, and "judgments that would have done credit to a Solomon." He restored to the Florentines most of their former liberties. But numbers of them were not content with a monarchy. Besides, a good many were still bitter over the war.

Into this stirring drama now steps a fourth character. Mention has already been made of him: Ippolito de' Medici.

Ippolito felt that he and not Alessandro should have been made head of the family. He claimed not only priority of age, but nobler birth, his mother having been a noblewoman while Alessandro's was a servant, perhaps even a slave. He became Alessandro's worst foe and headed the faction against him.

Varillas says:

When Ippolito understood that Pope Clement had decided that Alessandro was to be made heir to the riches and greatness of the House of Medici, a great change took place in him. He was seized with immense anger and grief, as it seemed to him that, being older and a nearer relative of the Pope and better endowed by nature that so rich an inheritance and so brilliant a marriage should be his; either not knowing, or refusing to believe, the secret rumors, that Alessandro was the son of Clement.

The Pope made Ippolito a cardinal, but this so little contented him that he disdained the high honor, preferring Hungarian dress to the red hat.

An interesting light is thrown on the quarrel by Ambassador Soriani, who was an eyewitness. He says:

The Duke Alessandro shows that he has a good mind and that he has the tact to accommodate himself better to the nature and will of the Pope than the Cardinal Ippolito de Medici. Therefore, His Holiness has made it evident to me that he loves the Duke more than the Cardinal, and expects very much more from him. Many times in conversation with me, he has told me that he intends to make the Duke head of the Medici family and to let him govern Florence as his ancestors have done.

The most Rev. Cardinal Ippolito de Medici was twenty years old on March 23, 1531. He has a good mind and has given some little time to study, so that in comparison with the other cardinals, he cannot be considered as ignorant. He is indeed of vivacious, one might almost say, of a restless nature, but perhaps it comes from his youth.

He is very envious of the Duke because it seems to him that the

Pope did him a great injustice in putting the Duke at the head of the government of Florence. He thinks himself of a better social class than the Duke whose mother is a slave. The quarrel between the two gives great displeasure to His Holiness who is disgusted with the Cardinal for disturbing his plans.

This question of the respective characters and merits of the duke and of Ippolito is still a subject of dispute among historians. By some Alessandro is painted as a just and able young man; by others he is held to be a creature who would have disgraced even "the worst epochs of Roman villainy."

Ippolito readily found a number of influential Florentines to support his claims. He continued his plotting until he was forced to leave Florence for Rome, where he found refuge, and where his home became a center for all those who fled from Duke Alessandro.

Several attempts were made on the duke's life, after which he disarmed friend and foe. He garrisoned the towns and built the fortress of San Giovanni to dominate the city. Many of his enemies he caused to be stripped of their wealth and sent into exile.

At last Ippolito decided to make a direct appeal to the emperor Charles V, who was on his way to attack the great African pirate, Barbarossa.

But Ippolito never reached him; he died on the way, poisoned, it is said, by the emissaries of Alessandro.

Alessandro's troubles multiplied. To make matters worse, the Pope died, thus depriving him of his ablest counsellor. Alessandro, in order to pacify the people, began to give them fetes after the manner of the old Roman emperors. This only helped to give him the reputation of a libertine—a reputation that was not unjustified. It was a dissolute age and Alessandro was a part of it, but his enemies magnified those faults that would have been condoned in another ruler. When his mother died, quite naturally, it seems, he was accused of starving her to detah to get her out of the way.

At last the enemies of the duke took their case to the emperor. The latter summoned Alessandro before him, whereupon Alessandro defended himself so ably that he rose higher in the imperial favor. Charles not only promised him his full support, but decided to hasten his daughter's marriage to him.

In June, 1536, the emperor visited Florence in great state, and on the 16th of that month the marriage was celebrated in gorgeous style in the old palace of the Medicis in the presence of the kings and queens of the leading countries of Europe.

This marriage, by the way, helps to throw some light on the better side of Alessandro's character. Charles V was just, devout, and much beloved. Later he voluntarily renounced his vast empire to follow a life of solitary meditation and Christian devotion. Is it logical to believe that he would have given his daughter to a monster such as Alessandro has been painted, especially after Clement died?

That Alessandro was a despot there is no doubt whatever, though some of the blame must be placed on his adviser, Francesco Guicciardini, an able historian of Machiavellian tendencies.

Enters now the villain, Lorenzino, better known as Lorenzaccio (The Wicked). Lorenzino, who has been described as "half-poet, half-madman," and who had been threatened by the Pope with hanging if ever he showed himself in Rome, for having out of sheer wantonness, knocked off the heads of some precious statues, felt that since Alessandro was illegitimate he, as the eldest offspring of the younger branch of the family, was the rightful heir. He began to plot. To further his intrigues he cultivated the good graces of the duke.

This was not difficult as he had qualities that pleased the duke, especially his capacity for vice. Both soon became boon companions, going about the streets dressed as minstrels and serenading the Florentines. Sometimes both would ride on the same horse through the town.

When the enemies of Alessandro learned of Lorenzino's real feelings toward the duke, they decided to use him as the instrument of their vengeance and promised him the dukedom if Alessandro were put out of the way.

Lorenzino readily fell in with this plan. Among his friends was a soldier named Michaele who was nicknamed Scoronconcolo because of his wild and turbulent disposition. A giant in physique, this ruffian was devoted body and soul to Lorenzino.

One day when Lorenzino said to him, "I want you to kill the man I hate most on earth," Michaele readily agreed. Accordingly, Lorenzino invited the duke to his home, promising him a rendezvous there with a beautiful Venetian, already married, of whom Alessandro was enamored: Signora Ginori.

Alessandro left the palace masked, accompanied by his two faithful guards, Giacomo and Bobo. Arriving at Lorenzaccio's gate, he sent the men to wait for him at a wine shop and slipped in unseen. At the door he was received by Lorenzaccio. All the servants had been dismissed. Hidden within was Michaele.

The duke gave his coat to Lorenzaccio. The latter urged him also to lay his sword aside, and taking it, hid it in another room. He then left, saying he was going in search of the lady and would return soon. Before leaving, he signaled Michaele that the coast was clear for the attack on the duke.

The duke, left alone, went over to the fire to await Signora Ginori, but feeling drowsy, threw himself on a couch and was soon fast asleep. Hours passed, and Lorenzaccio returned. To his chagrin he found the duke still alive. Michaele had lost his nerve.

Deciding to lose no more time, Lorenzaccio crept into the room, sword in hand. He plunged the weapon into the back of the sleeping ruler.

But the wound was not fatal. Alessandro, leaping to his feet, shouted, "Traitor," "Assassin," and seized his attacker in a desperate grip.

Both went to the floor. The duke bit Lorenzaccio's thumb so hard that he yelled with pain. Michaele rushed to his aid, and lunged at the duke, but in the tangle of bodies struck Lorenzaccio instead, wounding him on the cheek and nose.

This caused Lorenzaccio to yell the louder, whereupon Michaele, drawing his dagger, plunged in into the duke's side and twisted it all the way around. As the duke fell, Michaele drew his sword across his throat, almost severing the duke's head.

The two hastened to remove the blood from their hands. It was then that Lorenzaccio made a chance remark that apprised Michaele of the rank of his victim, which so terrified Michaele that he rushed from the house and confessed. As to Lorenzaccio, he lost his nerve also, and mounting a horse, galloped out of the city.

Alessandro's bodyguards, tired of waiting, at last burst into

Lorenzaccio's home and found the body. They hastened to tell the prime minister, Cardinal Cibo, who, fearing the effect of the news on the populace, kept it secret and buried the duke privately.

A council was at once summoned. Alessandro's son Julian was named as his successor, but as he was only five years old, he was set aside in favor of Cosimo, a member of the younger branch and a near relative of Lorenzaccio.

One of Cosimo's first acts was to seek vengeance on Lorenzaccio, who, safe in France, declared that he had killed Alessandro because of an insult the latter had offered to his sister Laodomia. Later he assumed a Brutus-like pose and alleged that he had saved his country from a tyrant.

For eleven years he eluded the emissaries of Cosimo, but finally overtaken in Venice, he was stabbed to death.

Margaret, Alessandro's widow, married the Duke of Parma and became a powerful figure in European politics. She was made regent of the Netherlands by her brother, King Philip of Spain.

The tomb into which Alessandro had been hurriedly thrust was that of his nominal father, the Duke of Urbino, under Michelangelo's famous statue, "Il Penseroso." For a long time this was disputed by historians. To settle this question, the Italian government ordered the tomb opened in 1875.

Charles Heath Wilson, who was present, said that the two dukes were lying head to foot, that they were embalmed, and that Alessandro's body was clothed in an embroidered shirt. He also said that the latter was easily recognized by his hair, his mulatto cast of features, and the traces of wounds about his head and body.

Alessandro might have gone far but for his untimely death. Charles V was planning to make him general-in-chief of his armies in Italy.

REFERENCES

Bronzino's portrait of Alessandro in the Uffizzi Palace in Florence, shows him with woolly hair and thick lips—undoubtedly of African descent.

Gino Capponi says, "His mother was a mulatto slave and he had the dark skin, thick lips, and curly hair of a Negro."

Cotterill says:

"The reconciliation of Pope Clement VII with Charles V after the sacking of Rome, resulted in the siege and capture of Florence. Thereupon, Charles imposed on this city as its regent, the mulatto bastard above-mentioned, Alessandro the Moor, who married a daughter of the Emperor and received the title of the Duke of Florence.

"Alessandro was a dark-skinned boy of about thirteen years with the thick lips and woolly hair of a Negro. . . . His father was almost indubitably Pope Clement."

G. F. Young says:

"Alessandro, then about thirteen, appears in Florence. His woolly hair and Negro-like appearance had already caused him to be called the Moor. This boy's origin was a secret. Born during the time the family was in exile, he was in reality the son of Clement himself, but the latter had hidden and kept the boy out of sight as long as he could.

"There is no doubt of this, though none cared at the time to contradict the Pope's assertion that Alessandro was the son of Lorenzo [Duke of Urbino] and as such, he is mentioned in history; historians contenting themselves with saying that he was reputed to be so but was more probably Clement's son.

"Moreover, the historian, Ammirato, states that afterwards, when Clement and Alessandro were both dead, Cosimo I told him positively that Alessandro was Clement's son." (Cosimo I was Alessandro's successor.)

Clarice de Medici, a legitimate member of the family, hated Alessandro and would shout "Negro" and "Bastard" whenever she saw him. Catherine despised him too, but later disputed the title to his wealth with his wife Margaret.

Alessandro was not the only one of the Medicis to show a Negro strain. Cosimo III appears by his portrait to have been even more Negroid, while Cosimo's son, Gian Gastone, bears a striking resemblance to Dumas père. (For their pictures see C. H. Russell's *Regiae Familiae Mediceorum Etruriae*, pp. 18 and 44.)

Charles II of England was a Medici on his mother's side. G. F. Young says of him, "His dark hair and swarthy complexion showed traces of the Medici blood."

Catherine de' Medici, Queen of France, Alessandro's supposed sister, also had a son, the Duc d'Alençon, who was to all appearances a mulatto. (For sources, see *Sex and Race*, Vol. III, p. 224. 1944.)

Among the existing portraits of Alessandro are the following: one by Andrea del Sarto in the Museum of the Marquis de Cerralbo in Madrid; one by an unknown artist in the Silver Museum of Florence; one by Bronzino, and another by Vasari, in the Medici Museum; one by Sangallo in the National Museum of Florence; one a fresco by Vasari in the Palazzo Vecchio at Florence; one in the Museum of Pisa.

Benvenuto Cellini, who made ten dies for Alessandro, mentions him frequently in his autobiography and says, "It was believed for a certainty that Duke Alessandro was the son of Pope Clement." (*Memoirs of Cellini*, Chap. 18, p. 190. 1845.) Ammirato, a historian of the times, says that after Clement and Alessandro died Cosimo, Alessandro's successor, told him that Alessandro was Clement's son. (*Ammirato, lib.*; Gonf. 1347.) Since priests and popes were not supposed to have children their offspring were called "nephews.") (Farmer and Henley, *Slang and Its Analogies*, Vol. V, p. 28.) But it was not uncommon for a Pope to have children. Paul III, successor of Clement, also had a son, who was named Pier Luigi.

Alessandro's children married into the Italian nobility and had distinguished offspring.

Varchi, B., *Istoria Delle Guerre Della Republica*. Fiorentina, 1723.

Nestor, G., *Hommes Illustrés de la Maison de Medici*. Paris, 1564.

Cotterill, *Italy from Dante to Tasso*. New York, 1919.

Young, George Frederick, *The Medici*, Vols. I and II, pp. 493–514. New York, E. P. Dutton & Co., Inc., 1909.

La Châtre, *Histoire des Papes, etc.*, Vol. VII–VIII, p. 133. Paris, 1842.

Reumont, A. de, *La Jeunesse de Catherine de Medicis*, trans. by Bachet, p. 134. 1866.

Capponi, Gino, *Storia della Republica di Firenze*, Vol. III, p. 167.

Noble, M., *Memoirs of the Medicis*, p. 214. London, 1797.

Sandoval, *Vida y hechos de Carlos V*, Vol. II, p. 324. Pamplona, 1614.

Gauthiez, P., *Jean des Bandes-Noires*, p. 177. Paris, 1901.

Van Dyke, P., *Catherine de Medici*, p. 15. 1923.

Cellini, B. de, *Memoirs of Cellini*, Vol. I, Chaps. 16 and 18. 1845.

Vaughan, H. M. *The Medici Popes*. London, 1908.

Otetea, A. *François Guichardin (Francesco Guicciardini)*, pp. 290–304. 1926.

ADDITIONAL REFERENCES

Beach, Mrs. Hicks (Susan Emily Christian), *A Cardinal of the Medici*. New York, The Macmillan Company, 1937.

Cust, Robert H. Hobart. *The Life of Benvenuto Cellini*, Vols. I and II. London, The Navarre Society, Ltd., 1935.

Abraham Hannibal

✳❧

RUSSIAN GENERAL AND COMRADE OF PETER THE GREAT
(d. 1782)

HISTORY CONTAINS FEW FIGURES more extraordinary than Abraham Hannibal. Stolen from his parents in Africa and sold into slavery, he became general-in-chief of one of the leading white empires of his day. His great-grandson became one of the world's greatest poets, while other of his descendants became members of the leading royal families of Europe.

Destiny was kind to Hannibal from the beginning; instead of being sent to America, where he would have been at best a house servant, he was taken to Turkey. At that time, while Africans were languishing in slavery in America, some of their brothers, also from the jungles, were the pampered pets of European royalty, especially at the court of Russia.

Still a child, Hannibal was sold as a slave to Sultan Selim IV at Constantinople, where he attracted the attention of Count Raguinsky, the Russian ambassador. Wishing to take an unusual gift to the czar, Raguinsky secured Hannibal either by kidnapping or as a gift, and took him back to Russia.

Merry, vivacious, and intelligent, the ten-year-old boy captivated Peter the Great, who adopted him immediately. With Christina, Queen of Poland, as his godmother, Hannibal was baptized into the Christian faith. Peter gave him his own name, but the boy, whose real name was Ibrahim, wept so bitterly at the change that thereafter he was called Abraham, the Christian equivalent of his own name. Hannibal was later added as a tribute to his military skill. However, his parents, who later appeared on the scene, claimed that he was descended from the great Carthaginian and that his real name *was* Hannibal.

The lad showed special talent for mathematics and engineering and Peter sent him to Paris to study. There, as the czar's protégé, he was received in the highest circles. His exotic appearance won him the favor of the ladies of the gay court of the Duke of Orléans, who was then regent; indeed the duke himself offered Hannibal a high position if he would transfer his allegiance to him. But Hannibal, though preferring the gayer and more cultured French atmosphere, remained loyal to his master, even though at this time Peter, preoccupied with the affairs of state, had quite forgotten Hannibal who, finding himself without money, thought of returning on foot to Russia.

While Hannibal was pursuing his studies war broke out between France and Spain. He accepted a commission in the French army, serving with valor until he was wounded in the head. Soon afterward he returned to Russia where he became an officer in the engineers' corps, winning rapid promotion on his own merits.

About this time his people in Africa, discovering his whereabouts, sent a rich ransom for him, but he refused to leave his benefactor. Peter appointed him tutor in mathematics to the crown prince, later Peter II. As this post gave him great influence with the future ruler, he became of considerable importance to those engaged in court intrigue. As a result of this, fortune was to turn against him after the death of Peter the Great for the next sixteen years.

On Peter's death in 1735 the throne was seized by his wife, Catherine I, grandmother of Peter, the real heir, who was set aside, the chief power being in the hands of Prince Menshikov.

Menshikov, who was of humble origin, having started as a common soldier, wanted to marry his daughter to the young Peter. Knowing Hannibal's influence with Peter, he tried to bribe him. Hannibal, who had sworn to Peter the Great that he would protect his grandson, refused, and Menshikov, to stop his influence with the prince, sent him on a military mission to Siberia. Then to lengthen his stay he ordered him to take the exact measurements of the Great Wall of China, which was 1,500 miles long. Menshikov hoped that Hannibal would not survive the hardships of this undertaking.

Hannibal remained in Siberia until the death of Catherine in 1737. Learning that young Peter had ascended the throne, that Menshikov had been exiled, and that Dolgouriki, a former favorite of Peter the Great, was in control, he decided to return. But at Tomsk he was arrested. Dolgouriki feared his influence with Peter no less than Menshikov—and he was held there until Peter's death two years later.

Peter was succeeded by Anna the Bloody, a niece of Peter the Great. Once more Hannibal started for St. Petersburg, but when he reached it he was compelled to go into hiding, as he was suspected of belonging to the faction that wanted to put Elisabeth, daughter of Peter the Great and rightful heir, on the throne. Hannibal escaped, thanks to his friend Field-Marshal Munich, who smuggled him out of the city and sent him to inspect the fortifications on the Swedish border. This duty done, he was sent to a little village near the city of Reval where he spent the next twelve years of Anna's reign, almost forgotten.

On Anna's death, Elisabeth came to the throne, and grateful to Hannibal for his unswerving loyalty to the family of Peter the Great, she showered honors on him. Among her gifts were ten villages with thousands of white serfs. She wished him to remain at court, but remembering what his influence there had once cost him, he declined, and asked permission to return to Reval, where he was made commander.

But his retirement was short. He was one of the empire's leading engineers, and when a dispute arose with Sweden over the boundary in 1752, he was appointed head of the Russian commission to settle the matter. Still later, he was appointed commander-in-chief of the army. But in spite of all these honors, the title he cherished the most was "The Negro of Peter the Great."

Hannibal had other troubles, too—domestic ones. He had married a very beautiful woman, the daughter of a Greek captain named Dioper. During his long absences she had found consolation elsewhere and had presented to him a daughter who showed no African blood. Hannibal sued for divorce and the ensuing trial was one of the most celebrated of its day. It dragged on for fifteen years while scientists discussed at great length the question of whether the offspring of a black and white couple could be "pure" white. Hannibal finally won, whereupon the unfaithful wife, seeking to justify her actions, said, "That Negro is not of our race," She was punished severely. In addition to the court's censure, she was forced to do public penance and to spend the remainder of her life in a convent. As for the white daughter, Hannibal kept her in his house, gave her a good education, and left her considerable property but never permitted her to come into his presence.

While the case was pending, he married a titled German woman, Regina von Schellberg, by whom he had eleven children, all bonafide mulattoes, five of whom were sons, and all of whom attained distinction. The eldest, Ivan, was a naval commander who was victorious over the Turks at Navarin and was also the hero of the battle of Chesma. Later he was Governor of Ukraine and founded the city of Kherson. After a quarrel with Potemkin, the powerful favorite of Catherine the Great, he retired to his estates.

Another son, Joseph, was a naval commander and a navigator. His daughter, Nadejda, married Count Pushkin, whose grandfather had been privy counsellor to Peter the Great and whose father had borne the scepter at the coronation of Catherine the Great. Her son, Alexander Pushkin, was the famous poet.

Hannibal continued in favor under Catherine the Great, who appointed him to draw up plans for a canal linking St. Petersburg with Moscow. Finally he retired to his estates, immensely rich, and died there in 1782, over ninety years old.

Pushkin, who was born seventeen years after Hannibal's death, and who, in preparation for his book *The Negro of Peter the Great*, had gathered details from those who had known his illustrious ancester, describes him as "A pure Negro—flat nose, thick lips, woolly hair."

D. M. Wallace, British ambassador to Russia, says of him, "Hannibal, who died with the rank of Commander-in-Chief, was a Negro."

REFERENCES

Negroes always enjoyed favor at the Russian court. Peter III once kept the British ambassador waiting while he entertained himself with his sprightly little Negro Narcissus. His wife, Catherine the Great, in her *Memoirs* charged that Peter cared for Narcissus more than he did for her.

Eugene Schuyler, American diplomat, writing as late as 1883, said, "Negroes were also in esteem as indeed they have been of recent years. Volynsky sent from Astrakan a couple to Catherine in order to ingratiate himself with her, and Peter [the Great] had several."

One of the confidential agents of the last czar, Nicholas, was a Georgia Negro. George Thomas, who, coming to Russia from the United States as a valet, remained there and became one of the leading restaurant and cabaret owners. His night club was the rendezvous for Russian aristocracy.

Nicholas II also had a corps of fifteen Negroes of exceptional blackness. Of magnificent height and build, they were dressed in gorgeous exotic robes and jewelry. They were popularly known as the czar's bodyguard, but, as a former English army officer and interpreter, Owen Colmer, who lived in Russia twenty-four years, told me, their real purpose was to adorn the dining room. They were cared for by the czar and were married to Russian women.

According to *Notes and Queries* (Oct. 30, 1852, p. 411), the czarina of Russia sent to England in 1769 to buy Negro boys as attendants.

Pushkin, A. S., *The Negro of Peter the Great*.

Wallace, D. M., *Russia*, p. 271. New York, 1877.

Schuyler, E. S., *Peter the Great*, Vol. II, p. 438. New York, 1884.

ADDITIONAL REFERENCES

Adams, Russell L., *Great Negroes: Past and Present*, p. 5. Chicago, Afro-Am Publishing Co., 1963, 1964.

Fleming, B. J., and Pryde, M. J., *Distinguished Negroes Abroad*, pp. 166–170. Washington, D.C., The Associated Publishers, 1946.

Kemp, Ruth, "Alexander Pushkin." *Negro History Bulletin*, pp. 57–59, 61–62 (December, 1940), Association for the Study of Negro Life and History, Washington, D.C.

Pankhurst, Richard Keir Patrick, *An Introduction to the Economic History of Ethiopia from Early Times to 1800*, pp. 423–426. London, 1961.

Pushkin, Aleksander Sergeevich, *The Captain's Daughter and Other Tales*, trans. by T. Keane, pp. 419–466. London, New York, Toronto, Hobber & Stoughton, 1915.

International Literature, pp. 68–108.

Antonio Vieira

PORTUGAL'S GRANDEST PERSONAGE
(1608–1697)

FATHER ANTONIO VIEIRA is often acclaimed as Portugal's greatest orator; its greatest preacher; its greatest missionary; its greatest prose writer; one of the leading statesmen of his time; one of the world's greatest linguists; and to crown all, one of the noblest and most unselfish souls in the history of mankind.

Popes, kings, the great ones of Europe, sought his company and wanted to confer the highest honors on him. But he refused them. He could have been another Cardinal Richelieu, perhaps even a Pope, but he chose to remain a humble priest; instead of the salons of princes he prefered the huts of the wretched Indian and Negro slaves in whose passionate defense he made scores of powerful enemies.

"Vieira," says Larousse, "was a man of profound knowledge and one of the most vigorous spirits that Portugal has ever produced. Versed in the study of the ancient languages, he wrote Latin with the talent of Erasmus; spoke and wrote the principal languages of Europe and had learned, as if it were play, all the idioms of Brazil. He was in addition an exact and scrupulous historian, something rare in his day, and in his reports upon his missions in Brazil he has shown a great elevation of sentiments and ideals."

"He is superior to all the great writers of Portugal by the universality of his powerful gifts," says Carel. "The grandeur and the extreme variety of his deeds cast a brilliance upon the 17th Century, illuminating it entirely." He continues:

What a picture would his life present, could we but retrace it with colors worthy of it; what unheard of vicissitudes; what great events was he not, turn by turn, actor in and witness of? Preacher to the king of Portugal and of the most savage tribes of the New World, we see him now borne in triumph in the midst of 100,000 barbarians as the arbiter of peace and war; now persecuted; now outraged by his fellow-citizens; thrown a prisoner in the hold of a ship—one might say the tribulations and the zeal of a new Paul. But, like Paul, he appealed to the justice of Caesar and he comes from the hold of the ship but to go into the chapel of the kings of Lisbon, to thunder according to the fine expression of his biographer, "against the hunting down and the sale of men, with accents worthy of a Chrysostom or a Bossuet." Great orator and pacifier, conquering 1800 miles of country, he is charged with heresy and thrown for 26 months into the dungeons of the Inquisition. His enemies wish to dishonor him, and so stifle his voice. But Pope Clement X takes him out of their jurisdiction. His preaching at Rome excites a general applause and an admiring public proclaims him "the prince of Catholic orators of his time." But neither the favor of the Pope, nor Queen Christina can make him fix his home in the Eternal City, and like a prophet of old he returned to the solitudes of the New World to die there full of days and of merit in the midst of his beloved savages.

Vieira was born of Portuguese parents either in Lisbon or Bahia, Brazil, on February 6, 1608. His grandfather, who was in the service of the Count of Unhao, fell in love with a Negro woman who also worked there, and married her after a scandal. Of this union Christopher Vieira Ravasco, the father of Vieira, was born. Later Ravasco served in the household of John IV and was raised to the nobility. He married Maria Azevedo, a maid of honor. Before going to the palace, Ravasco served as a secretary in the Civil Court of Appeal at Bahia, where, according to some, Vieira was born.

Another account has it that Vieira was born in Lisbon and that his parents took him to Bahia when he was eight years old. One thing is certain, however: he had his elementary education in Brazil and was a dunce at school.

The fault, however, seems to have been with the teachers and their method of instruction rather than with their pupil. Vieira, whose individuality was pronounced, could not respond to their dry-as-dust knowledge. Finally, he was placed among the Jesuits, for whose teachings he had a liking.

Suddenly such a great change occurred in him that some historians attributed it to the miraculous intervention of the Virgin, who, they said, had appeared to him. The slothful schoolboy was transformed into an intellectual prodigy. His penetration, his quick perception, his sureness of grasp, his keen intelligence, vivacity, and ready wit amazed everyone. So remarkable was his mastery of all subjects that he was given his degree in theology without ever having taken a regular course in it—something exceedingly rare.

At fifteen he became a Jesuit novitiate, and later a professor of rhetoric. At eighteen he had composed commentaries on the *Metamorphoses* of Ovid and the tragedies of Seneca, as well as several commentaries on the historic books of the Bible and the Song of Solomon.

At twenty-five he was professor of dogmatic theology, a position he held until he was thirty-two. In the intervening years he had been working hard to alleviate the lot of Indian and Negro slaves.

Political events were to change the course of his life. Portugal not only proclaimed her independence from Spain, but in Brazil she was victorious over Holland, thanks chiefly to the brilliant generalship of a former Negro slave, Henri Dias. The Brazilian viceroy, Dom Jorge de Mascarenha, sent a delegation to the King of Portugal to congratulate him on both these events, and Vieira was appointed its head.

He arrived in Portugal at a critical time. The cause of independence was languishing. The country needed a leader, who with his fire, eloquence, and patriotism would keep enthusiasm alive. But where to find him? When Vieira made his congratulatory address at court, the king and almost everyone else present felt that this newcomer from America was the much-needed individual. The king appointed him as his spokesman to the people, a task that Vieira performed so well that soon all Portugal was in a frenzy of patriotism.

John IV next sent him as the head of a mission to the leading courts of Europe to seek recognition of Portuguese independence and to combat Spanish influence. Thanks to his tact, his persuasiveness, and his ability to preach in all the leading European languages with eloquence undimmed, he performed the delicate task with skill.

Among those with whom he had to deal was the shrewd Cardinal Mazarin, successor to Richelieu. At the Congress of Münster, before the representatives of the leading powers of Europe, he successfully opposed the plenipotentiaries of Spain and won full recognition for his country. His grateful king thereupon urged him to accept the prime ministership and a bishopric.

Vieira declined both honors. He planned, as soon as affairs were settled in Portugal, to return to Brazil to fight the battles of the downtrodden Negroes and Indians.

But for the next ten years he was detained in Portugal. During this period he was its most important figure. His humility, devotion, and unselfishness were such that the king came to regard him as his own son. He reformed the kingdom, aided in the development of the colonies, improved the army and navy, and kept alive the war against Spain, being in turn, legislator, financier, soldier, and sailor.

To aid commerce, Vieira had a law passed forbidding the seizure of the goods of merchants. (Spain had written confiscation into all the Portuguese codes.) At that time, too, the nobility, the clergy, and the military held all the honors, while the merchants were regarded with contempt. Vieira enhanced their standing by having titles conferred on some of the leading traders and shipbuilders. He abolished discrimination against Jewish merchants and newly converted Christians and their children; created a national bank for Portugal; founded a powerful company for trade with Brazil; and labored to establish a company for the East Indies that would bind them still closer to the mother country—but here opposition was too great. Later, when Portugal began to lose her vast East Indian possessions, his opponents saw their error.

Vieira also reduced waste by the rich and alleviated the misery of the poor by bringing about a more equitable distribution of taxes. He said in an address to Parliament, "Taxes are the flesh and blood of the people. They must be equally distributed among all. The war we have to maintain puts us in an abnormal situation, and in face of such pressing needs, liberality on our part becomes merely justice."

For the war against Spain he drew up a plan of campaign which, according to military experts, was worthy of the ablest general and which led to the victories of Elvas, Ameixal, and Castello Roderigo. In every way he was the most brilliant figure in the kingdom.

His political foresight was almost uncanny. When France recaptured Dunkirk, and John IV, his ministers, and courtiers went to chant a *Te Deum* in honor of the occasion, Vieira protested. "Your Majesty," he said, "it is an occasion for sorrow rather than felicitation. The Dutch now maintain a fleet before Dunkirk to assure passage of their vessels in the English Channel. They are the allies of France and are going to use that fleet against us. When I was in Amsterdam I noticed their inclination that way. Now they can do whatever they wish at Pernambuco. Without shedding a drop of blood they can prevent our revictuallment." Holland, at that time, was mistress of the seas.

When asked what should be done, Vieira said, "We must get fifteen frigates with thirty pieces of cannon each."

The other counsellors opposed his project, declaring that there was no danger. Six months later, however, it was discovered that the Dutch had fortified themselves at Tamarica, Brazil, and were again threatening Portugal. The fleet suggested by Vieira was then seen as a necessity.

But the war with Spain had depleted the treasury. When the ministers declared they could find no money, Vieira said, "With this patched, rusty old cloak of mine I will do so." Going among the merchants he had befriended he secured the same day the equivalent of $300,000, which was enough for the purpose.

During these years he lived simply, giving to the poor all that exceeded his bare needs and presenting at court a shabby figure in his patched frock and shoes in contrast to the rich laces and brocades of others. He refused to accept any pay for his services to his country. On his mission to Holland he had been entrusted with a large sum of money. Later, the king, finding that Vieira had taken nothing for himself, sent him a large sum by the Marquis of Niza, bidding him use it for the renewal of his library. But Vieira declined, saying that his breviaries were in good order. "I serve my country," he said. "I do not let my country serve me."

Once when an emissary of a nobleman came to him with 6000 pieces of gold, asking his support for a certain cause, Vieira, who had already decided to support him, said, "Tell your master he may count on me, but as for his gift, I am going to show my forbearance by giving you a chance to leave peaceably instead of throwing you out as the insolence of his offer warrants."

He did much to reform the clergy and to show what it meant to be a real servant of Christ. At Maragnon, when the hospital lacked beds, he promptly gave up his own. While his frock or his shoes could yet be patched he refused to buy others. When unjust accusations were made against him he kept silent. "On entering my chamber," he said, "I saw my crucifix, and recalling that my Master kept silent, I resolved to do the same."

In his addresses to Parliament he spoke freely to the deputies, telling them that many of the present evils were due to the fact that some of them sought place and honor, instead of letting the honor and the place seek them.

But always uppermost in his mind were the Indians and the Negroes in Brazil, and at last he announced his departure. The king begged him to remain, but he went nevertheless.

In Brazil he attacked slavery, for which the planters mobbed and nearly killed him. When his friends counselled prudence he replied, "If, to please the mob, we approved injustice today, this same mob tomorrow, on reflection, will declare us unworthy of our ministry."

He saw his duty and he did it, come what might. On Easter Sunday he preached a sermon against slavery in its very stronghold, that is, before the viceroy, his ministers, and the leading slaveholders and slavedealers.

Taking as his text Matthew IV, on the temptations of Christ and how Christ had resisted the offers of the devil, he excoriated slavery.

Souls are cheap today. Between the promises that Satan made formerly for a single soul and the price that he pays today for a mass of them, what a difference! There is no other country in the world where the Devil would obtain a better bargain today than amongst you. He has no need to offer you kingdoms, or cities, or even hamlets. He has only to show you one or two slaves to have you fall in adoration at his feet.

For a Negro, your soul!

This Negro will be your slave during his life, but in return your soul will be my slave during all eternity. Such is the pact Satan has made with you.

As they writhed under his words, he continued:

Ah, those riches! Ah, your mansions, your opulence, your fine robes and mantles—if one were to wring them, how much blood of your unhappy slaves would drip from them.

You will ask me who will do your work if you free your slaves, but I reply: Better far is it that your wives should do their own work, fetch their wood and water and go to heaven like the Samaritan than to have them served like queens here on earth and go to hell like Jezebel.

Go to Turkey, go to hell, if you will. There is not a Turk or a demon in hell who will not tell you it is a damnable thing to deprive a human being of his liberty. Moreover, your own common sense tells you that.

Then he began to plead their better natures:

Give to the sky this triumph; to hell this humiliation; to our country this remedy; to the Portuguese nation, this example of generosity; to ourselves this glory in the eyes of the universe. Let the pagans know that God was not in error when he chose us to be the conquerors and the preachers of His gospel in Brazil. Show to the world that there is still truth; that there is still the fear of God; a soul, conscience and salvation.

In his oratory what clearness, what passion! He touched the hearts of all and wrung penitence and promises from many. But he knew that a mere appeal would not end slavery. He had a tribunal elected to examine carefully claims of both proprietors and slaves—one that would give judgments, subject to no appeal.

He had all the Indians captured in war set free, and all those who had been inherited as slaves were given the choice of leaving their masters or of staying with them. As for his "brothers, the blacks," he was able to do little for them since the slave holders held on to them too firmly. Furthermore, he was forced to yield in the case of those Indians captured from cannibal tribes.

Next he plunged into the immense forests of the Amazon where he saw the slave hunters at work. This so stirred him that he decided to go to Portugal and seek an order from the king abolishing these terrible manhunts.

Arriving in Lisbon, he painted a vivid picture of the wealth of Brazil to the king and his cabinet; of the numbers of Indians and the possibility of their being made into useful citizens; and then of the greed and cruelty of the slave hunters, who were ruining everything.

The king readily gave him the desired power. Returning to Brazil, he checked the marauders, and going 1800 miles into the wilderness, he began civilizing the Indians, teaching them agriculture, lessening war among them, and improving Brazilian commerce.

He won such power over the Indians that in 1659 when Holland declared war on Portugal and the planters thought the only way to prevent the Indians from aiding the enemy was to make immediate war on them, he went among the Indians and easily obtained from them a promise of allegiance to Portugal, which was faithfully kept.

Returning to Pernambuco, Vieira devoted himself to the cause of the Negro slaves. Pointing out that the blacks had once saved Brazil from Holland, he denounced their treatment as the worst ingratitude. The infuriated slave holders provoked a riot against him, threw him, chained like a slave, into the hold of a ship, and "exiled" him to Portugal.

He arrived there to find his friend John IV dead. John's son Alphonso, a dissolute minor of low morals, was on the throne with his mother as regent.

The queen dowager received Vieira cordially and invited him to preach in the royal chapel. In a fiery sermon he told of the treatment of the Indians and the Negroes, and of their protectors, the missionaries. "Once," he said, "our ships went out, taking preachers in the name of Christ; now they return with them to Portugal in the name of the devil."

So great was the effect of what he said that the queen ordered the immediate recall of the governor and decreed so severe a punishment for Vieira's enemies that Vieira found it necessary to plead for them.

Vieira had planned to return to Brazil at once but he found that his services were urgently needed at home. The young king was scandalizing everyone by his debauchery. Vieira was named head of a delegation to check him.

The king yielded and exiled his favorites. But when he came into his majority, he vented his full wrath on Vieira, denouncing him to the Portuguese Inquisition because of one of his sermons, "The Reign of Christ on Earth Consummated."

The Inquisition threw him into a dungeon where he remained from October 2, 1665, to December 24, 1667.

It investigated his conduct and teachings, only to find them flawless. As a last resort it dug into his ancestry, hoping to prove that his swarthy skin, frizzled hair, and Negroid face were due to Jewish or Moorish lineage, in which case he could be thrust out of the Church as a heretic.

His parentage was carefully traced. Noblemen and peasants were summoned to tell what they knew about it. But the worst that his enemies could prove was that he was of West African ancestry, which was not considered heretical, because these pagan blacks had not refused Christ, but on coming to live among Christians, had readily accepted his teachings.

Soon after this investigation Alphonso died, and Philip II, a friend of Vieira's, came to the throne. The Inquisition, a docile instrument of political power, not only freed him but tried to honor him by endorsing the disputed sermon. Vieira had determined to crush the Inquisition, however. He prepared a scorching indictment of its methods, and sent it to Pope Clement X, who then ordered the Portuguese Inquisition suppressed.

In 1669 Vieira was again preaching to the royal family. Then he was sent on an important mission to Rome, where the Pope kept him for the next six years. This was the period of his most brilliant eloquence. He preached often before the Pope and the Sacred College of Cardinals, his language preserving the same independence as when he was addressing humble whites, Negroes, and Indians.

Whenever he spoke at St. Peter's Cathedral it was crowded. Once, according to Carel, eighteen cardinals, together with members of Italian nobility and strangers of distinction, were forced to fight their way through the crowd to reach the seats reserved for them.

Pope Clement consulted with him at length on how to end the injustices of the Spanish Inquisition and his advice served greatly to modify the activities of that oppressive body.

Queen Christina of Sweden, then living at Rome, was enamored of him and spoke of him as being her father confessor, an honor which he, nevertheless, had not accepted. At her salon he met some of the leading scientists and learned men of Europe, who praised him for his eloquence, the universality of his knowledge, and his modesty.

But he longed to return to Brazil, preferring his humble Indians and Negroes to the company of the great. He was then nearly seventy, and he hoped to spend his last days among them.

At last he wrung a reluctant consent from the Pope to go. Queen Christina tried to retain him by letters, prayers, tears—in vain. He sailed from Portugal on January 27, 1681.

At his departure Clement showered upon him every mark of his tender solicitude. To make sure that his friend would not be molested again, the Pope issued an order exempting him from "all jurisdiction of the venerable Inquisition-General for every kind of cause, even specific." This meant that no one could sit in judgment on him save Clement himself. No higher mark of the Pope's confidence was possible.

In Brazil, despite malaria and the loss of one eye, he continued his appointed task with his usual energy. Toward his eightieth year he was so lame that he walked with great difficulty. Then, to his sorrow, he saw that the Jesuits were aiding in the exploitation of the blacks and the Indians. He protested and this brought him into sharp disfavor with the order to which he had been so loyal.

The Jesuits struck at him through his brother, Bernard Ravasco, one of the highest judges in the colony, accusing Bernard of murder. When Vieira protested to the governor-general, that official retorted, "The assassination needed only your presence to make it complete. You are a perpetual troublemaker." Later the governor-general and his friends were found guilty of this murder.

Vieira's nephew Gonsalo went to Lisbon to protest to King Philip, who blamed Vieira for everything and refused to listen. Undaunted, Vieira continued to speak out, until in his zeal he broke one of the rules of the order, namely, that no one was to show any particular favor in private life to any particular member of the order. During a conversation, he spoke strongly in favor of a certain priest, naming him as the one best fitted to go to Rome to plead with the Pope against slavery. For this he was deprived of a voice in the counsels of the Jesuits.

Vieira, however, sent a delegation to the Pope, who not only quashed the ruling but extolled Vieira. But the old fighter was not to be cheered by the decision. He died on July 18, 1697, a month before the return of the delegation. His last words were, "God is the Master. Let Him do with me what seems best to Him."

With his death Brazil realized his value. All classes and races joined in mourning for him. When the Pope's verdict arrived it was read aloud to the people in triumph by his friends.

His body was taken to Lisbon. The king, the dignitaries of the Church, the nobility, and the members of Parliament came in state to the pier to receive the ship that had brought his body. He was buried with great pomp at San Roch, the wealthiest church of Portugal, and a statue was commissioned in his honor. In scholarly circles he was hailed as "The Cicero of Lusitania."

"No modern philanthropist," says Brucker, "equals Vieira in his zeal and his eloquence for the weaker races. In poverty Jesus Christ instituted a new sacrament, and Vieira, by putting himself in the place of the poor, thus transformed himself into them by a sort of consecration."

Vieira taught not only simplicity in daily life, but also in writing and speaking. He said:

To preach in order to make a great name, that is the spirit of worldliness. But never hesitate to say what ought to be said, even if the price of doing so is losing one's reputation. That is the true spirit of Christ. What if your hearers do not like it? That is their affair. Does the doctor worry about the particular taste of the patient when he wishes to cure him? What if the medicine be bitter, provided it cures? Similarly what if our words hurt, if they be necessary to improve conditions. It is for that that we are doctors of the soul.

The style of the preacher, he said:

Ought to be clear and distinct. Never fear that because you are easily understood, you are lacking in dignity. The stars are very distinct and very clear; they are not the less elevated for that. They furnish a guide to the peasant for his planting; to the sailor for his ship; to the astronomer a subject of study and observation. The peasant and the sailor both understand the stars without being able to read or write, while the astronomers, in spite of all their knowledge, always find something beautiful and infinite about them. So should be our sermons; stars, which all can see, yet which but few know how to measure.

Vieira's addresses were abundantly illustrated with examples drawn from everyday life. A speech, for instance, ought to be like a tree:

As the tree has its roots, trunks, branches, leaves, twigs, flowers, fruits, so ought also a sermon to have. It ought to have deep roots because it is founded on the gospel of Christ; it ought to have a trunk, that is to say, it ought to deal with a single subject; and the branches ought not to be bare but ornamented with leaves, which are the words; there should also be twigs, with which to punish errors; there must be flowers, that is thoughts new and delicate; finally, there must be fruit, because the fruit is the goal of every sermon.

Thus in such a tree, which we may truly call "The Tree of Life," there ought to be the usefulness of the fruit; the beauty of the flower; the vigor of the twigs; the ornament of the leaves; the nervure of the branches, but the whole arising from a single trunk and having its roots, not in the air, but in the profundity of the Word of God. Such ought to be our sermons. But they are not. What wonder if they do not bear fruit!

These translations give but a faint idea of his eloquence, for his sermons were pyrotechnic displays. He acted them with all the vividness of his tropical imagination. To show up the devil and man's wickedness, he would actually indict God, whom he would picture as sitting before him on a stool in the pulpit. Then taking up charge after charge, he would absolve God and place the blame on the devil. His fellow preachers, envious of his great popularity, accused him of sacrilege and clowning. But no one was ever known to sleep at his sermons. They were far too lively.

Soon after his death his writings appeared in fifteen volumes. As a writer he is linked with Camoëns, Portugal's greatest poet. "If," says Lobo, "our language were to be lost and with it all our works with the exception of the Lusiades and the works of Vieira, the prose and the poetry of Portugal in all its native purity and its freshness would revive."

Carel says of his style:

His soul, with its generous ardor, gave to his thoughts as well as to his style that communicative warmth, that which genius alone could not. There lies the great charm of Vieira. Passion animates and colors all his writings. The truth! That is the muse that inspires him; there is the very soul of his eloquence. At the same time his heart, which was devoted to the good of humanity, found in his religious convictions a superhuman energy. Betrayed, persecuted, banished, he never yielded. And with the force of his eloquence he changed defeats into triumphs. When he seemed beaten, he arose and uttered one of those sublime cries which struck terror among his triumphant enemies. Never was Vieira more eloquent than in a struggle. Like to the great commanders, there came to him sudden inspiration—illuminations of genius.

Nunes said, "Vieira unites vigor with grace; boldness of conception and correctness of the design with the powerful originality of a Michael Angelo."

On July 18, 1897, on the 200th anniversary of his death, ceremonies in his honor were held in Portugal, Brazil, and Rome. At the Church of San Roch in Lisbon, where he used to preach, literary and scientific societies of all kinds were represented, as well as the king, the Pope, and Parliament.

REFERENCES

J. L. D'Azevedo says, "The future nobleman [Vieira's father] had as his mother a mulatto servant in the house of the Counts. (*Historia de Antonio Vieira*, Vol. I, p. 9. Lisbon, 1918.) See also the testimony of the witnesses regarding Vieira's ancestry in the appendix in the second volume of this work.

Lobo, F. A., *Padre Antonio Vieira*. Coimbra, 1897.

Carel, E., *Vieira*. Paris, 1879.

Silva, *Diccionario Biographico Portugez*, Vol. I, pp. 287–293, and Vol. XXII, pp. 369–383. Lisbon, 1858. (For bibliography and iconography.)

Robertson, J. P., and W. P. Robertson, *Letters on Paraguay*, Vol. II. London, 1839. (For the activities of the Jesuits.)

John VI of Portugal

John VI

KING OF PORTUGAL AND MAKER OF MODERN BRAZIL
(1767–1826)

ON NOT MANY SOVEREIGNS does opinion diverge so widely as on John VI, King of Portugal, Algarve, and Brazil. Some historians call him weak, indecisive, and indolent; others hail him as one of the ablest and wisest rulers in history.

The real verdict, it appears, depends upon what are considered the essential qualities for rulership. If ruthlessness and double-dealing are among them, then John VI was less than a weakling compared with his great adversary, Napoleon; but if peace and a desire to cultivate the arts of peace are preferable, then John ranks above Napoleon, for John created while Napoleon destroyed.

By nature few were less fitted than John VI for the warlike times in which he lived. A devout Christian, he tried to rule by enlightenment and love, perhaps because of which he was a failure at politics. But these qualities helped make him one of the best-loved monarchs in history. And even his worst enemies agree that his private life, in a dissolute age, was unimpeachable.

Born on May 13, 1767, John VI came to power as regent in 1792, when his mother, Queen Marie, lost her mind. His ambition was to restore Portugal to her former glory. Through the encouragements of Prince Henry the Navigator in the fifteenth century, she had been the first maritime power to achieve real supremacy. She commissioned explorers and navigators, the first great pioneers—Marco Polo, Magellan, Cabral, Vasco de Gama—who circumnavigated the globe and claimed for her vast possessions on which the sun did not set. India, Brazil, West Africa, and the South Sea Islands were hers. For a brief period in the sixteenth century she was the leading country of the world.

The year 1588 was the turning point. The impulsive but courageous young king, Don Sebastian, invaded Morocco and was defeated and slain by its ruler, Abdel-Malik. Don Sebastian left no heir and Philip of Spain seized the throne. A long war followed, which so weakened Portugal that England took away much of her trade and some of her possessions.

After independence was won from Spain in 1640 Portugal revived under John IV, but after him the country was afflicted with profligate rulers, one of whom, John V, had more mistresses than even Louis XV of France.

Later there was the great Lisbon earthquake of 1785, which practically wiped out the best in Portuguese culture. When John VI, then Prince of Brazil, became regent, he found that though the country had revived somewhat under the able leadership of the Marquis de Pombal, the masses of the peasantry, illiterate and steeped in ignorance, had been reduced to great poverty by an exploiting clergy and an equally greedy nobility. John, who had been carefully trained by some of the leading savants of the time, among them the great mathematician Franzini, set about the task of reform.

He dug canals and built several great roads; established military and naval schools; founded a number of academies, free schools, and libraries; sent students to be educated in the leading universities of Europe; improved the museums of natural history and botany; created a school of charts which soon became the equal of that in Paris; encouraged agriculture, commerce, industry, mining, and metallurgy, and all branches of art and science. In the archives of the marine and the colonies at Lisbon are to be found a number of plans drawn after his orders for the improvement of the rich colonies of Portugal in Africa and India. Carrying his improvements into Brazil, he founded thirteen new towns there. Thanks to his energies a new era of Portuguese development was beginning when the French Revolution exploded.

John, fearing the influence of the Revolution on his people, joined England and Spain against France, but soon withdrew his aid. Then came Napoleon, "walking on the heads of the kings of Europe." John, in his corner of the continent, decided to play a middle course. He granted France and England equal commercial rights, a step which angered both countries. Napoleon, charging him with partiality to Britain, forced him to close his ports, inflicted a heavy fine on him, and seized several of his colonies.

With the Treaty of Amiens came a lull in the Napoleonic Wars. When they started again, Napoleon ordered John to close all his ports to England, who, in turn, offered him the alternative of war or an alliance. John succeeded in gaining a brief period of neutrality, during which he again devoted himself to the improvement of his kingdom.

Napoleon, however, had decided to rule all Europe. The first dynasty he intended to overthrow was the Braganzas, John's family; the next, the Bourbons. As a preliminary to ousting the Bourbons, he made an alliance with them and issued an edict from Versailles: "The House of Braganza has ceased to reign."

Napoleon's war with Prussia, however, saved John for a year. In October, 1807, orders came from Napoleon to close all Portuguese ports to England and to imprison all British subjects and confiscate their properties. England, thereupon, descended on Portugal and bottled up a large part of her fleet in the Tagus. At the same time Marshal Junot with an army of 30,000 Frenchmen and Spaniards was marching on Lisbon with orders to take John, dead or alive.

In this dilemma John was offered safe conduct to Brazil by George III of England, and hoping to preserve his dynasty and his kingdom, he accepted.

Moreover, John had always had a longing for the tropics. Was that the call of his African blood? His proudest title was "Prince of Brazil." He would go to this country of eternal summer, away from the intrigue and strife of Old Europe, and there create the dream empire which he had tried to build without success in Europe.

With his court, his servants, and 13,000 of his leading subjects he sailed for South America. And none too soon. Marshal Junot was only six miles away from Lisbon.

After a difficult voyage of three months John arrived in Brazil and received a very warm welcome. But he had come to a land that was primitive. Up to this time Brazil had largely been a goal for European adventurers who exploited the natives, accumulated wealth as rapidly as possible, and returned to Europe to enjoy it.

Economically, and in nearly every other way, Brazil was in virtual bondage to the mother country. All manufacture, save of sugar and rum, was illegal. Learning of any kind was forbidden to all but a select few. Except for approved religious books, the importation of literature was strictly prohibited.

It also suffered from underpopulation. The immense region had, exclusive of the Indians, only 3,600,000 souls, most of whom were Negro slaves. As for the remainder, they were largely of mixed European, Negro, and Indian strain.

John began by giving Brazil a government such as no other colony in the New World then enjoyed. De Santarem has summarized his activities there as follows:

Having given the Brazilians permission to exercise all kinds of industrial manufacture, he established military and civil tribunals; councils of administration; a prefecture of police; a police force; a treasury; a council of finance; a bank; a royal printery; a powder factory. Then he instituted at Minaes Geraes, under the presidency of the captain-general, a council for the civilizing of the Indians.

He gave prizes to those who introduced useful plants into Brazil; established a military hospital, and schools of anatomy, surgery, and medicine. He created a Royal Academy for the instruction of mathematics, physics, chemistry, metallurgy, natural history, and the military sciences. He opened to the public his own library and founded a public library at Rio de Janeiro. He improved the Botanical Garden at Lagoa and sent there a large number of plants brought from Cayenne and Asia.

To this ruler Brazil was indebted for the large number of tea trees planted in the Botanical Garden and at Santa Cruz. Through funds provided by him the learned mineralogist Napion was able to do research and write the first essays on the resistance, elasticity, and hardness of metals, as well as on the principal woods of Brazil.

A liberal in the matters of religion and trade, John proclaimed religious freedom in Brazil and created a free port at Goa. He encouraged immigration and brought in colonists from the Azores to whom he gave land, money, and implements for agriculture.

He established towns in the interior, which contributed much to the civilizing of the Indians, and brought 100 Swiss families to Brazil to settle, giving them land free from taxation.

To encourage the farmers, he ordered that estates, especially sugar plantations and their crops, should not be seized outright for debt, but rather only a part of their incomes. He developed interior communications by opening great routes into the interior and finishing those that had been begun. He ordered renewed exploration of the great rivers, Madeira, Tapajós, Kingu, and Arinos, and by so doing, opened navigation from Villa Bella as far as Pará. Navigation of the Cuiabá through the Arinos and through the Tapajós was also opened and couriers established on these routes. In this region John founded thirty-one new towns.

He also encouraged mining and established a fine iron foundry at Morro de Pilar, under the direction of the learned metallurgist, Ferreira de Cama, and another at Ipanema. To encourage the building of houses in Rio de Janeiro he exempted those of more than one floor from taxes for twenty years, and those of one floor for ten years.

He built the superb theatre of St. John; an immense building to house the treasury and the mint; and magnificent barracks. In Bahai he build beautiful gardens; public promenades; a Stock Exchange; and a library. At Pernambuco he erected breakwaters to protect the port of Recife. He encouraged manufacture by suppressing all duties on raw materials.

Passionately fond of music, he brought fifty singers from Lisbon, nearly all Italians and increased the number of musicians in his palace orchestra to 100.

He invited novelists, dramatists, and musical composers to Brazil, one of whom was the celebrated Marcus Portugal, thus aiding in developing the natural talent of the Brazilians for these arts.

To encourage painting he brought from France in 1816 a colony of artists, headed by Lebreton of the Academy of Fine Arts; Debret, the historical painter; and Taunay, a landscape artist.

All of this was not accomplished without friction, however.

John had to contend with the rivalry that had long existed between the Portuguese and the native Brazilians. The former, being from the mother country, regarded themselves superior, while the latter regarded the newcomers as intruders.

In John's wake, moreover, a host of needy adventurers had come, eager to exploit anyone. John also had marital and political quarrels with his wife Charlotte Joachine de Bourbon, sister of Ferdinand VII of Spain. She was unfaithful to him. "The morals of the Court," says Armitage, "were at the lowest ebb. The private character of the Regent [John VI] was unimpeachable, but the infidelities of his consort were so notorious that her Royal Spouse lived apart from her in consequence." Nevertheless, while the rulers of Europe were engaged in ruinous wars, John VI was building in Brazil a kingdom that was to give him such prestige that he was able to win nearly all of his demands at the Vienna Peace Conference in 1815.

On March 20, 1816, on the death of his demented mother, John came into power in his own name with the title "King of the United Kingdom of Portugal, Brazil, and Algarve." The leading powers of Europe sent their ambassadors to Rio de Janeiro to congratulate him. The same year he arranged a marriage between his son and heir Dom Pedro and Archduchess Leopoldina, daughter of Emperor Francis I of Austria, father-in-law of Napoleon.

Portuguese affairs were now to demand John's closer attention. Ravaged by the war that had been fought there between Wellington and Napoleon, Portugal was in a very wretched state. Junot had pillaged the country of immense quantities of gold and art, and the English had been almost as greedy. Victorious England had made Lord Beresford governor of Portugal, to the discontent of the people.

To aggravate matters, Portugal was now in reality a colony of Brazil. The head of the government was in Rio de Janeiro, thus making it the first and only American country ever to rule over a European one. Documents needing the king's signature had to be sent to Brazil, thus causing a delay of months. The Portuguese clamored for John's presence, until Lord Beresford had to come to Brazil to urge him to return.

John, who had found Brazil a paradise, hated to leave. Moreover, the Brazilians were pleading with him to stay. He delayed his departure until the European powers sent him a sharp note. He finally sailed on April 6, 1821, for Europe with the deepest regret.

John was welcomed in Portugal with extravagant joy. Conditions had changed with the war, however. One result of it was the clamor for greater rule by the people. Parliament prepared a democratic constitution, which John signed. This was opposed by the queen and her son, Dom Miguel. Civil war followed but John was later successful and the queen was banished.

No sooner was this settled than other troubles arose. Brazil having enjoyed rule over Portugal, as it were, objected to returning to the status of a colony. To the regent Dom Pedro, son and heir of John, it gave the alternative of becoming emperor of an independent Brazil or of being ousted. Pedro, in this crisis, reluctantly chose the former. He had sworn eternal loyalty to his father and had even sent him a letter written in his own blood to that effect. But John had foreseen this event. His last words whispered to Pedro on his leaving for Europe were, "Whatever happens, do not let the government of Brazil pass out of the hands of a Braganza." John signed the Act of Independence with heavy heart. The loss became the great anguish of his life until his death on March 30, 1826. He loved Brazil more than any other land on earth and had hoped to return there some day.

De Santarem says of John VI:

He was endowed with a prodigious memory and cited often and to the point historical facts, notably those of his own country. . . . He acquired a great deal of precise knowledge of the principal countries of Europe and on those who directed the cabinets. He was well informed on the intrigues of their courtesans, and knew the details of their private lives.

We, who have known this king, and have talked with several statesmen of his cabinet, can certify that his opinion was always of the wisest; that he was endowed with a profound knowledge of men and affairs and that we were often astonished by the facility with which he grasped the most difficult situations. John VI was beloved by all the sovereigns of his time, and received from them many proofs of their friendship and esteem. He was the first of the dynasty of Braganza to to whom England sent the Order of the Garter. The czar of Russia, and the kings of France and Denmark also sent him their decorations. John welcomed strangers with great affability and gave them magnificent presents.

REFERENCES

As regards his personal appearance, John VI was stout and unprepossessing. As proof of his Negro strain, we have, in addition to his portrait, a precise account from Laura, Duchess d'Abrantès, wife of Marshal Junot, French ambassador to Portugal. Speaking of a uniform of her husband's to which John had taken a fancy, she said:

"The first valet of the Prince Regent [John VI] came to ask if the French ambassador would kindly lend him his hussar's uniform so that the tailor of His Royal Highness could be enabled to make him one like it, as well as for the young prince, Dom Pedro.

"As I did not know the Prince of Brazil [John VI] then, I could not laugh at thus imagining him decked out in the uniform of a hussar, with his great abdomen, his thick legs, his enormous head with its Negro hair, which moreover was quite in harmony with his thick lips, his African nose, and the color of his skin." (Abrantès, Duchess d', "*Mémoires Secrètes,*" p. 220. Paris, 1837. *Memoirs of Napoleon,* Vol. I, pp. 290-304. London, Universal Classic Library, 1901.)

The wife of John VI, who was the sister of the King of Spain, seems also to have been Negroid, according to this French duchess, who says that the queen's skin was brown and her hair "dry and woolly."

Since the King of Portugal was Negroid, it follows that members of his nobility also were. The Duchess of Abrantès speaking of the Duchess of Alafoes, John's aunt, said, "Her skin is dark, so very dark that one would hardly ever take her for a European . . . a grand dame of such remarkable beauty that she could well say: 'I am brown, but comely: Oh Daughters of Zion.' "

The duchess also said that on entering Portugal she was struck by the Negroid appearance of the people. "The Portuguese," she says, "have thick lips, Negroid noses, and black hair which is often woolly."

Spain and Portugal both had a Negro strain, not only from the Moors, but from Negro slavery, which began in 1441 and lasted until the emancipation in 1773.

Nicolas Clenard (1495-1542), a Belgian traveler who visited Portugal, said that the bulk of the population was Negroid. This has been denied by later writers but it certainly was true of southern Portugal. In the northern parts whites of Teutonic stock predominated.

Of the number of Negroes in Portugal a century after the introduction of slavery, M. W. Williams says:

"The rural lands were converted into extensive estates held by absentee landlords and worked by large armies of black bondsmen recently brought from Africa. Soon the population of Algarve was almost completely Negro and by the middle of the 16th century, blacks outnumbered whites in Lisbon, itself. As the intermarriage between the races went on from the beginning, within a few generations Ethiopian blood was generally diffused throughout the nation, but it was notably pronounced in the south and among the lower classes." (*People and Politics of Latin America*, p. 100. Boston, 1930.)

John VI was a descendant of John IV, who, in turn, was a lineal descendant of the illegitimate son of John I. John VI's father, Pedro III, who was also strikingly Negroid in appearance, married his niece Marie Françoise, John's mother. The Negro strain in the Portuguese royal houses may thus be traced through a long period prior to John. The famous Prince Henry the Navigator, who married into the English royal family, was probably also of Negro descent. Charles II of England married a Braganza.

ADDITIONAL REFERENCES

People and Politics of Latin America, p. 100. Boston, 1930.
Santarem, Viscount de, *Biographie Universelle* (see "John VI"). 1858.
Armitage, John, *History of Brazil*. London, 1836.
Oevras, Count de, *Memoirs of the Court of Portugal*. London, 1827.

Chevalier de St. Georges

Chevalier de St. Georges

DAZZLING BLACK NOBLEMAN OF VERSAILLES
(1745–1799)

THE ADVENTURES of Chevalier de St. Georges were so astonishing, his talents so superlatively brilliant, that an account of his life reads like an incredibly romantic novel with a perfect hero.

He was the most dazzling and fascinating figure at the most splendid court in Europe. As a violinist, pianist, poet, musical composer, and actor, he was phenomenal; as a swordsman he so far eclipsed the best of his time that in his prime none could match him; as a marksman none could pull a trigger with such unerring aim; as a soldier and commander he performed prodigious feats on the field of battle; as a dancer, swimmer, horseman, and skater he was the most graceful in a land supreme for its grace and elegance; in the matter of dress he was the model of his day, setting the fashions of England and France; a King of France, a future King of England, and royal princes sought his company; and to crown all, he possessed a spirit of rare generosity, kindliness, and rectitude.

Chevalier de St. Georges was born in Guadeloupe, West Indies, on Christmas Day, 1745. His mother was a black woman of extraordinary beauty named Naomi; his father was the rich Marquis Jean de Boullogne, governor of the island, later King's Counsellor, Grand Chancellor of France, and High Treasurer of the Order of the Holy Spirit.

At the age of thirteen St. Georges went to France. According to one report he was a runaway; according to another his father, proud of his offspring's precocity, took him there to study. The latter version is probably true, for the best tutors in Paris were engaged for him. His mornings were devoted to the study of music, literature, science, and similar subjects; afternoons were spent in fencing, marksmanship, riding, and physical exercises, in all of which the West Indian lad excelled his fellows.

At fifteen he had defeated the best amateur swordsmen in Paris and at seventeen there was no professional in that city to equal him. When only twenty-one he defeated Faldoni, the renowned fencing champion of Italy. His prowess in other branches of sports was also remarkable.

Without a rival out-of-doors, he became also the star of drawing rooms, fetes, and spectacles. He played the violin, improvised verses, and in the favorite pastime of the period, conversation, he was one of the most sparkling. His witticisms were keen but never offended the sensibilities of ladies. He was never coarse or vulgar.

At twenty he was appointed esquire to the Duchess of Orléans, wife of the brother of Louis XVI, and became the confidant of the duke himself and of his son, the Duke of Chartres. Then he entered into the whirl of the brilliant life of the Court of Versailles, where his physical charm, his talents, and his taste in dress made him the most striking figure in that scintillating throng.

During this time he wrote plays and musical compositions, some of which became the most famous of the day. "St. George," says Larousse, "was a master on the violin, and a story is told of him so remarkable that it borders on the improbable; he played one evening a bit of music with his whip, a fact certified by several present. This whip became famous; the handle is ornamented with a great number of precious stones, and the nobleman declared that each stone in the dazzling collection represented a woman who loved him." Among those who fell under his charm was the wife of his patron, Madame de Montesson, Duchess of Orléans.

In a similar vein of praise, *Biographe de Musiciens* says:

None could equal him at running; in the dance he was the model of perfection; he could mount horses bareback and break the wildest of them; he skated with perfect grace and distinguished himself among the best swimmers. Trained by Leclair for the violin, he acquired on this instrument a skill equal to that of the best French violinists of his time and shone at concerts with his playing and his concertos alike.

To the added delight of the gay French aristocracy, he brought a band of colored musicians from the West Indies which he trained himself and which became a leading attraction at Versailles.

In winter it was considered one of the most thrilling sights at Versailles to see St. Georges skate on the large artificial lake. Tall, lithe, and graceful, he would skim over the ice with the ease of a swallow, describing marvelous rhomboids, flowers, portraits, and sometimes "whole lines from Racine."

According to Jean de Beauvois, who knew him:

As soon as St. Georges appeared in any circle, a murmur, to which all had long been accustomed, circulated through the room. They recognized him; and the expression of an unforgettable joy shone on his handsome brown face. The women, on seeing him, had the appearance of hiding behind their fans, as if to convey a secret to one another, while the men, the most distinguished in nobility, mentality, and intelligence, came forward to shake his hand. In an instant he had become the lion of the assembly.

He was a master at everything, and his conduct was so perfect withal that his enemies could find but one thing to pin their meanness on, and that was his birth and racial descent.

Visiting London with the Duke of Chartres, St. Georges' social success there equaled that in Paris. The Prince of Wales, afterwards George IV, welcomed him as a special guest. In the most elegant salons hosts and hostesses and their guests fought for the honor of entertaining him; people called him "the most seductive of colored gentlemen." The prince himself, enthusiastic over the accomplishments of his guest, wished to decorate him with the Order of the Bath, but St. Georges had the modesty to refuse.

When St. Georges arrived in England he adopted the English hat and shoes, and discarded the French broidered jacket and culotte for the English pantaloon and frock coat. He gave to these garments a style of his own which at once became the prevailing mode. Lords copied his dress. Indeed, it has been said that St. Georges was the forerunner of the English Beau Brummell. To France, in turn, St. Georges brought the English style, which replaced the French one.

After three months St. Georges returned home, by no means richer than when he had left it. Extremely generous, he had spent lavishly, and the only sum he brought back with him was 200 guineas that he had won from the Prince of Wales on a bet that he could jump a wide ditch in Richmond with his knees closed. Among his expenditures were fabulous sums spent on fetes and games.

English engravers strove for the honor of doing his portrait, and dozens were made of him, several of them showing him in the company of the Prince of Wales. One showed him doing a favorite trick of his—shooting off pistols with both hands at two swallows and bringing both birds down. Another showed him in a comic duel with the chef of the Prince de Conti. St. Georges, who was an epicure, had found fault with the chef's dishes, and the latter, in a fit of rage, had seized a sword and attacked him, whereupon the famous swordsman picked up an *écumoire*, or iron strainer, and proceeded to disarm his enemy.

"This master of arms, whom they surnamed the inimitable and the invincible, never had a duel," says Larousse. "No one dared risk one with him. Indeed his historic duel with the Count de la Morlière was only a comedy."

The count, offended by a remark, had challenged St. Georges, and the encounter took place under the bridge of St. Marie. But the count proved so poor an opponent that St. Georges seized him bodily, put him across his knees, and spanked him like a child to the great amusement of the onlookers.

The only man before whom St. Georges is said to have quailed was another colored man, Alexandre Dumas, father of the novelist. The latter, in his *Memoirs*, asserts that St. Georges evaded a duel with his father, pleading illness. At that time, however, Dumas, a master swordsman himself, was twenty-two, while St. Georges was near fifty.

Despite St. Georges' prestige and position he was sometimes taunted about the dark color of his skin. On one occasion while walking on the Rue de Bac, a pedestrian, trying to be funny, called him a *moricaud*, the French equivalent of "darky." St. Georges seized the offender, rubbed his face in the gutter, and laughingly remarked, "There you are now! As black as I am."

A more serious instance of racial discrimination against him occurred in 1776. At that time the Royal Academy of Music was under the direction of the city of Paris. St. Georges, who was the director of a musical company, wished to make the Academy a national theatre, and because of his influence, easily assembled a group of capitalists to finance the project. But incited by his enemies, several of the performers, headed by Mlles. Arnould, La Guimard, and Levasseur, sent a petition to the queen, Marie Antoinette, in which they indignantly declared that their "honor and privileges were opposed to their submitting to the dictation of a mulatto." The queen upheld them and the project fell through.

Up to that time Marie Antoinette had been one of the warmest friends of St. Georges. Several reasons have been given for her stand in the affair. One is that St. Georges was too friendly with the Duke of Orléans, brother of the king and the king's leading opponent; the other is that the queen's vanity as a woman had been hurt by St. Georges' too marked attention to another woman.

On still another occasion St. Georges was snubbed because of his color and illegitimacy. When sent by the Duke of Orléans to a group of emigrés, discontented nobles who had left the court, they refused to receive him.

According to some writers, it was the queen's support of color discrimination that drove him into the ranks of the republicans. It is also said that he imbibed his republicanism from the Duke of Orléans, "Philippe Egalité." Both assertions are wrong, as St. Georges' correspondence shows. The truth is that he was a democrat at heart though reared as an aristocrat. A man of color, he had been born among the common people, and in sympathy he remained one of them.

Despite the queen's conduct toward him St. Georges did all in his power to warn her and the king of the coming revolution. One day while skating at Versailles he came close to the box in which the queen was sitting and with his skates scratched on the ice the word "peril" in German, hoping that she might thereby realize the imminent danger. A few days later Marie Antoinette, in a touching scene, expressed to him her deep regret for having sided against him.

When the Revolution came, St. Georges threw himself heart and soul into the people's cause. Going to the West Indies, he raised a regiment of black cavalry, which he called the Black Legion. As lieutenant-colonel, he appointed another prominent young nobleman, Count de Pailletérie, later General Alexandre Dumas.

With their dashing cavalry, St. Georges and Dumas soon distinguished themselves by saving Lille for the republicans after the defection of General Dumouriez, an ex-royalist leader. In the war with the Prussians St. Georges proved himself as brilliant on the field of battle as in the salon.

Later, however, when the Revolution got out of hand, even his impeccable conduct did not suffice to save him from suspicion. He was thrown into prison and came near having his head chopped off, the fate suffered by the king, Marie Antoinette, his patron, the Duke of Orléans, and thousands of others of the nobility. His life was saved in the nick of time. Just as he was being led up to the guillotine, the counterrevolutionists, having triumphed, rushed up and saved him.

After this experience St. Georges retired from public life. His father had left him an annuity equivalent to $150,000, but the Revolution had swept this away. He suffered extremely from poverty, and died on June 12, 1799, from bladder trouble and neglect.

The news of his passing revived all the old interest in him. E. M. von Arndt, the noted German poet, patriot, and traveler, who knew him well and happened to be in Paris at the time, wrote:

St. Georges, the great Georges, died a few days after my arrival. St. Georges, the representative and favorite of the French nation. . . . St. Georges was dead and so great was public interest that the news made people forget the battles of Verona and Stockhart. All the day they talked about nothing else but that. In all the theatres, promenades, cafes and gardens resounded the name of the great, the amiable St. Georges. In the streets they stopped to exchange the news. For three, four days, his name echoed in all the newspapers. They lauded his skill in all the arts, his fine manner, his force, his generosity and gaiety, and generally concluded with these words: "He was the perfect Frenchman, that is to say, the most amiable of mortals. He was the Voltaire of equitation, music, dancing, and skill in the use of weapons."

In truth, St. Georges is an astonishing figure in the eyes of a German, whose education is so silly that he considers skill in bodily exercises as one of the little supplementary things of life. St. Georges was the handsomest, the strongest, and the most agreeable man of his times (he died at the age of 58). He was a faithful friend, a good citizen, a man of society, full of so many charms and virtues that any single one of them would have caused us to mourn his death. He was the Alcibiades of his time, he loved pleasure, but never abused it. Oh! such marvellous gifts merit immortality and a people with a keen and ever ready recognition of beauty as the French will admire him eternally.

Talleyrand, Napoleon's great chancellor, declared that St. Georges was the most accomplished human being he had ever met. Perhaps his only defect was that he stammered slightly.

Like Dumas, the novelist, St. Georges gave pensions from his private purse to several poor people. Larousse says, "He distinguished himself among the personages of his time, selfish, wicked, and corrupt for the most part, by a generosity and a rectitude of character very rare. To the end of his days he did good and he had a special list of poor people, whom he supported entirely."

Biographie Universelle says, "He was unselfish and benevolent. He suffered privations to relieve the unhappy, and several indigent old people were his pensionaires as. long as his money lasted."

His nobility of character never shone brighter than in the manner in which he received his humble black mother, once a slave, when she came to Paris. Taking her into the most brilliant salons, he presented her to his aristocratic friends, letting it quietly be known that whoever attempted to snub her would in turn be snubbed by him. "Who refuses her, refuses me," he said.

Biographie de Musiciens gives a list of his works, principal among which were the "St. Georges Minuet," two operas, several symphonies, and a comedy, *Fille Garçon.* His plays, according to several critics of the day, lacked originality, and were a failure, but his concertos, which became the rage of the day, possess genuine merit. As a technician of the violin, he is considered one of the most brilliant in the history of music.

Neither King Arthur nor Lancelot nor any traditional figure of chivalry was more gallant than he. His conduct at all times was exemplary, and for that portion of humanity which admires nobility of character and excellence in attainment, he will ever remain a model.

Chevalier de St. Georges was Prince Charming come to life.

REFERENCES

As regards the match between St. Georges and Faldoni, the latter says of St. Georges, "I do not believe that his equal as a fencer is now living," but gives the impression that in their match he was the victor. Vigeant, however, produces evidence to show that it was Faldoni who was beaten. (*Reminiscences of Henry Angelo*, Vol. II, pp. 398–399. For St. Georges' bout with the celebrated Chevalier d'Eon, a man who posed as a woman, see p. 421; and for his affair with Captain Telfer, pp. 308–309.)

Durozoir says that St. Georges' hair was "woolly" and that "his color was much darker than that of the average mulatto."

R. Lesage says, "St. Georges was admired on his promenades and in spectacles, and was sought after in the salons, in spite of his woolly hair and dark skin."

Lionel de Laurencie wrote an excellent article on him, particularly his musical ability, in the *Musical Quarterly* of Boston.

A street in Paris—Rue St. Georges—is said to have been named in his honor.

St. Georges is reported to have had a child by the Marquise de Montalembert, whose husband had a private theatre that gave intimate performances for the nobility. G. Capon says, "Here was to be seen Monsieur de St. Georges who, to skill in fencing, added dramatic ability and who, moreover, won the favors of the Marquise de Montalembert, née Marie Josephine de Commarieu, daughter of the Inspector-General of the domains of the Crown. One even spoke of a child born from this illicit union in 1785. . . ." (*Les petites maisons galantes de Paris*, p. 14. Paris, 1902.)

Angelo, Henry, *Reminiscences*, Vol. II, pp. 308–309, 398, 421.

Arndt, E. M. von, *Bruchstücke einer Reise durch Frankreich im Frühling und Sommer*, Vol. II, pp. 36–37. 1799.

Beauvoir, Jean de, *Chevalier de St. Georges*, 2 vols. Paris, 1890.

Bachaumont, *Mémoires de, May, 1779*. Paris, 1890.

La Boessière, *Traité de l'art des armes*. Paris, 1818.

Larousse, *Grand Dictionnaire Universal de 19e Siècle*, Vol. XIV, pp. 68–69. 1875.

Michaud, *Biographie Universelle* (see "St. Georges").

Musical Quarterly (Schirmer's), Jan. 1919, pp. 74–85. Boston.

ADDITIONAL REFERENCES

Angelo, *Angelo's Picnic or Table Talk*, pp. 21–25. London, John Ebers, 1834.

Daressy, Henry, *Archives des Maîtres d'Armes*, pp. 183–212. Paris, Maison Quantin Publishers, 1888.

Duyeyrier, Anne Honoré Joseph, *Le Chevalier de Saint-Georges*, a play. Paris, 1840.

Duncan, John, "The Chevalier de Saint-Georges: Musician-Patriot." *Negro History Bulletin* (March, 1946), pp. 129–130, 142. Association for the Study of Negro Life and History, Washington, D.C.

————, *The Negro's Literary influence on Masterpieces of Music*, pp. 134–137 (March, 1958), Washington, D.C.

Fleming, B. J., and Pryde, M. J. *Distinguished Negroes Abroad*, p. 63. Washington, D.C., The Associated Publishers, 1946.

Maill, Bernard, *Pierre Garat*, pp. 95–97. London, 1913.

"Le Chevalier de Saint-Georges," *Biographies from Tuesday Magazine*, pp. 60–67. New York, Toronto, London, Bantam Pathfinder Ed., 1966, 1967, 1968.

"The Chevalier de Saint-Georges" in *Negro History Bulletin* (December, 1937), p. 7, Washington, D.C.

Jean-Louis

WORLD-FAMED SWORDSMAN AND DUELIST
(1785–1865)

DURING THE FRENCH REVOLUTION boys of tender years were taken into the army for training, as later were the Ballila under Mussolini. The colonel of a regiment was inspecting a company of these boys on a morning in 1796 when he started angrily and stopped before a dark bushy-haired Negro.

It was not the lad's color that had caused the officer's wrath, however. At the time there were even Negro generals in the French army. It was the boy's physique. Very small for his eleven years he stood shakily on thin legs. Certainly the army was no place for him.

"Step forward," commanded the colonel. The quaking little Negro obeyed. "Who had the idea of enlisting this little abortion?" asked the colonel.

The boy listened in dumb dismay. Being in the regiment meant everything to him.

The colonel was about to order his discharge when a captain, touched by the lad's pathetic look, said, "Won't you give him a chance, colonel? The poor little devil has neither father nor mother. He arrived in France from Haiti two or three years ago and has been having a hard time ever since. He came to the barracks some days ago and was adopted by the regiment. Really, he is a fine lad. All he wants is a chance to serve France."

The colonel shrugged his shoulders. "Impossible. He'll never reach the size of our smallest grenadier." Then touched by the lad's forlorn appearance, he asked him his name.

"Jean-Louis."

The voice was so firm it astonished the colonel. "I suppose," he said, "you brought with you your heathen voodoo practices from the West Indies?"

"No, monsieur, I read my Bible every day." He went on to say that he was a Protestant.

"A Protestant, eh?" The colonel's favorable impression of Jean-Louis' character increased. France is a Catholic land and it took some courage to be a Protestant. "Very well," he said, "but it's a pity. You have the spirit but not the body. I wager that in the next two years he won't grow a quarter of an inch."

"One can always try, my colonel," answered the captain.

"Try to grow? How?"

"We can send him to D'Erape, our master-of-arms. What he has done for others he can do for this boy."

"If he does it will be a miracle. Well . . . let him go, we'll see."

Thus began the career of perhaps the greatest swordsman and duelist in history.

At the first trial under D'Erape the colonel's worst opinions proved justified. Jean-Louis could not stand up under the physical strain. But two things impressed D'Erape: the boy's spirit and his quick recovery from fatigue.

A week later, thanks to nourishing food, he had more life. Furthermore, he showed such intuitive skill in fencing that D'Erape was delighted. "Bravo," he said, "you have already grasped the chief essential of fencing. You have already done better than many of the cocksure greenhorns I have been working on for months." From then on he took him under his own private care. "Someday," he said, "that boy is going to astonish the world."

At seventeen Jean-Louis, now tall and sturdy, was the first swordsman of the garrison. He was sent into active service and for the next ten years fought in Italy, Russia, Prussia, and Austria.

The year 1814 found him in Madrid as master-of-arms of his regiment, the 32nd, in the Third Division. In this division there was also a regiment of Italians recruited by Napoleon in Italy, between whom and the Frenchmen in Jean-Louis' regiment there existed much animosity. Street brawls between the two were frequent. One night there was a fight in which more than a hundred were engaged and in which several were killed.

Finally the general in command decided that the only way to end the feud would be to let them fight it out. Sending to the master-of-arms of the Italian regiment, Giacomo Ferrari of Florence, then Italy's most famous swordsman, he bade him select fifteen of his best men. Jean-Louis was also commissioned to select his fifteen best.

On the appointed day the garrison, 10,000 strong, was drawn up on the parade ground to see the fight. Ferrari arrived with fourteen of his best swordsmen. Jean-Louis came alone. On receiving the order, he had named himself fifteen times, sure that he would be more than a match for that number of Italians.

A roll of drums and the duel began. Ferrari and Jean-Louis were the first to engage. Ferrari, confident that he was invincible, began quietly, almost caressingly. Suddenly he uttered a wild, piercing cry and darted on Jean-Louis. It was a Florentine ruse that had brought death to many of his opponents. But the cry ended in a roar of rage. Jean-Louis, unfrightened, had parried the blow and in a lightning thrust passed his blade through the fleshy part of Farrari's shoulder.

Ferrari, declaring that it was nothing, attacked again. This time Jean-Louis' sword darted under Ferrari's guard and through his left side, near the heart. Ferrari's blade fell from his hands, he spun about, and fell dead.

Ferrari's fourteen remaining comrades, eager to avenge his death, wanted to attack Jean-Louis all at once.

Taking a bare two minutes' rest, Jean-Louis engaged the next opponent. The latter bounded in, there was a click of swords, and another Italian fell dead, pierced through the heart.

A third, engaging, met the same fate. Soon all but two of the Italians were dead or wounded. The friends of Jean-Louis bade him rest but he declared he was not tired. And in truth he was not. The whole affair had taken less than forty minutes.

The colonel, thinking that the affair had gone far enough and fearful for Jean-Louis' life, tried to stop him. "Master," he said, "you have valiantly maintained the honor of the 32nd. In its name, I thank you."

But Jean-Louis, carried away by the heat of battle, brandished his sword impatiently at the suggestion and in the gesture wounded a man of his own regiment in the leg.

In an instant he had dropped his sword and was beside the wounded man. When he saw that the wound was slight, he said, "You see, my colonel, the only one of the 32nd who was hurt is by one of his own comrades."

The colonel, feeling that this was an omen to stop the fight, said, "Jean-Louis, this is a warning that enough blood has been spilt. Shake hands with the two surviving comrades of the First."

Jean-Louis obeyed and a great cheer went up from both regiments. Napoleon, in recognition of this exploit, sent him the Legion of Honor.

Jean-Louis now became one of the most popular men in the French army and one of the best beloved, for in addition to his skill he was modest and good-natured. Vigéant, a famous writer on fencing who knew him intimately, said, "Jean-Louis' face which appeared hard at first meeting, hid a soul of great goodness and generosity." Of a merciful disposition, he tried to spare his opponents' lives. "Fencing," he would say, "is the art of conciliation."

After serving in various parts of France Jean-Louis retired from the army in 1830 and settled in Montpellier, where he founded what became the most famous fencing school of the times, and where he developed a method of his own, which came to be taught in the French army and in nearly all the fencing schools of France.

Several schools in France were named after him and tournaments were given in his honor, one of them at Metz in 1850. The most distinguished members of the nobility came to take lessons from him. In the famous bout between Count de Bondy and Lafaugère he served as umpire. He was now not only wealthy but a leading social figure as well. At that time a champion swordsman had all the athletic prestige that a world's heavyweight champion now does, plus social recognition.

Jean-Louis married Mlle. Veillard, daughter of a Montpellier physician, by whom he had a daughter, who was so skilled with the sword that once, dressed as a man, she defeated a leading fencer.

In 1865 he lost his beloved wife. Her death and the fact that he was blind in both eyes from cataracts afflicted him greatly. He died on November 19 of the same year at the age of eighty.

Writers on dueling laud Jean-Louis for his encounter with the Italians at Madrid. Some hail him as the foremost exponent of the art of fencing in the nineteenth century.

REFERENCES

Frédéric Régamey, leading painter of fencers and the art of fencing as practiced at that time, has executed three or more portraits of Jean-Louis, one of which shows him in his fencing school and another umpiring the bout between Lafaugère and the Count de Bondy.

Vigéant, A. *Un Maître d'Armes, (Jean-Louis).* Paris, 1883.

————, *Bibliographie de l'Escrime.* Paris, 1882.

————, *L'Almanach de l'Escrime.* Paris, 1889.

————, *Ma Collection de l'Escrime.* Paris, 1892.

Surdun, J., *Notice sur Jean-Louis.* Montpellier.

Merignac, E., *Historie de l'Escrime,* Vol. II, p. 579. Paris.

Durue, *L'Escrime dans L'Armée,* p. 18. Paris, 1888.

Hilton, H., *The Sword and the Centuries,* pp. 323–327. London, 1901.

Steinmetz, A. *Romance of Duelling,* pp. 300–301. London, 1868.

ADDITIONAL REFERENCES

Daressy, Henri, *Archives de Maîtres d'Armes,* pp. 213–214. Paris, Maison Quantin Publishers, 1888.

Aleksander Sergeevich Pushkin

THE FATHER OF RUSSIAN LITERATURE
AND APOSTLE OF FREEDOM
(1799–1837)

To ALEKSANDER SERGEEVICH PUSHKIN belongs the unique distinction of welding together and elevating a great European language. Before his day the Russian language was half-formed, and disdained, being used chiefly by the enslaved serfs and the masses. The educated and the elite spoke and wrote in French.

When a Russian uses his language he is more indebted to Pushkin than Anglo-Saxons are to Shakespeare. But for him, Tolstoi, Dostoevski, Gogol, Gorky, Lenin, and other famous Russian writers might have written in French instead of in Russian. Pushkin, in the fullest sense, is "The Father of Russian Literature."

Pushkin was born in Moscow on June 7, 1799, and was descended on his mother's side from Abraham Petrovitch Hannibal—"The Negro of Peter the Great." On his father's side he belonged to one of the thirty-one leading families of Russia. A Count Pushkin was a privy counsellor to Peter the Great. A later one bore the sceptre at the coronation of Catherine the Great.

Though reared as an aristocrat, Pushkin was at heart a man of the people. His sympathies from his earliest youth were with the masses of his oppressed and downtrodden countrymen. Slavery was then quite as bad in Russia as in the United States. Pushkin's *niania*, or white "mammy," Arina Rodionova, told him the folklore of "the common people" and fired his imagination with stirring tales from Russian history. His great favorite among the

French writers was Voltaire. Still later he became absorbed in Byron and even came to be called "The Russian Byron." But what he liked most, next to hearing about the exploits of his famous ancestor, General Hannibal, was to wander among the serfs on his father's estate and the humble folk of Moscow and listen to their folktales and songs. These people, in turn, came to idolize him.

At twelve he entered the Imperial Lycée at St. Petersburg where his bold independence, his witty epigrams and outspoken opinions of men and things, however high, made him the despair of his teachers who said of him, "Very lazy . . . inattentive in class . . . immodest . . . rather capable . . . witty (more the pity) only for boasting . . . makes very mediocre progress . . . thoughtless, flighty, untidy, negligent; but good-natured and polite; has a special passion for poetry." Three years later, at the age of fifteen, he became Russia's leading poet. His first poem, "Reminiscences of Tsarskoye Selo," read before Derzhavin, up to that time Russia's leading poet, sent the latter into such transports of delight that he praised Pushkin to the skies and said, "This is he who will replace Derzhavin." (The latter was then very old.)

Perhaps the most remarkable thing about this poem was that it was written not in the conventional French but in Russian. Russia had at last a great poet using her own language! As one writer says, "With one cut of the sword Pushkin had freed Russian literature from the ties that were keeping it enslaved."

The poem was soon circulating everywhere. In slave huts and royal palaces alike it was being recited, creating the beginnings of a common bond among the Russian people. By the time he was eighteen Pushkin was the most talked of writer in Russia. Impulsive and lively, so much so that he was called "The Cricket," he spared no one, not even the czar, in his witty, satiric verses. He wrote of Alexander I: "As a brave captain he ran at Austerlitz and trembled in 1812." He made so many enemies that one of his friends said, "Over the poet, Pushkin, hangs not only a cloud but a thundercloud." As a result he engaged in many duels, in all of which he was fearless. In one of these he let his opponent, Zubov, fire at him while he calmly ate cherries.

The masses, on the other hand, worshipped him, and learned his poems by heart. They were enchanted by his verse because he was a master at taking their most ordinary feelings and transmitting them into words of living beauty. They recited his love poems everywhere, illiterate men and women and slaves and women of the high nobility alike because he was the love bard par excellence.

He represented love in so many aspects and in such beautiful forms and always with such loftiness and tenderness, that he left as ineffaceable a stamp upon Russian literature as did Goethe's refined women and Hugo's deep humanity upon world literature. After Pushkin it was impossible for Russian poets to speak of love in the ordinary sense of the word.

His poems also breathed the spirit of liberty. Around him were autocracy and slavery. Forty million of his countrymen were chained to the soil as their ancestors had been from time immemorial. These unfortunates were whipped, branded, and sold like cattle. They were sold from estate to estate and whole families were torn apart in the process. "Serfdom" was the name of this system, but it was slavery at its worst.

Pushkin, touched to the depths by their misery, boldly declared the serfs were men and brothers, not chattels—the first Russian writer of note to say this.

His vehicle for freedom was poetry, which he considered the most exalted expression of the human spirit. "He proclaimed," as one of his admirers said, "the right of human personality to be free. From the very first words of his poetic creations, he unequivocally declared himself a champion of freedom." Later, to emphasize his sympathies with the oppressed, he wore the blouse and the wide-brimmed straw hat of the serf.

His poems had such effect on the slumbering spirit of freedom in the masses that he became the target of the censors whose duty it was to scan every line of printed matter for seditious content. Agitators of every kind were exiled to the icy wastes of Siberia, a punishment worse than death.

Undaunted by this, Pushkin continued to write fearlessly. His defiant "Ode to Liberty" stirred the people.

> Oh shake and shiver, tyrants of the world,
> But lend an ear ye fallen slaves,
> Gain courage and rise!

Finally the police descended on him in 1820 and he was arrested. Out of consideration for his family he was exiled to southern Russia where he continued to write and hope for a victorious revolution:

> Ye winds, ye gales, plough up the waters,
> Break the pernicious barriers down!
> Where art thou tempest, freedom's symbol?
> Above the captive waters burst!

When he wrote a stinging satire against Prince Vorontzoff, the governor of the province, he was sent back to Moscow as a prisoner and was paroled to his family, which was hereafter held responsible for him. Quarreling with his parents, he left them and went off to live among the serfs and peasants on a far-off estate where he devoted himself to his writings.

His next political involvement came in December, 1825. Inspired by his writings, a secret society of which he was a member made an attack on the new czar, Nicholas. Several of the members were executed, and others were sent to Siberia. Pushkin escaped only because he was away at the time.

His name, however, had been discovered on the books of the society, and the czar, anxious to win him over, sent for him. The two masters in their respective domains met on a cold day in 1826 in the czar's palace.

The czar asked, "Were you a friend of the conspirators against me?"

Pushkin, his back to the fire, his manner not showing the proper respect due to the Czar of All the Russias, replied frankly, "That is true, Your Majesty. I loved those so-called conspirators deeply, and I shall ever love and esteem them."

"What would you have done had you been in St. Petersburg on the 14th of December?" Nicholas asked.

"I should have been in the ranks of the rebels," was the fearless reply.

"That would have caused us great sorrow," replied the czar. "We are grateful for all you have done for Russia, and wish you to be always near us. We name you Imperial Historian."

Realizing that this would fetter his pen even more, Pushkin declined, but finally, impressed by the czar's evident solicitude for him, accepted. Nicholas, however, had a double motive. He could, while advancing Russian literature, keep this fiery young man under his own eye.

When Pushkin left, Nicholas said to one of his generals, "We have just been talking with the wittiest man in Russia."

In this new post Pushkin's literary star rose even higher. Editors fought for his manuscripts at the then enormous figure of four dollars a line. But Pushkin, with his hatred of intrigue and artificiality, could hardly have entered a more unfavorable environment. "When I meet fools and hypocrites," he once said, "it is all I can do to keep from biting them."

His sharp wit and his favor with the czar brought him many powerful enemies. When these attacked him, he struck back with his rapier-like pen and tongue. Unable to retort in kind, they made fun of his ancestry. Pointing to his crisp, curly hair, his dark skin, and full lips, they would say, "There goes the Negro, a descendant of cannibals." Others called him "a black man, badly whitened," and said that his liveliness was inherited from the African monkeys which had fathered his ancestor, Abraham Hannibal.

Pushkin's reply was to join them in the attack against himself. In self-caricature he repeated the bad things they were saying about him. He wrote of himself: "An ever-idle scapegrace, a hideous descendant of Negroes, brought up in savage simplicity. . . . Knowing naught of the sufferings of love, I pleasure the young beauties with the unbridled furies of my African passion." There was more than a little truth in this last, as his love affairs were legion.

Unable to dent him with their mockery, his enemies decided to strike at him through his wife Nathalie, "the first beauty of the day," with whom the czar himself was in love. Two of his chief enemies, Counts Benkendorff and Ovaroff, cabinet ministers, circulated anonymous letters saying that Nathalie was being unfaithful to him with the czar. One such letter, written on November 4, 1836, by Count P. V. Dolgorukov said that Pushkin had been "unanimously elected Acting Grand Master of the Order of Cuckolds."

Pushkin, believing that the letter originated with Baron Heckeren, the French ambassador, sent a challenge to his son, Baron D'Anthès. He could not challenge Heckeren himself because of his age and his position. D'Anthès also had been paying attention to Nathalie, while in love with Nathalie's sister Ekaterina. The matter was settled when D'Anthès declared that he was showing attention to Pushkin's wife only in order to win her sister and Pushkin withdrew his challenge.

This reconciliation, however, did not please Pushkin's enemies who continued to besmirch him with gossip, some color to which was given by the fact that D'Anthès, though married to Nathalie's sister, continued to be attentive to Nathalie. The anonymous letters continued to arrive, and finally Pushkin sent another challenge to D'Anthès which the latter was now forced to accept.

The two met on a morning of biting wind and snow in February 1837. D'Anthès, firing first, struck Pushkin in the abdomen before Pushkin could fire. A few minutes later, Pushkin fired, hitting D'Anthès but not seriously. Pushkin died two days later.

A great cry of anguish went up from Russia. One newspaper in announcing his death said, "The sun of our poetry has set! Pushkin is dead! Dead in the prime of life, in the midst of his great career. We cannot say any more about it, and no more need be said. Every Russian heart knows the full value of this irretrievable loss, and every Russian heart is bleeding: Pushkin! Our poet! Our joy! Our national glory. . . . It is impossible to be reconciled to this thought."

People besieged the Kazan Cathedral to see his body and so great was public indignation that the czar, fearing a revolt, ordered a private funeral to which only a few of the poet's intimate friends would be allowed. But even this was changed. The body was taken away secretly at night and buried outside St. Petersburg in the cemetery of the Svyatogorsky monastery, near Mikhailovskoye. D'Anthès and his father were driven from Russia, and Pushkin's persecutors were hunted out and exiled. But even this did not quiet the people, and the czar, in an effort to still public clamor, forbade further mention of Pushkin.

Among Pushkin's principal works are *Boris Godunof, Euguene Onegin, The Ode to Liberty, The Prisoner of the Caucasus, The*

Stone Guest, The Captain's Daughter, and *The Negro of Peter the Great.* These and others of his works will live as long as literature endures because they express so many shades of emotion and human aspiration. Pushkin, the fiery, the passionate, the irritable, the generous, the enthusiastic, the witty, the faithful friend, the honest adversary, the bitter foe of falsehood and injustice, was one of the completest human beings who ever lived.

"He is the echo of the world," says Eichenwald, "an obedient and melodious echo, which moves from realm to realm, passionately responding to everyone so that no one significant tone in the life of the universe may vanish without leaving a trace.

"There was such a limitless amount of beauty in his soul that it could find relief, consonance, and inner rhyme only in the virility of nature and in the boundlessness of human existence. His all-responding soul was like a many-stringed instrument, and all the universe playing on it, extracted the most marvelous songs.

"Pushkin, the great Pan of Poetry, listened eagerly to the call of the sky, the earth, the throbbing of the heart. . . . A giant of the spirit, full of burning curiosity, full of restlessness and sounds, Pushkin embraces all, sees, and hears everything. Without boundaries or limits, knowing no distance or past, always in the present, everywhere alive, a contemporary of overnight, he moves about space and above time, from age to age, and nothing is alien to him."

Modern Russian writers are enthusiastic in their appreciation of Pushkin. Professor I. Luppol says:

Pushkin created the Russian literary language, was the founder of modern Russian literature and made humanity the richer for his immortal works.

Pushkin's name is inseparably bound up not only with literature but also with the whole Russian culture, the culture which the great Russian people built up in a struggle with a harsh nature and with the no less harsh forms of social relationships which shaped its history.

Pushkin is our Voltaire, our Shakespeare, our Goethe. . . . It was the great Pushkin who, in the dawn of our literature, taught us this human pride, this knowledge of one's own dignity.

Professor V. Kirpotin says:

. . . one of the most remarkable geniuses of the world, whose works have established themselves firmly in the international treasure-house of culture. . . . Today he is dear and familiar to everybody. Pushkin's name and his immortal poetry are on the lips of all the working people. In our time the whole Land of the Soviets is with Pushkin.

And I. Lezhnev:

Pushkin's works represented the epitome of all the preceding development of Russian poetic thought. Pushkin was and is an inexhaustible source of its further development. The pure and copious well-spring of Pushkin's works nourished Russian literature throughout the 19th century and continues to do so even at present. For the greatest writers of the country, both past and present, Pushkin was the starting point and it was to him they constantly reverted.

Lenin defined the boundaries of the modern Russian language with the words, "From Pushkin to Gorky."

Maxim Gorky himself says of Pushkin's poems:

I read them all at once. I was seized with that greedy feeling one experiences when one happens upon an amazingly beautiful place— one wishes to run through it all at once. This is what one feels after a wearisome walk along mossy hillocks in a swampy forest one suddenly comes across a dry glade bathed in sunshine. For a moment one looks at it in wonder and then with glee one runs and runs and each time the foot touches the soft grass of the fertile land one's heart is filled with peaceful joy. . . . The sonorous lines of his poetry are so easily remembered; they adorn gaily everything they deal with. All this made me happy, it made my life light and pleasant. His poetry sounded like the ringing of a new life.

REFERENCES

That Pushkin was of Negro ancestry is so well known that it is taken for granted in Russia. Not so in Anglo-Saxon lands, however, and from time to time there are writers who will say that his ancestor Hannibal was "an Abyssinian and not a Negro"—for instance, Professor E. J. Simmons of Harvard University. But this contention is not worth taking seriously. Not only are some of the most pronounced Negroid types, as the Chankalla, to be found in Ethiopia, but it would be extraordinarily difficult to find a native Ethiopian, regardless of rank, who would be able to pass for other than a Negro in America. And for the Negro strain to have remained so pronounced in Pushkin after three generations, it must have been marked in the beginning.

Moreover, as Simmons himself says, "Unlike Browning or Dumas, Pushkin took his African ancestry very seriously. On more than one occasion he referred poignantly to his Negro descent. He thought and dreamt about the founder of his family in Russia, traced his physical appearance to him and felt that this strain of African blood gave him a unique position in society." (*Pushkin*, p. 11.)

Finally Pushkin wrote of himself, "Potomok Negrov bezobrazny" (an ugly descendant of Negroes).

Descendants of Pushkin have married into the royal families of Germany, Russia, Luxemburg, Italy, and England.

One of his daughters, Natalie, Countess of Merenberg, married Prince Nicholas of Nassau. Their daughter, the Countess de Torby, was the wife of Grand Duke Michael, a brother of Nicholas II of Russia. (Ruvigny, Marquis de, *The Titled Nobility of Europe*. London, 1914.)

Nadjeda, a daughter of the Grand Duke Michael and the Countess de Torby, was married to George, Marquess of Milford Haven, great-grandson of Queen Victoria. (*Burke's Peerage*, Vol. II, p. 1675. London, 1936.)

When this last marriage occurred, the feature section of the Hearst Sunday supplement discussed the sensational question of whether a coal-black child with kinky hair, thick lips, etc., might not yet be born into the English royal family.

Charles Josa says further of the descendants of Pushkin: "A son of the poet, alive during the time of the Duma, was grand marshal of the Moscow nobility. He went each morning to walk upon the Red Square, which used to attract to the place many natives and strangers who used to crowd around the marshal and compare admiringly the resemblance between himself and the statue of his father which stood there. In 1890 a General Prince Pushkin, grandson of Pushkin, was commander of the Russian troops in Poland."

The Grand Duke of Hesse was a descendant of Pushkin. Mme. Grete Stueckgold, former prima donna of the Metropolitan Opera, who knew the Grand Duke, told this writer that the Negro strain was evident in him.

On the centenary of his birth Pushkin's memory was honored by national celebrations. This curious fact is worth noting: It was a white woman, Harriet Beecher Stowe, whose writings lit the torch for Negro freedom in America; it was a Negro, Aleksander Sergeevich Pushkin, who did the same for white emancipation in Russia.

Descendants of Pushkin still live in Russia. See *Sex and Race*, Vol. III, p. 23, for information about one of them.

For a portrait of Pushkin from life showing his Negro strain more clearly than any other, see *Sex and Race*, Vol. I, p. 218. 1941.

Flack, J., *Un grande Poëte Russe*. Paris, 1894.
Haumant, E., *Pouchkine*. Paris, 1911.
Semenoff, E., *Alexander Pouchkine*. Paris, 1889.
Wallace, D. M., *Russia*. New York, 1877.
Pushkin, a Collection of Articles and Essays on the Great Russian Poet. USSR, 1939.
Simmons, E. J., *Pushkin*, pp. 11, 12.

ADDITIONAL REFERENCES

Adams, Russell L., *Great Negroes: Past and Present*, p. 119. Chicago, Afro-Am Publishing Co., 1963, 1964.

Brasol, Boris Leo, *Poushkin, the Shakespeare of Russia*. New York, 1931.

Simmons, E. J., and Cross, Samuel Hazzard, eds., *Centennial Essays for Pushkin*, Cambridge, Mass., Harvard University Press, 1937.

Duncan, John, "The Negro's Literary Influence on Masterpieces of Music." *Negro History Bulletin* (March, 1948), pp. 134–137, Association for Study of Negro Life and History, Washington, D.C.

Fleming, B. J., and Pryde, M. J., *Distinguished Negroes Abroad*, pp. 171–178. Washington, D.C., The Associated Publishers, 1946.

Haynes, Elizabeth Ross, *Unsung Heroes*, pp. 105–113. New York, Du Bois and Dill, 1921.

Kemp, Ruth, "Alexander Pushkin." *Negro History Bulletin* (December, 1940), Association for the Study of Negro Life and History, Washington, D.C.

Lambert, Lydia, *Pushkin, Poet and Lover*. Garden City, N. Y., Doubleday and Company, 1946.

Magarshack, David, *Pushkin: A Biography*. New York, Grove Press, 1967, 1969.

Smidovich, Vikenti Vikentyevich, *A. S. Pushkin: A Biographical Sketch*, trans. by H. G. Scott. Moscow, 1937.

Wolkonsky, Prince Serge, *Pictures of Russian History and Russian Literature*, pp. 205–213. Boston & New York, Lamson, Wolffe and Company, 1898.

Joachim Murat

JOACHIM MURAT, who assumed the name of Joachim Napoleon, and was later King of Naples, came from the Department of Lot, in the Auvergne, France, a region known for the Negroid strain in its inhabitants, many of whom are descended from the Moors who settled in that region after they had been driven out of Spain. It is estimated that more than a million of these people of African ancestry migrated to that region. This is the same part of France from which came Bernadotte, King of Sweden, and Pierre Laval, twice Premier of France, both of whom were dark-skinned and were commonly said to be of Moorish ancestry. In fact, Murat himself claimed descent from a Moorish king, and Frederic Masson, noted writer on Napoleon's cavalry, said it was commonly believed that he was of that ancestry.

The most striking proof of Murat's Negro strain comes from Laura, Duchess d'Abrantès, famous writer of the times, who knew Murat intimately and was moreover well acquainted with evidences of Negro strain. She had lived in Portugal with her husband Marshal Junot, French ambassador, at a period soon after the Negro slaves there had been freed and there was still an abundance of mulattoes.

She says of Murat, "There was a great deal of the Negro in his face. His nose, it is true, was not flat, but his lips were thick. This nose, although straight, lacked distinction, thus giving him in keep-

89

ing with the rest of his features, at least the appearance of a half-breed." She uses the word *métis*, which, in addition to meaning "half-breed," is often used in France for "mulatto." Indeed it is the same thing.

Next to Napoleon himself Murat was the most spectacular figure of the Napoleonic era. Indeed, but for him there might have been no Napoleon of such greatness. Napoleon thought so much of him that he gave him his favorite sister, Marie Caroline, in marriage.

Arriving in Paris, the young Murat found work as a pot washer. Then he joined the army and found such favor with Napoleon that the latter made him one of his aides-de-camp. In Egypt, where he served directly under the command of General Dumas, a mulatto born in Haiti, he distinguished himself and was made general of a division. Devoted body and soul to Napoleon, after they returned to France he urged Napoleon to make himself dictator. When Napoleon hesitated, he drew his sword and declared he would not sheathe it until Napoleon was dictator of France. A few days later, with sixty of his guards, he burst into the National Convention in Paris, as Cromwell had done in the English Parliament, dominated it, and kept his word to make Napoleon supreme. "Good citizens," he said to the 500 members, "the Convention is dissolved," and he drove them all out. In reward, Napoleon appointed him the next most powerful man in France, and married his youngest sister, Marie Caroline, later Queen Caroline, to him. He also made him Governor of Paris and later for his victories over the Germans made him, successively, a Marshal of the Empire, Grand Duke of Berg and Cleves, and Grand Admiral of France. Finally when the Bourbons were ousted, he made him ruler of Naples, one of the richest countries of southern Europe.

But the two were later to be enemies. During the disastrous campaign in Russia where he was in command of the cavalry, Murat deserted his post to return to Naples, upon which Napoleon sent him a most insulting letter. Thereafter, he worked as hard to pull down Napoleon as he had to build him up.

The loss of Murat's services contributed much to Napoleon's final downfall, an admission that Napoleon himself later made. His presence at Waterloo, Napoleon said, would have inspired the

French and discouraged the English. In the hundred or so battles in which he had fought, Murat had been so dashing, so courageous, and so victorious, that he was invested with invincibility by his men. He could be seen always in the forefront of the fight, conspicuous in his gorgeous uniform and snow-white plumes.

But it was not Murat's fault that he was not at Waterloo. A month before he had returned to France. The Allies, once having succeeded in isolating him from Napoleon, turned against him and in face of the strong coalition he was forced to flee. In France he offered his services to Napoleon, who contemptuously refused them.

After the capture of Napoleon, he went to Corsica and sailed from there with an expedition to recover his kingdom. A storm scattered his ships and he was forced ashore at Pizzo, Italy, with only thirty men. Captured, he was court-martialed five days later and shot.

Murat had four sons. One of them, Napoleon, came to the United States and married a grandniece of George Washington. Another, Lucien, married a Baltimore society woman. He returned to France when Napoleon III came to the throne, and was recognized as a prince of royal blood.

REFERENCES

Abrantès, Duchess d', *Mémoires Secrètes*, Vol. II, p. 238. Paris, 1835.
Masson, F., *Cavaliers de Napoléon*, p. 289. Paris, 1921.
See *Encyclopaedia Britannica* for bibliography on Murat.

George A. P. Bridgetower

MUSICAL GENIUS AND COMRADE OF BEETHOVEN
(1789–1860)

GEORGE AUGUSTUS POLGREEN BRIDGETOWER was one of the most brilliant violinists in history. Kings and princes, great composers and art lovers, social leaders, and even his rivals were enthusiastic in his praise. Among these was Beethoven.

Prices that would be considered high for ringside seats at a world championship fight today were paid to hear him. He was the private musician and personal friend of King George IV of England; Beethoven wrote a sonata for him and had him for an accompanist; and Samuel Wesley, famous organist and composer of hymns, eulogized him.

When he drew his bow across the violin, he affected his hearers so deeply that he seemed to them to be more of a miracle than a man. The strains that emerged from his instrument seemed to come from some remote corner of the universe; there was such sweep, certainty, and haunting beauty in them that his hearers felt transported.

Bridgetower was born in Biala, Poland, in 1789, of an African father and either a German or Polish mother. His father, known as "The African Prince," was an accomplished musician and linguist.

Most famous artists have to work long and hard to win success. It was not so with Bridgetower. His first public appearance was in Paris when he was not yet ten years of age, and from that day he won the music lovers of his time.

To that concert had come the musical elite of Paris, attracted by the story of this little colored pupil of Giornovichi, whom the papers described as a prodigy. Bridgetower's technique surpassed all reports, and his audience was enraptured. The *Mercury* of France said:

A remarkable debut which has greatly interested the music lovers of Paris is that of the young Negro from the Colonies, Mr. Bridgetower.

He has played several concertos with a clearness, ease and execution, and even a sensibility, rarely found in one so young (he is not yet ten). His genius, as true as it is precocious, is one of the best retorts that one can make to the philosophy of those who would deprive others of his color of the opportunity to distinguish themselves in the arts.

The leading salons of Paris vied for the honor of hearing and entertaining him. His father became one of the most sought-out individuals in the French capital.

Father and son next went to England, where Bridgetower's fame had preceded him. The first engagement was at Windsor Castle, where he had been invited to play before King George III, the royal princes, and the court. Again the young Negro genius scored.

The Prince of Wales was so delighted that he invited the Bridgetowers to be his special guests and took the lad under his protection, placing him in his own private orchestra.

Bridgetower gave many private recitals for the prince and his friends. He was often at court, and the close friendship between him and the Prince of Wales continued after the latter became king.

Some of those who sought the prince's favor used to approach him through Bridgetower. A letter from Dr. Crouch, noted composer, to Bridgetower, reads in part, "As I find that you are frequently in company with the Prince Regent, could you do me the favor to mention my oratorio to His Royal Highness?"

In the meantime, Bridgetower's popular triumphs continued. At

Bath, where he appeared a few months after his arrival in England, the record price of five guineas a seat ($26) was paid.

The Bath *Morning Post*, December 8, 1799, said:

The young African Prince, whose musical talents have been so much celebrated, had a more crowded and splendid concert on Sunday than has ever been known in this place.

There were up to 550 persons present and they were gratified by such skill on the violin as created general astonishment as well as pleasure.

Ruzzuni [noted violinist] was enraptured and declared that he had never heard such execution before, not even from his friend, La Motte. The exquisite playing of Master Bridgetower, his taste and execution on the violin, is equal, perhaps superior, to the best professors of the present, or any former day. The Covent Room, Recesses and Gallery were thronged with the very best company and scores went away without being able to hear him.

Those who had that happiness were enraptured with the astonishing ability of this wonderful child, for he is but ten years old. He is a mulatto. The greatest attention and respect was paid by the nobility and gentry present to his elegant father, who is one of the most accomplished men in Europe, conversing with fluency and address in several languages.

After conquering the provinces, Bridgetower returned to London. His first appearance was at the famous Drury Lane Theatre. Seats were sold at a record price and thousands were turned away. The king, the Prince of Wales and their retinues were present.

This performance was another triumph. The *Post Adviser* said, "He gave the utmost satisfaction in his performance," and the *London Chronicle*, "He performed with great taste and execution."

This extraordinary Negro boy became the idol of the music lovers of London. Social invitations from the most fashionable hosts and hostesses in the land poured in on him and his father. At the Handel Concertos, held not long after, he was the center of attraction.

No composition seemed too difficult for him. On May 23, 1805, when a grand concert was given for him under the patronage of the Prince of Wales, he conducted the orchestra "with the coolness and the spirit of a Cramer to the astonishment of all." (Cramer was the leading conductor of the period.)

After studying under Attwell and Haydn, the famous composer, Bridgetower went to Dresden to see his mother, taking with him letters of introduction from the Prince of Wales to people in the highest musical circles. He was now approaching manhood and is described as being of medium height and dark complexion, with dark brown, curly hair, soulful brown eyes, and a rather broad nose.

He took that center of German culture by storm, and was introduced by Prince Lichnowsky to Beethoven. The great composer fell into raptures over him on the spot, giving him a letter of introduction to Baron Alexander de Wexlar, a leader of Austrian society, in which he said of Bridgetower, "A very skillful virtuoso and master of his instrument. He plays his concertos and quartets excellently and I wish you could procure him some acquaintances. . . . I know that you, yourself, will thank me for having procured you this acquaintance."

Beethoven thought so much of him that he composed a sonata for him, which he later called the *Kreutzer Sonata*. The story goes that Beethoven had intended naming the great sonata for Bridgetower, but a young lady of whom Beethoven was very fond, Countess Guiccardi, showed too great an interest in the famous young violinist, which so angered Beethoven that impulsively he scratched off Bridgetower's name and susbtituted that of Rudolphe Kreutzer of Paris, another violinist. Such is the account given by Ries in his *Notizen*.

Bridgetower had scored a triumph with that composition. Beethoven had promised him he would write it for one of his concerts, but the composer was so busy that he did not give it to Bridgetower until 4:30 on the morning of the concert and then in a script that was quite illegible.

The concert was to take place at 8 A.M. But Bridgetower was equal to the occasion. His interpretation of the sonata was so perfect that Beethoven leaped to his feet, and hastening to Bridgetower, embraced him, crying, "Once more, my dear fellow."

Later in Vienna he often accompanied Beethoven to the salons of the rich, and with his warmth of touch and his fascinating eccentricities in playing contributed greatly to Beethoven's popularity, according to Beethoven himself.

In Vienna the aristocracy turned out in force to see him and he became the idol of the Austrian capital. Among those present at his first concert were the Emperor of Austria and his court; Prince Esterhazy; Prince de Liechtenstein; Prince Lobowitz; and the British ambassador.

Visiting Rome, Milan, Paris, and other cities, he rode on the crest of popularity. Back in London, he became a greater rage than ever, and commanded a higher price than any other musician of his day.

His successes continued for many years, and he remained in the service of King George IV until the latter's death. After the king's death, he retired from public life. He died on February 29, 1860, in comparative poverty and obscurity and was buried at Kensal Green Cemetery, London.

As with most geniuses, money had meant little to him, and he spent it as easily as he earned it. Much of it went toward aiding deserving musicians. Because of his close friendship with the king, he might have enjoyed many personal favors, but his influence was used only on behalf of his friends.

Samuel Wesley wrote of him:

George Bridgetower, whom they used to denote the African Prince, is justly to be ranked with the first masters of the violin. He practiced much with the celebrated Viotti, and imbibed largely of his bold and spirited style of execution.

It was a rich treat for the lover of the instrument to hear him perform the matchless and immortal solos of Bach, all of which he perfectly retained in memory and executed with the utmost precision and without a single error. Indeed, whatever the composition, or whoever the author, whose music he undertook to perform, he treated them in so perfect and masterly a manner as to yield entire and universal delight and satisfaction to every auditor.

Bridgetower also wrote several compositions, two originals of which are preserved in the British Museum. They are a "diatonica Armonica for the Piano" and a ballad, "You Call Me Fickle."

REFERENCES

Thayer, A. W., *Beethoven*, Vol. II, pp. 8–12.
Musical Times of London, May, 1908.

ADDITIONAL REFERENCES

Adams, Russell L., *Great Negroes: Past and Present,* p. 139. Chicago, Afro-Am Publishing Company, 1963, 1964.
Fleming, B. J., and Pryde, M. J., *Distinguished Negroes Abroad,* pp. 160–165. Washington, D.C. The Associated Publishers, 1946.
St. Laurent, Philip, "The Negro in World History: Geo. A. P. Bridgetower." *Tuesday* Magazine, 1968.

General Alexandre Dumas

General Alexandre Dumas
("Alexandre the Greatest")

DASHING COMMANDER OF NAPOLEON'S CAVALRY
(1762–1806)

So FULL OF ROBUST ADVENTURE is the life of General Alexandre
Dumas that it reads more like that of a fabulous knight of romance than even of a Napoleonic commander.

Dumas reminds one of Richard the Lionhearted of England,
who fought the Turks in Palestine for the tomb of Christ. Like
Richard, Alexandre was a giant in size and strength, and one of
the bravest of the brave.

Coming on the scene at one of the most critical and dramatic
periods of history, he played an important role, during which he
rose from a sergeant to general-in-chief in twenty-two months.
Anatole France was so fascinated by the story of his life that he
dubbed him "Alexandre the Greatest." Dumas' story goes back to
the day when a certain great nobleman, tiring of the gay, empty
life at the court of Louis XV, decided to get away from it all and
went to settle in the far-away island of St. Domingue, now Haiti.

On his arrival there he was warmly welcomed by the rich planters, who were glad to have one of such rank in their society. But
the nobleman, the Marquis de la Pailletérie, shunned them and
went to live among the Negroes, little knowing at the time that in
so doing he was to add a thousand glories to his name.

The marquis, completely breaking with his past, took a consort from among his dark-hued neighbors, one whose bright,

flashing eyes, supple figure, and merry laughter had captivated him. She was Marie Dumas. Perhaps he married her, perhaps he did not. It is believed, however, that humble Marie became Madame la Marquise.

A year later a son, Alexandre, was born. In color he was very dark. For eleven years the couple lived happily together, and then Marie died. The Marquis, grief-stricken, remained in the West Indies eight years longer and then returned to France, taking Alexandre.

And what a son was Alexandre! In three years he had become the talk of Paris. Standing six feet two in his bare feet, he was endowed with strength to match. He performed feats of incredible physical prowess; as a swordsman he eclipsed all in France save one, another Negro, the Chevalier de St. Georges.

Raising his right leg, the young nobleman could support two men on his calf and hop around the room with his burden. Placing four fingers of his right hand in the muzzles of as many muskets, he would lift them all with his arm extended. Once, while on horseback, he saw a soldier misbehaving, and swooping down on him, he caught him by the back of his coat, held him at arm's length as he would a contaminated object, and rode off with him to the guardhouse.

Generous, kind-hearted, but hot-headed and quick to resent insults, Dumas got into many quarrels. He was forever challenging opponents. At twenty-two he fought a duel and won. A year later he fought three duels in a single day, receiving a wound in one of them that later gave him much trouble. When his son, the great novelist, made one of his heroes, D'Artagnan, challenge three men the same day, he was merely using his father as a model.

One of the young man's quarrels was with his father. This, however, was to be his making. When the marquis took another wife, Dumas hotly objected, and decided to leave his father's home. "I have but one request, young man," said the marquis coldly. "Do not take my name around with you to dishonor it." And the future general, to show his scorn, rejected his father's title and name, and took another that was to become illustrious for three generations —that of his mother.

On June 2, 1786, a few days later, he enlisted as a private in the Army of the Rhine. Several republicans of St. Germain brought suit to prevent his entry because he was a nobleman, but he was allowed to remain.

Immediately Dumas distinguished himself. One day while reconnoitering with four men, he found himself cut off from them with thirteen of the enemy against him. Spurring his horse into their midst he fought so vigorously that the thirteen surrendered. Tying all of them up, Dumas led them back to camp on a single string. For this he was made a regimental sergeant-major, cited for bravery by his commander, and invited to dinner.

This was the period of the French Revolution, and a number of free Negroes from the West Indies had come to France to offer their services to the people. They served as a unit known as "La Légion Américaine," (The American Legion), later as "The Black Legion," and at their head was the famous Chevalier de St. Georges.

The latter, eager to get Dumas, offered him a second lieutenancy, but the officer of a white regiment, Colonel Boyer, equally desirous of having him, offered him a lieutenancy. Not to be outdone, St. Georges offered him a captaincy, and so the bidding went on until Dumas gained a lieutenant-colonelship under St. Georges.

At this time Dumas met the daughter of a hotel-keeper, Marie Labouret, and as he was going off to war, he married her at once. Two weeks later he won distinction again, when he and St. Georges saved Lille from the royalist sympathizer, Dumouriez, by a brilliant dash. In July of the following year he was made a brigadier general; September 3 of the same year, a general; five days later he was appointed commander of the Eastern Pyrenees; two months later he was put in command of the Army of the Alps; and early in the following year he was promoted to the command third in importance, that of Commander of the Army of the West—all this in less than two years.

Dumas was always doing something spectacular. One day in the Alps, while reconnoitering with fourteen men, he learned that two squadrons of enemy cavalry were approaching. Instead of sharing the alarm of his men, he bubbled with glee. Hiding his companions behind a hedge, he said, "You'll laugh. It's up to you now to amuse the Austrians. Stay hid! Don't move! I'm going to look for them. When I return, let me pass and then shoot all who follow me."

Sword in hand, he spurred his horse to a gallop and went out alone to meet the Austrians. At the turn he met the advance guard in the narrow path. With three sweeps of his great sword he felled the first three. Four others behind instinctively stopped their horses. He did not give them time to turn. In a second he was on them, stabbing, sabering, overturning them. Saber strokes to the right! Saber strokes to the left! With a blow of his fist he smashed a head. Three more strokes, three more corpses. The survivors fly in panic before this madman who seems invulnerable. Now they meet the others and return. On the ground they see several corpses and before them the single man responsible for all that carnage. This man awaits them a moment, allows them to approach within speaking distance, then shouts, "Bonjour, messieurs," and is off at a gallop.

"Now it's your turn," he calls to his men in the bushes. After him come the Austrians. A volley and the first comers drop from their horses; the others coming on, stumble over these. By this time Dumas' men have reloaded. Another volley and others fall. Before this invisible enemy, sheltered by the bushes from the cavalry attack, the Austrian commander gave the order to retreat. Dumas then returned to his men and led them safely back to camp.

In Paris, meanwhile, the National Convention had been urging Dumas to make an attack on the main body of the Austrians, but he took his time, studying thoroughly the topography of the region. When, a few days later, he did attack, he won a brilliant victory, accomplishing one of the most astonishing feats in military history: the capture of Mont Cenis, one of the highest peaks in the Alps.

Mont Cenis was assailable only from three sides; the fourth was so well protected by nature that the Austrians took no further precaution than putting up a stockade. Dumas decided to attack there. Feigning an assault on the other three sides, he set out one night with 300 men to capture the peak.

"Understand," he warned his men, "he who slips is a dead man.

Nothing can save him if he falls from such a height. It will, therefore, be useless to call for help. His cry will not be heard, and may imperil our enterprise by giving the alarm."

Three men fell, but there was no sound save the hurtling of their bodies against the jagged rocks. Up the dizzy heights the little band climbed, surprising and overcoming the enemy.

France was elated by the victory. The National Convention in a special bulletin said, "Glory to the conquerors of Mt. Cenis and Mt. St. Bernard. Glory to the invincible Army of the Alps, and those who have led them to victory. We do not know how to describe to you, dear comrades, the enthusiasm that has been created by your brilliant feat of arms. We rely upon you with great confidence and upon the energy and genius of brave General Dumas."

On another occasion, like Horatius of old, Dumas defended the bridge at Brixen, single-handed, winning the title of "Horatius Cocles of the Tyrol" from Napoleon. He was in pursuit of the Austrians and as usual had out-distanced all his men but one, named Dermoncourt, later a general. The Austrians, seeing only two men in pursuit, stopped to defend the bridge. Dermoncourt was struck down, falling under his horse. "Having no longer to defend my own body," says Dermoncourt, "I could look back in the direction of the general; he had stopped at the bridge of Brixen and was holding it alone against the whole squadron. Because of the narrowness of the bridge the men could not come upon him except two or three at a time, the general sabering them as they came up."

Dumas killed eight of them and wounded others but he was near the end of his strength, for he had received three wounds in the head, thigh, and arm; numerous small cuts; and eight bullet holes through his uniform. Besides his horse was killed. His men arrived just in time to save him.

This exploit resounded through the nation, and medals were struck, depicting the action of a single man stopping a whole troop of cavalry.

Soon afterward Dumas was transferred to Italy where he fought under Napoleon. Here again he was instrumental in winning a victory. One day a spy was brought into camp. Search as they would, they could find nothing on him. Then Dumas arrived. Calling four men, he ordered them to shoot the spy. Asked why, Dumas replied, "To get the message he has in his stomach." To save his life the man confessed that he had a message stowed away there—in a pellet. A purgative was administered and a message found disclosing just when the enemy would come to the relief of Mantua and by what route.

The result was that the French won a victory in which, as usual, Dumas distinguished himself. But Marshal Berthier, his commander and rival, did not mention him in his dispatches to Napoleon.

However, he was soon to come to the notice of Napoleon in another way. While pursuing the Austrians, his horse was killed under him. Crawling into a valley he found a number of guns the retreating Austrians had thrown away. With these he shot down twenty-five of the enemy, finally making his way back to camp on an Austrian horse. "He entered so weak and worn," says Dermoncourt, "that I cried, 'General, are you wounded?' 'No,' he said, 'but I have killed too many, too many.' And he fainted away."

Napoleon sent him a brace of pistols made at Versailles as a souvenir and soon afterward sent him to capture the rich province of Treviso. Later, he was appointed governor of this province, a function which he performed so well that when he was to be removed, the Italians begged Napoleon to let him stay. When he did leave they gave him a fine coach-and-four as a present.

Dumas, though fierce on the field of battle, was very gentle away from it, so much so that his tender-heartedness proved more than once embarrassing to him and on one occasion came near costing him his life. At Bayonne a revolutionary mob hooted him because he closed the windows of his quarters rather than see heads being chopped off by the guillotine. "Oh, Monsieur de l'Humanité," they mocked, "come to the window."

At another time, when he saw a guillotine being erected to cut off the heads of four men who had been accused of refusing to hand over a church bell to be melted into bullets, he ordered the execution halted, took the prisoners in charge, gave their captors a personal receipt, and then freed the men. For this he was recalled to Paris by the Convention, which was lopping off heads on its own account, but he succeeded in clearing himself.

In the Egyptian campaign the impulsive general was comman-der of Napoleon's cavalry. Among those serving under him were two of Napoleon's brothers-in-law, Murat and Leclerc. Dumas dis-tinguished himself at the Battle of the Pyramids and in the taking of the Grand Mosque, but his plain speaking during this campaign was to prove his undoing. A republican at heart, he viewed with dis-favor Napoleon's imperial ambitions and took no pains to conceal his attitude.

The break between the two came soon after the destruction of Napoleon's fleet at Aboukir. There, cut off from France and harassed by the heat, some of the generals grew impatient. One day when several of these met in Dumas' tent to eat melons, they complained bitterly against Napoleon for having brought them to Egypt. Napoleon, hearing of this, blamed Dumas as the instigator, a charge that Dumas hotly denied. When Dumas announced his intention of returning to France, Napoleon begged him to stay on, but insisting that his wounds, particularly the old one he had re-ceived in dueling, necessitated his departure, Dumas made prepa-rations to leave.

A sudden revolt of the Egyptians brought about a temporary revival of friendship between the two men. Dumas by his courage and promptitude again saved the day for the French and Napoleon in gratitude sent for him. Greeting Dumas before the assembled officers, Napoleon said, "Good morning, Hercules—it is you who have beaten the hydra. . . . Gentlemen, I shall have a picture painted of the taking of the Grand Mosque. Dumas, you have al-ready posed as the principal figure." The picture was painted—but a blond cavalier was shown in Dumas' place, for by that time Dumas had left Egypt.

Landing at Tarentum in the kingdom of Naples, Dumas was taken prisoner by the Italians, who, unknown to him, had retaken the city.

He was kept a prisoner for two years during which time several attempts were made to poison him.

When he returned to France he tried to reenter the army but Napoleon ordered that his name should never be mentioned in his presence again. He even refused to pay Dumas for the time he was held prisoner, though the Neapolitans had been made to pay heavily for it. Recalling the time when he had once embraced the diminutive Napoleon, Dumas said bitterly, "To think that I had him in my arms and how easily I could have strangled him!"

Dumas wrote Napoleon:

In 1793 I was commander-in-chief of the Republican armies. I am the oldest general officer of my rank; feats of daring performed by me have greatly influenced the tide of affairs. I have always led the defenders of my country to victory. Tell me, who then received more marks of your esteem? And yet, now I see officers of all grades, junior to me, unreservedly employed while I am left inactive.

In a letter to the Minister of War, he said:

Throughout the unfortunate and difficult time I was never beaten: on the contrary, my enterprises were invariably crowned with success. . . . I was the companion of the Consul-General [Napoleon] in nearly all his Italian and Egyptian wars and no one contributed more to his triumphs and the glory of his arms than did I; his letters, which I have in my possession, testify no less to the respect in which he held me than in his friendship.

That friendship had been a close one. One day when Dumas was at dinner with Napoleon, Josephine being present, the two generals made an agreement that the one who had a son first should stand godfather for the other. Dumas was the first, but the two had already quarreled. Later that son was to have so great a name that he dimmed for a time even that of Napoleon. And a Napoleon of a later day was pleased to have a Dumas as a traveling companion.

Even after General Dumas' death, Napoleon visited his grudge on Dumas' widow. He ordered that she should not be permitted to pass through the gates of his palace at the Tuileries.

At the age of forty-four Dumas died of stomach trouble, his ailment being largely the result of his hardships at Naples. But for his quarrel with Napoleon, to what heights might he not have risen? At thirty-five, when he was a general, Napoleon was only a major. And it was only by an extraordinary twist of fate that Napoleon came to succeed Dumas as commander-in-chief of the French Army.

This happened in 1793 when the Revolution had got out of hand and the Convention at Paris, seeking someone to restore order, sent for Dumas. The latter was then living at Villers-Cotteret, fifty miles from Paris, and at that time, a return journey of two days. Dumas, receiving the order by courier, set off at once for Paris, but the affair was so urgent that the Convention could not wait for him and selected Napoleon, who succeeded so well in quelling the riots that the Convention kept him in the post intended for Dumas.

Napoleon who was both soldier and politician turned this coup into personal profit and became ruler of France. Whether Dumas would have done the same had he arrived in time is to be doubted. He was a republican at heart, and first and foremost a soldier, self-effacing and honest. In Egypt when he found hidden gold valued at two million francs, he turned it over to Napoleon.

Napoleon, in his way, admired Dumas. He told him on one occasion, "What I like about you, Dumas, is not only your courage but your humanity. I know in the Tarentaise you rescued from the guillotine three or four poor devils who did not wish to let their church bells be melted down."

Dumas' early victories contributed greatly toward keeping France republican and thus in paving the way for Napoleon. No wonder, therefore, that Dumas was so bitter against Naploeon.

Anatole France says:

The greatest of the Dumas's . . . was the son of the Negro woman. . . . General Alexandre Dumas de la Pailletérie, the conqueror of St. Bernard and Mt. Cenis, the hero of Brixen. He offered his life sixty times for France; was admired by Bonaparte and died poor. Such a life is a masterpiece beyond all comparison. One is proud to have such a man as an ancestor.

Dumas' statue stands in the Place Malsherbes, Paris, near those of his son and grandson. His name is also on the Arc de Triomphe.

REFERENCES

In the *Almanach National*, An. II. Napoleon is cited as a "major" —Dumas as a "general."

Marquis de la Pailletérie, Dumas' father, was the first nobleman in the suite of Prince de Conti.

General Dumas was five French feet and ten inches tall; or six English feet two and two-fifths inches.

Napoleon had at least twelve other Negro generals, all of whom served in France, namely: André Rigaud, Martial Besse, Antoine Cloulatte, B. Leveille, Pierre Michel, Magloire Pelage, Villatte, Chanlatte, Barthelmi, and Adjutant-Generals Alexandre Pétion, J. B. Belley, and Etienne V. Mentor.

Dumas, Alexandre, père, *Mémoires*, Vol. I. Paris, 1863.

France, Anatole, *La Vie Littéraire*, Ser. I, p. 29. Paris, 1889.

Hautriue, Ernest d', *Un Soldat de la Révolution*. Paris, 1897.

Napoleon, *Correspondance*, Vol. IV, pp. 52, 453. Paris, 1860.

ADDITIONAL REFERENCES

David, Placide, *Sur Les Rives du Passe*, pp. 39–70. Paris, La Caravelle, 1947.

Fleming, B. J., and Pryde, M. J., *Distinguished Negroes Abroad*, pp. 70–77. Washington, D.C., The Associated Publishers, 1946.

Maurois, André, *The Titans*. New York, Harper and Brothers, 1957.

Shaw, Esther Popel, "The Three Alexandres (Dumas)." *Negro History Bulletin* (December, 1940), pp. 59–61. Association for the Study of Negro Life and History, Washington, D.C.

Alexandre Dumas, Père

THE WORLD'S GREATEST ROMANCER
(1802–1870)

NATURE AT TIMES endows one man with the energy and gifts of so many other individuals combined that he soars above the average mortal as an eagle does the ostrich. While these prodigies move through life with scintillant ease, the others plod heavy-footed along, and are left with two alternatives: either to thrill in admiration or to rage in envy.

To this type of a multitude of talents in a single body belongs Alexandre Dumas, père, the greatest, the most prolific, the most jovial writer the world has ever known.

Born wretchedly poor and almost friendless, Dumas educated himself to the point where he became the educator of tens of millions of human beings the world over. A self-trained writer, he produced more literature than anyone who ever lived, earning with his pen more than $10 million in the currency of our day. And yet, he found time enough to win fame as a soldier, duelist, hypnotist, cook, gourmet, entertainer and bon vivant, champion of human rights, excavator of buried cities, and gallant. Dumas perhaps held the record of his day as a lover. He rose to such a conspicuous position in the eyes of the world that whatever he did was news and was heralded far and wide.

Kind-hearted and lavish as nature herself, this extraordinary man gave away great sums of money; created a private pension system for those who had served him and his faithfully; built a castle in which he kept open house for the world; spent more millions than he earned—and left life as poor as he had started out.

Dumas, père, was the son of General Dumas, another extraordinary figure who rose from a sergeancy to the post of general-in-chief in the armies of France in twenty-two months.

When his father died broken-hearted in 1806, following a quarrel with Napoleon, Dumas was only five. Madame Dumas gave him such education as her wretched means could afford. Deciding on a musical career for him, she placed him in charge of a violinist, but Dumas was so devoid of musical talent that after three years of study, he could hardly tune his instrument. As for mathematics, he was never able to get beyond the multiplication table. Indeed, his fondness for adventure and the open air prevented his taking serious interest in study of any sort.

His mother finally decided that the priesthood would be the best career for him, and a near relative of hers offered to pay the expense involved. But on the morning he was to leave for the seminary, a girl cousin of his laughed so heartily at the idea of his becoming a priest that Dumas ran away to the woods and hid, staying there for days with his friends—the poachers.

Despite his scholastic shortcomings, Dumas loved reading, and eagerly devoured every bit of printed matter he could lay his hands on. When not reading, he was out shooting rabbits or chatting with his poacher friends.

His first job—that of messenger boy in a notary's office—gave him plenty of time for reading. One day, hearing that *Hamlet* was to be performed in a nearby town, he went to see it, coming away so thrilled that he proceeded to learn the entire role of Hamlet by heart. After this he tried his own hand as a playwright. His first play, *The Mayor of Strassburg*, met with some slight success.

This encouraged him to write other plays. But he used so much of his employer's time at this that he was discharged. His elder cousin, Deviolané, who was always predicting that Dumas' absorption in literary work would make a vagabond of him in the end, took malicious satisfaction in what happened and called him an "idle scoundrel." Later, when Dumas published his first book,

Nouvelles Contemporaines, and only four copies were sold after an outlay of several thousand francs, Deviolané's triumphant "I told you so" seemed justified.

Dumas' next position was in another notary's office, where he worked for room and board. His employer was in the habit of spending weekends in Paris and a powerful longing came over him to go there too. From the monotonous provincial town to which poverty tied him, Paris looked like heaven. He made up his mind to go while his employer was away.

But how to get to Paris on an empty purse? He settled the matter by going poaching, like Shakespeare. An excellent shot, Dumas killed enough birds and hares to get money for his fare.

That visit to Paris opened his eyes to the fact that there was no future for him in a small town. Once more in Villers-Cotteret, there was the problem of getting enough money to return to Paris and pay his keep there until he found a way of earning a living.

It was then that Lady Luck came to his rescue. One evening, while playing for drinks at a café, he won 600 glasses of absinthe. As he did not drink, he sold them and with the proceeds went to Paris.

There he tried in vain to get help from several persons who had been indebted to his father. At last, thanks to his excellent handwriting, he obtained work as a copyist in the household of the Duke of Orléans, later King Louis-Philippe, at a salary of 1200 francs ($240) a year.

In the meanwhile he was reading voraciously, particularly history and mythology. Then he wrote a comedy, *La Chasse et L'Amour*, which had considerable success in a small theatre. This was followed by others in a similar vein—until one night he heard a woman spectator say, "This sort of thing will never keep the theatre going." He determined to do better, and wrote a play, *Christine*, which pleased the repertorial committee of the Théâtre Français, but was received with scorn by Picard, the leading comedian of the day. Picard, after glancing through it, sent for Dumas and asked him caustically whether he had any occupation other than that of writing. When Dumas said that he was a clerk, Picard snapped, "Go back to your desk, young man, and stay there."

Dumas, thanking Picard sarcastically for his advice, immediately wrote another play, *Henry III*, which was readily accepted by the Théâtre Français, and rehearsals began.

But as opening night approached, two misfortunes occurred. His beloved mother fell ill, and the duke discharged him for neglect of his work. Undaunted, Dumas decided to make the duke sorry for having discharged him and invited him to attend the premiere.

The duke replied that he was giving a party that night and could not possibly be there. Undiscouraged, Dumas suggested that he bring the entire royal party to the play, but again the duke declined. Dumas, not to be beaten, then suggested that the duke advance his dinner by one hour and the theatre would postpone its opening for the same time. Persistence won out and the duke agreed to appear at the play with his guests.

As for his mother's illness, Dumas divided his time between rehearsals and her bedside.

On opening night, he discovered that he hadn't a clean collar and couldn't afford to buy one. He promptly cut one out of white cardboard and wore that.

The play was an instant success. The audience clamored for the author, and Dumas, in his cardboard collar, came out and took his curtain calls. The next morning his name, hitherto unknown, was the talk of Paris. He hurried to his mother, followed by a train of porters carrying so many baskets of flowers that there was hardly place in her room for them.

Dumas was paid a large sum for the rights to his play. Then he did two things characteristic of him. Seeking out his skeptical cousin, Deviolané, he flourished in his face the bank notes he had just received; then, going to a restaurant, he insured himself against supperless days by buying a meal ticket good for a year, on which the restaurant promptly failed. But the duke, took him back and gave him work that permitted him plenty of leisure.

Only twenty-six, he was now one of the leading figures of the gay capital. He was admitted into the best circles, where his color was in his favor. Society gossiped about his African passions and his tropical sensuousness. Dumas, quick to capitalize on the situation, lived the part.

He wrote other plays, some fifty of them. But he was always in financial hot water as he spent money faster than it came in. When the public grew tired of his plays, he found himself swamped with debts. Then he took a long-planned step. He started writing historical novels. He would do for French history what Sir Walter Scott had done for Scottish history.

Shortly after this he met Auguste Maquet, his lifelong collaborator. Taking a short sketch of Maquet's, Dumas breathed life into it and produced *The Chevalier Harmenthal*, which proved an instantaneous success. This was followed by his most famous works, *The Three Musketeers*, *The Count of Monte Cristo*, and *The Black Tulip*.

The children of his brain who populated these books became so popular that they were discussed in cafés and salons as if they were living personages. Indeed, there were those who insisted that they were real. So great a sensation were his books that soon he was the most talked of man in France. Kings and princes sought his company. It was while touring Italy as the guest of Prince Napoleon that the idea of one of his most famous books, *Monte Cristo*, occurred to him. When his yacht arrived off Algiers he was given a royal salute of twenty-one guns.

Dumas decided he needed his own theatre and opened one. The Historique. A queue formed at the box office the night before the opening, a thing hitherto unknown, and which proved profitable to street vendors, who sold food and bedding to the crowd. All the next day until the box office opened, there was feasting and merry-making on the sidewalk. For the next several years Dumas packed his theatre nightly.

A giant in size, Dumas possessed exuberance and mental powers to match. For more than thirty years he wrote incessantly, snatching only some four hours of sleep nightly. One of his best books, *Chevalier de Maison Rouge*, was written on a wager. He made a bet that he could write it in seventy-two hours including time required for food and sleep. He finished it in sixty-six. And it was written in his very beautiful hand without erasures.

His energy seemed inexhaustible. He lived at top speed, yet neither age nor high living seemed to affect him. At the age of sixty he would come home after a whole night of entertainment and sit down to write, while his son, and others half his age, would go to bed. He wrote with the same impetuous ardor his father had shown in battle.

He could not keep pace with the demand for his work. For each letter of the alphabet he wrote, he received one centime, or about half a dollar for a word of ten letters, a sum equal to several times the present rate. Each time he stopped to put on his shoe, it cost him $100. He wrote and published more than 1200 books and plays, and about four times as many articles for the newspapers. His travel articles described Europe and North Africa to the world.

As for adventures, he had so many that it is not possible to give even a brief description of them in a short sketch. He fought several duels in which he was invariably the victor. He took a leading part in the Revolution of 1830, going after the sorely-needed gunpowder at Soissons with the dash and daring of his most noted figure, d'Artagnan. In Italy he helped the Garibaldians in their fight for freedom against Austria, and then gave a large sum for the excavation of Pompeii, he himself directing the work. In short, he lived his characters.

And while the people liked Dumas for his books, they liked him even more for himself. He radiated good humor and made people laugh wherever he went. Even when alone writing, he would laugh uproariously with the characters he was creating, splashing as joyously in the literary element as a bird in its bath. Of his gaiety, he wrote, "I carry it about with me wherever I go—I don't know why it is but it is so—an atmosphere of stir and life which has become proverbial." He was the life of every party—"always crazy, always excellent." No prominent festivity was considered complete without him.

Once he appeared at a costume ball dressed as a greased pole. At dinner parties he appeared resplendent with rows of decorations bestowed upon him by foreign rulers. He knew the value of publicity and how to get himself talked about. He was the Barnum and the Hercules of literature in one. Other literary men envied this unschooled "upstart" who, at almost one bound, had leaped to the foremost place in the public eye. Balzac, the great novelist, always contemptuously referred to him as "the Negro." Others said that he was only a figurehead and that his collaborators did all the work. Dumas admitted that he had collaborators but "only as Napoleon had generals." A rival, hearing that he was going to write another book, said, "Monsieur Dumas, are you really going to write a novel this time?" "Oh yes," he laughed, "I have to this time. My valet wrote the last one but the scoundrel demanded so much that I had to discharge him." To another he gaily replied, "Oh me, I am only a trademark."

His wit was equal to all occasions. Once, while in a theatre with a fellow playwright whose play was being acted, Dumas saw a man fast asleep and twitted his friend about it. The next night both were in the same theatre, and again they saw a man asleep. It was one of Dumas' plays this time. The playwright flung back, "Ah, Monsieur Dumas, I see your plays also send people to sleep."

"Oh no," laughed Dumas, "that's the same fellow we saw last night. He hasn't waked yet."

Dumas scorned all convention. He gave his fancy free rein and could be counted on to do the unexpected, a reason why his characters are so alive. Unlike his distinguished son, Dumas fils, the word "duty" did not exist for him. Once when the Duke de Chartres, as a preliminary to inviting him on a trip to Italy, asked him what were his arrangements for the winter he replied, "Arrangements? I never make any. I'm like a bird on the branch of a tree. If there is no wind I stay there. If a wind comes I open my wings and go wherever it takes me."

Many of his doings were considered amazing even in liberal-minded France. Once at a royal dinner party, when irked by his stiff shirt, he tore open the collar and bared his massive chest. A distinguished lady once called on him to find three beautiful women, nude, draped about his table while he wrote. He married a beautiful actress, Ida Ferrier, in the French House of Lords with two noblemen as witnesses, for by birthright he was Marquis de la Pailletérie. His women friends were selected lavishly from the galaxy of beauties that swarmed around him like moths to a light.

His friend Lamartine wrote him, "The world has sought perpetual motion, Dumas, you have done better; you've created perpetual amazement." His enemies, nearly all of them literally men, used his oddities to discredit him, but the masses considered him a privileged character. Whatever Dumas did they considered well done.

He scattered money about as the wind scatters the leaves of autumn. In his own words, "Whatever my hand grasps it holds tightly except money, which flows through it like water." He built a castle in the suburbs and called it Monte-Cristo. People whom Dumas never met would come in to spend the weekend. Once a friend asked to be introduced to a guest who was sitting near him at the table. "Introduce him?" asked Dumas laughingly. "Why, I have never met the gentleman myself."

Monte-Cristo, built and maintained at a fabulous cost, probably did more than anything else to ruin Dumas financially. When the Revolution of 1848 brought about the collapse of the theatrical business, Dumas found himself bankrupt and was forced to flee to Brussels along with other refugees.

His generous nature would not permit the prosecution of men who had wronged him, and he never sought to avenge himself against his enemies. When a subscription for a memorial to Balzac was taken up, he was the first contributor. When a man whom he had befriended swindled him out of a large sum of money and was being sought, Dumas declined to help the police. "The fellow," he said, "is a scoundrel but it is no business of mine to find a rope to hang him with." When his Negro valet, "Alexander the Great," dressed himself in Dumas' finery and strutted along the boulevards posing as the great writer, Dumas got another valet, and calling Alexander in, informed him that the new man was to wait on them both, and that his sole request was that he should not take the new valet on his walks. His valuables were never kept under lock and key. On his dressing table he kept a heap of gold coins to which anyone might have helped himself.

His extraordinary good and forgiving nature is perhaps best illustrated by the following incident. One wintry night he returned home unexpectedly to find one of his best friends, Roger de Beauvoir, who had been one of the witnesses at his wedding, usurping his place in the family bed. Unclad, Roger de Beauvoir dashed out on Dumas' approach into the sitting room, which was unheated.

Dumas, aware of everything, greeted his wife as if nothing had happened, and then sat down to write while Roger de Beauvoir shivered and stifled his coughs as best he could in the cold room. Then Dumas, laughing heartily, opened the door and bade the frozen lover come in and be warmed. He fixed him comfortably in an armchair with blankets and then crawled into bed with his wife, but thinking that Roger was not comfortable enough, took him into the bed beside Madame Dumas.

Next morning while she was still asleep Dumas said gaily, "Roger, shall we two old friends quarrel over a woman even though she is a lawful wife? That would be stupid." Extending his hand to his rival over his wife's belly, he added, "Let's be reconciled like the Romans of old over this public place." And he shook Roger's hand cordially.

When one of his passing mistresses told him she was pregnant, he replied, "I am not so presumptuous as to believe myself the author of this miracle, but if he brings into this vale of tears a head of kinky hair I'll have to be convinced."

Dumas never worried about his color, although many of his friends, particularly the English-speaking ones, were anxious to prove that he wasn't a Negro, but a quadroon. In his own memoirs Dumas tells how, when he drew his pistol on the commandant of Soissons, where he had gone to get powder for the rebels, the commandant's wife advised her husband to yield as the Negroes were attacking the place. Dumas said that he was puzzled at this for a long time, since he was the only Negro there. Later, however, he discovered that the woman had lived in Haiti and had witnessed a massacre of the whites by the blacks.

Dumas had a little Negro page named Alexis of whom he was very fond. A friend of his had presented Alexis to him hidden in a huge basket of flowers. Colored Americans who visited France were cordially received by Dumas, among them the great Negro tragedian Ira Aldridge, to whom he gave a dinner at "Les Réservoirs," Versailles.

Luckily for the world, Dumas was born in France and not in America, where he would have been circumscribed and might have used his genius in the struggle for elementary liberty like his notable Negro contemporary, Frederick Douglass.

Dumas numbered among his friends and admirers most of the great men of his period, including Lamartine, Eugène Sue, de Musset, Rossini, Goethe, King Louis Phillippe, Pope Gregory XVI, Delacroix, St. Beuve, Chateaubriand, Heine, and Victor Hugo.

Once Victor Hugo acted very spitefully toward him but Dumas promptly forgave him and later defended Hugo, which so touched Hugo that he wrote Dumas, "I love you more every day not alone because you are one of the brilliant lights of my century, but because you are one of its consolations."

Heinrich Heine, on his death bed, had Dumas' novels read to him, and wrote Dumas, "Your first name and your last name are currency worth more than gold and silver."

Toward the end, when Dumas' overworked brain began to weaken, he took an interest in cooking and became the most renowned chef of his time. None could equal him in preparing a hare, a chicken, a sole, or a sauce. Bouilhet, the poet, wrote Gustave Flaubert:

Everybody rushes to the doors to see Dumas, without his hat, his hair standing out. It is a real event, a revolution. He is recognized, a queue forms at the hotel entrance where I order luncheon for my guests. We take an absinthe in the café and then go to the kitchen. Dumas, in shirt sleeves, puts his finger in the pie, makes a dream of an omelet, roasts the chicken at the end of a cord, (they are keeping the nail here reverently), cuts an onion, stirs the kettle, throws twenty francs to the scullery-servants and seizes the grateful cook around the waist. It's immense! What youthfulness! He was as happy as a boy on his holiday. And what a mouth . . . I have rarely seen anyone eat with such zest. He drinks less. We embraced each other several times. Excepting him and me everybody was tipsy. What's best of all is that the mistress of the hotel sold, at a high price, the remains of the omelet and the chicken. A good manager! One thing not to be denied, and which I didn't believe before was so genuine, is the immense popularity of this jolly fellow!

As late as 1931 the Paris daily *L'Intransigeant* asked its readers whom they considered the greatest gourmet of modern times. Dumas was named first, and King Leopold I of Belgium second.

Innumerable are the anecdotes told about Dumas. When his beloved friend the Duke of Orléans died, Dumas, always with a sense of the dramatic, fell into the arms of Prince Jerome Bonaparte, crying, "Permit me to weep over a Bourbon in the arms of a Bonaparte." (The two were rival royal families.)

When told that his novels were a violation of history, Dumas retorted, "It is permissible to rape history on condition that you have a child by her."

When someone shouted at him, "Your father was black." Dumas flung back, "And my grandfather was a monkey." As the crowd roared, he added, "Now that I have amused you all with wit of a good quality, I must bid you good-day as I have work to do."

In his declining years he was tenderly cared for by his son, who, also starting at the bottom of the ladder, made a fortune independently of his father. Dumas, fils, always saw to it that his father's vest pockets were filled with gold pieces as the old man had a horror of poverty towards the last.

In 1870, at the age of sixty-eight, he died, his great fame suffering temporary eclipse in the genius of his son.

At the unveiling of his statue in Place Malsherbes, Paris, Edmond About said:

This statue is that of a great madman, who into all his good humor and astonishing gaiety, put more true wisdom than this is to be found in the hearts of all us here. It is the likeness of a prodigal, who after squandering millions in a thousand generous ways, left without knowing it, a king's treasure!

"He was not France's; he was not Europe's; he was the world's!" said Victor Hugo.

A journalist of the time said of him:

During half a century Europe swore by him; the two Americas sent fleets of packet-boats to fetch his novels; his dramas were played in Egypt to delight the old age of Mehemet-Ali; his writings have been read in Chernandagor and in Tobolsk. With his hand he blackened mountains of paper; he has had a hundred theatrical pieces performed and published a thousand volumes. He became a soldier in order to take part in street fights; he commanded a legion; has taken part in twenty duels, fought as many law suits, chartered ships, and distributed pensions from his private purse. He has danced, hunted, loved, fished, hypnotized, cooked, made ten millions, and spent much more.

Michelet wrote, "A man? No, he is an element like an inextinguishable flame or a mighty American river."

Lucas Dubreton in *The Fourth Musketeer* says of Dumas:

He fills an enormous place like that which Homer's heroes occupied on the field of battle. An American newspaper that arranged a list of the famous men of the nineteenth century put his name by the side of Napoleon's. Figures have an eloquence all their own. From 1870 to 1884, 2,845,000 volumes and 80,000,000 subscription parts were sold, 600 of his works were reprinted by various journals, without counting the countries which had no copyright arrangement with France and so pirated and spread them in many tongues. His favor has not waned since then, and as Edmond About said, if all the readers of the 'Three Musketeers' and 'Monte Cristo' assessed themselves one centime each, the statue of Dumas would be of solid gold.

The fittest tribute one can pay Dumas is to repeat what Dumas said of Shakespeare. "Shakespeare," he said, "is the one who next to God has created the most." But for every character of Shakespeare's there are at least three of Dumas'. And his personages are just as real as Shakespeare's. Who, having once met d'Artagnan, Porthos, Athos, or Aramis, Abbé Faria, Cagliostro, Cardinal Richelieu, the Duke of Buckingham, My Lady of Windsor, Edmond Dantes, and a score of his other characters can ever forget them?

Many of Dumas' most sincere admirers have found it necessary to apologize for, or to explain, his exuberance and his utter disregard of dogma and taboo—but for a man like this, no excuses are needed. Dumas was a truly free individual, such a one as most of us, deep down in our hearts, would like to be but cannot.

Dumas opposed slavery and wrote a letter to the Bishop of Autun thanking him for his fight against it. He said, "There may even be relatives of mine who even now are forming part of the cargoes of slave vessels."

One remark of Dumas' deserves special mention here. He said, "When I discovered that I was black I determined to so act that men should see beneath my skin." There was once considerable color prejudice in Paris because of the horrible war between blacks and whites in Haiti.

Peerless, good-hearted colossus of brain and brawn, one can truly say of Dumas to all the world, "Here was a man! Whence comes such another?"

REFERENCES

One of Dumas' great desires was to visit the United States but he was dissuaded by his friends and especially his publishers. His books were best sellers in the United States and his publishers feared for the result if his American admirers saw him in the flesh. The *Imperial Dictionary of Universal Biography* says, "He is understood to have abandoned on sound advice the desire he once cherished of visiting the birthplace of Washington and Franklin and the land of republican equality. Such a resolution is to be deplored as the world would have rung with indignation at insults being offered to a man of genius on account of his colour and a case of prejudiced outrage so extreme might have produced a salutary reaction." (Vol. 2, p. 116. 1863.)

Dumas, Alexandre, *My memoirs*, 6 vols. New York, 1907–1908.

Michaux, A., *Souvenirs sur Alexandre Dumas*. 1885.

Parigot, H., *Alexandre Dumas*. Paris, 1902.

Spurr, Harry A., *The Life and Writings of Alexandre Dumas*. New York, Stokes, 1902.

Pléon, A., *Un Romancier Populaire Compiegne*. Paris, 1900.

Gorman, Herbert Sherman, *The Incredible Marquis*. New York, Farrar and Rinehart, Inc., 1929.

New York Tribune, April 17, 1910.

Biographie Universelle "Dumas, Alexandre, père." (has vast bibliography on Dumas).

Imperial Dictionary of Universal Biography, Vol. II, p. 116. 1863.

ADDITIONAL REFERENCES

Adams, Russell L., *Great Negroes: Past and Present*, p. 120. Chicago, Afro-Am Publishing Company, 1963, 1964.

Cook, Mercer, *Five French Negro Authors*. Washington, D.C., The Associated Publishers, 1943.

Fitzgerald, Percy Hetherington, *Life and Adventure of Alexander Dumas*. London, Tinsley Bros., 1873.

Fleming, B. J., and Pryde, M. J., *Distinguished Negroes Abroad*, p. 78. Washington, D.C., The Associated Publishers, 1946.

Gribble, Francis Henry, *Dumas, Father and Son*. New York, Dutton Press, 1930.

Haynes, Elizabeth Ross, *Unsung Heroes*, pp. 237–445. New York, Du Bois and Dill, 1921.

Lesser, Allen, *Enchanting Rebel*. New York, Beechhurst Press, 1947.

Lucas-Dubreton, J., *The Fourth Musketeer*, trans. by Maida Castelitun Darrton. New York, Coward-McCann, Inc., 1928.

Marcelin, Frédéric, *La Confession de Bazouité*, pp. 163–185. Paris, Société d'Editions Littéraires et Artistiques, 1909.

Maurois, André, *The Titans*. New York, Harper Brothers, 1957.

Miltoun, Francis, *Dumas' Paris*. Boston, L. C. Page and Company, 1904.

Saunders, Edith, *The Prodigal Father*. London, New York, Toronto, Longmans, Green and Company, 1951.

Sewell, Eugene P., *Balzac, Dumas, "Bert" Williams, Poetry, and a Short Story*, pp. 14–32. Chicago, 1923.

Shaw, Esther Propel, "The Three Alexandres (Dumas)." *Negro History Bulletin* (December, 1940), pp. 59–61, Association for the Study of Negro Life and History, Washington, D.C.

Todd, Ruthven, *The Laughing Mulatto*. London, Rich and Cowan, Ltd., 1940.

Underwood, Edna Worthley, *The Taste of Honey*, pp. 62–68. Portland, Me., Mosher Press, 1930.

Alexandre Dumas, Fils

REMAKER OF THE MODERN FRENCH STAGE
(1824–1895)

ALEXANDRE DUMAS, fils, last of the great Dumases, was the foremost French dramatist of the nineteenth century, and one of the world's most original thinkers.

To him perhaps more than to any other writer belongs the honor of bringing realism to the stage. His genius completely changed the course of the French theatre, turning it away from empty romance and oratory to life, to serious thought, and to purpose.

Dumas' unvarying theme was love, and he ranks as one of the greatest analysts of that passion. No secret of love life was hidden from him. Like a deep-sea diver, he explored the recesses of the human heart and held up his discoveries to the gaze of the world.

His early youth was marred by a great sorrow, which acting on his extremely sensitive nature did more than anything else to make him take up the theme in which he was a master. He was to learn later that when life has a great destiny for us it sometimes begins by hurting us deeply.

Yet Dumas' sorrow was one that is considered ordinary by millions of individuals. It was only illegitimacy. His mother was a humble dressmaker, Marie Labay. The elder Dumas, at that time, was just out of his teens, and was earning less than $5 a week.

At boarding school the boys taunted the shy and intensely proud

123

Alexandre about his birth. That might have been their revenge because he was smarter than the cleverest of them. When he was nine his father, who had not yet reached the height of his fame, gave him his name but the wound to his spirit remained incurable.

The elder Dumas took the boy everywhere—into the salons of the elite, the dens of the underworld, to Russia, Germany, Spain, Italy, and North Africa, where he astonished everybody by his vivacity, precocity, and wit.

In these circumstances he grew up to be a brilliant idler. Then one morning he awoke to find himself penniless, homeless, and $10,000 in debt. In the financial collapse of his father, he had fallen also.

What was there in the world for him to do? His position is best told in his own words:

> I found myself sitting sadly on a cane-seated chair before a white wooden table in a miserably furnished room of the hotel where I had taken refuge. I had been driven out of my elegant apartment with everything seized and sold.
>
> I gave myself up to bitter reflection and mechanically I opened the drawer of the table. Inside were some stamped papers and a pad of writing paper evidently forgotten there by the last occupant. I took out the pad, and as I had no occupation, and did not know what else to do, I decided to become an author, and started to write.

Success was not to be won easily. Time and time again he threw aside his manuscripts and decided never to write another line. His first work—a book of poems—attracted hardly any attention. Later, however, the book collectors paid a fabulous price for copies of this edition.

His next work, *The Sins of His Youth*, had better luck. It treated of the underworld of Paris of which he and his father had tasted deeply, and of his own experiences.

This was followed by *Camille*, his masterpiece. As a novel, *Camille* went well, but when he turned it into a play (later its more successful form), his early difficulties seemed endless.

Again it was a question of money. While penniless in Marseilles he decided to turn the book into a play in the hope of selling it. At one sitting he dashed off the first three acts "without an erasure," and hurrying off to Paris, finished the remainder in five days.

After much difficulty he found a producer. But when it was ready for a showing, the censors barred it. When he won over the censors, the theatre failed. When he got another house, the leading lady died.

Next he tried to interest Lecont, the leading actor of the day. Lecont kept the manuscript a few days and returned it, greasy and smelly with tobacco, with the comment, "Never would I play such rot."

Dumas, heartbroken, flung the manuscript into the bottom of an old drawer, feeling that that was the end of it. But fate was yet to have its fling. Months later, as he was walking on the boulevards, he met a friend, who invited him to have a drink. While seated there on the terrace, Bouffé, an actor, saw him and stopped to speak with him.

The conversation turned to the rejected play and Bouffé, saying he was to take Lecont's place, promised to do what he could about the play.

Months passed and Dumas heard nothing. Then he received a call from Bouffé. The theatre at which the latter played was in desperate need of a good play to save it from bankruptcy and *Camille* was accepted as a last resort.

Its success was instantaneous and lasting. *Camille* remained popular well into the twentieth century. Sarah Bernhardt, Desclée, and other world-famous actresses and actors have played it. It became an opera, and later a motion picture, with Rudolph Valentino in the role of Armand. Still later it was played by Greta Garbo.

Dumas soon became the most talked of playwright in Paris. His father was earning millions. Both stood at the top of their literary world. Each loved the other tenderly and yet no two men could have been less alike. The elder Dumas was gay, jolly, always in good humor, an expansive and easy-going soul.

The younger was reserved and inclined to haughtiness, a stern moralist, an apostle of duty. He believed that his mission was to reform mankind and lead it into the path of right living. Most of all, he believed in fidelity to the marriage vow. He insisted that a husband had a right to punish with his own hand any man who had taken his wife.

The elder delighted people with his wonderful tales; the younger lashed them for their sins and called them to repentance.

The father said of the son, "Alexandre loves preaching over-much." The son said of his father, "My father is a big child that I had when I was very little."

Later, when the elder squandered the greatest fortune ever earned by a writer, the younger took care of him like a mother.

The younger Dumas was witty too, but in a manner entirely different from his father. Unlucky was the one who ran up against him. It was like a striking a buzz saw with a bare hand.

Once, in a noted club, a flippant young count, proud of his ancestry, thought he would have some fun with young Dumas.

"Monsieur Dumas," he began, "I understand your father is a quadroon?"

"Yes," replied Dumas.

"And your grandfather was a mulatto?"

"Yes."

"And your great-grandfather was a Negro?"

"Yes."

"Good," said the count, laughing. "Will you tell us what was your great-great-grandfather, then, M. Dumas?"

"Sir," was the acid reply, "he was an ape. My ancestry began where yours ends."

His plays are filled with biting observations such as the following:

"A woman's past is like a coal mine: do not go into it with a light or there'll be an explosion."

"She is one of those women who spend their lives in lining with soft padding the ditch into which they intend their virtues shall fall, and who, furious at waiting on the edge for someone to push them in, throw stones at other women who pass."

"One can always live with a wife, provided he has something else to occupy his time."

"She had spread all those diamonds over her mother who accompanied her and who resembled the constellation of the Great Bear, not only in brilliance, but in form."

Dumas, fils, won higher literary honors than his father, and in certain learned circles is regarded as the abler of the two. As a thinker, he was undoubtedly profounder. He knew human nature thoroughly and had mastered the theatre as few before or since. He knew that all that touches the flesh interests us; he realized the imperative need of love in the lives of all. He was fearless in depicting these truths, thus his characters are alive. Of a deeply sympathetic nature, his cry of pity for fallen womanhood resounded over the world. The French Academy elected him to membership by a vote of twenty against eleven.

The elder Dumas had coveted this honor and the failure to get it had hurt him deeply. When the son rose to make his first address to the Academy, he scored it for what he considered its neglect of his father.

Seeing also with deep pain that his own reputation was overshadowing that of his illustrious father, he tried to correct this impression by praising his father above himself. He said to them:

It was under the sun of Africa, of African blood, born of a Negro virgin, that was formed the one from whom thou wert to be born— the one who as soldier of the Republic stifled a horse between his knees; broke an iron helmet with his teeth; and defended alone the bridge of Brixen against a vanguard of twenty men.

Rome would have borne him in triumph and made him a consul. France, calmer and more economical, refused education to his son, and this son, reared in the forest, under an open sky, driven by need and the force of his genius, invaded one day the great city and strode into the field of literature as his father strode into the field of battle, overturning all who did not make way for him.

Then commenced the cyclopean task that lasted forty years. Tragedy, history, travel, romance, thou has thrown them all out from the vast alembic of thy brain; thou hast peopled the whole world of fiction with new creations. Thou hast caused to crack with the volume of thy work the newspaper, the book, the theatre, all of which have been too narrow for thy powerful shoulders. Thou hast enriched France, Europe, America, the world. Thou hast enriched the publishers, the translators, the plagiarists. Thou hast made them million-aires, whilst for thyself thou hast nothing left. . . .

Then one day there comes a break. Thou hast become Dumas, the Father, for the respectful, and Father Dumas for the insolent. In the midst of all this fools' clamor thou hast perhaps heard this phrase:

"Decidedly, his son has more genius than he."

How thou oughtest to laugh! Oh, well, no! Thou wert happy like to the first father, believing, perhaps, what was said.

Dear, grand old man, simple and good, thou wouldst give me thy glory as thou gavest me thy gold, when I was young and idle. Let others of my age and value declare that I am thy equal, bearing only thy name, if they wish. But it is necessary for posterity to know that whatever happens it will be forced to count with thee. Know well, it will read our two names, one below the other, as they appear in age, and let me here record that I have never seen in thee but my father, my friend, and my master.

Later he was elected president of the Academy, the highest possible intellectual honor for a Frenchman. The next highest honor, Grand Cross of the Legion of Honor, was also conferred on him. He died on November 27, 1895, at the age of seventy-one, enjoying the great esteem of the French nation to the end.

Buffenoir gives the following picture of him:

Recently in the rue D'Amsterdam we met this distinguished dra-matist, and as he strode along he looked like a victor in life. Truly, he has the air of a master. He is very far from having lost the poise and carriage of his youth. Tall, upright, firm and strong, he has the air of a gentleman born—the look a little haughty, the mustache provokingly turned up, the step and the calves firm, with cane in air, he walked as a conqueror in this Paris of which he is the son—this Paris in which he is known to all.

That day I saw more than twenty persons turn and say: "It is Alexandre Dumas." A woman who sold papers murmured his name aloud and cried: "Yes, it is he. What a fine and handsome gentleman!" I returned later and saw the same thing each time Dumas went on foot. He reigned in the streets by his presence as he reigned in the theatres with his plays.

Faguenot said, "A combatant, a man firm in dispute and stub-born in attack, reply and retort. You noticed this at first glance for he possessed a soldier's stride, a military mustache, and a manner of lifting his head like a conquistador."

Alphonse d'Alain wrote:

With the death of Alexandre Dumas, fils, is extinguished the glory of this immortal trio which filled Europe with glory for a full century.

The Ancestor: General of the Republic, the Hercules, the colossus, the giant, the valiant soldier; typifying action.

The Father: the story-teller, par excellence, the master romancer, typifying imagination.

The Son: the subtle and faithful observer, typifying Reason.

Future centuries will write the name of Dumas, fils, in the book of immortality beside that of the best masters of French literature and of the world.

In the Place Malsherbes, Paris, his monument stands near those of his father and grandfather.

REFERENCES

Almeras, Henri F., *Avant La Gloire*. Paris, 1902.
Buffenoir, H., *Hommes et Demeures Célèbres*. Paris, 1914.
Duquesnel, F., *Souvenirs Littéraires*. Paris, 1922.
Hermant, A., *Alphonse Daudet; Alexandre Dumas*, Paris, 1903.
Gribble, F. H., *Dumas, Father and Son*. New York, 1930.

ADDITIONAL REFERENCES

Duncan, John, "The Negro's Literary Influence on Masterpieces of Music." *Negro History Bulletin* (March, 1948), pp. 134–137, Association for the Study of Negro Life and History, Washington, D.C.

Fleming, B. J., and Pryde, M. J., *Distinguished Negroes Abroad*, pp. 84–87. Washington, D.C., The Associated Publishers, 1946.

James, Henry, *Notes on Novelists*, pp. 362–384. New York, Biblo and Tannen, 1969.

Maurois, André, *The Titans*. New York, Harper Brothers, 1957.

Marcelin, Frédéric, *La Confession de Bazoutté*, pp. 163–185. Paris, Société d'Editions Littéraires et Artistiques, 1909.

Saunders, Edith, *The Prodigal Father*. London, New York, Toronto, Longmans, Green and Company, 1951.

Shaw, Esther Propel, "The Three Alexandres (Dumas)." *Negro History Bulletin* (December, 1940), pp. 59–61, Association for the Study of Negro Life and History, Washington, D.C.

Ira Aldridge

GREATEST OF THE OTHELLOS
(1810?–1867)

IRA FREDERICK ALDRIDGE, one of the world's greatest actors, was born in the early years of the nineteenth century, probably 1810. As regards his birth and early life there are two conflicting stories.

According to the first, he was born in New York City, the son of an African prince and a colored American woman. This prince, so the story goes, was the sole survivor of a revolt in Africa in which his father, the king, and other members of his family were slain. Rescued by missionaries, the prince was taken to America and trained for the ministry, eventually becoming an excellent preacher.

With the aid of the missionaries, the prince sent Ira to Glasgow University to be educated for the ministry. But enamored by the stage, he left the church to become an actor.

The second version, and more likely the true one, is given by J. J. Sheahan, who knew Aldridge, in *Notes and Queries*. At that time, any dark Negro who distinguished himself was usually said to be of royal origin. The story of the princely birth is very clearly the work of press agents.

Sheahan says:

That his ancestors were princes of the Pulah tribe, and much more that may be read in a work entitled Memoir and Theatrical Career of Ira Aldridge, the African Roscius, published many years ago by

Onwhyn, Catherine Street, Strand, belongs to the region of romance, there can be little doubt. The father of the subject of this notice was the Rev. Daniel Aldridge, Calvinistic Minister of Green Street Chapel, New York, his congregation being of the coloured race. This gentleman died in September, 1840. Ira, his son, was born at New York in 1807, and was destined for his father's sacred profession; but the fates would have it otherwise. At an early age he imbibed a strong taste for declamation; later on he became the "star" of a goodly private company of coloured amateurs, and in the end he would be an actor. This just mentioned body of sable artists displayed their histrionic talents in a large room or loft over a blacksmith's shop, before audiences of their own complexion. Besides Mr. A. [Aldridge] I have met with one or two members of that sable troupe. Our youthful Thespian managed to "scrape an acquaintance" with the late James Wallack, then manager of a theatre at New York, and when that gentleman resolved upon returning to England, he conceived the idea of introducing young Aldridge to his fellow country people and thus making money by him. Arriving at Liverpool, Wallack was silly enough to state that his protégé had been his servant in America; a rupture and a newspaper war ensued and "the Child of the Sun" was left to his own resources in a strange land, and without much money in his purse. He soon found his way to London where he "starred" in the characters of Othello, Zanga, Gambia, Bertram, Oronooko, etc., at the Royalty, Coburg, and other theatres. He then took to the provinces and in time became a splendid actor, drawing large audiences in all the great towns of Great Britain and Ireland, and occasionally revisiting London. In April, 1833, he appeared as Othello at the Theatre Royal, Covent Garden, Miss Ellen Tree being the Desdemona. At the close of the first performance Mr. Sheridan Knowles, the great dramatist, rushed into his arms, exclaiming, "For the honour of human nature let me embrace you." His success was now complete. . . .

To the above may be added certain interim details as the fact that he had, previous to his success in London, such bitter disappointments and so many refusals from managers to play the part of Othello that he returned to America in 1830, but getting even less consideration from the American managers, he went back to England, determined to win.

After his London triumph, letters of congratulation poured in on him, one of the most enthusiastic being from Edmund Kean, one of the greatest of all Shakespearean actors. Seats to his performance sold out weeks in advance and in four days he earned as his share of the receipts $9500, a sum worth at least five times that now. Everywhere he was hailed as "The African Roscius" (Roscius was a Roman slave who became a famous actor, in the days of Julius Caesar).

So masterful, so perfect in every detail was his acting that several critics declared that Shakespeare in creating the role of Othello, "the noble Moor whom the full senate of Venice called all-in-all sufficient," might have had him in mind.

In physique too Aldridge fitted the part. He was well over six feet, with a well-developed body and a carriage of great dignity. His voice was equally remarkable. He would put so much fire and realism into his acting that some in his audience wept aloud, while others rose in their seats demanding the punishment of Iago.

Madame Malibran, leading prima donna, was so impressed that she wrote him, "Never in the whole course of my professional career have I witnessed a more powerful and interesting performance." Lady V. Beecher, the most noted tragedienne of the time, said, "During my professional, as well as my private life, I never saw so correct a portraiture of Othello amidst the luminaries of my day."

But great as his successes were in England, they were minor compared with those on the Continent. Arriving there in 1852, he played for the next three years at the head of a troupe in the chief towns of Germany. Duke Bernhard, ruler of Saxe-Meningen, and brother of Queen Adelaide of England, made him a Chevalier of the Royal Saxon Ernestinischen House Order, and presented him with the Verdienst Gold Medal.

King Frederick William IV of Prussia was so delighted that he ordered the Gold Medal of Science and the Arts struck in his honor. The only other personages to be so honored were Humboldt, the naturalist and philosopher; Spontini, the composer; and Liszt, the composer and musician.

In Austria-Hungary his triumphs continued. The Imperial Histrionic Conservatory of Pesth elected him to membership and gave him the Large Gold Medal. The Imperial and Archducal Creche Institution, whose members were leaders of the nobility and great artists, gave him life membership. Accompanying the notification was a complimentary letter from the Emperor of Austria-Hungary in the emperor's own hand.

In Switzerland the city of Berne presented him with the Gold Medal of Merit. In Belgium further honors awaited him, also in Sweden, where he went at the invitation of the king. In Russia, as the guest of the czar, he played before the court in the imperial palace, and so impressed the czar that he gave him the First Class Medal of the Arts. He was elected a member of the Versamlung, and also a life member of the Russian Imperial Academy.

In Asiatic Russia he was equally honored. In Bessarabia the highest possible honor was conferred on him: Associate of the Order of Nobles.

As Sheahan says, he "had honours conferred upon him by almost every crowned head in Europe, besides valuable presents from nobles. His villa residence at Upper Norwood was literally crammed with costly articles of every description received by way of presents."

Aldridge was also a success in "white" roles as Lear, Macbeth, and Shylock, receiving often as high praise as in Othello. In *King Lear* he was so perfect that Théophile Gautier, celebrated French critic, declared that Cordelia, Lear's own daughter, would have taken him for a white man and her father.

Gautier, who saw him in Russia, thought he was greater than any other actor of his day. "He was the lion of St. Petersburg," says Gautier, "and it was necessary to engage a seat several days in advance. . . . Aldridge's entrance was magnificent . . . with his eyes half-closed, as if dazzled by the African sun, he was Othello himself, as Shakespeare had created him. He had that nonchalance, that Oriental attitude, that desinvolture of a Negro that no European is able to imitate. . . . He produced an immense effect and received interminable applause."

In the role of Lear Aldridge created a greater effect even than as Othello, thought Gautier. "A thick white paint covered his cheeks," he says, "and a great white beard enveloped the rest of his face, descending to his chest. . . . Cordelia, herself, would not have guessed that she had a Negro for her father. . . . An astonishing fact: Aldridge though at the height of his physical power did not betray by a single movement that he was a younger man; the voice, the step, the gestures were all those of an octogenarian."

At St. Petersburg Aldridge outshone Samiloff, the leading Russian actor and one of the foremost of that time. "Samiloff's representations of Shakespeare," said Gautier, "were attended but not so much as those of Aldridge. The truth is that Samiloff could not disguise himself as a Negro."

The St. Petersburg correspondent of *Le Nord* (Dec. 15, 1850) said similarly:

The scene in the third act when the sentiment of jealousy is aroused in the ferocious Moor, is the true triumph of Aldridge. At the first word of the wily insinuation, you see his eyes kindle; you feel the tears in his voice when he questions Iago, then the deep sob which stifles it, and finally when he is persuaded that his wretchedness is complete, a cry, or rather a roar, like that of a wild beast starts from his abdomen. I seem to hear that cry yet; it chilled us with fear and made every spectator shudder. Tears wet his cheek; his mouth foamed and his eyes flashed fire. I have never seen an artist identify himself so perfectly with the character he represented. An actor told me that he heard him sob after his exit from the scene. Everybody— men, women, and children—wept. Boileau was right in saying to actors: "Weep yourself, if you would make others weep."

The most remarkable fact about this is that Aldridge was declaiming Shakespeare in English to a Russian audience.

In France Aldridge was warmly welcomed, and especially by his friend, Alexandre Dumas, the novelist. Everywhere he was lionized by rich and poor alike. In Russia two of his greatest friends were Tolstoi and Shevchenko, poet of the Ukraine. No American actor, before or since, has been so well received, so highly honored, in Europe.

Death came suddenly for the great actor. In 1867, at the height of his triumphs, while on his way to Russia to accept an invitation from the czar, he was taken ill at Lodz, Poland, and died soon afterward on August 7.

Aldridge was married twice. His first wife was Swedish, Countess Pauline Brant; his second, an Englishwoman of good family connections, who had fallen in love with him after witnessing his performance in *The Slave*, and came to compliment him at its close.

A short biography published by Agence Kuschnik, Paris, contains a remarkable collection of excerpts from the critics of that time. It says:

> The letters of felicitation that Ira Aldridge received from all parts, gathered together, formed an enormous volume. . . . Tragedian and comedian together, Ira Aldridge was in both of an undeniable superiority. He possessed all the intellectual and physical endowments of his art. . . .
>
> As a tragedian his powerful and massive style could, when necessary, carry him away in formidable outbursts of anger and passion. Then the black shadows of his face became doubly blacker under the feelings he portrayed. One could say a second night descended on his physiognomy. Never did a white face attain such a degree of expression.
>
> As a comedian, he was exhilarating. The ebony shone; the coal glowed. His mask was the faithful mirror of the thoughts that agitated him. There was never a more terrible frown than his; never a more winning smile.

This book cites a Danzig critic:

> Ira Aldridge is the greatest dramatic artist we have ever had. In a little over two years he has conquered all the sympathies of the public. The critics of Berlin have completely exhausted themselves in praising this lion of the day. His Othello, Macbeth, and Shylock leave him without a rival in the annals of the theatre.

And a Viennese critic said, "Ira Aldridge is without a doubt the greatest actor that has ever been seen in Europe. . . . It may well be doubted whether Shakespeare, himself, had ever dreamed for his masterpiece, Othello, an interpretation so masterly, so truly perfect."

REFERENCES

Additional details on Aldridge's career are given by C. H. Stephenson in *Notes and Queries*, November 9, 1872, together with a poem of twelve verses on William Tell, famous Swiss patriot by Aldridge, which attained great popularity.

Aldridge had a son and two daughters by his second marriage. The son, after winning much success as a pianist, died young.

The elder Lauranah, after a successful career in grand opera, was stricken with rheumatism and became an invalid. The younger, Ira (Montagu Ring), worthily kept alive the name of Aldridge.

While still a child she won a scholarship and was accepted by the celebrated Swedish singer, Jenny Lind. She appeared in several recitals, and in later years became a successful composer and teacher of voice. Her selections are played by military bands and in leading theatres. In her home in Kensington, London, she had preserved a good many of her father's souvenirs, where I had the pleasure of seeing them.

Gautier, T., *Voyage en Russie*, Vol. I, pp. 254–258. Paris, 1867.

Appleton's Encyclopedia, "Ira Aldridge."

Encyclopedia Americana, "Ira Aldridge."

Illustrated London News, July 3, 1858.

Notes and Queries, 4th S.X., August 17, 1862, London.

Ira Aldridge. Paris, Kushnick, 1866.

Trommer, M., *Ira Aldridge, American Negro Tragedian, and Taras Shevchenko*. New York, 1939.

ADDITIONAL REFERENCES

Adams, Russell L., *Great Negroes: Past and Present*, p. 130. Chicago, Afro-Am Publishing Company, 1963, 1964.

Bruce, John E., *Was Othello a Negro?* New York, 1920.

Durilin, S., "Ira Aldridge," trans. by E. Blum. Reprinted from *Shakespeare Association Bulletin*, Vol. XVIII, No. 1, pp. 33–39 (January, 1942).

Fleming, B. J., and Pryde, M. J., *Distinguished Negroes Abroad*, p. 125. Washington, D.C., The Associated Publishers, 1946.

Gautier, Théophile, *Russia*, pp. 229–232. Philadelphia, John C. Winston Company, 1905.

Hughes, Langston, *Famous American Negroes*, pp. 23–25. New York, Popular Library, Inc., 1962.

Malone, Mary, *Actor in Exile: The Life of Ira Aldridge*. Toronto and New York, The Macmillan Company and Crowell-Collier Press, 1969.

Marshall, H., and Stock, M., *Ira Aldridge: The Negro Tragedian*. New York, The Macmillan Company, 1958.

Rollins, Charlemae Hill, *They Showed the Way*, pp. 6–11. New York, Thomas Y. Crowell Company, 1964.

Schomberg, A. A., *List: Showing the Theatres and Plays in Various European Cities Where Ira Aldridge, the African Roscius, Acted during the Years 1824–1867.* New York, New York Public Library, 1932.

"The Radical," in *The Negro as Artist*, Vol. II, pp. 39–42. Boston, Adams and Company; New York, The American News Company, London, 1867.

José T. De Sousa Martins

MEDICAL AND SANITARY EXPERT OF PORTUGAL
(1843–1897)

José Thomaz De Sousa Martins, Portugal's most honored physician and one of its leading medical writers, was born at Alhandra, Portugal, in 1843, of mixed Negro and Portuguese parentage. He studied at the National Lyceum of Lisbon and at the Medico-Chirurgical Institute of that city, where he received his medical diploma in 1866.

In 1876, after having served as substitute professor in general pathology at the Faculty of Medicine in Lisbon, he was appointed to head that department. In 1875 he was named by the government as head of a commission to take steps to ward off Asiatic cholera, which had invaded Europe. He was appointed member of many other high commissions as well. In 1897 he represented Portugal at the International Conference on Sanitation in Vienna.

He was a member of many leading medical and scientific societies in Portugal and other lands: the Pharmaceutical Society of Portugal; the Society of Medical Sciences, of which he was elected president at the July 31, 1897, session, a post he did not fill because of his death; corresponding member of the Royal Academy of Sciences of Lisbon; the Institute of Coimbra; the Royal Academy of Medicine in Belgium; the Royal Academy of Medicine in Madrid; the Spanish Anthropological Society; the Spanish Gynecological Society; the National Academy of Medicine and

Surgery at Cadiz; the Provincial Academy of Medical Sciences in Luxembourg; the Royal Society of Public Medicine of Belgium; the Vasco da Gama Institute in Nova Goa; foreign associate of the French Hygenic Society; regular member of the Geographical Society of Lisbon; and founder of the Association of Journalists and Portuguese writers. He also wrote several books on pneumonia, pneumo-gastritis, and the heart, as well as on quarantine and sanitation, on which he was probably the leading European expert of his times. In addition, he was a collaborator on the *Medical Gazette* of Lisbon, the *Journal of the Portuguese Pharmaceutical Society*, the *Journal of the Society of Medical Sciences of Lisbon,* the *Portuguese Medical Review,* the *Occidental Review, Contemporary Medicine,* the *Illustrated Daily*, and the *Popular Encyclopedia.*

An expert pharmacist with a first-class degree from the Medico-Surgical School, he was appointed a member of the commission to revise the *General Pharmacopeia* of Portugal in 1875. For his services against cholera Greece conferred on him the order of Commander of St. Jago and the Saviour.

In 1897 the government of Portugal ordered a medal struck in recognition of his services. King Carlos I in presenting it said to him, "You are the most brilliant luminary of my reign."

On his death the same year, a grateful country erected a splendid monument to him in the Campos de los Martires, Lisbon. This was later taken down and a more imposing one placed in front of the Faculty of Medicine in Lisbon. In a mural by Veloso Salgado in the great hall of the building he is shown as one of the twelve leading physicians in Portuguese history.

On the centenary of his birth, April 7, 1943, the Faculty of Medicine and some of the leading physicians of Portugal held a memorial service for him. Professor Moreira eulogized him as a healer of the sick, a humanitarian and an educator. Sousa Martins, he said, had died from tuberculosis induced by overwork with the sick. "Battlefields," he said, "are not the only places to claim their victims. Science and the clinics also have their martyrs."

He also praised him as the best Portuguese expert on phthisis, as a tender man and an exemplar for his colleagues, a protector of young doctors, a slave to the sick without regard to class, and extremely charitable to the incurable. His funeral was magnificent, a merited consecration.

Sousa Martins was great in science, great as a teacher and in the clinic, imposing as an orator. A charming, moving speaker, his famous orations were unforgettable experiences; his was a warming, illuminatingly divine flame.

Bethencourt Ferreira said:

Sousa Martins was so perfectly brilliant in his many faceted aspects that we can all find him a fortifying example.

He always brought his noble and cultivated mind to bear upon the basic social problems. He was always wise and modest, without any of that prejudice of talent which characterizes so many of the quasi-great.

Antonio José d'Almeida said:

He was a man of exceptional talent; a man of brilliant speech whose words could have all the soothing beauty of gold dust in a breeze, or the cutting quality of tool steel. I see him now lying quietly and graciously in the cemetery of the little town of Alhandra. . . . Perhaps the Pantheon would be the more glorious spot for the great Sousa Martins; yet all of us feel that Alhandra, his birthplace, is more fitting.

"He was one of the great giants of contemporary Portugal," says Bethencourt Rodrigues.

Many stories are told of Sousa Martins of which this is the best known:

One day a well-known old lady of very aristocratic family called him in because she had a pain in her chest. Proper diagnosis demanded an auscultation.

The old lady was swathed in many layers of lace and garments, which she slowly began to remove piece by piece. The doctor, noticing the many clothes, decided that he would have a long wait for his auscultation if he left it to her to disrobe. So with his own hands he began to unfasten the old woman's clothes.

She put the wrong interpretation on the physician's actions, however, and jumping up, she rang a bell. A maid suddenly appeared. Pointing to a glass pitcher of water on a nearby table, the modest old lady said, "Please give the doctor a drink of water. And don't go away. I think he's going to need some more."

Sousa Martins, who had already risen, divined the intentions of his prudish patient, sipped a little water, made a hurried examination, wrote a prescription, and asked for his hat. Just as he was about to go the old lady anxiously asked "And when are you coming back, doctor?"

"I . . . I'm returning on a day when I'm very thirsty," retorted Sousa Martins, stalking out.

REFERENCES

One of Sousa Martins' most distinguished colleagues was a full-blooded Negro from Benguela, Angola, Portuguese Africa, Dr. Carlos Joaquim Tavares, who was physician to King Carlos I and his family. (Esteves Pereira, *Portugal*, Vol. VII, pp. 32–33. 1915.) For a portrait of Dr. Tavares, see *Sex and Race*, Vol. I, p. 225. 1941.

Pereira, Esteves, *Portugal*, Vol. VII, pp. 32–33. 1915.

Monteiro, Sousa, and fifty-three colleagues of Sousa Martins, eds., *Sousa Martins: In Memoriam*. Lisbon, 1904.

Medicos Portugueses Revista Bio-Bibliographica, Vol. I, No. 3, May, 1926.

Imprensa Medica Centenario Do Nascimento Do José Tomaz De Sousa Martins (Centenary Edition on the Birth of Sousa Martins), Ano. IX, No. 5, March 10, 1943.

ADDITIONAL REFERENCES

Barros, Eudes, *Dezesete (Romance Historico)*. Rio de Janeiro, Irmaos Pongetti, 1938.

Claudio J. D. Brindis de Sala

🌿🌿

GERMAN BARON AND COURT VIOLINIST
(1852–1911)

CLAUDIO JOSÉ DOMINGO BRINDIS DE SALA, "King of the Octaves," belongs to that cluster of meteoric geniuses who dazzle the earth with their brilliance and lift mankind up to heights of rapture and admiration. Few of the world's great violinists have equaled him in the passion of his style, his ecstatic frenzy, and his eccentricity.

Fame and applause such as is the lot of few artists came to him. Kings, commoners, the beautiful people, poured out their grateful tributes to him.

Brindis de Sala was born in Havana, Cuba, on August 4, 1852, of unmixed African parentage. His father Claudio, a musician and composer who had delighted the aristocratic salons of Havana with his violin playing and dancing, was his teacher.

At the age of ten young Brindis de Sala achieved much success at a recital in Havana, after which his father took him to Paris where he won the first prize at the Paris Conservatory. Following this success the young violinist made a tour of Europe, appearing in the principal concert halls. At Milan, Turin, Florence, London, Berlin, he was almost mobbed by music lovers, who hailed him as "The Black Paganini" and "the leading violinist of the century." He was not yet fourteen.

Le Siècle of Paris, said, "He is an artist of great talent, who, in all the concerts he has given in Paris and abroad, has received the greatest applause; one would say that some hand surpassing human powers was drawing from the instrument notes that seemed to come straight from the skies."

In Berlin he was called "King of the Octaves." Weber, the great critic, said of him, "No better player has ever appeared before an audience, and dominated it so completely."

The *Courrier* of Florence said:

The esteemed gentleman, Brindis de Sala, is a young Negro, perfectly black, a son of Cuba, of extraordinary talent with a fine sympathetic face and who speaks six or seven languages. He played last night in the interval at the Opera, two selections on the violin: the young Negro astonished the audience and swept it off its feet with enthusiasm. He possesses an admirable activity; holds his bow with remarkable lightness and at the same time with an energy characteristic of the fire and impetuosity of his race.

The *Gazeto dei Teatri de Milano*, said:

Two nights in the Manzoni Theatre the celebrated violin artist, Brindis de Sala, has delighted us with the magnificent sound of his instrument. He is a sympathetic Negro, with a lively, intelligent and penetrating glance, and of elegant and cultured manners . . . this concert artist merits the fame that has preceded him. He drew from the violin the sweetest sounds and most passionate accents, and, even in the most difficult variations conserved a sureness, a good taste, and a purity of intonation, truly enviable.

In 1875 he went to Haiti as the director of the Musical Conservatory there, after which he made a tour of Central America and Venezuela and returned to Cuba, with many decorations.

Visiting Europe again, he was invited to the courts of some of the leading monarchs. The delicate hands of princesses applauded him and pinned roses in the lapels of his bemedaled dress suit, while kings affixed still more decorations there. France gave him the Legion of Honor.

Berlin was the scene of his greatest triumph. Emperor William I bestowed on him the coveted Order of the Black Eagle, made him a German citizen, raised him to the rank of baron, and graced his marriage to a noble woman with his presence.

But combined with his artistic fire was a wanderlust that made it impossible for him to live a domestic life. In spite of the entreaties of friends, he left Germany for the West Indies and South America, where a careless life combined with his eccentricities started him downward. Once, in Mexico City, while probably drunk, he wrecked the choicest room in his hotel, "just to leave a remembrance in my having been in the land of the hidalgos," he said.

For money he had the contempt of the born artist. Once when a rich mine owner offered him 800 francs in gold to play for his guests at a soiree, he demanded 1000 and would not accept less though he was penniless and had not eaten that day. That night, however, when the party was at its height, he walked in, played for the guests in his most brilliant style, and disappeared before anyone could thank him.

For one so whimsical and heedless of money there is usually but one end. He sank lower and lower, forgotten by the brilliant circles in which he once moved. He fell a victim to tuberculosis and alcohol, and on June 2, 1911, his body was discovered in a miserable hovel in Buenos Aires.

Unknown, he was taken to the morgue and placed on a slab between a suicide and a thief. About to make an autopsy, the medical students noticed that he wore a corset. Wondering who this vagabond could be who was corseted like a society beau, they searched his clothing and discovered a German passport with the name: Chevalier de Brindis, Baron de Sala.

Within its pages was a touching souvenir of the time when he walked as an idol amid scented salons and when his elegance in dress had earned him the name of "The D'Annunzio of the dress suit and the four-in-hand."

To his funeral came one society woman who had loved him in his better days. Her flowers were the only tribute on his pauper grave in the Cemetery de Oeste.

In 1930 his body was brought to Havana by the Cuban government and interred with honors.

Three of the children born to his German wife became violinists at the German court and were last heard of in Germany in 1932. He also had an illegitimate daughter in Buenos Aires and another in Mexico City.

REFERENCES

The elder Brindis de Sala was also unfortunate. Active in the cause of Cuban emancipation, he organized a battalion called Leales Morones (Loyal Blacks) for this cause. Arrested for conspiracy, he was thrown into a dungeon where he was incarcerated for six years until freed by General Conchas, whom he had hypnotized with his music.

In 1877 the conductor of a train in Cuba attempted to eject the younger Brindis de Sala from a first-class coach. Negroes, who at the time were still slaves, were permitted to ride only third-class. But the passengers who knew him shouted, "Leave him alone. He is the great artiste, Brindis de Sala."

For Brindis de Sala, the Elder:

Enciclopedia Universal Ilustrada.
Anglo-African Review, June, 1859, p. 191.
Calcagno, F., *Diccionario Biografico Cubano*, 1878.
Academia Nacional de Artes y Letras, Anales, Vol. XV, pp. 331–350; Vol. XIX, pp. 74–78. Havana, 1930, 1937.

ADDITIONAL REFERENCES

Guillen, Nicolas, "C. J. D. Brindis de Sala." *Cuadernos de Historia Habanera*, No. 3, Municipio de la Habana, Havana, 1935.

Reed, Gladys Jones, "Distinguished Negroes of the West Indies: Brindis de Sala, Negro Violinist." *Negro History Bulletin*, p. 79 (January, 1941), Association for the Study of Negro Life and History, Washington, D.C.

Samuel Coleridge-Taylor

ENGLAND'S "GREATEST MUSICAL SENSATION"
(1875–1912)

ONE EVENING in Croydon, London, a frail Negro boy of seven stood on the sidewalk gazing eagerly into a parlor where a music lesson was in progress. He had been playing marbles with his companions, but hearing the music, had left them taking with him his marbles and his violin, which he carried habitually as a girl her doll.

The music teacher, attracted by the youngster's interest, and seeing his violin, invited him in. He came after much coaxing.

At the end of a violin duet the boy was urged to play and he rendered the difficult selection that had just been given with such feeling and correctness that the delighted music teacher offered to give him lessons free.

In this way began the musical career of Samuel Coleridge-Taylor, England's musical phenomenon of the early part of the twentieth century.

The teacher was Joseph Beckwith, whose son was to be leader of the Handel Society Orchestra under this Negro lad.

Coleridge-Taylor, though very brilliant, did not win success easily. Few who climbed to the top had so hard a struggle. His first handicap was poverty. Soon after he was born on August 15, 1875, his father, Daniel Hughes Taylor, a native African, abandoned him and his mother to return to Africa. Taylor, an unusu-

146

ally able and brilliant doctor, had received the rare distinction of being elected to the Royal College of Physicians and Surgeons at the age of twenty-two, but the color prejudice he encountered in everyday life was too much for his sensitive nature.

Young Coleridge-Taylor, who was also very sensitive, was also greatly affected by color prejudice. His white companions dubbed him "Coaley" and one of them once set his mop of thick, frizzly hair on fire just to see whether it would burn. An added difficulty was the high standard he had set for himself. Aiming at nothing less than perfection, he threw almost everything he wrote into the fire for years.

At school he led in music. He was the only colored child there. Whenever visitors came to the school he was asked to entertain them. This he did by playing the piano or the violin and by singing. He had a treble voice "remarkably sweet and true."

On leaving school he found that continuance of his musical studies was out of the question. He must go to work. But here also, he was faced with another difficulty. Employment was scarce in England; his color made it scarcer yet for him.

His mother tried to solve the problem by apprenticing him to a piano tuner. She thought that thus his musical ability would be served at the same time he was making a living. But to the gifted youth it was like harnessing a thoroughbred horse to a lumber wagon. At this critical period a wealthy Londoner, Colonel Waters, offered to pay all expenses of his musical education.

Friends of Colonel Waters tried to discourage him. They told him that the Negro's brain development was arrested at an early age and that since Coleridge-Taylor was "but one removed from the African jungle" he might revert there, psychically at least. Had not his father given up everything and returned to Africa? Therefore spending money on the son was as good as wasted.

Coleridge-Taylor was sent to the Royal College of Music where the director, Sir George Groves, refused to accept him at first. At the end of the first year the lad had made such little progress that what had been said of his African ancestry seemed justified. But this was later discovered to be due to the fact that he was being conducted along a path not his own. Coleridge-Taylor was a trailblazer, not a follower; a creator, not an interpreter. At last he came under the care of one who understood him, Sir Charles Stamford, and he leaped ahead.

The more he progressed, the greater grew his dissatisfaction with himself. Sir Charles had but to express the slightest disapproval of a composition and it went into the fire. When friends remonstrated that he might be destroying a work of future value, he replied, "The best place for unsatisfactory compositions is the fire." But his friends were right. One of these manuscripts, his "Melody in F," snatched out of the fire by a friend of his, later became one of his most popular works. This symphony was one of four he had finished after four weeks of labor. But he thought nothing of that because music came as spontaneously to him as song to a nightingale. He said once, "There are times when I could set a butcher's bill to music."

His persistence and his high ideals were soon to bear fruit. He won the coveted Lesley Alexander Prize two years in succession. Far-seeing eyes in British music were being directed toward him.

Another marked influence in his life was his close association with Paul Laurence Dunbar, who was then in London. Dunbar did much toward helping the young English Negro to find himself racially.

Some of the leading composers now began to take notice of him, among them Sir Edward Elgar. Sir Edward, on being asked by Dr. Herbert Brewer to write a composition for the Three Choirs Festival, recommended Coleridge-Taylor instead. "He is the cleverest fellow going among the younger men," said Elgar.

Coleridge-Taylor thereupon wrote his "Ballade in A Minor." Two leading composers, Sir Arthur Sullivan and Sir Hubert Parry, who heard it in advance, praised it highly.

The festival was to be given at Gloucester with Coleridge-Taylor himself conducting the three choirs. As it was advertised that the conductor was an Anglo-African, the audience expected a white man. What was its surprise to see instead a dark-skinned Negro, quick-moving, slight of build, with an enormous head of high, thick, frizzly hair, broad nostrils, flashing white teeth, and a winning smile.

The audience, a highly critical one, waited breathlessly. Negroes had been unheard of as composers. What sort of composition was it going to be? The moment was dramatic, intense.

The music began! The opening bars and the audience was won! The arresting character of the theme, the strange barbaric beauty, the boldness and the originality, thrilled the music lovers. It was clear that a new star of the first magnitude had risen in music.

The applause was thunderous. He was called again and again to the footlights. The next morning the story of his life appeared in many of the leading dailies of England, the Continent, and America with embellishments.

He had come up to Gloucester unknown; he left it famous.

London wanted to hear him and he was engaged to conduct his "Ballade" at the Crystal Palace where he achieved even greater success. As for his next work, *Hiawatha*, it showed still greater genius and placed him on a solid foundation.

Joseph Bennett wrote, "Certainly the man of the hour is Coleridge-Taylor. He has written, as everybody knows, a work called "Hiawatha's Wedding Feast." Let us see how that stands at the present time. It is to be performed this week at Norwich, and three weeks later at the North Staffordshire Festival." He goes on to name seven other places.

Being greatly in need of money, and like most artists, a poor businessman, he sold the entire rights of *Hiawatha* for $1250. Later he was chagrined to see the publishers making a fortune out of it.

Invitations to the highest social circles, and offers to conduct orchestras and to teach, poured in on him. At one concert he gave at the Albert Hall, England's largest auditorium, thousands were turned away. At the close of the performance he was recalled so many times that he left the building. Someone had to go to fetch him back as the audience refused to go.

Critics spoke of him in unmeasured phrases as:

He shows the hand of a master, marvellous indeed. Unique in music as Swinburne was in poetry. His flow of melody is unfailing and the brilliancy of his orchestration and the fertility of his imagination are astounding. Not less surprising is his originality. From first to last, every page of his score is stamped with the composer's originality.

Others called him "the greatest musical sensation," while some placed him "in the sublime class with Beethoven, Brahms and

Wagner." Others spoke of his "prolific imagination, melodic charm, grace, dignity, and sonority and weird, rushing barbarity."

Jaeger called him "a heaven-sent musician," and Herbert Antcliffe wrote of him in the *Musical Quarterly*:

When we analyze the work to discover the qualities which make it so distinguished, we are able to discern only the one supreme and indefinable one which we call genius. Schubert wrote nothing simpler or more melodious, and neither he nor Weber produced more beautiful and richly balanced tones from the orchestra, while not Hayden nor Mozart was more direct in his structural methods.

There were also those critics who saw nothing whatever in him. One of them was heard to remark after the success of his first piece, "He's only a damned 'nigger.' He'll never do anything more."

Another well-known critic tried to disparage him. In one of Coleridge-Taylor's repertoires was a "Te Deum," which was credited to an unknown composer. The critic in question praised the "Te Deum" enthusiastically and took the occasion to belittle the orchestration of the famous "Ballade" by suggesting to Coleridge-Taylor that if he would learn balance in orchestration, he should study the "Te Deum." It happened that the orchestration of that very piece had been done by Coleridge-Taylor too.

Orders for scores from leading producers and actors poured in on him. He wrote the music for Sir Herbert Beerbohm Tree's *Herod*, for Israel Zangwill's *God of War*, and *Faust*, and others, meanwhile conducting the Croydon Conservatory Orchestra, the Croydon Orchestral Society, the Westmoreland Festival, and the Rochester Choral Society, as well as being Professor of Composition at the Trinity College of Music, Professor of Theory and Harmony at the Crystal Palace School of Music and Art, and elsewhere.

As a teacher he was one of the most popular and beloved, infusing into his students his own instinctive love of music.

In 1903 he visited America. Each appearance was a triumph. Years before, however, Afro-Americans, proud of his success, had been forming Coleridge-Taylor clubs. At Norwalk, Connecticut, he conducted the Litchfield Choral Union Festival on its twentieth anniversary with 450 white singers on the stage; and in Baltimore, Maryland, the United States Marine Band, a corps from which Negroes were zealously barred. Theodore Roosevelt entertained him at dinner in the White House and American society, white and colored, lionized him. His subsequent American tours were equally felicitous.

Despite these successes, color continued to be an important psychological factor to him. Whereas in his early youth he used to say that he was a British subject first and a Negro next, now he became passionately a black man and the champion of his people. He wrote much to the open columns of the English papers refuting scientific and other falsehoods against them and protesting against their exclusion from the higher social and artistic life.

Negro themes and Negro spirituals attracted him. He wrote a stirring composition on Toussaint L'Ouverture; an *African Suite*; *Songs of Slavery*, among which is the "Quadroon Girl"; and twenty-four "Negro Melodies."

Was this change due to the fact that he had at last proved to the world and to himself that color was only an incident?

Tormented by the demon of work, Coleridge-Taylor gave himself no rest. Worse, too, he was frail. The fog and chill of England proved too much for his lungs and he died of acute pneumonia on September 1, 1912, at the age of only thirty-seven.

In his short life he had written eighty-two opus numbers in addition to anthems, organ and violin melodies and piano solos. He considered *A Tale of Old Japan*, his last work, his masterpiece, but *Hiawatha* is the better known.

In physiognomy he bore a striking resemblance to Beethoven, which strengthened his belief that Beethoven was also of Negro descent. In demeanor he was of the rarest modesty. One who knew him well described him as merry, laughing, never ruffled when among friends but shy at gatherings. Almost all of his life, prior to his marriage, had been spent in the company of his mother. As for his own compositions, he never included them in his programs and audiences had to beg him for them. His colored American admirers bought the house in which he lived at Croydon as a memorial and presented it to his widow, Mrs. Jessie Coleridge-Taylor.

As Coleridge-Taylor was the first modern Negro to achieve fame as a composer, he is often spoken of as being preeminently a Negro in his works. But the wide sweep of his creations proves that he was universal in sympathy and feeling; that like the other titans of music, he was of all times and all peoples. Alfred Noyes very truthfully said of him:

> Greater than England or than Earth discerned
> He never paltered with his art for gain
> When many a vaunted crown to dust is turned
> This uncrowned king shall take his throne again.
> Nations unborn shall hear his forests moan
> Ages unscanned shall hear his winds lament
> Hear a strange grief that deepened through his own
> The vast cry of a buried continent.

On his monument in the Bandon Hill Cemetery, London, is an epitaph, also by Noyes:

> Sleep crowned with fame, fearless of change or time
> Silent, immortal, while our discords climb
> To that great chord which shall resolve the whole. . . .
>
> Silent, with Mozart on that solemn shore
> Secure where neither waves nor heart can break
> Sleep till the Master of the world once more
> Touch the remembered strings and bid thee wake
> Touch the remembered strings and bid thee wake.

REFERENCES

Sayers, W. C. B., *Samuel Coleridge-Taylor*. London, Cassell, 1915.

ADDITIONAL REFERENCES

Adams, Russell, *Great Negroes: Past and Present,* p. 141. Chicago, Afro-Am Publishing Company, 1963, 1964.

Du Bois, W. E. B., *Darkwater*, pp. 193–202. New York, Harcourt, Brace and Howe, 1920.

Fleming, B. J., and Pryde, M. J., *Distinguished Negroes Abroad*, pp. 130–138. Washington, D.C., The Associated Publishers, 1946.

Haynes, Elizabeth Ross, *Unsung Heroes*, pp. 127–149. New York, DuBois and Dill, 1921.

Henessy, Maurice, *Our Pioneers*. Lagos, Nigeria, Crownbird Publishers, 1951.

Lotz, Philip Henry, *Rising Above Color*, pp. 38–49. New York, Association Press; Fleming H. Revell Company, 1943.

Lovingood, Penman, *Famous Modern Negro Musicians*. New York, Press Forum Company, 1921.

Phillips, Theodore De Witt, *The Life and Musical Compositions of S. Coleridge-Taylor*. Unpublished thesis, 1935.

Sosthene H. Mortenol

FRENCH NAVAL CAPTAIN AND COMMANDER
OF THE AIR DEFENSES OF PARIS
(1859–1930)

SOSTHENE HÉLIODORE MORTENOL was born in Guadeloupe, West Indies, on November 29, 1859. His father, a struggling storekeeper, sent him to elementary school at Pointe-à-Pitre, where, for excellence in his studies, he was awarded a scholarship endowed by the colony to provide further education in France.

He entered the lycée at Bordeaux to prepare for entrance into the Naval Academy. Lacking scientific training and discovering that, after three more years in college, he would be unable to enter the Naval Academy because of age requirements, he gave up his plan and started instead to prepare for matriculation into the famous military college of St. Cyr, which he entered four years later and from which he was graduated with honors, being the third highest in his class. But for a zero in gymnastics, he would have been first.

From St. Cyr he went to the Polytechnic School from which he emerged two years later as a second lieutenant, and chose the navy although he knew that promotion was slower there than in the army.

He saw active service in Madagascar in 1884, and again in 1896. From 1891 to 1892 he commanded the second flotilla in the China Sea; from 1898 to 1900 he was in command of torpedo boats *Aviso* and *Alevon*, stationed off the coast of Toulon and Brest; finally, in September, 1912, he was appointed captain.

In the meantime he had distinguished himself as one of the most competent artillery officers in the French Navy. In 1907 the squadron of torpedo boats which he commanded in the China Sea won the first prize. Later he commanded target practice on some of the leading battleships of the French Navy. He had also won several medals. In 1895 he was made a Chevalier of the Legion of Honor, and in 1911 an Officer of that order. He had also been awarded the Medal of Madagascar and the Gold Medal of Cambodia; had been made an officer of the Order of Anjouan; officer of the Dragon of Annam; and officer of the Crown of Prussia, which last had been conferred on him by Kaiser Wilhelm II of Germany for having saved a German torpedo boat and its crew on the west coast of Africa in 1909.

When war was declared in 1914 he was in command of the battle cruiser *Carnot*, which formed part of the squadron that defended the great naval port of Brest. As senior officer he had been, from time to time, in command of this squadron.

In 1915, when German air raids over Paris were at their worst, General Gallieni, military governor of Paris, selected Mortenol to combat the zeppelins. Gallieni had met him years before and had traveled with him to Madagascar on board the cruiser *Favert*, of which Mortenol was then second in command.

Mortenol performed his duties as aerial defender of Paris to the utmost satisfaction of his superiors for the remainder of the war. He built up a competent defense of artillery and airships, and thanks to his vigilance, Paris was never once surprised as London was.

His flotilla of airships was on the alert night and day and always the approach of the enemy was signaled. Attacks were always beaten off and had he at first been able to get the 105s he demanded instead of 75s, the German airships might never have been able to reach the city at all. Mortenol not only successfully fought off zeppelins, but also, by means of mathematical calculations, discovered the lair of the Big Berthas that were bombarding the city, and destroyed them.

Two documents testify to the able manner in which Captain Mortenol performed his vital task. The first was a bill introduced into the Municipal Council of Paris by M. Raoul Brandon, for the naming of a street in his honor, and which reads in part:

When Marshal Gallieni undertook the defense, one of his greatest problems was how to protect the city from bombing by enemy airships. He organized the very severe service of the D. C. A., whose command he confided to a native of Guadeloupe, a member of the Negro race, Captain of the Navy, Mortenol.

As you recall, gentlemen, these airplane attacks were liable to occur during the day as well as at night; thus the organization and operation of the defense of the capital demanded vigilance every minute of the twenty-four hours, but Captain Mortenol never failed. Always vigilant he kept his service on the alert so well that Paris was never surprised. His successive chiefs, Gallieni, Guillaumat, and Dubail have testified that his devotion to duty at all times procured the maximum of security.

In the first months of the war the aerial defense of Paris consisted of only ten 75's. Besides, the science of aviation was still in its infancy. Its utilization as an arm of combat on a great scale, seemed hardly possible. In 1918, however, thanks to the energy and enterprise of Captain Mortenol, who was always vigorously supported by the military governor of Paris, this defense had increased to one hundred and ninety-two 75's and 105's, which were distributed in the fourteen sectors of Paris.

Those under his command—aviators, gunners, range-finders, and look-outs—were about 10,000. The military airplanes—non-existent, or nearly so, in 1914—numbered under Captain Mortenol 205, being divided in 15 homogenous squadrons.

All this was the work of Captain Mortenol and I believe that his role in the great task of watching over the capital in the most tragic hours of its destiny justifies the homage in his memory that I solicit of you.

The second document is from the government when naming him Commander of the Legion of Honor.

Superior officer of the highest merit. At his post day and night to watch over Paris. Performed with rare devotion and enlightened competence the functions of Commander of the D. C. A. The Cross of Commander is the just recompense for a well-filled career and for excellent services rendered.

None who took part in the World War performed an arduous task with greater devotion than Mortenol. Extremely modest, he retired after the war, refusing to profit in any way by his fame.

Though often urged by his fellow Negroes to become a candidate for Parliament, he preferred to live quietly at his home at 5 Rue François-Coppée, until his death on December 22, 1930. His last request was for a quiet burial—without speeches or flowers—a wish that was observed.

REFERENCES

I knew Captain Mortenol well, having visited him at his home several times. It was with the greatest difficulty that one could learn anything of his career from him; he would not give his picture for publication. When I said that his naval career was unusual for a Negro, he quickly answered that there had been other Negroes who had held high command in the French Navy, one of whom was an admiral, he said.

Captain Mortenol was slight in build, below the average size, with woolly hair, and of unmixed Negro type. He said that he had been to America several times while in command of ships, and that he had been refused service in bars, restaurants, and elsewhere at Norfolk, Virginia, and New York City, while his subordinates had been served. He was very amiable and lively, enjoying excellent health up to the time of his death. At the age of seventy-two, he climbed daily to the fifth floor of the building in which he lived, and he attended a dance a few days prior to his sudden demise. He nearly always attended Negro social functions in Paris. The colored residents of Paris always felt that Mortenol should have been made a rear admiral (the duties of which he had more than once performed), and hinted at prejudice, but this may have been due to the fact that promotion in the navy is slow, and that Captain Mortenol, unfortunately, reached the age limit just at the time when war had accelerated advancement. Whatever his feelings were, he never expressed them.

Professor Isaac Béton of Paris, also a Negro and a native of Guadeloupe, is preparing a biography of him. A photograph in *Le Monde Colonial* shows Captain Mortenol in company with Marshal Foch, General Pershing, and other Allied leaders; another in *L'Illustration* shows him with his staff and his aerial defense map (March 22, 1919).

Blaise Diagne

AFRICAN BAREFOOT BOY WHO BECAME A
FRENCH CABINET MINISTER
(1873–1934)

THE RISE OF the lowly to high positions is always noteworthy. It becomes even more so when it includes a jump from an African village to a cabinet membership in one of the most cultured countries of the world.

Blaise Diagne performed this feat. Born in 1873 on the rocky little isle of Gorée, off Dakar, French West Africa, his opportunities were almost nil. There was no chance for an education. However, the French language was spoken about him and he decided to master that. He studied it and became so proficient in it that visitors to the colony employed him as interpreter. Obliging and alert, he made many friends.

He finally worked his way up to interpretership in the customs service. Taking an examination later for junior clerk, he passed it with honors and for the next twenty-two years served as a customs official in various towns of Africa and France. In 1914, he was appointed Controller of Customs for French Guiana, South America.

The same year his people elected him to the French Parliament, thus making him the first native African to have that distinction. This was accomplished despite the opposition of many leading white merchants and officials, who had been accustomed to name a white representative from Bordeaux.

In Parliament Diagne soon commanded respect. His patriotism was unquestionable and his poise and restraint made a favorable impression even on his opponents. Whenever he spoke, which was not often, everyone listened. Unlike some of his colleagues who spent much time talking of the commercial interests of their particular friends, Diagne thought only of France and of his people in Africa.

His great opportunity came in 1917 when the First World War was in its most desperate stage and the outlook for the Allies dark. Russia had capitulated, leaving Germany free to hurl her armies along the Western Front. America, though officially at war with Germany, was not ready. France, bleeding and almost prostrate, was fighting with her back to the wall. Where should she turn to next for help?

The answer was Africa. Oh, for more of those valiant blacks, who, rushing to the front in taxis during the crucial days of August, 1914, had turned the tide in favor of the French, sweeping back the Germans from the Marne.

Premier Clemenceau sent his recruiters into the jungles in search of fresh manpower. But everywhere, in Senegal, in Upper Senegal, the Congo, the Sudan, Dahomey, Ivory Coast, the blacks, instead of responding, revolted.

The situation was critical. Prime Minister Clemenceau thought of Diagne. He was the only man in the French Empire capable of handling the situation. He had the confidence of the Africans. Clemenceau created a special post for him in his cabinet: Commissioner-General of African troops, and sent him to West Africa.

Diagne accepted the post for two reasons: He knew that of the exploiting white powers in Africa, France showed the least color prejudice; and he felt that if the blacks came to the rescue of France it would make her more liberal.

But when he arrived in Africa he ran full tilt against color prejudice. The white Governor of Senegal resented the holding of such a high post by a Negro. Instead of coming to receive him in person as the occasion demanded, the governor sent a minor official with a small detachment of black troops to do the honors. Diagne did not mind the slight to himself, but feeling that it was the dignity of France itself that had been slighted, refused to go ashore, and sent a telegram to Clemenceau telling what had happened. Clemenceau replied with a sharp message to the governor bidding him receive Diagne with full military honors or resign.

Diagne, on landing, plunged into the jungle and into the midst of the hostile blacks with only a few friends. He soon won them over. Eighty thousand answered his call, more than twice the number Clemenceau had asked for. All had been done in three months and without friction. Clemenceau was overjoyed.

When Diagne returned to France Clemenceau offered him the Legion of Honor. Diagne declined saying that he had only done his duty and that that was reward enough. Such a thing was unheard of, the Legion of Honor being a highly sought decoration. Even President Poincaré himself could not shake Diagne's determination to accept no reward.

Diagne's black troops brought new terrors to hand-to-hand combat in the trenches. Captain Eichacher, a German, describes one of their attacks thus:

On they came. First singly at wide intervals. Feeling their way like the arms of a horrible cuttle-fish. Eager, grasping, like the claws of a mighty monster. Strong, wild fellows, their log-like, fat, black skulls wrapped in pieces of dirty rags, showing their teeth, like panthers, with their bellies drawn in and their necks stretched forward. Some with bayonets on their rifles. Many armed only with knives. Frightful their distorted dark grimaces. Horrible their unnaturally wide-open, blood-shot eyes. Eyes that seemed like terrible things themselves. Eyes that seemed to run ahead of their owners, unchained, no longer to be restrained.

On they came like dogs gone mad and cats spitting and yowling with a burning lust for human blood with a cruel dissemblance of their beastly malice. Behind them came the first wave of the attackers in close order, a solid, rolling black wall, rising and falling and heaving, impenetrable and endless. . . .

Our artillery sent them its greeting. Whole groups melted away. Dismembered bodies, sticky earth, shattered rocks were mixed in wild disorder. The black cloud halted, wavered, closed its ranks and rolled nearer and nearer, irresistible, crushing, devastating.

So much for Diagne's troops. Diagne himself was often with them in the front lines, braving enemy fire to look after them. He saw that they were properly fed and clothed and arranged for pensions for invalids and their transportation home.

After the war a Paris periodical, *Les Continents*, questioned his integrity, claiming that he had accepted a dollar a head, or a total of $80,000, for the men he recruited.

Diagne sued the editor. Clemenceau, testifying for him, said that Diagne had insistently refused compensation of any kind and that "the question of money or any other reward for recruiting had never been raised." Minister of War Painlevé took the stand and told how Diagne had stopped the African revolts by his sheer force of personality. Diagne was completely cleared. The editor received a suspended sentence of six months and was heavily fined.

Diagne was an ever-active and uncompromising foe of color prejudice. In 1919 when some white American tourists had two African officers ejected from a sight-seeing bus, Diagne protested against it in Parliament and Premier Poincaré issued an order against any color discrimination in France under penalty of prosecution.

Diagne rose in Parliament again in 1922 to denounce the taking away of the light-heavyweight championship from Siki, Senegalese boxer. Siki, an ex-dishwasher and war veteran with a distinguished record, had won the title from Georges Carpentier. The fight was a benefit one, and, it seems, had been intended only as an exhibition bout. Siki, it is said, for the privilege of appearing with Carpentier, had agreed to being "knocked out." But in the ring, Siki went berserk and knocked out Carpentier in a battle that was one of the great sensations of the ring. The referee, saying that Siki had fouled, declared Carpentier the winner, which so angered the spectators that the referee was forced to change the decision and give the title to Siki. But the French Boxing Federation, which had the final word, took the title from Siki on which Diagne charged racial discrimination.

The matter became a big issue in France. Diagne said in the Chamber of Deputies, "If I speak of this prize-fight here, it is because I fear that in the future similar men will be called to judge military championships, and that they will decide against others simply because of their color. They have acted over Carpentier as if he had really won. It is unthinkable that they should take away Siki's title simply because he is black." The title was restored to Siki.

Diagne was not without his critics, some of whom were sincere and others motivated by jealousy. He was called by some a traitor for having brought the Africans to fight for France and a tool of the rich white colonial interests. Others, however, praised him as having done more than any other to strengthen the position of colored peoples in the French Empire.

Full justice to Diagne's ability can only be rendered by considering the fact that politics is a difficult game in France. Whereas there are only two political parties in America, there are always several in France, thus only a politician of extraordinary shrewdness can attain the pinnacle—the French Cabinet, in which Diagne became Under-Secretary of State for the Colonies in 1931.

The basis of Diagne's policy was the belief that the blacks had more to gain by aligning themselves with France and by being French than by opposing her and thinking in racial terms. Consequently, when he was president of the first Pan-African Congress held in Brussels and Paris, he maneuvered it into virtual futility. When Marcus Garvey, Back-to-Africa leader, questioned him in this connection, Diagne answered, "We French natives wish to remain French since France has given us liberty and since she has unreservedly accepted us upon the basis of her own European children. . . . No propaganda, no influence of blacks or of whites, can take from us the pure sentiment that France alone is capable of working generously for the advancement of the black race."

Indeed, Diagne's own position lent considerable strength to his argument. There were hundreds of white men under him in his ministry on Rue Oudinot, where he himself was helping to shape the destinies of a great nation. His appointment was a bitter blow to the colonial aspirations of the German nationalists, who saw that it tightened France's hold on the former German colonies in Africa. Other nations with black subjects were apprehensive also lest their blacks ask, "If France, why not us too?"

In 1931, while Paul Renaud, Minister for the Colonies, was in Indochina, Diagne acted for him. In that capacity, he officiated at the dedication of the Mount Vernon House that had been built at the Inter-Colonial Exposition, with the American ambassador and other American residents of Paris present. One French daily, recalling how certain Americans had tried to establish a color line in Paris, said that the Americans would no doubt have felt more at ease if Monsieur Diagne had come as a coachman and not as the representative of France.

Diagne was one of the most effective speakers in Parliament. His delivery was without pose, he spoke clearly and to the point in a French that was worthy of a member of the Academy. He was extremely popular in West Africa, so popular, in fact, that many predicted he might become another Samory or Mahmadou Lamine. In 1918 he was too ill to return to Senegal for elections; nevertheless, he polled 7343 votes of 8000 cast in his district. The three greatest things in life, he once said, were Dignity, Love, and Justice.

Diagne was very popular too with the Parisians. Once, when he entered the amphitheatre of the Sorbonne to officiate at the presentation of prizes to the cleverest schoolchildren of France, the audience rose to its feet and greeted him with long and loud applause.

Diagne had great pride of tribe. He belonged to the Woloffs, who were of ancient lineage. Now and then he would say in jest that the West Indians and American Negroes were parvenus. "I am the original tree; you are but the branches," he said on one occasion.

But in his conduct Diagne was unassuming. While Mayor of Dakar he pointed out a little barefoot urchin reminiscently and said, "That little one there—it's I."

Some of his compatriots and others accuse him of having played the game of the French imperialists against his own people. But as the result of his influence, Senegal flourished. Agriculture was developed and schools and hospitals built.

By his French wife Diagne had several children, one of whom was France's leading football player, and another became an officer in the medical corps. He himself was a swordsman of ability. While head of the customs service in Madagascar he challenged a white man who had insulted him to a duel and came off the victor. The white man, Boujassy, was wounded in the hand.

Diagne was tall and slim with a carriage whose erectness showed no signs of the burden of his years. He walked in long, active strides that attested to his abundant vitality.

REFERENCES

It is often erroneously said that Diagne was the first Negro to become a cabinet minister in Europe but Prussia once had an unmixed African who was a state counsellor, while Portugal had both Negro cabinet ministers and ambassadors.

Diagne was the first African to become a French cabinet minister but not the first of Negro ancestry to be one. Others preceding him were: Alcide Delmont, a Martinique mulatto, and one of the leading lawyers of France, who was in the first two Tardieu cabinets; Severiano de Herédia, an unmixed Negro of Cuban descent, who held the portfolio of Public Works in the Rouvrier cabinet; and Henri Leméry of Martinique who was under secretary of state under Clemenceau and later minister of justice under Doumergue in 1934.

This writer met and talked with Diagne several times in his home, in his office on Rue Oudinot, and in the Chamber of Deputies.

ADDITIONAL REFERENCES

Gouvernement général d'Afrique Occidentale Française, *Fêtes du Cinquantenaire du Soudan Français*, speech by Blaise Diagne, pp. 51–53. Gorée, December, 1933.

Gueye, Lamine, *Itinéraire Africain*, pp. 51–63. Paris, Présence Africaine, 1966.

Padmore, George, *Pan-Africanism or Communism?*, pp. 119–123, 134, 197. London, Dennis Dobson, 1961.

SOUTH AND
CENTRAL AMERICA

Commentary and Notes
on References

THE PART THAT AFRICANS PLAYED in the making of South and Central America is still a neglected aspect of history. In order to understand the African in South and in Central America, one must look especially at this area and in general at North and South America, the West Indies, and then at developing Europe and the ideas that brought this development into being. In looking at the Africans it is necessary that we honestly examine the interpretations of the role that they played in shaping the destiny of this hemisphere.

A lot of romance and pure nonsense came from many interpreters who were long ago academically accepted. It is high time that serious questions be asked about their interpretations, and the concept of a "mild" slave system, especially in Brazil.

For instance, Frank Tannenbaum interprets Gilberto Freyre in *Brazil: An Interpretation* (New York, Alfred A. Knopf, 1945):

The settling of the western hemisphere by peoples coming from Europe and Africa was an adventure on a grand scale, involving diverse people, varying cultures, millions of human beings, and hundreds of years. The common element was the New World, though strongly dissimilar in physical features and cultural type. But the student discerns, in many an analogous design, patterned by the newcomers as they established themselves in the strange and unexplored regions. It is natural, therefore, for Gilberto Freyre to draw revealing similarities between the history of Brazil and the United States.

Then Tannenbaum goes on to say:

Like everything that he writes, this volume has a freshness and a lucidity that endow the reader with insight and understanding of the complex instrumentalities for life and labor contributed by man in his new world. Freyre finds in the development of Brazil, for example, the impact of the frontier and the dominion of the plantation so typical of our own South. The disparity, implied rather than expressed in the study, is the divergent position of the Negro within the two areas. For the Negro—and especially the Mulatto—had an access to the culture of Brazil, and a role in social life, unknown in the United States. In politics, in the arts and in society, the Mulatto found the door ajar even if not fully open, and a markedly different social milieu has come into being. Even under the Empire, the Negro and the Mulatto—and, socially, the attractive Mulatto women—found an acceptance unthinkable in the North American scene.

Freyre quotes from Ewbank this revealing picture:

I have passed black ladies in silks and jewelry, with male slaves in livery behind them. Today one rode past in her carriage, accompanied by a liveried footman and a coachman. Several have white husbands. This first doctor of the city is a colored man; so is the President of the Province.

The young Afro-Caribbean scholar Tony Martin, in his article "The Black Man in Brazil: A Challenge to the Honest Historian," calls for a whole new approach to the history of Africans in the New World, especially in Brazil. He opens his article by saying:

A lot of rewriting of Black History will have to be done over the next few years if a true picture of the Black Man's experience in the New World is ever to emerge. One of the areas where most violence has been done to the available evidence is Brazil, where a host of travellers and historians, many of them highly-esteemed members of their professions, have over the years weaved a web of nonsensical mystification around the concept of the "mild" treatment of slaves in Brazil, as opposed to the "harsh" treatment meted out to the unfortunate Black persons who happened to find themselves in the West

Indies or North America. The "favorable" experience of the Black Man in Brazil has been extended by these pundits to an alleged absence of racial discrimination in contemporary Brazil, which is conveniently contrasted with the situation in racist North America.

To account for these "differences," explanations have been sought in the alleged ameliorating influences of the Catholic Church, the Portuguese propensity for violating the virginity of Black women, the residue of Black blood coursing through Portuguese veins, relics of the Moorish conquest, and the "different" species of African who found his way to Brazil.

The determining factor in the economic and cultural survival of the New World was the African. His labor developed the plantation system, which laid the basis for the economic system that we call capitalism.

There were several competing slave systems in the New World. In order to understand the effects of these various systems on the personality of the Africans, we have to look at each one individually. In Cuba and Haiti often the Africans were a majority in the population. This is also true of certain portions of Brazil. Therefore the system operated differently in these areas, and although it was still slavery, the African had some cultural mobility.

In South America and in the West Indies the slave master did not outlaw the African drum, African ornamentations, African religion, or other things dear to the African, remembered from his former way of life. This permitted a form of cultural continuity among the slaves in the West Indies, Cuba, and South America that did not exist in the United States.

In the Portuguese area, in the West Indies, and often in South America the population owner would buy a shipload or half a shipload of slaves. These slaves usually came from the same areas in Africa, and they naturally spoke the same language and had the same basic culture. Families, in the main, were kept together. If a slave on an island was sold to a plantation owner at the other end of the island, he could still walk to see his relatives. This made for a form of cultural continuity among the slaves in South America, Cuba, and in Haiti. Because of this cultural continuity the slave revolts in South America and the West Indies were more successful than the slave revolts in the United States. Slavery was still harsh in all of these areas, which accounts for the numerous slave revolts.

Haiti and Cuba, during this early period, were dominated by their "mother countries." Wars were started within these countries to liberate them from their European masters. Africans made a meaningful contribution toward the early liberation of Cuba, Haiti, and other areas of South America; they fought with Simon Bolívar for the freedom of South America, and fought valiantly to free Haiti from the domination of the French.

Africans were not strangers to the Spanish and the Portuguese before the settlement of the New World. These Europeans had been mixing freely with Africans for hundreds of years. This mixing continued in South America and in the West Indies. It continued to the point where, with justification, South America can be called, mainly, a mulatto continent. In this context the careers of men like Henrique Dias, in Brazil, Manuel Carlos Piar, in Venezuela, Vicente Guerrero, in Mexico, and Bernardino Rivadavia, in Argentina, are not contradictions. These men developed as a logical consequence of certain conditions and attitudes that the Europeans had before the settlement of the New World.

The careers of Rafael Carrera, liberator of Guatemala, and Dom Pedro II, the Magnanimous, of Brazil, are also related to these conditions and attitudes.

Carlos Gomes and Machado de Assis were cultural figures with no political partiality. Carlos Gomes was hailed in Europe by Guiseppe Verdi for the originality of his opera music. He was the first composer of the New World to be accepted into the musical circles of Europe.

Machado de Assis was to Brazil what Aleksander Pushkin was to Russia: he was the father of Brazilian literature. He was among these nineteenth-century New World writers who broke away from the European tradition in literature and produced a new and vital literature that reflected the excitement and the agony of a new nation and society being born.

J. H. C.

Henrique Dias

EX-SLAVE WHO BROKE THE POWER OF HOLLAND
(1605–1662)

NEGRO SLAVES, as military leaders, have played an important part in the present political alignment of the New World. Toussaint L'Ouverture and Dessalines weakened the power of France in the Caribbean, and thereby brought about the sale of the Mississippi Valley to the United States; Vicente Guerrero drove the Spaniards from Mexico and his antislavery policy caused Texas to enter the American Union; and Henrique Dias broke the power of the Dutch in South America, thus making easier the rise of the English-speaking peoples in North America.

Dias lived nearly a century and a half before Toussaint L'Ouverture. Though Toussaint probably never heard of him, the great Haitian could well have used him as a model. Also born a slave and of unmixed Negro parentage, Dias, without military training and almost illiterate, defeated two of Holland's ablest generals trained in the best schools of Europe. One of these was the celebrated Count Maurice of Nassau, brother of Frederick Henry, King of Holland.

Dias was born at Pernambuco, Brazil. Holland was then the world's leading power. With mastery of the seas, she was crowding out Portugal, her leading rival, from the markets of the world. She had a monopoly on all the trade in the region south of the Tropic of Cancer, that is, Central and South America, Africa, India, the

Philippines, and Australia. The English tried to capture some of this trade, but the Dutch defeated them in several battles, even sailing up the Thames and burning shipping.

The Dutch, having secured a foothold in North America in what is now the state of New York, decided to gain another in South America. Selecting Brazil, which had been Portugal's for more than a century, they landed there with a powerful force under Count Maurice and easily defeated the Portuguese. At Porto Calvo Count Maurice defeated Count de Bonjola, Portuguese commander, and made himself master of all northern Brazil.

Portugal dispatched a powerful fleet with a large army to Brazil, but on the voyage across, the plague killed more than 3000 soldiers. The remainder were forced to land in Africa, where still more died. When the expedition arrived in Brazil it was easily beaten by the Dutch. Of the ninety-three ships that started from Portugal only two ever returned. "These victories," say D'Urban and Mielle, "so inflated the courage of Count Maurice that he began to regard Brazil as a theatre too small for the exercise of his valor."

The Brazilians, now forced to live under Dutch rule, longed for freedom, and revolted under two of their leaders, Vieyra and Negreiros, but their scanty forces were easily beaten by Count Maurice in every fight. It was at this seemingly hopeless juncture that Dias entered the fight as a leader. Hitherto he had been only a common soldier.

As such he had distinguished himself, however. At Iguarussa early in the struggle, with only thirty-five other black men, he had turned the tide of battle in favor of the Portuguese.

In 1635 he had been among the prisoners captured by the Dutch at Fort Buen Jesus, but the Dutch, taking him for a slave of one of the white prisoners, had guarded him loosely and he had escaped. Rejoining the Portuguese, he had again distinguished himself at Porto Calvo, June 9, 1639.

In this battle, in which the Portuguese were surrounded by the Dutch, Dias, with only eighty black men, fought his way to liberty through the ranks of the enemy.

When the Dutch had captured all of northern Brazil, Dias went south where the Portuguese were still resisting and offered his services to the governor, Mathias de Albuquerque. While here, he saw that the Indians were fighting under their own leader. Why, he asked, should not the blacks do likewise?

He suggested this idea to the governor, who gave him permission to raise a corps of slaves and free Negroes. Enlisting 500 of them, he trained them thoroughly and went off to meet the hitherto victorious Count Maurice. At Arecise he defeated him with great loss. In ten successive battles he repeated this success, inspiring all, white and black, by his example. King Philip IV of Portugal, in recognition of these services, placed him over all the other black men and mulattoes in the colony, and gave him the highest decoration, the Order of Christ, together with a salary sufficient to maintain his rank.

Count Maurice was recalled and the leading Dutch commander of that period, Count Sigismond, took his place. Portugal, at the same time, sent out her ablest general, Baretto de Menenes, with a large fleet, but this, like the other, also met disaster. The Dutch destroyed it and captured Menenes.

Count Sigismond, with a greatly strengthened force, assailed Pernambuco and captured it after defeating all the Portuguese leaders, including Dias. Once again, however, Dias rallied the black men, and meeting Count Sigismond in one of the most stubborn engagements of that war of twelve years, defeated him. With his seasoned European troops, Count Sigismond attacked Dias twice with impetuosity and twice Dias beat him off with incredible valor.

Dias now besieged the Dutch general in Pernambuco. Sigismond made a sortie, hoping to surprise him, but the latter, ever vigilant, made a counterattack and pursued the Hollanders to the gates of the town, killing nearly all of them.

Dias' greatest exploit was the capture of Cinco Pontus. This was an apparently impregnable fortress near Pernambuco which commanded the whole city and neighborhood. It was well provisioned and garrisoned by an army of 5000 men, and protected by high, massive walls and deep and wide ditches with twelve feet of water. As provisions were supplied by the Dutch ships, it was impossible to reduce the fort by famine. Each attack upon it was immediately punished by a bombardment of the town and the surrounding Brazilian territory.

Dias decided to capture this fortress and sent his plan of attack to the commander-in-chief, who thought so well of it that he gave Dias a free hand.

"Tomorrow," assured Dias, "you shall see our flag waving over the fortress of Cinco Pontus."

Bidding his men take only their knives and pistols and a tightly-bound bundle of wood each, he left for the fort at two o'clock in the morning. In the dark they arrived at their destination undisturbed. Silently and rapidly they threw the wood in to the deep trench, making an easy passage over the water, then with this same wood piled against the wall, they climbed over easily into the fort, Dias leading.

The garrison was asleep. Before it could be aroused Dias had gained the greater part of the fortress.

The Dutch, rallying, resisted desperately. Dias received a wound which shattered the bones of his left arm above the wrist. Learning that it would take some time to adjust the bones and arrange the dressing, he bade the surgeon cut off the hand. "It is of less consequence to me than a few moments' time just now," he said, laughing grimly. "The five fingers on this other hand will be worth that many hands."

This done, he rushed into the thickest of the fight, and although the Dutch had the advantage of artillery and rifles, he defeated them, capturing the garrison with its stores of provisions and ammunition. When the smoke cleared the Portuguese flag was floating over the battlements, as Dias had promised.

Menenes, the commander-in-chief, could hardly believe the good news. Seeking out Dias, who was lying on a camp bed weak from loss of blood, he overwhelmed him with praise.

Dias was taken to Portugal at the command of King John IV, who received him with great distinction and bade him ask for anything he wished. Dias, thinking of his men first, asked that the regiment be perpetuated and that pensions be given his soldiers. Later a town called Estancia was built near Pernambuco for them at the king's orders. In addition, he raised Dias to the nobility and struck a medal depicting the capture of the fortress in his honor.

Driven out of Pernambuco, the Dutch finally yielded. With peace restored, Dias, who was as modest as he was brave, kept in the background. Others pushed themselves forward and he and his brave men were soon forgotten. Worse, Brazil, impoverished by the long war, reduced them to slavery again on an even more oppressive scale. The Indians, who had also played a very important role in victory, were treated even worse and were once again raided by slave hunters.

Dias lived seventeen years longer and died in neglect and poverty at Pernambuco June 8, 1662. His memory, however, was perpetuated in a regiment composed entirely of Negroes, which lasted until the Brazilian Civil War of 1835. It was commanded by the descendants of Dias and up to that time did not "ally itself with the whites, wishing thus to perpetuate the memory of a race which is honored in the colony."

French, Spanish, and Portuguese encyclopedias speak in highest terms of Dias. Pinheiro Chagas has written a short sketch of his life. Several Italian writers of the seventeenth century have also praised his bravery and his military skill, among them Brandano, who has devoted considerable space to him.

According to the Abbé Gregoire:

To cleverness in military tactics and in strategy, he joined the most audacious courage and disconcerted the Dutch generals. In a battle when the superiority of some of his soldiers began to fail, he threw himself into the midst of them, shouting: "Are these the valiant companions of Henrique Dias?" His speech and his example infused them with new vigor, and the enemy that already believed itself victorious he charged with an impetuosity that forced it to turn back and dash precipitately for the town. Dias forced Arrecife to capitulate; Pernambuco to yield, and destroyed entirely the Dutch army.

The American Brigadier-General A. S. Burt, in his appraisal of the Negro as a soldier, says:

The story of Dias' organization of a black regiment officered entirely by men of his own race, his brilliant campaigns against the Dutch, make one of the important chapters in the history of the western hemisphere; for this man emancipated his country from the hard hand of a stubborn, masterful race; and his countrymen have deservedly placed him in the class with Bolivar, Washington and Toussaint L'Ouverture, the great liberators and founders of states in the Western world.

In resources, Brazil is one of the richest and most highly favored countries. It is as large as the United States and France combined. Had this immense territory remained in the power of Holland, the Dutch might have been strong enough to retain New York and other parts of New England. In short, but for Dias there might not have been a United States, or, at best, a less powerful one.

REFERENCES

Another important Negro leader against the Dutch in this struggle was General Luiz Barbalho Bezerra, who for his services was made Governor of Rio de Janeiro by the King of Spain. Barbalho fared better than Dias, very likely because he was born in Portugal, and though a Negro, was looked on as white. He died in 1644. (Coelho de Senna, N., *Africanos no Brasil*, p. 42. 1933; also *Diccionario de Pernambucanos Celebres*, pp. 620–25. 1882; *Enciclopedia Universal Ilustrada*, Vol. VII, pp. 646–647.)

D'Urban, and Mielle, J. F., *Histoire-Général de Portugal*, Vol. IV, pp. 470–471. Paris, 1829.

Grégoire, H., *Littérature des nègres*, p. 96. Paris, 1808.

Chagas, P., *Brazileiros Illustres*, pp. 21–23. Porto, 1892.

Brandano, A., *Historia della Guerre di Portogallo*, pp. 181, 329, 364, 393, etc. Venice, 1689.

Brito Freyre, Fde. *Nova Lusitania*, pp. 480, 610, 762. Lisbon, 1675.

Macedo, J. M., *Anno. Biog. Brazileiro*, Vol. II, pp. 533–538. Rio de Janeiro, 1876.

Pombo, Rocha, *Historia do Brazil*, Vol. IV, p. 548. San Paulo, 1918.

Revista do Instituto Arquelogico, Historico etc., Vol. XXIX, pp. 76–88; Vol. XXXIX, pp. 231–245. 1928–1929, 1943.

Pereira da Costa, F. A., *Diccionario Biographico Pernambucanos*, pp. 410–418. 1882.

Biographie Universelle, "Dias, Henrique."

Child, M., *The Oasis*. Boston, 1834.

Burt, A. S., "The Negro as a Soldier." *Crisis Magazine*, pp. 22–25 (February, 1911).

ADDITIONAL REFERENCES

Romas, Arthur, *The Negro in Brazil*, trans. by Richard Dattee, pp. 161–162. Washington, D.C., The Associated Publishers, 1939, 1951.

Willis, Dorothy J., "Henrique Dias: A Brave Soldier." *Negro History Bulletin*, p. 98 (February, 1941), Association for the Study of Negro Life and History, Washington, D.C.

Woodson, Carter G., "Henrique Dias." *Negro History Bulletin*, p. 7 (November, 1937), Association for the Study of Negro Life and History, Washington, D.C.

Manuel Carlos Piar

HERO OF VENEZUELAN DEMOCRACY AND MARTYR TO THE
CAUSE OF TRUE DEMOCRACY

(1782–1817)

MANUEL CARLOS PIAR, Venezuelan general and rival of Bolívar,
was born in Curaçao, Dutch West Indies. His parents, says Gil
Fortoul, Venezuelan historian, were "Ferdinand Piar and a
mulatto woman, María Isabel Gomez."

Piar received a good education and went into business, but not
succeeding in that, he went to Venezuela in 1810 to throw in his
lot with the insurgents against Spain, and was made a second
lieutenant.

Four years later his brilliant qualities as a military leader came
to the notice of General Marino, who took him as his aide. At this
period, however, came one of the darkest moments in the struggle
for independence. The rebels were scattered and Bolívar went
abroad in search of help and support. When he returned, Piar
joined him, and Bolívar, recognizing his ability, made him a general and sent him to take command in Maturín.

In this post Piar distinguished himself in battle after battle and
carried out Bolívar's slogan of "War to the Death." As cruel as
he was brave, Piar killed without quarter every captured Spaniard.

One of his merciless onslaughts was against the Spanish monks
of Caruache in the Caroni River territory, who were well supplied
with food and other essentials needed for his campaign. When the
monks refused to hand over their goods, he had twenty-two of

them shot. With these supplies, he strengthened his army, and though outnumbered, attacked the Spanish forces at San Felix, May 11, 1817, and won a crushing victory. True to the policy of war to the death, he had every Spaniard shot, though he spared the Creoles.

The victory at San Felix against such odds came at a time when the revolutionists needed encouragement most, and Piar's name was not only mingled with Bolívar's but was placed by some above it. As a general, Piar was equal, if not superior, to Bolívar. In statesmanship, however, he was Bolívar's inferior.

Now began a struggle between the two for supremacy. In addition to military jealousy, there was the question of "race." Bolívar belonged to a caste that looked down on Negroes, though he himself not only seemed to have no prejudices of this kind, but had been one of the most prominent in decrying them. In one of his addresses he had pointed out the African strain not only in Venezuela but in the Spaniards in Spain. He went further. He married his adopted daughter Felicia to Laurencio Silva, one of his favorite generals and an unmixed Negro. Bolívar himself is said by several writers to have been of Negro ancestry, much attenuated.

The upper class, however, boasted of its *sangre azul*, or blue blood, and despised Negroes and mulattoes, who were then furnishing most of the soldiers in the fight for independence. Gil Fortoul estimates that in 1811, the year after the fight began, there were 406,000 people of color as against 12,000 whites and 200,000 Creoles. A considerable portion of these Negroes were slaves.

Piar, as a man of color, wanted all caste and color distinctions wiped out. He opposed those practiced not only by the Spaniards but also by the native Venezuelan whites. He wanted, he said, "a republic of free and equal men," and accused Bolívar of giving only lip service to this principle.

Bolívar to placate him and to retain his much needed services made him a general-in-chief and placed him second in command. Piar, however, resolute in his belief in equality for the blacks and very likely too in the thought that he was superior to Bolívar as a military leader, began inciting the Negro officers to revolt, which was serious since most of the men in the army were of Negro ancestry. Bolívar, learning of this, sent for him and tried in every way to win him over. Piar refused to yield and offered his resignation, which Bolívar reluctantly accepted.

Piar, in leaving Bolívar, said he was returning to his native Curaçao, but instead of doing so remained in Venezuela, stirring up the army against Bolívar, who then ordered him to rejoin his command. Piar refused, and going to Maturín, where he was very popular, began to organize a revolt. Bolívar issued an order for his arrest and court-martial. Found guilty, he was sentenced to be shot. One of the judges who condemned Piar was an unmixed Negro, Colonel Judas T. Pinango, later a general. Piar, defiant to the last, died with the same courage he had shown on the battlefield. He was only thirty-five.

Since Piar, next to Bolívar, had been the most popular man in the army, Bolívar found it necessary to issue an explanation to the soldiers as to why Piar had been executed. Piar, he said, was planning to start a civil war—a proceeding, which, he said, was not necessary since "the odious difference of class and color had been abolished forever" in Venezuela. This was not wholly true. While individual blacks of ability were permitted to rise to high positions, the great mass of mixed-bloods and Negroes was exploited and looked down on. As for those blacks who rose to power, they were regarded as inferiors by the white upper class and rejected socially.

By nearly all historians Piar is regarded as a malcontent, intensely jealous of Bolívar. Some even declare that he was not of Negro ancestry and only said he was to win favor with the Negro officers and men. That he was jealous of Bolívar and felt himself superior was no doubt true, but that he was also inspired by a higher motive is even more true. As a mulatto, he was snubbed by the upper classes in spite of his rank. He wanted, as he said, equality with not only the Spanish exploiters but the native white caste as well.

Bolívar had made a very definite promise to Alexandre Pétion, President of Haiti, to free the slaves of Venezuela. When Boívar had come twice to Pétion for aid and the latter had given it, Pétion had urged that step. "How," said Pétion, "can you free a country if you do not free all the people in it?" Slavery, however, was not abolished in Venezuela until twenty-four years after Bolívar's death.

Bolívar, in spite of his power and popularity as well as his promise to Pétion and his wish to keep it, was faced with a situation similar to that of certain fathers of American independence. Washington and Jefferson, though at bottom opposed to slavery, did not take an open stand against it, not wishing to cause discontent and even possible revolt among the upper classes of the South. Piar, on the other hand, had taken the bull by the horns.

REFERENCES

Gil Fortoul, J., *Historia Constitucional de Venezuela*, Vol. I, pp. 258, 362, 312–365. 1907.

Larrazabal, *Simon Bolívar*, pp. 75–100. 1918.

Baralt, R. M., *Resumen de la Historia de Venezuela*, Vol. I, pp. 512–526. 1841.

Lemly, H. R., *Bolívar*, pp. 131–150. 1923.

Ybarra, T. R., *Bolívar*, pp. 135–136. 1929.

ADDITIONAL REFERENCES

Whitridge, Arnold, *Simon Bolívar: The Great Liberation*, pp. 86–88. New York, Random House, 1954.

Vicente Guerrero

MEXICAN LIBERATOR AND PRESIDENT
(1782–1831)

VICENTE GUERRERO, a mulatto ex-slave, was the George Washington and Abraham Lincoln combined of Mexico. He freed his country and then freed its slaves.

Guerrero was born at Ixtla, Mexico, in 1782 of mixed white and Negro parentage with an Indian strain. His father, Juan Pedro Guerrero, and his mother, Guadelupe Saldena, were both of humble origin, the lowest of the low, degraded by law, custom, and prejudice. No Negro woman could wear any kind of ornamentation, jewels, trinkets, or linen.

Guerrero started life as a mule driver. Unlike Abraham Lincoln, he hadn't the slightest opportunity to learn to read or write. He was nearly forty before he knew a letter of the alphabet. But within his breast was an unquenchable desire for freedom and a spirit of love and justice for his fellow man. Therefore when the struggle for Mexican independence began in 1810, led by a valiant priest, Hidalgo, he was one of the first to enlist. The upper-class Mexicans who oppressed the Indians and the Negroes were, in turn, oppressed by Spain. They could not trade with foreign countries and Mexican manufacture was forbidden. When Hidalgo planted grapevines to make his own wine, government officials tore them up. Wine had to be imported from Spain, with a high tax. At this time, also, Mexico was ordered to pay a tribute of an additional $45 million to Spain. The grievances of the American colonists against George III were insignificant compared to those of Mexico against the King of Spain.

Declaring Mexican independence, Hidalgo had called upon all his countrymen to follow him. Guerrero distinguished himself so well in the first battle that he was made a captain.

In the first stage of the struggle the Mexicans were successful, but Spain, sending reinforcements from home, soon crushed the insurgents. One by one the leading Mexicans—Hidalgo, Allende, Aldama, Jiminez, Mina—were slain or made prisoner. The remainder accepted the king's pardon—all except Guerrero, who fought on.

Villaseñor says of him, "Forsaken by fortune, betrayed, without money, without arms, with only his will-power left, he was at this time of desolation and despair, the only supporter of the cause of independence, displaying valor, prudence, profound sagacity, indefatigable activity and heroic constancy."

"Even in the darkest days of the long revolution," says Rives, "he was the leader of a little body of unconquered men, who kept alive the cause of independence."

The government, in an effort to win Guerrero, sent his father Pedro to offer him lands and wealth. But Guerrero scorned the offer. He had pledged himself no rest until the hated Spaniard had been driven into the sea.

Spain sent her best general, Iturbide, against him. Guerrero defeated him in two battles. Iturbide, who secretly had resolved to desert Spain and make himself master of Mexico and had been winning over the army to himself by bribes, now made overtures to Guerrero, promising to revolt against Spain provided he had Guerrero's support. The latter, not seeing through his duplicity, consented.

Joining hands, the two defeated General Santa Ana, Spanish commander. Iturbide was named President of Mexico, Guerrero stepping aside though he was the more popular of the two.

As ruler, Iturbide showed his true colors. He proclaimed himself emperor and with the landed classes continued the exploitation of the masses of ignorant natives who had born the brunt of the struggle for independence.

Guerrero thereupon declared war against Iturbide, captured him, and had him shot. Another was elected president with Guerrero as vice president. But the struggle between the landed classes and the masses went on. The opposing sides carried on their activities through freemasonry, which had lately been introduced into Mexico. The rich were in the Scottish rite; the poor, the York rite. Guerrero was head of the Yorks.

At the next presidential election the candidates were Guerrero and Pedraza, the former backed by the common people, the latter by the rich. Pedraza won, ten electors declaring for him against eight for Guerrero.

Revolt over the nation followed. The Yorks issued a proclamation naming Guerrero president. It said, "The name of the hero of the South is echoed with indescribable enthusiasm everywhere. His valor and constancy combined have engraved themselves upon the hearts of the Mexican people. He is the image of their felicity. They wish to confide to him the delicate and sacred task of the executive power." Finally the government surrendered and Guerrero became president in April, 1825.

Guerrero at once set about improving the conditions of the masses, composed of Indians, half-breeds, and Negroes. He ordered schools to be built, established free libraries—reading had been forbidden—proclaimed religious liberty, established a coinage system, suspended the death penalty, and took other steps far in advance of his time.

His most important act was the abolition of slavery. Though inspired by the Constitution of the United States, he went further than that document. He ordered the immediate release of every slave in Mexico. The estimated number of Negro slaves was 10,595 blacks and 1050 mulattoes, with Guerrero's native state containing the largest number. The remainder were Indians and half-breeds, some of whom had a Negro strain.

The Mexican constitution, which is as liberal a document as has ever been penned, was much of it the work of Guerrero. One of its clauses read, "All inhabitants, whether White, African, or Indian, are qualified to hold office."

Guerrero's emancipation proclamation was put into effect almost without resistance because it did not entail great economic loss to the rich, except in one state, namely Texas.

The Texans were chiefly Americans who had migrated into Mexico with their slaves to escape antislavery agitation in the United States. They made it clear that they would not give up their slaves without a struggle and Guerrero, who was busy fighting his enemies in Mexico City, was forced to leave them alone.

Later Texas revolted and joined the American Union partly because of the emancipation decree of this Negro president. The Texans knew that the temper of the Mexican masses was against slavery and that they would be forced to give in sooner or later.

Guerrero's rise to the presidency increased the oposition of the wealthy and the landed classes and they used every means in their power to pull him down. Bancroft says, "They could not bear the sight of one of Guerrero's race occupying the presidential chair and ruthlessly destroyed a government whose only faults were excessive clemency and liberalism." Strode says, "Because of his lack of education, his country manners and his reputed Negro blood, he was held in contempt by the upper-class society of the capital. The conservatives chose to regard him as a triple-blooded outsider."

He might have won their approval, however, had he been willing to become their tool and give them a free hand with the masses. This he would not do and tried to win them over to his side by liberal arguments and generous dealing, which proved a total failure. Uniting against him, they drove him from office.

Guerrero, as in the days when he was fighting for independence, took once more to the mountains, where for the next four years he defeated every force sent against him even though his strength had been undermined by a bullet that had lodged in his chest while fighting Iturbide. Finally his rival, General Bustamente, took him by treachery. He gave a ship captain, Picaluga, a friend of Guerrero, $13,000 to lure Guerrero to his ship. There Guerrero was made prisoner and executed after a mock trial.

His death was followed by nationwide revolt. Bustamente was driven from the presidency and saved his life only by flight. Picaluga was executed.

A pension was paid Guerrero's window; honors were conferred on other members of his family; and cities and a state were named in his honor. In 1842 his body was removed to Mexico City and interred there.

Parkes says, "Guerrero was an uneducated man of mixed Spanish, Indian and Negro descent of a singularly generous and kindly disposition."

"Guerrero," says Bancroft, "was possessed of a gentleness and magnetism that inspired love among his adherents; while his swarthy face, resonant voice, and flashing eye made him an object of profound respect even among his enemies."

REFERENCES

Negroes played a more important role in Mexico than is generally known. For information on this, see Chapter Six, "Mexico," *Sex and Race*. Vol. II.

Larousse Universel calls Guerrero, "esclave mulatre" (mulatto slave): so, too, does *Biographie Universelle* (see "Guerrero"). *Webster's New International Dictionary*, 2nd ed., Vol. III, p. 317, calls him "mulatto president of Mexico." See also *Colored American*, September 5, 1840, where in an article reproduced from the *Anti-Slavery Almanac* he is mentioned with other South American generals as a Negro.

Guerrero's most trusted friend was Colonel Juan del Carmen, a full-blooded Negro, who is described by Villaseñor as being "very black, of horrible appearance, and extraordinary bravery."

Rangel, J., *General Guerrero*. 1868.

Villaseñor y Villaseñor, A. *Biografías de los Heroes y Caudillos de la Independencia*, pp. 401–409. 1910.

Loyo, L., *Vicente Guerrero*. 1925.

Collection of material by and about Vicente Guerrero, New York Public Library.

Sprague, F. S., *Vicente Guerrero, a Study in Patriotism*. 1939.

Carriedo, I. B., *Estudios Historicos*, Vol. II, pp. 49–55. 1847.

Gutierrez De Lara, *The Mexican People*, p. 54. 1914.

Bancroft, H. H. *Works: History of Mexico*, Vols. IX–XI. 1914.

Parkes, H. B. *A History of Mexico*, p. 165. 1938.

Strode, H., *Timeless Mexico*, p. 124.

ADDITIONAL REFERENCES

Sterne, Emma Gelders, *Benito Juarez*, pp. 25–26, 30–33, 36, 40, 42, 43, 51, 54–55. New York, Alfred A. Knopf, 1967.

Bernardino Rivadavia

FIRST PRESIDENT OF THE ARGENTINE REPUBLIC
(1780–1845)

BERNARDINO RIVADAVIA was one of South America's greatest and noblest statesmen. A native of Buenos Aires, he was one of the leaders in repelling the English when they tried to seize that country in 1806 and again in 1807. He distinguished himself in several engagements and received the high commendation of the Spanish viceroy, Liniers.

He was also one of the leaders for Argentine independence. As a member of a secret committee working toward that end, he saw his opportunity when Napoleon invaded Spain and so weakened her that she would not be able to send an expedition to faraway Argentina. Taking advantage of this, the Argentines ousted the Spanish viceroy when Napoleon captured Cadiz in 1811 and established their own local government. They did not cut themselves off from Spain, however, due to English and French designs on their country.

Rivadavia was made secretary of war and was later sent to England to try to encourage an understanding between her and Spain about Argentina. England at that time was fighting Napoleon in Spain. Soon after Rivadavia's arrival, however, the French were beaten in Spain and the Spanish king, Ferdinand VII, came back to his throne. Rivadavia was now left to deal with Ferdinand himself, but could not come to an agreement with him. The king demanded submission; Rivadavia wanted independence.

Bernardino Rivadavia

One of his missions in leaving Argentina was to seek a prince of one of the royal houses of Europe to be King of Argentina. Ferdinand refused to let one of his family go. Rivadavia next tried the House of Orléans but Louis XVIII of France also objected; and so did the Braganzas of Portugal. His mission to Europe was not entirely unsuccessful, however. He induced the King of Spain not to send an expedition against Argentina.

In 1820, after an absence of six years, he returned to Argentina, which had, in the meantime declared its independence. He was made secretary of state.

This task was very difficult, external troubles and, even more, acute internal ones making it so. The native-born Spaniards, who lived chiefly in Buenos Aires, the capital, center of wealth and of such culture as then existed in the republic, wished to be dominant and to have Buenos Aires practically rule over the rest of the nation. Their party was called Unitarios. Opposed to them were the Federalists, who were chiefly in the provinces and wanted an equal voice in the government, or something like states' rights in the United States. Feeling ran high between the two parties and

there were several armed clashes. At the same time relations between Argentina and Brazil were so disturbed that war threatened.
In 1826, however, the Unitarios were able to form a central government and Rivadavia was elected the first president.

Thanks largely to the years he had spent in Europe, he was then
the most cultured man in Argentina. To this was added great
integrity and a spirit of broad humanity. With great visions for his
country's future he set about with greater zeal than ever to work
for its progress. He decreed freedom of speech and of the press;
abolished the slave trade; instituted commercial freedom; encouraged immigration; organized the archives; set the finances of
the country and the banking system in order; and established the
representative system on a more democratic base.

Keenly interested too in advancing his country culturally, he
founded more and better schools, including the University of
Buenos Aires, of which the Spaniards had been merely talking of
founding for many years. He founded an engineering school and
brought scholars from Europe to be teachers and professors. He
encouraged literature, built libraries, founded literary societies,
and had Argentine poetry printed at government expense.

He built a botanical garden; a new system of drainage; laid the
foundations of the Cathedral of Buenos Aires; and built highways
into the interior. One of these, the Calle Rivadavia, forty-two
miles long and said to be the longest street in the world, is named
after him. But his most renowned work is probably the establishment of a charitable organization, the Sociedad de Beneficia,
for aid to the poor and the needy, which is still doing splendid
work.

His time in office was short, however, due largely to the above-
mentioned efforts. Argentina was then largely a wild, rough land.
The people of the interior were mostly cattlemen, farmers, and
peasants unappreciative of education and culture. The mass of the
population were illiterate and were chiefly *mestizos*, born of
Spanish fathers and Indian mothers. Next in number were the
mulattoes, born of Spanish fathers and Negro slave mothers. The
white population, including those born in Europe, were hardly
more numerous than the unmixed Negro slaves. As a result there
was a great outcry against Rivadavia for his expenditures for

national improvement. Added to this was continued trouble with Brazil, which soon afterward broke into war. In the face of these difficulties he resigned after a little more than a year in the presidency. Going to Europe, and refusing to return even for vindication, he died in Spain in 1845. In 1857 his ashes were brought to Argentina and buried in the Plaza Once. Towns and other parts of the republic were named after him and on his centenary, his birthday, May 20, was made a public holiday.

Rivadavia's seven years of control of Argentina laid the base of that country's progress and started it off toward being the rich and powerful nation it is today.

John M. Forbes, American diplomatic agent who knew Rivadavia well, said of him that he "was the champion of moral influence; the enemy of prejudice; the enlightened and honest statesman; patriotism his motive and guide; his shield and reward the approbation of a pure and elevated conscience."

Saldias, Argentine historian, says:

Rivadavia descended from the presidency because of the passions and the demagoguery of his era. He fell amid a silence that he was foremost to preserve. He left everything to posterity which is free from the prejudices that dwarf men and the injustices that belittle nations. His name symbolizes an era which left in the republic the brilliant vestiges of free government. No one has surpassed him there as a statesman and administrator, and after the lapse of seventy years what he accomplished as a constitutional reformer is still the most desired thing of the nations of South America. . . . Posterity will do him justice.

REFERENCES

L. L. and J. S. Bernard, say, "Rivadavia, one of the greatest figures in Argentine history, was a mulatto." (*Proceedings National Academy of Science*, Vol. V. No. 3, p. 316. 1928.)

Luis Alberto Sanchez: "Rivadavia, the first president of Argentina, was undoubtedly a mulatto." (*Antioch Review*, Fall of 1942, p. 360.) His portrait bears out this fact.

Until the last half-century, the majority of the Argentine population was of mixed blood, with the Indian strain dominant, Negro next, and white last. An Argentine source as cited by J. W. White (*Argentina*, p. 124, 1942), says that in 1852 less than 3 percent of the Argentine population was white. There were 553,000 *mestizos*, 110,000 mulattoes, 100,000 Indians, 15,000 native-born whites, and 7,000 Europeans.

Even in Buenos Aires less than a third of the population was white. Of its 76,000, there were 33,000 *mestizos*, 26,000 Indians, Negroes, and mulattoes, and 17,000 whites, of which 5,000 were Europeans.

Negro slavery was abolished by the dictator Rosas, a successor, but one, of Rivadavia. But even during slavery there was little color prejudice which explains why mixed-bloods like Rivadavia and San Martin were able to have such influence there.

Argentina is today predominantly white due to the flood of immigration from Europe, principally Italy and Germany, which began in the second decade of this century. In 1936 over 36 percent of the population of Buenos Aires was foreign-born. The Indian population is now almost extinct and unmixed Negroes are few.

Due largely to American and Nazi influence color prejudice has increased in Argentina but it is still vastly less than in the United States. There are some Argentines who, because of their national jealousy of Brazil, affect to look down upon her because of her large Negro population.

Galvan, Moreno C., *Rivadavia, el Estadista Genial.* Buenos Aires, 1940.

Lamas, A., *Rivadavia.* Buenos Aires, 1915.

Picirilli, R., *Rivadavia y su Tiempo.* Buenos Aires, 1915.

Saldias, A., *Historia de la Confederacion Argentina*, Vol. I, pp. 261–262. 1892.

Enciclopedia Universal Ilustrada, Vol. VI, p. 881. 1926.

Koebel, W. H., *Romance of the River Plate*, Vol. II, pp. 357–360. 1914.

Rafael Carrera

LIBERATOR OF GUATEMALA WHO WAS WORSHIPPED
AS A GOD BY THE INDIANS
(1814–1865)

RAFAEL CARRERA, dictator of five Central American republics and first President of Guatemala, is an amazing figure among the founders of the republics of the New World. Whereas all the others fought for progress and greater freedom for the masses, he upheld the opposite. But it was in so doing that he brought about the independence of his native land.

The other side of the story is that what he really opposed were radical laws, which though aimed at freeing the people, had been introduced so sharply and suddenly that a population which was more than 95 percent illiterate was not prepared for them. By proponents of this view he is regarded as the champion of religion and stability. The Pope of Rome in recogniation for what he had done in this respect commended him highly and sent him his highest decoration. Finally, any appraisal of Carrera must take into consideration the rape of his wife by members of the opposing force. This fact seemed to have influenced his whole career.

When he was nine years old, in 1823, five of the former Spanish provinces of Central America, Guatemala, Honduras, El Salvador, Nicaragua, and Costa Rica, formed the Central American Union. This Union, however, was dominated by the conservative element, which included the clergy, the old Spanish aristocracy, the landlords, and the monied class in general. This coalition was later known as the Conservative Party.

Opposing them was the Liberal Party, at whose head was General Francisco Morazán. Seizing power and wishing to root out the old injustices under which the Indians and the lower classes were exploited, Morazán promulgated what was known as "The Livingstone Code," under which the properties of the clergy were confiscated, the monasteries closed, freedom of religion proclaimed, civil marriages legalized, and the Catholic archbishop banished. This code also provided for schools, wider education, and trial by jury.

The Indians, who composed most of the population, opposed these reforms. For three centuries the priests had been working among them and had unbounded influence over them. Totally illiterate, religion was their chief, perhaps only, consolation. This religion was a mixture of Catholicism and the worship of Ekchuah, "The Black Christ," whom they had been worshipping long before the coming of the white man and to whose shrine at Esquipultas they still go annually by the thousands. The clergy, in opposition to the laws of the Liberal Party, agitated among the Indians, who began an unorganized resistance, which was strongest in Guatemala.

To make matters worse, there was an epidemic of cholera at this time which spread terror through the country. To prevent panic, the Liberals ordered that the church bells should not be rung for funerals, that burials should be prompt, private, and without processions. They also sent doctors and medicine among the Indians. At this, it is said, the priests, seeing their opportunity for revenge, told the Indians that the Liberals were trying to poison and destroy their people—an allegation that the superstitious Indians fully believed, especially when they saw the doctors washing their instruments in the rivers. Rising against the government, they killed several officials.

On this, Galvez, the Governor of Guatemala City, sent an official with a troop of cavalry to hear their complaints but they surrounded the soldiers and killed them to a man. Galvez, in return, sent a larger force which burned the Indian villages and ravished the women, Carrera's wife among them.

Carrera, who up to this point had spent most of his time minding his own herd of pigs, now swore a great oath not to lay down his gun until the Liberal Party had been swept from Guatemala.

He was then twenty-three and as illiterate as the rest of his people.

Gathering the Indians, he went from village to village, killing the Liberal judges and officials. In this, his chief aide was a renegade priest named Lobo, at whose instigation he issued a proclamation restoring the power of the church and against all strangers, except Spaniards. To sign his name, he used a rubber stamp. His fame as a highwayman spread through Central America.

Hearing now that there were dissensions in the Liberal ranks, Carrera thought the time had come to strike at Guatemala City, the enemy stronghold, and from his lair in the mountains sent his emissaries among the Indians, promising them the plunder of the city.

An ignorant half-naked rabble answered his call. Men, women, and children came, 20,000 strong, armed with clubs, poles with knives attached, and rusty muskets and pistols. Shouting their battle cries, "Long Live Religion" and "Down with Foreigners," they marched on the capital, Carrera at their head. He was as ragged as the rest. Around his battered sombrero was a cotton cloth with pictures of the saints.

Frightening both friend and foe, the rabble entered the city and marched straight for the cathedral, while the upper classes barricaded themselves in their homes. One leader of the mob, breaking into the home of a general, took his uniform coat and placed it on Carrera, who with his old sombrero and ragged trousers presented a ludicrous figure.

Services began in the cathedral, the Indians marveling at the statues and the undreamed-of glitter and splendor. John L. Stephens, American envoy sent to the scene by President Van Buren, said, "Probably since the invasion of Rome by Alaric and the Goths no civilized city was ever visited by such an inundation of barbarians." Carrera alone had the power to control the mob. The Indians regarded him as a god, calling him "Our Lord" and "Son of God." Anxious to avoid bloodshed, he sent priests with crucifixes through the streets to calm the Indians.

Galvez, the governor, asked Carrera for a parley and Carrera agreed to leave the city for $11,000, a thousand of which was for himself and the rest for his men. The sum, which seemed an immense fortune to Carrera and his followers, was paid. In addition, Carrera was made Governor of the province of Mita. He had then no aspirations to be ruler.

He had not forgiven the Liberals, however. Actually, he had always been opposed to them. When they had come to power, he was a drummer boy in the army, and refusing to serve them, he had broken his drum and gone off to the mountains to mind pigs. He was then fifteen. Now he kept an eye on the Liberals and from time to time sent them hints of what he might do. He had an army of 4000, he said, and would march on the city again. The Liberals, on their side, were plotting to seize him. He once narrowly escaped assassination. One of his lieutenants, Moureau, who was said to be in the pay of the Liberals, had him bound to a tree and was about to shoot him when Laureano, Carrera's brother, arrived and saved him.

The Liberals then tried to buy him off, giving him a large sum and $5 to each of his men to surrender their guns. Carrera, however, continued to send them imperious warnings.

This went on until General Morazán, dictator of the Union of Central America, arrived at Guatemala City with a strong, well-armed force. He invited Carrera to the conference, which broke off suddenly when Carrera insisted that the Liberals were betraying the Indians. Carrera again took to the mountains where he lived as a bandit. Morazán sent federal troops against him there and then began what was known as "The Morazán-Carrera War," which lasted from 1838 to 1842.

Unable to capture Carrera himself, Morazán offered a reward for him, dead or alive. Anyone who brought in his head would receive $1500, a large tract of land, and pardon for any crimes committed. When this also failed, he attacked Carrera in the mountains, surprised him, and killed 400 of his men. Carrera, badly wounded, barely managed to escape. Thereafter, Carrera was constantly beaten but would never yield. At last Morazán promised him peace if he surrendered his arms. Instead of the 1000 guns he had promised to yield, Carrera, however, gave up only 400.

In the meantime, he had gained even greater power over the Indians, and feeling that the time had come to end Liberal power once and for all, he assembled his forces and marched to the city. Morazán met him outside the gates and in the bloody battle that followed was beaten.

Entering Guatemala City, Carrera now installed himself in the government palace. The upper classes either fled or catered to him, while the common people and the clergy hailed him as a hero. At a bull fight, says Stephens, "All eyes were turned on him as when a king or an emperor enters his box in the theatre in Europe. A year before he was hunted in the mountains under a reward for his body 'dead or alive' and nine-tenths of those who now looked upon him would have shut the city against him as a robber, murderer and outcast."

Stephens, who interviewed him at this time, gives the following personal impression of him:

Carrera at the time of my visit was more absolute master of Guatemala than any kind in Europe of his dominions and by the fanatic Indians called "the Son of God" and "Our Lord." . . .

He was about five feet six inches in height with straight black hair, an Indian complexion and expression without beard, and did not seem to be more than twenty-one years old.

Considering Carrera a promising young man, I told him he had a long career before him and might do much good to his country; and he laid his hand upon his heart and with a burst of feeling that I did not expect said that he was determined to sacrifice his life for his country. With all his faults and his crimes no one ever accused him of duplicity or of saying what he did not mean: and, perhaps, as many self-deceiving men before him, he believed himself a patriot.

I considered that he was destined to exercise an important, if not controlling influence in the affairs of Central America and trusting that hopes of honorable and extended fame might have some effect upon his character I told him that his name had already reached my country and that I had seen in the newspapers an account of his entry into Guatemala with praises of his moderation and his exertions to prevent atrocities. He expressed himself pleased that his name was known and such mention made of him by strangers and said that he was not a robber and a murderer as he was called by his enemies. He seemed intelligent and capable of improvement. . . .

My interview with him was much more interesting than I had expected; so young, so humble in origin; so destitute of early advantages, with honest impulses, perhaps, but ignorant, fanatic, sanguinary and the slave of violent passions, wielding absolutely the physical force of his country and that force entertaining a natural hatred to the whites.

Now in absolute power, Carrera repealed the Livingstone Code, which provided for civil marriages and trial by jury. He brought back the Catholic archbishop, permitted the Jesuits to return, and restored the monasteries and the titles of nobility. As was said, the Pope sent him his highest decoration for his services to the faith. He also decreed the independence of Guatemala from the rest of Central America.

But Carrera's troubles were not yet over. In 1842 Morazán tried to revive the Central American Union and attacked him, but again Carrera defeated him, and capturing him in Honduras, had him executed. Another formidable opponent also arose in the person of William Walker, a white American filibusterer who had made himself President of Nicaragua and had ambitions to rule all Central America. Carrera, marching against Walker, defeated him and had him shot. After this Carrera became the dominant figure in Central America, the presidents of the four other so-called republics, El Salvador, Costa Rica, Nicaragua, and Honduras, taking orders from him.

Stephens, who called on him for the second time, wrote:

Carrera had passed through so many terrible scenes since I saw him that I feared he had forgotten me; but he recognized me in a moment, and made room for me behind the table next to himself. His military coat lay on the table and he wore the same roundabout jacket; his face had the same youthfulness, quickness, and intelligence; his voice and manners the same gentleness and seriousness and he had been wounded again.

Carrera, who had since learned to write, made out the American diplomat's papers with his own hand, a fact which, says Stephens, he seemed prouder of than his victories over Morazán.

In 1848, after being in power for eight years, he resigned. It seems he did not at any time want to rule. Rivera Paz was made president but he was not strong enough and the Liberals came back into power. Dissensions followed and there was talk of inviting Carrera back. On this the Liberals issued a decree of banishment against him, but unable to maintain their power, they were swept out and Carrera agreed to return. He continued as president until 1854 when the Constituent Assembly named him "Supreme and Perpetual Ruler." His power was absolute and he had the right to name his successor. He continued thus until his death in 1865, having ruled for thirty years.

Carrera lacked not only education but liberality as we know it today. His evident desire to help his people and advance them was too much mixed with religious superstition, which is always a clog. Nevertheless, he did give to the Indians and the masses a vision of better things and a taste for education and enlightenment. In any case, the events which he had set in motion prepared the way for reform. Guatemala today is one of the most advanced of the Latin-American republics.

Against the popular view of Carrera is that of one who had much dealing with him: Colonel R. De Puydt, Belgian chief of the Commission of Explorations. Belgians had settled in large numbers in Guatemala and had a colony of their own there. De Puydt lauds Carrera and calls him a friend of white people. He was, he says, "the protector of religion, property, and the security of the family." He adds:

One is compelled to accept as a friend of the whites one who restores their property and their rights to them; one who maintains the laws, divine as well as human; one who reestablishes peace and order; one who is a natural protector of our Catholic populations; one who by the largest concessions and unhoped for privileges endeavors to draw them around him in order to consolidate with them the shifting bases of an edifice which his powerful hand had made firm.

At his death the Liberals returned to power, reestablished their laws, and again banished the Catholic archbishop.

REFERENCES

The population of Guatemala under Carrera was about 512,000, most of whom were Indians, very slightly mixed with white. Negroes did not number over 1000, half of whom were unmixed blacks who called themselves Caribs, and still do.

As for Carrera, he is sometimes called a mulatto and sometimes a *zambo*, that is, half-Negro, half-Indian. *Enciclopedia Ilustrada* says that his father was a Negro and his mother an Indian. (See "Carrera," Vol. XI, p. 1325.) *Encyclopedia Americana*, in its sketch of him, says the same. On the other hand, C. L. Jones, in his authoritative work, *Guatemala, Past and Present*, p. 42 (1940), says that Carrera's parents were listed in the parish register as mulattoes. He adds, "One of his few apologists deduces from the available records that the boy [Carrera] inherited at the most 17 and a half percent of Negro blood. The rest he estimates at 10 and a half Indian and 72 percent white."

The American diplomat Stephens, evidently thinking that it was less humiliating to deal with an Indian than with a Negro ruler, said of Carrera, "His friends, in compliment, call him a mulatto; I, for the same reason, call him an Indian, considering that the better blood of the two." (*Incidents of Travel in Central America*, Vol. I, p. 224.)

The character El Supremo in C. S. Forrester's popular novel *Captain Horatio Hornblower* is undoubtedly Carrera.

Stephens, J. L., *Incidents of Travel in Central America*, Vol. I, pp. 224, 247–249; Vol. II, p. 137. 1848.

De Puydt, R. *Compagnie Belge de Colonization Amérique Centrale— Report*, pp. 119–129. 1844. (Included in this is also an article from *Courrier Belge*, November 14, 16, 1842, on Morazán and Carrera.)

Montufar, L., *Resena Historico de Centro America*, 7 vols. 1887.

Cinta, R. A., *Guatamala*. 1899.

Leysbeth, N., *Historia de la Colonización a Santo Tomas*. Guatemala, 1938.

Zamora, Castellanos P., *Vida Militar de Centro America*, pp. 189–196. 1924.

ADDITIONAL REFERENCES

Jones, C. L., *Guatemala, Past and Present*, pp. 42–46, 203, 246. Minneapolis, University of Minnesota Press, 1940.

Carlos Gomes

❧

FIRST GREAT OPERATIC COMPOSER OF THE NEW WORLD
(1836–1896)

ANTONIO CARLOS GOMES was the first native of the New World to write an opera that received recognition in the highest musical circles of Europe. The immortal Giuseppe Verdi, after hearing Gomes' masterpiece at La Scala, Milan, hailed him as his successor.

Gomes was born at Campinas, São Paulo, Brazil, and began his musical education at an early age. His father, who was a music teacher of note and head of the city's band, took him into the band at the age of ten, where he taught him to play all the instruments. To make sure, however, that he would be independent of music for a livelihood, he also had him taught tailoring.

This bit of caution was not necessary, however, because Gomes was so gifted musically that at the age of twenty his first opera, *Alte Noite*, was a success.

Going to Rio de Janeiro, he devoted himself entirely to composition and his two operas, *A Noite do Castello* and *Joanna de Flandres,* won him such acclaim that the Emperor of Brazil, Dom Pedro II, offered to pay his expenses for study in Europe. Dom Pedro also gave a letter of introduction to King Ferdinand of Portugal, who, in turn, sent him to Maestro Lauro Rossi, director of the Conservatory of Milan. Since, however, foreigners were not permitted to enter this school, Rossi took him as a private pupil.

Gomes was so brilliant that in the following year, 1866, he passed the examination for the degree of Maestro Compositori, with highest praise from the examiners. This course usually took four years and Dom Pedro had provided funds for that length of time.

Gomes' first work after graduation was *Se Sá Minga*, which was based on Italian folk tunes. This became so popular that parts of it were hummed all over Italy. His next work, *Il Guarany*, based on an Indian theme by José de Alencar, was even more successful. Performed at La Scala, Milan, then the home of opera, before outstanding representatives of the music world, it received tremendous applause. Among those present was the aged Giuseppe Verdi, who said, "This young man has genius. He begins where I end." The King of Italy in recognition bestowed on Gomes the Order of the Crown of Italy.

Il Guarany definitely placed Gomes in the ranks of the immortals and his path continued upwards with other successful plays as *Forca, Salvator Rossi, Maria Tudor, O Condor, Colombo,* and *Lo Schiavo.* This last, an attack on slavery in Brazil, was hailed as "the opera of emancipation, par excellence" and earned him the title of "Maestro of Abolition." The work was dedicated to Princess Isabel of Brazil for her work in the cause of abolition.

In 1876 America heard more of him when he wrote the hymn for the first centennial of American independence which was performed at the Centennial Exposition at Philadelphia, where his sovereign and benefactor Dom Pedro was a guest. In 1893 he came to the World Columbian Exhibition at Chicago where he directed an orchestra of 114 pieces playing his own compositions on Brazilian Day. His triumph on this occasion was the most complete. Press and public raved over him.

Gomes married Adelina Peri, daughter of an old family, by whom he had five children, one of whom, Itala Gomes de Carvalho, wrote the story of his life. In 1895 he returned to Brazil to become director of the Conservatory of Belém, Pará, where he died the following year.

Monuments have been erected in his honor in Rio de Janeiro and other cities. In the city of his birth, Campinas, the Italians of São Paulo built a magnificent one. In 1936 the centenary of his birth was celebrated throughout Brazil.

REFERENCES

Gomes was a mixture of Negro, Indian, and Caucasian. Pradez, writing in 1872, said of him, "The first great musician Brazil has ever produced is a colored man." (*Nouvelles Etudes sur Brésil*, p. 29.)

Vas de Carvalho, I. G. A., *Vida de Carlos Gomes.* 1937.
Vieira Sonto, L. F., *Antonio Carlos Gomes.* 1936.
Revista Brasileira de Musica, Vol. III. 1936.
Coelha de Senna, N., *Africanos no Brasil*, p. 37. 1938.

ADDITIONAL REFERENCES

White, C. C., "Antonio Carlos Gomez." *Negro History Bulletin* (February, 1941), Association for the Study of Negro Life and History, Washington, D.C.

Dom Pedro II, "The Magnanimous"

BRAZILIAN EMANCIPATOR
(1825–1891)

DOM PEDRO II, de Alcántara, surnamed "The Magnanimous," shared with Queen Victoria the honor of being the best-beloved monarch of the nineteenth century.

He was born in Rio de Janeiro, Brazil, the son of Pedro I, Emperor of Brazil and King of Portugal, and Archduchess Caroline Josephine, daughter of Emperor Francis I of Austria. Thus he was a lineal descendant of three of the most ancient royal houses of Europe: the Braganza, the Hapsburg, and the Bourbon.

By his own marriage and those of his children, he was later allied with both the royal houses of France, as well as with the English, German, and Swedish royal families.

Dom Pedro's fame, however, rests not on his blue blood but on his extraordinary qualities of heart and mind. He came to the Brazilian throne at the age of six when his father returned to rule Portugal. Exceptionally brilliant, he made such progress in his studies and had so wide a knowledge of his country that at fifteen he was considered fit to rule and was crowned emperor.

Many difficult problems confronted him from the start. Among them were a determined effort on the part of certain leaders to make Brazil a republic; an epidemic of yellow fever, which swept off thousands and weakened national morale; and a long and costly war with Rosas, dictator of Argentina. No sooner had that war been won than there was a naval dispute with Britain to be followed by another long war with Lopez II, tyrant of Paraguay, in which Dom Pedro was also the victor.

During these trying years Dom Pedro, however, succeeded in pushing the development of his country until, next to the United States, it was the foremost country of the New World. His program of road construction was so great that for a long time after his death half the roads and all the railroads in Brazil were those built in his time. He introduced the telegraph; established a steamship line between Brazil and Europe; erected academies of art; built colleges and schools, and instituted free and compulsory education. He organized the army; built a fleet of warships, and so generally improved the country that in the fifty years of his reign the population increased at a greater rate than in the four centuries preceding him. It grew from 5,250,000 to 14,000,-000, exclusive of Indians.

He ruled with great liberality and wisdom. He abolished the old colonial abuses; protected the Indians and induced them to adopt civilized ways; reduced the clashes between them and the whites; and in general brought a spirit of greater liberty and democracy to his vast, wild, and undeveloped empire.

He invited artists and men of learning to Brazil, gave them positions of honor, and paid them from his own purse. When Richard Wagner, noted German composer, was exiled from Bavaria, he offered him a suite in his own palace. Sending for Joseph White, great Negro artist, he made him court violinist. Charles Darwin, famous naturalist, wrote of him, "The Emperor has done so much for science; every savant owes him the highest respect." W. E. Gladstone, the British prime minister, with so notable an example as Queen Victoria before him, said of Dom Pedro, "He . . . is a model to the Sovereigns of the world in his anxiety for the faithful and effective discharge of his duties . . . a pattern and a blessing to his race."

Under his rule Brazil won a worldwide reputation and was regarded as an earthly paradise. Alexandre Dumas, fils, Negro president of the French Academy, said truly of him, "Happy Monarch! Happy People!"

Dom Pedro was an intellectual prodigy. He spoke and wrote English, French, Spanish, Italian, German, Latin, Hebrew, and

Portuguese. He discussed the natural sciences and the arts with experts of his time, was an able astronomer, an accomplished musician, a poet of distinction, and a skilled painter.

As if to crown his magnetic personality and remarkable mental gifts, he was of magnificent physique—six feet four inches tall and beautifully proportioned from head to foot. Everywhere he went, in Europe, the United States, and his own land, he was the center of admiring attention.

This handsome giant of unbounded energy knew all the capitals of Europe first-hand, requiring an interpreter in none of them. Five o'clock in the morning was not too early for him to start a fourteen-hour day of sightseeing. Meeting a young Brazilian on the streets of London before dawn one morning, he exclaimed, "Admirable youth, to be up so early!"

He invariably refused an escort, preferring to mingle with the crowd. He entered places informally and few ever dreamed that the handsome stranger with whom they were chatting was an emperor. On leaving the French Academy where he was introduced by Dumas, he took his hat and coat and walked to his hotel like an ordinary citizen. In the United States, where he was the guest of honor at the Centennial Exhibition in 1876, he was received with acclaim wherever he went. The American press and public hailed him as "the crowned democrat."

At home in Brazil he rose at six in the morning, beginning the day's work at seven. Every morning he held an audience in his palace for the poor and received any of his subjects who had a grievance. Everyone, however humble, was allowed to approach him without formality. "Welcoming my family" he called it.

He lived simply, though he was one of the world's richest men. His residence was the old mansion of the viceroy, and when someone proposed a palace be built for him, he said, "What, when there are yet not enough schools?" When Brazil was finally victorious over Paraguay, a large sum was collected for the purpose of erecting a monument to him, but Dom Pedro used it to build new schools. "The finest monument in the world," he said, "is a school-house. If I were not an emperor I should choose to be a school-master. There is no grander or nobler occupation in the world than that of directing minds and preparing men for the future good of the human race."

His farsighted policies attracted foreign capital to his land; his foreign debts were paid promptly, winning him international respect and confidence. He made long journeys into the interior of Brazil, one of which took him up the Amazon, which he opened up to the ships of all nations.

In all of his activities, however, his greatest concern was the slavery that still existed in his empire. There were over three million Negro slaves. One of his first acts on coming to the throne was to stop the importation of slaves, thus earning the enmity of the great landowners, who hoped by establishing a republic to get rid of him. But unflinching in his determination to wipe out this evil, he was instrumental in passing a law by which all children born of slave parents were freed. He himself set an example by liberating all slaves belonging to the state. All these freedmen were given positions according to their ability. When he toured the United States in 1876, he had seen the wretched condition of the freedmen there and the Ku-Kluxism and night-riding and decided to prevent similar conditions in his own land when emancipation came.

So that there should be no loss to the slaveholders, he established an abolition fund out of which $400 was paid for each slave freed. In this way he hoped to end slavery in five years, but at the end of that time only a million were freed. He decided that a more radical step would have to be taken and he told his people and parliament so. Finally in 1876 a compromise was made whereby all the slaves would be freed in fourteen years, on January 1, 1890, in honor of his jubilee.

But he soon grew dissatisfied with this arrangement. Fourteen years was far too long to tolerate this evil. It must end in five years, he said, and ordered his prime minister, Baron de Cotegipe (a mulatto), to draw up a bill to that effect. The bill was defeated and he dissolved parliament. The step was far too radical, said the legislators. Slavery, they knew, must eventually end, but most of the slaveholders wanted a semi-bondage and in this they had strong support among the people. These latter were known as the emancipationists. Opposing them were the abolitionists, who wanted full but very gradual freedom, with efficient protection for the freedmen.

Dom Pedro found himself in conflict with both groups. His plan called for a much earlier emancipation. When his bill was defeated, he made a direct appeal to the people, which brought him much support and nominal success with the new parliament. In his opening address to it, he announced his intention to introduce "an Emancipation Bill for the purpose of gradually abolishing slavery in our country in consonance with the wishes of the Brazilian people." But his cabinet, unable to make progress with the measure, resigned.

Dom Pedro thereupon summoned a new parliament, introduced his bill, and took the floor himself on its behalf. His enemies in parliament and the nation denounced him as a tyrant for so doing but this did not stop him. However, the best he got was a law to free the slaves entirely in from ten to seventeen years. Insisting on a shorter time, he secured only a law to abolish flogging.

Regardless of the threats against his life, he appealed once more to the people and succeeded in getting a reform of the election laws by which he at last obtained a parliament obedient to his will in 1888. The same year slavery was declared ended forever in Brazil. Dom Pedro could at last look the world in the face.

The news was received with jubilation over the civilized world. Impressive ceremonies were staged in Paris, London, and New York. But Dom Pedro's crown of glory was to prove his crown of thorns as it had been with two other emancipators, Abraham Lincoln and Alexander II of Russia. The slaveholders, declaring that Dom Pedro had overstepped his constitutional authority, plotted against him, led by Marshal Fonseca, commander-in-chief of the army.

When the conspiracy gained momentum, Dom Pedro was in Europe. Sixty years of age and ailing from malaria and liver trouble, he had been sent there by his physicians. The government was in the hands of his amiable and beloved daughter, Princess Isabel, and her husband, Count d'Eu. Had he been in Brazil, revolt might have been prevented. The plotters were demanding his abdication.

He returned at once but it was too late. He was resting at his summer home in Persopolis, thirty miles away, when he was called hurriedly to Rio. There he found his ministers assembled and ready to put down any attempt to oust him from the throne, but knowing that the rebels were strong and that resistance meant civil war, he said, "I will be no party to the shedding of the blood of my people. If it's my abdication they want, they shall have it." When the abdication papers were brought to him, he signed them quietly.

The insurgents treated him with great respect and placed him on a ship for Portugal. His parting words were, "My greatest desire is to receive the news in Europe that all has taken place without bloodshed." A vain hope! Anarchy reigned in Brazil for the next ten years. A few months after his abdication, Marshal Fonseca, leader of the revolt, had to flee for his own life.

Dom Pedro lived in Lisbon for a short time, thence he went to Cannes, and later to Paris, where he settled permanently. Here he became a popular and beloved figure, though he remained as quiet and as unpretentious as ever. The Brazilian government offered him $4,000,000 to set himself up in state in Europe, and an annuity of $160,000 a year, but he refused both sums, feeling that his people needed the money more than he did. He lived instead on his own income of $20,000 a year, much of which went to support the needy friends who had followed him into exile.

Two years later, on December 5, 1891, the end came for the illustrious exile. Gathered around his bed in the Hotel Bedford were his relatives, most of whom were of the leading royal families. Queen Victoria, who admired him greatly, sent a wreath and a representative to the funeral service, and the Queen of Spain, a near relative, came to meet the bier at Madrid on its way to Lisbon for interment in the Pantheon.

Dom Pedro dearly loved his native land and to the last he had hoped to be recalled. On his dressing table was found a small bag with the words, "This is earth from my native land. I wish it to be placed in my coffin should I die abroad."

The press of the civilized world, with rare unanimity, lauded him. The London *Times* devoted a whole page to him. So did the London *Standard*, which said:

The history of the vast region which for more than half-a-century he ruled so wisely and so well, forms, therefore, the larger and brighter portion of the biography of the Monarch. To his firmness, tempered with prudence—his concessions to reasonable demands on the one hand, and his foresight on the other in refusing to yield the "reforms" for which he saw the country was not ripe—was due to the fact that while political ferment often ran high in the Brazils, it never until the final and unlooked for collapse, approached the point of revolution. State after state, to the north and south of his empire, had suffered endless changes, drifting from anarchy to despotism, ruined in credit, and with resources undeveloped. But the only Monarchy in the New World had from the time Dom Pedro undertook to guide its destinies steadily advanced in wealth and in the good opinion of Europe.

Speaking of the way in which the emperor had abdicated rather than cause civil war, the *Standard* continued:

This tenderness is characteristic of the man. The knowledge that the Emperor was far more sincerely devoted to the cause of freedom and of true reform than were the military conspirators, who, while they vapored about the liberty of the rights of man, were, in truth, acting as the instruments of a ring of slave-holders, who had vowed to be avenged on the author of the Decree of Emancipation, made the sympathy expressed for the Imperial Exile especially strong in England. The countrymen of Wilberforce were not likely to entertain any feeling but that of indignation at the deposition of a ruler against whom the gravest complaint could be alleged was that he had determined to remove from his kingdom the reproach of being the only Christian country in which men could still claim property in their fellows.

The London *Globe* said:

He was learned; he was patriotic; he was kind and merciful. . . . Here was a Sovereign who was conspicuously better than his subjects, or indeed the average of mankind; and it would not be a difficult matter to make out a plausible case for ascribing his failure and his faults to his virtues. . . .

Victor Hugo, who admired Dom Pedro greatly and considered him a most illustrious man of great learning and intelligence and with a natural kindliness to match, said, "One image rests ineffaceable: that of a sovereign dethroned, who had done his duty, spotless in character, marching towards exile as a philosopher, foreign to the passions of this world without expressing ever a complaint."

REFERENCES

The Negro strain in Dom Pedro might have been about a sixteenth or less. In any case, there are Americans with less than his who are now called Negroes in America and treated as such. Pedro inherited his Negro strain more recently from his grandfather. (See "John VI" in this volume.)

His family, the Braganza, had a Negro strain at least as far back as John I, the Great. (1385–1433). For marriages that the Braganzas have contracted with the other royal houses of Europe, consult the *Almanac de Gotha* and F. V. Wrangel's *Les Maisons Souveraines de L'Europe*. Stockholm 1888, 1889. In the latter volume, see "Bragance et Portugal"; also p. 703.

Dom Pedro was related by blood to three of the leading royal houses of Europe, and by marriage to both of the royal houses of France. His grandsons were the Duke of Chartres and the Prince de Joinville, direct heirs of Louis XVI of France; another grandson of his was the Prince of Saxe-Coburg-Gotha. Albert, Queen Victoria's husband, came from this family but was not related by blood to Pedro. Dom Pedro was, however, related to the Napoleons. His mother was the sister of Napoleon I's second wife, which made Napoleon his uncle, by marriage, and Napoleon's son, his first cousin.

Mosse, B., *Dom Pedro II*. Paris, 1899.

Montiero, T., *La Chute d'un Empire*. Paris, 1914.

Kidder, D. P., and Fletcher, J. C., *Brazil and the Brazilians*. Philadelphia, 1857.

L'Abolition de L'Esclavge au Brésil, Proceedings of a banquet held in Paris, July 10, 1888.

Cooper, C. C., *The Brazilians*. London, 1917.

ADDITIONAL REFERENCES

Ramos, Arthur, *The Negro in Brazil*, trans. by Richard Pattee, pp. 12–14. Washington, D.C., The Associated Publishers, 1939, 1951.

Machado de Assis

FIRST GREAT WRITER OF BRAZIL
(1839–1908)

To JOAQUIM MACHADO DE ASSIS belongs the honor of placing the young literature of his country on a foundation of such dignity and literary excellence that it won universal recognition.

Born of poor parents in Rio de Janeiro, he had many difficulties. Fortunately for him, however, he was a typesetter, and while setting up manuscripts he studied them for style and literary content. Meeting some of the writers and talking with them, he decided to become one himself.

Unable to attend classes to further his ambitions, he read omnivorously and wrote comedies, short stories, poems, and news articles, putting into them all a feeling characteristic of himself. This, at first, proved a handicap because the editors, unused to this new quality in literature, rejected his manuscripts. His persistence won, however, and long before his death in 1908 some of those who rejected him would have thought it a great honor to be his publisher.

His most distinctive qualities are charming simplicity, gentleness, and modesty, and a delicate, reflective soul, truly in love with the beautiful. There is also a deep pessimism, which is softened, however, by his inherent kindliness. As Goldberg says:

The world weariness appears in the very reticence of his style. He writes at times as if it were one of the vanities of the vanities, yet one feels that a certain inner guide lay behind this outer timidity. His method is the more leisurely one of indirection.

The real Machado de Assis stands apart from all who have written prose in his country. Señor Costa, in his admirable book upon the Brazilian novel, has sought to present his nation's chief novelist by means of an imagery-drawn architecture. . . . Machado [is] the sober, elegant Ionian column. . . . Sobriety, elegance are surely the outstanding qualities of the noted writer.

Machado de Assis belongs with the original writers of the nineteenth century. His family is the family of Renan and Anatole France; he is their younger brother, but his features show their resemblance.

Oliviera Lima, in his lectures on Brazilian literature at Harvard University, said:

By his abounding talent as a writer, by his profound literary dignity, by the unity of a life that was devoted to the cult of intellectual beauty and by the prestige exerted about him by his work and by his personality, Machado de Assis succeeded, despite a nature that was averse to acclaim and little inclined to public appearance, in being considered and respected as the first among his country's men of letters, the head, if that word can denote the idea of a youthful literature which already possessed its traditions and cherishes, above all, its glories.

Another critic, Verissinio, says:

To say that in our literature Machado de Assis is a figure apart, that he stands with good reason first among our writers of fiction, that he possesses a rare faculty of assimilation and evolution which makes him a writer of the second Romantic generation, always a contemporary, a modern, without, on his account, having sacrificed anything to the latest literary fashion or copied some brand-new esthetic, conserving his own distinct personality . . . is but to repeat what has been said many times already. All these judgments are confirmed by his latest book, wherein may be noted the same impeccable correctness of language, the same firm grasp upon form, the same ascendancy, form, and originality of thought that makes him the only thinker among our writers of fiction.

One of Machado de Assis' finest poems is "Mosca Azul" in which he shows the intangible, elusive quality of life, the near impossibility of our being able to place our finger on anything and call it our very own, even our dreams. This is all the more so when we examine and analyze the things that we like too closely.

"Mosca Azul" was a blue fly with "wings of gold and carmine" that flew and buzzed glittering in the light of the sun—brighter than the gem of a grand Mogul. A humble toiler, seeing this fly, is enraptured at her colorful beauty and asks her who she is. She replies, "I am life, I am the flower of grace, the paragon of earthly beauty—I am glory, I am love." The toiler, as he continues to gaze at her, has a dream of the most wonderful and ecstatic splendor. He sees a great palace, with the costliest furnishings and jewels, and a hundred radiantly beautiful, voluptuous women, with himself the king of it all. But the impulse comes to him to pry into the why and wherefore of what is giving him so much pleasure and stretching out his calloused hand, he seizes the fly. Its wings are crushed, it dies, his beautiful dream vanishes, and life in all its reality returns to him.

In "Circulo Viciosi" (Vicious Circle) he depicts the emptiness of glory and the discontent of those who hold exalted positions:

Dancing in the air, a restless glow-worm wailed: "Oh that I might be that radiant star which burns in the eternal blue like a perpetual candle." But the star cried, "Oh that I might be the transparent light, that, at the Gothic window of a Greek column, the beloved, beautiful one, sighingly contemplated." But the moon, gazing at the sun, said peevishly: "Wretched I! Would that I had that vast undying refulgence which resumes all light itself." But the sun, bowing its rutillant crown, sighed, "This brilliant heavenly aureole wearies me. I am burdened by this vast blue canopy. . . . Why was I not born a simple glow-worm?"

Among his principal works are *Chronicas; Contos Fluminenses; Critica Litteraria; Critica Theatral; Historia de Meia Noite; Historia Romanticos; Historia Sem Data; Resurreicao;* and *Phalenas.* His chief novels are: *Helena; Don Casmurro; Yaya Garcia;* and *Memorias Posthumas de Bras Cubas.*

In 1909, on the first anniversary of his death, commemorative exercises for him were held at the Sorbonne in Paris, Anatole France presiding. In 1939, on the centenary of his birth, the Brazilian Ministry of Education published a volume of general information and miscellany about him.

REFERENCES

Instituto Nacional do Livro, *Exposicao Machado de Assis* (Extensive bibliography) Rio de Janeiro, 1939.

Matos, M., *Machado de Assis.* 1939.

Maya, A., *Machado de Assis.* 1942.

Pontes, E., *A Vida Contradictoria de Machado de Assis.* 1939.

Orban, P., *Litérature Brésilienne.* Paris, 1914.

Goldberg, I., *Brazilian Literature*, pp. 142–164. New York, 1922.

ADDITIONAL REFERENCES

Andrade, Mario De, *Aspectos da Litteratura Brasileria*, American edition. Rio de Janeiro, 1943.

Caldwell, Helen, *The Brazilian Othello of Machado de Assis.* Berkeley, University of California Press, 1960.

Machado, José Bettencourt, *Machado of Brazil.* New York, Bramerica, 1953.

Pierson, Donald, *Negroes in Brazil*, p. 215. Carbondale and Edwardsville, Southern Illinois University Press; London and Amsterdam, Feffer and Simons, Inc., 1942.

Pujol, Alfred, *Machado de Assis.* São Paulo, Typographia Levi, 1917.

Sayers, Raymond S., *The Negro in Brazilian Literature.* New York, Hispanic Institute in the United States, 1956.

Weyl, Nathaniel, *The Negro in American Civilization*, p. 244. Washington, D.C., Public Affairs Press, 1960.

THE WEST INDIES

Commentary and Notes
on References

THE TERRIBLE DRAMA OF SLAVERY and resistance played itself out in the West Indies with a great flair that did not, at first, involve the Africans. In his book *Capitalism and Slavery* Dr. Eric Williams reveals that:

Slavery in the Caribbean has been too narrowly identified with the Negro. A racial twist has thereby been given to what is basically an economic phenomenon. Slavery was not born of racism: rather, racism was the consequence of slavery. Unfree labor in the New World was brown, white, black, and yellow; Catholic, Protestant and pagan.

The first instance of slave trading and slave labor developed in the New World involved, racially, not the Negro but the Indian . . . the immediate successor of the Indian, however, was not the Negro but the poor white. These white servants included a variety of types. Some were indentured servants, others were convicts, sent out by the deliberate policy of the home government, to serve for a specified period.

For long-range development of the plantation system the Indian and the poor whites were not reliable. The Indians escaped in large numbers; some of the poor whites had no particular skill or physical stamina. These conditions led to the intensification of the drive to get more slaves from Africa. And so the African now had his place, though he did not ask for it, in the broiling sun of the sugar, tobacco, and cotton plantations of the New World. From the very beginning the Africans began to revolt against this condition.

The revolt of the Maroons in Jamaica under the leadership of Captain Cudjoe is extraordinary, but not unique. This is one of the best-documented slave revolts in history. A simplified version of the story is in the book *Distinguished Negroes Abroad* by Beatrice J. Fleming and Marion J. Pryde (1946).

The revolt in Haiti under the leadership of Toussaint L'Ouverture and the splendid array of rebels who followed in his footsteps are better known, and the literature about this most successful of all slave revolts is extensive.

In what is considered to be the best book on the Haitian Revolution, *The Black Jacobins* by C. L. R. James, the following capsule history of that revolution is given:

In 1789 the French West Indian colony of San Domingo supplied two-thirds of the overseas trade of France and was the greatest individual market for the European slave trade. It was an integral part of the economic life of the age, the greatest colony in the world, the pride of France, and the envy of every other imperialist nation. The whole structure rested on the labour of half-a-million slaves.

In August 1791, after two years of the French Revolution and its repercussions in San Domingo, the slaves revolted. The struggle lasted for 12 years. The slaves defeated in turn the local whites and the soldiers of the French monarchy, a Spanish invasion, a British expedition of some 60,00 men, and a French expedition of similar size under Bonaparte's brother-in-law. The defeat of Bonaparte's expedition in 1803 resulted in the establishment of the Negro state of Haiti which has lasted to this day.

The revolt is the only successful slave revolt in history, and the odds it had to overcome is evidence of the magnitude of the interests that were involved. The transformation of slaves, trembling in hundreds before a single white man, into a people able to organize themselves and defeat the most powerful European nations of their day, is one of the great epics of revolutionary struggle and achievement.

Toussaint L'Ouverture, the slave who freed Haiti, also helped, indirectly, to free a large part of what is now the United States from French colonial rule. He rose to power during the age of revolution and successfully led one of the great slave revolts in history. The success of this revolt and the drain on the French treasury caused by their attempt to suppress it were the underlying reasons Napoleon had to sell the Louisiana Territory to the United States. The aftermath of this revolt rendered more certain the final prohibition of the slave trade in the United States.

For additional information on the Haitian revolt and the political aftermath, I suggest the following books: *The Rise of the Colored Races* by Keith Irvine (1970), pp. 241–284; *Distinguished Negroes Abroad* by Beatrice J. Fleming and Marion J. Pryde (1946), pp. 187–205; and *Black Democracy* by H. P. Davis (1939).

Louis Delgrès was to the island of Guadeloupe what Toussaint L'Ouverture was to Haiti. The little-known revolt led by Louis Delgrès spread to other islands dominated by France. This revolt, along with the uprising in Haiti, forced the French into adopting a more enlightened policy in the Caribbean area.

When Richard Hill was born in Jamaica in 1795 the Haitian revolution had entered its second phase and the plantation owners of the West Indies were in fear for their lives. His own father literally weaned him on antislavery feeling, and it influenced the rest of his life. His fight against slavery and for a better system of justice in Jamaica is a main factor in the nineteenth-century struggle for nationhood on this island. His historical writings about Jamaica are still being read.

While Afro-American women were participating in slave insurrections, and fighting to save some semblance of their families under the slave system of the United States, Mrs. Mary Seacole of Jamaica trained herself to be a nurse and was preparing to serve in the Crimean War. In the cholera epidemic in Jamaica in 1852 she joined the government health service and helped to lay the basis for the nursing profession on the island.

In the Cuba of today Antonio Maceo is one of the new national heroes. He was first and foremost a Cuban nationalist who opposed the oppressive rule of Spain. The story of Antonio can be found in most of the books about Cuba's long struggle to free herself from Spain.

Santo Domingo was a troubled island from the time when Christopher Columbus decided that it was here he would find the gold to pay off his debts to the Queen of Spain and acquire the means of financing his future adventures in the West Indies. In the many attempts to dislodge Spain from the island that came much later, Ulises Heureaux was the most able of the patriots who used his skill and cunning to establish home rule and give Santo Domingo an independent political personality. This he did, while asking no quarter and giving none. He was, in all truthfulness, a tyrant. His greatest achievement is that he held a troubled nation together and guided it to the threshold of the twentieth century.

Sir Conrad Reeves's singular distinction is that he was one of the great legal minds in the British Empire during the last years of the nineteenth century. In many ways he was a cultured Englishman who assumed that his position as Chief Justice of Barbados had elevated him above his blackness. In his court he favored neither black nor white. He ordered justice and dispensed mercy in each case, depending on its merits.

Edward Wilmot Blyden is distinctive among the personalities that are treated in this section of the book. From the beginning of his awareness of self, and to the last day of his life, he was a black nationalist. The study of Edward Blyden throws new light on African world history in the second half of the nineteenth century. Blyden became the intellectual focus of English-speaking Africa during this period. Concepts such as the African personality, Pan-Africanism, and what is now called negritude owed their early development to the stimulus of Edward Wilmot Blyden.

He was a West Indian by birth, and African by adoption. This did not narrow his world view. He was astute in his knowledge of America, Europe, and Asia. He traveled extensively in West Africa and made his home in Liberia. In 1877 he became Liberia's first ambassador in London. In 1905 he opened a legation in Paris. He advocated repatriation years before Marcus Garvey was born. The first full-length biography of Dr. Blyden, *Edward Wilmot Blyden: Pan-Negro Patriot, 1832–1912* by Hallis R. Lynch, was published in 1967 by the Oxford University Press. His master work, *Christianity, Islam and the Negro Race*, first published in 1887, was reprinted in 1967 by the University Press in Edinburgh, Scotland. In 1971 *The Selected Published Writings of Edward Wilmot Blyden*, edited by Hallis R. Lynch, was published by the Humanities Press, New York.

Félix Eboué was one of the most outstanding of the French West Indians who rendered service to colonial France. He served in Africa most of his life, and helped to save French West Africans from being overrun by the Germans during the Second World War. He died before the end of that war and did not learn that he had, in many ways, helped to prepare French West Africa for independence.

J. H. C.

Captain Cudjoe

❧

NOTHING IS FURTHER from the truth than the popular belief that the African in the New World was in love with slavery and submitted calmly to it. The fact is that he rebelled against it from the United States to Argentina times without number.

This is especially true of Mexico, Cuba, Haiti, Surinam, the Virgin Islands, Brazil, and Venezuela. Among the most valiant of these Negro rebels were the Maroon Negroes of Jamaica, West Indies. For 140 years they defied the white slaveholders and finally forced them to seek a treaty of peace.

The greatest of the Maroon leaders of this island was Cudjoe, an illiterate, ragged, barefooted, undersized, and unshapely Coromantee. Of seemingly inexhaustible energies, Cudjoe possessed all the qualities of a born commander. He defeated the British in every encounter, and had he been able to get arms and ammunition, he would doubtless have done to them what Dessalines did to the French in Haiti, that is, drive them from the island.

The slaveholders seemed powerless against his attacks. Before planning a raid on their plantations, he had his spies mingle freely with the slaves in the markets and on the plantations, learning when to strike and where, then sallying out by night and even by day, he attacked with such deadly thoroughness that he left in his wake burnt mansions and cane fields and the bodies of the whites and their faithful slaves. With the arms and ammunition thus obtained, he staged other raids.

By 1730 he had grown so strong that some of the old English settlers thought it best to abandon their plantations and return home. It was commonly said, "General Williamson [the British Commander] rules Jamaica by day and Captain Cudjoe by night."

At last the government decided to make a supreme effort to capture him. It built forts and outposts near the Maroon settlements and brought in hundreds of Central American Indians to track down the rebels. At the same time a force of 1000 soldiers, white and black, under Captain Lemelia, was sent against Cudjoe.

But Cudjoe was equal to the occasion. Sending one of his spies to tell the British that he would be found at a certain distant spot, he marched stealthily down the mountains to meet the enemy and took up a position overlooking a deep pass through which the foe had to come.

Dividing his force into four parts, he stationed one of each high up on the extremities of both sides of the pass.

Captain Lemelia, believing Cudjoe to be many miles away, came on with relaxed vigilance. Tired from dragging the cannon uphill, his soldiers straggled into the pass. Cudjoe, waiting until the narrow pass was filled with men, signaled to his own men at the entrance to fire. A hundred British fell, struck in the back. When the others turned in the direction of the fire, Cudjoe's men at the other end again struck the enemy in the rear until the shooting from all sides of the rocks became general. This crisscross fire coming from everywhere so demoralized the foe that abandoning guns and supplies, they fled down the mountains.

Cudjoe during the next four years continued his victories but the superior arms of the slaveholders began to tell at last. They attacked one of his camps on a high mountain and killed nearly everyone.

This made him decide to move to another part of the island and take his women and children with him. To screen this bold move, he left men around the old camp to blow horns and discharge guns to make the enemy think he was still there. So successful was he that it was not until months later when he had staged a great raid on the part of the island to which he had gone that the truth was known.

For another four years the tornado that was Cudjoe raged, leaving slaughter and destruction in his wake. Once more the government, in desperation, planned an expedition against him.

Every able-bodied man on the island was pressed into service, but when the expedition was about to start, someone asked who would protect the women and children if all the men went off. What would happen if the slaves seized the occasion to revolt? The Jamaican slave could not be trusted. As for the faithful slaves, the Maroons hated them even more than they did the whites, and they were likely to be struck down by some unseen hand at any time.

Faced with this dilemma, the governor, Sir Edward Trelawney, decided there was but one course: to seek a treaty of peace with Cudjoe. He sent Colonel Guthrie with a mission to offer Cudjoe independence and a tract of land.

R. C. Dallas, a British commander, describes the meeting thus:

Colonel Guthrie advanced unmolested with his troops through situations in which the Maroons might have greatly annoyed him even with the large force he then had under him. Making, however, the best disposition of his troops that the nature of the ground would permit, he marched on with confidence, and judging of the distance he was from the Maroons by the sound of their horns, he continued advancing till he thought he could make them hear his voice that he was come by the governor's orders to make them an offer of peace which the white people sincerely desired.

An answer was returned declaring that the Maroons wished the same and requesting that the troops might be kept back.

Several Maroons now descended, and among them it was difficult to discover the chief himself. Cudjoe was rather a short man, uncommonly stout, with very strong African features and a peculiar wildness in his manners. He had a very large lump of flesh upon his back which was partly covered by the tattered remains of an old blue coat of which the skirts and sleeves below the elbow were wanting. . . .

Around his head was tied a scanty piece of white cloth so very dirty that its original color might have been doubted. He wore no shirt, and his clothes, such as they were, as well as the part of his skin that was exposed, were covered with the red dirt resembling ochre. He had on a pair of loose drawers that did not reach to his knees and a small round hat with the rims pared so close to the crown that it might have been taken for a calabash.

Such was the chief, and his men were as ragged and as dirty as himself: all were armed with guns and cutlasses. Cudjoe constantly cast his eyes toward the troops under Colonel Guthrie. He appeared very suspicious and asked Dr. Russell many questions before he ventured within reach.

At last, Dr. Russell offered to change hats with him as a token of friendship, to which he consented and was beginning to converse more freely when Colonel Guthrie called aloud to him, assuring him of a faithful compliance with whatever Dr. Russell promised. He said that he wished to come unarmed to him with a few of the principal gentlemen of the island, who should witness the oath he would solemnly make to them of peace on his part with liberty and security to the Maroons on their acceding to it.

And so peace was made. Cudjoe and his men were given a large grant of land free from all taxation in perpetuity, and permission to hunt anywhere on the island, except within three miles of a white settlement.

REFERENCES

Captain Cudjoe had a very important effect on Jamaica's population. He frightened away white settlers and gave the island an unsafe reputation for white people, thus leaving the blacks in the majority, which they have been since. Today the island is 90 percent Negro and Negroid, although with its high mountains and extraordinarily fine climate it is one of the healthiest places in the tropics for Europeans. But for Captain Cudjoe it might have been like Cuba, which although less mountainous and thus much hotter, has a preponderant white and mixed-white population.

Dallas, who also fought against the Maroons of Surinam, describes the Jamaica Maroons, thus:

"In their person and carriage, the Maroons were erect and lofty indicating a consciousness of superiority. Vigor appeared upon their muscles and their emotions displayed agility. Their eyes were quick, wild and fiery, the whites of them appearing a little red, owing, perhaps, to the greenness of the wood they burned. They possessed most, if not all, of the senses in a superior degree. They were accustomed to discover from habit in the woods objects which white people of the best sight could not distinguish, and their hearing was so wonderfully quick that it enabled them to elude their most active pursuers.

"In character, language and manners, they resembled those Negroes on the estates of the planters that were descended from the same race of Africans, but on closer inspection displayed a striking distinction in their personal appearance, being blacker, taller, and in every respect, handsomer.

"They were seldom surprised. They communicated with one another by means of horns, and when these could scarcely be heard by other people, they distinguished the order the sounds conveyed. It is very remarkable that the Negroes had a particular call upon the horn for each individual by which he was summoned from a distance as easily as he would have been spoken to had he been near."

The descendants of the Maroons still live in their towns on the island, all except the Trelawney Maroons, who revolted in 1796 and were transported, 500 of them, men, women, and children, to the cold climate of Nova Scotia, Canada. Later most of them were shipped to Sierra Leone, Africa. But descendants of these Maroons are still to be found in Nova Scotia, mixed with the American Negroes who aided England in the Revolutionary War.

Dallas, R. C., *History of the Maroons*, 2 vols. Longman and Rees, 1803.

Proceedings of the Governor and Assembly of Jamaica in Regard to the Maroon Negroes. 1796.

Brymer, D., Royal Society of Canada, *Proceedings*, 2 series, Vol. I, Sec. 2. Ottawa, 1893.

ADDITIONAL REFERENCES

Black, Clinton, *History of Jamaica*, pp. 84–87. London and Glasgow, Collins Clear-Type Press, 1958.

Fleming, B. J., and Pryde, M. J., *Distinguished Negroes Abroad*, pp. 181–186. Washington, D.C., The Associated Publishers, 1946.

Harper, Alvin T., "An Introduction to the Maroons." *Negro History Bulletin*, pp. 4, 22–23 (October, 1948), Association for the Study of Negro Life and History, Washington, D.C.

Toussaint L'Ouverture

❧

THE NEGRO OF WHOM NAPOLEON WAS JEALOUS
(1743–1803)

IN 1743, IN A SLAVE HUT on the plantation of Count de Breda in St. Domingue, or Haiti, was born a male child whose civil status was that of an ox. For the next forty-eight years he remained thus, almost untaught; then, at a time when others are nearing the grave, he rose to be dictator of the colony, establishing a record for political and military ability that has rarely, if ever, been excelled. His high-born masters, some of them descendants of kings, trained in the best universities and military academies of France, became part of his retinue. All of this was accomplished in less than six years. No romance ever written can excel the true story of Toussaint Breda, surnamed L'Ouverture.

Toussaint came on the scene when slavery was at its worst in Haiti. This richest of French colonies had an annual export trade of two and a half billion gold francs and imports that totaled only half of that sum. Its 40,000 white inhabitants lived in luxury. Determined to maintain and make the most of their power, these whites repressed with rigorous severity the rising ambitions of the 30,000 freedmen and the 450,000 slaves, the creators of their wealth.

When one of the freedmen, Lacombe, presented a petition in 1789 asking that he be seated in the local legislature, he was hanged after a mock trial for this "crime." The freedmen were

Toussaint L'Ouverture

mostly mulattoes, who constituted a caste superior to the blacks. They were, for the most part, children of white men, some of them of noble birth, and humble black mothers. These mulattoes, some of whom were educated in France, owned a quarter of the real estate of the colony and had black slaves who toiled for them. Because of their ancestry, however, they had no social standing, and on the whole, like the slaves, had no rights that a white man was bound to respect.

During the French Revolution, when citizens in the mother country were slaughtering the nobility, the mulattoes, thinking the time opportune to win their rights, sent two of their number, Oge and Chavannes, to the Convention in Paris, to ask for them. On their return the two delegates were seized by the whites who broke their arms, legs, thighs, and backs on the wheel, and turning up their faces to the broiling sun left them thus till they died. Their bodies were then quartered and hung up at important crossroads as a lesson.

These injustices stirred Toussaint to the depths and he felt that he was destined to remedy them. He had read in the works of

Abbé Raynal, a great foe of slavery and a contemporary of his, a passage which seemed addressed directly to him. It ran:

Nations of Europe, your slaves have need neither of your generosity nor your counsel to break their chains. They need but a leader. Where is this man? He will appear. Have no doubt of that; he will raise the standard of liberty; his companions will rally around him. More impetuous than the torrent, they will leave everywhere the ineffaceable traces of their just resentment.

Toussaint knew, however, that the time to strike was not yet and prepared himself for the day. While tending cattle, he read authors who inspired him for his "divine" mission, as Plutarch, Epictetus, Caesar, Saxe, and Raynal. So diligent and obliging was he that the overseer, Bayou de Libertat, made him his coachman. This post served him well. From the box he would listen to the conversation of the whites, learning of their plans and their way of thought. Rising still higher in esteem, he was made overseer of all the blacks on the estate.

In this post he was so humble, devout, and eager to please that in time he was held up as a model for all the slaves on the island. His exterior was but a mask, however. Underneath was an iron determination that one day, all, including his master, should be taking orders from him.

Ever the words rang through his mind, "A great man will arise!" with the echo, "You are that man!"

The atrocious treatment of Oge and Chavannes was the signal for a double revolt: one, of the mulattoes under General Beauvais; the other, of the slaves under Bouckmann, Biassou, and Jean-François. On the night of October 30, 1791, the blacks arose, and setting fire simultaneously to thousands of cane fields, butchered the whites as they fled from their blazing mansions.

Though Toussaint helped to engineer the revolt, he was too humane to approve the slaughter of helpless women and children. Thereafter he came out openly in favor of revolt, and so modest and patient was he that although he was the most capable of the leaders, Negro or mulatto, he accepted calmly the minor title that Biassou, the black leader, had conferred on him, "Doctor in the

Armies of the King." Diminutive, desiccated, toothless, and nearly fifty, he looked less like a leader than any of his compeers.

But the others, knowing his ability and his popularity with the blacks, were jealous of him even in the innocuous post they had given him. Jean-François, one of the three great black leaders, threw him into prison.

In the meantime, the whites of Haiti, finding themselves powerless, sent to the slaveholders in the neighboring colony of Jamaica for aid. These British whites, on arriving, succeeded in making an alliance with the mulattoes, who, as was said, were many of them slaveholders and oppressors of the blacks. The result was that the blacks were overwhelmed. The Black Code and slavery were restored and the black leaders fled to the Spanish part of the island where all were given high posts, except Toussaint. Loyal to the King of France and a monarchist at heart, he refused to join in any attack on the French part of the island. It was only after the monarchy in France had been overthrown and a republic established that he did join the other Haitian black leaders in their attack on the French part of the island.

Made a colonel, he soon began winning victories for Spain against France. The French, eager to have him back now, made him flattering offers, intending to use him as a means of driving the Spaniards off the island, but Toussaint refused to serve republicans. He said, "The world has always obeyed a king. I could not live under any other form of government."

But he was destined to leave the Spaniards. His military successes aroused the jealousy of the other black leaders, Jean-François and Biassou. The former, an able man, but selfish and a lover of pomp and power, had been made a grandee of Spain, the highest rank of Spanish nobility, which entitled him to call the King of Spain "cousin" and to wear his hat in his presence; the latter, Biassou, also able, but cruel and too fond of drink, had been made a field marshal. The two plotted against Toussaint, who now decided that the best course was to return to the French part of the island.

Once again there, he found an extremely complicated and treacherous situation. Not only was there a three-cornered fight between whites, mulattoes, and blacks, but there was intense rivalry among the black leaders for supremacy. In addition, there were the plottings of both the English and the Spanish to seize the French portion of the island.

Deciding to deal with the Spaniards first, he assembled an army under the powers granted him by the French governor, Polverel, and marching against the Spaniards, forced them to surrender their capital, San Domingo, and otherwise defeated them with such ease that Polverel exclaimed in admiration, "Ce bigre-la fait l'ouverture, partout," hence his surname.

Turning his attention next to his own part of the island, Toussaint decided to restore order out of the chaos there; to repress any excesses by whites, mulattoes, or blacks; and to establish a government in which all, regardless of color, could live in peace. When the mulattoes revolted and captured the French governor, La Veaux, he marched against them, defeated them, and freed La Veaux. The latter, in gratitude, made him a general and lieutenant-governor of the colony and assured him that he would henceforth not act without first consulting him. Toussaint smiled inwardly at these honors. He had already made his own secret plans regarding La Veaux.

He next turned his attention against the English. Deciding that they had overstayed their invitation, he attacked their commander, Sir Thomas Brisbane, with a mixed army of blacks, whites, and mulattoes, and compelled him to take refuge in Fort St. Nicholas.

Now virtual master of the colony, he decided to get rid of the white officials and sent them, one by one, to France, ostensibly on missions. Next, he suggested to La Veaux himself that he was needed in France. He took the hint and left.

In his place Toussaint appointed Raymond, a Negro, who had been sent from France, as one of the commissioners. Toussaint felt that the blacks preferred a Negro as governor.

To assure the mother country of his loyalty, he sent his stepsons, Placide and Isaac, to France to be educated. Napoleon, however, fearing Toussaint, sent an official to the colony on the pretext that it was necessary because the English were still there. On this, Toussaint attacked the English at St. Nicholas, forced their commander, Lord Maitland, to surrender, and drove them from the colony.

This done, he set in motion his reforms. He issued a general pardon to his white, black, and mulatto opponents, and urged all to unite for the good of the colony. He invited the former planters who had taken refuge in Jamaica and the United States, assuring them of the return of their lands and that their former slaves would work for them for five years for one-fourth of what was produced.

Among those who accepted his offer was his former overseer, Bayou de Libertat. Toussaint received him in his palace, surrounded by a brilliant retinue of white and colored subordinates. Bayou de Libertat, overjoyed at seeing his former coachman again, hastened forward to embrace him. But the diminutive Toussaint, stepping back with dignity, said, "Gently, overseer. There is today a greater difference between me and you than there formerly was between you and me. Return to the plantation, be inflexible, but just; make the blacks work and so add to the prosperity of yourself and the administration."

Toussaint devoted himself energetically to the development of the colony. He built roads, one of them 180 miles long; reinforced the forts; reorganized the army; improved agriculture; built schools for the liberated blacks, on whom he imposed discipline; proclaimed free trade; and in less than two years placed San Domingo on a sounder financial footing than it had ever been.

Under his rule Haiti rose as if by magic out of the chaos of the few years previous. Everyone, white or black, responded to his wishes. He ruled as a benevolent despot, appointing only the most capable and honest men, white, black, or mulatto, to important positions.

He maintained a brilliant retinue of 1500 followers of all colors; owned large estates and stables with hundreds of thoroughbreds. From all who approached him he demanded the strictest formality. Those in his most intimate circles were chiefly white men and women. He insisted that these white women dress circumspectly. No low-necked dresses were permitted. On one occasion when a young white girl appeared at his court in a dress too low at the neck, Toussaint drew his handkerchief and covered her bosom with it. "Modesty," he reprimanded her, "ought to be the chief virtue of your sex."

But Toussaint's troubles were by no means over. There was a revolt in his own ranks, the blacks. Numbers of them opposed to working again for white people revolted under Toussaint's one-eyed nephew, General Moyse, who had been commissioned to see that the former slaves worked. Moyse said, "Whatever my uncle may do I will not be the hangman of my race. He urges me to oppress my fellow blacks in the name of France, but I will love the whites only when they give me back my eye." Moyse's followers massacred 200 whites.

Marching against him, Toussaint captured him and had him shot along with thirteen other rebel chiefs.

The mulattoes, charging that Toussaint had betrayed them to the whites, revolted next. Led by General Rigaud, a veteran of the American Revolution, they were at first victorious, but Toussaint finally defeated them and Rigaud, Pétion, and other mulatto leaders fled to France. He now made a new constitution in which he named himself governor of the colony for life with the right to name his successor.

This step angered Napoleon, to whom Toussaint was still but "a rebellious slave." The honor of France, he declared, had been "outraged" by this menial. Toussaint, too, had said that to Haiti he was "a black Bonaparte," a comparison that caught on among Toussaint's admirers in France. Some of them, enemies of Napoleon, went even further. They said, "Of the two Bonapartes, the black one is the greater."

Napoleon decided to crush him. The aristocratic refugees from Haiti, as well as the mulatto leaders, were urging him to do so. They charged Toussaint with plotting with England and the United States and said he intended making himself king.

On the other hand, Colonel Vincent, a white Haitian, advised Napoleon strongly to the contrary. To send an expedition against Toussaint, he said, would be an act of extreme folly. Toussaint, he said, had not only restored prosperity to the colony, but was loyal and the fittest man for the post:

At the head of this rich colony, is a man, the most active and indefatigable that can be imagined. It may be truthfully said that he is everywhere, and precisely at the spot where sound judgment and danger would say that his presence is most necessary; his great moderation; his power, peculiar to himself of never needing rest; the advantage he has of being able to resume the labor of the cabinet after laborious journeys; of replying to a hundred letters daily and habitually fatiguing five secretaries. More still, the skill of amusing and beguiling everybody, carried even to the point of deceit, makes him a man so superior to all around him, that respect and submission go to the point of fanaticism in a very great number of persons. It may be affirmed that no man of the present day has acquired over an ignorant mass the boundless power obtained by General Toussaint over his brethren in San Domingo; he is the absolute master of the island and nothing can counteract his wishes whatever they are, although some distinguished men of whom, however, the number among the blacks is very small, fear the extent to which his ambition goes.

Napoleon was obdurate. He had just made peace with England and this left him a large army for which he had little use now. Sending these men to Haiti was one way of employing them. Moreover, he intended to make himself emperor, and since many of these soldiers were republican at heart, they would be in the way. There was another consideration too. His beautiful sister Pauline with her incessant love affairs was making him look ridiculous. He would dispatch her husband, General Leclerc, in command of the expedition and she with him.

This expedition of eighty-three ships and 35,000 picked men sailed from France in December, 1801. With it were four Negro generals, two of whom were the mulatto leader, Rigaud, and the black leader of Guadeloupe, J. B. Belley. As for Pauline, she refused to go and Napoleon had her carried aboard. After this expedition there followed two others, making a total of 60,000 men.

Napoleon had given orders to Leclerc to act treacherously with Toussaint in order to get him into his power. "You will treat with Toussaint," he said in his written orders, "you will promise him everything he asks in order that you may get possession of the principal points in the country." That done, he was to make him prisoner and send him to France. As for the other black and mulatto leaders, they too should be used to gain control and then imprisoned. When this had been done, a condition just short of chattel slavery should be restored.

But the wily Toussaint saw through Napoleon's plan even before Leclerc landed. On the morning of January 29, 1802, from a hilltop overlooking Cape Samana he counted Napoleon's eighty-three ships. He said, "All France has come to Haiti. She comes to reduce the blacks to slavery. But we shall die first."

Against this large well-equipped force Toussaint had only 20,000 trained blacks. But he was undaunted, and like Hannibal of old, never lacked an apt illustration to inspirit his men. Holding up a glass bowl of water to the blacks, he threw into it a handful of corn, some grains of which, previously charred, were black. The white grains quickly sank to the bottom but the black grains, made lighter by roasting, floated. "See," cried Toussaint, "the blacks are on top! That's where we will be if we unite!"

Leclerc, reaching Cape Haitien, ordered its commander, fiery Christophe, to surrender. In reply, he set fire to the town and joined Toussaint in the mountains. Everywhere the French landed they were greeted with smouldering ruins.

One by one, however, Toussaint's generals, Dessalines, Christophe, Maurepas, surrendered to Leclerc till at last Toussaint alone held out. Declaring he would fight on even if he had to use Leclerc's own men, he continued until he had only 1200 men left, and even attacked Leclerc's army of 11,000 with this handful. Finally, when these were nearly all gone he agreed to surrender, and swearing loyalty to France, was permitted to retire to his estate. The other black and mulatto leaders were given high posts in the government.

Toussaint, however, had not yet played his last card. Leclerc's troops were being decimated by yellow fever, and he knew that sooner or later Leclerc would weaken and then would come his opportunity. He began to plot with the British.

Leclerc, in power now, decided to seize Toussaint. He had General Brunet invite him to his home for a conference, assuring him of a safe return and then had him tied like a common thief and carried aboard a ship bound for France. As his feet left the soil of Haiti forever, Toussaint cried, "In seizing me you have only cut down the tree of liberty. It will spring afresh; its roots are deep and strong."

Prophetic words these were!

When Toussaint reached France, Napoleon sent General Caffarelli to interrogate him about 32,000,000 francs in gold that he had heard Toussaint had hidden in the hills. But to all importunities Toussaint replied, "I have lost other treasures." Or he would say, "My conscience is my only treasure."

Napoleon ordered him to be imprisoned at Fort Joux, high in the Alps, and gave special orders that he was to communicate with no one save his jailer and a domestic. Toussaint pleaded to see his wife and children, but Napoleon was obdurate. His money, his watch, his papers, were all taken away at Napoleon's orders, and no writing paper was permitted him. In his cell, well above his reach, was a little barred window that looked out on the eternal snows.

Napoleon allowed him the equivalent of a dollar and a half a day for maintenance, later reducing this by half. A wooden chair and bed of straw were the only furnishings in his cell. (Napoleon denounced the English as stingy when they allowed him $200 a day at St. Helena.) Perhaps in irony, Napoleon had General Rigaud, Toussaint's mulatto rival, put in an adjoining cell. Rigaud, however, was more favored; he was permitted to converse with a black general, Martial Besse, also a prisoner.

Hoping to learn the secret of the supposed treasure, Napoleon had Toussaint subjected to torture. Nine months later, on April 27, 1803, the valiant black chief died of apoplexy and pneumonia and was buried at St. Pierre at the foot of the fort. Later his remains were transferred to Chartreuse Cemetery at Bordeaux by his stepson, Placide, where a small monument was erected in his memory by his French admirers.

Toussaint was one of the outstanding figures of an age that produced notables like Washington, Napoleon, Nelson, Murat, and the Duke of Wellington. Certain French writers place Toussaint L'Ouverture above Napoleon in military as well as in administrative genius. Chateaubriand says, "The Black Napoleon—whom the White Napoleon imitated and killed."

Gerbal writes, "Bonaparte was angered. He could not admit

that a Negro could be so intelligent; he regarded all that passed at San Domingo as a personal affront. . . . Toussaint was a victim of the rising despotism of Napoleon who could not pardon a Negro for having elevated thoughts and having dared to do what he had done himself."

Biographie Universelle states that Napoleon might have copied Toussaint. It says, "His political administration was such that Napoleon, in a larger sphere, appeared to have taken him for a model."

Auguste Comte, in his *Calendrier Positiviste*, ranks him with Buddha, Plato, Charlemagne, and Washington. Wordsworth and Lamartine, great white poets, eulogized him. To Wendell Phillips, however, he owes his finest tribute. The latter said in a memorable speech:

> You think me a fanatic tonight, for you read history not with your eyes but your prejudices. But fifty years hence when Truth gets a hearing the Muse of History will put Phocion for the Greek, and Brutus for the Roman, Hampden for England, Fayette for France, choose Washington as the bright, consummate flower of our earlier civilization, and John Brown, the ripe flower of our noon-day, then dipping her pen in the sunlight, will write in the clear blue above them all, the name of the soldier, the statesman, the martyr, TOUSSAINT L'OUVERTURE.

Wendell Phillips based his stand on the fact that while Washington and the others had been born free and had had resources, greater or lesser, to start and continue their early careers, Toussaint rose from the very depths of society. He was a slave who had to pick up stealthily even the mere rudiments of education and then forge his weapon of victory against a mighty, well-trained power from the crudest materials.

Having done all this untaught, and how far might he not have gone had he had Washington's advantages; or had he even been born in France and to a great extent free from color prejudice? History, three centuries hence, might not put Toussaint above Washington but it will certainly class him as one of the ablest and most phenomenal figures of all time. Born under Islam, even as a slave, he would have been another Kafur, Tarik, or Mahmud of Ghazni.

Toussaint is often pictured either as a monster or a saint. Both these views are wrong. Like every other man who rose to great prominence, he was a mixture of good and evil, and in his case, the good was predominant. He acted hypocritically at times, like all statesmen, but he was inherently just, courteous, and humane. Had he been a saint, he would have remained a slave, obedient to his master and Haiti would not have been free. He had to deal with tricky, ruthless men, white and black, and candor and open dealing would merely have put him at their mercy. His task called for cunning, deception, ruthlessness, in a word, statecraft, and he was abundantly endowed with it. When the mulattoes opposed him he massacred 10,000 of them. Terrible in combat though he was, he was magnanimous in victory. This his white enemies, were not—nor his Negro aides or opponents, with the exception of Pétion.

The United States of America owes him a great debt. Because of events he set in motion, the power of France in the New World was broken, hastening the sale of the Louisiana territory, or nearly half of what is now the United States, for a trifling sum.

REFERENCES

Toussaint L'Ouverture, it seems, after a stable government had been assured to Haiti, had hoped to found an empire on the west coast of Africa somewhere in the region of Dahomey. From there he intended to attack the slave trade.

For this purpose, according to Gragnon-Lacoste, he had placed in the safekeeping of an American consul, Stevens, better known as Edouard Girard, the sum of 6,000,000 francs in gold. This sum, the writer charges, was appropriated by Girard. After Girard's death there was considerable litigation over the money, which finally went to the founding of the Girard College in Philadelphia, an institution from which people of Negroid descent were barred.

Placide, one of Toussaint's stepsons, married the daughter of the Marquis de La Caze and had a daughter who was sixty-nine years of age in 1892. She lived in Dordogne, France, where she was highly respected by her neighbors, and on a pension from the French government. The last child of Toussaint, Marie Asselin Dessables, died at Lagrac, France, January 23, 1859, at the age of eighty-five. Years after

Toussaint's death, his estates, valued at 1,125,000 gold francs, went to his supposed heirs, the Legros of Haiti.

Napoleon, while looking out on the blank ocean from the rocks of St. Helena as Toussaint had done on the snows of the Alps, regretted his treatment of Toussaint. He wrote, "It was one of my greatest follies. I should not have sent an army to Haiti. I ought to have contented myself with governing the island through Toussaint L'Ouverture." Napoleon not only lost Haiti as a result, but his army too. Incidentally, the heir to the throne he had built, Prince Napoleon, was ambushed and killed by Negroes in the Zulu War of 1869.

De La Croix, Pamphile, *La Révolution de St.-Domingue*, 2 vols. Paris, 1820.

Rainsford, M., *St. Domingo*. London, 1801.

DuBroca, M., *La Vie de Toussaint*. Paris, 1801.

Napoleon, *Correspondence of Napoleon*, October 31, 1801.

Gragnon-Lacoste, T. P., *Toussaint L'Ouverture*. Paris, 1877.

Métral, A. M. T., *Histoire de L'Expedition des Français*. 1825.

Beard, J. R., *Life of Toussaint L'Ouverture*. London, 1853.

Stephen, J., *Bonaparte in the West*. 1803.

Cousin d'Avallon, C. Y., *Toussaint L'Ouverture*. 1802.

Elliott, C., *Heroes Are Historic Men*. 1855.

Lamartine, A.M., *Toussaint L'Ouverture* (a dramatic Poem). 1857.

Benjamin, R. C. *Toussaint L'Ouverture*. 1888.

"Toussaint L'Ouverture au Fort de Joux." *Nouvelle Revue Rétrospective*, Vol. XVI, pp. 241–58. Paris, 1902.

Nemours, A., *La Captivîté et de la Mort de Toussaint L'Ouverture*. Paris, 1929.

Ardouin, *Etudes sur L'Histoire de Haiti*. Paris, 1855.

"Letters of Toussaint L'Ouverture and Harold Stevens." *American Historical Review*, Vol. XVI, pp. 67–101. New York, 1911.

Biographie Universelle, "Toussaint L'Ouverture." 1854.

Phillips, Wendell, *Toussaint L'Ouverture*.

Intermédiare des Cherchers et des Curieux, Vol. XXVI, p. 263. 1892.

Korngold, R., *Citizen Toussaint*. Boston, 1944.

ADDITIONAL REFERENCES

Adams, Russell, *Great Negroes: Past and Present*, p. 13. Chicago, Afro-Am Publishing Company, 1963, 1964.

James, C. L. R., *A History of Pan-African Revolt*, pp. 7–20. Washington, D.C., Drum and Spear Press, Inc., 1969.

Leyburn, James G., *The Haitian People*, pp. 24–30 (main part). New Haven, Conn., and London, Yale University Press, 1966.

Moran, Charles, *Black Triumvirate*. New York, Exposition Press, 1957.

Phillips, Wendell, "Wendell Phillips' Eulogy of Toussaint L'Ouverture." *Negro History Bulletin*, p. 74 (January, 1941), Association for the Study of Negro Life and History, Washington, D.C.

Reddicic, Ruth, "Toussaint and Haiti." *Negro History Bulletin*, p. 75 (January, 1941), Association for the Study of Negro Life and History, Washington, D.C.

Redpath, James, ed., *Toussaint L'Ouverture: A Biography and Autobiography*. Boston, 1863.

Redpath, James, *New York Tribune* (daily), March 12, 14, 1863; *Semi-Weekly Tribune*, March 12, 1863.

Scherman, Katharine, *The Slave Who Freed Haiti*. New York, Random House, 1954.

Vandercook, John W., *Black Majesty*. New York, Scholastic Book Services, 1928.

Woodson, Carter G., "Toussaint L'Ouverture." *Negro History Bulletin*, p. 7 (May, 1938), Association for the Study of Negro Life and History, Washington, D.C.

Dessalines, "The Ferocious"

LIBERATOR OF HAITI AND ITS FIRST EMPEROR
(1758–1806)

BYRON, in his tribute to Bonnivard, a Swiss patriot who died miserably in a dungeon, wrote:

> Eternal Spirit of the chainless Mind!
> Brightest in dungeons, Liberty! thou art
> For there, thy habitation is the heart—
> The heart which love of thee alone can bind
> And when thy sons to fetters are consign'd—
> To fetters and the damp vault's dayless gloom
> Their country conquers with their martyrdom
> And Freedom's fame find wings on every wind.

This is precisely what happened in the case of Toussaint L'Ouverture. His martyrdom stirred his countrymen to a supreme effort to be free of France forever.

Their leader was Jean Jacques Dessalines, who also had been born a slave. In the fight for freedom he had been second to none except Toussaint, while in courage and daring he was inferior to no one. At Crete-à-Pierrot, when besieged by 12,000 French soldiers under General de La Croix, he had refused to surrender though he had only a thousand men. When lack of food and ammunition made it impossible to hold on any longer, he and 600 survivors had fought their way out, inflicting terrible slaughter on a force that outnumbered them twenty to one.

La Croix wrote in later years:

The retreat that the commander of Crete-à-Pierrot had the courage to conceive and execute was a remarkable feat of arms. We were surrounding his fort with 12,000 men; he escaped without losing half of his men, leaving us only his dead and wounded. Our losses were so great that they distressed the captain-general and he forced us to minimize them, which he himself also did in the official reports.

In character, Dessalines was, however, quite unlike Toussaint. Impulsive, untameable, he made a bad slave. He was always trying to escape or was disobeying the overseer so that his body was a mass of scars from the slave driver's whip. In short, he had none of Toussaint's calmer, more humane qualities, and despised learning because it was of the whites.

He was not only illiterate but selfish and unprincipled. After the fall of Toussaint, he had become one of the most active tools of Leclerc in restoring slavery of the blacks. Leclerc wrote Napoleon that Dessalines "is at present the butcher of the blacks." In the rising of the blacks following the treachery to Toussaint, Dessalines saw his opportunity to shift masters once more, and leaving the whites, went back to the blacks.

While acting as governor of the southern part of the colony, and while subduing the rebels there, he played a double game and managed to leave much arms and ammunition in their hands, looking forward to a day of revolt, which he would lead. Fever was decimating the white troops and Dessalines knew that as they dwindled, so would the strength of the blacks increase.

On November 1, 1802, Leclerc died and Count de Rochambeau, son and heir of the American Revolutionary hero of that name, took command. He had arrived some time before with 10,000 men, another of Napoleon's expeditions to the colony. Rochambeau now announced that he was going to be even more severe than Leclerc, which was indeed difficult. Leclerc used to tie the prisoners back to back and throw them into the sea to save the ammunition it would take to shoot them. Once he treated 1200 captives thus.

But Rochambeau was to learn that when it came to using terror, he had a master in Dessalines. At their first encounter, Rochambeau was the victor in the early part of the day, but before night Dessalines had turned the tide against him, and captured a large part of the French Army. His first act was to hang 500 of the French.

From then onwards, Dessalines defeated the French in every battle and finally chased Rochambeau and the surviving 6000 men of the 60,000 that Napoleon had sent to Haiti in to the city of Port-au-Prince, where he besieged him. Rochambeau surrendered soon afterward on condition that he and his men be permitted to leave for France, a condition that Dessalines accepted in November, 1804. What had largely influenced Dessalines was the knowledge that the English were waiting outside the harbor to make prisoners of all the French.

Haiti was free at last! The glorious work begun by Toussaint L'Ouverture had been accomplished.

Dessalines, now absolute master, was elected president. He began the new year with a proclamation of independence. To create a flag for the new republic, he tore the white out of the French flag, leaving the red and the blue to represent the blacks and the mulattoes. He also abolished the French name, St. Domingue, and took the ancient Indian one of Haiti. Hoping to insure peace, he issued two decrees. The first was, "Never again shall a white man set his foot on this territory with the title of master." The second was that all Negroes, regardless of complexion, should be known as black. This was an attempt to wipe out the strife between mulattoes and blacks. He further ordered a general massacre of all white people.

Dessalines excused this atrocity by saying that he was only imitating the whites. After thirteen years of one of the most ferocious and pitiless struggles in the annals of war, the hearts of both French colonists and blacks were dead to pity. Rochambeau had used every sadistic method he could invent to kill the blacks: burying them alive, stifling them slowly to death with sulphuric fumes, and starving them. To get his bloodhounds to disembowel the blacks, he trained the animals, deprived of food, to disembowel dummies stuffed with food.

On the other hand, it is refreshing to note that Madame Dessalines opposed this policy and succeeded in saving many lives, one of whom was the French scientist Descourlitz, who had taken refuge in her home.

Not content with the title of president, Dessalines soon proclaimed himself emperor, in imitation of Napoleon, it was said. But the truth is he preceded Napoleon in so doing by two months.

As emperor, Dessalines tried to begin well. In his political creed he embraced all nations and welcomed all white people except the French and the former slave masters. But rivalry between mulattoes and blacks, jealousy of him by other leaders, and discontent among the people who felt that they were not getting the freedom they had bought so dearly created a problem too great for his untutored soul. Lacking the innate sagacity of Toussaint; vain, self-seeking, unscrupulous; never hesitating to betray a friend if it suited his purpose, he knew of but one way to solve a situation: brute force. He ordered a massacre of all who opposed him, mulattoes and blacks alike. He became one of the most odious tyrants.

As for the public treasury, it became his private purse and that of his friends of the moment. His political policy in his own words was, "How to pluck the chicken without making it squawk"—the equivalent of the old saying, "Politics is the art of extracting honey without disturbing the bees."

He continued his misrule until friend and foe alike hated him and plotted against him. Finally he rode out to review his army one day in 1806 to find the men ignoring him. In rage he demanded why he was not being shown the honors due their emperor. In answer an officer snatched a gun from a private and sent a bullet through his heart. The men, instead of being aroused, quietly left the parade ground, and left him lying there. An old peasant woman later took up the body and buried it.

Dessalines will long remain a model of ferocity and terror; of courage and audacity; of resourcefulness and daring nonchalance. His character has perhaps been best summed up by Schoelcher, noted French abolitionist, who said:

Dessalines, whose instinctive military qualities enabled him to play a grand role in San Domingo, was a barbarous force, but nevertheless, a force. Impetuous, violent, hardened to pain, he had always been a slave rebel, often a fugitive one, and he had many times been flogged with that atrocious cruelty which had become natural to the slave masters. His whole body was covered with scars from the atrocious corrections that his indomitable temper had brought upon him. Later, every time he changed his uniform, he threw his eyes down upon himself to exclaim with fury: "For these marks I'll wage a war of extermination against all whites."

He was of audacious courage, bold, and like Murat, seemingly invulnerable. Although he was always in the thickest of the fight, he was never wounded. When he went into battle it was like a workman preparing himself for his work. He put off his coat, rolled up his sleeves, and with his arms bare as the blade of his sword, he was a blaze of fire, intrepid, and at the same time full of resource. But victorious, he made nothing of it; he thought of nothing but amusement and the dance. His life was passed between the contra dance and the combat.

He did not wish to borrow anything of the whites. He repelled all civilization; he would not consent to learn anything beyond merely making some marks which represented only his name. He affected to speak only Creole, and not to understand French, and although born in San Domingo, he vaunted himself as being only a savage African.

Dessalines, in short, was a product of his times. Had he not seen, too, the fate of Toussaint? It was only by outdoing the whites in cruelty he could have freed Haiti. It was fire against fire—that of Dessalines against Napoleon's and his lieutenant, Rochambeau.

Dessalines liked only one white person, a man who had owned him for a short time and had treated him well. He made him his butler and said he would have promoted him except for the fact that he was a great drunkard.

Dessalines was of short stature but very well built. Those who knew him said that his eyes actually sparkled with the ferocity within. A monument stands to him on the Champs de Mars, Port-au-Prince.

REFERENCES

Dubroca, L., *Vida de J. J. Dessalines*. Mexico, M. De. Zuniga y Ontiveros, 1800, 1806.
Biographie Universelle, "Dessalines."

ADDITIONAL REFERENCES

Adams, Russell L., *Great Negroes: Past and Present*, pp. 12–15. Chicago, Afro-Am Publishing Company, 1963.

Bellegarde, Dantes, . . . *Dessalines à Parle*. Port-au-Prince, Haiti, Société d'Editions et de Librarie, 1948.

Brutus, Timoleon C., *L'Homme d'Airain*. Port-au-Prince, Haiti, Imprimerie, N. A. Theodore, 1946–1947.

Dubroca, Louis, *Leben Des J. J. Dessalines*. Leipzig, J. C. Heinrichs, 1805.

James, C. L. R., *A History of Pan-African Revolt*, pp. 12–17. Washington, D.C., Drum and Spear Press, Inc., 1969.

Laurent, Gerard M., . . . *Six Etudes sur J. J. Dessalines*. Port-au-Prince, Haiti, Imprimerie Les Presses Libres, 1950.

Leyburn, James G., *The Haitian People*, pp. 32–42 (main section). New Haven, Conn., and London, Yale University Press, 1966.

Lherisson, Louis Carius, *Poor Dessalines*. Port-au-Prince, Haiti, Imprimerie A. A. Heraux, 1906.

Moran, Charles, *Black Triumvirate*. New York, Exposition Press, 1957.

Pattee, Richard, *Jean Jacques Dessalines, Fundador de Haiti*. Havana, Imprenta Molina y Cia, 1936.

Alexander Pétion

HAITI'S FIRST AND NOBLEST PRESIDENT
(1770–1816)

GENERAL ALEXANDER PÉTION was Haiti's first president and her best beloved ruler. At a time when war, bloodshed, and massacres were the order of the day, Pétion distinguished himself by a humanity and forbearance rare in history. The devastating warfare between the whites and the blacks grieved him immensely, and the bloody conflicts between the mulattoes and the blacks broke his heart. Yet, as a military commander, he was the equal of anyone, white or black, engaged in that fierce struggle. It was said of him, "He never caused anyone to shed a tear."

He was the son of Sabès, a rich French planter, and a free black woman, being in this respect more fortunate than any of the other three great black leaders—Toussaint L'Ouverture, Dessalines, and Christophe—all of whom were born slaves. Pétion also was given a fair education by his father.

When he was twenty-one a double insurrection broke out: that of the slaves under Biassou, Jean-François, and Toussaint L'Ouverture; and that of the freedmen, chiefly mulattoes, under General Beauvais, a mulatto. Pétion joined Beauvais and so distinguished himself that he was made a general of artillery. He later assisted Toussaint in fighting the English. It was his brilliant capture of La Coupe that forced the English out of Port-au-Prince.

Pétion, unlike most of the other mulatto and black leaders, was for driving the French out of Haiti altogether and making the country independent. He knew that as long as the blacks remained under French rule and were economically weak they would be exploited and there would be strife. Toussaint, on the other hand, was not only patriotically French but a royalist at heart. After the decree of emancipation issued by the Convention at Paris, he had deserted Spain and returned to the French.

After white rule had been overthrown by Toussaint, a struggle for supremacy arose between mulattoes and blacks. The former charged that Toussaint, inflated by his exalted position and the homage of his former masters, was depriving them of their rights. Furthermore that he was exploiting the ex-slaves for his own benefit and to win the favor of the whites.

Toussaint, on his side, asserted that the mulattoes objected to him because of his color. He said that their leader, General Rigaud, "refuses to serve under me because I am black. Mulattoes, I see to the bottom of your souls. You are ready to rise against me. I am leaving Port Republican for the Cape, but I leave an eye and an arm: the eye to watch, the arm to strike."

Civil war broke out between the blacks under Toussaint and the mulattoes under Rigaud. Toussaint's lieutenant, Dessalines, ruthlessly ordered a massacre of the mulattoes. When Toussaint was accused of this crime, he said, "I told Dessalines to prune the tree; not to uproot it."

Pétion, feeling that Toussaint was being used as a tool by the whites, left him and joined Rigaud. Later when Toussaint was treacherously captured by them and sent to a dungeon in the Alps, Pétion explained why he had left his old companion-in-arms. "I could not support General Toussaint against what I considered the best interests of the Haitian people," he said. "How could Toussaint ever have counted upon the sincerity of the whites, he, their former slave, when I have not the friendship of my own father simply because I have African blood in my veins?"

In the war between mulattoes and blacks that followed, Pétion again distinguished himself. He defeated Dessalines at Grand Goave, and captured Port-au-Prince. His most notable exploit, however, was his entry into Jacmel, in open boats under heavy shellfire. The city was being closely besieged by Toussaint himself with 20,000 men.

Pétion held his city for months, then with only 1900 men, fought his way through Toussaint's large army. When the mulattoes were finally defeated by Toussaint, and the latter was confirmed as commander-in-chief in Haiti by Napoleon, Pétion left for France with the other mulatto leaders. En route, he was captured by the English and held a prisoner in England for three months.

On being freed, he went to France where he devoted himself to the study of military tactics and artillery. Later Napoleon promoted him to general and sent him with Leclerc's expedition to Haiti. In offering him the post, Napoleon had personally assured him that the sole purpose of the expedition was to protect Haiti from the English and establish there a rule of highest equity for all, regardless of color. Pétion was to learn only later that Napoleon had issued secret orders to Leclerc to restore slavery.

The expedition arrived, and Toussaint was beaten. Pétion succeeded in making a sort of peace between the French and the Haitian leaders, some of whom, as Dessalines, were given high command by the French. To Pétion had been entrusted the task of disarming the guerrillas and others still in revolt.

It was at this time that Leclerc, thinking himself firmly in the saddle at last, started to restore slavery. Seizing the mulatto chief Rigaud, he shipped him off to a dungeon in the Alps, doing the same soon afterward to Toussaint. It was then and only then that mulattoes and blacks awoke to what Pétion had long been preaching to them, namely, the folly of their rivalry.

On the capture of Toussaint, Pétion took an oath that he would not rest until Haiti was free. He sought out Dessalines, who was now leader of the blacks.

The impetuous chief, recalling his defeat at the hands of Pétion, refused to listen at first but was finally won over by Pétion's logic.

The two leaders talked long. Pétion revealed all that he had learned while he was serving with the French and also his plans for Haitian independence, urging Dessalines to revolt at once. The latter fearing, however, that the other black and mulatto leaders were still loyal to France, bade him wait awhile.

Pétion had decided to strike as soon as possible, however, and revealed his plans to his officers, winning their enthusiastic approval.

A few days later a French officer in passing Pétion's camp attempted to change his tired horse for one belonging to one of Pétion's officers. When the latter objected, the Frenchman threatened him with dire punishment. Pétion, who was standing nearby, remarked, "So you mean to have us all drowned, eh?" (Drowning was the usual way of getting rid of prisoners in order to save powder and burial.)

The French officer hastened to report to General Clausel, the commander, who sent for Pétion. The latter, feeling that General Clausel intended to make him prisoner, worked out a plan of escape in advance. He went, and while Clausel was questioning him closely, a messenger arrived from Pétion's camp saying that an officer had struck another, that the camp was in an uproar, and Pétion's presence was needed to restore order. Clausel bade Pétion go but told him to return as soon as order was restored.

Again in his camp, Pétion urged his men to immediate revolt and they agreed.

Pétion's first move was to attack the French at Haut de Cap, an important military post, from which he drove them. On this, the French commander, General Lavalette, sent a message to him urging him to return to the French, and his rank would be restored. Pétion flatly refused. "We have resolved to live free," he said, "or die in the attempt."

Christophe and Dessalines, the black leaders, soon followed his example. Pétion, despite his superior military training, served under Christophe, and later under Dessalines. When the latter, recognizing his superior skill, offered him supreme command, he refused. He knew that since the majority of the men were black, the cause of harmony would be better served by having a black leader.

In this final phase of the struggle for independence Pétion distinguished himself. He defeated the French general, Kerverseau, on the plains of Mirebalais, then going to the rescue of two other Haitian generals, he rallied the remnants of their forces, welding all into a strong force, and attacked the French at Port-au-Prince and captured that city after a brilliant assault. This marked the end of the struggle. Haiti was free!

Dessalines was now named president. Pétion, whose military skill had been the chief factor in victory, effaced himself for the black chief. But Dessalines soon afterward established an absolute monarchy, and followed it with a massacre of the white people, and later of the mulattoes and their black sympathizers. He also monopolized public funds for the benefit of himself, his favorites, and his mistresses, and reared on the foundations of the liberty he had so ably built an abominable tyranny. At last he was shot dead by his own men on the parade field.

Two figures now loomed for the presidency: Pétion, who had reared the standard of liberty against Dessalines; and Christophe, leader of the blacks, extraordinarily able in some respects, valiant and firm, but illiterate, autocratic, and unscrupulous. Like Dessalines, he had also been a butcher of the blacks under Leclerc. Again Petion stepped aside and Christophe was chosen. But Christophe soon set up an absolute monarchy, the State of Haiti, in the north of the island, and called himself Henry I.

Pétion, in the south, proclaimed the Republic of Haiti and was elected president. He governed with mildness and justice and many of Christophe's people, tired of his tyranny, deserted to him. Christophe, to get the money to carry out his grandiose schemes, had instituted a system of labor that was slavery in all but name.

The two were soon afterward at war, with one or the other in the ascendancy. In the first engagement Pétion was beaten. Rallying his forces, Pétion broke and dismembered Christophe's army, but instead of pursuing him, he let him go. Finally he defeated Christophe in a great battle during which the cream of Christophe's army deserted to Pétion. Retiring to his part of the island, Christophe disturbed Pétion no more. In 1820 with the mob howling for his blood, Christophe killed himself.

But Pétion's troubles were not yet over. Rigaud, the old mulatto leader, freed from prison, returned to Haiti. Ambitious and designing, he sought supreme power, and Pétion, to keep the peace, offered to make him second in command. Disdaining service under a former subordinate, Rigaud revolted. But his death a year later left Pétion in comparative peace.

Pétion now devoted his energies to building up the nation, which had been ruined by thirteen years of bloodshed. He founded a government with freedom for all, regardless of color; placed the army on a much sounder footing; encouraged agriculture; established schools; paid off the public debt; filled the treasury; restored foreign trade; protected the whites; and improved, by his diplomacy, the relations between mulattoes and blacks.

With his wise administration he ushered in the Golden Age of Haiti which lasted for twenty years after his death.

Pétion's ideals were of the loftiest. He wanted freedom for all peoples. In nothing was this more striking than in his attitude toward Bolívar, great South American liberator. When the latter was beaten and had been refused asylum by other countries, Pétion welcomed him and a number of Haitian volunteers who accompanied him, and twice gave him money, arms, food, and a printing press to continue the struggle. Bolívar, in a letter dated February 8, 1816, generously credited Pétion with being "the author" of Venezuelan liberty, and his grateful countrymen later erected a monument to Pétion in their capital.

Pétion's advice to Bolívar was even more significant than his help. Recalling how a liberated United States had retained its slaves, he advised Bolívar that his first move should be the freeing of the slaves in his native land. "How," he said, "can you free a country if you do not free all the people in it?"

In 1815 a grateful nation named Pétion president for life. He died three years later, stricken with fever, at the age of forty-eight. It is said that disappointed at being unable to rid Haiti of her greatest bane, the rivalry between mulattoes and blacks, he deliberately chose death by refusing to take any medicine or nourishment. Poet, dreamer, perfectionist, he had hoped to create conditions wherein men would have nothing to fear.

The black leaders had tried to do this too, and had failed, but Pétion had persisted to the last. After the defeat of France, Dessalines had ripped the white out the French flag, leaving the red and the blue to represent mulatto and black. Later Dessalines had inserted a black stripe and placed it vertically to mark the supremacy of the blacks, but Pétion took out the black and replaced the red and blue, horizontally, to denote the equality of black and mulatto.

Pétion went so far in his policy of conciliation and his desire to avoid bloodshed that at times he seemed weak. When Napoleon, in bravado, later sent out delegates to demand the submission of the island, Christophe, the black leader, had those sent to him shot; Pétion received them courteously and offered to pay an indemnity to those French whites whose property had been unjustly seized.

Haiti lamented his death loud and long. The people cried in the streets, "Our father is dead," and went into voluntary mourning for three months.

Pétion was noted for his bravery. Like Toussaint, Christophe, and Dessalines, he always set an example of the highest courage. Once while he was playing draughts in a house, a loaded shell fell through the roof. All dashed precipitately out except Pétion, who stopped to pick up the "men" his opponent had thrown away.

He was often called the "George Washington of Haiti." Tall, well built, every inch a soldier, and strikingly handsome, "he carried himself like one who feels he is born to a great destiny."

REFERENCES

There were other important Haitian leaders but I have confined myself to biographies of only three of them: Toussaint, who paved the way; Dessalines, who accomplished independence; and Pétion, who stabilized it.

Saint-Remy, *Pétion et Haiti*, 5 vols. Paris, 1854–1857.
Vaval, D., "Alexander Pétion." Revue *Société d'Histoire et de Geographie d'Haiti*, Vol. III, No. 7, 1932.
Enrique de Tovar y R. Pétion, *Haiti y La America Bolivariana*, Vol. VIII, pp. 124–135. Santiago de Chile, Acad. Chilena de la Historia, cuarto trim. de 1941.
Biographie Universelle, "Pétion."

ADDITIONAL REFERENCES

Delencour, François, Stanislas Ranier, *Alexandre Pétion Devant L'Humanité*. Port-au-Prince, Haiti, en vente chez l'auteur, 1929.

Lamour, Saladin, *Justification de la Conduite Politique D'Alexandre Pétion*. Port-au-Prince, Haiti, Imprímerie de T. Bouchereau, 1850.

Leybourn, James G., *The Haitian People*, pp. 51–64 (main section). New Haven, Conn., and London, Yale University Press, 1966.

Manigat, Lesie François, *La Politique Agrarie du Gouvernement D'Alexandre Pétion*. Port-au-Prince, Haiti, Imprimerie La Phalange, 1962.

Mesa Rodriquez, Manuel Isaias, *Alejandro Pétion y la Independencia Americana*. Havana, Instituto Civico-Militar; Seccion de Artes Graficas, Centro-Superiro Tecnologico, 1943.

Prévost, Julien, . . . *La Comte de Limonade*. Cap-Henri, Haiti, P. Roux, 1815.

Schomberg, Arthur Alfonso, *Military Services Rendered by the Haitians in the North and South American Wars for Independence*. Nashville, Tenn., A. M. E. Sunday School Union, 1921.

Vastey, Pompee Valentin, *Le Cri de la Patrie*. Cap-Henri, Haiti, P. Roux, 1807.

Louis Delgrès

GUADELOUPE PATRIOT WHO DEFIED NAPOLEON
(1772–1802)

LOUIS DELGRÈS, the Toussaint L'Ouverture of Guadeloupe, was born at St. Pierre, Martinique, and was sent by his father to be educated in France, where he received a careful military education. A brilliant student, he graduated with high honors, and during the French Revolution served with such distinction that he was promoted to colonel at the age of twenty-seven.

In the meantime, the repercussions of the Revolution were being felt in the French colonies in the West Indies. Even as the whites of France were seeking economic emancipation from the nobility, so the slaves of the islands were seeking emancipation from their white masters. In Haiti they had revolted and in Guadeloupe the 106,000 blacks had risen against the 13,000 white colonists, and after killing many of them had fled to the swamps and the woods, where they resisted bravely, choosing death rather than surrender.

This struggle continued, and when the Revolution had succeeded in France, the Negroes sent five of their delegates to the National Convention there, asking for recognition. One of the delegates was J. B. Belley, an unmixed black, later to be made an adjutant general by Napoleon. An ex-slave, Belley made such a ringing appeal to the Convention that he drowned all opposition. The assembly, swept off its feet by his eloquence, voted to abolish slavery at once, not only in Guadeloupe but in Haiti as well.

To enforce its order the Convention sent two commissioners, Hugues and Chrétien, to Guadeloupe with instructions to abolish all color and class distinctions. In the meantime, however, the English, profiting by the revolution in France, had seized Guadeloupe, on which the Negroes rose under a mulatto, Colonel Magloire Pelage, and drove them out. Soon afterward General Baco arrived from France with reinforcements. With him as aide-de-camp was Delgrès.

With slavery abolished in the island, order was restored and the ex-slaves became peaceful cultivators of the soil. But this did not last long. Napoleon, lacking money to carry out his grandiose schemes of conquest in Europe, decided to bleed the colonies and to restore a condition that was chattel slavery in all but name. For this purpose he sent his brother-in-law, General Leclerc, to Haiti and General Richepanse to Guadeloupe.

True to his orders, Richepanse disarmed the blacks and began a reign of terror. All justice disappeared. Negroes were hunted down like wild beasts; the scaffold worked without cessation; cruelty was pushed to the exteme and the revolting tortures of the days of slavery—the wheel, the stake, and the iron cage were restored.

Among those most disturbed by the event was Delgrès. Though a mulatto and a member of the upper class, he protested, on which General Richepanse ordered him to surrender his command and to have his men give up their arms. Delgrès replied by going over to the blacks and inciting them to greater revolt.

The odds were against him and he knew it. Richepanse had 7000 of Napoleon's seasoned veterans, well equipped, while his men were chiefly recruits. Rallying the blacks, he issued an appeal to the liberty-loving people of France and the world. It was entitled "An Appeal to the Entire Universe. The Last Cry of Innocence and Despair." It said, "The most odious practices of tyranny are being surpassed in Guadeloupe today. Even our former tyrants permitted a master to free his slaves. In this century of advanced thought and philosophy there still exist men who are so unjust and so powerful, and so far away, too, that they cannot think of black men except as slaves."

On May 12, 1802, Delgrès was attacked by a strong French force under Magloire Pelage, a mulatto, who had now been made a general by Napoleon, and by the white commander, General Gobert. His troops fought bravely. Gobert had a horse killed under him while Pelage was nearly captured. Even the black women fought with Delgrès and carried off the wounded. But outnumbered, he was forced to retreat, until on May 28 he was driven into Fort Manotuba were he decided to make a stand. Knowing that it would be his last, he said that he asked of posterity only remembrance and a tear for his brave men.

In the attack the next day he was badly wounded, and knowing that the end was near, he resolved to sell his life and those of his men as dearly as possible. His aide-de-camp, Claude, also wounded, and lying on a cot near him, had decided to do the same.

He ordered a trail of gunpowder to be strewn from the foot of his bed to the powder magazine and two blazing charcoal stoves to be placed one at his leg and the other at Claude's. He also ordered that when the French entered the fort and were well within it, a rifle should be fired outside his door.

When all was ready, word came to him that six white prisoners were in the fort. His magnanimous reply was, "Set them free; there will be enough victims without them."

The blacks fought heroically but the French entered finally. At the sound of the rifle outside, Delgrès kicked over the charcoal stove. Soon there was an explosion that shook the earth and blew friend and foe to bits. The mangled body of Delgrès was found fifty yards away.

REFERENCES

LaCour, Al., *Histoire de Guadeloupe*, Vol. III. Basseterre, 1855–58.
Boyer-Peyreleau, E. E., *Antiles Françaises,* Vol. III. Paris, 1825.

Richard Hill

❧

SCIENTIST, JUDGE, AND CHAMPION OF HUMAN RIGHTS
(1795–1872)

RICHARD HILL, antislavery agitator and naturalist, was born on the island of Jamaica, the son of a well-to-do English merchant and an African woman. At the age of five he was sent to England to be educated.

His father, a resident of the island, strongly opposed slavery, and on his death bed made young Hill swear that he would not rest until it had been abolished. That promise Hill faithfully kept, even though it deprived him of his greatest pleasure—the study of nature.

His studies completed, he returned to Jamaica. Soon afterwards he visited Cuba and the United States, studying slavery in those lands. After a short stay in Canada, he went to England to secure the assistance of the Anti-Slavery Society, where he met Wilberforce, Buxton, Clarkson, and other leading agitators.

Together with them, he presented a petition to the House of Commons for the removal of the civil disabilities of the free colored people of the island, and the freeing of the slaves. Hill was received with deference by the House, and Canning, the greatest British statesman of the time, made his last speech in favor of Hill's petition.

For the next few years Hill remained in England, and though greatly handicapped by lack of funds, continued the fight, supporting himself by contributing literary and scientific articles to the leading newspapers and periodicals. By pen and voice he worked tirelessly to enlighten the English people on the true conditions in Jamaica and to arouse them against slavery.

He was next appointed by the Anti-Slavery Society to go to Haiti to study social conditions and to report on the natural resources of the island, which was then under the single rule of President Boyer. Hill spent nearly two years there, studying the soil, animals, plants, fishes, and insects, as well as the effect of freedom on the natives. He took back with him several notebooks filled with valuable information, as well as many drawings because he was an artist also.

Returning to England, he continued his fight against slavery until the emancipation in 1834, after which he went to Jamaica to aid in the period of adjustment. Here he was appointed head of the special magistrates appointed for the settlement of disputes between ex-slave and former master, a post he filled for thirty-eight years.

During this period he devoted his leisure to a study of the anthropology of the West Indies and to its plant, bird, fish, and insect life. He wrote books and articles on them. Two of his books, *A Naturalist's Sojourn in Jamaica* and *The Birds of Jamaica*, were published in collaboration with Gosse. He was also a corresponding member of the Zoological Society of London, the Zoological Society of Leeds, and the Smithsonian Institution of Washington, D. C.

By the journals of the Academy of National Science of Philadelphia, the Lyceum of Natural History of New York, and other scientific societies, in botanical circles in America and Europe, he was often quoted as an authority. Charles Darwin was among those who gratefully acknowledged the influence of his data on their scientific studies.

Hill's botanical knowledge was of great value when cholera swept the island in 1857. He advised the use of bitter-bush (*Eupatorium nervosum*), a native plant, which was a successful remedy that saved many lives.

He was also a historian, his best-known works being *Lights and Shadows of Jamaica History* and *Eight Chapters on the His-*

tory of Jamaica, the latter a work which deals in part with the settlement of the Jews there and the activities of the pirates, whose lair it once was.

Hill was tall and of commanding appearance. Frank Cundall, head of the Jamaica Institute, says, "All who knew him bore testimony to his generosity, philanthropy, modesty, even temperament and unfailing forgetfulness, his kindness of heart, his piety and his catholicism."

Two American missionaries, James Thome and J. H. Kimball, who went to the West Indies to observe the effects of the emancipation, say similarly:

He is a colored gentlemen and in every respect the noblest man, white or black, whom we met in the West Indies. He is highly intelligent and of fine moral feelings. His manners are free and unassuming and his language in conversation fluent and well-chosen. He is intimately acquainted with English and French authors and has studied thoroughly the history and character of the people with whom the tie of color has connected him. He travelled two years in Haiti and his letters, written in flowing and luxurious style, as a son of the tropics should write, were published in England and have been copied in the anti-slavery journal in this country [America].

He is at the head of the special magistrates, of whom there are sixty in the island, and all the correspondence between them and the governor is carried on through him. The station he holds is a very important one and the business connected with it is of a character and extent, that, were he not a man of superior abilities, he could not sustain them. He is highly respected by the government in the island and at home, and possesses the esteem of his fellow-citizens of all colors. He associates with persons of the highest rank, dining and attending parties at the government house with all the aristocracy of Jamaica. . . . Though the African sun has burnt a deep tinge on him, he is truly one of Nature's noblemen. His demeanor is such, so dignified, yet so bland and amiable that no one can help respecting him.

John Bigelow, American diplomat and writer, was also highly impressed by Hill:

It was my privilege shortly after my arrival to make the acquaintance of one of the most highly cultivated men I have ever met, upon whose complexion the accident of birth had left a tinge which betrayed the African bar on his escutcheon. I refer to Mr. Richard Hill, of Spanishtown. He is a brown man, about forty-five years of age, I judged, and was educated in one of the English universities where he enjoyed every advantage which wealth could procure for his improvement. He enjoys an enviable reputation as a naturalist and has published a volume on the birds of Jamaica, illustrated by his own pencil, which displays both literary and scientific merit of a high order.

The British government, wishing to honor him, offered him the governorship of the island of St. Lucia, but he declined it.

REFERENCES

Bigelow, John, *Jamaica in 1850*, p. 24. New York, 1851.

Thome, J. A., and Kimball, J. H., *Emancipation in the West Indies*, pp. 104--105. New York, 1838.

Griffey, William Almon, *A Bibliography of Richard Hill: Negro Scholar, Scientist, Native of Spanishtown, Jamaica*, pp. 220–224. Metuchen, N.J., 1932.

Cundall, F., "Supplementary Bibliography of Richard Hill." *The American Book Collector*, pp. 46–48 (January, 1933).

ADDITIONAL REFERENCES

Gosse, Philip Henry, and Hill, Richard, *A Naturalist's Sojourn in Jamaica*. London, Longman, Brwn Green and Longmans, 1851.

Hill, Richard, *Lights and Shadows of Jamaica History*. Kingston, Jamaica, Ford and Gall, 1859.

Mary Seacole

MRS. MARY SEACOLE, heroine of the Crimean War, and one of the most adventurous and true-hearted women of her times, was born in Kingston, Jamaica, of a Scottish army officer and a Negro woman who kept a boarding house principally for army officers.

Growing up among officers, she was so fascinated by military life that she hardly felt at home in any other environment. Add to this the fact that she was a born nurse with a most compassionate heart and a love for travel and you have one who is destined to be "an angel of the battlefield." She wrote in later life, "I am not ashamed to confess—for the gratification is after all a selfish one—that I love to be of service to those who need a woman's help. And whenever the need arises, in whatever distant shore, I ask no greater privilege than to minister to it."

As a child she nursed the cats and dogs of her neighborhood. When she grew older she extended this care to human beings, and in time became known as "The Yellow Doctress."

At twelve she was sent to England and returned years later, her views on life considerably broadened and her desire to be a nurse as great as ever. In later life she wrote of this, "I had from early youth a yearning for medical knowledge and practice which has never deserted me." With no medical college available, she took lessons from the doctors at the hospital and in the army; thus in the great cholera outbreak on the island in 1852 she was able to be of very great service. In the meantime, she married a man named Seacole, who was sickly and who died soon after the marriage.

From Jamaica she went to Panama, where cholera was also raging. Fearless of danger, she went everywhere, dispensing her own remedy, which proved so effective that she became the heroine of the city, even of the prejudiced white Americans there.

At a Fourth of July banquet given by the Americans she was the guest of honor. One of them, in toasting her, regretted that she had not been born white and laughingly suggested that she should be bleached to make her so. He added, "Well, gentlemen, I expect that there are only two things we are vexed for. The first is that she ain't one of us, a citizen of the great United States, and the other is that Providence made her a yellow woman. Gentlemen, let's drink to the health of Aunty Seacole."

Mrs. Seacole replied, "I must say that I don't altogether appreciate your friendly kind wishes with regard to my complexion. If it had been dark as any Negro's I should have been just as happy and useful, and as much respected by those whose respect I value, and as to the offer of bleaching me, I should, even if it were practicable, decline it without any thanks. As to the society which the process might gain me admission into, all I can say is, that judging from the specimens I have met here and elsewhere, I don't think I shall lose much in being excluded from it. So, gentlemen, I drink to you and the general reformation of American manners."

Returning to Jamaica, she was of great service there in the yellow fever outbreak of 1853. In 1854 the Crimean War, with England, France, and Turkey against Russia, broke out and she decided to go there.

Going to England, she offered her services to the War Office but she was rebuffed. The battlefields were no place for a woman, it was felt, and the great Florence Nightingale and her nurses were also being strongly rejected. The army finally yielded in the case of Miss Nightingale but continued adamant against Mrs. Seacole. She tried the War Office, the Quartermaster General, the managers of the Crimean War Fund, and Miss Nightingale's own organization, but all turned her down.

In vain she presented a letter of strong recommendation from a retired army officer, which seemed to indicate that she was better qualified for nursing in the diseased Crimean area than any of the English nurses. This letter said, in part:

I have had many opportunities of witnessing her professional zeal and ability in the treatment of aggravated forms of tropical diseases.

I am, myself, personally much indebted for her indefatigable kindness and skill at a time when I am apt to believe the advice of a practitioner qualified in the North would have little availed.

Her peculiar fitness, in a constitutional point of view, for the duties of a medical attendant, needs no comment.

At the time cholera was raging among the troops in the Crimea and Mrs. Seacole probably knew as much about its cure as any doctor of her times.

Almost heartbroken at the wall of prejudice facing her, she wrote:

Was it possible that American prejudices against color had some root over here? Did those ladies shrink from accepting my aid because my blood flowed beneath a somewhat duskier skin than theirs? Tears streamed down my foolish cheeks as I stood in the fast thinning streets; tears of grief that any should doubt my motives—that Heaven should deny me the opportunity that I sought. Then I stood still, and looking upward through and through the dark clouds that shadowed London prayed aloud for help.

Then an idea came to her. If she could not enlist as a nurse, she would go as a sutler, one who followed the army selling liquor and provisions to the men. Her mother had kept a boarding house for officers. She would go to the front and do the same. At once she had cards printed:

British Hotel

Mrs. Mary Seacole (late of Kingston, Jamaica), respectfully announces to her former friends and to the officers of the Army and Navy generally that she has taken passage on the screw steamer, Hollander; and that she declares her intention to start a rest and nursing home.

Her entire capital for this bold scheme was only the equivalent of $4000. Of this plan, she writes:

> Heaven knows, it was visionary enough. I had no friends who could help me in such a project, nay, who would understand why I desired to go and what I desired to do when I got there. My funds, although they might, carefully handled, carry me over the three thousand miles and land me at Balaclava would not support me there long; what to persuade the public that an unknown Creole woman would be useful to their army from Sebastopol was improbable an achievement to be thought of for an instant.

Investing her little capital in supplies, she left England and after many difficulties reached the port of Scutari in Turkey, where she met the noble Florence Nightingale and then pushed on to the front where the most terrible conditions prevailed. Men were dying like flies from disease, neglect, and gross mismanagement. Both the British and the French commanders, Lord Raglan and St. Arnaud, while very brave, were incompetent. Cholera and dysentery were masters of the battlefield. W. H. Russell, war correspondent of the London *Times*, painted a most heartrending picture of the scene. Of the hospital, he said, "It was a charnelhouse—a sight enough to drive one mad—a stench, a scene of horrors which sickened me." Calthorpe said, too, "The field of battle is a dreadful sight but the hospitals far more terrible."

Mrs. Seacole, without waiting for the arrival of Miss Nightingale, went into this place of horrors, comforting the men, and with deft, accustomed hands rearranged their bandages. A medical officer, seeing her working thus unauthorized, started to drive her out, but stopping to watch her and noticing her skill, thanked her instead. He said in admiration, "That dame knows her work a jolly sight better than some of the M.D.'s and the K.C.B.'s." At the touch of a woman's hand, the men had grown quieter too.

After great difficulties from overcharging and thieves, Mrs. Seacole finally got her supplies ashore and set up her canteen-hotel-hospital, which was welcomed as a godsend by officers of all ranks. She prepared wholesome food for them and nursed the sick and wounded, one of whom was Count Gleichen, Queen Victoria's nephew. Aiding her was her daughter Sally.

She did not stop there, however. Out on the battlefields she went amid flying shot and shell to aid the wounded. On one occasion while probing in a man's mouth for a bullet that had lodged there, he died, closing his jaw on her thumb and dislocating it. She gave her services and supplies free to those who could not pay. Officers and men loved her and called her "Mother Seacole."

Expecially noteworthy were her services to the labor battalions. Inspector-General of Hospitals Sir John Hall in a letter from Headquarters Camp, Crimea, dated June 20, 1856, said:

I have much pleasure in bearing testimony to Mrs. Seacole's kindness and attention to the sick of the Railway Labourers' Army Work Corps and Land Transports Corps during the winter of 1854 and 1855. She not only [nursed], from the knowledge she had acquired in the West Indies, but, what was of as much or more importance she charitably furnished them with proper nourishment which they had no means of obtaining except in the hospital and most of that class had an objection to go to the hospital, particularly the Railway labourers and the men of the Army Works Corps.

W. H. Russell, the London *Times'* war correspondent, wrote of her:

In their hour of their illness, these men in common with many others, have found a kind and successful physician. Close to the railway, halfway between Balaclava and Radikoi, Mrs. Seacole, formerly of Kingston, Jamaica, and of several parts of the world such as Panama and Chagres has pitched her abode—an iron storehouse with wooden sheds and outlying tributaries—and here she doctors and cures all manner of men with extraordinary success. She is always in attendance on the battlefields to aid the wounded and has earned many a poor fellow's blessing. . . . I have seen her go down under fire, with her little store of creature comforts for our wounded men and a more tender or skilful hand about a wound or a broken limb could not be found among our best surgeons. I saw her at the assault on the Redan, at the Tehernava, at the fall of Sebastopol, laden, not with plunder, good old soul! but with wine, bandages and food for the wounded or the prisoners.

When Sebastopol fell after a long siege, she was not only the first woman to enter it but the first to do so with succor for the besieged. She wrote, "For weeks past I had been offering bets to everyone I would not only be the first woman to enter Sebastopol from the English lines but that I would be the first to carry refreshments into the fallen city."

She remained in the Crimea until sometime after the war, having stood the hardships better than Florence Nightingale, who had been ordered home because of illness. Tenderhearted as she was, Mrs. Seacole seems to have felt some nostalgia that the war was over and with it her adventures. Her comment on victory was, "It was something like right that we said the play was fairly over, that peace had rung the curtain down, and that we, humble actors in some of its most stirring scenes, must seek engagement elsewhere."

In 1857 she returned to England, penniless, wounded, and sick. She wrote:

Let me in a few words, if possible state the results of my Crimean campaign. To be sure I returned from it shaken in health. I came home wounded, as many others did. Few constitutions, indeed, were the better for those winters before Sebastopol and I was too hard worked not to feel their effects, for a little labour fatigues me now— I cannot watch by sick beds as I could—a week's want of rest knocks me up now. Then I returned bankrupt in fortune. Whereas many in my position may have come back to England rich and prosperous, I found myself, poor, beggared. . . . So few words can tell what I have lost.

How different had she been from the other sutlers, or canteen owners! Russell wrote of them, "They are a wealthy race, these social vultures—many of them king vultures, respectable birds of prey—with kempt plumage and decent demeanour."

But Mrs. Seacole had gained more than money. She had won the love and respect of the English people. Considerable feeling arose against those whose prejudices had prevented her official enlistment in her errand of mercy. *Punch*, noted London weekly, wrote a poem about her and linked her name with Florence Nightingale's. And when it was known that she had no money, noble and grateful hearts rose to respond. A public subscription was started to reimburse her.

Heading it were some of the biggest names in England who had seen her devotion and sacrifices on the battlefield. They were: Major-General Lord Rokeby; Prince Edward of Saxe-Weimar; the Duke of Wellington; the Duke of Newcastle; Rear-Admiral Sir Stephen Lushington; Major F. Rea; and Sir William Howard Russell, the *Times* war correspondent.

Her autobiography, published in 1857 by a leading London firm, had an extensive sale. It was dedicated by permission to Major-General Lord Rokeby.

In the introduction of this book Russell wrote:

I should have thought that no preface would have been required to introduce Mrs. Seacole to the British public, or to recommend a book which must from the circumstances in which the subject of it was placed, be unique in literature.

If singleness of heart, true charity, and Christian works; if trial and sufferings; dangers and perils; encountered boldly by a helpless woman on her errand of mercy in the camp and on the battlefield, can excite sympathy or move curiosity, Mary Seacole will have many friends and many readers.

She is no Anna Commena who presents us with a verbose history but a plain truth-speaking woman who has lived an adventurous life amid scenes which have never yet found a historian among the actors on the stage.

I have witnessed her devotion and her courage; I have already borne testimony to her services to all who needed them.

She is the first who has redeemed the name of sutler from the suspicion of worthlessness, mercenary baseness and plunder, and I trust that England will not forget the one who nursed her sick and who sought out her wounded to aid and succor them and who performed the last office for some of her illustrious dead.

Alexis Soyer, the renowned chef who went to the Crimea to reform the diet of the soldiers, speaks in magnificent praise of her and gives a picture of her immense good nature, cheerfulness, and generosity.

Mrs. Tom Kelly also wrote:

Mother Seacole set up her store-dispensary hospital and became historic by right of good deeds, which is almost the rarest claim . . .

even in an enlightened century Mother Seascole stands out preeminent and cannot be passed over. She had the secret recipe for cholera and dysentery and liberally dispensed the specific, alike to those who could pay and those who could not. It was bestowed with an amount of personal kindness, which though not an item of the original prescription, she evidently deemed essential to the cure and innumerable sufferers had cause to be grateful for the "sovereign'st thing of earth" for their ills as well as for her "gentle deeds of mercy."

Here are some excerpts from Mrs. Seacole's autobiography:
On the Christian life:

I have stood by receiving the last blessings of a Christian; and closing the eyes of those who had nothing to trust to but the mercy of God who will be far more merciful to us than we are to one another, and I say decidedly that the Christian's death is as glorious as is his life. You can never find a good man who is not a worker; he is no laggard in the race of life.

On color prejudice, deploring the tendency of white Americans to bully colored peoples, she says:

Against the Negroes, of whom there were many in the Isthmus, and who almost invariably filled the municipal offices and took the lead in every field, the Yankee had a strong prejudice; but it was wonderful to see how freedom and equality elevate men and the same Negro, who perhaps in Tennessee would have cowered like a beaten child or dog beneath the American's uplifted hand, would face him boldly here, and by equal courage and superior physical strength cow his oppressor.

Of the coldness and hostility she sometimes met in the streets of London while traveling as a child with her Negro servant, Francis, she said, "I am only a few shades duskier than the brunettes whom you all admire."

On what she saw in Greece:

Some people, indeed, have called me quite a female Ulysses. I believe they intended it as a compliment but from my experience of the Greeks, I do not consider it a very flattering one.

On money:

I have never thought exclusively of money, believing rather that we were born to be happy and that the surest way to be wretched is to prize it overmuch.

Mrs. Seacole returned to Jamaica and died there in 1881. Few women had faced death in all its forms more than she: from cholera, yellow fever, shipwreck, and on the battlefield. In 1843 she nearly lost her life in the great fire of Kingston which burned down her home; and in Panama she narrowly escaped being stabbed by a thief; in the Crimea a flood swept away a quantity of her supplies and herself, but fortunately she was a good swimmer. Her whole life was one long battle with death.

In any list of the world's great women Mrs. Seacole's name is today conspicuous by its absence. But in the days to come when worship of a white skin shall be no more and human worth, regardless of color, shall be the standard of value, she will find a place in the list of those worthy to be held up as a model for all time.

REFERENCES

A copy of Mrs. Seacole's book is in the British Museum and another in the Jamaica Institute.

Punch's poem to her was of six verses of which the following are the last three:

> She gave her aid to all who prayed
> To hungry and sick and cold
> Open hands and heart alike ready to part
> Kind words, and acts, and gold.
> And—be the right man in the right place who can
> The right woman was Dame Seacole.

The Jamaica Institute also has a bust of her by Count Gleichen, nephew of Queen Victoria, and two of her Crimean War medals.

Seacole, Mary, *Wonderful Adventures of Mary Seacole in Many Lands*. London, J. Blackwood, 1857.

Russell, W. H., *Letters from the Battlefield*, Vol. II, p. 187.

Kelly, Mrs. Tom, *From the Fleet in the Fifties*, pp. 161–162. 1902.

Soyer, Alexis, *Culinary Campaign*, pp. 231–234, 269. 1857.

Morris, Helen, *Portrait of a Chef*, pp. 165–169, 202. 1939. (This book has a picture of Mrs. Seacole in her canteen.)

Antonio Maceo

"THE LION, THE CENTAUR, THE INVINCIBLE"
(1848–1896)

ANTONIO MACEO was the last of the spectacular patriots of history. With his horsemanship, whole-souled vivacity, and daring in the face of tremendous odds, he attracted worldwide attention. On that December morning of 1896 when the news came that he had been treacherously slain, indignation and profound regret filled the hearts of lovers of liberty and justice the world over. No one since, fighting in freedom's cause, so captivated the world's imagination as Maceo.

Maceo was born in the province of Santiago de Cuba in 1848, of a mulatto father, Marco Maceo, and a black ex-slave mother, Marianna Grajale. Very poor, he began as a driver of oxen on a sugar plantation and was not able to read or write until he was twenty years old. When the first Cuban insurrection broke out in 1868, he was the first to join. When it failed, ten years later, he was the last to yield.

During this war he did something characteristic of him. As a boy on the plantation of Don Leandro he had seen the latter order his slave driver to strip a female slave to the waist and then had her so brutally beaten that she died.

One of his first acts, when he had an armed band, was to go to Don Leandro's mansion and punish him in the same way.

Maceo's skill as a leader soon won him promotion to a generalship. When the Ten Years' War, as the first revolt was known, came to an end, he held out in the eastern provinces for months, creating terror among the Spaniards by his daring raids. Several times he was surrounded, but when called on to surrender, he would give the order to charge. "That's the way brave men surrender," he would say.

When the Spanish commander offered him money and a high position to yield, he replied with scorn, "Those who, like me, fight for the sacred cause of liberty, will break their weapons when they are not strong to win."

Resolutely refusing to accept any compromise or treaty with Spain, he left for Jamaica. For the next seventeen years he became a roaming agitator for independence, visiting Mexico, Costa Rica, the United States, and Spanish Honduras, making friends, studying languages and military tactics, and reading the best literature in his spare moments. Finally, with the fever of Cuban independence burning in his blood, he returned to his native land. Starting another insurrection, he was captured and imprisoned, but escaping, he fled to New York.

In 1894, while leaving a theatre in New York, a Spaniard fired a bullet into his back. It could not be extracted and remained there until his death. In New York he succeeded in getting money, arms, and ammunition, and left for Cuba. Spanish spies, learning that he was going to make a dash for the Bahamas, offered the captain of the ship $25,000 to steer toward a Spanish warship.

Maceo discovered the plot, and forced the captain to land him in Cuba. Before leaving the ship, he tied the captain and his two accomplices to the mast, stove in the brig, and shot the three traitors to death.

In Cuba he found that the revolt started by José Martin and General Gomez was languishing. Springing into action, he pledged that in three months he would make his way across the island and strike against the Spaniards at Havana.

With his followers on hardy Cuban ponies and with no impediments but their rifles, machetes, and cartridges, he began a vigorous onslaught, driving the enemy before him, burning plantations and spreading destruction.

Spain, in alarm, sent out her ablest commander, Field Marshal Campos, with 10,000 additional men. Campos had tremendous prestige as a fighter and a statesman. He had subdued the first Cuban revolt. In Spain he was known as "the king-maker" because he had returned the Bourbons to the throne.

Undaunted, Maceo's raiders swept over Puerto Principe, across the *trochas*, past the rich and fertile provinces of Santa Clara and Matanzas, dodging past the Spanish columns, dashing at outposts, burning plantations, destroying mills, laying waste every field and crop, blowing up railways, cutting telegraph lines, punishing and blackmailing the loyalists, terrorizing the rural population, and spreading alarm even in garrison towns.

At last he met the brave old Marshal Campos, and Maceo outmaneuvered him so completely that the Spanish king-maker had only just time to return by sea to Havana before Maceo himself appeared close to the capital of the island, carrying fire and sword into the wealthiest and the most loyal territory of Cuba.

One after the other he defeated Spain's best generals—Cledes, Lugue, Cornell, Echague, Deods. Campos was recalled and Weyler, known as "Butcher Weyler," was sent in his place.

Weyler, finding that force was unsuccessful, tried to stir up color dissension. A majority of the Cuban insurgents were Negroes. Maceo's men were nearly all blacks. As Franc Woodward, an American newspaper correspondent, said, "The party of General Maceo is spoken of as the black party. It is composed exclusively of the darker-complexioned Cubans, although there are many white officers."

Knowing that there was ill-feeling between mulatto and blacks, Weyler tried to get the blacks to desert to him, offering them full equality with the whites and high government posts. They rejected his offer with scorn. Weyler and his 200,000 men had no better luck against Maceo's 20,000. As a last resort, Weyler built wide fortifications of barbed wire, cement, and bombs, known as *trochas*, across the island from coast to coast.

But Maceo had pledged to lead his men into Havana, *trocha* or no *trocha*. He not only crossed the most formidable one, that defending the capital, but with only 500 men drove on to Havana, which was garrisoned by a force a hundred times stronger than his. This extremely brave but foolhardy attack was to cost him his life. On December 7 he encountered a greatly superior body of the enemy and with his usual daring ordered his men to attack. Scorning danger, he himself went openly along the lines, directing the fire. A ball struck him in the neck and he fell, mortally wounded.

His men fell back. The Spaniards came up. A bugler stooped over him, and seeing the diamond ring on his finger, reached out for it. The dying Maceo asked feebly, "Cuban or Spaniard?"

"Spaniard," said the bugler, plunging his machete into Maceo's throat. Maceo's last words were, "Long live Cuba."

That Maceo was betrayed to the Spaniards by his own physician, Zertuchas, was popularly believed. The latter was said to have led him into an ambush for a price. He alone escaped and was later found safe behind the Spanish lines while every one of Maceo's men with him at the time was killed or wounded.

Maceo's body was later recovered by his men. The news of his death, telegraphed to Spain, caused great rejoicing there. Well it might, for thereafter the struggle lagged until the American intervention. Dr. Willard S. Bowen, correspondent of the *New York World*, wrote from Havana, "The town is filled with Spanish soldiers. They have nothing to do since the death of Maceo."

Charles E. Chapman considers Maceo the greatest of all the Cuban leaders. Gomez, head of the Cuban army, he says, "showed great military abilities in his conduct of affairs but the skill and courage of Maceo were so astonishingly great as to capture the attention of the entire world."

Cummings compares Maceo to Sheridan and Stonewall Jackson. He says:

He was as swift on the march as either Sheridan or Stonewall Jackson, and equally prudent and wary. He had flashes of military genius when a crisis arose. No one has ever questioned his patriotism. Money could not buy him; promises could not deceive him. His devotion to Cuban freedom was like the devotion of a father to his family. All his energies, physical and intellectual, were given freely to his country.

In his *Life of Maceo* Lucciardi declares that while he does not wish "to discredit the bravery" of General Gomez, "Maceo merited the title of general-in-chief as a right because he was the real soul of the revolution."

"Of all its heroes," he says, "none can be compared with him. He consecrated his life to the triumph of the idea of independence, and he fell gloriously—a victim of ardent patriotism. Maceo knew how to die as did the heroes of old."

The sincerity of Maceo's patriotism is perhaps best illustrated by the fact that although he was heralded by the press of the world as the leading figure of the revolution, he did not seek supreme command.

When a friend of his once said to him, "You are by right the general-in-chief. You are not only the leading spirit, but you were the last to surrender in the last war," Maceo replied, "My sword can never compete with that of General Maximo Gomez." When the Spanish press charged that he was trying to establish a black republic, Maceo retorted, "I am neither black nor white. I am a Cuban." He knew that it would be fatal to his cause, especially in the United States, if ever the Cuban revolution became known as a black insurrection against white people. At bottom, it really was, however, since most of the oppressors were white. (Later, when independence was won, the Cuban Negroes had to stage a great revolt to win a measure of liberty from their white and near-white compatriots.)

One editor who knew Maceo well, said of him:

He was always of the sunniest disposition, closely attaching all people to him—a man of the strictest moral integrity. He never drank wine, he never smoked and that in a land where tobacco is as common as potatoes in Ireland, and he never played cards.

In Havana, he was always dressed in the most finished style. His massive frame—he was about five feet ten in height, and unusually broad shouldered—was displayed to advantage in frock coat, closely-buttoned, and he usually wore a silk hat. Among his men he dressed as one of them.

On the spot where he fell at Punta Bravura, fifteen miles from Havana, a splendid mausoleum stands in his memory.

REFERENCES

General Gomez, the white leader, and the first President of Cuba, was also of Negro descent, according to Sir Harry Johnston. Gomez was a native of Santo Domingo. (*Negro in the New World*, p. 51. 1910.)

Hernandez, E., "La Personalidad de Antonio Maceo," in *Acad. Naci. de Artes y Letras*, Vol. XV, pp. 92–207. 1920.

Cabrales, Gonzalo, ed., *Epistalario de Heroes*. Havana, El Siglo, 1922.

Chapman, C. E., *History of the Cuban Republic*. New York, 1927.

Rubens, H. S., *Liberty—The Story of Cuba*. New York, 1932.

Argenter, J. M., *Antonio Maceo*. Vera Cruz, 1896.

Lucciardi, E., *Un Héro Révolutionnaire*. 1902.

Collado Diaz, L., "En el Centerario de Maceo." *Ejercito Revisita Official*, July-September, 1945.

ADDITIONAL REFERENCES

Adams, Margaret J., "Antonio Maceo." *Negro History Bulletin*, p. 83 (January, 1941), Association for the Study of Negro Life and History, Washington, D.C.

Cabrera, Luis Rolando, *El Centenario de Maceo*. Havana, Molina y Compania, 1945.

Carbonell y Rivero, Nestor, . . . *Proceres: Ensayos Biograficos*, pp. 163–168. Havana, Montalvo y Cardenas, 1928.

Carbonell y Rivero, Miguel Angel, . . . *Antonio Maceo*. Havana, Imprenta "La Prueba," 1924.

Cortina, José Manuel, *Antonio Maceo: Discurso Pronunciado in la Extraordinaria de la Camara*. Havana, Imprenta de A. Miranda, 1916.

Costa, Octavio Ramon, . . . *Antonio Maceo, El Heroe*. Havana, Imprenta "El Siglo XX," 1947.

Estenger, Rafael, ed., *Homenaje a Maceo*. Havana, Editorial Selecta, 1945.

Fergusson, Erna, *Cuba*, pp. 165–177. New York, A. A. Knopf, 1946.

Fleming, B. J., and Pryde, M. J., *Distinguished Negroes Abroad*, p. 218. Washington, D.C., The Associated Publishers, 1946.

Frealing, Pearl Adams, "Antonio Maceo." *Negro History Bulletin*, pp. 123–124, 143 (March, 1944), Association for the Study of Negro Life and History, Washington, D.C.

Horrego Estuch, Leopoldo, . . . *Maceo, Estudio Politico y Patriotico*. Havana, Imprenta "El Siglo XX," 1947.

Jerez Villarreal, Juan, *Hierro y Marfil*, pp. 29–39. Havana, Carasa y Cia., Impresores, 1930.

Maceo, Antonio, . . . *Cartas Ineditas del General Antonio Maceo con Una Introduccion por el Dr. Alfredo Zay.* Havana, Imprenta La Mercantil, 1916.

Miro y Argenter, José Ignacio, *Muerte del General Antonio Maceo.* Havana, Rufino Hernando Liberia, 1897.

————, *Apuntes de la Vida de Antonio Maceo Grajales.* Veracruz, Tip. de "Las Selvas," 1897.

Piedra Martel, Manuel, *Compansas de Maceo en la Ultima Guerra de Independencia.* Havana, Editorial Lex, 1946.

Rodriquez Morejon, Gerardo, . . . *Maceo, Heroe y Candillo.* Havana, Cultural SA La Habana, 1943.

Sanguily y Garritte, Manuel, *Defensa de Cuba,* pp. 59–69. Havana, Oficina del Historiador de la Ciudad, Municipio de la Habana, 1948.

Santovenia y Echaide, Enterterio Santiago, . . . *Maceo Palabras Preliminares de Joaquin Martinez Saenz.* Havana, Buro de Publicidad y Servicio social de ABC, La Habana, 1940.

Woodson, Carter G., "Antonio Maceo." *Negro History Bulletin,* p. 4 (December, 1937), Association for the Study of Negro Life and History, Washington, D.C.

Ulises Heureaux

IRON-FISTED DICTATOR OF SANTO DOMINGO
(1845–1900)

AMONG THE MANY colorful tyrants ruling in the republics of Central and South America, none was more fascinating than Ulises Heureaux, dictator of Santo Domingo, affectionately known as "Lilis."

A rare combination of astuteness and audacity; ability and unscrupulousness; ferocity and kindliness; ambition and disinterestedness, Heureaux guided the destinies of his country with an iron hand in a velvet glove. Like the Romans of old, he spared neither friend nor foe and killed both "with the greatest respect."

With an unbroken stream of lead, he restored order among his turbulent countrymen and maintained peace for twenty years—a record. In the twenty-one years preceding him there had been twenty-four presidents and twenty-six revolutions.

Santo Domingo, Columbus' favorite colony, after long prosperity had been reduced to chaos and bankruptcy in 1865 by the long wars with Spain and the adjoining republic of Haiti. Hordes of adventurers, wholly disinclined to pursue commerce or agriculture, pillaged the republic. Ambitious and domineering leaders, whose passions ran riot, murdered their opponents, only to be assassinated in turn. At last the Dominicanos sought relief by attempting to join the United States, but the proposal was defeated in the American Senate. Heureaux came on the scene at this point.

Born in 1845, the illegitimate son of a Haitian merchant, Heureaux was first employed in his father's store, but finding this life too drab, he joined the insurgent forces who were attempting to oust the Spaniards. He did so well that at the age of eighteen he was appointed a general. Generals in the Dominican Army were quite as numerous as colonels in Kentucky, but Heureaux deserved his promotion. He was really brave and his valor was conspicuous. For instance, he enjoyed letting himself be surrounded by a band of Spaniards and then hacking and shooting his way out with pistol and machete on horseback.

After the defeat of the Spaniards Heureaux returned to his father's shop but soon deployed to the Haitian border where he became a horse thief on a large scale. Following a boundary dispute between the two republics Heureaux was given a minor post in the customs service, but love of excitement took him into politics—the best field for ambition that his country had to offer.

Almost illiterate but endowed to an extraordinary degree with that suavity, flourish, and manner so dear to the Latin heart, as well as with good looks, he soon became a prominent figure. At that time there were three parties: the Blues, led by General Luperon: the Reds, by General Baez; and the Greens, by General Gonzalez. Colors were employed since political issues were lacking, and under these colors the candidates would spout forth all the burning platitudes about liberty, patriotism, and the rights of man that one hears in more advanced lands. The loudest demagogue had, as in more civilized lands, the masses with him. Also, in order to get on the bandwagon, prominent leaders would shift their allegiances overnight. Opportunism was the order of the day; treachery and murder were its handmaidens.

Heureaux supported Luperon and aided him in defeating two presidents. But he did not take his allegiance seriously, and when Luperon attempted to seize power for a third term, he found his flashy subordinate barring the way, and was forced to step aside in his favor.

Affable, generous, corrupt, but exacting and firm, Heureaux soon became the idol of the masses—and to a great extent, of those who longed for peace. One of his first acts was to change the constitution so as to make himself an absolute monarch in all but name—a trick of present-day dictators. His next step was to rid the country of a swarm of presidential aspirants. Some were bought with lucrative sinecures, open bribes, or plain flattery. Irreconcilables were shot, often without the semblance of a trial.

One of the latter was General Marcheno, once his most trusted friend. In 1892 and 1894 Marcheno had negotiated loans totaling $7,000,000 from certain European powers. Heureaux disposed of this sum in short order, his private account and that of the republic being one. After Marcheno was defeated for the presidency, Heureaux, suspecting him of treachery, promptly had him shot. Heureaux' patriotic pose on this occasion surpassed that of Brutus. He gave Marcheno a magnificent funeral, marched in the procession as chief mourner, and shedding real tears, declared that the republic had lost one of her ablest sons, and he, his best friend.

He had his own brother-in-law killed with shocking cold-bloodedness. Heureaux invited him to the National Palace, entertained him regally, and at the close of the dinner asked his guest how he liked the meal.

"Finest I have ever had, Señor El Presidente," said his relative.

"Glad you liked it for it's your last," remarked El Presidente, adding in his genial way, "Won't you have some more liqueur and another cigar?"

Then Heureaux coldly revealed details of a plot in which his brother-in-law was implicated, ordered him out into the courtyard, and had him shot without further ado.

Heureaux was at his best in playing his opponents against each other. When he found out that his Minister of War, General Ramon Castillo, was planning to join with General José Estay, Governor of the province of Macoris, in a plot against him, Heureaux sent his agents to start trouble between the two, and they did so well that before long Estay took a potshot at Castillo, missing him, however, and killing a child instead. Civil strife followed, and Heureaux summoned both to appear before him.

Estay obeyed immediately, but Castillo hesitated for weeks. Finally Heureaux sent him word that Estay was being held a prisoner and asked him to come and file charges against him.

Heureaux meant to kill both, and told Estay, in the meantime, to pretend that he was a prisoner so that Castillo would walk into the trap. Estay readily consented and entered a cell. The next scene of the grim farce was enacted when Castillo arrived. Heureaux received him at the palace with an exquisite bow of solicitude, and announced his intention of shooting Estay. Asking his guest whom he recommended for Estay's post, and for the positions held by Estay's friends, Castillo, naturally, named his fellow plotters. Heureaux, writing down their names as if they were already as good as appointed, said, "Come to the Ministry of War at three this afternoon to lodge your complaint against Estay. He hasn't long to live."

Castillo arrived promptly at three and was received with music and full military honors. He was taken to the cell where Estay lay shackled. Soon the two enemies were screaming recriminations at each other to the secret delight of Heureaux. Castillo, pounding the table angrily, shouted, "I want you to know that I'm here to ask questions, not to answer them." At this Heureaux winked approvingly as if to say, "That's the way to talk to him."

Estay, voluntarily in chains, thought the wink was meant for him, and became even more convincing in his act, especially when Heureaux kept his promise to him and ordered the guards to shackle Castillo and toss him into another cell. Estay now expected to be released but the smiling Heureaux bade him be patient a little longer as the denouement was near. "Soon," he said, "you will witness our final joke on Castillo."

Two days later when Heureaux had rounded up all of Castillo's friends, he ordered that the two prisoners be taken to Fort La Punta. They arrived on a gunboat, and when midnight came, were manacled and led into the courtyard where Heureaux awaited them. Castillo was placed against the wall, an execution squad marched up, took aim, fired, and he was dead.

Estay, thinking that the comedy was over, cried out approvingly, "That's the way to treat him, Señor El Presidente."

Estay had hardly spoken when Heureaux, in his politiest tone, said, "Your turn next, señor." The firing squad, swinging about, shot him dead too.

But the farce was not yet over. Heureaux, in full view of all, knelt in the moonlight, and raising his voice to the heavens, theatrically lamented, "Hear me, oh God, in this horrible nightmare in which I see my friends for the last time: I did this for Santo Domingo, our beloved country, and I call upon you as a witness." Straightening out the crumpled, blood-stained lapel of Castillo's coat, he wailed, "Oh, my poor friend. You were looking for it and now you got it."

On another occasion, hearing that one of his own staff was plotting against him, Heureaux invited him to his palace, wined and dined him admirably, and then invited him for a horseback ride. Presently they came to a spot where laborers were shoveling dirt. Heureaux reined his horse as if in great curiosity, whereupon his guest asked, "What are they doing there?"

"Strange you should ask," answered Heureaux airily. "That's your grave." The man was executed on the spot and flung into his waiting grave.

Many of Heureaux' prisoners disappeared mysteriously. It was generally said that they were shot at night on the lower floor of Fort La Fuerza, and handily tossed into the sea to be devoured by sharks.

Some of his opponents who fled abroad were executed. Among them was Eugenio Deschamps, a journalist who was shot dead on the streets of Port-au-Prince.

Iron discipline was maintained in the army and in Heureaux' little navy. Deserters were sent in groups of twos and threes to be publicly executed in the squares of the leading towns as a lesson.

Heureaux was adept at diplomacy and often used it to win over his foes. Arriving in the town of La Vega on one occasion, he noticed preparations for some festivity being made in the adjoining home. Upon inquiry, he learned the daughter of General Lozano was to be married. Lozano was the chief supporter of General Moya, Heureaux' chief opponent.

As Heureaux watched from his balcony, he saw an elderly woman ride up on a spirited silver-gray horse, together with her escort. Learning that it was the mother of the bride, he called his aide-de-camp, General Losoi, and said, "Fetch me a man capable of committing any crime from theft to murder."

When the desperado arrived, Heureaux instructed him: "Take Señora Lozano's horse and hide him where even the mosquitoes can't find him."

The next morning when the señora and her party were about to leave, her horse was gone, and no suitable mount could be found for her. Her husband was waiting impatiently for her in the next town. Then Heureaux rode up, dismounted, and with a sweeping bow, presented his own superb black horse and grandiloquently informed her that henceforth it was hers. The señora demurred, but finally accepted. She was immensely pleased with the animal and impressed by Heureaux' gallantry. To her husband she effused, "You see how friendly the president feels toward you." A few days later Heureaux was a guest at the Lozano mansion, and General Moya's movement, losing its chief supporter, collapsed.

Heureaux' resourcefulness was equal to every occasion. One day he was disturbed by the noise of a mob under his office windows and learned that it was the bakers, shoemakers, carpenters, and other craftsmen who had come to complain against their masters. Declaring that it was a plot of one of his enemies, Heureaux refused to address the crowd. Labor strikes, he insisted, had nothing to do with his government. Finally he was persuaded to speak a few words. Stepping out on the balcony, he raised his hand for silence and said, "Gentlemen, I pledge you that all of your just demands will be granted." Then he turned to General Lolo, his Minister of Police, who was in the courtyard below, and shouted, "Take down the names of all the bachelors."

There was an instant hubbub. Why only the bachelors? A whisper ran thruugh the assembly and in an instant it dispersed. (In Santo Domingo the majority of the unions between the sexes were common-law ones, and 60 percent of all births were illegitimate. Heureaux rightly divined that the majority of the strikers were "living in sin," and knew that they feared that their names might be published.)

Heureaux generally proved more than a match for Europeans, to whom he either owed money or had sold concessions, and who sometimes demanded excessive indemnities for real or fancied insults. Much of the financial trouble of the republic was due to the last cause. Once a Danish merchant demanded $10,000 for alleged violation of contract. When told by his consul that he would be fortunate to get $40, he readily agreed to settle for that sum.

Heureaux sidestepped all demands, just and unjust. When the Dutch firm of Westendorf sent a mountain of a man named Den Tex Bond from Amsterdam to collect a debt, Heureaux evaded the huge Hollander until the latter cornered him one day. Heureaux listened politely, and then running his fingers over the beefy shoulders and vast girth of Bond, asked nonchalantly, "Tell me, Señor Den Tex, how much do you think your government would want for a corpse the size of yours?" The Dutchman left on the next boat.

The story of how he tricked Spain and aided Cuba in her fight for independence is a classic in Latin America. When the Cubans sent a delegation to ask his aid in their struggle for freedom, Heureaux received its members publicly and pompously announced that as the head of a neutral state, he could do nothing. "Cuba," he said, "is my mistress, but Spain is my wife." After the meeting was over, he had one of the delegates brought privately to him. "I will give you," he said, "five hundred rifles, fifty thousand cartridges, and two thousand dollars. Remember, this is a gift from Ulises Heureaux. Whatever you do, do not let the President of Santo Domingo hear of it."

When the Spanish consul told him that General Rodriguez, a Cuban agent, was about to leave for Cuba with a shipload of arms and ammunition, Heureaux readily consented to aid in his capture. Warning Rodriguez secretly to leave from another port, Heureaux ordered his men to load another vessel with a shipment of arms and shells; to mark the cases with Rodriguez' initials and "C.L." (Cuba Libre); and to set sail from Rodriguez' original destination. Steaming out in a gunboat with the Spanish consul abroad as a guest, Heureaux then ostentatiously "captured" the planted ship. The Spanish consul sent home a glowing report of the affair, and the queen regent of Spain bestowed on Heureaux the Grand Cross of Isabella la Catolica in recognition of the act, while Marshal Campos, Spanish commander in Cuba, gave him a fine Arab horse. And all the time Rodriguez' weapons were decimating the Spaniards.

Heureaux always had difficulty making ends meet. To keep his hundreds of military chiefs loyal, he was compelled to pay them lavishly. His mistresses were a major item of expense. He had so many that it was commonly said that there was but one town in the republic that could not boast of having one of his sweet-hearts. He bought them gowns of the latest Parisian make and heaped jewels upon them. He did not stint himself either. All his clothes were tailored in Bond Street. Expensive wines, rich banquets, full-blooded horses, gifts to beggars—these were but a few of the many items that kept the national treasury empty.

Unable to get any more foreign loans, he printed inconvertible paper money. To help stabilize his coinage, he clipped all foreign coins that came into the country, thereby reducing the chances of their being taken out.

On one occasion, when harder pressed than usual for money, he confiscated the cash box of a European branch bank doing business in Santo Domingo City. The bank president, to whom he had appealed, had refused to extend any further loans to him. The government of the bank in question sent out an emissary to inquire into this affair. When the envoy, who later became a noted diplomat, arrived with his wife, Heureaux sent a gunboat to escort him into the harbor.

Before the reception committee departed, Heureaux gave his secretary of state, who was in charge, a gorgeous bouquet with a costly necklace wound around the stem, with instructions as following: "When you present this bouquet, watch the faces of Señor X and his wife very closely. If they look pleased, deliver it as is; if not, tell them the necklace was merely intended as a holder for the flowers and bring it back to me."

The bouquet was presented intact, and Heureaux knew the calibre of the man with whom he was to deal. That evening, at a sumptuous dinner, the impeccably-mannered host had no difficulty in settling the affair of the looted bank. Foreign delegates who came to chide him usually softened under his gifts, glibness, and champagne.

Heureaux was so firmly entrenched that other candidates found it hopeless to run against him. One of his opponents correctly summarized the situation, when he said, "My friends, this Republic is founded on the free and unrestricted suffrage of its citizens. It is the boast of the Dominicano that he may vote for whomsoever he pleases. You are therefore free to vote for me, but I certainly would not be your friend if I failed to warn you that those who do not vote for President Heureaux might as well leave the country."

Heureaux, however, was extremely popular with the masses. He captivated women with his grand manner, and returned the compliment by showing deference to old ladies.

While on his way to Santiago one time he heard that two of his generals, Patino and Espaillat, were planning to waylay him and assassinate him. Sending ahead, he had them arrested and promptly sentenced to death by court-martial. The execution was to be carried out that evening.

Upon his arrival at Santiago, he found the town in mourning over the impending death of two of its most popular citizens. A delegation of local Freemasons, headed by the father of one of the condemned men, came to plead with him. Heureaux, gravely polite, informed them that he was a Mason himself, but said that he felt sure that they would agree with him that the welfare of the state transcended that of Masonry. A group of merchants came to intercede, followed by another, consisting of the most beautiful girls of the town. Heureaux praised the beauty of the delegation, uttered charming platitudes about the fair sex, but remained immovable. At last came a tottering old woman— Donna Eloisa Espaillat, mother of condemned General Espaillat. She attempted to throw herself at his feet, but Heureaux caught her, and before she could utter a word, gallantly said, "Señora, I could refuse you nothing. They are free." Everybody was happy, the town made merry, and Heureaux was the hero of the day.

Like all dictators, Heureaux never missed a chance to show his solicitude for the sick. Arriving in Damas village once, he found everyone in deep distress over the sudden illness of the daughter of one of the prominent townsmen, Señor Carite. The doctor had to be fetched from many miles away and had not yet appeared. Heureaux hurried to the house, felt the child's forehead, and noticed that she had a fever. Calling for coconut oil, castor oil, and honey, he mixed these up with a liberal dose of English mustard. Then he rolled up his sleeves and started massaging the child's body with this concoction, using a shoe brush as he continued. Presently the child relaxed. She was dead. To the stupified onlookers, Heureaux, with grave composure, remarked, "*Y que!* If the *muchachita* had not died, you would have seen how a sure-fire remedy works."

Extremely punctilious in matters of etiquette, he never failed to notice breaches committed by others. He had his own method of correcting them. Once in the ante-chamber of his palace he saw one of his lieutenants seated on a chair, lazily tilting it backwards. Calling the man, he sent him to the cabinet maker's to inquire about the price of similar chairs. When he returned and reported the price, Heuraux said, "Since they are so expensive, I know that in the future you will not tilt them against the wall."

What was most disconcerting to his enemies was Heureaux' unruffled urbanity, even under the most aggravating circumstances. For instance, one St. Andrew's Day—when it is the custom for the Dominicanos to indulge in such pranks as dumping buckets of water on pedestrians from upper windows, squirting water at them with syringes, throwing perfumed-filled eggs, and even stones and knives—he was on the way to his office, accompanied as usual by a single attendant, when some young girls up on a balcony emptied a pail of water on him, drenching him from head to foot.

To make matters worse, he had ordered this kind of thing stopped because so many people had been hurt in the past. Heureaux, however, raised his panama hat, politely said, "Thank you, laides," and went on his way as dignified as ever.

When he told his cabinet of the incident, they suggested he use force to enforce his order. Heureaux, perceiving that his order against the fete had failed, was quick to sense the sentiment of the people, and replied, "Gentlemen, one must either tolerate or repress the populace. In the latter case, machine guns are the only effective weapon. If you suggest the latter, I will handle the guns myself, but you recall the last suppression your ordered. People are still wearing mourning because of it. I am for joining in the celebration."

The cabinet agreed, and Heureaux, ordering a large quantity of perfume, was soon in the streets squirting it right and left. St. Andrew's Day that year was the maddest and most enjoyable in the history of the republic.

In spite of innumerable plots and scores of attempts on his life,

Heureaux seemed to bear a charmed life. One conspirator, Jiminez, who received considerable support in the United States, landed on the coast with an expedition and was successful for a time, but was finally vanquished and sought refuge on British soil. Another was Horacio Vasquez, a close friend of Jiminez, who was supported by Ramon Caceres, later president. He proved to be Heureaux' nemesis.

The Vasquez plot spread into the interior at a time when Heureaux was starting thither. Just before he reached the town of Moca, news came that Caceres was planning to waylay him and kill him. Heureaux, arriving there, bade the governor arrest Caceres. But the latter secretly warned Caceres to flee. Knowing that he was a dead man unless he killed Heureaux first, he decided to act.

Heureaux went about town openly without an escort, confident that the conspirators would never dare attack him on the streets. Before leaving Moca, he rode over to the store owned by the provincial treasurer, dismounted, stopped to give a coin to a beggar, and went inside. When he came out, Caceres and his men were there. They opened fire. The first ball struck Heureaux in the chest. Drawing his revolver, he shot. Death filmed his eyes— the bullet went wild, puncturing the heart of the beggar he had aided but a moment before. After pumping his body full of bullets, the conspirators remounted their horses and galloped away.

Heureaux was buried in the cathedral near the tomb of Christopher Columbus. The people mourned for him. At least he had kept peace. The next sixteen years (1900–1916) were disturbed ones. There were thirteen presidents, several of whom were assassinated. Peace was not restored until the American occupation. The Dominican legislature renamed a state Pacificador, thus perpetuating the title that had been conferred upon Heureaux: "Pacificador de la Patria."

Machiavelli said that the art of governing was in knowing how to extract the honey without disturbing the bees. Dessalines said that it was in being able to pluck the chicken without making it squawk. But Heureaux robbed the Dominicanos of even the pin feathers and made many of them like it.

A white American whom Heureaux had aided said, in a eulogy

at the funeral, "He was a Negro, but his methods were white. He had a black skin and a white heart."

Sumner Welles, American Minister to Santo Domingo, gave the following description of Heureaux:

Tall, with splendid carriage, his body was beautifully proportioned, being that admirable welding often found in the African race, of a suave almost feline surface under which there rippled the muscles and sinews of an unusually powerful resilient frame. His physique was . . . untirable and his nerves ever under the most perfect control, due in part, no doubt, to his life-long abstinence from both alcohol and tobacco. His sole weaknesses, if they can be so termed, were those of the savages, his domination by his sexual passions, which were never satiated, and his lust for blood. Courageous in the highest degree, confident in his own powers, astute with native shrewdness, possessed of the innate suspicion of the savage, polished with the veneer of civilization which he had acquired, rapacious, merciless, pitiless, filled with unquenchable daemonic energy he was.

A bon vivant and a pagan at heart, Heureaux always lived in the present. Once a friend of his, interceding for a number of condemned men, asked him, "What will history say of this?" His reply was, "To the devil with history—I won't be there to read it."

REFERENCES

Castro, Victor M. de, *Cosas de Lilis*. Santo Domingo, Imprenta "Cina de America," 1919.

Schoenrick, O., *Santo Domingo*. New York, 1898.

Welles, S., *Naboth's Vineyard*, 2 vols. New York, 1928.

Day, S. de F., *Cruise of the Scythia*. London, 1899.

Cestero, T. M., *La Sangre*. 1913.

ADDITIONAL REFERENCES

Berges Bordas, Gustavo E., . . . *Otras Cosas de Lilis*. Santo Domingo, Imprenta Montanvo, 1921.

Sir Conrad Reeves

CHIEF JUSTICE OF BARBADOS
(1821–1902)

WILLIAM CONRAD REEVES was born at Bridgetown, Barbados, the son of Thomas Reeves, a Negro doctor (according to others, a shoemaker), and a slave named Peggy.

Born with a thirst for knowledge, young Reeves eagerly devoured every morsel of literature he could get on the little island. His guardian, a paternal aunt, sent him to a private school, where he made rapid progress and attracted the attention of Prescod, editor of the leading newspaper, who gave him employment. Reeves learned shorthand, mastered the details of newspaper work, and rose to be managing editor.

He was also the island's leading orator. His friends, recognizing his ability and seeing a brilliant future ahead for him, raised enough money to send him to England to study law. At the Middle Temple in London he was one of the most brilliant students in its history. In 1863 he was admitted to the bar.

On his return he was soon the island's leading lawyer. Later he entered politics, was elected to the legislature, and was appointed solicitor general. In 1876 he came very prominently to public notice when he opposed the governor, Sir John Hennessy, on the question of the constitutional rights of the natives of the island. Hennessy had proposed confederation with the other West India islands, for which he was regarded by some as a benefactor of the masses and by others as an autocrat who was trying to deprive this old colony of Britain of the degree of self-government it had.

In 1878 Sir Conrad was to come even more to public notice. The governor, in an attempt to strengthen the position of the Crown, tried to introduce two additional members into that portion of the legislature appointed by the government, a step that would permit the government to outvote the representatives elected by the people. Sir Conrad opposed this attempt so ably and so vigorously that he stood out more than ever as the leading person on the island. His grateful compatriots held public exercises in his honor and presented him with a purse of a thousand guineas.

Other honors followed. He was named attorney general and later Queen's counsel, one of the highest honors conferred on a British lawyer, and then chief justice. In 1881 he was knighted by Queen Victoria.

His usefulness continued until his death at the age of eighty-one. *National Biography* said of his appointment as chief justice, "The promotion was a rare recognition of worth in a black man and was well-justified in the result."

Sir Conrad's manner, according to general report, was that of the typical British aristocrat of his times, that is, somewhat haughty. Once in an address at Harrison College, with the white governor of the island present, he said, "Here am I on Olympus looking down on you ordinary mortals." This attitude was even more marked in dealing with people of his own color. It is said that he refused to let his daughter marry the leading physician on the island because the latter was too dark. This daughter was later married twice to white men. Professionally, however, he lived up to the best British legal tradition. On the bench he was not influenced by color, one of his greatest merits being his ability to distinguish the common good amid the complex antagonisms of the white, black, and mulatto classes on the island. He was noted also for his clear, well-worded judgments. Some of these were collected by his successor, Sir Thomas Greaves, and published as a model. Small of stature, but full of dignity and rectitude, Sir Conrad is a legal mind worthy to be ranked with the best in the British Empire.

REFERENCES

All, or nearly all, of the chief justices of Barbados have been native whites or near-whites. Sir Conrad, the first black to be one, was the most distinguished of all except Sir Arthur Piggott, who rose to be attorney-general of England and Wales.

Dictionary of National Biography, Vol. XXIII. 1920.

Froude, J. A., *The English in the West Indies*, pp. 124–125. 1888.

Edward Wilmot Blyden

❦

EDWARD WILMOT BLYDEN, Arabic scholar, student of African affairs, writer, diplomat, educator, and one of the most forceful thinkers of the nineteenth century, was born at St. Croix, Danish West Indies.

Imbued from his earliest years with the spirit of African patriotism, and proud of Africa's imprint on his face, he decided to devote himself to Africa's advancement and left his tiny island in the Caribbean at the age of seventeen for the United States to fit himself for the task, but finding color prejudice there too strong, he decided to leave for Africa. An African colonization society paid his passage to Liberia, where he entered the high school of the Foreign Missions of the Presbyterian Church. A brilliant pupil, he was not long in becoming principal of the school.

Soon afterward he was appointed a professor in the newly-founded College of Liberia. In 1864 he was also appointed secretary of state of Liberia, combining the duties of this office with his educational work. At the same time, he studied languages, among them Arabic, Latin, Greek, French, German, and several African dialects. This last was to give him an insight into the African mind, such as perhaps no one before him had ever attained.

In 1871 he resigned his professorship and left for a tour of Europe, chiefly in order to learn something of the culture of the Old World. After this he went to Sierra Leone, West Africa, where on two different occasions he was selected as the one best fitted to lead government missions into the interior. His reports of these missions were published in full in the *Proceedings of the Royal Geographical Society*, of which he was a member.

In 1877 he was appointed Liberian Minister to the Court of St. James, and was received by Queen Victoria at Osborne. While in England he became the personal friend of several of the most prominent Englishmen of his times, as the Marquis of Salisbury, prime minister; Lord Brougham, antislavery leader; W. E. Gladstone, prime minister; Dean Stanley; and Charles Dickens. He was also elected to membership in several leading literary and scientific clubs, among them the Athaenum, and the Society of Science and Letters of Bengal, of which he was a vice president. In all these circles he used his influence untiringly for the advancement of Africa.

One important result of his African studies and experiences was the decision to become a Mohammedan. Though reared as a Christian, he decided that Islam was a far better and more liberal religion for black people than Christianity. His views in this respect are set forth in his scholarly work "*Islam, Christianity and the Negro Race.* He threw himself into the task of persuading Negroes that Islam was the better faith for them. Going among the Mohammedans of West Africa, he founded schools and spread knowledge. Later, when he visited Turkey, the sultan received him as a guest and gave him his highest decoration in recognition of his services to Islam.

As a speaker and a conversationalist, Blyden was one of the best of his times. In the most learned circles of London, Berlin, Paris, Vienna, and Rome, he shone by his wide knowledge, linguistic ability, and magnetic personality.

Casely Hayford, distinguished Gold Coast lawyer and author, summarized Blyden's work thus:

Edward Wilmot Blyden has sought for more than a quarter of a century to reveal everywhere the African unto himself; to fix his attentions upon original ideas and conceptions as to his place in the economy of the world; to point out to him his work as a race among the races of men; lastly and most important of all to lead him back unto self-respect. He has been the voice crying in the wilderness all these years, calling upon all thinking Africans to go back to the rock whence they were hewn by the common Father of the nations—to drop metaphor, to learn to unlearn all that foreign sophistry has encrusted in the intelligence of Africans. Born in the West Indies some seventy years ago, and nurtured in foreign culture, he has yet remained an African and today he is the greatest living exponent of the true spirit of African nationality and manhood. . . . Edward W. Blyden is a leader among leaders of African aboriginal thought.

Edward Clodd, noted writer on evolution, wrote Mary Kingsley:

I have written to Dr. Blyden. . . . I do not know whether I told you he was as black as the ace of spades. If this will alarm Saville, you had better have him elsewhere, but his manners are perfect and he is a perfect type of the kindly, thoughtful Negro.

Blyden is quite out of the ordinary, a man, head and shoulders above all the other educated Africans, and I enjoy his company immensely. I know so well the sure, slow way that form of mind moves, and the absolute reality of belief it holds. I really want you to see a big black man's mind, as I know you will, if you see Blyden. I have to say "if" because if he is—you cannot say frightened, because in his way you cannot frighten a Negro—but if he doesn't take to a person, he is silent, civil, but to put it mildly, uninteresting.

A monument stands to Blyden's memory at Freetown, capital of Sierra Leone.

ADDITIONAL REFERENCES

Agbebi, Mojola, *Inaugural Sermon Delivered at the Celebration of the First Anniversary of the "African Church."* Yonkers, N.Y., Edgar F. Hanortn, 1903.

Blyden, Edward Wilmot, *The Aims and Methods of a Liberal Education for Africans.* New York, G. Young, 1920.

———, *Aftrican Life and Customs.* London, C. M. Philips, 1908.

———, *From West Africa to Palestine.* Freetown, Sierra Leone, T. J. Sawyer, 1873.

————, ". . . Mohammedanism and the Negro Race." *Methodist Quarterly Review*, 4th Ser., Vol. XXIV, No. 7 (January, 1877), New York.

————, "Self-Government in Trial," in Joan (Coyne) Maclean, ed., *Africa: The Racial Issue*, pp. 155–160. New York, H. W. Wilson, 1954.

Brotz, Howard, ed., *Negro Social and Political Thought 1850–1920*. New York, Basic Books, 1966.

Cromwell, John Wesley, *The Negro in American History*, pp. 235–239. Washington, D.C., The American Negro Academy, 1914.

Davis, Stanley A., *This Is Liberia*, pp. 104–107. New York, William-Frederick Press, 1953.

Holden, Edith, *Blyden of Liberia*. New York, Vantage Press, 1966.

Lynch, Hollis R., *Edward Wilmot Blyden*. London, Ibaden, New York, Oxford University Press, 1967.

Schieffelin, Henry Maunesell, ed., *The People of Africa*. New York, A. D. F. Randolph, 1871.

Félix Eboué

GREAT STATESMAN OF FRANCE, AFRICA,
AND THE WEST INDIES
(1884–1944)

FÉLIX EBOUÉ, born at Cayenne, French Guiana, December 26, 1884, was a key figure in the Second World War. But for his statesmanship in Africa, the forces of Hitler and Mussolini might have succeeded in breaking through the Allied line at El Alamein, Egypt, in one of the most critical phases of the war. Such a step might have given all Egypt and Africa to the Fascist forces and turned the tide of war in their favor before America entered.

When France fell in August 1940, and was given over to Hitler, plans were laid by the betrayers of the French people to hand over the African colonies also. Eboué thwarted this by not only revolting against Pétain, Laval, and others of the Vichy regime, but by succeeding in winning over most of the other governors, who were white, to the cause of General de Gaulle. It was through the territory governed by Eboué that the supplies that started the defeat of Hitler and Mussolini went.

The task Eboué had set for himself from the start of his career was a grueling one and was doubtless instrumental in hastening his death. A brilliant student, he won a scholarship in his native Guiana to study in Bordeaux, France. Later he entered the school of Colonial Science for preparation as a colonial administrator and then he went to the famous military college of St. Cyr, near Paris, where he studied military tactics and strategy.

In 1907, or 1911, he was appointed Governor of Ubangi-Shari territory in Central Africa, where because of his desire to advance the African people he spent little time in his luxurious colonial mansion but traveled through hundreds of miles of virgin territory away from the outposts of civilization to learn of the people and their life. He studied their language, dialects, customs, folklore, and music. In this last field he had a great collaborator in his wife, a gifted musician. Together they collected and wrote down the native compositions, especially the drum language and the whistle language, which they later published. Few if any ethnologists had a greater knowledge of African life than Eboué. By the time of his death he had spent a total of over thirty years chiefly in its interior.

In 1930 he was appointed Secretary-General of the Soudan, and in 1931, Secretary-General of Martinique. In 1936 he was named Governor-General of Guadeloupe, and then made Governor of Chad territory in 1939. Secretary for the Colonies, Georges Mandel, seeing that war with Germany was imminent, chose him for that strategic post, a trust that fully justified itself.

When France fell in August, 1940, and Eboué refused to side with Vichy, he was denounced as a traitor, stripped of his Legion of Honor and other decorations, and sentenced to death in absentia. However, in November, 1940, General Charles de Gaulle appointed him Governor-General of Equatorial Africa, a territory of over a million square miles and 6,000,000 souls.

Egon Kaskeline, a European war correspondent, writing in 1942, ably summed up the effect of Eboué's decision to side with the Allies during the war. As a result, he says:

Free France had been recreated in the heart of Africa with who knows what destiny in the history of French democracy. When in September, 1940, General de Gaulle came to visit the Free French colonies, there could be no doubt about the personality who should be the head of the colonial administration. Félix Eboué was appointed governor-general of Free French Africa.

Free French Africa has ever since proved to be an important cornerstone in the United Nations' defense system. A network of modern airports has been established there, and in these days of military crisis in the Middle East the air transport lines through Africa have proved to be of immense usefulness. Hundreds of British and American planes have been ferried across the Atlantic and then flown across the continent to the Egyptian battle-front, to the Middle East, and to India. Fort Lamy in the Chad region has become one of the aerial turntables of Africa.

Had Eboué gone over to Vichy, this would not have been possible. Kaskeline continues:

The Free French administration in Africa has also endeavored to shorten the transport lines for heavy war material which cannot be sent by air. With the Mediterranean Sea practically closed for United Nations convoys, war materials and other supplies must be shipped on the 12,000 miles route around the Cape of Good Hope. So two trans-African roads constructed by the Free French now cross 1,700 and 2,000 miles respectively of African veldt, forest, swamp and desert, a great deal of it built of stone and operable during the rainy season. The military critic of the London News Chronicle recently emphasized the increasing importance of land transportation across the African continent, facilitating the delivery of supplies to strategic points in normal or even shorter time. Ships and transports landing at West African ports run only a sixth of the risk involved in rounding the Cape of Good Hope. Thus is Free French Africa playing a major role in the active war effort.

In addition, Eboué provided more than 15,000 crack African troops who attacked the Italian flank in Libya and also prevented the Libyan Army of Marshal Graziani from joining with the Italian forces in Ethiopia under the Duke D'Aosta. But for this feat, victory in Ethiopia would certainly not have come when it did, if ever.

During this crucial period of the war more than 150 British planes used the Chad base every day. In every way Eboué was an important figure during the most crucial stages of the war.

A democrat at heart, a servant of the people, modest and humble but very competent, Eboué was beloved not only by the natives but by those white subordinates who at first resented taking orders from a black man. He did all that he could to advance the natives and to prepare them for a fuller share in the government of the colony. He started a mass program of education and founded schools in which the best features of African life were grafted onto modern European education. He undertook large-scale public works which were of great service in the war and was instrumental in the natives' getting higher prices for their products.

His death on May 17, 1944, in a Cairo hospital was a great shock to Africa, France, and many in the other allied nations.

R. W. Merguson, the *Pittsburgh Courier*'s war correspondent, who visited him in Africa, says:

> I first saw Eboué in the palace at Lake Tchad in the Sudan— refined, dignified, and reflecting the highest type of French culture. He received me informally with an extended hand of friendship and, at the same time lifting his large white helmet with cordial hospitality. . . .
>
> Félix Eboué is a man of black complexion, stockily built, whose hair is tinged with grey, for he is nearly sixty—58 years of age to be exact —and the heat of the tropics ages one much faster. When I saw him I had the immediate impression of a dominating force, a mental storehouse of knowledge for the acquisition of which years of travel was necessary.
>
> Eboué was nattily dressed in an immaculately white tropical suit. His warm personality is one that is pleasing to contact and one which bespeaks a man of action, energy and determination. He is jovial, conversant, and well-informed on world affairs. I might say that he knows America well. I found the General with a keen interest in current topics and he manifested a deep concern about the American Negro. . . .
>
> The troops of Eboué, at the moment, are on the march. They are moving from the Sudan to join forces with other units of the French forces under General Giraud and the Allied forces which are battling away at German defenses in Lybia and Tunis. He is bringing up the famous Senegalese, who are universally known for their bravery and utter contempt for death. Contingents have already met the enemy.
>
> As was presaged, the world has heard of this remarkable man way from the heart of Central Africa. In collaboration with General DeGaulle of the Fighting Free French, Eboué is making history and his name will be emblazoned on its pages so the future generations will read with pride of the work he did to help free Africa from the thralldom of foreign domination.

REFERENCES

Eboué, F., *L'A. E. F., et la Guerre*. Discours pronouncé devant le Conseil d'Administration, December 1, 1943, also November 10, 1941, Brazzaville.

Kaskeline, E., "Félix Eboué and the Fighting French." *Survey Graphic,* pp. 522, 523, 548, 549–550 (November, 1942), New York.

The New York Times, August 29, 1940; May 18, 1944.

Merguson, R. W., *Pittsburgh Courier,* February 6, 1943.

ADDITIONAL REFERENCES

Alvarez-Pereyre, J., "Félix Eboué: First Negro Governor of French Equatorial Africa." *Negro History Bulletin,* pp. 27–30 (November, 1949), Association for the Study of Negro Life and History, Washington, D.C.

Eboué, Adolphe Félix Sylvestre, *La Nouvelle Indigène pour L'Afrique Equatoriale Française.* Paris, Office Français d'Edition, 1945.

Fleming, B. J., and Pryde, M. J., *Distinguished Negroes Abroad,* pp. 95–104. Washington, D.C., The Associated Publishers, 1946.

Gamache, Pierre, *Geographie et Histoire de L'Afrique Equatoriale Française,* pp. 288–290. Paris, F. Nathan, 1949.

Maran, René, . . . *Félix Eboué, Grand Commis et Loyal Serviteur.* Paris, Editions Parisiennes, 1957.

Maurice, Albert, *Félix Eboué, Sa Vie et Son Oeuvre.* Bruxelles, Institut Royal Colonial Bdge.

Saurat, Denis, *Watch Over Africa.* J. M. Dent & Sevsltt, 1941.

Ulrich, Sophie, *Le Gouverneur Général Félix Eboué.* Paris, La Rose, 1950.

THE UNITED STATES

Commentary and Notes
on References

✯✯

WHEN THE MOORS were expelled from Spain, they returned to Morocco, where the emperor El Mansur arranged with them to invade Equatorial Africa, the old empire of Songhay. This invasion broke up the structure of the last great empire in Western Africa. And the chaos that followed set up Africa for the future European slave trade.

The slave trade prospered, and Africans continued to be poured into the New World. Figures on the subject vary, but it has been established that during the years of the African slave trade, Africa lost from 60 to 100 million people. This was the greatest single crime ever committed against a people in world history. It was also the most tragic act of protracted genocide.

The first Africans who came to the New World were not in bondage, contrary to popular belief. Africans participated in some of the early expeditions, mainly with Spanish explorers. The best-known of these African explorers was Estevanico, sometimes known as Little Steven, who accompanied the de Vaca expedition during six years of wandering from Florida to Mexico.

There existed in Africa prior to the beginning of the slave trade a cultural way of life that in many ways was equal, if not superior, to many of the cultures then existing in Europe. And the slave trade destroyed these cultures and created a dilemma

305

that the African has not been able to extricate himself from to this day.

There were in the Africans' past, rulers who extended kingdoms into empires, great armies that subdued entire nations, generals who advanced the technique of military science, scholars with wisdom and foresight, and priests who told of gods that were kind and strong. But with the bringing of the African to the New World, every effort was made to destroy his memory of ever having been part of a free and intelligent people.

In the United States, in the fight to destroy every element of culture of the slaves, the system was cruel. No other system did so much to demean the personality of the slave, to deny his personality, or to ruthlessly sell family members apart from each other. The American slave system operated almost like the American brokerage system. If a person bought twenty slaves at the beginning of the week, and found himself short of cash at the end of the week, he might, if the price was right, sell ten. These ten might be resold within a few days. The family, the most meaningful entity in African life, was systematically and deliberately destroyed.

The publication of William Styron's novel *The Confessions of Nat Turner* (1967) and the dissenting reactions of a number of black writers that were published in the book *William Styron's Nat Turner: Ten Black Writers Respond* (1968) has caused new interest in the life of Nat Turner and slave revolts in general. In addition to the two books already mentioned, Herbert Aptheker's *Nat Turner's Slave Rebellion* (1966) provides new insight into the most famous of all the American slave revolts. The roots of these revolts are deep in the history of this country.

In the United States, especially during the American Revolution, the African slave often took the place of a white person who decided that he did not want to fight, and fought with the promise that he would get freedom afterward. Thousands of Africans fought in the American Revolution with this promise. And a little-known incident in our history is that thousands of Africans fought with the British when the British made the same promise and the African believed them. Apparently it depended on who got to him first.

The African was a major contributor in the making of the New World; the economy of the New World rested largely on slave labor. For many years one-third of the trade of the New World was with the small island of Santo Domingo, which later became Haiti. Haiti and the other Caribbean islands also influenced the economic system of Europe.

The first large-scale intercontinental investment of capital was in slavery and the slave trade. Many Europeans invested in ships and in the goods and services taken from these African countries and thus became independently wealthy.

But the slave revolts continued. By the end of the seventeenth century, the picture of slavery began to change drastically. Economic necessity, not racial prejudice, originally directed the African slave trade to the New World. As early as 1663 a group of white indentured servants rose in revolt. And some slaves took the Christian version of the Bible literally and believed that God meant for them to be free men—slaves such as Gabriel Prosser in Virginia, who led a revolt of 40,000 slaves in 1800. In 1822 in Charleston, South Carolina, a carpenter, Denmark Vesey, planned one of the most extensive slave revolts on record, but he was betrayed and put to death with many of his followers. And in 1831 Nat Turner led the greatest slave revolt ever to occur in Virginia.

Further, in order to understand the African in the New World, it is necessary to look honestly at the African. It is even more necessary that we look honestly at the interpretations of the role that the Africans have played in shaping the destiny of this hemisphere.

The fact that slave revolts occurred at all is remarkable. The fact that a large number of these revolts were successful in their early stages is more remarkable. The slaves never accepted their condition passively. In his book *American Negro Slave Revolts* (the best book on the subject) Dr. Herbert Aptheker records 250 slave revolts.

The protracted fight against the slave system was continued by the escaped slaves and the "free" blacks in the North. The most outstanding of all the escaped slaves was Frederick Douglass.

The career of Frederick Douglas is the greatest dramatic proof of the contributions of the people of African descent to the democratic tradition of this country. From his early life until his death, on February 20, 1895, this great black American was concerned with the universal struggle for freedom of people everywhere. "Under the skin," he once observed, "we are all the same, and every one of us must join in the fight to further human brotherhood." The story of his life is mainly the story of a lifelong effort to further human brotherhood. Born a slave, he lifted himself up from bondage by his own efforts, taught himself to read and write, developed great talents as a lecturer, editor, and organizer, became a noted figure in American life, and gained an international reputation as a spokesman for his people. He was an advocate of women's rights, labor solidarity, and full freedom for all regardless of race, creed, or color. Douglass represents the highest type of progressive leadership emerging from the ranks of the American people.

Of all the books written about Frederick Douglass, the most extensive is the four-volume work by Philip Foner. Still, the best insight into his life comes from him, and in his words. His book, *The Life and Times of Frederick Douglass*, is one of the greatest documents of a life in this country's literature.

Black inventors in general are shamefully neglected in the story of the industrial development of this country. Two new books, *Black Pioneers of Science and Invention* by Louis Habor (1971) and *Black Inventors of America* by McKinley Burt, Jr. (1971), have gone a long way toward correcting some of these "sins of omission." Jan Matzeliger is one of the black inventors whose life is included, in great detail, in these new books.

The play and the motion picture *The Great White Hope* revived interest in the black prizefighters who came to public attention early in this century. Most of the attention is devoted to Jack Johnson, the subject of the play and the movie. Unfortunately, another good fighter, Peter Jackson, has been forgotten. Jackson fought some of the best fighters of his day without becoming the heavyweight champion. He seemed always on the edge of the big breakthrough, but some of the major white fighters of his time avoided him.

Charles Chesnutt and Paul Laurence Dunbar in their day reached a larger general reading audience than any of the black writers who came before them. Dunbar was the author of four novels, several volumes of poetry, a drama, and a half-dozen collections of short stories. His novel *The Sport of the Gods* has recently (1971) been reprinted in paperback. This book is considered to be the first protest novel by an Afro-American writer.

Bert Williams, the great comedian, left behind three large notebooks, but was never able to finish a book about his life and the troubled years of his career when he tried to make a name for himself in roles other than as a comedian. There have been many articles written about him, as well as a full-length treatment of his life in the play *Star of the Morning* by Loften Mitchelle, and Ann Charters' excellent biography *Nobody* (1970). He was one of the brightest stars during the golden age of the American theatre. The book *Bert Williams, Son of Laughter*, written about him in 1923 by Mabel Rowland, is interesting, but it leaves a lot to be desired.

Booker T. Washington stood astride the life of black America in the period between 1895 and 1915. The history of this period is mainly the history of this man and how others reacted to him. His famous "Atlanta Cotton Exposition Address" in 1895 is still being debated. As an educator, as a man, and as an American he was not without greatness. He still has some important things to say to our times. There are many books about him, with varying degrees of good and bad in their interpretations of his life and career. I have found Hugh Hawkins's *Booker T. Washington and His Critics* (1962) very useful in providing new insight into this man and his impact on America in general and black America in particular.

William Monroe Trotter is the black radical who for a number of years was lost from history. The writer Lerone Bennett, Jr., figuratively brought him back to life in his book *Pioneers in Protest* (1968). (See Chapter 15, "The Last Abolitionist.") The first full-length book about his life. *The Guardian of Boston,* by Stephen R. Fox, was published in 1971.

W. E. B. Du Bois died in 1963 on the eve of the famous March on Washington. For over fifty years he was the intellectual leader

of black America. In the last five years there had been a revival
of interest in his life and thought. Nearly all of his books, long
out of print, have been republished. A number of new books
about him have appeared. *Black Titan: W. E. B. Du Bois* (1970)
an anthology by the editors of *Freedomways*, is the most extensive collection of articles on Dr. Du Bois that has been published to date.

The following books are also of some interest: *W. E. B.
Du Bois, Propagandist of the Negro Protest* by Elliott M.
Rudwick (1968), *W. E. B. Du Bois: Negro Leader in a Time of
Crisis* by Francis L. Broderick (1966), and *A. W. E. B. Du Bois
Reader*, edited by Andrew G. Paschal (1971).

The recent publication (1970) of a paperback edition of
Garvey and Garveyism by Mrs. Amy Jacques Garvey, followed
by a reprint of Mrs. Garvey's earlier work *The Philosophy and
Opinions of Marcus Garvey,* proves, if proof is needed, that we
are now in the midst of a Marcus Garvey renaissance. In nearly
all matters relating to the resurgence of black people, in this
country and abroad, there is a reconsideration of this man and
his program for the redemption of people of African descent
throughout the world. The concept of Black Power that he advocated, using other terms, is now a reality in large areas of the
world where people of African origin are predominant. Several
books on Marcus Garvey are in preparation. *Black Power and
the Garvey Movement* by Theodore G. Vincent (1971) is the
last book on this subject to be published. In this book Mr. Vincent shows that the origins of the black nationalism of Stokely
Carmichael, the Republic of New Africa, and the black radicalism of the Black Panther Party can be traced to the Garvey
movement.

Hubert Harrison was one of the great minds of the age of black
radicalism that saw the emergence of Marcus Garvey, A. Phillip
Randolph, Richard B. Moore, and other awakening black
thinkers during the early part of this century. He is still not
fully rediscovered or appreciated. His many articles have not been
brought together in an anthology and his speeches are only partly
collected. His life begs for an astute biographer who can see and
understand the impact that he had on his time. He was one of

the first supporters of Marcus Garvey in this country and he was instrumental in introducing Garvey to his first large audience in Harlem. His book *When Africa Awakes*, published in 1920, had a profound effect on the Garvey movement and the concept of African redemption.

Ernest E. Just was one of the first American scholars of African origin to make an international impression, during the first two decades of this century. At the age of thirty-one, he was named the first Spingarn Medalist by the National Association for the Advancement of Colored People. About six months later, in 1916, he obtained his Ph.D. at the University of Chicago. After 1924 he became a world figure when leading biologists of Germany considered him the best fitted scientist-biologist to write a treatise on fertilization. His later thesis on the cytoplasm of the cell was so far-ranging that experts said he was twenty-five years ahead of his contemporaries in biological comprehension.

Dr. Charles Drew, an outstanding researcher in blood plasma preservation, described Dr. Just as a "biologist of unusual skill and the greatest of our original thinkers in the field." He was seen as producing "new concepts of cell life and metabolism which will make him a place for all time."

Dr. Just wrote two major books and over sixty scientific papers in his field. He was for many years head of the Department of Biological Sciences at Howard University. Like all men of profound learning, Dr. Just was modest. His reputation for integrity, experimental ability, and loyalty was the highest possible. Scientists from all over America and Europe sought him out and studied his work. He also engaged in research at the Kaiser Wilhelm Institute for Biology in Germany. At times he was a guest at the Marine Biological Laboratory at Naples, and at a similar institution in Sicily. In 1930 he was one of the speakers at the Eleventh International Congress of Zoologists at Padua, Italy. The same year he was elected vice president of the American Society of Zoologists.

Dr. Just was a native of North Carolina. Before his death in 1940, he was a much-honored member of the world's scientific community.

A short biography of Dr. Ernest Everett Just is included in a recently published book (1970), *Black Pioneers of Science and Invention* by Louis Haber.

Arthur A. Schomburg, a Puerto Rican of African descent, is responsible for the founding of the world's most important library on the life, culture, and history of African people the world over. In this century he was one of the pioneer book collectors and a founding member of the Negro Society for Historical Research. His work helped to lay the basis for the Black Studies programs in a large number of present-day institutions. See the article "The Schomburg Collection" by Jean Blackwell Hutson in the book *Harlem: A Community in Transition* (1969).

For a number of years the black artist in America was ignored. Henry O. Tanner was no exception. This in spite of the fact that his paintings have been bought by galleries all over the world. Some of his most famous paintings are "Christ Walking on Water," "The Destruction of Sodom and Gomorrah," and "The Flight into Egypt." Henry O. Tanner died in Paris in 1937.

George Washington Carver is the best-known black man of science of our time. His public life and research were based at Tuskegee Institute in Alabama. From this base his discoveries became known to the world. In 1939 he was awarded the Theodore Roosevelt Medal for Distinguished Research in Agricultural Chemistry. In 1940 the International Federation of Architects, Engineers, Chemists, and Technicians gave him a citation for distinguished service. In 1941 the University of Rochester conferred on him the degree of Doctor of Science. Before his death in 1943 he established the George Washington Carver Foundation for Agricultural Research. The following books contain short biographies of George Washington Carver: *They Showed the Way* by Charlemae Hill Rollins (1964), *Black Pioneers of Science and Invention* by Louis Haber (1970), and *Great Negroes: Past and Present* by Russell L. Adams (1963).

Before Joe Louis, Jack Johnson was the only black American to hold the title Heavyweight Champion of the World. He was throughout his career a controversial figure. The new interest in him, motivated by a play, *The Great White Hope*, and a movie of the same name, has not removed this controversy. There are a number of books about him, good and bad; the latest are: Finis

Farr's *Black Champion: The Life and Times of Jack Johnson* (1964) and *Jack Johnson Is a Dandy: An Autobiography* (1949) by Jack Johnson.

Matthew A. Henson was the last of the great black explorers. Henson, like the early black explorer Estevanico, helped to increase the world's knowledge of the unknown. Henson had been a companion of Admiral Robert E. Peary, the famous scientist and explorer, on many expeditions. Therefore, it was only natural that he should accompany the admiral on his expeditions to find the North Pole. There are a number of books about the life of Matthew Henson, among them Floyd Miller's *Ahdoolo: The Biography of Matthew A. Henson* (1963) and Henson's own *A Black Explorer at the North Pole* (1969).

There were a number of black concert singers before Roland Hayes, but he was the first one to achieve international attention and acclaim. His career extended over half a century and his journey was from the cotton fields of Georgia to the royal palaces of Europe. The story of Roland Hayes is included in every book about the contribution of black Americans to the music and culture of this country, but there is no adequate full biography. The following books show some insight into his life, his songs, and what he achieved: *Angel Mo' and Her Son Roland Hayes* by McKinley Helm (1947) and *My Songs: Afroamerican Religious, Folk Songs* by Roland Hayes (1948).

Carter G. Woodson has been called "The Father of Negro History" because more than any other man before and after his time he formalized an approach to the history of African people in Africa and in the rest of the world.

In his career as an educator, he served as principal of the Douglass High School, supervisor of schools in the Philippines, teacher of languages in the high schools of Washington, D.C., and dean of the school of Liberal Arts at Howard University and West Virginia State College. Ever a seeker for more knowledge, he earned the B.A. degree in 1907 and the M.A. degree in 1908 from the University of Chicago, and the Ph.D. degree in 1912 from Harvard University. A year of study in Asia and Europe, including a semester at the Sorbonne, and his teaching and travels abroad gave him a mastery of several languages.

Convinced by this time that among scholars the role of his own people in American history and in the history of other cultures was being either ignored or misrepresented, Dr. Woodson realized the need for special research into the neglected past of his people. The Association for the Study of Negro Life and History, founded in Chicago on September 9, 1915, is the result of this conviction. In the same year appeared one of his most scholarly books, *The Education of the Negro Prior to 1861*. In January of the following year, Dr. Woodson began the publication of the scholarly *Journal of Negro History,* which despite depressions, the loss of support from foundations, and two World Wars has never missed an issue.

For his scholarly works and publications, Dr. Woodson is accorded a place among ranking historical schools of the nation and the world.

As an artist-activist Paul Robeson was a generation ahead of his time. On June 23, 1956, the San Francisco *Sun Reporter* noted in an editorial that "Robeson as far as most Negroes are concerned occupies a unique position in the U.S., or the world for that matter. He says the things which all of us wish to say about color relations, and in the manner in which he says these things attracts the eye of the press of the world."

In a career extending over thirty years, he has shown himself to be a sensitive artist, an indomitable advocate of freedom, dignity, and the brotherhood of man. This was reflected in his public life, as he refused to let his voice be silenced and insisted on being heard. Paul Robeson, the man, has become a legend in his own time. Yet his personal odyssey is inseparable from the life and struggles of the Afro-American community and the monumental changes which have taken place in the world over the last half-century. The books about Paul Robeson range from good to bad. The best new information on his life and career is in the special issue of *Freedomways* magazine devoted to Paul Robeson (Vol. II, No. 1, First Quarter, 1971). The bibliography compiled by Ernest Kaiser for this issue contained in essence the most important materials that have been published about Paul Robeson in the last twenty years.

The life of Charles Clinton Spaulding is important because

he represented a business approach that is now called Black Capitalism. This concept is no longer popular with the young black radicals of today. But one cannot honestly look at the total picture of black America without considering men like Charles C. Spaulding. This man rose from dishwasher to be president of a multimillion-dollar corporation. His is a classic American success story. Like Paul Coffee before him, he used his wealth to help people who were less fortunate. The life of Charles C. Spaulding does prove, if proof is needed, that a black American, in spite of adverse circumstances, can succeed in the difficult world of high finance. Short biographies of Dr. Spaulding have been included in the following books: *Great Negroes: Past and Present* by Russell L. Adams (1963) and *The Negro Vanguard* by Richard Bardolph (1961).

Marian Anderson, who retired only a few years ago, is one of the best-known concert singers of this century. Soon after the great conductor Arturo Toscanini said that "a voice like hers is heard only once in a century," many doors, previously closed, were opened to her. Probably the greatest experience was on Easter Sunday morning in 1943 when she sang to an audience of 75,000 from the steps of the Lincoln Memorial. In her autobigraphy, *My Lord, What a Morning*, published in 1956, she has written about this occasion and other great moments in her life. Additional information on her life is included in the books *13 Against the Odds* by Edwin R. Embree (1944) and *Men and Women Who Make Music* by David Ewen (1949).

In the history of the profession of prizefighting, Joe Louis is one of the best known, and according to some sports writers, the greatest prizefighter of all times. To black Americans he was more than that. He was for many years the symbol and the keeper of their manhood. He came to public attention during the 1930s when the spirits of black Americans were as low as the depression that held sway over the nation. Joseph Louis Barrow became an amateur boxing champion, then turned professional in 1934. In 1937 he became the heavyweight champion of the world and retired as undefeated champion in 1949. He defended his championship twenty-five times. From 1934 to 1949 he fought seventy-one professional fights and suffered only two defeats. Some of the many books about him are: *Joe Louis, the Brown Bomber* by Gene Kessler (1936), *Joe Louis: A Picture Story of His Life* by Neil Scott (1947), and his autobiography *My Life Story* (1947).

J. H. C.

Estevanico

DISCOVERER OF ARIZONA AND NEW MEXICO
AND PIONEER EXPLORER OF THE SOUTHWEST
(d. 1540)

To THE NEW WORLD with the Spanish conquistadores came many unmixed Negroes, some of whom distinguished themselves in various ways in its exploration and conquest.

Among the most romantic of these was Estevanico, whom fortune permitted, in spite of his enslaved condition, to play a leading role in the opening-up of the Southwest. He was one in a party of the first three to cross the North American continent from the Atlantic to the Pacific. At least two American states owe their beginnings to him.

Of Estevanico's history prior to his arrival in the New World all that is known is that he was a native of Azamor, Morocco, and that he was very black with thick lips. He is first heard of when he and other Negroes arrived in Florida with the ill-fated expedition of Pánfilo de Narváez in 1527.

At that time Florida and the Southwest were believed to be as rich in gold and precious stones as Mexico and Peru, from which the Spaniards had wrung fabulous wealth. A tale had come to Mexico City of the Seven Golden Cities of Cíbola situated in what is now Arizona and New Mexico. It was said that in these cities whole streets were given over to goldsmiths; the roofs of the houses were of gold; and the doors studded with precious stones. Incredible tales they seem now but the civilizations of

317

Mexico and Peru, which had been undreamed of in the Old World prior to Columbus, gave credence to them.

Pánfilo de Narváez left Spain on June 17, 1527, for Florida, with 600 men. But storms and desertions soon reduced his force by half. Tall, red-bearded, one-eyed de Narváez, pushed on however, and finally landed at St. Clement's Bay, north of Tampa Bay, Florida. In a deserted Indian hut one of his men found a golden ornament. De Narváez, hailing the find as the first fruit of the millions in gold awaiting him in the interior, gave the order to march.

Into the forests and swamps of Florida, his men plunged. But after three months of weariness, hunger, and attacks by Indians, they found nothing, whereupon they returned to the coast and set sail westwards, arriving at Apalachicola Bay. Thence they sailed toward the Texas coast, traversing the mouth of the Mississippi at least fourteen years before its reputed discoverer, De Soto.

Caught soon afterwards in a storm, they were cast ashore off the Texas coast where they were killed by the Indians. Only four members of that expedition were ever heard of again, Cabeza de Vaca, Castillo de Maldonado, Donates de Carranza, all white, and the latter's Negro slave, Estevanico. Captured by the Indians, all were enslaved.

For the next six years they experienced a most cruel bondage. They were forced to do all the drudgery of the tribe. Quite naked, they suffered from sores on their bodies caused by stones, thorns, and brushes. Year after year they planned to escape, but something always arose to frustrate them. Their male captors were in the habit of going away in the prickly pear season at the time others would arrive with objects for barter. They planned to escape with the latter, but when success seemed near, there was a quarrel over a woman; the tribe separated, taking one of the four.

Finally, all four succeeded in escaping. Traveling westwards, they roamed from the Mississippi to California, traversing the land of the cactus and the ranges of the buffalo, being the first from the Old World ever to see that animal.

With their knowledge of Indian life they now became medicine men, and as such were well treated and even feared. At last, after three more years of almost unparalleled hardships, they arrived at a Spanish slaving post in California, having wandered more than 2500 miles from Tampa Bay. The story of this journey as told by Cabeza de Vaca is one of the most thrilling in the entire history of adventure.

Their return to Mexico City was a sensation, the more so as they brought back news of the Seven Golden Cities of Cíbola, of which they had had abundant confirmation from the Indians. From all accounts these cities possessed riches compared with which those taken from Mexico and Peru were paltry.

The viceroy of Mexico, Antonio de Mendoza, immediately prepared an expedition to go in search of them. The important considerations were a leader who knew the country, the language, and the ways of the Indians, and was honest as well. Estevanico seemed such a one in every respect and the viceroy gave him 300 Indians for the task. It is probable that there were several Negroes among them; at least the Indian legend on the subject seems to confirm this. Estevanico and his savages, Mendoza felt, would not make off with the captured treasures of Cíbola.

Estevanico was illiterate. Two priests, Marco and Onorato, went as recorders. The latter died a few days after they set out.

Leaving Mexico City, the party traveled in a northwesterly direction. The journey proved a veritable triumph for Estevanico. Everywhere he was received with honor, thanks to his size and strength, his dark skin, his daring, bravery, and bluff, as well as his good nature and ready wit, his reputation as a medicine man, and his knowledge of Indian life and lore. The most beautiful virgins were given him as presents. These he accepted and incorporated into his retinue, much, it is said, to the displeasure of the chaste Father Marco, who, soon after they crossed the Rio Grande, dropped behind, letting Estevanico blaze the way.

According to certain writers, it was Estevanico's acceptance of, and freedom with, the women that caused Father Marco to lag behind, but it seems that the latter also acted from motives of prudence and advantage, as Estevanico was easing the way splendidly. Father Marco was none too squeamish himself. He had taken part in the conquest of Peru and the barbarous treatment of the Indians there by Pizarro.

The following is the reason for the parting, according to Castenado, the historian of the Coronado expedition, which followed immediately that of Estevanico's:

It seems that after the friar I have mentioned, and the Negro had started, the Negro did not get along well with the friars because he took the women that were given him and collected turquoises and got together a stock of everything. Besides, the Indians in those places got along with the Negro better, because they had seen him before. This was the reason he was sent on ahead to open up the way and pacify the Indians so that when others came along they had nothing to do except to keep an account of the things for which they were looking.

Father Marco and Estevanico parted "one Passion Sunday after dinner," with the understanding that if Estevanico heard tidings of a fair country he would send back a small cross; if the country were rich he would send a cross "two hand-fuls long"; and if it were richer than Mexico, he would send back a great cross.

With his emblem of power, a rattle gourd decorated with two bells and two feathers, one red, the other white, Estevanico forged his way northward, hearing as he went yet more wonderful tales of empires in the interior; of buildings that were five stories high; of peoples who were well clothed; and beyond, of other cities even richer. That he had only 300 followers did not daunt him. He possessed the true spirit of the conquistador and meant to win or die. Optimistic by nature, present conditions made him even more so. Was it not he, the former slave, whom the viceroy had chosen to lead this important expedition? By virtue of the tribute and the presents of women showered on him, was he not a conqueror? In his enthusiasm he saw riches far beyond those captured by Cortez and Pizarro. Already he saw his bearers struggling under loads of golden breastplates; doors studded with jewels; great idols of gold with eyes of burning rubies; bracelets and sacrificial knives of gold. In the heat of his optimism he sent back to Father Marco a cross so large that it took four men to carry it and a message urging him to hurry on as he had heard of "the greatest thing in the world." He added that he was not yet at a town, but was thirty days' march from the first of the golden cities.

At last, Estevanico arrived on a mountaintop from where he saw what appeared to be a city with great battlements and buildings that looked taller than even those of the Old World. He again dispatched messengers to Father Marco to urge him on, and sent envoys ahead to the city with presents and his emblem of power to proclaim that a great black chief had come from the south with a message of peace and to heal the sick. But the chief of the "city" wanted none of Estevanico or his medicine. He sent back to say that the medicine was no good and that if Estevanico knew what was good for him he'd stay out. This served but to excite the black chief, who gave the order to march.

He arrived at the "gates of the city" early the next morning. Once more the chief of the Hawikuh, as these Indians were known, sent a messenger warning Estevanico away, but brushing them aside he walked in boldly.

What happened after this is conjecture. Some writers say he was met with a shower of arrows and spears, and that his followers, seeing him fall, ran away panic-stricken to Father Marco. Another version is that the Indian chief asked him how many brethren he had and he replied many, so they killed him to prevent him from telling them about the Indians, and that his body was cut up and a piece sent to each of the fourteen or fifteen headsmen and his dog was killed later. One fact is certain, however. The expedition was attacked, and many of its members killed, among them Estevanico.

Father Marco thought it best to return to Mexico but decided he must at least have a glimpse of the city. By giving all his belongings to the frightened guides he persuaded them to take him to the top of a mountain from where he could see it.

What he saw confirmed all that Estevanico's messenger had reported. Afar in the golden haze of the morning lay what appeared to be a great city. Returning to Mexico, the worthy father spread the news.

Mexico City was thrilled, the size and wealth of Father Marco's city increasing with each telling. An expedition was organized, Coronado, the governor, himself leading it in golden armor. Accompanying was Father Marco.

Several months later the expedition reached the town of the Hawikuh. In the battle that followed the Indians were defeated.

But the marvelous city turned out to be only a miserable village. The historian of that expedition said, "When we first saw the village that was Cíbola such were the curses that some hurled at Friar Marco that I pray God may protect him from them. It is a little crowded village, looking as if it had been all crumpled up together."

Why had Father Marco been so deceived? The Hawikuh were cliff-dwellers and these cliffs and other weird natural formations with their many colors when tipped by the sunlight really looked like some wonderful city. They still do.

The expedition, still hopeful, continued the search for the other six cities until it arrived near the northern borders of what is now Kansas. Nothing of immediate value was found. Thanks, however, to the credulity and optimism of Estevanico, a vast region that was later to be the home of millions of American citizens had been discovered.

Estevanico's journey had taken him through what is now New Mexico and Arizona. Herbert E. Bolton, in *The Chronicles of America*, says:

Estevanico, this African, was one of the earliest explorers of North America and had wandered over a greater part of its wilderness than any man before him or than any many long after him. The Arab was one of a fearless race, loving freedom, no doubt, as his tribesmen of the Moroccan desert today love it, and only in the desert could he enjoy it. Lifted again out of the thrall of slavery, which had fastened on him again after this great journey from Florida, and given three hundred savages to discover the cities of argent traceries and turquoise doors, he had made his tour like an Oriental chieftain or like a Moorish prince before the conquest with pomp and display and the revels of power. Gifts were brought him and tribute was exacted. His tall, dusky body soon flaunted robes dyed with the colors of the rainbow. Tufts of brilliant feathers and strings of bells dangled from his arms. He carried a magical gourd decorated with bells and with one white and scarlet feather; and sent it ahead of him to awe the natives in each town where he demanded entrance. A score, perhaps, of Indians formed his personal retinue and bore on their shoulders the provisions, and the feathered ornaments accumulated on the road. Flutes of reed, shellfifes and fish-skin drums played his march against the sunlit mesas. And an ever-increasing harem of gayly-bedecked young women swelled the parade of Estevanico, the black Berber chief, on his way to the city in silver and blue. Perhaps, as has been suspected, the belled and feathered gourd was "bad medicine" to the Indians of Hawikuh, for when Estevanico presented it with the announcement that their lord had come to make peace and cure the sick, the Indians became enraged and ordered the interlopers out of the country on pain of death. Estevanico, disdaining fear, went on. Just outside the walls of Cíbola, he was seized. "The sun was about a lance high" when the men of Hawikuh suddenly launched upon his followers. Some of those, who, fleeing, looked back, thought they had seen Estevanico fall beneath the thick hail of darts.

The legends of the Zuni Indians confirm the visit of Estevanico and call him the precursor of the white men. They speak of him as being bold, cheerful, and ready:

It is to be believed that a long time ago when the roofs lay over the walls of Kya-ki-me, when smoke hung over the house-tops, and the ladder-rounds were still unbroken, then the Black Mexicans came from their abodes in Ever-lasting Summer-land. . . . Then and thus was killed by our ancient right where the stone now stands down by the arroyo of Kya-ki-me, one of the Black Mexicans, a large man with chili lips [lips swollen as if from eating chili peppers]. . . . Then the rest ran away, chased by our grand-fathers and went back towards their country in the land of Everlasting Summer.

REFERENCES

Cabeca de Vaca, *Narrative of Nunez Cabeca de Vaca*, reprint. 1922.

Hodge, F. W., *Spanish Explorers in the United States*, p. 333. 1925.

———, *The First Discovered City of Cíbola*.

Hosmer, J. K., *A Short History of the Mississippi Valley*, pp. 25–27. New York and Boston, Houghton, Mifflin and Company, 1901.

Colonial Records of Florida, Vol. II, No. 5, p. 323.

Bolton, H. E., *Spanish Borderlands*, p. 16. 1919–1921.

———, *Chronicles of America*, Vol. XXV.

Bancroft, H. H., *History of the Pacific States*, Vol. XII, p. 32. 1888.

Bandelier, A. F., *History of the Southwestern Pacific*, pp. 107–108. 1891.

Hakluyt's Voyages, Vol. IX, pp. 120, 125, 128, 130, 139, 162, 305. 1904.

ADDITIONAL REFERENCES

Bishop, Morris, *The Odyssey of Cabeza de Vaca*. New York and London, The Century Company, 1933.

Hughes, Langston, *Famous Negro Heroes of America*. New York, Dodd, Mead, 1958.

Lowery, Woodbury, *The Spanish Settlements within the Present Limits of the United States, 1513–1516*. New York and London, G. P. Putnam's Sons, 1901.

McWilliams, Carey, *North from Mexico*, pp. 22–23. Philadelphia, Lippincott, 1948.

Nordholt, T. W. Schulte, *The People That Walk in Darkness*, trans. from *Het Volk dat in Dusterius Wandelt* (1956), p. 20. © Van Loghum Slaterus, first pub. in English: London, Burke Publishing Company, Ltd., 1960.

Plen, Abel, *Upon This Continent*, pp. 13–15. New York, Creative Age Press, 1949.

Terrell, John Upton, *Estevanico the Black*. Los Angeles, Westernlore Press, 1968.

Winship, George Parker, "The Coronado Expedition" in *U.S. Bureau of American Ethnology, 14th Annual Report, 1892–1893*, pp. 329–613. Washington, D.C., 1896.

Wright, Richard Robert, "Negro Companions of the Spanish Explorers." *American Anthropologist*, Vol. IV, pp. 217–228 (April-June, 1902), New York.

Nat Turner

LEADER OF AMERICA'S GREATEST SLAVE REVOLT
(1800–1831)

NAT TURNER was the leader of a revolt that put more terror into the hearts of the oppressors of the black man than any other event since American slavery had begun. And he started out with only seven followers, six fewer than John Brown in his immortal raid on Harper's Ferry. He succeeded in so alarming the slaveholders that it was necessary for the United States to call out a portion of its navy to their rescue.

Nat was born a slave on the plantation of John Travis of Southampton County, Virginia. He was an unmixed Negro with strongly marked African features, short and powerfully built, and according to Anglo-Saxon standards, unattractive. But from his piercing black eyes there shone genius and an undaunted soul —what Byron called "the eternal spirit of the chainless mind."

A born lover of freedom, as surely as were Robert Bruce, Oliver Cromwell, George Washington, Patrick Henry, Simon Bolívar, and Garibaldi, he experienced what none of these patriots had, namely, the lash of the slave whip. But even that could not tame him. What right, he demanded of himself, with ever-increasing bitterness and vigor, had white men to treat him like an ox simply because he was black when an indomitable soul within told him he was as good as they.

Revolt was born in his soul. He thought of his father who,

brought as a slave to America, had escaped and had somehow made his way back to Africa. He tried to escape too, but was caught and brutally flogged.

This experience maddened him all the more against his master and all white people. But it made him more sensitive to the sufferings of his fellow slaves. Deeply religious, he told himself that God had caused him to fail because he had tried to escape alone. He resolved that when he left the next time, he would be taking the other slaves with him. Thereafter he spent his waking moments planning how to do this.

His conduct up to the time of his escape had been exemplary. He was never known to drink, swear, or steal. Very intelligent, he had learned to read with so much ease that he later said he did not know when he started to do so. Once when as a little child a book with pictures was given to him to stop him from crying, he began spelling out the names of the objects. He was also skilled at making pottery and knew how to make gunpowder.

A born mystic, his Sunday School teachings made him even more so. His feet trod the earth but his spirit roamed in regions beyond earthly confines. As Mohammed, the camel driver, driver, "heard" the spirit bidding him go forth to preach the doctrine of the One God; as Constantine the Great "saw" a sign in the sky bidding him conquer for Christendom; as Joan of Arc "heard" voices in the forest bidding her arise and drive the English from France; just as surely Nat Turner "heard" voices as he walked behind the plough bidding him arise and free his people. "Such is your luck," said the voices, "such you are called to see. Let it come rough or smooth. You must surely bear it."

He saw "visions" as did St. John in the Revelation forecasting his own, living mission. In the sky he saw black hosts and white ones battling and shutting out the light of the sun. The thunder rolled, blood flowed like a river, and then came shouts of victory. The blacks had won because they had God and the right on their side.

At times he "saw" Christ stretched on a cross the whole breadth of the skies. On the leaves of corn were drops of blood— Christ's blood, shed for all men, white and black alike. In the woods and on the leaves "appeared" letters and numbers and the figures of men. He fasted, prayed, read his Bible, and withdrew from his fellow slaves. His hallucinations increased.

On May 12, 1828, the "Holy Spirit" appeared to him and told him that the yoke of Jesus had fallen on him and that he must be prepared to fight against the serpent. When the time came, he would see a sign in the sky; until then, there should be a seal on his lips.

Three years later in February, 1831, the sign came. There was an eclipse of the sun. The sky was darkened just as his vision and the Bible had "predicted." From heaven he "heard a voice" saying, "Arise and slay the enemies of God with their own weapons." He was so affected that for days he trembled as if with ague.

He had been telling himself for years that he needed disciples and now he felt their need more than ever. All that time he had been observing his fellow slaves closely and felt that at least four of them could be trusted. Now that "the seal" had been removed from his lips, he told all to the four.

These recommended three others, making a total of seven. At noon, Sunday, August 31, 1831, the seven, Henry, Hercules, Nelson, Sam, Will, Jack, and Nat, went off for a barbecue in the woods, taking a pig, a bag of potatoes, and a jug of cider. Nat could play the guitar, and as he passed his master's mansion, he strummed a spiritual while the others sang. Such carefree mortals, Master Travis felt, certainly were not up to mischief.

The conspirators spent all day in the woods, laying their plans and taking a solemn oath that they would gain liberty or die. They planned to attack the whites in Southampton County, capture it as Washington had done during the Revolution, and retreat to Dismal Swamp. There they would establish headquarters and assemble their forces for a bigger blow.

They would strike that night. Cromwell, Washington, Garibaldi, and Bolívar started out with an army of trained soldiers, equipped with good weapons. Nat Turner and his valiant band of six had only farm implements as their arms.

They returned at midnight. The master and his family were sound asleep. Planting a ladder against a window, Nat mounted it, sneaked into the mansion, and opened the front door for the others. Taking all the weapons they could find, they tiptoed up to the master's bedroom.

Now for the reckoning with the man who had been so cruel to them.

Creeping into the room, Nat struck Travis on the head with a hatchet. The blow glanced off, and Travis leaped to his feet, blood gushing from the wound. When he shouted for help, Will brained him.

Mrs. Travis came running in—she met the same fate. When Nat and his men left the house, the other four members of the family, including the baby, were no more.

Nat told himself that it was a wicked thing he had done. But he silenced his conscience by recalling how the white people had stolen his people from Africa and how they had mistreated them ever since. He knew also that if the whites got the upper hand, they were going to wreak awful vengeance on guilty and innocent alike.

Mounted on Travis' horses, the seven galloped off to the next plantation where they killed everyone. Nat was no longer a plain slave. He was now General Cargill.

Before morning dawned, he had collected an army of fifty. Riding ahead with a mounted guard, he surrounded each mansion, holding it besieged until his foot soldiers arrived to complete the slaughter. In this way some fifty white persons were killed without the loss of a single man by the attackers.

The neighborhood was sparsely settled by whites. Not far away was Jerusalem, the county seat. Nat meant to surprise the inhabitants and kill them before the news of his invasion could reach Richmond or Peterburg. He would seize arms, ammunition, and money.

He gave the order to march. Every white person met on the way was killed. When the men came to the gate of the Parker plantation, someone suggested that they go in, kill the master, and pick up more recruits.

Nat objected. Time was pressing. They must hurry on to Jerusalem. But the majority thought otherwise, and Nat reluctantly yielded. Forty of the men started off for the mansion six miles away. Nat, with the remainder, stayed behind to block the roadway.

Hours passed and the men did not return. Nat started off in search of them. While he was away, a body of armed white men appeared. The rebels were just retreating when Nat and the other returned.

The whites, sure that they could bluff the Negroes, shouted to them to drop their guns on penalty of a whipping. Nat, reminding his men that they were no longer creatures of the banjo or the shakedown, but soldiers of Christ fighting for the right, gave the order to fire. When the smoke cleared, the whites were fleeing in disorder leaving behind several of their number, dead or wounded.

Nat dashed after them, cutting them down. The survivors ran into a strong body of white reinforcements. In the encounter that followed, Nat's force was beaten and he fled with twenty others. Still determined to attack Jerusalem, he urged his men to follow him, but they hesitated. He then picked up twenty more men and attacked the plantation of Major Ridley. When he reached the plantation of Dr. Hunt the next day, he found the whites there organized, and after a skirmish, he was forced to retreat. Telling his men to scatter, he instructed them where to meet that night. No one came, however. Nat was alone. Knowing that it was the end, he took to the woods.

In the meantime the news had reached Richmond and the United States government had been appealed to. It sent two warships, the *Warren* and *Natchley*, to the scene with 800 marines. The Virginia State Militia was also summoned in force.

An indiscriminate slaughter of the blacks began. Fully a hundred were killed the first day alone. Others were tortured for secrets they were supposed to know.

Six hundred men with bloodhounds started after Nat. Digging a hole under a pile of fence rails in the woods, he hid there for eight weeks.

At last he was cornered by accident. He had left some fresh meat in his hiding place, and while he was away, a dog, attracted by its scent, came in and ate it. The next day the dog, who happened to be out with a group of slaves, came back. Nat was in the hole and the dog barked wildly. The slaves came up to investigate, and Nat, thinking that they had come in search of him, begged them not to betray him.

Learning who he was, they fled in terror, running straight to their master to tell the news. A posse of 1000 armed men set out to look for him. They finally discovered him on top of a tree, where he had taken refuge. When they threatened to shoot, he came down and gave himself up.

A few days later he was brought to trial. Nat faced his accusers with courage. Thousands came to catch a glimpse of the man who had spread the fear of insurrection in all the slave states. Nat boldly acknowledged his deeds and told of his hope of freeing his people. His lawyer, Gray, said, "Clothed with rags, covered with chains, yet daring to raise his manacled hands to heaven, with a spirit soaring above the attributes of men, I looked at him, and my blood froze in my veins."

He was hanged on November 11, 1831, walking serenely to the gallows, convinced to the end that he had obeyed the dictates of the voice within—the voice of God and the right.

His revolt brought many sleepless nights to the slaveholders and the whites in all the slave states for years to come. How could they be sure that on their plantation there was not another Nat Turner waiting for a chance to butcher them?

Nat Turner, with his talents suppressed by servitude, is surely a case of one who was capable of being of great service to America and to humanity but whose genius, ignored by a most brutal system, was diverted into an instrument of ruthless slaughter and revenge. Between fifty-five and sixty-one whites were killed in the outbreak he led.

REFERENCES

The rebels made no attempt to violate the white women. R. R. Howison says, "It is remarkable that through the whole series of assaults not one female was violated. Remembering the brutal passions of the Negro we can only account for this fact by supposing the actors had been appalled by the very success of their hideous enterprise." (History of Virginia, Vol. II, p. 443. 1848.) The more likely answer to this is that Nat and his followers hated white people too thoroughly for that, as did the Haitians in their massacre of the French, who also killed the white women but did not rape them.

Gray, T. R., *Confession, Trial, and Execution of Nat Turner.* 1881.
Drewry, W. S., *Slave Insurrections in Virginia.* 1900.
Carroll, J. C., *Slave Insurrections in the United States*, pp. 129–140. 1938.
Magazine of American History, June, 1891.
Dictionary of American Biography, "Nat Turner." 1936.

ADDITIONAL REFERENCES

Adams, Russell L., *Great Negroes: Past and Present*, p. 22. Chicago, Afro-Am Publishing Company, 1963, 1964.
Aptheker, Herbert, *Nat Turner's Slave Rebellion.* New York, Humanities Press, 1966.
———, ed., *A Documentary History of the Negro People in the United States*, pp. 119–125. New York, The Citadel Press, 1951.
Clarke, John Henrik, ed., *William Styron's Nat Turner: Ten Black Writers Respond.* Boston, Beacon Press, 1968.
Higginson, Thomas Wentworth, *Nat Turner's Insurrection. 1831.* Boston, Lee and Sheppard Co., 1889.
Johnson, F. Roy., *The Nat Turner Slave Insurrection.* Murfreesboro, N.C., Johnson Publication Company, 1966.
Logan, Rayford, "Nat Turner, Fiend or Martyr." *Opportunity*, Vol. IX, 1931.
Nye, Russel Blaine, *A Baker's Dozen*, pp. 233–253. East Lansing, Michigan State University Press, 1956.
Rollins, Charlemae Hill, *They Showed the Way*, pp. 132–137. New York, Thomas Y. Crowell Company, 1964.
Turner, Lucy Mae, and Turner, Fannie V., "The Story of Nat Turner's Descendants." *Negro History Bulletin*, pp. 155, 164, 165 (April, 1947), Association for the Study of Negro Life and History, Washington, D.C.
Walker, Gerald, *Best Magazine Articles 1966.* New York, Crown Publishers, 1966.

Frederick Douglass

FREDERICK DOUGLASS was not only one of the greatest Americans, colored or white, but he was one of the most inspiring figures in the entire history of the human race. Plutarch contains no figure of more heroic proportions.

None of America's most famous white men had as hard a time as he. None of them came up from such depths of degradation and seeming hopelessness. Lincoln with all his immense difficulties was at least born free and there was never any law against his learning to read or acquiring an education, as there was against Douglass, whose social status until he was past twenty-three was that of an ox or a mule. He had to win his freedom, a very formidable task, before he could reach even near to where Lincoln started. Had he been born white with such great natural gifts as he possessed, what further heights might he not have reached?

No child living in any civilized or semi-civilized country today can encounter the handicaps Douglass faced. Born in one of the darkest periods of slavery on an estate owned by Colonel Lloyd in Talbot County, Maryland, his life was one of extreme hardship from the beginning. Hunger, as he said, was his constant companion. His share of corn mush, which a dozen children ate like pigs out of a trough on the kitchen floor, was so scant that he was pinched with hunger. He used to run races against the cat and the dog to reach the bones that were tossed out of the window, or to snap up the crumbs that fell under the table. He never tasted white bread, and the great desire of his childhood was to have one of those hot biscuits that were taken to his master's table every day. He suffered intensely from the cold, his only garment, summer and winter, being a long shirt. He had neither shoes nor hat.

While a baby, he was taken away from his mother and put under his grandmother's care. Later he was passed on to his Aunt Katy, who treated him badly. So did the poor whites, among whom he lived. They were ignorant and cruel and would take out on the slaves their spite against the upper-class whites.

As for his mother Harriet, she loved him but she was a slave on a plantation twelve long miles away. To get a glimpse of her little boy she sometimes stole away after the day's labor and hurried so as to get back in time for work at sunrise. She died when he was eight years old.

Of a sensitive nature, the lad was very much affected by the sufferings of his people. He saw old men beaten to death by cruel masters, and young and beautiful colored girls tortured by jealous and hysterical mistresses. Everybody around him seemed to wish to have the privilege of beating someone else.

"As I grew older," he said, "I became more and more filled with a sense of wretchedness. The unkindness of Aunt Katy, the hunger and the cold I suffered, and the terrible reports of wrongs, and outrages which came to my ears, together with what I daily witnessed led me to wish that I had never been born. I used to contrast my condition with that of the blackbirds in whose wild and sweet song I fancied them so happy."

At the age of ten, when life seemed gloomiest, relief came. He was sent to live with the Auld family, relatives of the manager of the plantation. Mrs. Auld, who was rather tenderhearted, took a fancy to him. She gave him his first pair of trousers, and made him the playmate of her little son, Thomas. Instead of the damp dirt floor of a cabin, he now had carpets to walk on.

The boy's great ambition was to learn to read, and he begged Mrs. Auld to teach him. Not knowing that she was breaking a state law, she gladly complied. But one day she told her husband, who scolded her sharply and forbade any more lessons.

"Teach him to read," shouted Auld wrathfully, "and you'll unfit him to be a slave. Learning will spoil the best nigger in the world. He should know nothing but the will of his master and learn to obey that. The next thing you know he'll be wanting to write and then he'll be running away with himself."

Auld's order almost broke the heart of the young slave. But it was a turning point in his life. It made him realize, as nothing else could have, the value of education. He made this solemn vow: "Knowledge I mean to have."

Thereafter, anything with print on it became precious to him. He treasured bits of old newspapers as others do bank notes. How he envied all those who had access to books!

From these bits of paper he spelled out the words as best he could, while hiding. Sometimes he used cunning to get his white playmates to help him. Whenever Mrs. Auld caught him she would snatch away the book or paper, stamping and storming "in the utmost fury." But he did not give up, and after three years of this catch-as-catch-can method he could read.

He learned to write in a manner no less ingenious. While firing a boiler in a Baltimore shipyard, he saw that the carpenters marked letters on the timber according to the part of the ship for which it was intended. Starboard pieces would be marked "S," larboard, "L," and so on.

Between shovelfuls of coal he would copy the letters on any available material, and later, to learn their names, would challenge white boys to see who could make a similar letter the most accurately.

"With my playmates for my teachers," he said, "fences and pavements for my copybooks, and chalk for my pen and ink, I soon learned to write." Appropriating used copybooks, he copied the lessons in margins and empty spaces. At night, in the kitchen loft, with a flour barrel as a desk, he copied from the Bible and the hymn book, running the risk of being soundly thrashed if caught. Lincoln's solitary struggles to educate himself, arduous as they were, were easy compared to those of Douglass.

An important event in the life of young Douglass was the secret purchase of a *Columbian Orator* with money earned by shining shoes. Over and over again he read the mighty orations of Pitt, Fox, and Burke until his ambition flamed at white heat.

About this time an event occurred which brought what seemed to him the crowning humiliation of his wretched life. His master, Colonel Lloyd, died, and he was sent for to be evaluated with the rest of the estate. He, in whom such noble thoughts burned, to be treated like one of the cattle on the estate!

His new master, Captain Thomas Auld, to make matters worse, was selfish, brutal, and very religious. His piety did not prevent him from going among the slaves during their prayer meetings and showering blows on them.

Auld's wife was also not only unkind but stingy. She gave the slaves barely enough food to keep them alive. To make sure that they would steal none she kept the key to the meat house in her pocket. Douglass says, "Bread and meat were mouldering in there while I was famishing."

Driven by hunger, the young slave would sneak away to friends on a nearby estate for something to eat. For this he would be severely beaten. He did not conceal his resentment after his floggings, which led Auld to decide that he needed breaking in. Accordingly, he sent him to Covey, a poor renter, to whom masters sent their stubborn slaves to have the spirit beaten out of them.

Douglass went not unwillingly, expecting at least that he would get a square meal now and then. Covey was a round-shouldered, bull-necked man, above middle height, ferocious and strong, and with a thin, wolfish face. At once he put Douglass to doing field work. Three days later, on some pretext, he beat Douglass so severely that his back was a mass of wounds.

A few days later he again beat him savagely because a team of unbroken oxen Douglass was driving crashed into a gate. Thereafter, overwork the lash were Douglass' daily lot. As for study, that was out of the question. The dark night of slavery had closed in on him—he was at the level of the brute creation.

Longingly he would watch the ships sailing by, bound for free lands, and wish he were on them. Only his burning resolution to escape at the first opportunity kept him alive.

In spite of the cruelty he suffered, his spirit remained unbroken. One day Covey, in a greater fit of anger than ever, seized him by the leg to tie him up in order to beat him and he pushed Covey away. The latter's cousin, Hughes, came rushing up to help Covey but Douglass, with his six feet of brawn, charged Hughes and sent him flying, then, regardless of the consequences, turned on Covey and gave him the thrashing of his life.

To strike a master meant death, but after what he was experiencing, even death seemed welcome. However, to his great surprise, nothing came of the affair. Covey, knowing that it would hurt both his reputation and his income if the story were known, said nothing. He never tried to beat Douglass again.

Six months later Douglass was hired out to a less brutal master, but, still untamed, he incited his fellow slaves to revolt, for which he was tied to a horse and dragged fifteen miles to jail where, after several weeks, he was released at Auld's request.

He was then sent to a shipyard to learn caulking. His orders were to obey all the carpenters, who would send him on dozens of errands, kicking and beating him when they considered he did not move fast enough. On one occasion he was knocked down and kicked in the eye, as a result of which he could not see for days.

Another time four of his tormentors jumped on him at once. "Dear reader," says Douglass in his autobiography, "you can hardly believe this statement, but it is true, and therefore I write it down; no fewer than fifty men stood by and saw the brutal and shameful outrage, and that one's face was beaten and battered most horribly, and no one said, 'that's enough,' but some-one shouted, 'kill him, knock his brains out.'" After this, Auld took him away from the shipyard, not from sympathy but because his property was being damaged.

Douglass was now allowed to hire himself out with orders to turn over his wages each Saturday. Able to move about now with much more freedom, he began to plan his escape. If only he could reach Philadelphia, ninety miles away! But how was he to get there? The regulations on the railroads and steamships were so strict regarding Negroes that it was difficult for even a free one to buy a ticket. To get one he would have to show his "free" papers to the ticket agent.

Douglass at last got hold of a sailor's uniform and a passport. To avoid buying a ticket, he waited until the train had started and then caught it. He had taken the further precaution of learning sea lingo and imitating a sailor's walk. However, the description on the passport was that of one much darker than he. Fortunately for him the conductor merely glanced at it. Then another thought worried him: suppose some white man who knew him should be on the train. This was just what happened. There were two such: one a German ship carpenter with whom he had once worked, and another with whom he had talked only two days before. Both, however, to his great relief, made no move to betray him.

The next day he arrived in New York. But he was not yet free. There was the Fugitive Slave Law. Slave masters had Negro spies in the North to report runaways and the judges who received $10 a head for each slave returned to the South, readily issued orders returning them there.

He found work shoveling coal. He was now twenty-one, and hoping to find work at his trade, he went to the shipyards at New Bedford, Massachusetts, but color prejudice was very strong in the North and he was forced to take a job blowing the bellows in a foundry.

The bellows was to be pumped continually in order to keep the furnace at a heat that would make the metal run. Since this was purely mechanical, he was determined to use the time to better his education, and nailing a newspaper or other printed matter to a post, he would read as he worked the bellows.

Up to now he had no surname. He had been known only as Frederick. He now decided to call himself Douglass after the hero of Walter Scott's *Marmion*. He also married a freedwoman, Anna Murray.

With freedom he had an increasing desire to help those still in slavery. This determination grew as he read *The Liberator*, published by William Lloyd Garrison, famous abolitionist, whose motto was, "Color prejudice is rebellion against God."

His opportunity came three years later. He was attending an antislavery meeting in Nantucket when someone said that an escaped slave was present. His name was called and shouts came back for him to speak.

Douglass got up in great confusion. He had never spoken in public before. His first words were stammering but soon his nervousness was lost in his tale and he was pouring out a story such as an antislavery audience had never heard before. Its force and fervor held everyone present spell bound.

When he was finished there was a rush to him. Parker Pillsbury, who was present, says, "The crowded congregation had been wrought up almost to enchantment as he turned over the terrible apocalypse of his experience in slavery."

Emotion fairly boiled over when Garrison arose and thundered, "What I want to know is: Have we been listening to a thing, a piece of property, or a man?"

"A man! A man!" shouted the audience.

"Shall such a man be sent back to slavery from the soil of Old Massachusetts?" demanded Garrison, swept away by the storm of enthusiasm. "No, a thousand times, no! Sooner let the lightnings of Heaven blast Bunker Hill monument until not one stone shall be left on another."

The abolitionists, quick to realize the worth of this escaped slave, engaged him on the spot. What better than to have a slave of such intelligence and commanding personality and conviction to plead the cause of his own people!

Douglass took the field and at once it became clear that a newer, greater, and more relentless foe than ever before had arisen against slavery. Across the Northern states he thundered. Raging mobs attacked him in Faneuil Hall, Boston, and at Harrisburg, Pennsylvania. At Richmond, Indiana, he was rotten-egged. But everywhere he showed the spirit he had shown against Covey, the slave killer. At Pendleton, Indiana, when a mob tore down the platform on which he was speaking, he fought back until his arm was broken and he was battered into unconsciousness, but the same night, with his arm in a sling, he was again on the platform. During the Draft Riots in New York, when the greatest massacre of Negroes probably known in American history occured, he faced frenzied white mobs with the same courage.

As for Jim Crow in the North, he never yielded to it. When the conductor of a train in Massachusetts wanted to send him to the Jim Crow section, he refused. The conductor sent for the train hands to oust him but he held onto the seat so firmly that it came loose and he was thrown off the train still holding it.

One winter night while on a steamboat plying between Boston and New York, he was shut out on deck although entitled to a berth. A compassionate white steward, wanting to admit him, hintingly said, "You're an Indian, aren't you?" "No," replied Douglass resolutely, "only a damned nigger."

Everywhere his courage was as firm as the pigment in his skin, though he was constantly running the risk of being caught and returned to his master in the South. At first he used a false name and gave a wrong place of birth, but when the pro-slavery faction denounced him as a fraud, he boldly published his autobiography with full details.

His book had a wide sale and put the slavers on his track. He fled to England where he had long been wanting to go to carry on the fight. On the way over, however, his zeal almost cost him his life. An antislavery speech he made aboard the ship so incensed a party of Southerners that they tried to throw him overboard and might have succeeded had not members of the crew and other passengers interfered. This dastardly attack on the high seas brought him immense publicity in England and world-famed figures as Cobden, Brougham, Peel, and Disraeli invited him to their homes.

He literally swept England off its feet. Leonine, majestic, lithe, graceful, and peerless in his eloquence, he stirred audiences with his clear, expressive voice like a bugle sounding the charge. Some acclaimed him the greatest living orator. Some white Americans living in London were proud to call him countryman while others tried to win his friendship, hoping to be introduced into aristocratic and influential circles. Among the latter, he said, was one white minister, who seeing him speaking with Lord Morpeth in the House of Parliament, came up to him and asked him for an introduction to the lord. But, says Douglass, in America "he would scarcely have asked such a favor of a Negro man."

While in England at this time, indignation at his treatment increased when he applied to George M. Dallas, the American minister there, for a passport to visit France and was refused one on the ground that he was not a citizen of the United States. The

Supreme Court of the United States had held that a Negro could not be a citizen. Douglass wrote directly to the French minister in London and immediately received the necessary permit to go.

He was offered a home in England, but true to his resolve, he declined. "America," he said, "is my home and there I mean to spend my life and be spent in the cause of my outraged brethren." His English friends thereupon gave him $20,000, of which $750 was to purchase his freedom and the remainder to found a newspaper.

His liberty now purchased, Douglass went to Rochester, New York, and started his paper, *The North Star,* later *Frederick Douglass' Paper*, through which he fought not only for the emancipation of the slaves but full equality for Negroes. In this he was opposed by many of the abolitionists who felt that in their attack on slavery they already had a big enough fight. He says, "They did not want a Negro newspaper and even the Negroes ridiculed me." Undismayed, however, he persisted. Later, Rochester was to be very proud of him.

On the lecture platform he worked closely with the white abolitionists, especially Wendell Phillips, Theodore Tilton, and John Brown. When the last begged him to join in his raid on Harper's Ferry, however, he refused. He saw the futility of the attempt and wisely decided that his life could be used to better advantage than in such a quixotic attempt.

In spite of this he found himself involved. His name was found among John Brown's papers and to avoid arrest he fled to Canada, and then again to England. What he feared most was not implication in the raid but disclosure of his activities as a station master on the "Underground Railway," a system of freeing slaves by aiding their escape from the South and smuggling them into Canada.

In England he was received with even greater acclaim but his heart was in America and he longed to return. Then sentiment in the North swung in favor of John Brown. The latter was no longer "a traitor and a fanatic" but a martyr, a hero. Douglass, feeling that he would be safe, returned and when the Civil War broke out, threw all his energies into it. His slogan was "Union and Emancipation; Abolition or Destruction."

Consistent with his policy of equality, he demanded that colored men should be used as soldiers and not merely as servants and laborers. Northern color prejudice opposed him, and Lincoln, whose declared goal was to save the Union even if it were necessary to retain slavery and color discrimination to do so, obeyed the popular will. But Douglass went on fighting for the use of Negro soldiers until the need for men became so urgent that the Union Army had to use them. Lincoln later admitted, no less than four times, that the Negroes furnished the balance of power which decided the conflict in favor of the North. For instance, in a letter to Charles G. D. Robinson in Ausust, 1864, he said:

Drive back to the support of the rebellion the physical force that the colored people now give and promise us, and neither the present nor any coming administration can save the Union. Take from us and give to the enemy the hundred and thirty, forty, or fifty thousand colored persons now serving as soldiers, seamen and laborers, and we can no longer maintain the contest.

The party who could elect a President on a War and Slavery Restoration, would of necessity lose the colored force; and that force being lost, it would be as powerless to save the Union as to do any other impossible thing.

Douglass helped to raise the 54th and 55th Massachusetts Regiments, his sons, Charles and Lewis, being the first to enlist. He himself was promised the post of assistant to General Thomas by Secretary of War Stanton, but Stanton never kept his promise, although Douglass reminded him of it several times.

With colored soldiers now in the Army, Douglass' next task was to see that they were fairly treated. The South was hanging all colored prisoners. As Horace Greely said, "Every black soldier now goes to battle with a halter about his neck." Douglass insisted that the North should retaliate on such occasions. He demanded equal pay for the colored soldier with the white, and the same opportunity for promotion.

He fought stubbornly and went often to the White House. At first Lincoln regarded him as a pest. Later, when the Negro soldiers proved their worth, Lincoln learned to appreciate him, and in the darkest moments of the conflict, sent for him to ask his advice.

In spite of this an attempt was made to bar him from Lincoln's second inaugural ceremony on account of color. Fairbank, a white man who was present, relates the episode thus: "Douglass was stopped at the door. 'Hold on, you can't go in,' someone said. Another interposed and said: 'This is Frederick Douglass.' Douglass replied for himself: 'I don't want to go in as Frederick Douglass, but as a citizen of the United States.'"

At this point Lincoln, noticing the trouble, came over, and with his long arms outstretched over the heads of the crowd, said, "How do you do, Frederick? Come right in!"

Lincoln wanted to know what Douglass thought of his inaugural speech. "Mr. Lincoln," replied Douglass, "I must not detain you with my poor opinion. There are a thousand waiting to shake your hand."

"No, no!" insisted Lincoln, "you must stop a little. There's no man in the country whose opinion I value more than yours. I want to know what you think of it."

"Mr. Lincoln," responded Douglass, "that was a sacred effort."

With the Civil War won, Douglass' next fight was to have the freedmen made citizens. Lincoln was opposed to this, as was his successor Andrew Johnson. Lincoln had said in a speech at Charleston, Illinois, September 18, 1858, "I am not, nor have ever been, in favor of making voters or jurors of Negroes, nor of qualifying them to hold office." The Civil War had perhaps modified his views on this but very little. He strongly favored colonization of the blacks outside of the United States. In 1862, when a deputation of Negroes called on him at the White House, he advised them to encourage their people to leave America because of the physical differences between black and white. "This," he said, "is a reason why, at least, we should be separated."

In 1862 Lincoln proposed an amendment to the Constitution for settling Negroes outside the United States and had Congress give him $600,000 to colonize Negroes on the Ile de Vache off the cost of Haiti. The attempt was not only a miserable failure but more than a hundred Negroes lost their lives on that desolate island. Still, after the Civil War, he proposed to General Grant to send the Negro veterans to dig the Panama Canal where they would have perished like flies as did the French. As Douglass pointed out, had the free Negroes followed Lincoln's advice and left the country, the Union forces would not have had their invaluable services.

Had Lincoln lived, Douglass would probably have had greater difficulties with him than he did with his successor, Andrew Johnson, whose Reconstruction policies had been largely outlined by Lincoln. Under Johnson's plan, the freedmen would have become peons, this in an attempt to coax the South back into the Union. Douglass fought this new kind of slavery with as much vigor as he had fought the old. He demanded the ballot for the Negro. American liberty, he said, depended on three boxes: the ballot box, the jury box, and the cartridge box.

"From the first," he says, "I saw no chance of bettering the condition of the freedman and become a citizen. I insisted that there was no safety for him or anybody else in America outside the American Government. I set myself to work with whatever force I possessed to secure this power for the recently emancipated millions."

Douglass' proposal was ridiculed even by most of the abolitionists. Garrison himself had to be won over to the idea by Wendell Phillips. Thanks to Douglass, the Negro was thus enfranchised decades before he otherwise would have been.

With the winning of the ballot for the Negro, Douglass' chief task was done. There were honors, such as they were, in store for him. He served as U.S. Commissioner to Santo Domingo; Minister to Haiti; member of the Legislative Council of the District of Columbia; presidential elector of New York; and Marshal of the District of Columbia, in which capacity he officiated at the inauguration of President Garfield. At one Republican convention, he was among those named for the presidency.

Later he went on the lecture platform, where his addresses on "Self-Made Men" thrilled black and white auditors alike. On Memorial Day, 1871, he was one of the principal speakers at Arlington Cemetery, with President Grant present. In 1876 he was the orator on the occasion of the unveiling of the Freedmen's Monument in Washington, President Grant, his cabinet, and other dignitaries attending. Copies of this speech were sold by the hundreds of thousands in America and England.

Whenever and wherever he was announced as a speaker, audiences were thrown into commotion. When he rose to speak, he was an impressive figure with his noble head covered with bushy gray hair. Tall, upright, every inch of his robust frame seemed to radiate vitality and purpose. Even before he uttered a word, his audience had been won over. He spoke in a voice low-pitched but full, slowly, deliberately, with majestic cadence and great ease, every gesture dignified and poised.

George L. Ruffin wrote of him at this period:

He has by his own energy and force of character commanded the respect of the nation; he was ignorant, he has, against law and by stealth entirely unaided, educated himself; he was poor, he has by honest toil and industry become rich and independent, so to speak; he, a chattel slave of a hated and cruelly wronged race, in the teeth of American prejudice and in face of nearly every kind of hindrance and draw-back has come to be one of the foremost orators of the age, with a reputation established on both sides of the Atlantic; a writer of power and elegance of expression; a thinker whose views are potent in controlling and shaping public opinion; a higher officer in the National Government; a cultivated gentleman whose virtues as a husband, father and citizen are the highest honor a man can have.

He and Mrs. Douglass were regular guests at social functions given at the White House by President Cleveland. His declining years were spent on his property, Cedar Hill, at Anacostia, D.C. —land formerly owned by an aristocrat who had stipulated that "neither mulatto, Negro, nor Irishman" should ever own a foot of his estate.

Here, surrounded by his books and many souvenirs, he devoted himself to the study of music, of which he was passionately fond. Many national and international persons of note visited him, and he became known as "The Sage of Anacostia."

Of many interesting stories about him, the following deserves mention. After the Civil War he visited Talbot County, the scene of his early privations, and saw, among others, his heartless former master, Thomas Auld, now penniless and dying of paralysis. Douglass greeted him with touching sympathy, and when Auld addressed him as "Marshal" Douglass, Douglass replied, "Not Marshal Douglass—just Frederick." This splendid gesture was construed as subservience by Douglass' enemies among the colored people, many of whom never forgave him for marrying his white secretary after the death of his first wife, a colored woman. Auld's death was mentioned in newspapers in America and England because he had once owned Douglass.

Although he was received as a privileged character almost everywhere in the North, this did not prevent his being snubbed by some whites—and some Negroes too. Once two colored dining-car waiters refused to serve him because of color. He says of this:

In their eyes I saw Fred Douglass, suddenly, and possibly undeservedly, lifted above them. The fact that I was colored and they were also colored, had so long made us equal that the contradiction now presented was too much. After all, I have no blame for Sam and Garrett. They were trained in the school of servility to believe that only white men were entitled to be waited upon by colored men.

While the rank and file of our people quote with much vehemence, the doctrine of human equality, they are among the first to deny it and denounce it in practice.

In spite of his advanced age, the Grand Old Man plunged with characteristic vigor into the fight for suffrage for all American women. But the end was at hand. On February 20, 1895, the seventy-eight-year-old orator addressed a woman's suffrage convention, returning home in the best of spirits and, apparently, the best of health. Leaving the dinner table, he paused in the hallway to relate an incident that had occurred at the meeting. He was telling it in his usual animated way, when suddenly he dropped to his knees, his hands clasped.

Mrs. Douglass thought he was only reenacting part of the scene. But he sank lower and lower, and stumbling gently to the floor, breathed his last.

The press of the civilized world burst out in resounding praise of him. Memorial services were held over the nation. The city of Rochester voted to suspend business during his burial. Later a monument was erected to him there. It cost $10,000, of which

New York State paid $3,000 and the Republic of Haiti, $1000. Theodore Roosevelt was the orator at the unveiling.

The Chicago Western Newspaper Union said of him:

Physically, mentally, and morally, Mr. Douglass was a grand specimen of manhood, and any race might be proud to claim him as a representative. . . . As an orator and a thinker, he ranked with the best in the land; though born a slave and excluded from the advantages of education, he had a command of the English language that was marvelous in its perfection. Sneered at, hissed, mobbed, stoned, and assaulted, he stemmed the tide and came off conqueror. When it was dangerous even for white men to speak the truth on the question of slavery, he did not equivocate or palliate evil with soft words. He lifted his voice like a trumpet and told the people of their transgressions.

The *Narragansett Times* said:

As for scholarships, he was the peer of the ablest. He had evidently been a reader of the best English literature; he never lacked for a good, apt and elegant illustration; his mind was well-stored and a grand dignity presided over the man. This dignity gave him character with the world.

Slave, fugitive, crusader, champion, achiever of truest success, wielder of vast usefulness, commander of the world's respect, yet with all of his honors, humble, gentle, as are all the truly great.

In his immense ascent from the lowest depths where the masses were reached not even by the faintest gleam of hope to the heights of meritorious and even majestic triumph, in his noble aspiration and upward mountings, his final complete and serene success, the life of this man affords one of the most satisfying illustrations of high human realization that appears in the history of the whole world.

Theodore Tilton said, "I knew the noblest giants of my day and he was of them, strong amid the strong."

And Paul Laurence Dunbar wrote:

> . . . he was no soft-tongued apologist;
> He spoke straight forward, fearlessly, uncovered.
> The sunlight of his truth dispelled the mist
> And set in bold relief each dark-hued cloud.
> To sin and crime he gave their proper hue
> And hurled at evil what was evil's due.

REFERENCES

Many are the incidents told about Frederick Douglass in the literature of the period, for instance, in books by (or about) Alexis Soyer, world-famed chef; Margaret Fuller, Marchionness of Ossoli; Princess Helene von Racowitza, one of the most celebrated women of her times, who knew him well; and Frederika Bremer, a noted writer on American life and manners.

Princess Racowitza says, "Two names stand out above all in my mind's eye—Ottile Assing and Fred Douglass." Ottilie Assing, she says, was "a German woman of 'splendid education and fine manners' " who used to receive escaped slaves from the South. She hid Douglass for two years, helped in his education and "taught him the most perfect manner." She also fell in love with him and hoped that he would marry her. Von Racowitza says:

"Good Ottilie's ageing heart, as was natural was centered upon the dark, handsome Fred—the handiwork of her spirit. She respected his bonds of wedlock but no doubt hoped that when death released him from his colored spouse he would lay his freedom at her feet.

"The poor thing was disappointed. Fred Douglass whose hair was now snow-white, contrasting with the dusky color of his skin, lost his wife through death but he offered his hand to a younger white woman who had been his secretary when he was in the service of the State.

"My friend, Ottilie, who had hitherto been so brave, now in her despair, committed suicide in Paris, whither she had journeyed in the anguish of her soul. She poisoned herself on a lonely bench and in this way miserably ended a life which had been so full of good and noteworthy deeds." (*Memoirs*, pp. 368–372. 1911.)

Frederika Bremer tells of her visit to Douglass' home and of his first wife. The latter, she says was "very dark, stout and plain but with a good expression. His daughter, Rosetta, takes after her mother. The governess is a white lady who lives in the family." (*Homes of the New World*, Vol. I, p. 585. 1853.)

Douglass, Frederick, *Life and Times of Frederick Douglass*. New York, Pathway Press, 1941.

Holland, F. M., *Frederick Douglass, the Colored Orator*. New York, Funk and Wagnalls, 1891.

Washington, Booker T., *Frederick Douglass*. Philadelphia and London, G. W. Jacobs and Company, 1907.

Douglass, H. P., *In Memoriam*. Philadelphia, 1897.

Thompson, J. W., *An Authentic History of the Douglass Monument.* Rochester, N.Y., Rochester Herald Press, 1903.

Curtis, C. K., *Fighters for Freedom.* New York, 1933.

Pickett, W. P., *The Negro Problem: Abraham Lincoln's Solution.* New York, 1908.

Dana, R. H., "Nullity of the Emancipation Proclamation." *North American Review*, Vol. MCCCXXXI, pp. 128–134, 1880.

ADDITIONAL REFERENCES

Adams, Russell L., *Great Negroes: Past and Present*, pp. 26–28. Chicago, Afro-Am Publishing Company, 1963, 1964.

Bontemps, Arna, *Frederick Douglass: Slave–Fighter–Freeman.* New York, Knopf, 1959.

Brawley, Benjamin G., *Negro Builders and Heroes*, pp. 61–66. Chapel Hill, The University of North Carolina Press, 1937.

Carroll, Howard, *Twelve Americans: Their Lives and Times*, pp. 263–299. New York, Harper, 1883.

Cromwell, John Wesley, *The Negro in American History*, pp. 139–154. Washington, D.C., The American Negro Academy, 1914.

Douglass, Frederick, *Narrative of the Life of Frederick Douglass, an American Slave.* Boston, 1845.

———, *Life and Times of Frederick Douglass.* Hartford, 1887.

Gregory, James Monroe, *Frederick Douglass, the Orator.* Springfield, Mass., Willey Co., 1893.

Grimke, Francis James, *The Works of Francis J. Grimke*, Carter G. Woodson, ed., Vol. I, pp. 34–71. Washington, D.C., The Associated Publishers, 1942.

Lotz, Philip Henry, ed., . . . *Rising Above Color*, pp. 58–65. New York, Association Press, 1943.

Monroe, James, *Oberlin Thursday Lectures, Addresses and Essays*, pp. 57–94. Oberlin, E. J. Goodrich, 1897.

Pickens, William, *The New Negro*, pp. 71–102. New York, The Neale Publishing Company, 1916.

Quarles, Benjamin, *Frederick Douglass.* Washington, D.C., The Associated Publishers, 1948.

Rankin, Jeremiah Eames, *Frederick Douglass.* Washington, D.C., Howard University, 1895.

Rollins, Charlemae Hill, *They Showed the Way*, pp. 46–52. New York, Thomas Y. Crowell Co., 1964.

Sears, Louis Martin, "Frederick Douglass and the Mission to Haiti 1889–1891." *Hispanic American History*, Vol. XXI, No 2 (May, 1941).

Washington, Booker T., *Frederick Douglass*. London, Hodder and Stoughton, 1906.

Jan Ernest Matzeliger

INVENTOR WHO GAVE SUPREMACY IN THE SHOE INDUSTRY
TO THE UNITED STATES
(1852–1889)

IN SPITE OF HANDICAPS which exceed those of the oppressed in
almost every other land, there are always individual Negroes in
the United States who are not content to settle down to a color-
line job but strive to play a man's part in achievement, regardless
of all discouragements. These individuals are to be found in almost every field, including the very difficult one of scientific
invention.

In at least one branch of industry, America owes its supremacy directly to a Negro, Jan Ernest Matzeliger. A pioneer in the
art of shoemaking, he enriched America and other nations by
billions of dollars, made a dozen or more millionaires, created
work for hundreds of thousands, and contributed enormously to
what is regarded as one of the distinctive features of civilization,
namely, the wearing of shoes. Massachusetts, center of the
world's shoe trade, has been a particular beneficiary of his
ingenuity.

Matzeliger was born in Dutch Guiana, South America, of a
Dutch father and a Negro mother. Mechanically inclined as a
child, he entered the government machine shops of the colony at
the age of ten as an apprentice.

Ambitious to learn more, he left for New York City when his
apprenticeship expired. Handicapped by his color and his lack of

funds, he nevertheless contrived to learn a good deal about machinery.

At the age of twenty-five he went to Lynn, Massachusetts, and thanks to the more liberal environment there, he found employment in the factory of M. H. Harvey, where he operated a McKay machine for turning shoes. There his attention was naturally directed to shoe machinery. Noting the time-wasting method of lasting shoes by hand, he decided to invent a machine to do it.

Such a machine had been the fond dream of many an ingenious youth eager to make a fortune. Inventors had burned barrels of midnight oil and promoters had spent hundreds of thousands of dollars in the endeavor to change the lasting of shoes from hand to machine methods, as Blake and McKay had changed the sewing of the uppers.

When Metzeliger announced his intention, his white fellow workers laughed at him derisively. That a Negro should succeed where some of the best white inventors had failed seemed ridiculous. They boasted, moreover, that whatever else was done by machinery, nothing could ever supersede hand-lasting. The lasters felt secure in their position. These skilled craftsmen were the gentlemen of the shoe trade, earning from $20 to $40 a week, a very good wage then.

Securing a room over the old West Lynn Mission at the corner of Ann and Charles streets, where he would be safe from too curious eyes, Matzeliger worked nights studying, experimenting, and drawing.

With no other capital but his meager wages, he was forced to make use of such material as he could get hold of. He used mainly pieces of wood and old cigar and packing boxes. For six months he toiled strenuously until he had constructed a model which, though crude, gave him confidence that he was on the road to success.

Although he tried to work in secret, the hand-lasters learned of his efforts and sometimes dropped in to laugh at the odd-looking combination of sticks in the form of a machine. One of them, in racial contempt, dubbed it "the niggerhead machine," the name by which it was popularly known later.

Even Matzeliger's friends advised him to give up what seemed to them a foolish undertaking, and insisted that after a long day's work at the factory he should have rest and recreation. One man, however, thought he saw some good principles in the collection of sticks and offered Matzeliger $50 for it. But Matzeliger, reasoning that if it was worth a $50 first offer, it probably would have a much higher value elsewhere, refused to sell.

He now planned to make a model in metal. Gathering odd bits of iron, he worked patiently, filing and fitting the parts unaided. Four years later he perfected a machine that would work. He was offered $1500 for his invention of pleating the leather around the toe, which sum he again refused. Greatly encouraged by the widespread interest his model created, he started to build a better one. Perfection was his aim. For another six years he worked on his invention until a more simplified machine had been constructed.

With his new model it was easy for him to convince practical men that his invention would work successfully. A company was formed, consisting of himself, those who had advanced him money from time to time, and some others with large capital. It was soon found necessary, however, to build another machine, different in construction, which, when completed, worked almost to perfection.

One of the special merits of the invention was that the pincers for pulling the upper were positively closed by a smooth movement and did not tear even the most delicate leather.

Today, according to experts, no better method of handling loose tacks for fastening the upper to the sole has ever been invented. The twist and pull of the pincers reproduced exactly the peculiar and almost inimitable skill with which expert hand-lasters treat difficult upper leather in their lasting of shoes. No other machine has been invented that is capable of manipulating and shaping a shoe on all styles of lasts, and it is practically impossible to make shoes to meet commercial requirements without using Matzeliger's machine. After twelve years of persistent pursuit of a single idea, he had won.

With this new invention, the United Shoe Manufacturing Company rapidly drove competitors out of the shoe business until, a few years later, it controlled 98 percent of the shoe machinery business.

A tremendous expansion in the shoe industry followed. Shoe stocks proved a gold mine to investors. Earnings increased more than 350 percent while wages increased but 34 percent and the price of footwear decreased.

The machine was set up in factories but there were stubborn and prolonged strikes against it by the hand-lasters. One veteran laster said, "The machine revenges Matzeliger by singing as it works: I've got your job! I've got your job!"

F. A. Gannon says:

Sales of shoes abroad increased approximately $16,000,000 annually. United Shoe Machinery Company machinery and shoe experts were sent around the world and American shoe manufacturing methods were adopted farthest north in Norway, in tropical Central America, in England and all the countries of Europe, in Africa, Australia and even in China, Japan and the Philippines.

The United Shoe Manufacturing Company constructed a model manufacturing plant in Beverly, Massachusetts. It was built of reinforced concrete and employed 5000 persons at a high average wage. Nearby recreational buildings, including a country club, a gun club, and motorboat club, were constructed, and a band and an athletic team organized—all for the benefit of the employees. The health of shoe workers under the new working conditions improved immensely, and tuberculosis, their worst menace, was greatly decreased.

One of the stockholders, Colonel McKay, left $5,000,000 to the engineering department of Harvard University.

And what about Matzeliger? The amazing young genius was not to enjoy his triumph. Close confinement and overwork had undermined his health. He was stricken with tuberculosis and died two years later, in September, 1889, at the age of thirty-seven.

In his will Matzeliger left a few shares of his stock to the North Congregational Church, a white congregation that had befriended him. Years later this church, finding itself in financial difficulties, remembered the bequest and sold the stock for $10,860. A tablet in this church commemorates the inventor.

The Consolidated Hand Lasting Machine Company, in its bulletin, said of him:

The conviction is forced upon us that this man of iron will, this man of nerve, who could not be turned from his course, knew whereof he spoke and builded better than he knew, very much better than his most sanguine friends hoped for. Such men do away with old methods and institute new and better ones. Such men make missionaries and martyrs. Without such men we should be without material progress.

What Edison is to artificial lighting, Matzeliger is to footwear. This great Negro genius needs no monument. Almost every shoe worn by civilized men is his memorial.

REFERENCES

Though Matzeliger was mocked about his color, and his machine called "niggerhead" in derision, he came to be considered white as the great value of his machine grew. However, his death certificate listed him as a "mulatto." Also Waldemar Kaempfert, noted scientific writer, says he was "a poor half-breed son of a Dutch engineer and a native black woman. . . . This messenger from a foreign land solved in principle the final problem of making shoes by machinery." (*Popular History of American Invention*, Vol. II, pp. 429–450, 1924).

Gannon, F. A., *A Short History of American Shoe-Making.* 1912.
McDermott, C. H., *History of the Shoe and Leather Industries*, pp. 61, 106–07.

ADDITIONAL REFERENCES

Adams, Russell L., *Great Negroes: Past and Present*, p. 51. Chicago, Afro-Am Publishing Company, 1963, 1964.
Aptheker, Herbert, *A Documentary History of the Negro People in the United States*, pp. 744–745. New York, The Citadel Press, 1951.
Haber, Louis, *Black Pioneers of Science and Invention*, pp. 25–33. New York, Harcourt, Brace and World, Inc., 1970.

Kaplan, Sidney, "Jan Ernst Matzeliger and Making the Shoe." *Journal of Negro History*, Vol. XL, pp. 8–33 (January 1958).

Rollins, Charlemae Hill, *They Showed the Way*, pp. 93–96. New York, Thomas Y. Crowell Company, 1964.

Peter Jackson

GALLANT KNIGHT OF THE PRIZE RING
(1861–1901)

PETER JACKSON, "Black Prince Peter," is, by reputation, the most graceful, most gentlemanly figure who ever stepped into the prize ring. Six feet one and a half, weighing 192 pounds, sinewy, handsome, he had a body that would have delighted a sculptor of ancient Greece. And his manners were equally pleasing.

Jeffrey Farnol, the boxing expert, who knew him, said:

Perhaps for his size the most finished and beautiful boxer ever seen; magnificently shaped from head to foot, his every move graceful; also, he was incredibly quick and very sure. He was both, in looks, manners, and behavior, the very best of his type, delightfully modest and thoroughly sportsmanlike.

Wignall says:

Peter trod as daintly as a cat; the pristine energy of savage haunts was in his style; his eye was like a panther's. The head was carried on a powerful neck that rose like a pyramid from the broad shoulders. Every line of the figure from the jaunty head to the nimble feet was clean-cut and graceful and the whole gave an astonishing impression of the lithe activity and superb strength.

Nat Fleischer, boxing authority, says:

He was a sharpshooter, scientific, a two-fisted fighter. The most feared of his time, he is rated among the ring Immortals because he possessed every asset of a great champion even though he never gained the world crown.

Peter Jackson was born in the Danish West Indies, not in Australia, as is generally believed. He went to Australia at the age of six with his parents, had his early training there, and was so beloved by the Australians that they claimed him as their own.

An excellent swimmer with a magnificent style, he gave swimming exhibitions and attracted the attention of Jem Mace, former champion of England, who trained him as a boxer. He had some reverses at first, being knocked out by Bill Farnon in 1884 in three rounds, but finally he defeated the Australian champion, Tom Lees, and was given the title.

With no opponents worthy of him there, he yearned for America, where there were plenty of fighters, and arrived in California in 1888, bringing with him the massive gold belt of the Australian championship. At San Francisco the sportsmen marveled at him and were eager to match him with other fighters, but one look at him and the white fighters scurried like rabbits to cover behind the color line. They knew that Jackson's fists had the driving force of a trip-hammer. His favorite blow was the one-two—a right to the stomach and a left between the eyes.

There was but one Negro fighter in America near worthy of him: the original George Godfrey, and a match was arranged between the two. But Jackson beat him with such form and captivating ring grace that the more sportsmanlike whites began ridiculing the white fighters for taking refuge behind the color line until Jack McAuliffe, the leading heavyweight on the Pacific Coast, agreed to fight him for $3000.

They met before the California Athletic Club and fought with bare knuckles as was the custom then. Jackson simply toyed with McAuliffe. To give the sports a run for their money, he allowed him to stay to the twenty-fourth round and then drove home his famous one-two. When the right to the stomach had doubled up McAuliffe, Jackson straightened him up with a left between the eyes before he fell.

The victory drove the white American fighters still farther behind the color line, John L. Sullivan most of all. The Australian sportsmen, indignant at the treatment of their favorite, ridiculed

Sullivan, telling him that by refusing to fight Jackson, he was no longer world champion but only white champion.

Sullivan, arrogant and unpopular with the fighting fans, but at times good-natured, announced that he could whip Jackson, and therefore it wasn't necessary to try. Sullivan was probably stronger than Jackson. It is said that he once lifted a trolley car back on its tracks after six men together had failed to do so. Jackson, on the other hand, was three inches taller, weighed a pound more in fighting trim, was three years younger, and a more scientific boxer. Sullivan trained on whisky, while Jackson drank little.

The sporting papers took up Jackson's cause, but Sullivan was too difficult to catch. When Jackson would be leaving London for New York, John L. would be leaving New York for London. A cartoon of the times showed the two meeting in mid-Atlantic on ships going in the opposite direction with Jackson shaking his fist at John. This was the nearest that Jackson ever got to the championship.

In England Jackson was warmly welcomed. The English remembered two other great Negro fighters, Tom Molineaux and Bill Richmond. Jackson's elegant manners captured them too, and they arranged several matches for him.

England at that time was still the principal center of boxing. To be English champion was almost equivalent to being champion of the world. There was a tradition, too, that only Englishmen and Irishmen made good fighters. Jackson shattered that belief. He defeated all comers, among them Jem Smith, the English champion, whom he knocked out in two rounds. Soon there was no worthy opponent for him in England, and none in America who dared meet him.

Jackson by now had made such a reputation that the true sportsmen in America were clamoring for his return. He came and a match was arranged for him with Patsy Cardiff, the Peoria Giant. The match was a slaughter. Jackson played around with him until the tenth round, then finished him with his deadly one-two.

This victory increased the cry against Sullivan. Patsy Cardiff had once fought Sullivan to a draw. The English and the Australian papers redoubled their ridicule of Sullivan, but fear of humiliation at the hands of a black man was too great for the Boston-born Irish-American. At least his persistent dodging of Jackson amounted to that in the opinion of those who were eager for such a match.

At last, a leading white boxer, James J. Corbett, later to be world champion, agreed to fight Jackson. Corbett, called Gentleman Jim because of his graceful manner, was five years younger than Jackson but had the disadvantage in height and weight. He was an inch shorter and fifty pounds lighter. But what he lacked in build and strength was amply compensated for in skill. Corbett was a born strategist and one of the most scientific fighters of all time. In the very fine points of the game he was probably Jackson's superior. Moreover, unlike Sullivan and most of the other fighters, he shunned liquor and trained with Spartan discipline.

The two met on a night forever to be famous in ring history, May 21, 1891, before the California Athletic Club for a fight to the finish with five-ounce gloves. The purse was $10,000. Odds were against Corbett.

When the gong sounded, Jackson came straight at the delicate-looking Corbett and it looked like his finish. All felt that his meeting with the black giant was suicide. Corbett saw that his only hope was to keep away from Jackson, and he ran, dodged, and ducked, with Jackson in pursuit, until the spectators hooted.

Corbett, in his account of the fight, says, "No matter in what direction I would dash, this big black thing was on top of me trying to one-two me to death." At last, in the sixteenth round, Jackson caught up with Gentleman Jim and landed his favorite blow. Corbett successfully blocked part of it, but the tail-end, catching him sideways, sent him reeling like a drunken man. To all it seemed as if the fight was over, but Corbett, thanks to his strict regimen, was able to rally. Clinching, he hung onto Jackson so desperately that the referee had great difficulty in tearing him away.

But Corbett had not only skill but brains. He had been observing where Jackson was in the habit of landing his blows, and as the fight progressed, learned how to avoid them. When the bout dragged into the twenty-eighth round, Jackson no longer seemed the certain victor. He had turned his right ankle. In the next round, Corbett broke through Jackson's guard, but he still dreaded that lightning one-two, and worked cautiously.

In the fortieth round the odds were almost even. It had become an endurance contest. Two of Corbett's ribs were broken, but he stuck it out gamely. In the sixty-first round Corbett "was somewhat fortunate when the referee declared it a draw."

This fight, the most noted up to that time and for long after, was a turning point in ring history. It introduced new tactics and methods of training. The gentlemanly and chivalrous nature of the two opponents gave the public a taste for other than bruisers. Corbett gained great prestige by the fight. Later he defeated Sullivan. Many insisted that Sullivan would not have made as good a showing against Jackson as Corbett had.

Soon afterwards Jackson returned to England. He was in time to meet a boxer whose name was on everybody's lips: Frank Slavin, an Australian, who had been trained by Jackson's own teacher, Jem Mace. Slavin was a magnificent athlete, and next to Sullivan, the most powerful hitter in the world. He was square-jawed, ferocious, brutal, and feared no one. He despised black men. Certain that the white race was superior, he was, unlike Sullivan, eager to prove it. Best of all, he made a perfect match for Jackson, being almost the same in age, height, and weight.

The fight was staged at the National Sporting Club in London, May 30, 1892, with the leading sportsmen present, among them the Prince of Wales, afterwards Edward VII. As Slavin stepped into the ring, he shouted, "To be beaten by a nigger is a pill I will never swallow."

The betting was two to one in favor of Slavin. "He was the stronger and more powerful; his devastating right was world-famous, and then, moreover—he was white," says Farnol.

When the gong sounded, the two faced each other cautiously. Then Slavin shot out a terrific right at Jackson, which, had it caught him, might have finished him. But Jackson danced nimbly out of his way. Crouched like a panther, alert and dangerous, he kept Slavin at bay with his long reach, shooting out his wonderfully straight left with a feline swiftness that defied duplication and never missed its mark.

Slavin, hoping to ruffle Jackson, taunted him, but Jackson boxed coolly and gracefully, winning every round up the fifth, and letting Slavin tire himself out. In the sixth round, however, Slavin smashed one through that caught Jackson under the heart. He reeled and Slavin drove in another. All seemed over for Jackson, when the gong saved him.

When they came out again, Slavin was sure of victory. Wishing to show his backers something spectacular, he rushed at Jackson to finish him, but Jackson, refreshed, kept out of his way and waited for his chance. In came in the tenth round. As Slavin charged madly in, Jackson flashed through his famous one-two. And the fight was over.

Slavin was still standing, however, his hands at his sides. He had been knocked out on his feet!

Then something happened that made ring talk for a long time to come—something that sent Jackson's popularity soaring even higher. Seeing his opponent helpless, he did not want to hit him again, and when the referee insisted otherwise, Jackson said, "Sorry, Frank," and gave him a few light taps that sent him to the floor. He then picked up Slavin and carried him tenderly to his corner.

Frank Harris, famous English editor and author, says of Jackson in this respect, "The colored man, Peter Jackson, like Corbett, was very much of a gentleman: he told me he always hated to knock anyone out and thought the referee should stop the fight when the complete superiority of one fighter was established." He says also that Jackson "was a much better specimen of the prize-fighter than Slavin; certainly the best character I ever saw in the ring. . . . I soon got to know Peter Jackson personally and liked his quiet and modest ways. . . ."

Jackson's victory over Slavin served even more to put him on the shelf. Corbett, now the champion, showed no eagerness to fight him again even though the proudest fact in his life was his fight with Jackson and how he had been able to stand him off for sixty-one rounds. Fleischer says that that fight made so great an impression on Corbett that it was one of the last things he referred to on his death bed. He said, "To think I held the greatest ring warrior sixty-one rounds." Corbett often said that Jackson could box, could fight, "could do anything any mortal man ever did with his brains, hands and feet. What a fighter! . . . Indeed, Peter the Great." A match was finally arranged between the two in 1893 but nothing came of it.

Disgusted at the treatment he was receiving, Jackson took to drink. Since nothing could be gained by staying either in England or America, he went back to the West Indies but soon afterwards returned to London where he gave exhibition bouts in dance halls and later opened a boxing school.

American sportsmen, however, did not forget him and begged him to return. He did so in 1898 and was matched with James J. Jeffries. Jackson knew that his fighting days were over. Six years of drink and indulgence had finished him. And he was thirty-seven. But he needed the money and he wanted to oblige his friends. He and Jeffries met at the Pavillion in San Francisco.

Jeffries was taller, stronger, heavier, and sixteen years younger but less agile and less graceful. Jackson, knowing that his only hope against the giant Jeffries was a quick finish, came out at him and landed his famous one-two, following it with a punch under the heart. But the blows had no more effect on Jeffries than a massage. All was over for "the Black Prince." In the third round Jeffries finished him with a right to the temple.

The victory helped Jeffries greatly. It was felt, as one writer says, that "anyone who could beat even a shadow of Old Peter had something in him." Later, when Jeffries became champion, he too drew the color line.

Jackson returned to Australia where he gave himself up to drink and became a physical wreck. He lived in back rooms and ate only when someone gave him food. Tuberculosis did the rest.

He was buried in the Toowong Cemetery in Roma, Queensland. His friends erected a monument over his grave with the words: "This was a man."

REFERENCES

Miles, H. G., *Pugilistica*. Edinburgh, 1906.
Wignall, T., *Story of Boxing*. London, 1923.
Corbett, J. J., *The Roar of the Crowd*. New York, 1925.

Farnol, J., *Epics of the Fancy*. London, 1928.

Hales, A. G., *Black Prince Peter*. London, Wright and Brown, 1931.

Harris, Frank, *My Life*, Vol. XXXIII, pp. 178–179. Nice, 1927.

Fleischer, Nat, *Black Dynamite: Story of the Negro in Boxing*, Vol. I, pp. 123–172. 1938.

———, *All Time Ring Record Book*, p. 198. 1941.

ADDITIONAL REFERENCES

Fleischer, Nathaniel S., and Sama, Andre, *A Pictorial History of Boxing*. New York, Citadel Press, 1955.

Golding, Louis, *The Bare-Knuckle Breed*. New York, A. S. Barnes, 1954.

Johnston, Alexander, *Ten—And Out!* New York, Washburn, 1936.

Paul Laurence Dunbar

PAUL LAURENCE DUNBAR came on the scene at a time critical
for his people. The spasm of sympathy aroused for them during
the Civil War was almost dead. The Northerners, having resumed
their commerce with the ex-slaveholders, were trying to woo
them. Slavery in the South had returned in a new guise with the
consent of the North and the white press and pulpit. North and
South were generally justifying it by trying to prove that while
the ex-slaves were not exactly apes, they were somehow not quite
human.

It was then that Dunbar took up the challenge. In love with
his people, but not so much as to be blind to their faults, he
interpreted them in song and story with such compelling genius
that a large portion of white America stopped to listen, and was
finally led to regard the black man as a human being first, and
an African next. It is no exaggeration to say that Dunbar endowed the so-called Negro with humanity in the eyes of hundreds of thousands of his white fellow citizens.

None of the world's great poets had a more difficult time. His
early financial difficulties equaled those of Camoëns and Burns,
but he had an additional difficulty that neither Burns nor
Camoëns had to encounter—the handicap of color.

Dunbar's father Joshua and his mother Matilda both came

of the humblest stock and both had a love for literature. The father fled from slavery into Canada but came back to join the Union Army. After the war he married Matilda at Dayton, Ohio. Paul was born in 1872.

He wrote his first poem when only seven years old. At school he won high praise for his diligence and his behavior. In 1891 he was graduated from high school with honors, although since the death of his father seven years before he had been working to support himself and his mother.

On leaving high school, he was forced to work as an elevator boy because of color prejudice. But with a soul attuned to the infinite he set about his menial and poorly paid task cheerfully. Prejudice, he decided, would not dominate his soul. With the spirit of John Bunyan at his last, or Mohammed at his camel driving, he composed verses, as he worked. His cheerfulness and courtesy won him friends among his elevator passengers.

A year later there was a literary reunion at Dayton. Through one of his teachers, Mr. Truesdale, he was selected to give the address of welcome. To avoid opposition it was kept a secret; his name was not printed on the program.

When the time came, Dunbar walked quietly to the platform and amid general astonishment was introduced by John Clark Ridpath, the historian. Dunbar's address, in its metrical fluent English and its cultured delivery, convinced all that they were listening to a cultivated genius. At its close he vanished during the applause.

The next morning three of the editors who were present called to see him where he worked and talked with him between elevator trips. One of them, Dr. Matthews, published one of Dunbar's poems with excerpts from others, which were extensively reproduced in America and England. James Whitcomb Riley congratulated him and quoted his poem "Drowsy Day." Dunbar now planned to publish some of his poems but the printers wanted $125, an impossible sum for one who was earning only $4 a week. After much discouragement, a friend of his guaranteed the amount, and the book, *Oak and Ivy*, appeared. He sold enough copies among his friends to clear the debt. Soon afterwards he secured employment in the Dayton courthouse with more pay and more leisure. At this time one of his admirers, Charles Thatcher of Toledo, offered to send him to college but Dunbar gracefully declined. He did not wish to be so indebted to anyone.

Wanting to buy a home for his mother, he gave paid readings from his works. These became popular, for Dunbar used to act out his poems. "His lithe form, graceful as a gazelle, glided about the stage when he gave his recitations with a rhythm of movement which showed that his whole being responded to the music of the orchestra and the beauty of his own conception. Every emotion depicted in his lines came out in his face."

While in Detroit he was invited by his friend Thatcher to appear before the West End Club, a white society. Among those present was one Dr. Chapman, who had just returned from the Southern states and was voicing his disapproval of Negroes everywhere.

Regarding Chapman's presence as a challenge, Dunbar selected his most stirring poem, "An Ode to Ethiopia," and put so much fire and feeling into it that he trembled.

> Go out and up! Our souls and eyes
> Shall follow thy continuous rise
> Our ears shall list thy story
> From bards who from thy root shall spring
> And proudly tune their lyres to sing
> Of Ethiopia's glory.

Chapman left that meeting discomfited.

At the World's Fair at Chicago in 1893, Frederick Douglass gave him a post with the Haitian exhibit and paid him out of his own pocket. On "The Colored Folk's Day" at the fair, Dunbar scored a rousing success.

After this came many trying days, however. The home he was buying for his mother proved a terrible drag. He complained:

> Every door is barred with gold
> And opens but to golden keys.

The devoted Thatcher came to his rescue then, but there were days when he thought of suicide. At the darkest moment, however, another admirer, Dr. Tobey, employed him to read to his patients in his hospital at Toledo. Encouraged, Dunbar got out another book: *Majors and Minors*, Thatcher and Tobey aiding him.

He tried to sell his book himself but, like a true artist, he had no great salesmanship abilities, especially as the public saw in him only "a nigger book agent." Then came another and greater turn of fortune. Colonel Robert Ingersoll, then the foremost figure on the American platform, was so pleased with his verses that he wrote of them, "I am astonished at their depth and subtlety. Dunbar is a thinker. 'The Mystery' is a poem worthy of the greatest. It is absolutely true and proves that its author is a profound and thoughtful man. Dunbar is a genius."

This was his making. The press found him good copy now. William Dean Howells, then the leading American critic, praised him highly in *Harper's Weekly*. "This little contrified volume is full of a new world," he wrote. Recognition, as Dunbar said, came "like the sun which suddenly slips from behind a cloud to flood the whole world with glory."

Publishers who had ignored him sought him out. Orders poured in. Once, on returning home after a short absence, he found his table snowed under with letters containing money orders and congratulations.

On Independence Day, 1898, Dr. Tobey invited fifty influential friends to hear him. Dunbar recited his "Ships That Pass in the Night." The governor of the state, who was present, said, "Of all things I have ever heard I have never listened to anything so impressive."

With his manager he started on a recital tour, delighting and impressing audiences, colored and white, everywhere. Hospitality was showered on him, and being neither retiring nor exclusive, he enjoyed himself. "Wherever beauty, pleasure and music met he made a feast." He drank heavily.

He was sometimes snubbed by the ignorant and the boorish on account of color, even by some of those whose battles he was fighting. Once a Negro waiter, trained in the school of white race prejudice, hesitated to wait on him in one of the leading hotels of Albany, New York, where a suite of rooms had been reserved for him. Nevertheless, some of the most stubborn Negrophobes capitulated to his charm. At a meeting for the furtherance of Negro education, a white man who had come to oppose the project after hearing him donated $1000. Perhaps his greatest triumph was winning the praise of Jefferson Davis, defeated President of the Confederacy.

With money pouring in, Dunbar paid off his debts and gave a house to his mother. In 1897 he went to England where John Hay, the American ambassador, one of his warmest friends, introduced him into the leading literary clubs. At one of these, the Savage Club, which was noted for its critical and hostile attitude toward incompetent speakers, he scored a veritable triumph. Everywhere in England his appearance was a success. But the English tour ended unpleasantly. His manager, it is said, decamped with the funds, leaving him stranded.

He returned to America and Ingersoll secured him a post in the Library of Congress at $720 a year. He now attempted a novel, *The Uncalled*. But it was poorly written. He wrote for the Washington dailies with better success. On March 6, 1898, he married his first love: Alice Ruth Moore.

The same year he left the Library. Work in the day there and writing at night were undermining his health, which was far from robust. He made another recital tour of the Southern states and won even greater applause. One of his best poems, recited at Tuskegee Institute, was written in twenty-four hours. Theodore Roosevelt and Henry M. Stanley sent their congratulations.

But his health continued to decline. An attack of pneumonia sent him to Colorado to recuperate, where as often as strength permitted, he gave recitals, sometimes in wealthy homes.

Among his admirers in Denver was a millionaire, Major W. C. Daniel, who aided him. Dunbar, feeling that "all the favors were coming from one side only," desired to end the acquaintance. He continued it only on the advice of his friends.

Deciding to settle down, he bought a home in Washington, D.C., on his return. President McKinley, as proof of his esteem, made him a colonel so that he could ride in his inaugural parade, but his health grew worse and he drank more heavily. This, as in the case of Poe and Baudelaire, alienated his friends and others dear to him, including his wife.

Of his separation from her he wrote, "Something within me seems to be dead. There is no spirit or energy left in me. My upper lip has taken on a droop."

He lingered on, hoping like Baudelaire for death. He wrote:

> Because I have loved so vainly
> And sung with such faltering breath
> The Master in infinite mercy
> Offers the boon of death.

The end came two years later on February 9, 1906, at the age of thirty-four.

As a lyrical poet, Dunbar ranks with the best. His "When Malindy Sings," and his "Angelina" are as ecstatic as Shelley's "Skylark," with the added merit of being more realistic. For those who understand dialect, his "When the Cone Pone's Hot" is as mouth-watering as Lamb's "Dissertation on Roast Pig." His "Cabin's Tale" and "The Soliloquy of a Turkey at the Approach of Christmas" are as humorous, fresh, and sparkling as anything of their kind in English poetry.

Few phases of life escaped Dunbar. Even Shakespeare did not note more thoroughly the little things of life. And, like Shakespeare, his genius illuminated them.

Dunbar loved his people as did Burns. Like Burns, he idealized the lives of the so-called common people and gilded their humble tasks until they felt it a joy to live. His was the supreme gift of taking the drab and commonplace and evoking joy, beauty, and meaning from them. His verses seemed to take the burden from the shoulders of the weary and leave them refreshed. As Professor Scarborough said:

Every phase of Negro life has been caught by his pen as by a camera. The simplest and homeliest life threw upon his brain indelible pictures that he transformed to liquid notes of song, sparkling with grace and vivid imagination. The life of the fireside, the field, the cabin, the wood, the stream, all gave him happy themes for his gift to play upon. The peculiar traits of his people, their quaint characteristics, their propensities and inclinations, all received a loving tender tribute at his hand as he wove them into immortal verse."

Howell says of his dialect poems:

There are divinations and reports of what passes in the hearts and minds of a lowly people, whose poetry had hitherto been inarticulately expressed in music, but now for the first time in our tongue, literary interpretations of a very artistic completeness.

Dunbar is often spoken of as a "Negro poet." But this is true only in the sense that Burns was Scottish, Shakespeare was English, or Omar Khayyám was Persian. In his sympathies and his outlook he was as universal as they.

Who but one transcendent of race could have written:

> The rain streams down like harp-strings from the sky
> The wind that world-old harpist sitteth by
> And ever as he sings his low refrain
> He plays upon the harp-strings of the rain.

Or:

> A crust of bread and a corner to sleep in
> A minute to smile and an hour to weep in
> A pint of joy to a peck of trouble
> And never a laugh but the moan comes double
> And that is life.
> A crust and a corner that love makes precious
> With a smile to warm and the tears to refresh us
> And joy seems sweeter when cares come after
> And a moan is the finest of foils for laughter
> And that is life.

Or:

> Though oft through fateful darkness do I reach
> And stretch my hand to find that other hand
> I question of the eternal bending skies
> That seems to neighbor with the novice earth
> But they roll on and daily shut their eyes
> On me as I one day shall do on them.
> And tell me not the secret that I ask.

ADDITIONAL REFERENCES

Adams, Russell L., *Great Negroes Past and Present*, p. 122. Chicago, Afro-Am Publishing Company, 1963, 1964.

Aptheker, Herbert, ed., *A Documentary History of the Negro People in the United States*, p. 759. New York, The Citadel Press, 1951.

Bone, Robert A., *The Negro Novel in America*, pp. 38–43. New Haven, Conn., Yale University Press, 1958.

Boyd, Rubie, *An Appreciation of Paul Laurence Dunbar*. 1930.

Brawley, Benjamin, *The Negro in Literature and Art in the United States*, pp. 64–75. New York, Duffield and Company, 1929.

———, *Paul Laurence Dunbar, Poet of His People*. Chapel Hill, The University of North Carolnia Press, 1936.

Brawley, Benjamin G., *Negro Builders and Heroes*, pp. 158–166. Chapel Hill, The University of North Carolina Press, 1937.

Cook, Will Marion, . . . *In Dahomey*. London, Keith, Prowse and Company, 1902.

Cunningham, Virginia, *Paul Laurence Dunbar and His Song*. New York, Dodd, Mead and Company, 1947.

Daniel, Theodora W. "Paul Laurence Dunbar and the Democratic Ideal." *Negro History Bulletin*, pp. 206–208 (June, 1943), Association for the Study of Negro Life and History, Washington, D.C.

Haynes, Elizabeth (Ross), *Unsung Heroes*, pp. 41–59. New York, DuBois and Dill, 1921.

Heydrick, Benjamin Alexander, ed., *Americans All*, pp. 209–232. New York, Harcourt, Brace and Company, 1941.

Lotz, Philip Henry, ed., *Rising Above Color*, pp. 90–97. New York, Association Press, 1943.

Marcus, Shmuel, *An Anthology of Revolutionary Poetry*. New York, Active Press, 1929.

Rollins, Charlemae Hill, *They Showed the Way*, pp. 59–62. New York, Thomas Y. Crowell Company, 1964.

Bert Williams with George Walker at right

Bert Williams

KING OF LAUGHTER
(1875–1922)

EGBERT AUSTIN WILLIAMS, foremost American comedian of his times, was born with a sense of humor. In situtions where the average human being experienced only monotony and boredom, he saw humor and side-splitting laughter. He said that as a child in his native Antigua, British West Indies, during the insufferably long and tiresome sermons of the minister of his church, instead of going to sleep as many others did, he would not only keep awake but have plenty of fun by conjuring up comedies around the preacher's bald spot, or a fly or a mosquito that was annoying some pious sister in the congregation.

It was, he said, a good way to keep awake: "Such simple subjects would suggest whole slap-stick comedies to me, and I would find myself shaking the pew with uncontrollable laughter."

The young lad was at his best as a mimic. On returning from church, he would imitate every gesture of the preacher, heightening the picture with touches of his own. The result was so effective that his mother more than once boxed his ears for his lack of reverence. As for music, he could play almost any instrument by ear, his forte being the banjo.

At the age of twelve, Bert went to California with his father. The latter had lost his money and was in poor health. Bert was ambitious and wanted to go to college after finishing high school, but was compelled by poverty to go out and earn a living instead. Turning naturally to entertaining, he went from café to café in San Francisco, singing minstrel ditties and passing the hat. Later he met some Hawaiians, who took a liking to him and taught him to play the ukulele.

As a boy in Antigua, he was particularly interested in the mannerisms of a certain type of peasant, and now he shifted his attention to a similar type of Afro-American—the humble, shiftless, slouch Negro who could neither read nor write but who had a certain hard, and not altogether inaccurate, philosophy of life. Williams studied this type as patiently as Fabre did his insects, observing and imitating their slightest gestures. Whenever he discovered some new twist of dialect or expression, he rejoiced as a miner would over a newly-found nugget. In fact, his finds were worth a gold mine later, though at the time all he got out of them were hearty laughs from the original subjects themselves.

Knowing that one of mankind's greatest afflictions is self-pity, and that the most effective laughter can be evoked from mole hills that we make into mountains, he portrayed his Negro as a victim of life, of his sharp-tongued wife, or as a loser in a crap game, or in a similar misfortune. Luck was always against his hero. (Charlie Chaplin later created a similar tragicomic figure who was white.) But even while poking fun at his hero, Williams managed to create a deep sympathy for him by making him lovable. One of his greatest hits was built around a character who was a regular Jonah and would sing, "I'm a Jonah man . . . a good, substantial, full-fledged, real, first-class Jonah man." And unlike many other comedians, Williams never resorted to smut, low wit, or burlesque to win his audiences.

In spite of his natural-born wit, he did not win success easily. He sang in cheap music halls, barely earning enough to take care of himself and his parents. He thought it a wonderful stroke of luck when he got a steady job in a San Francisco music hall at $7 a week, though he had to make from seven to ten appearances a day. Then fortune came his way: he met a sprightly young American black, Walker, in whom he recognized an immediate affinity, though Walker could neither dance nor play. Walker, moreover, was even financially worse off than himself. He had only sixty cents and a bulldog. Nevertheless, he groomed Walker as a partner.

Together they made up a sketch and offered it at Koster and Bial's music hall, where a new comedy, *The Gold Bug*, was about to open. They were turned down flat but when *The Gold Bug* proved an instantaneous flop they were sent for in desperation. They were a sensational success. Even more, their play was epoch-making because they sent the white minstrels in blackface into oblivion. White audiences up to this time had demanded the latter. Barnum, knowing of this prejudice against the Negro performer, had once blackened and painted a Negro and passed him off as a white man when his white minstrel suddenly fell ill. Williams and Walker left the theatre that night made men, with a contract for a salary larger than they had ever dreamed of.

After successes over the nation, they left for England but were total failures there. Their Negro humor was totally lost on English audiences. Returning to America, they scored fresh triumphs with *In Dahomey*, but feeling that they could still penetrate the funny side of the English, they returned. Once again, the American Negro dialect with its subtle humor proved too unfamiliar and they were leaving when a bolt of luck as if from the blue struck: King Edward VII, wishing to give some novel entertainment for the birthday of his son, the Prince of Wales, sent for them to come to Buckingham Palace. They made the king and the royal family laugh so heartily that as if by magic they were transformed into the leading comedians of the British Isles.

No theatre was now large enough for them. The king invited them to the palace, entertained them at dinner, and had them teach him the cakewalk and initiate him into the mysteries of "craps," with all the twists and expressions peculiar to the game. Williams says that the king was an excellent pupil.

Queen Alexandra also gave her approval to the cakewalk, and some of the smartest figures in London society came daily to the studio which Williams and Walker opened, between the hours of ten and eleven in the morning, for dancing lessons. The Duke of Connaught, the king's uncle, and other leading noblemen and social figures took them to their homes and clubs for golf, tennis, and dinner. In Scotland the Waverly Lodge made them Master Masons.

At their first appearances at Buckingham Palace an incredibly funny incident occurred for which Williams himself vouches. Jesse Shipp, the Negro stage director, was at the palace arranging the setting and having considerable difficulty getting his English help to understand what he wanted, when a stout man came in and asked him what was wrong. Shipp, thinking the man was one of the servants in the palace, replied that everything was wrong with the English from the handling of baggage onwards. The supposed servant who was none other than King Edward himself quietly enjoyed it all. Williams says:

After being presented to King Edward and meeting him on several occasions, he told me of the incident and how much he enjoyed Shipp's unrestrained criticism. I was grateful that the thing happened where the monarch was a man of such great intellect and possessed of such a decided sense of humor and of the fitness of things; that we were not in Georgia, say, nor in Texas, under similar circumstances.

On their return to America, Williams and Walker were more than ever the leading attraction of the day. They staged *Bandanna Land*, *Abyssinia*, and other musical shows, with tremendous success. Finally, Walker fell ill. Williams, then appearing in *Mr. Lode of Koal*, shared his earnings with him and cared for him tenderly until Walker died in 1911.

Playing alone, Williams' popularity continued and he was starred in many leading revues. He joined the Ziegfeld Follies, then the top-notch production of its kind in America, and was its leading star and its highest paid actor for ten years. He had reached the height of the ambition of most actors—to see their names blazing in huge letters on Broadway.

As "Mr. Nobody," he saved the reputation of the Follies more than once. Seats for his performances were sold weeks in advance.

It is impossible to convey the essence of his humor by any kind of description. Rennold Wolf describes one of his scenes. It is when his bosom friend Bud drives him from his house:

"Now get out of here, and don't ever let me see your ugly face again."

"You don't mean that, does you, Bud," asks Williams wistfully. "Yes, go," replied Walker.

In the moment that followed this scene, says Wolf:

Williams proved what a really good actor he was, for, with his wonderful faculty for pantomime expression, he rang a note of pathos as true as ever did Joseph Jefferson in Rip Van Winkle. Slowly he walked away and as he reached the door he said: "All right, I'll go." It seemed a trivial bit of acting, and it came in the midst of the broadest fun, yet in that moment he brought tears to the eyes of many in the audience. And in an instant later he roused them to laughter again by drawling in his inimitable way: "But I will return."

Prohibition furnished Williams with abundant material. One of his greatest hits was his telling of the rapid depletion of his stock of liquor with no means of getting a fresh supply. It was entitled, "Ten Little Bottles." The verses appear in his biography by Mabel Rowland.

The leading critics of the day praised him in superlatives. The *Theatre Magazine* said:

Bert Williams has long enjoyed the reputation of being a vastly funnier man than any white comedian now on the American stage. He is spontaneously and genuinely funny. Nature has endowed him with a comic mask and he succeeded in obtaining with voice and gesture, ludicrous effects that are irresistible."

The *Record Herald* said:

And you know as you know in everything else that this masterly pantomimist and eloquent ballad singer does, that if he put a shade more gravity into his acting he would be pathetic, even tragical in an altogether legitimate way. Of course, it is not within the limitations of his task to do so, but the consciousness of what he could do and would be doing were his skin white, gives a mournful cast to reflections on his great gifts. He is, however, the drollest, most expert buffoon on the American stage.

Jack Lait: "Bert Williams makes us glad that the slaves were freed. He is a man of another race who can lampoon us and cartoon us in our own follies and weaknesses and make us like it."

R. J. Coady: "He is the only actor I know who can express

melancholy, if only for an instant, and then suddenly cause wild outbursts of laughter in his audience."

Bert Williams' most famous story was "When Martin Comes." Of this, Heywood Broun has said:

No man in the theatre of our day could tell a story so well. He had in his repertoire at one time a tale about a Negro parson and a haunted house. This was the story built about a refrain: "We Can't do Nothin' till Martin Comes." You may remember that it was said by the first cat which came out of the fireplace and paused to eat the live coals. It was a friendly little cat. The next cat was the size of a St. Bernard dog and after it had dined and spat out the sparks, it asked: "When are we goin' to begin?" "We can't do nothin' till Martin comes." The next one was as big as a Shetland pony, and like the others, it ate fire and inquired, plaintively: "When are we goin' to begin?" And the answer came, chorally: "We can't do nothin' till Martin comes." It was at this point that the Negro preacher rose and said: "When Martin gits hyah, you tell him ah was hyah but ah'm gone."

For all the humorous fantasy of incident and the whip-like finish, Bert Williams did not tell the story as a comic anecdote. By voice and pantomime he lifted it to the stature of a true ghost story. We could see the old Negro, feverishly turning the pages of the Bible; the cats from the fireplace took form before our eyes. Sparks dripped from their jaws and the wind howled outside the cabin. All this was built for us by a tall black man, his face clownishly blackened by burnt cork, who stood still in the center of the stage and used no gesture which travelled more than six inches.

The memory of the happening remains with us so vividly that sleeping in a haunted house is one of the all too numerous things we are afraid to do. Of course we laughed at the message which was left for Martin, but it was more or less defensive laughter because we knew in our heart that the preacher of the story had out-stayed us by at least one cat.

Bert Williams enjoyed full popularity to the end. In 1921 his health began to break, and though advised by his doctors to take a rest, he insisted on keeping to his contract when he thought of the possible loss to his producers. While playing in Chicago the same year, he fell seriously ill, but he appeared nevertheless, getting out of bed to go on the stage. Soon he suffered a complete breakdown.

Blood transfusions were made in vain, and he died in New York on March 4, 1922, at the age of forty-seven. Tens of thousands of persons, colored and white, came to view his remains and attend his funeral.

In addition to being one of the greatest pantomimists of all time, Bert Williams was one of the most warmhearted and generous of mortals. He aided liberally not only his fellow actors, white as well as black, but struggling students of law, medicine, singing, painting, and sculpture. To a German carpenter who had aided him in his earlier days, he was most generous. As with all true artists, his only use for money was the good he could do with it.

Fond of peace and harmony, he would often rather submit to injustice than push for his rights. He was perhaps the most plagiarized artist of his time, yet he never brought a law suit against any imitator. Like all great comedians, he had a serious side and loved the finer things. He had read many of the masterpieces of literature; could discuss Darwin, Voltaire, Kant, Goethe, and Oscar Wilde, and took a deep interest in the occult sciences. He was tall and handsome with a finely developed physique kept in trim by athletics. He was a clever boxer and took lessons regularly from Joe Gans, world's lightweight champion.

Next to the stage, he was most interested in the history of Africa and of his own people in America and the West Indies. After all, he was a Negro, and as such in America, even at the height of his fame, he suffered much. Though he had been entertained by English royalty and nobility, and was often a guest in the homes of many of America's leading citizens, there was no such hospitality for him "on the road." Often he was compelled to stop in mean and inferior hotels. He once said, "They keep me out of a hotel where loafers are admitted without question so long as they are white. Then a professor, or a doctor, or a lawyer will invite me to his house. It's a great, sad, little world." He took it all as a true philosopher. "It's no disgrace to be colored, but it's so inconvenient," he would say.

Some white actors tried to bar him and frequently objected to his appearing with them on the same stage. Once, while he was with the Follies, a number of them told Florenz Ziegfeld that he would have to choose between Williams and themselves. Ziegfeld replied,

"Go if you want to. I can replace every one of you, except the man you want me to fire."

Although Bert Williams did more toward winning a place on the stage for Negroes than anyone who had preceded him; although he overcame the prejudices of many a producer and unlocked the door that had been closed to colored faces for centuries; and although he was the innovator of mixed white and colored casts; he was very much misunderstood by a great many Negroes. Already the subject of ridicule, the latter felt that he was only increasing their burdens. What he was really doing, however, was taking all the bad things that had been said about them, and in his own gentle and humorous way, transforming them into a lesson that showed the white people that the very same bad things were generally true of them too. Instead of scolding the whites as others were doing, he corrected them by gentle ridicule and their own laughter. As Booker T. Washington once modestly observed, "Bert Williams has done more for the race than I have. He has smiled his way into people's hearts. I have been obliged to fight my way."

The posthumous comment on Williams is eloquent.

Miss Patterson said:

Bert Williams was a kingly figure. A king of comedy. . . . When he appeared it was as though a herald proclaimed "The King approaches." There was a silence, attention, expectation, that were never disappointed. However trivial his theme and however anaemic the material provided him, he held court and received tribute. . . . I like to think of those evenings in England when "In Dahomey" captured the London play-goer and the black King was more than once commanded to appear before the white one. King Edward VII enjoyed the drollery of the comic King.

Florenz Ziegfeld, the famous producer, said:

I like the man as well as any man I ever met and better than most men, for he had so many fine qualities. I admired him as an artist tremendously because he was a great artist. In fact, he was so great that it was impossible for him to do anything badly. Had he lived and opportunity come for him to do serious work, I really believe no one on our own stage could have excelled him, just as in his own line, no one ever came near equalling him.

I am sure if Bert Williams had suddenly found himself deaf and dumb, he would have been able to command the high place that he held in the theatre just the same because of his thorough mastery of pantomime. I have seen him silently rise from his chair while a group of us were sitting, and go to a door, admit a lady in pantomime, bring her down to a table, converse in gesture, order a whole dinner with various bits of comedy to the waiter, pay the check and escort her out. It would be a perfect gem in its completeness. He could turn his back on the audience and convey more than thousands of actors can do with every trick known to the business.

David Belsaco, whose name is a classic in the American theatre, said:

He was one of the simplest, kindest, most amiable and most likeable men that I have ever known—and I have known many. He was a delightful entertainer. He was a sincere and careful artist. He was a genuine comedian. . . .

Williams truly was funny himself—he had at once a quick sense and a profound faculty of humor. His mind saw life at a comic angle and what he saw he faithfully reproduced.

Upon the stage, however, his artistic method was so perfect that it completely concealed his artistic mechanism, making all which he said and did appear to be wholly unpremeditated while he seemed entirely conscious of the comicality of his words and actions, thus enhancing their effect. His individuality was as strong as it was comic and engaging as it was strong.

His audiences laughed at him and at his strange, grotesquely serious proceedings, but also from the first moment when they saw him, they liked him. . . .

To see and hear him was to be instantaneously amused: to have the mind diverted and drawn away from any saddening thoughts of the pain and mutability of human experience.

REFERENCES

Rowland, Mabel, ed., *Bert Williams: Son of Laughter*. New York, The English Crafters, 1923.

Wolf, Rennold, "The Greatest Comedian on the American Stage." *The Green Book Album*.

ADDITIONAL REFERENCES

Adams, Russell L., *Great Negroes: Past and Present*, p. 132. Chicago, Afro-Am Publishing Company, 1963, 1964.

Charters, Ann, *Nobody: The Story of Bert Williams*. New York, The Macmillan Company, 1970.

Fletcher, Tom, . . . *100 Years of the Negro in Show Business*. New York, Burdge, 1954.

Rollins, Charlemae Hill, *They Showed the Way*, pp. 146–149. New York, Thomas Y. Crowell Company, 1964.

Sewell, Eugene P., *Balzac, Dumas, "Bert" Williams*. Published privately, 1923.

Booker T. Washington

❦

EX-SLAVE, AMERICA'S LEADING EXPONENT OF
INDUSTRIAL EDUCATION
(1858–1915)

LIFE AT TIMES seems to delight in irony. It will place certain
individuals at the foot of the ladder where there seems to be no
hope for them, and harass them to within an inch of their lives,
then some day lift them high above those who started with the most
favorable advantages. Striking modern examples of this among
white people are Lincoln, Rockefeller, Carnegie, Henry Ford,
Lloyd George, Mussolini, Hitler, Stalin.

But life sometimes goes to greater extremes. It digs a pit at the
foot of the ladder and boots a man into it, where he is spat on by
the lowest of the low, when it seems there is no hope for him, then
it starts him upward until he is elevated far above his scorners to
receive the world's applause. Of this latter type history affords no
more brilliant example than Booker T. Washington.

It is true that slaves, white and black, have risen to rulership in
many countries, especially Islamic ones. As regards Negroes in the
Latin-American countries, it would be difficult to find one where
they have not risen to very high positions. No less than twelve of
the Latin-American nations have had Negro presidents, some of
them former slaves. Even under the French in Haiti, where slavery
was at its worst, mulattoes sometimes rose to positions over white
people. The Haitian master also would sometimes send his mulatto
son to be educated in France, where, if he distinguished himself,

he might be invited to be the guest for days of even the king himself. In America, on the other hand, no matter how capable a black or a mulatto was, the highest he could expect was to be a valet, a coachman, or an artisan. Anglo-Saxon civilization has been the most procrustean, most inflexible of all, where Negroes are concerned. Even as I write, eighty years after the emancipation, no man of known Negro descent occupies even a third-rate government position in the United States. It is the same in South Africa. Great Negroes ceased to exist there when the Anglo-Saxons finally got full control. Negro genius was (and still is) crushed in the United States. The result is that while white men of even ordinary talent may rise, and have risen, to the presidency, only Negroes of the most extraordinary ability and determination could rise into the niche they later carved out for themselves.

Washington's own story, together with a knowledge of his times, will show that with the exception of Frederick Douglass, his handicaps were far greater than any other American who rose to fame.

He was born in slavery on a Virginia plantation of a totally illiterate mother and a white father, who, by all accounts, took no more notice of him than a male fish of its fry.

Although living in a civilized, Christian land, young Washington's condition was far more wretched than it would have been in Africa, from which his mother's parents had been torn. His bed was the bare ground of a hut, covered with leaves and a few rags. His table was the same place. Food was eaten from the pot with his fingers. Of palatable, nourishing food, he had none. He only heard of it from those who served at the master's table.

His entire wardrobe consisted of a single shirt made from the coarsest part of the flax. Putting on a new garment, he said, was like donning one made of pin-points. From the age of six he worked all day carrying water to the men in the field, and as soon as he was strong enough to hold a hoe he became a field hand himself.

As for education, that was out of the question, even after the emancipation when learning to read was no longer outlawed. Not a Negro for miles around could read. When he saw white boys and girls going to school and saw himself chained to the soil, he thought that being able to go to school must be like the heaven to which his masters told him he would go if he remained a faithful, cringing slave on earth.

At the age of ten a change for perhaps the worse came. His mother and his stepfather moved to Malden, West Virginia, where in spite of his tender years he was sent to work in a salt factory at four in the morning. About him were debased and illiterate whites and Negroes who were far removed from the atmosphere in which his hungry soul lived. Learning to read was out of the question here too. At last, however, he did, through his mother's stinting of the family, get a secondhand spelling book but not a single Negro around him knew a letter of the alphabet and he did not care to ask any of the whites, who were unfriendly, to teach him. When a colored boy who could read came to the community, he seemed as great a phenomenon to Washington as a two-headed calf! He said, "How I used to envy this man! He seemed to be the one young man in all the world who ought to be satisfied with his attainments."

A school for Negroes was finally opened in a nearby town but his stepfather would not let him go—he wanted his wages—so he went at nights after a hard day's work. Later, by an arrangement with the management of the factory, he was permitted to go in the day by starting his work at six in the morning, working till nine, and then returning to work after school.

The school, however, was miles away and he would arrive late. He tried putting the clock in the factory ahead but was finally caught by the foreman. Then, as if to make matters still worse, his stepfather sent him to work in a coal mine, thereby stopping him altogether from going to school.

This seemed to be the death of all his hopes. "Once a miner, always a miner," he heard it said. He said of this time:

I used to try to picture in my imagination the feelings and ambitions of a white boy with absolutely no limit to his aspirations and activities. I used to envy the white boys who had no obstacles placed in the way of their becoming a Congressman, Governor, Bishop or President, by reason of the accident of birth or race. I used to picture the way that I would act under the circumstances; how I would begin at the bottom and keep rising until I reached the highest pinnacle of success.

But it was indeed at a bottom of a coal mine that he was to hear of the solution to his problem. One day there he overheard two Negro miners talking about a school somewhere in Virginia where poor but worthy students could get an education while earning a living. If there was such a school, he meant to find it.

But several years were to pass before he could go. At last, with a small satchel holding his few belongings, he started off for the place of his dreams—Hampton Institute. It was 500 miles away, and he had barely enough money to pay coach fare for the first stage of the journey. He arrived at the first stopping place late at night. But, although it was winter, the innkeeper, a white man, indignantly refused him food and lodging, and slammed the door in his face. To keep himself from freezing, he walked about all night.

By walking and begging rides, he at last reached Richmond, Virginia, tired, dirty, penniless, friendless. He went from door to door, pleading for work in exchange for food, but no one heeded him. The sight of cuts of roast meats, chicken pies, and other food in restaurant windows made him feel more famished than ever. He says:

I must have tramped the streets until after midnight. I became so exhausted that I could walk no longer. I was tired, I was hungry, but I was everything but discouraged. Just about this time when I reached extreme physical exhaustion, I came upon a part of a street where the board-sidewalk was considerably elevated. I waited for a few minutes till I was sure that no passer-by could see me, and then crept under the sidewalk and lay for the night on the ground with my satchel for a pillow. Nearly all night I could hear the tramp of feet over my head.

Years later a banquet was given in his honor within a few yards of this spot.

The next morning, still hungry but refreshed, he found work on a ship that was being unloaded. With Hampton Institute as his goal, he continued to sleep under the sidewalk in order to save room rent. Weeks later he reached Hampton Institute, but he was so ragged and dirty that he was refused admittance. For days he loitered about, seeing others well fed and well clothed being admitted. He begged for a chance—any kind of chance. At last he was sent to sweep a room. Feeling that his whole future depended upon getting that room clean, he swept and dusted it four times over. When a teacher came to inspect it, a Northern white woman with an eye for dust, and saw how well it had been done, she admitted him to the school.

Poverty dogged him during the entire term. His clothing was almost in rags but he kept it clean. His only pair of socks he washed at night. But so determined was he on getting an education that these privations seemed trifling to him.

His studiousness, his deportment, and his absolute honesty won him the highest regard of his teachers. Once, while working in a restaurant, he found a $10 bill under a table where a customer had dropped it. Although he needed money desperately, he turned it over to the proprietor of the restaurant, who pocketed it, saying that since it was found in his place it was his.

After graduation from Hampton Institute, he went to work as a waiter in a hotel in Connecticut. The proprietor, thinking him experienced, sent him to wait on a party of several persons, but he was so confused that he left the dining hall, and was later reduced to busboy. Years later he was a guest at this hotel and the proprietor used to boast that Washington had once worked for him.

Returning to Malden, he received an appointment in the colored school, where he taught hygiene, farming, cattle raising, and general literature, not without considerable opposition from the white people. This was during the period when the Ku Klux Klan was ruthlessly attacking Negroes and friendly whites, burning homes, schools, and churches. Those were terrible days, when no aspiring Negro's life was safe. Washington, because he was black, called them not his "black" days but his "white" days. The exploiters of Negro labor, seeing that education would place Negroes less in their power, were preventing it by force.

But undaunted he continued. The great need of his racial group was education and his goal was to teach them. When offers came to him to enter politics or the ministry, where the pay was higher, he refused. In doing this he hoped to set an example. He saw others, with little or no education, setting themselves up as teachers and preachers in order to escape the manual work for which they were better fitted. As for politics, he decided it was turning his people away from the fundamental task of perfecting themselves in the industries at their doorsteps; from securing property; and generally from becoming stable citizens.

Deciding at this time to equip himself still more for teaching, he went to Washington, D.C., and spent eight months there in a teacher's school. On his return to Malden, the white people wishing to change the capital of the state to Charleston, a more central location, sent a delegation to ask him to enlist Negro support for the project. He did this for three months, winning so much distinction as a speaker, that he was again urged to enter politics. But although better equipped for it than perhaps any other Negro in the state, he refused.

Soon afterward he accepted an offer to teach at Hampton Institute, and not long after that a call to take charge of Tuskegee Institute.

This school had been founded through the efforts of a white man, Lewis Adams, who had the state legislature appropriate $2000 for it. His object, it is said, was to create a strong Negro vote in his favor.

Arriving at Tuskegee, Washington found that the school was only a rundown plantation with a stable and a hen house. He was the only teacher and he opened the school in these two buildings with thirty students. To make it worse, there were no funds for improvements—the $2000 had been voted only for teachers' salaries.

There were other and even more irritating difficulties—those with his own people, most of whom looked on the race question, and even their own condition, as something to be solved by God alone. Washington, by stressing the gospel of work rather than one of prayer, drew down on himself the wrath and opposition of a noisy and largely illiterate Negro clergy. Washington said, "Sentimental Christianity which banks everything in the future and nothing in the present is the great curse of the race."

What seemed the greatest heresy of all was his advocacy of agriculture—fieldwork. He said, "There is as much dignity in tilling a field as in writing a poem." But the ministers and others replied that tilling the soil savored strongly of sin. Did not the

Bible say man was forced to do field work because he had sinned? Furthermore, did not the white overlords to whom they looked up shun all labor and fatigue, while the poor white "trash," whom everyone scorned, hoed corn and picked cotton? Wasn't heaven something like how the upper-class whites lived? Anyway, what good was emancipation for Negroes if they were to be no better off than poor whites? Accordingly, Washington was denounced as an infidel, an anti-Christ, and the people were warned to stay away from him.

He also had to face the hostility of the whites, who at the mention of Negro education pictured instead of fields of cotton and potatoes, a crop of "darkies" with silk hats, high collars, imitation gold lorgnettes, showy walking sticks, kid gloves, fancy boots, and loud clothing. The white storekeepers, who later found Tuskegee Institute a godsend, refused to give Washington credit. Whites and Negroes alike tried to hinder him.

Borrowing $200 from a friend, with his salary as security, he opened the school formally on July 4, 1881, with an enrollment of thirty pupils. He meant to educate these pupils from the ground up; to impress upon them not only the utility, but also the beauty and dignity of labor; to make them feel that doing the common things of life in an uncommon way was an essential part of all education. He told them, "No one cares for a man with empty head and pocket, no matter what his color."

He planned to teach them how to utilize air, water, steam, and other forces and thereby avoid drudgery. With his thirty pupils he cleared the land, cut down the timber, sawed the lumber, and erected the school buildings. This policy of self-sufficiency he adhered to ever after. Of the numerous buildings at Tuskegee, only four were not erected by the students.

In Tuskegee village Washington found the same conditions as in his birthplace in Franklin County, Virginia. The 2000 black inhabitants were wretchedly poor and ignorant. Children were left to grow up like weeds; everybody's crops were mortgaged. Some of the blacks barely regarded themselves as human. One of them once said to Washington, "There was five of us sold at the time, myself, my brother, and three mules."

He taught the girls of these families to cook, sew, and keep house so that they might become better fitted for their tasks as wives and mothers. He taught trades to the boys and practical living to adults. He went among friendly whites and blacks, North and South, soliciting funds with which he erected more buildings. Andrew Carnegie sent him $20,000 for a library. Slowly but surely, Tuskegee Institute and its energetic founder were making themselves known.

He continued thus for the next fourteen years when a note of high appreciation came: he was invited to be the principal speaker at the Cotton States International Exposition at Atlanta, Georgia, in 1895.

That invitation was fraught with explosive possibilities from the side of the blacks as well as from that of the whites. The problem of racial adjustment was a very serious one. The industrial economy of the North had not long before beaten in war the agricultural one of the South. The North, however, had come to see that the South was a fine field for investment with its cheap, abundant labor, and had invested accordingly there. But to reap the highest profits it was necessary to give the former slaveholders as free a hand as possible with the blacks: Therefore in 1877 the North withdrew the army stationed there for the protection of the freedmen.

Left alone, the ex-slaves were soon reduced to a condition which for some was worse than slavery. The master had been responsible in some measure for the slave, but now, since the latter was an alleged employee, he was not. Furthermore, exploitation was free now, not only to the master, but to any white person.

The chief instrument for the intimidation of the former slaves was the racial hatred of the oppressed white masses, which was fanned to fury by the white press and pulpit. Lynchings and massacres, rare when the blacks were chattels, became common and went unpunished. Daily the position of the Negroes grew worse, and with it grew the volume of protest from the more tenderhearted whites in the North and South.

The situation called for rare diplomacy. It demanded a leader who knew how to reconcile the vested interests and the consciences of the more compassionate whites. Such a one would have to be persuasive enough to convince capital that by advancing the Negro, dividends on agricultural and industrial investments would be increased. Such a leader must also be able to assure the white masses, not only in the South but in the North, that an educated Negro would never become a menace to their jobs and that Negroes would be taught to regard themselves the perpetual inferiors of white people, especially socially. In short, what was wanted was the wiping out of the crudities of color injustice and a glossing over of the other evils in order to give the appearance that the Negro was getting fair play even though a rigid color line was being maintained. To the liberal whites, North and South, Booker T. Washington appeared to be the man to handle this situation.

The day before he spoke at the Atlanta Exposition a white farmer correctly diagnosed his position to him thus: "You have spoken before the Northern white people, the Negroes in the South, and to us white people in the South, separately. But in Atlanta, tomorrow, you'll have before you the Northern whites, the Southern whites, and the Negroes all together. I am afraid you have put yourself in a difficult situation."

When he reached the auditorium, Washington was very nervous. He desired to say something that could cement friendship between white and black and bring about cooperation between them. He knew he would have to be careful to avoid anything that would make the whites feel that so-called social equality would ever be a result of that cooperation. He realized that the Southern whites wanted to be assured that even if the Negroes gained a better position economically, the whites would still retain their former superiority and that there would never be a possibility of Negroes marrying among them. At the same time, he knew that many of his listeners would resent anything that might suggest stopping the concubinage of black women. As for the Negroes, he would have to choose his words carefully in order not to make them feel that he was selling them out to the whites.

An immense crowd came to hear him and he rose to the occasion. He made an address that was a masterpiece of diplomacy from first to last. Skillfully avoiding any accusation against the whites, he painted a rosy picture of the future for the whites, and of the profit they would reap, provided they gave the Negroes a freer chance to develop themselves. He said:

Nearly 16,000,000 of hands will aid you in pulling the load upward, or they will pull against you the load downward. We shall constitute one-third and more of the ignorance and crime of the South, or one-third its intelligence and progress; we shall contribute one-third to the business and industrial prosperity of the South, or we shall prove a veritable body of death, stagnating, repressing, retarding every effort to advance the body politic.

Playing on the sectional feeling of his Southern auditors, he continued:

The wisest among my race understand that the agitation of questions of social equality is the most extreme folly and that progress in the enjoyment of all privileges that will come to us must be the result of severe and constant struggle rather than artificial forcing. No race, that has anything to contribute to the markets of the world, is ostracised for any length of time. It is important and right that all privileges of the law be ours, but it is vastly more important that we be prepared for the exercise of these privileges. The opportunity to earn a dollar in a factory just now is worth infinitely more than the opportunity to spend a dollar in an opera house.

James Creelman, reporter for the *New York World*, said of the speech:

When Professor Booker T. Washington stood on the platform with the sun shining over the heads of his auditors into his eyes and with his whole face lit up with the fire of prophecy, Clark Howell, the successor of Henry Grady, said to me: "That man's speech is the beginning of a moral revolution in America. . . ."

The eyes of the thousands present looked straight at the Negro orator. A strange thing was to happen. A black man was to speak for his people with none to interrupt him. As Professor Washington strode to the edge of the stage, the low, descending sun shot fiery rays through the windows into his face. He turned his head to avoid the blinding light and moved about the platform for relief. Then he turned his wonderful countenance to the sun without a blink of the eyelids and began to talk.

There was a remarkable figure; tall, bony, straight as a Sioux chief; high forehead, straight nose, heavy jaw and strong determined mouth with big, white teeth; piercing eyes and a commanding manner. The sinews stood out on his bronzed neck and his muscular right arm swung high in the air with a lead pencil grasped in the clenched brown fist. His big feet were planted squarely with the heels together and the toes turned out. His voice rang out clear and true and paused impressively as he put over each point. Within ten minutes the multitude was in an uproar of enthusiasm—handkerchiefs were waved, canes flourished, hats were tossed in the air. The fairest women of Georgia stood up and cheered. It was as if the orator had bewitched them.

And when he held his dusky hand high above his head with fingers outstretched wide apart and said to the white people of the South on behalf of his race, "In all things that are purely social we can be separate as the fingers, yet one as the hand in all things essential to material progress," the great wave of sound dashed itself against the walls, and the whole audience was on its feet in a delirium of applause, and I thought of that moment of the night when Henry Grady stood among the curling wreaths of tobacco smoke in Delmonico's banquet hall and said: "I am a Cavalier among Roundheads."

I have heard the great orators of many countries but not even Gladstone himself could have pleaded a cause with more consummate power than did this angular Negro, standing in a nimbus of sunshine, surrounded by the men who had fought to keep his race in bondage.

A ragged, ebony giant squatting on the floor in one of the aisles watched the orator with burning eyes and tremulous face until the supreme burst of applause came, and then the tears ran down his face. Most of the Negroes in the audience were crying, perhaps without knowing just why.

At the close of the speech, Governor Bullock rushed across the stage and grasped the orator's hand. Another roar of approval greeted this demonstration and for a few minutes the two men stood facing each other, hand in hand.

The speech astounded the nation. The *Boston Transcript* said, "The speech of Booker T. Washington seemed to have dwarfed all the other proceedings and the Exposition, itself. The sensation that it caused in the press has never been equalled." President Grover Cleveland wrote him a letter of congratulation.

The crowning "glory" of that speech was that the whites and Negroes in the South could in social matters be "separate as the fingers," yet be "one as the hand" in essential things. This was one of the most specious bits of nonsense ever uttered by a man. No two human beings, except a child in its mother's womb, can ever be closer, more intimate, than the fingers on one hand. They are ever in the closest possible contact. Yet the exploiters of the Negro in the South and all the segregationists, North and South, ate it up greedily because they felt that this great leader of the Negroes had surrendered the Negroes to them.

Self-respecting Negroes and those engaged in fighting Jim Crow laws were furious. They called Washington's speech "The Atlanta Sell-Out." Washington, they said, was following not only the line of least resistance, but of no resistance at all.

Washington too was conscious that it was a surrender. He wrote later:

I do not deny that I was frequently tempted during the early years of my work to join in the general denunciation of the evils and injustices I saw about me. But when I thought the matter over I saw that such course would accomplish no good and that I would do a great deal of harm. . . . The salvation of the Negro race in America is to be worked out not by abstract argument, not by mere denunciation of wrong but by actual achievement of constructive work.

The Atlanta speech projected Washington into the national spotlight. The next morning he was stopped by so many on the street who wanted to congratulate him that he had to return home to escape them. Offers for speaking engagements poured in on him, one of them for $50,000. Not wishing to interrupt his life's work at Tuskegee, he declined them all.

The same year another unusual honor was conferred upon him. Georgia, the last state of the Union to ratify the Thirteenth Amendment to the Constitution, appointed him one of the judges of award in its department of education, a post that entitled him to pass not only on the work of Negroes, but whites as well.

Thereafter he spoke at the leading Northern universities—Harvard, Yale, Amherst—and even at some of the Southern ones. At Chicago he addressed 16,000 persons in the Auditorium; President McKinley, the members of his cabinet, and several foreign ambassadors were present. He received a tremendous ovation which reached its height when McKinley arose and bowed to him.

Honors of one kind or another came to him fast. Harvard gave him an honorary Master of Arts. President Theodore Roosevelt invited him several times to the White House. Friends, seeing that he was overworked, paid his expenses for a European tour in 1899. On the ship he was the most talked of passenger. In England Queen Victoria invited him to tea; the nobility feted him; some of the most distinguished persons in politics, letters, and the arts invited him to their homes; and the King and Queen of Denmark had him to dinner in their palace. In America, however, he was subject to insult with impunity by even the most debased whites. In the South he had to travel enclosed either in a compartment or in a filthy Jim Crow car. To many he was always only a "nigger" with all that that term implied. Even his surrender and subservience did not win him favor with a certain element of whites, who objected to seeing a Negro receiving any kind of honor. When he dined with President Theodore Roosevelt at the White House, it created a national storm. And when toward the end of his life a white ruffian attacked and beat him in the hallway of a New York apartment house, that hoodlum was made a hero and offers of legal aid were showered on him from all parts of the nation. The more liberal whites, as President Taft, sided with Washington, however, and voiced their indignation at the attack. Washington, true to his nature, forgave the man, and did not prosecute him.

During these years Tuskegee Institute had been growing greatly. In 1901, its twentieth anniversary, it had a staff of 110 officers and instructors, and 1400 students, some of them from Africa, Cuba, Puerto Rico, Jamaica, and South America. It owned 2300 acres of land, 1000 of which was under cultivation by students; 66 buildings; and 30 industrial departments—representing a total value, together with the school's annual endowment, of $1,700,000. At his death, fourteen years later, it was considerably greater.

His interests and activities were many and varied and requests for all manner of services poured in on him. In 1906, when the white mobs of Atlanta, Georgia, the scene of his greatest triumph, descended on the Negro section, plundering, burning, killing, and wounding hundreds of defenseless Negroes, he was on the scene, going among the smoking ruins and speaking words of encouragement to the victims and securing succor from the city authorities. Into his life so much was crowded, that it was no wonder that he died of overwork while still in his fifties.

The press of America and the civilized world eulogized him. Theodore Roosevelt wrote:

Booker T. Washington was a great American. For twenty years before his death, he had been the most useful as well as one of the most distinguished of American citizens of any race.

Eminent though his services were to the people of his color, the white men of our republic were almost as much indebted to him both directly and indirectly.

As nearly as any man I have ever met, Booker T. Washington lived up to Micah's verse, "What more doth the Lord require of thee than to do justice and love mercy and walk humbly with thy God?" He did justice to every man. He did justice to those to whom it was a hard thing to do justice. He showed mercy not only to the poor and to those beneath him, but he showed mercy by an understanding of the shortcoming of those who failed to do his race justice. . . .

I profited very much by my association with Booker T. Washington. I owed him much along many different lines. I valued greatly his friendship and his respect. And when he died, I mourned his loss as a patriot and an American.

Washington's fame, now that we are able to look at it in a more detached light, stands on a firm foundation. Whatever may be the viewpoint regarding what he said, or inferred, about a Negro's "place," the fact remains that he helped hundreds of thousands to rise out of the rut of centuries to a level where they were able to get a better vision of their rights as human beings.

As for the American whites, he probably did even more for them than for Negroes. Though the whites generally considered him as one of a despised caste, he was, nevertheless, one of their leaders. Washington was of that intensely practical type, peculair to America, who set about getting what is needed without delay. The very incarnation of the spirit of American go-get-ism, he breathed efficiency—high-powered efficiency—and the doing of things as quickly and as perfectly as possible. The sweeping of that room at Hampton was typical of the thoroughness of the man. He delighted in telling this story, and its effect on the nation was far-reaching. As to his philosophy, which he always drove home with apt anecdotes, it equaled Franklin's in homely wisdom, and surpassed it in wit.

Among those who profited most from his work were some of his greatest despisers, the white farmers of the South, to whom he taught new methods of farming and stock-raising.

Washington's contribution to the education of young people is of worldwide significance. He gave this a more practical trend. He educated them to earn a living in a definite way as soon as they were graduated, instead of having to flounder in search of any kind of unskilled work. As an exponent of industrial education he deserves a place among the immortals of education. In 1945 he was elected to the American Hall of Fame.

In view of the manner in which Washington had bowed to segregation, even to condoning it, this significant final act about the real man must be noted. In proportion as he gained strength, he became radical. In his last article, which was published in the *New Republic*, December 4, 1915, two weeks after his death, he attacked segregation, calling it unjust, unnecessary, and inconsistent.

REFERENCES

Washington, B. T., *Up from Slavery*. New York, Al. Bert Company, 1901.

———, *My Larger Education*. Garden City, N.Y., Doubleday, Page and Company, 1911.

Thrasher, M. B., *Tuskegee*. 1901.

Scott, Emmett J., and Stowe, Lyman B., *Booker T. Washington, Builder of a Civilization*. Garden City, N.Y., Doubleday, Page and Company, 1916.

Matthews, V. E., ed., *Black Belt Diamonds Savings of Booker T. Washington*. 1898.

Washington, E. Davidson, comp., *Quotations of Booker T. Washington*. Tuskegee, Ala., Tuskegee Institute Press, 1938.

ADDITIONAL REFERENCES

Abbott, Lyman, *Silhouettes of My Contemporaries*, pp. 258–281. Garden City, N.Y., Toronto, Doubleday, Page and Company, 1921.

Adams, Russell L., *Great Negroes: Past and Present*, pp. 110–111. Chicago, Afro-Am Publishing Company, 1963, 1964.

Boone, Theodore Sylvester, *The Philosophy of Booker T. Washington*, Fort Worth, Tex., Manney Printing Company, 1939.

Brawley, Benjamin G., *Negro Builders and Heroes*, pp. 147–157. Chapel Hill, The University of North Carolina Press, 1937.

Cromwell, John Wesley, *The Negro in American History*, pp. 195–212. Washington, D.C., The American Negro Academy, 1914.

Fauset, Arthur Huff, *For Freedom*, pp. 86–104. Philadelphia, Franklin Publishing and Supply Company, 1927.

Graham, Shirley, *Booker T. Washington*. New York, Messner, 1955.

Hagedorn, Hermann, *Americans: A Book of Lives*, pp. 87–109. New York, The John Day Company, 1946.

Haynes, Elizabeth (Ross), *Unsung Heroes*, pp. 63–84. New York, DuBois and Dill, 1921.

Hubbard, Elbert, . . . *Booker T. Washington*. Aurora, N.Y., The Roy Crofters, 1908.

Lotz, Philip Henry, ed., . . . *Rising Above Color*, pp. 74–81. New York, Association Press; Fleming H. Revell Company, 1943.

Meier, August, *The Emergence of Negro Nationalism: A Study in Ideologies*, pp. 85–104. M.A. thesis, Columbia University, 1949.

————, *Negro Thought in America, 1880–1915*. Ann Arbor, University of Michigan Press, 1963.

Miller, Kelly, *The Everlasting Stain*, pp. 253–270. Washington, D.C., The Associated Publishers, 1924.

Rollins, Charlemae Hill, *They Showed the Way*, pp. 141–142. New York, Thomas Y. Crowell Company, 1964.

Riley, Benjamin Franklin, *The Life and Times of Booker T. Washington*, New York, Chicago, Fleming H. Revell Company, 1916.

Shaw, John W. A., *A Tangled Skein*. Boston, A. Mudge and Son, 1904.

Spencer, Samuel R., *Booker T. Washington and the Negro's Place in American Life*. Boston, Little, Brown, 1955.

Washington, Booker Taliaferro, *The Story of My Life and Work*. Toronto, J. L. Nichols and Company, 1901.

William Monroe Trotter

❦

MOST UNSELFISH OF THE NEGRO LEADERS
(1872–1934)

WILLIAM MONROE TROTTER, the most persistent, uncompromising, and unselfish crusader against racial injustice since Frederick Douglass, was born of parents who had been slaves. His fighting spirit was encouraged by his father, a Civil War veteran, who taught him that he had a right to enter any public place and that he should always insist on that right. He was also told that he should try to excel whenever he came into contact with white people. If beaten in a fight with a white boy, he would get another whipping when he came home. For this ideal of fullest rights for his people, he later sacrificed wealth, political preferment, friends, the ordinary comforts of life, and finally, life itself.

No other Afro-American leader of his time was as courageous as Trotter. There were worlds of difference between him and his prominent contemporaries, some of whom were ready to compromise in order to be able to enjoy comforts that the people for whom they were supposed to be speaking were very far from attaining. Unlike most of the other Afro-American leaders also, Trotter had started life with a certain degree of affluence, and had been able to get an education with little or no financial difficulty. His father, who was recorder of deeds under President Harrison, was earning about $10,000 a year.

As a youth Trotter was exceptionally bright. At fourteen he led his class in grammar school at Boston, Massachusetts, and was its president and valedictorian. At Harvard University he won four important scholarships and was graduated *magna cum laude*. So excellent was his record that Harvard conferred a Master of Arts on him without further studies.

At the university he had also distinguished himself as a member of the Debating Club and was elected to Phi Beta Kappa, being the first Afro-American to win that distinction. He was also president of the Harvard Total Abstinence Society.

Finding it impossible to get suitable employment on graduation because of his color, he entered the real-estate and mortgage business in 1897 and was so successful that he soon became the second wealthiest Negro in Boston. But ever concerned about human rights, he did not confine his activities to making money. True to his ideals of racial equality, he founded *The Guardian*, a militant newspaper, in 1901, as well as the New England Suffrage League in 1903.

At this time arose a new Negro leader with a program which Trotter felt was a challenge to all that he stood for. This was Booker T. Washington, who was preaching to Negroes the doctrine of duty and the concentration on trade, agriculture, and self-development, rather than the seeking of citizenship rights.

Washington's gospel, as enunciated by himself, was not wholly one of surrender, however. Viewed from a certain angle it was practical. But what mattered to Trotter was how what Washington said was being construed by all those who were eager to keep the Negro in his so-called place. It practically meant that since the white people were "the Negro's best friends," he should always yield to them and let them decide what was best for him. In short, subservience.

Trotter knew further that many of these white "friends" had the same superiority complex as white enemies, and that such "friends" usually insisted that in any clash of wills it was the Negro who should yield in the cause of peace and goodwill. As for the Negroes, he saw that since most of them took their cue from the whites and usually accepted the leader chosen for them by the whites, Booker T. Washington, doctrines and all, had become their hero.

His fighting spirit aroused more than ever, Trotter decided to show America that there was an element of Negroes who did not accept Washington as their spokesman. Washington was to speak in Boston and a large audience of both "races" came out to hear him. Trotter and his lieutenants stationed in different parts of the church heckled Washington and finally set off stench bombs which sent the audience coughing and sputtering outside. As for Washington and his friends on the platform, cayenne pepper liberally thrown there sent them gasping. A free-for-all fight followed in the aisles, and one of Trotter's men, a policeman, and others were hurt.

Trotter was thrown into jail. His trial attracted nationwide attention. Found guilty, he was sent to prison for thirty days but he gained his end, as his views on rights for Negroes had been given a publicity they could not possibly have had otherwise.

He came out of jail more determined than ever. *The Guardian* became more militant. Forgotten was money-making. Into the insatiable maw of his crusade for justice he poured first of all his ready money, then that from the sale of his properties. When this was not enough, he threw in the money from the sale of his wife's properties and then of his mother's. The simple truth is that since his editorial policies were not countenanced by the whites and he did not receive any approval from them, he did not receive much support from established Negro leaders or from the Negro masses.

But his efforts bore fruit in other directions. As a result of his arrest, some of the bolder Negro spirits organized the Niagara Movement. Later, and no doubt as a result of this movement, the National Association for the Advancement of Colored People came into being with a membership of whites and Negroes.

This organization attacked Booker T. Washington and spoke up for the rights of the Negro vigorously. But Trotter resigned from it. He distrusted the white people in it. He felt that since the chief financial support of the organization came from them, they would dictate its policies, which, in the final analysis, would be to the Negro's disadvantage. He founded the National Equal Rights League, an organization that lived up to its name.

To his "call to arms" the response was weak. But Trotter continued to act as if he had a mighty host behind him. When *The Birth of a Nation*, a rabid anti-Negro moving picture, appeared in Boston, he fought it so vigorously that he went to jail again. Nevertheless, he won his case and succeeded in establishing a censorship to curb this kind of propaganda in the state. He next followed the picture to Richmond, Virginia, capital of the Confederacy, and fought it there even against the clubs of the police.

During World War I Trotter resolutely opposed separate regiments for Negroes. White and black, he pointed out, had fought side by side at Concord, Lexington, and Bunker Hill, and were even then doing so in the French army. As for those Negro leaders who had accepted segregation on the condition that there would be Negro officers, he denounced them with withering scorn.

Trotter took his case to the White House. He had been going there to petition every President since Theodore Roosevelt. But Woodrow Wilson refused to see him. Three years before, he had bearded Wilson at the White House on the segregation of Negro federal employees, which had come in with the Wilson regime, and his outspokenness in contrast to the soft, well-chosen words of the rest of the Negroes in the delegation had so angered the haughty Southerner in Wilson that Wilson walked abruptly from the room. When rioting Negro soldiers shot up the white population of Houston, Texas, Trotter went to the White House and was largely instrumental in getting a reprieve for them.

In 1926, on the 150th anniversary of the Declaration of Independence, Trotter was again at the White House with a mammoth petition addressed to Calvin Coolidge, asking that the spirit of that famous document be applied to the treatment of colored citizens. He also petitioned Coolidge and the Judiciary Committee of the United States Senate to support an antilynching bill. His efforts in this direction served in no small measure to bring about the passage of the bill in the Senate, but it was defeated in the House.

Trotter's most notable exploit was his invasion of the Versailles Conference after the United States government had tried to block him from going there. As one of the most important issues before that conference was the right of minority groups as expounded by Woodrow Wilson, Trotter felt that the Negro ought to be considered with other oppressed groups. Accordingly, he appeared before the Foreign Relations Committee of the United States Senate to demand an additional clause in the Covenant of the League granting Negroes equal rights in America.

The Senators gave him no satisfaction. He announced that he

would take the matter to Versailles himself. The government refused him a passport but he engaged as a ship's cook and reached France.

His mission did not succeed but his story told to the peace conference received worldwide publicity and caused Woodrow Wilson, who was acting as the champion of oppressed minorities while under his own administration the oppression of American Negroes had noticeably increased, considerable embarrassment.

In all these activities Trotter found an able and untiring helper in his wife Geraldine, who had come from a refined, well-to-do colored family and had, like him, the vision of equal opportunity and justice for all Americans. She gave her money freely to the cause, and then her beautiful home, to suffer privations with her husband. She was associate editor of *The Guardian*. After her death in 1918, Trotter published her picture each week on the editorial page in loving memory.

Trotter attacked segregation no matter where he saw it and no matter in what guise. There was no beating about the bush with him. Whenever he spoke he made every nerve of his auditors stiffen against the evil he was attacking. Nor did he spare the white philanthropists who gave money for the building of colored Y.M.C.A.s, racial scholarships, and racial medals. These he denounced as so many bribes given by the ruling class to silence the more articulate members of the group, and as being fatal to the cause of the inarticulate Negro masses. Naturally, none of the medals, scholarships, and prizes that were given to Negroes for accomplishments, or more properly speaking for good behavior, ever fell to Trotter. For example, *Who's Who in America* carried the names of nearly 100 Negroes, the majority of whom were only of average worth, but Trotter was omitted.

In the matter of so-called voluntary segregation, Trotter was equally consistent. Declaring that this was born of forced segregation, he insisted that it strengthened the position of the white segregationists. In consequence of this, most of the other Negro leaders, with an eye to present advantage, thought him erratic, while the masses, in whom a segregated psychology had been instilled through the centuries, regarded him on the whole as a fool.

For instance, after he had spoken at a convention of the National Equal Rights League in Chicago about 1919, some colored women, ignoring his inspiring address, began to discuss him personally. One of them said that she thought him worthless because his clothes were shabby and soiled, and were quite a contrast to those of her pastor. Another added deprecatingly that she had seen him that morning in an ill-smelling, fifteen-cents-a-meal Greek restaurant. Here, however, was a cultured and talented man who, had he closed his heart to the injustices suffered by his people, might have been a millionaire.

As the years went on, Trotter's financial worries increased. During the depression of the 1930s he had extreme difficulty keeping his paper going. The Negroes, it was true, were beginning to appreciate him but not enough to support his work.

His health failed and he was still inconsolable over the loss of his wife, whom he seemed to miss more and more with the years. Then in 1934 came the knockout blow to this stout-hearted fighter: he lost control of his newspaper. With wealth, health, wife, and newspaper gone, there seemed nothing else to live for. He staggered up to the roof of the three-story building in which he was only a lodger; later his shattered lifeless body was discovered on the ground.

He had given his last *défi* to life itself—life which had remained deaf to his ideal.

Like every other born crusader, Trotter had something of the fanatic in him. The cayenne-pepper and stench-bomb attack on Washington proved that; but it should be noted that the opponents of the Negro with their lynching and Jim Crow laws were infinitely more intolerant. Finally, were it not for a spirit such as Trotter's—the spirit of the eternal rebel against wrong and injustices—the masses of men would still be slaves and serfs.

If those leaders who compromise with racial injustice in the hope of present gain either for themselves or their group are following the better path, then the sacrifices of William Monroe Trotter have been in vain, and he deserves the name so often given him of fool and obstinate dreamer. But if an American citizen whose skin is dark is entitled to the same rights as one whose skin is fair—for this was, simply, Trotter's stand—then unborn generations will revere him.

They will revere him not because he alone had the vision of an America in which there would be no color injustice, not because he worked harder than others to achieve it, but for the persistency and purity of his ideals.

ADDITIONAL REFERENCES

Aptheker, Herbert, ed., *A Documentary History of the Negro People in the United States*, pp. 881–883. New York, The Citadel Press, 1951.

Fox, Stephen R., *The Guardian of Boston*. New York, Atheneum, 1970.

Harrison, William, "Valiant Trotter." *Negro History Bulletin*, pp. 34–36, 46 (November, 1947), Association for the Study of Negro Life and History, Washington, D.C.

William E. Burghardt Du Bois

William E. Burghardt Du Bois

SCHOLAR, EDUCATOR, AND FIGHTER FOR HUMAN RIGHTS
(1868–1963)

Dr. William E. Burghardt Du Bois, first American Negro to write books of scholarly merit, was born at Great Barrington, Massachusetts, of parents who, though poor, were of higher social standing than the average Afro-American of their time. Of remarkable intellectual brilliance from his early youth, he won scholarships that took him through Fisk and Harvard universities. He won his M. A. and Ph.D. degrees at Harvard and later studied at the University of Berlin.

His first works of importance were *The Suppression of the Slave Trade*, published in 1896, and *The Philadelphia Negro*, in 1899, the latter a systematic study of social conditions among the Negroes of that city. Both books were undoubtedly the first works of scientific importance on the Negro by an Afro-American.

From 1896 to 1910 he was professor of economics at Atlanta University, Georgia, where he was an important factor in helping not only his students but Afro-Americans think of their problems in a more organized, scientific way through *The Atlanta University Studies of the American Race Problem*, of which he was the editor. During this period he also wrote *The Souls of Black Folk*, which became a classic of its time and was widely quoted.

An uncompromising foe of injustice and Jim Crow restrictions, his righteous indignation burned at white heat against them, especially after he had seen the Atlanta Riot in 1906, when the white mob descended on the Negro district, ruthlessly slaughtering, destroying, and pillaging. He wrote a stirring denunciation of this massacre in which he attacked mob rule and the complacency of the white authorities. Thereafter, he became a most outspoken foe of lynching and mob rule in America. The year before that he had founded, together with William Monroe Trotter, the Niagara Movement, which demanded full citizenship rights for Negroes. It was a sort of meeting of the barons at Runnymede. No Magna Charta came out of it but its clear, unmistakable demands helped to crystallize in the minds of all what Negroes wanted. Later, largely as a result of the Niagara Movement, an organization that was destined to be the most important factor in the Negro's fight for justice came into being— The National Association for the Advancement of Colored People. Du Bois, one of its most active founders, became editor of its organ, *The Crisis*.

These activities brought him to the fore as the champion of Negro rights and the leading opponent of Booker T. Washington, who, as leader of the right wing, was stressing industrial education as the solution and soft-pedaling injustices. Washington was, in effect, advising Negroes to pay little, if any, attention to political and social rights and concentrate on industry to gain wealth and security.

Du Bois considered this policy suicidal. He saw that such wealth as the Negro might accumulate could not be guarded without political, legal, and social rights. If the Negro gave up the fight for these and surrendered his claims, even though they were only nominal, the white exploiters would eventually acquire a power over him that would make him a virtual slave again. And what was to prevent the mob from murdering Negroes en masse and plundering their homes as it had done at Atlanta and elsewhere?

He said that Washington had distinctly asked the black people to give up for the present at least, three things: political power, insistence on civil rights, and higher education of Negro youths, with the result that three things had occurred: the disfranchisement of the Negro; the legal creation of a distinct status of civil inferiority; and the steady withdrawal of aid from institutions of higher learning for the Negro. But, said Du Bois, three things were necessary: the right to vote; civic equality; and the education of youth according to ability. Hence, he said, "The black men of America have a duty to perform, a duty, stern and delicate—a forward movement to oppose a part of the program of their greatest leader."

In fact, Washington's own words gave strong support to Du Bois. He had said, "Education, whether of black man or white man, that gives one physical courage to stand up in front of a cannon and fails to give him normal courage to stand up in defense of right and justice, is a failure."

His editorials in *The Crisis* stirred the spirit of manhood in those Negroes capable of being stirred and made them more militant. At the same time, they drew the continuous fire of the white exploiters of the Negro in the South and their Northern sympathizers and even of those white liberals who felt that Negroes ought to be less insistent on their rights and be more grateful to white America for all the good they believed it had done them. Negro partisans of Booker T. Washington also attacked Du Bois as an agitator who was always stirring up trouble.

But he continued to speak out fearlessly. Under his able editorship, *The Crisis* became the first magazine of real merit among Negroes. And it was not only one of agitation. Its subtitle was: *A Record of the Darker Races*, and it lived up to it. It carried articles of historical and scientific information and excerpts of current opinion, native and foreign, on the race question, as well as portraits and illustrations. It gave light as well as heat and probably did more than any other Afro-American periodical or newspaper of its time to raise Negroes to a higher intellectual and more self-respecting level. In fact, no Negro publication of the time came near it in worth. As edited by Du Bois from 1910 to 1933, it was the best all-around magazine of information on the Negro. There has been nothing like it since.

He wrote other books, as *The Quest of the Silver Fleece, The Negro*, and *Darkwater*, which together with his editorials were widely quoted in America and abroad. When Booker T. Washington died in 1915, Du Bois became the foremost Afro-American.

In 1918, however, he took a step that was virtually equal to what he had objected to in Washington. In the July issue of *The Crisis* he wrote an editorial which practically advised the Negroes to surrender their rights while the war was on. He said, "Let us, while this war lasts, forget our grievances and close ranks, shoulder to shoulder, with our white fellow-citizens."

His adherents, even the most devoted ones, considered this a terrific letdown and protested bitterly. Forget our grievances, they asked. What about the East St. Louis riot, the greatest massacre of Negroes ever in America, had not that occurred during the war? And if the white oppressors were not disposed to give them their rights when they needed their services, were they likely to do so when the war was over and they needed them no longer?

This argument was not only logical but prophetic. Seven months after the end of the war, race riots swept the nation. In Chicago, Washington, D.C., Longview, Texas, and elsewhere, hundreds of Negroes were killed and thousands injured.

After the war Du Bois became militant again. He said that he had written the reactionary editorial because the War Department had begun to question his attitude toward the war. His opponents declared, however, that he had certain other material considerations for doing so.

For one of his universal outlook, it was natural to be concerned about the treatment of the darker peoples in other lands. In 1911 he was one of the speakers at the Universal Races' Congress held in London, which some of the world's leading sociologists and anthropologists attended. He was also organizer of the Pan-African Congress which brought together for the first time a group of thinking, influential Negroes of Africa, America, and Europe with several white leaders for a discussion of the problems of the Negro. The first conference was held in Paris and Brussels in 1919; there were later ones in Lisbon and New York, and then again in Paris in 1945.

After the First World War Du Bois went to Liberia where he represented the United States at the inauguration of President King. He also visited Sierra Leone and later made a tour of Russia and the Far East, returning by way of Hawaii.

Du Bois was an able and cultured speaker, and had he lived in France, he might have been awarded France's highest intellectual honor—election to the French Academy. The American race problem is considered a minor issue in world affairs and those who devote themselves to its solution, as Du Bois, however great their ability, do not receive commanding recognition unless they play the game of the whites, as did Booker T. Washington. Had Alexandre Dumas lived in America, he might have used his genius to attack the race problem instead of concentrating on novels that brought him world fame. As it was, Du Bois did attain enough prominence to make his work feared by the exploiting colonial powers in Africa.

His writings are rich in poetic quality and emotional appeal and in ecstasy, indignation, and biting sarcasm. His logic is often irresistible and he is at all times a superb master of the English language.

Following are excerpts from his writings:

The dangerously clear logic of the Negro's position will more and more loudly assert itself in that day when increasing wealth and more intricate social organization preclude the South from being, as it so largely is, simply an armed camp for intimidating black folk. Such waste of energy cannot be spared if the South is to catch up with civilization. And as the black third of the land grows in thrift and skill, unless skillfully guided in the larger philosophy, it must more and more brood over the red past and the creeping, crooked present until it grasps a gospel of revolt and revenge and throws its new-found energies athwart the current of advance. Even today the masses of the Negroes see all too closely the anomalies of their position and the moral crookedness of yours. You may marshall strong indictments against them, but their counter-cries lacking though they may be in formal logic, have burning truths within them which you may not wholly ignore. Oh, Southern Gentlemen! If you deplore their presence here, they ask, who brought us? When you cry: Deliver us from the vision of inter-marriage, they answer that legal inter-marriage is infinitely better than systematic concubinage and prostitution. And if, in just fury, you accuse their vagabonds of violating women, they, also, in fury quite as justly may reply: The rape which you gentlemen have done against helpless black women in defiance of your own laws is written in the foreheads of two million mulattoes, and written in ineffaceable blood. And, finally, when you fasten crime upon this race as its peculiar trait, they answer that slavery was the arch-crime and lynching and lawlessness, its twin abortion; that color and race are not crimes and yet it is they who in this land receive most unceasing condemnation, North, South, East, West.

Your country? How came it yours? Before the Pilgrims landed we were here. Here we have brought our three gifts of song and story, soft, stirring, melodious in an ill-harmonious and non-melodious land; the gift of sweat and brawn to beat back the wilderness, conquer the soil, and lay the foundations of this vast economic empire two hundred years earlier than your feeble hand could have done it. The third, a gift of the spirit. Around us the history of the land centered for thrice a hundred years; out of the nation's heart we have called all that was best to throttle and subdue all that was worst; fire and blood, prayer and sacrifice have billowed over this people and they have found peace only on the altars of the God of Right. Nor has our gift of the spirit been merely passive. Actively we have woven ourselves with the very warp and woof of this nation—we have fought their battles, shared their sorrow, mingled our blood with theirs, and generation after generation have pleaded with a headstrong, careless people to despise not Justice, Mercy and Truth, lest the nation be smitten with a curse. Our song, our toil, our cheer and warning have been given to this nation in blood brotherhood. Are not these gifts worth the giving? Is not this worth the striving? Would America have been America without her Negro People?

Even so is the hope that sang in the songs of my fathers well sung. If somewhere in this whirl and chaos of things there dwells Eternal Good, faithful yet masterful, then anon in His good time, America shall rend the Veil and the imprisoned shall go free. Free, free, as the sunshine trickling down the morning into these high windows of mine; free as yonder fresh young voices welling up to me from the caverns of brick and mortar below—swelling high song, instinct with life, tremulous and darkening bass. My children, my little children are singing:

> Let us cheer the weary traveller
> Cheer the weary traveller
> Let us cheer the weary traveller
> Along the heavenly way.

And the traveller girds himself and sets his face towards the morning, and goes his way. (*Souls of Black Folk*)

On the pale white faces which the great billows whirl upward to my tower I see again and again, often and still more often, a writing of human hatred vast by the very vagueness of its expressions. Down through the green waters on the bottom of the world where men move to and fro I have seen a man—an educated gentleman—grow livid with anger because a little, silent black woman was sitting by herself in a Pullman car. He was a white man. I have seen a great, grown man curse a little child who wandered into the wrong waiting room, searching for its mother: "Here you damned black——" He was white. In Central Park I have seen the upper lip of a quiet, peaceful man curl in a tigerish snarl of rage because black folk rode by in a motorcar. We have seen, you and I, city after city, drunk and furious with ungovernable lust of blood bring about murder, destroying, killing, cursing; torturing human beings because somebody accused of crime happened to be of the same color as the mob's innocent victims and because that color was not white! We have seen—Merciful God —in these wild days and in the name of Civilization, Justice and Motherhood—what have we not seen, right here in America, of orgy, cruelty, barbarism and murder done to men and women of Negro descent.

What then is this dark world thinking? It is thinking that as wild and awful as this shameful war was, it is nothing compared with that fight for freedom which black and brown and yellow men must and will make unless their oppression and humiliation and insult at the hands of the White World cease. The Dark World is going to submit to its present treatment just as long as it must and not a moment longer. (*Darkwater*)

Du Bois no longer stands alone as a Negro writer but he is still in the first rank. His *Color and Democracy*, published in 1945, was voted one of the best books of that year. His other principal works are: *The American Negro Family,* 1908; *Gift of Black Folk*, 1924; *Black Reconstruction*, 1935; *Black Folk Then and Now,* 1939; and *Dusk of Dawn,* 1940.

ADDITIONAL REFERENCES

Adams, Russell L., *Great Negroes: Past and Present,* p. 112. Chicago, Afro-Am Publishing Company, 1963, 1964.

Allen, Devere, ed., *Adventurous Americans*, pp. 192–202. New York, Farrar and Rinehart, 1932.

Brawley, Benjamin G., *The Negro in Literature and Art in the United States*, pp. 82–88. New York, Dodd, Mead and Company, 1929.

————, *Negro Builders and Heroes*, pp. 185–190. Chapel Hill, The University of North Carolina Press, 1937.

Broderick, Frances L. S., *Du Bois: Negro Leader in a Time of Crisis*. Stanford, Calif., Stanford University Press, 1959.

Embree, Edwin Rogers, *13 Against the Odds*, pp. 153–174. New York, The Viking Press, 1944.

Fauset, Arthur Huff, *For Freedom*, pp. 167–170. Philadelphia, Franklin Publishing and Supply Company, 1927.

Lacy, Leslie Alexander, *The Rise and Fall of a Proper Negro*, pp. 154–166. New York, The Macmillan Company, 1970.

Lotz, Philip Henry, ed., *Rising Above Color*, pp. 18–27. New York, Association Press; Fleming H. Revell, 1943.

Paschal, Andrew G., ed., *A W. E. B. Du Bois Reader*. New York, The Macmillan Company, 1971.

Rollins, Charlemae Hill, *They Showed the Way*, pp. 55–58. New York, Thomas Y. Crowell Company, 1964.

Rudwick, Elliott, *W. E. B. Du Bois: Propagandist of the Negro Protest*. New York, Aetheneum, 1968.

Rudwick, Elliott M., *W. E. B. Du Bois: A Study in Minority Group Leadership*. Philadelphia, University of Pennsylvania Press, 1960.

Tatum, Elbert L., *The Changed Political Thought of the Negro, 1915–1940*. Chicago, University of Chicago Press, 1942.

Marcus Garvey

"PROVISIONAL PRESIDENT OF AFRICA" AND MESSIAH
(1887–1940)

MARCUS GARVEY, "Back-to-Africa" leader, was the most widely known of all the agitators for the rights of the Negro and one of the most phenomenal. Arriving in the United States poor and unknown, within four years he became the most talked-of black man in the United States and the West Indies, and perhaps in the world.

He was born in Jamaica, West Indies, of very humble parents. His father was a breaker of stones on the roadway. He himself went to the denominational school and dreamed of doing great things. He read Plutarch and worshipped Napoleon. On Sundays he pumped the organ in the Wesleyan Methodist Church at St. Ann's Bay, of which his parents were members. Later Garvey became a Catholic.

Leaving school at sixteen, he went to work as an apprentice in the printing plant of P. Austin Benjamin in Kingston. Six years later he was the foreman. In the meantime he had been organizing the printers of the city and soon afterward led them in a successful strike for better pay.

An elocutionist also, he once won a first prize for his delivery of "Chatham on Liberty." Incited by this success, he began agitation for the political rights of the blacks of the island, who, though in the majority, were of lower social caste than the mu-

Marcus Garvey

lattoes. He went also among the West Indian laborers who were recruited for work in the neighboring republics and urged them to demand more pay and better working conditions. He was arrested for this in Port Limon, Costa Rica.

In 1911 he went to England, where he attended London University. He then visted the Continent and parts of North Africa, observing social conditions. In 1914 he returned to Jamaica and organized the Jamaica Improvement Association with himself as president and his first wife as secretary. Three years later he came to the United States with the intention of collecting funds for a school on the lines of Tuskegee Institute in Jamaica. But he stayed on in America. His first meeting was held in a Catholic hall in Harlem. The audience was small; his address was badly put together, and the response was weak. However, after he fell from the rostrum to the floor, it was said from hunger, he obtained a better hearing. From New York he traveled southward along the Atlantic seaboard to New Orleans.

His addresses on the race problem aroused the Negroes until by many he came to be regarded as another Moses. In March, 1917, he organized a movement, calling it the Universal Negro Improvement Association. He selected twelve disciples to assist him and announced that his aims were to establish a co-fraternity among Negroes the world over; to promote a spirit of love and pride; to assist in civilizing backward Africans; to establish schools and scholarships; and above all to found a strong Negro nation. As an organ for these aims, he founded a weekly newspaper, *The Negro World*. Contributions of from $1 to $25 were made by the thirteen persons at the first meeting.

To build his Negro nation and carry out his program of "Africa for the Africans," he said that ships were necessary and he founded The Black Star Line. Factories were to be established in the United States, the raw material of Africa and the West Indies was to be brought to America, manufactured there, and shipped back to those lands. The ships were also to be used to settle Negroes of the New World in Africa.

His program received wide publicity in the white press and was not long in running afoul of the ideals of most of the American Negro leaders, who declared it was sabotaging the fight here at home. This was all the more so when some of the most persistent enemies of the Negro hailed the Back-to-Africa program. Of course, these enemies knew that most Negroes would not be going to Africa, but the program shifted attention from injustices here at home and focused hopes for relief on Africa.

American Negroes had generally opposed any plan to uproot them and transplant them to Africa long before the emancipation. Had not this been advocated by some of their most violent foes, past and present? Lincoln, too, had tried it and his attempts had not only ended in failure but his colonization of Negroes on Ile de Vache off the coast of Haiti had cost the lives of more than a hundred of the Negroes taken there. Furthermore, had Lincoln been alive in Garvey's time he would probably have seen that colonization would not work.

Established bodies such as the clergy, the politicians, and the racial leaders saw in Garvey a tricky agitator who was trying to undermine them. Garvey's reply was that since Christian teaching for nearly two thousand years had failed to soften the hearts of the whites and improve the lot of the Negroes, for the Negroes to settle in a land of their own was the only solution.

Garvey's opponents at first had the upper hand and the Negroes shied away from subscribing to his steamship stock, $10,000,000 of which had been issued at $5 a share. Then came an affair in which he nearly lost his life that turned the tide in his favor. A half-demented Negro pushed into his dingy office in Harlem, accused him of swindling his money, and fired four shots at him, wounding him slightly. He rushed out into the street, the blood of martyrdom streaming from his face. Newspapers over the country carried the story and he was a made man.

Thereafter his steamship stock sold rapidly, the humblest Negroes becoming his most rabid supporters and making what sacrifices they could to buy. The West Indians in America, with their broader international outlook, flocked to him and two or three of them gave him $1000 each.

On August 1, 1919 (the anniversary of slave emancipation in the British colonies), he opened his first International Congress in New York, which became an annual event while his power lasted. These conventions opened with great spectacle. There was a huge parade through the streets of Harlem and banners were carried with such inscriptions as: "Africa Must Be Free"; "The Negro Fought in Europe, He Must Fight In Africa"; "Freedom For All."

On these occasions Garvey appeared in raiment that outdid Solomon in all his glory. He led the parade in a uniform loaded with tassels and gold braid that rivaled that of a British monarch. Beside him sat other officials as gaudily dressed. Though he was opposing British imperialism, he imitated its forms. Apparently he had never been able to throw off the impression British folderol and glitter had made on him in his childhood. Although he called himself a "president," he had his "Royal African Guards," and created dukes, as the Duke of Uganda, and the Duke of the Nile, and Knights Commander of the Most Noble Order of the Nile, etc., etc. Showman supreme, he applied the methods of Barnum to racial agitation and attracted the attention and support not only of primitive-minded Negroes but of many cultured whites and blacks who might otherwise have ignored him had he proceeded with less noise and ballyhoo.

During his conventions Madison Square Garden with its capacity of 25,000 was filled to overflowing. The platform contained hundreds of delegates from the American states, Central and South America, and Africa. In response to his appeals for funds came vast heaps of dollar bills, which had to be stuffed into suitcases like wastepaper to haul them off. (At that time bookkeeping had not been introduced into the "Universal Negro Improvement Association.") For the remainder of August the delegates met at Liberty Hall, the Garvey center in Harlem, a low-roofed, hot, zinc-covered building that held 6000 persons.

Garvey's successes stirred his enemies to greater activity, thereby increasing the wasp-like devotion of his partisans. Admirers and sycophants buzzed around him in swarms. He was hailed as the greatest man of all time, as another Moses and another Christ. "The two greatest G's in the world," said one of his admirers, "are God and Garvey." Like Napoleon, Mussolini, Hitler, and other dictators, Garvey himself was none too modest, and he too joined the chorus. The more he was praised, the greater became the frenzy of his followers, many of whom were virtually ready to sally out and attack the whites anywhere.

Among the many activities of Garvey's movement was the formation of an African Legion, the members of which carried guns and swords in the fervent belief that the day was near when they would be using them against the whites in Africa and elsewhere.

It was, in short, racial fascism. He seemed to have believed honestly that the best way to right the wrongs of his people was to retort by adopting the modus operandi of the racial imperialists he was fighting. In other words, for everything white they had, he would have something black. For instance, he promised "a Black House side by side with the White House in Washington." He himself declared that his movement was fascistic. He said, "We were the first Fascists. We had disciplined men, women and children in training for the liberation of Africa. The black masses saw that in this extreme nationalism lay their only hope and readily supported it. Mussolini copied fascism from me but the Negro reactionaries sabotaged it."

Opposition against him increased, while his followers became more fanatic. One of them sent a chopped-off human hand to A. Philip Randolph, editor of the *Messenger*, one of his leading opponents. Inside the movement, too, all was not harmony. In it were Negroes who were better educated than Garvey and with more practical, more liberal, and more advanced views, and who did not regard him as an oracle. Some of them were no doubt jealous, too, of the adulation showered on him. Others inside the movement denounced him as medieval, autocratic, and antimulatto. Some of his once most faithful supporters attacked him violently in print and founded counterorganizations. One of these, his lieutenant, Rev. J. W. Eason, known as "The American Leader," was shot to death as he was leaving a church in New Orleans by a fanatical Garveyite, at Garvey's instigation, it was charged.

His enemies concentrated their attack on his steamship program. Up to now it existed only on paper though he had collected huge sums of money for it. Under their pressure he bought a ship, the *S. S. Yarmouth*, which he rechristened *The Frederick Douglass* and "launched" with great ceremony in New York. This, however, was at the close of the First World War when ships were at a premium, being in demand for bringing back American troops from Europe. Once the troops were back, however, ships became a drug on the market and could be bought for a song. Indeed, the government burned or sank hundreds of its ships. The *Yarmouth* was rightly called "a floating coffin." He paid $165,000 cash for it and a year or so later sold it for junk at $1600.

This hulk was so wretched that when it was chartered soon after prohibition to take a cargo of whisky to Cuba in order to keep the whisky out of the clutches of prohibition agents, it broke down a few knots outside of New York harbor and came to final grief off the Florida coast and had to make its way into Miami with sails made of bed sheets.

He had no better luck with the *Kanawha*, an old yacht of the millionaire H. H. Rogers, which he rechristened the *S.S. Antonio Maceo*. It was bought for $60,000 and refitted at a cost of $25,000 but got no further than the coast of Cuba, where it fell to pieces. Another, a paddle-wheel, the *Shadyside*, bought for $35,000 for carrying passengers from New York to Albany, sank while lying at anchor, while a fourth, the *Orion*, which was to have been rechristened the *Phyllis Wheatley*, got him into so much legal trouble that it wrecked the movement itself.

With his steamship line headed for the rocks, he tried to build home enterprises such as laundries, groceries, a daily newspaper, and a printing plant (he already had a hotel and a restaurant). All failed except the printing plant, and this was finally dragged under by the debt accumulating from the others. Most of these failures were due to the fact that Garvey ran everything himself. He knew very little about business, and as his autocratic nature made it impossible for him to take advice, inexperienced managers to whom he could dictate and who would flatter him suited him best. There was some dishonesty, too. Some of the officials had joined the movement in order to exploit it. Bookkeeping was, at all times, loose.

Another handicap was that Garvey, in line with his grandiose ideas, had fancy paper salaries voted for his officials. Of course, these were intended only for show and the pay they were to receive was much below those figures, but when these officers were discharged or resigned, which happened in the case of most of them sooner or later, they brought suit for the paper salaries and won, thereby driving the organization deeper into debt.

Much of the opposition to Garvey, it must be said, was due to sheer jealousy. Here was a recently obscure alien who was collecting millions of dollars from Negroes, while other leaders, many of them college-trained, were having to rely chiefly on white philanthropy.

As a matter of fact, Garvey was the first black man who succeeded in making Negroes pay for Negro agitation. The secret of his support was that he appealed to that portion of the black masses too far down to be noticed by other leaders. He won the devotion of these by telling them that they were not only as good as the upper-class Negroes but that a black skin was just as good as a white one, and even better. They had every cause to believe that they could never hope for justice in America as long as their color was what it was, so when he told them this and said the only remedy was to get out, they believed him implicitly. And plenty of higher-ups sympathized too.

Much of the opposition, though, was honest and logical. Such opponents held that the Back-to-Africa program was diverting attention from the fight for justice here in America and disrupting its course. It was equivalent, some said, to the injunction not to lay up treasures on earth but to give up everything for a utopia in the hereafter. He opposed the joining of white trade unions by Negroes and those Negro organizations fighting for rights here at home. As for the Negro church, he practically rejected it and had his own rituals and Sunday services. Later, in his Liberty Hall, Christ and the Virgin Mary were canonized black.

Incredible as it may sound too, he endorsed the Ku Klux Klan, the most insidious foe of the Negro and American democracy. He called on the head of the Klan at Atlanta, Georgia, pledged him his support, and announced that he and the Klan had this in common: The Klan was fighting to make America a white man's land and he was fighting to make Africa a black man's country. He also allied himself with the pernicious Anglo-Saxon Clubs of America, sworn enemies of the Negro, and invited their leaders to his Liberty Hall platform, where they were acclaimed by his followers. He called what he and they were doing "The Ideals of Two Races." He had John Powell, head of these Clubs, speak to a huge crowd from his platform on October 28, 1925, where Powell praised and sold *White America* by Earnest Sevier Cox, a pseudo-history intended to prove that Negroes were an inferior race from the dawn of time. On page 414 of his *Philosophy and Opinions* he carried free a full-page ad of this vicious book. Cox, in return, wrote a pamphlet dedicated to Garvey, whom he called "a martyr for the independence and integrity of the Negro race."

Garvey had allied himself with these sinister organizations largely as one way of getting revenge on the American Negro leaders, nearly every one of whom were opposing him. In fact, he seemed to take a delight in opposing everything for which the American Negro leaders stood. During the Italo-Ethiopian War he frequently denounced Haile Selassie. His special target was Dr. W. E. B. Du Bois, who, in an article in *The Crisis*, had called him a "little, fat, black man; ugly, but with intelligent eyes and a big head." The Klan and the Anglo-Saxon Clubs had promised him congressional support to get his followers to Africa but used him only as a tool. Of course, they were willing to give him a free hand in Africa, where they had neither power nor interests, in exchange for the substantial benefits derived from the exploitation of Negroes in America.

His endorsement of the Klan was the last straw to his opponents. Eight of them signed a petition to the Department of Justice, citing cases of violence committed by the members of his organization, all of which, it was alleged, had been incited by Garvey himself. They quoted Section 3, Article 5, of the constitution of his organization as proof that it encouraged lawlessness. This section read, "No one shall be received by the Potentate and his consort who has been convicted of felony, except such crime or felony was committed in the interest of the Universal Negro Improvement Association."

This petition had almost immediate effect because in legal matters Garvey was very vulnerable, especially in his selling of stock in The Black Star Line, which was in a most wretched financial state. He had been carrying glowing full-page ads and publishing speeches in the *Negro World* offering stock in a "phantom" ship, the *Phyllis Wheatley*, on which he had only paid a deposit. It was not yet his and still bore its original name, the *Orion*.

His enemies, who had patiently been gathering the evidence against him for years, now turned it over to the federal government and he was indicted for using the mails to defraud.

The case came up in New York in May, 1923. He was defended on the opening day by a brilliant member of the bar, a Negro who was later appoointed as a federal attorney, but Garvey was so accustomed to ruling the roost that he could not stand having another speak for him, and discharging him, took over his own defense.

The trial up to his point had proceeded with dignity, but now it deteriorated into low comedy, which reflected indirectly upon black people as a whole. Garvey was completely ignorant of legal methods, and fully illustrated the adage: "He who pleads his own case has a fool for a client." Several times the judge found it necessary to tell the attorney-defendant that the court was not conducting a law school.

Garvey, the showman, ran riot, and there were times when even the judge joined the laughter. At times he would resort to the style of a backwoods attorney, apparently thinking that verbal fireworks would impress the jury. When witnesses for the prosecution appeared on the stand, he would pull old legal gags such as "Do you still beat your wife? Yes or no!" It was clear to all except defendant-counsel Garvey that he was fighting his way into the penitentiary.

The white press had an orgy of fun. It came out in the trial that the *Yarmouth* (or *Frederick Douglass*, as Garvey had renamed it) had sent an S.O.S. while taking its liquor cargo to Cuba, but, said the white press, the message had read "SOUSE. We are sinking and drinking." It was alleged the Negroes had taken to the lifeboats with a lifebelt in one hand and a bottle of whisky in the other. For three weeks the case made comic copy while self-respecting Negroes squirmed. Arthur Brisbane, the most noted editor of the time, wrote, "To jail Garvey would be to jail a rainbow."

Garvey took the stand on his own behalf and blamed his

troubles on his lawyers and his Negro captain. He also made a summation of his case which lasted for three hours and was undoubtedly the finest speech of his career. Justice, not sympathy, was his refrain. "I want no mercy, only justice," he said, and one felt that he meant every word. He went on:

I have served my people, my race and my God. I have wronged not even a child of my own race or any other. I would not betray my struggling race. If I did, I deserve to be thrown into the nethermost depths of Hell.

If I have committed any offense in truth, and it is a violation of the law, I say it is your duty to find me guilty, and let me have the full extent of the law. I ask no mercy. I ask no sympathy. I ask but justice based on the testimony given in this court.

Faultlessly dressed, now with a handkerchief in one hand and a glass of water in the other, now with a document or a slip of yellow paper handed him by his legal adviser fluttering in his fingers, he was impressive. He thundered, gesticulated, crouched, writhed, shot forth angry accusing fingers, shook his heavy shoulders. The perspiration fell in large drops from his stubbly beard as he swung his short, massive body from side to side. He was theatrical probably from platform habit but at times he was quite sincere. His followers wept. Friend and foe listened enthralled by the voice that sank at times to soft denunciation and then rose in thunders of wrath, scorn, and accusation.

The jury, after twelve hours, returned a verdict of guilty on one count, and the court inflicted the maximum penalty—five years' imprisonment, $1000 fine, and costs.

The sentence was considered very severe as at that time several worse offenders were given a year or less. Moreover, of the 35,000 or so Negro stockholders there had been only five or six complainants and these had appeared against him only after much urging.

There were reasons which had undoubtedly influenced the judge, Julian W. Mack. During the trial Garvey had indulged in several outbursts of anti-Semitism, and when called before Judge Mack after the jury had found him guilty, he shouted, "Damn the Jews." His unfortunate deal with the *Yarmouth* had been with a

Jewish firm and thereafter he had blamed all Jews for the affair. But both Judge Mack and the prosecuting attorney, Mattuck, were Jews. Judge Mack was also one of the directors of the National Association for the Advancement of Colored People, an organization then engaged in a bitter fight against the Ku Klux Klan, Garvey's ally.

During his release on bail, he appealed his case to the United States Supreme Court and resumed his activities. To show his strength, he founded another steamship line—the Black Star Corporation—and raised enough money to buy a modern first-class ship, which he called the *Booker T. Washington*, for $160,000. It sailed for the West Indies after a great sendoff in New York City but on its return was seized and sold for the many judgments that had accumulated against him.

The Supreme Court affirmed the verdict against him and he was taken to Atlanta Penitentiary, where he proved a model prisoner. Many attempts were made to get a pardon for him and in 1927 his sentence was commuted by President Coolidge and he was deported to Jamaica. There he entered politics and won a seat in the City Council, causing a considerable stir on the island by his articles in his newspaper *The Black Man*. In a libel case he was cited for contempt of court and sentenced to three months' imprisonment, and a heavy fine.

On his release he went to England and agitated there, but was generally ignored. With his determination to get a foothold in Africa as firm as ever, he petitioned the League of Nations for land. In Paris he addressed an audience well disposed toward his program. Nothing, however, came of his efforts in Europe and he returned to Jamaica. In 1931 he again returned to Europe and petitioned the League of Nations, again without result. His great organization, no longer news, became a shell. He spoke sometimes in Hyde Park but the English press ignored him until his death on June 11, 1940, in London.

Was Garvey honest? The answer to this depends on one's point of view. A leader may be thoroughly honest and yet appear insincere and dishonest to many. Garvey was a Messiah who had come to save a people who for centuries had been exploited by another "race," and, a Messiah without a Promised Land has about as great a chance for success as a political candidate who promises his constituents nothing. Moses had his Canaan; Jesus, his Heaven; Mohammed, his Paradise. The early Christians were no less simple in their beliefs than the Garveyites. It was amusing, to put it mildly, to listen to clergymen ridiculing Garvey about his dream-empire in Africa while they themselves held out the promise of a much vaguer heaven after death. If Garvey, like these Christians, had had the power of the law and the sword behind him, his paradise would have been accepted without a murmur. As it was, not even the fact that his paradise was planned for this earth saved it. It was called idiotic, though it wouldn't have taken his followers more than a little money to get there—which is more than can be said for these clergymen's heaven. As a matter of fact, some of Garvey's followers did go to Africa.

There can be no question as to Garvey's ability. He had all the potentialities of a Hitler or a Mussolini. His cause was just, but his methods were twisted, archaic, perverse. He undoubtedly wanted to help the downtrodden blacks but like every other autocrat believed that the end justified the means. Like all other messiahs too, he was a poet and romancer and knew how to soothe the sufferings of his followers with hopes of paradise. He could paint such halcyon pictures of this to his assembled cohorts that they would actually feel themselves already there. At one of his meetings in Carnegie Hall, New York, even two or three of the men went into hysterics, while the women shouted and shrieked. He furthermore gave his followers what they wanted even more than earthly goods: hope of revenge. "We will build," he said, "so strong a government in the Mother Land that when they lynch a Negro in Georgia or Alabama, we will have but to press a button and six white men will be lynched in Africa."

He also promised them, "Some day all the whites in Africa will be driven into the sea and the Negro race will become so strong that it will build a Black House side by side with the White House in Washington."

He even led his followers to believe that in Africa was a magic so powerful that it would pull airplanes out of the sky and turn machine-gun bullets to water. When one of his leaders told a gullible audience in Liberty Hall of this magic, which he called "the ancient mysteries of Africa," Garvey repeated the same in the *Negro World* in such a way as to endorse it. In short, his simpleminded followers believed in the Garvey heaven just as earnestly as educated Germans and Italians believed in the Hitler and the Mussolini ones. Since, therefore, hope and promise are about all that the rank and file of any movement have ever received from their messiahs, Garvey, according to this precedent, could not be said to have defrauded his followers. One fact was clear, too: He had profited little or nothing by the millions of dollars he had taken in. While no Gandhi in self-sacrifice, he lived more simply than many a Negro leader who had taken in far less money. His salary at no time exceeded $100 a week and for lunch he usually ate crackers and cheese. He never owned a car and he lived in an ordinary Harlem apartment. During his trial he was practically penniless, owning but $30 in the bank and 289 shares of his worthless stock. Of course, much of the money went for advertising himself, so much so that the judge in charging the jury said that if it had been proved that he hadn't stolen a penny but had misused the funds for publicizing himself, he was guilty.

As for the economic side of Garvey's program, it was doomed from the start even had it been conducted on sound business lines. It was based on racism, which runs counter to the law of gain, that is, buying in the cheapest market and selling in the dearest. This economic factor is above all racial, religious, and political dogma. It recognizes neither color nor creed. Blacks will spend their money among whites if it is to their economic advantage; and the converse. Furthermore, there is no proof that ever in history there existed a pure white, pure black, pure brown, or pure yellow civilization; rather all were mixed to a greater or lesser degree. Garvey's justification for a black empire was in rebuttal to an Anglo-Saxon cry for white supremacy, but since this latter was a fraud and delusion, his rebuttal was the same kind of monstrosity. If the Southern states with all their power and their laws have not succeeded in establishing a lily-white land, what hope would Garvey have of establishing an ebony-black one in Africa, where the whites already were in powerful control?

Moreover, any intelligent leader must realize that not race but economics is at the bottom of human conflict. The blacks of Africa were torn by strife among themselves long before the Pharaohs and were racked by tribal and national wars and barbarities precisely as were the American Indians, the Chinese, the Dayaks, and white Europeans.

Indeed, Garvey's organization even in its infancy had shown signs of this strife. He had planned to start in Liberia but he quarreled with the Liberian government even before he got there and he was forced to leave his sawmill and other equipment sent there to rot. Edwin Barclay, Liberian minister, interviewed by *The New York Times*, flatly announced that "neither Garvey nor any of those identified with him would be received in Liberia." It was alleged at the time that the Garveyites, once in Liberia, planned to seize control. Garvey's mission to Liberia years before had returned with two reports: one in glowing praise to be read to his followers; the other, a private one, painting an awful picture of the present regime, accusing it of corruption and slavery. One of Garvey's enemies, getting a copy of the secret report, had sent it to the Liberian president.

As for his career in the United States, it was one of strife from the start. Knowing nothing of Negro American history and psychology and the popular conditions of the struggle in the United States, he tried to impose his own way of seeing things, rather than working in harmony with the leaders here. A born autocrat, the acclaim and publicity he received also went to his head. Had he ever come to absolute power, he would have been another Robespierre. One of his leading opponents once said, "I, for one, would never have lived in Africa under his rule for he would have been the greatest head-chopping king that ever lived."

Moreover, he several times promised his followers that in Africa he would make them millionaires. To do that he would have had to continue the worst features of white imperialism now there. What he really did accomplish on the economic side was to take tens of millions of dollars from the poorest element of American blacks and hand it back to the capitalist whites by a more direct route than by which such money usually comes to them. To his stockholders he could well have repeated what his model, Napoleon, said to his faithful followers after Waterloo: "I found you poor, I leave you poorer."

As for the fascism of which he boasted, that was an abomination. If the injustices of color prejudice which had aroused him were disgusting, his solution was no better. On the other hand, it must be said that his movement was exactly the fruit that a soil poisoned by color prejudice might be expected to yield. In any case, the manifestations of ignorance in his followers were no worse and certainly more understandable than those of the better-educated whites with their Ku Klux Klans, Anglo-Saxon Clubs, and Black Legions.

There were certain benefits from his activities which cannot be ignored, however. He stirred the blacks in the New World and parts of Africa to feel that in spite of all the white man's vilifying of them they were human beings just the same. In other words, he gave them back their self-respect and opened for them windows of hope that would never be closed. Many could have been reached by no other message but his, that is, the promise of a land where they would no longer be pushed around and abused because of a difference of color.

And backing up his emotional appeal there was the good, solid information about themselves in his *Negro World*, which was edited by some of the brightest Negro minds. In this and certain other aspects he did good. And above all, he aroused millions of Negroes and whites in many lands to think of the "race" problem as they had never done before. Because of this he will be remembered and idealized more and more with the years. As in the case of other "strong" men, as the Muley Ismails, Napoleons, and Robert E. Lees, the evil he did will probably be forgotten and the good remembered.

REFERENCES

This writer knew Garvey well. He knew him as a boy in the West Indies; attended his meetings in the United States; talked with him; wrote for his newspaper (but was not a member); reported his trial for the press during the four weeks it lasted; visited him in Atlanta prison; and saw him in different years in London, and talked with him

there. It was at one of these talks in 1937 that Garvey boasted he was
the first fascist.

World's Work, December, 1920, pp. 153–166; January, 1921, pp.
264–270.

Literary Digest, March 19, 1921, pp. 48–51.

Current Opinion, March, 1921, pp. 328–331.

Garvey, M., *The Philosophy and Opinions of Marcus Garvey*, 2
vols. 1926.

Crisis Magazine, December, 1920, January, 1921, New York.

ADDITIONAL REFERENCES

Adams, Russell L., *Great Negroes: Past and Present*, p. 91. Chicago,
Afro-Am Publishing Company, 1963, 1964.

Cronon, Edmund David, *Black Moses*. Madison, University of Wisconsin Press, 1955.

———, *The Story of Marcus Garvey and the Universal Negro Improvement Association*. Madison, University of Wisconsin Press,
1955.

Drimmer, Melvin, *Black History*, pp. 324–510. Garden City, N.Y.,
Doubleday and Company, 1967.

DuBusdewarnaffe, Charles, Vicomte, . . . *Le Mouvement Pan-Nègre
aux Etats-Unis et Ailleurs*. Brussels, Goemaere, 1922.

Edwards, Adolph, *Marcus Garvey, 1887–1940*. London, New Beacon
Publishers, 1967.

Essien-Udom, E. U., *Black Nationalism: A Search for Identity in
America*, pp. 36–39. Chicago, University of Chicago Press, 1962.

Garvey, Amy Jacques, *Garvey and Garveyism*. Kingston, Jamaica,
1963; New York, Collier Books, 1970.

Harris, Robert, *Black Glory in the Life and Times of Marcus Garvey*.
New York, African Nationalist Pioneer Movement, 1961.

Henry, Edward Barnes, *The Predictions of a Great Race in Fulfillment*.
New York, 1953.

James, Cyril Lionel Robert, *History of Pan-African Revolt*. Washington, D.C., Drum and Spear Press, 1970; originally published as
History of Negro Revolt, 1938.

McKay, Claude, *Harlem: Negro Metropolis*, pp. 143–180. New York,
E. P. Dutton and Company, Inc., 1940.

Weinberg, Arthur Myron, ed., *Passport to Utopia*, pp. 214–222. Chicago, Quadrangle Books, 1968.

Hubert Henry Harrison

INTELLECTUAL GIANT AND FREE-LANCE EDUCATOR
(1883–1927)

THAT INDIVIDUALS of genuine worth and immense potentialities who dedicate their lives to the advancement of their fellow men are permitted to pass unrecognized and unrewarded from the scene, while others, inferior to them in ability and altruism, receive acclaim, wealth, and distinction, is common—yet it never ceases to shock all but the confirmed cynic. Those with a sense of right and wrong, of fitness and incongruity—whether they be wise men or fools—will forever feel that this ought not to be.

Shakespeare was so little regarded during his lifetime that no one bothered to record the details of his life, and today most of what is said about him is pure conjecture. Gregor Mendel, whose experiments were to revolutionize biology and agriculture, was practically unknown until sixty years after his death. Of course, there are some of genuine worth who do not die obscure and who do win gradual recognition while alive. But why are so many who we feel really ought to be up, down; and why are so many who certainly ought to be down, up?

Hubert Henry Harrison is the case in point. Harrison was not only perhaps the foremost Afro-American intellect of his time, but one of America's greatest minds. No one worked more seriously and indefatigably to enlighten his fellow men; none of the Afro-American leaders of his time had a saner and more effective program—but others, unquestionably his inferiors, received the recognition that was his due. Even today only a very small proportion of the Negro intelligentsia has ever heard of him.

Harrison was born in St. Croix, Virgin Islands, of apparently unmixed African descent. His birthday, April 27, was also that of Herbert Spencer, by whose philosophy he was profoundly influenced. At sixteen he made a tour of the world as a cabin boy, and at seventeen came to New York, where he worked as a hall boy in a hotel, as an elevator operator, and in similar positions. With an avid desire for learning, he spent his spare time reading and went to a public night school. He was the brightest scholar in a class composed almost wholly of white people. Professor Hendrick Karr, his instructor, said of him:

Harrison is the most remarkable Negro I have ever met. In the examination for the diploma—and it was rigid—he passed perfect at one hundred per cent—the only student in his class having that rating. He will be heard from in the future if learning has anything to do with success.

Shortly afterwards he took the competitive examination for the Post Office Service, and passed with ease. Unable financially to enter college, he spent his leisure hours absorbing all he could of sociology, science, psychology, literature, and the drama.

Harrison remained at the Post Office for four years. The routine of sorting letters was not for a man of his calibre. But in a land so color-conscious and alive with race prejudice, what opportunities, if any, were there for a youth whose skin had been dyed so deeply black by nature? The only outlet for his talent, ambition, sympathy, and deep sense of justice seemed to lie in concentration on the problems affecting himself and his people.

He saw that Negro leaders were treating their injustices as a purely racial question, and that their program was nebulous, consisting largely of complaint or advice to submit. The Negroes, these leaders would whine, had been brought to America against their will; they had supported the nation in all its crises—and just look how badly they were being treated for their pains! The remedy they suggested was work and submission, which they argued, would bring wealth.

Harrison, on the other hand, searched much more deeply. He realized that the Negro's ill-treatment transcended color differences; he knew that the black man in his time of ascendancy had exploited the white, and would do so again if the opportunity came. Color, he argued, was only the surface expression, and underneath it lay the world-old exploitation of man by his fellow man, which manifested itself now under the guise of tribal and national relationship, now under religion, political belief, sex, color, or anything else available.

His study of modern science and sociology enabled him to see that the Socialists had a clearer vision of this truth than either of the two great American political parties. Consistently, also, the Socialists were advocating the improvement of the economic lot of humanity, regardless of race or color. He thereupon joined the Socialists, who were few in number, but very militant. This latter feature pleased him most.

He showed such zeal that he rose rapidly to be one of the recognized leaders. His all-around knowledge; his grasp of economics; the logic of his thought; his fearlessness; his ability as a speaker, all brought increasing recognition to the party. He took an active part in promoting strikes, one of them at the Paterson, New Jersey, silk mills. It is true that the exploited white workers in those mills objected to working with Negroes, but Harrison, with his wider vision, saw that the cause of the black worker was also that of the white worker, and he hoped to make the white workers see that some day. With Elizabeth Gurley Flynn, Bill Haywood, Morris Hilquitt, and other party leaders, he labored for the emancipation of the workingman.

His activities were not confined to Socialist gatherings. He spoke wherever an audience could be had on subjects embracing general literature, sociology, Negro history, and the leading events of the day. He wrote also for such radical and antireligious periodicals as *The Call*, *The Truth-Seeker*, and *The Modern Quarterly*, being perhaps the first Negro of ability to enter this field.

While the older Negro leaders were taking generally a backward or a conservative point of view or agitating along purely racial lines, Harrison continued to speak of the Negro "problem" in its universal aspect, making it one with the protest of oppressed humanity everywhere.

He applied the latest scientific theories to the position of the Negro, and found much in Marx, Buckle, Spencer, Nietzsche, Schopenhauer, Lenin, Bertrand Russell, Dewey, and others to support his own ideas. At the Modern School (later located at Stelton, New Jersey) he was appointed adjunct professor of comparative religion, lecturing on the natural history of religion and expounding modern socialistic ideals and tendencies.

His views on religion and birth control were often opposed by Catholics and Protestants alike, and at his open-air meetings he and his friends were obliged to defend themselves physically from mobs at times. But he fought back courageously, never hesitating to speak no matter how great the hostility of his opponents.

He continued to work with the Socialists until he found that they too were becoming infected by color prejudice. Most of the original leaders were still sincere, but certain of them, tired of the struggle, were surrendering to the newer ones, who were either for barring Negroes from their ranks altogether, or for dealing with their wrongs pianissimo in the hope of attracting more adherents. The Socialists too, he felt, were becoming capitalistic-minded, at least in their attitude toward the Negro, and therefore, he was convinced, they could not be relied on to treat Negroes fairly should they ever come into power. He left them in 1917.

Retiring to Harlem among his own people, he founded the Liberty League together with its organ, a newspaper called *The Voice*. He continued his open-air addresses, stressing the economic side of the color question, which brought him much opposition from Negro press, pulpit, and politics. The Negro preachers, and sometimes their white colleagues, objected to his theories on evolution—which were Darwinian—and would summon the police to break up his meetings.

Nevertheless, crowds flocked to hear him. His auditors would stand hours at a time shifting from foot to foot, entranced. He had a way of presenting the most abstract matter in a clear and lively fashion, so that the least of his hearers were not only spellbound by his powerful delivery but also understood what the man was talking about. His vast knowledge and keen logic were a delight to the sophisticated.

For a livelihood he sold literature. So able was he in this respect that on one occasion he disposed of 100 copies of a book on sociology at $1 each within an hour on Lenox Avenue in Harlem. The feat was all the more remarkable in view of the fact that the purchasers were Negroes, who, as a group, were very little inclined to buy books.

Harrison also gave open-air addresses in parts of the city inhabited by white people. At Ninety-sixth Street and Broadway a large crowd of whites usually assembled to hear him, and at Wall Street, the world's money center, he had an even larger audience. Some of America's wealthiest men, attracted by his eloquence, would stop to hear his dissertations on philosophy, history, economics, and religion.

One of the men who was very much influenced by Harrison was Marcus Garvey, later the most prominent of Negro agitators. Garvey's emphasis on racialism was due in no small measure to Harrison's lectures on Negro history and his utterances on racial pride, which animated and fortified Garvey's views. Harrison's slogan became "Race First"—in opposition to his earlier socialistic one of "Class First." He explained this change by saying that since the Socialists were mostly Americans who had been reared in an atmosphere of color prejudice, they habitually thought "White First," hence, whenever their economic interests were involved they were usually ready to sacrifice the Negro. Thus, he reasoned, if Negroes thought in terms of "America First," or "Class First," they would be neglecting their own interests—at least until the time that the whites—socialist-minded and otherwise—underwent a real change of heart. Hence, he said, in self-defense, Negroes must think "Negro First."

Harrison's views profoundly influenced the Messenger Group, headed by A. Philip Randolph and Chandler Owen, two leaders who did more than anyone else to focus the attention of the government and of thinking whites on the injustices suffered by Negroes during the war. While the old leaders capitulated and urged the members of the race to submit while the war was on, these two brilliant young men spoke out fearlessly. Largely because of opposition from the War Department, The Messenger Group received nationwide publicity; by showing that progress toward obtaining justice lay not in barren agitation about race, or in dying and going to a white man's heaven, but in awareness and intelligent application of economic laws, it opened new vistas to the minds of thinking Negroes and not a few whites.

The Garvey movement and the Messenger Group, the first racial, the second economic in doctrine, had only radicalism in common and later became enemies. Both, however, represent eras in the progress of the Afro-American, and both were fructified by the spirit and teaching of Harrison.

In 1926 Harrison became a staff lecturer of the Board of Education of the City of New York. He gave a series of lectures at New York City College, making several addresses at New York University as well. Several times he was the principal speaker at the Sunrise Club, a fortnightly gathering of some of the most brilliant minds of the city. Fluent on almost any subject, he was best in topics dealing with world problems in relation to the darker races.

Under average height, Harrison was sturdily built. His head attracted instant attention, the more so as his forehead, which was a shade lighter in color than the rest of his face, seemed illuminated. It was unusually large and so fully rounded out in its upper portion that it seemed to bulge from pressure within.

His health was excellent, though at times he suffered from vertigo while speaking and had to steady himself. Small wonder, for he spent the night in reading, even after his strenuous three-hour lectures. He would retire at daybreak, sleep for two or three hours, and start the day all over again.

He made many enemies among the more conservative Negro leaders, especially those who derived support from wealthy whites. When he died, the two leading Negro magazines, *The Crisis* and *Opportunity*, ignored him, though at the same time, *The Crisis* gave space to the death of Tiger Flowers, Negro pugilist.

Harrison was not without his faults. The life of any leader, scrutinized detail for detail, does not look like the handsome image presented by ecstatic admirers after flaws have been removed and bits retouched. As the saying goes: "No man is a hero to his valet." The process of debunking history that has been going on since World War I has spared neither Jesus nor Washington—yet who would deny their essential greatness?

One of the charges made against Harrison was that he called

himself a "Doctor of Science," although he had not received that degree from a university. This charge seemed to be well founded —yet the fuss stirred up about it was out of all proportion to its significance, and handicapped him seriously. It is not for this writer to dwell upon the ethical implications of the case, yet in justice to Harrison it should be pointed out that in America especially, it is common for many who can barely read or write to adopt titles such as "Doctor" or "Professor," and this is particularly true among the Negro clergy, where "D.D.'s" are really superabundant. Often an individual who displays a certain amount of learning is addressed by a title, and in the Southern states that of "Colonel," for instance, is a form of courtesy. Harrison first entered a university as a lecturer, which, considering the fact that he had no formal education or prestige therefrom, would be regarded as quite an achievement by anything but a warped mind. There is no proof that he received a degree from the University of Copenhagen, as he said, yet it is obvious that he felt this ruse necessary in order to win favor in the eyes of those who worship degrees, holding them to be symbols of genuine scholarship. The sad commentary here is not so much on Harrison as on the academic system and the picayune minds it produces. Few graduates of any university excelled Harrison in erudition, and after a thorough investigation of the matter, it seems as if Harrison was not so much a delinquent as a victim of professional jealousy on the part of those who, by all rules of common decency, should have given a handicapped colleague a boost instead of a kick.

Inconsistencies in politics might be another point against Harrison. An ardent Socialist, he turned Democrat—a considerable change, to be sure. Yet when a principle for which one has labored hard and long fails economically, and when one has a wife and five young children to support, who can deny the reasonableness of practical considerations? If Harrison expected an appreciable material increase from his switch to the Democrats, it was not forthcoming. His enthralling oratory should have paid him well, yet, like so many scholars, he was so thoroughly wrapped up in his work that this aspect of the situation quite escaped him. Whatever money he received usually drifted to him as food to a polyp attached to the piles of a pier. Harrison's lifelong enemy, like that of most scholars, was poverty. Destiny sent him into this world very poor. And as if this were not enough, she gave him a critical mind, a candid tongue, a family to support; a passion for knowledge, and on top of all that, a black skin, and sent him to America. Surely, a more formidable string of handicaps would be hard to conceive.

Most of the enmity against Harrison was incurred by his devastating candor. In this respect he was an *enfant terrible*. He spoke out freely what he thought, and more often than not it was with such annihilating sarcasm and wit that those whom he attacked never forgave him. Before he began his attacks, he usually collected "the evidence," as he called it, consisting of verbatim utterances, verbal or printed, of the prospective victim. This type of ammunition was deadly. There was, however, no personal malice in Harrison's shafts. Like a true sportsman, he was willing to shake hands with an opponent as soon as he descended from the platform, and was surprised and hurt that the other was not.

In his personal contacts Harrison was kindly and good-natured, and both among the common people and the broad-minded intellectual whites he had many friends. He was happiest and at his best on a "soapbox" surrounded by admiring listeners and a heckler or two to match in a combat of wits. He would usually squelch these amid outbursts of laughter from his audience.

He momentarily forgot names, but his memory was astounding. In the course of his addresses he would reel off quotations from poets great and obscure, cite passages from Spencer, Darwin, Huxley, and other scientists and scholars without an error; in jokes and anecdotes he was to the point.

Unlike most persuasive speakers, he was also an able writer. At the age of twenty-four he was writing book reviews for *The New York Times*—a remarkable achievement for a beginner. He also contributed articles and reviews to the *New York Sun, Tribune, World*, and other metropolitan dailies, as well as for periodicals, including *The Nation*, *The New Republic*, and *Masses*. He was assistant editor of the last magazine for four years, and editor of Garvey's *Negro World* for another four years. Through this medium he did much to stimulate learning in various parts of the world. Every week he compiled a list of books on literature, science, drama, and learning in general as recommended reading. His best editorials and articles were published in two booklets: *The Negro and the Nation* and *When Africa Awakes*.

In his last years he suffered acutely from poverty. His clothes became shabby and his shoes heavily patched, quite in contrast to the appearance of many other Negro leaders, less sincere and less capable than he. All that he owned at the time of his death were his favorite books.

If the day ever dawns when mankind values truth and learning more than money and the superficial amenities of life, then men like Harrison will be at least assured of what nature freely gives to the animals in their haunts, namely, food and shelter. Then what is so glibly called civilization will really deserve its name. In the pursuit of an ideal surely no more can be demanded of one than to sacrifice literally everything, as Harrison did.

Harrison had many admirers. The following are some of the tributes paid to him while still alive:

New York University Daily News: "Dr. Harrison's address on 'India's Challenge to the Powers', was enlightening, authentic, and imposing."

Miss Ernestine Rose, librarian of the Harlem branch library, at which Harrison often spoke: "I appreciate very deeply Dr. Harrison's keen and intensely living mind; his wide and varied culture and his intellectual contribution to the expressed thought of his day."

The New York Times (September 11, 1922): "Hubert Harrison, an eloquent and forceful speaker, broke all records at the Stock Exchange yesterday."

Burton Rascoe, literary editor of the *New York Tribune* (June 4, 1923): "Mencken asked me to introduce him to Dr. Hubert Harrison, who sat next to me at the dinner, and very soon Dr. Harrison was the centre of the most serious discussion of the evening; for Theodore Dreiser, Heywood Broun, Ludwig Lewisohn, Charles Hansen Towne came over for the pleasure of talking with the distinguished Negro."

William Pickens, winner of the Ten Eyck prize for oratory at Yale University: "Here is a plain black man who can speak more easily, effectively, and interestingly on a greater variety of subjects than any other man I have ever met even in the great universities. . . . I know nothing better to say than that he is a walking encyclopedia of current human facts. . . . If you have brains you will give him the palm as an educational lecturer. . . . If he were white, and I say it boldly, he might be one of the most prominent professors of Columbia University, under the shadow of which he is passing his days."

Hodge Kirnon: "He was the first Negro whose radicalism was comprehensive enough to include racialism, politics, theological criticism, sociology and education in a thorough-going and scientific manner."

The obituary notices were striking. The *New York News* (December 31, 1927) said:

Thousands of New Yorkers will miss the philosophy of the most brilliant street orator that this metropolis has produced in the last generation. The soul of Hubert Harrison knew neither black nor white, race nor religion. If a more universal man has been created in our day we have not met him. His fund of philosophy, ready wit, his measured and melodious utterances disarmed all those who came to scoff, and turned them into his admiring followers. He was a potent and living example of the potential equality of the black man.

Rev. Ethelred Brown: "In Hubert Harrison we had a man so human, so natural, that because of this we forgot for a while that we stood in the presence of an intellectual giant."

The *Pittsburgh Courier*:

It was a revelation to see Hubert Harrison mounted on the street corner ladder and surrounded by a crowd of several hundred Negroes discussing philosophy, psychology, economics, literature, astronomy or the drama, and holding his audience spellbound. His achievement should prove an inspiration to many young Negroes, for despite the handicap of poverty, he became one of the most learned men of his day, and was able to teach the wide masses of his race how to appreciate and enjoy all the finer things of life, to glance back over the whole history of mankind, and to look forward "as far as thought can reach."

ADDITIONAL REFERENCES

Harrison, Hubert Henry, *The Negro and the Nation*. New York, Cosmo-Advocate Publishing Company, 1917.

———, ed., *The Voice of the Negro*, Vol. I, No. I (April, 1927), International Colored Unity League, New York.

———, *When Africa Awakes*. New York, The Purro Press, 1920.

Ernest Everett Just

PIONEER IN BIOLOGY
(1883–1941)

MAN'S OLDEST AND MOST absorbing passion, next to his concern for the immediate necessities of life, is the quest for his origins. From this search has come religion, philosophy, art, science, invention, in a word, civilization.

As late as the beginning of the nineteenth century thinkers endeavored to fathom this riddle chiefly by theological word-spinning. Today the method is experimental research, thanks to which cholera, smallpox, and bubonic plague have been wiped out in the civilized lands, while typhus, syphilis, tuberculosis, and even cancer, have been greatly checked. As a benefactor of humanity, the biologist ranks second to none.

Among the foremost of these was Dr. Ernest Everett Just, who was born in Charleston, South Carolina, and who from his earliest years showed exceptional brilliance in his studies. At Kimball Hall Academy, a white institution in New Hampshire, he completed a four years' course in three. Entering Dartmouth College, he made the highest marks of any student in Greek in his freshman year, and won the Rufus Choate Scholarship for two years. In 1907 he was graduated *magna cum laude*, being the only member of his class to win that distinction. In zoology and history he won special honors, and more in botany and sociology. In 1916 he received his Ph.D. from the University of Chicago, *magna cum laude*.

From 1907 to his death he taught biology at Howard University where he was head of the Department of Zoology. His vacations were spent in study at the Marine Biological Laboratory at Woods Hole, where he was a very popular and stimulating member of a group of noted biologists who met there annually.

His investigations dealt with fundamental biological problems concerning the cell, and from 1915 onwards he was a leading contributor to biological journals and was widely quoted, especially on such subjects as fertilization, artificial parthogenesis, cell division, hydration and dehydration in living cells, and the effect of ultraviolet rays in increasing chromosome number in animals and in altering the organization of the egg with special reference to polarity.

In polarity fertilization, on which great emphasis is laid by those scientists in search of the origin of life, his work was appraised by his contemporaries as among the most important in the field, while some place him first.

In 1925 he was selected by a group of German biologists as one of the contributors to a series of monographs which contained the latest knowledge in his field, thus further establishing his reputation in international science.

He also engaged in research at the Kaiser Wilhelm Institute for Biology in Germany, where he was a guest, as well as at the Marine Biological Laboratory at Naples, and at a similar institution in Sicily. In 1930 he was one of the speakers at the Eleventh International Congress of Zoologists at Padua, Italy, his topic being "The Role of Cortical Cytoplasm in Vital Phenomena." The same year he was elected vice president of the American Society of Zoologists.

In a treatise on cytology, edited by Dr. E. V. Cowdry of the Rockefeller Institute, he was co-author of the section on fertilization with Dr. Frank R. Lillie, dean of the Department of Zoology of the University of Chicago. He was also a contributor to Dr. Jerome Alexander's three-volume work on *Colloid Chemistry*; a collaborator of *Protoplasma*, a German journal devoted to the physical chemistry of the cell; to *Cytologia*, a similar paper published in Japan; one of the editors of *Physiological Zöology* and the *Biological Bulletin*, the latter the official organ of the

Biological Laboratory at Woods Hole; and one of the authors of *General Cytology*. His principal books are *Biology of the Cell Surface* (1939) and *Basic Methods for Experiment on Eggs of Marine Animals* (1939).

Dr. Just held membership in several leading scientific societies, among them the American Association for the Advancement of Science.

In 1914 he was awarded the Spingarn Medal which is given annually to the person of Negro descent who, in the opinion of the judges, had rendered the most distinguished service for the year. From 1920 to 1931 he was the Julius Rosenwald Fellow in Biology of the National Research Council.

Like all men of profound learning, Dr. Just was modest. His reputation for integrity, experimental ability, and loyalty was the highest possible. An excellent teacher, he exerted a far-reaching influence on research work not only among his students in the classroom, but on many older investigators in related fields. Discoveries of so fundamental a nature as his find their application in many other branches of biological work.

As head of the Department of Biological Sciences at Howard University, he rendered invaluable services to his racial group. It is safe also to say that had it not been for the color of his skin, he would have been head of a similar department in one of the nation's much larger and more influential universities, there to have enjoyed the prestige and the salary his merit deserved.

Karpman says:

He was a most tireless and persistent worker whose quality of work will match the highest. The total number of his contributions come to about sixty, averaging two a year during his scientific life, but they were models of scientific presentation—succinct, precise, direct with economy of words, withal most clearly expressed, reminding one of the late Jacques Loeb at his best. His work is of lasting value: nothing he has done will ever have to be done over again. His book, "The Biology of the Cell Surface," which synthesizes his life work, is a remarkable contribution of highest scientific order, of value and interest alike to scientists in general as well as to practising physicians and psychiatrists. . . . He knew the animal egg as few scientists knew their material. It was a knowledge so intimate, so deep, so clear-visioned as to comprehend even the minutest; in the intracacies of the workings of the cell he could envision a macrocosm within a microcosm. . . .

One would naturally expect that a man of such superior accomplishments and achievements would be richly rewarded. . . . He was a Negro. That one grain of melanin in his body locked all the doors of advancement and opportunity. Though the university with which he was connected during his life time has been most generous to him, it could not, in the nature of things, provide him with the opportunties a man of his calibre needed. It was like putting an eagle in a chicken-coop. . . .

The exquisite clarity and depth of Dr. Just's mind is revealed in his writings, for instance, in this passage from his *Biology of the Cell Surface*:

The realm of living things being a part of Nature is contiguous to the non-living world. Living things have material composition, are made up finally of units, molecules, atoms and electrons, as surely as non-living matter. Like all forms they have chemical structure and physical properties, are physio-chemical systems. As such they obey the law of physics and chemistry. Would one deny this fact, one would thereby deny the possibility of any scientific investigation of living things. No matter what beliefs we entertain, the noblest and purest concerning life as something apart from physical and chemical phenomena, we can not with the mental equipment which we now possess reach any estimate of living things as apart from the remainder of the physio-chemical world.

He points out, however, that:

Living matter has an organization peculiar to itself. Nowhere, except in the living world, does matter exhibit this organization. Life, even in the simplest animal or plant, so far as we know it, never exists apart from it. Resting above, and conditioned by non-living matter, life perhaps arose through the chance compounds which compose it. But who knows? A living thing is not only structure in motion. As static, it reveals the superlative combination of compounds of matter; as a moving event it presents the most intricate time-pattern in Nature. Life is exquisitely a time-thing like music. And beyond the plane of life, out of infinite time, may have come that harmony of motion which endowed the combination of compounds with life.

REFERENCES

American Men of Science, "Ernest Everett Just."

Who's Who in America, "Ernest Everett Just."

Arthur, George R., *The Crisis*, February, 1932.

Miller, Prof. Kelly, *Howard University Record*, April, 1925.

Karpman, B., *Journal of Nervous and Mental Diseases*, February, 1943.

ADDITIONAL REFERENCES

Adams, Russell L., *Great Negroes: Past and Present*, p. 59. Chicago, Afro-Am Publishing Company, 1963, 1964.

Just, Ernest Everett, *The Biology of the Cell Surface*. Philadelphia, P. Blackiston's Son and Company, Inc., 1939.

————, "The Necessity of the Egg Cortex for Fertilization." *Howard Review*, Vol. I, No. I, pp. 65–72, Washington, D.C., 1923.

Lindsay, Jack, *Marxism and Contemporary Science, or The Fullness of Life*, pp. 95–96. London, D. Dobson, 1949.

Ovington, Mary White, *Portraits in Color*. New York, The Viking Press, 1927.

Negro Yearbook. 1947.

Arthur A. Schomburg

Arthur A. Schomburg

"THE SHERLOCK HOLMES OF NEGRO HISTORY"
(1874–1938)

Arthur A. Schomburg, though dead, still ranks as the foremost bibliophile and collector of books on the Negro. In 1926 the Carnegie Corporation of New York paid him $10,000 for his collection of books, prints, manuscripts, and pictures, which was about a fifth of its intrinsic value.

He was born at San Juan, Puerto Rico, and was educated partly on that island and partly in the Danish West Indies. Interested from childhood in Negro history, he noted down every fact he could find on that subject, being especially prompted to do so because he saw the best of everything was reserved for whites and near-whites, with the blacks kept at the bottom.

His early researches were to serve him well in debates with his white classmates, some of whom would declare that the Negro had never accomplished anything of note and never would. On such occasions he was able to refute them successfully. As regards their own Puerto Rico, he would tell them of José Campeche, whose portraits, taken to Rome, created a sensation in art circles there; and of Rafael Cordero, a poor cigar maker, who was a pioneer in the education of whites and blacks on the island, and in whose honor a street in San Juan is named.

Such incidents inspired him to collect books and facts with increasing enthusiasm. This knowledge he gave freely to all who would listen.

In 1901 he came to New York City and found employment in the law office of Pryor, Mellis, and Harris, for whom he did excellent clerical work and research. In the case of *Johnson and Johnson*, for instance, which involved the question of the right to use the Red Cross label on absorbent and medicated cotton, Schomburg digested and indexed 4500 printed pages of the testimony. At the special request of Senator Brinkerhoff, he assisted in the discussion of the exhibits of the defense in Chancery. When he left the firm, its head, Pryor, later a Supreme Court Justice of New York, gave him a splendid testimonial.

While engaged in this work, he was also actively agitating for Cuban and Puerto Rican independence in New York, and was secretary of Las Dos Antillas, a club working for this cause. After Cuba had won her independence, he went on a scientific expedition to Central America and Haiti.

On his return, he entered the service of the Bankers Trust Company of Wall Street, where he remained for twenty-one years, becoming head of the mailing depeartment, with a large staff of white subordinates. His duties were difficult; nevertheless, his spare moments were devoted to his hobby. Indeed, it was during these years that he did his most important work in collecting and in writing.

While there he also helped in the founding of the Negro Society for Historical Research, and in 1892 was elected president of the American Negro Academy.

In 1924 he made a voyage to Europe that contributed immensely to research on Negro history. In Seville, Spain, he dug into the original records of the Indies which were loosely collected there, and thus was able to throw much new light on Negro history. American Negro slavery had originated in the Iberian peninsula.

While in Spain he also definitely established the fact that two of Spain's noted painters, Juan Pareja and Sebastian Gomez, were Negroes. On this voyage he also visited France, Germany, England, and other countries, making important additions to his collection.

For these and other discoveries Schomburg was highly complimented by John W. Cromwell, president of the American Negro Academy. Dr. Cromwell wrote him (June 17, 1928):

How can I adequately express to you my indebtedness for your rescue of Banneker from the seclusion in which he has been for one hundred and twenty years. Think of it, biographers, bibliophiles, enthusiastic devotees—Latrobe, Bishop Daniel A. Payne, the Banneker Institute, the noble army of admirers, and what-not, have all absolutely failed to cast down their buckets where they were and secure the refreshing waters you have drawn up! You are entitled to more than a vote of thanks for this one act. There can be no disputing the authenticity of the facsimile of a contemporaneous publication.

In the same letter Dr. Cromwell thanked him for the discovery of a manuscript of Lemuel Haynes, Negro pastor of a large white New England congregation before the emancipation. "The Lemuel Haynes manuscript," says Dr. Cromwell, "is also valuable. You possess some magnetic influence drawing you to these treasures that elude the eager quest of others."

In 1929 Schomburg retired from the Bankers Trust Company on a pension and went to Fisk University as curator. In 1931 he became curator of the collection which bears his name and which he enlarged until it is now the largest and finest of its kind, having more than 5000 volumes, a good many of them by Negroes; and thousands of pamphlets, old manuscripts, prints, and bound volumes of newspaper and magazine clippings. Some of the books are bound in hand-tooled leather and cost as much as $250.

The field of information covered is vast and varied. There are subjects such as Zulu nursery rhymes printed in the Bantu language; books on anthropology, folklore, sociology, customs of the Negro in the Congo, Guinea, Ashanti, the West Indies, and the wilds of South America; sermons on slavery by ex-slaves; travel, poetry, drama, and culture in general.

His researches are of immense benefit to present-day Negro historians, as well as to book lovers and collectors in other fields for whom he discovered at times rare and priceless volumes. For instance, he found for the Central New York Public Library a rare Gulistan. Foreign libraries also benefited by his finds.

Only those who knew him will ever be able to realize the depth of his love for his work. Untiring and conscientious, he had the persistency of a ferret. Once he found a clue, he never rested until the facts were fully and reliably developed. Learning, for instance, that a long-lost picture of Juan Pareja was somewhere in New York City, he traced it until he found it in the storeroom of a transfer company in Harlem, where the precious picture of this slave of Velásquez had long lain unrecognized. The *New York Sun* (January 4, 1927) said editorially of him, "The ambition that impels a man who has finished one day of hard or trying labor to attempt another exhausting effort is based on something more substantial than mere desire to achieve a tour de force. His will to express himself springs from a deeper motive than pure vanity."

He was a walking encyclopedia. Ask him almost any fact about the Spanish and the American Negro, and he would be almost sure to know something about it offhand. In 1926 he received a Harmon Award for his work on Negro education.

Schomburg also wrote extensively for magazines and newspapers and published a biographical checklist of Negro poetry, as well as *The Collected Poems of Phyllis Wheatley* together with an appreciation of her work; *The Life of Placido*, great Cuban poet and martyr; *Racial Identity—Helps to the Study of Negro History; Spanish Painters of the School of Seville;* and *Notes on Panama.* He was also one of the writers included in an anthology of Negro literature by V. F. Calverton in 1929.

One of his most important essays appeared in *The New Negro,* of which Alain Locke was editor. In this he made clear the goal for which he had so long been working and for which he had made so many personal sacrifices. With a family to support and with his continual outlay for books, he was often financially pinched. He said:

The American Negro must remake his past in order to make his future. Though it is orthodox to think of America as the one country where it is unnecessary to have a past, what is a luxury for the nation as a whole becomes a prime necessity for the Negro. For him, a group tradition must supply compensation for persecution, and pride of race is the antidote for prejudice. History must restore what slavery took away, for it is the social damage of slavery that the present generation must repair and offset. So, among the rising millions, we find the Negro thinking more collectively and more retrospectively than the rest, and apt, out of the very pressure of the present, to become the most enthusiastic antiquary of all.

There is the definite desire and determination to have a history well documented, widely-known at least within racial circles, and administered as a stimulation and inspiring tradition for the coming generations. The remote racial origins of the Negro, far from being what the race and the world have been given to understand, offer a record of creditable group achievement when scientifically and impartially viewed.

ADDITIONAL REFERENCES

Schomburg, Arthur, A., *Military Services Rendered by the Haitians in the North and South American Wars for Independence.* Nashville, Tenn., A.M.E. Sunday School Union, 1921.

————, "The Negro Digs up His Past." *Survey Graphic*, Vol. VI, No. 6, pp. 670–672.

Williamson, Harry Albro, *Arthur A. Schomburg, The Freemason.* New York, Williamson Masonic Collection, 1941.

Henry Ossawa Tanner

Henry Ossawa Tanner

"THERE IS NO American artist more talked of than H. O. Tanner," wrote Vance Thompson from Paris in 1900. "Perhaps this is because he is a mulatto and, in spite of the example of Dumas and De Heredia, we are still surprised when the artist reveals himself under a dark skin. And there may be another reason. Mr. Tanner is not only a biblical painter, but he has brought to modern art a new spirit."

Until his death thirty-seven years later Tanner was still the foremost painter of American birth resident in Paris. He undoubtedly did more toward retaining that high position in contemporary art won for America in France by Sergeant and Whistler than any other.

He was born in Pittsburgh, Pennsylvania, son of a bishop of the African Methodist Episcopal Church. At the age of thirteen he had already decided to be "a great painter." This inspiration had come when he saw an artist at work in the field. Gazing for a while in admiration, he had hastened home, and obtaining a piece of awning, painted his first picture on it. For a palette he used the back of an old geography book.

Like many another great artist, he had early difficulties. Poverty and lack of appreciation dogged him for a long time. His health, too, was not of the best and forced him to quit more than

455

once and to sell his pictures for a pittance. One of them that he once sold for $15 brought $250 a week later.

Drawing was difficult at first for him, despite the great urge within. His first lesson was most discouraging. Having saved $50, he arranged to take lessons with a leading painter at $2 a lesson. When he arrived at the studio, trembling with excitement, he was asked whether he could draw a straight line. Like the man who when asked whether he could play the violin replied, "I don't know. Give me one and I'll see," Tanner took his charcoal. For three hours he drew, or rather tried to draw, simple, straight, parallel, horizontal, and perpendicular parallel lines. Then he paid his $2 and left, his bright dreams of the morning completely shattered. Several days elapsed before his spirit returned.

Realizing that at $2 a lesson his $50 would not go very far, he began teaching himself, and did so well that he was accepted as a student at the Academy of Fine Arts, Philadelphia.

From the first he had difficulties with his teachers. He believed in independent expression; in putting on the canvas what was in himself.

In one of his economically darkest periods, this was to serve him ill. A fellow painter, generous but erratic, had taken him into his home free, on condition that he would renounce all other ideas of art save those of his benefactor. One day, however, a friend of the painter's visited him and complimented Tanner highly on his work, but said not a word about the work of Tanner's host. The next day, when Tanner returned from school, he found his canvasses, brushes, and clothes on the doorstep, and the door locked.

For a livelihood Tanner was now forced to go into the flour business. He would get up early to spend a little time with his art. The overwork caused an illness that interrupted his artistic work for several years.

Sometimes he did sell a picture. Of these he would say like a true artist, "I always felt like a criminal, for if they had seen that picture as I did, with all its faults continually staring at me, they certainly would not have purchased it."

Hoping to earn enough to continue his studies, he sent black-and-white sketches to New York publishers, but they were always returned. Finally he sold the sketch of a lion for $40, which permitted him to change his diet of corn bread and apple sauce. Soon afterward he sold another sketch for $80. Then, he was appointed art instructor at Clark University, which made his life easier.

Here he saved a little money and began to look toward Europe. In the hope of supplementing his savings he gave an exhibition. But it was a failure and consumed much of his savings. Then a friend lent him $75, which enabled him to leave for France.

In Paris he studied under John Paul Laurens and Benjamin Constant. During this period he ran very short of funds and was forced to practice the most trying economies. As a result he fell seriously ill from malnutrition and typhoid fever.

His great ambition, like that of many other artists, was to have a picture accepted by the Salon. One whose picture is hung at that great annual event is usually "made." But this dream did not come true for him until after five years. His "Daniel in the Lions' Den," hung at the Salon, received an honorable mention.

Recognition in America came at the same time. His "Raising of Lazarus" was exhibited at John Wanamaker's in Philadelphia, where it attracted much favorable attention.

The sun had begun to shine for him now. This picture was one of the sensations of the Salon the next year and was bought by the French government. Tanner, who was in the Levant at the time, received a letter from a friend saying, "Come home to see the crowds flocking around your picture." It was also hung in the Luxemburg Gallery. Tanner, as usual his own severest critic, wrote of it, "I lived several years in dread that the picture would look to others as it did to me and that it would lose the place it held in the Luxemburg."

Devoted to biblical subjects, Tanner went to Palestine for a living background for his ideas. "Moses and the Burning Bush," "The Scapegoat," "Christ and Nicodemus," "The Repentance of St. Peter," "The Immaculate Conception," and others were the result of this visit.

With success won, Tanner made France his home where, he said, he found an absolute cosmopolitanism and a recognition in the fine arts which barred no nationality, race, school, or variation of the artistic method. All that was asked, he said, was that art should be true, that it should set forth life.

He found there, also, a freedom from color prejudice that did not exist in America. For instance, when he revisited Chicago for an exhibition of his paintings at the Art Institute, where he had won the Harris Prize in 1906 for the best American painting of the year, he was given a guest membership in the Cliff Dwellers' Club, one of the country's leading societies of artists and literary men.

Tanner used to take his meals at the club. Once when it was ladies' guest night he came as usual for dinner, as did other members, and a certain miniature painter voiced his indignation that a Negro should be a guest at the club on such an occasion. "Didn't Tanner know that ladies were going to be present?" he demanded. This man, like a few others, usually kept out of the dining room when Tanner was there.

Among the prizes won by Tanner were the Walter Lippincott Prize; the Second Medal at the Universal Exposition, Paris, 1900; the Second Medal at the Pan-American Exposition, Buffalo, 1901, and at the St. Louis Exposition, 1906; and the Gold Medal at the Panama-Pacific Exposition at San Francisco, 1915.

Two of his pictures were bought by the French government, others by the Carnegie Institute of Pittsburgh, and his "Two Disciples at the Tomb" by the Chicago Art Institute. Others are in the leading art galleries of Europe and America.

Tanner was undoubtedly the greatest modern painter of religious subjects. Discarding worn-out traditions, he developed a technique of his own. To a vivid emotion he added a certain exact impressionism. There was a warm sympathy in his painting that placed him in the rank of Rubens, Rembrandt, Michelangelo, Murillo, and other great religious painters.

His fine sympathies are perhaps best brought out in his "Behold the Bridegroom Cometh." In this picture the Wise Virgin on the left is on her knees with her own lamp brightly burning at her side, trying to bring to life the smoking lamp of the Foolish Virgin. His purpose was to try to take off the cold, virtuous edge so often given to this parable, and to interpret it not only in the light of what Christians preach about the goodness of God but also what is expected of any humane individual.

The Independent, speaking of this quality, says:

It is this intense sympathy which has enabled Mr. Tanner to lift the veil for us and to present us modern living and convincing pictures of the storied past.

Daniel appears in the lion's den as convincingly free from danger as he seems free from fear. The mental exultation of the man is apparent in this wonderfully posed figure and we are not surprised to see that these very real lions, as they pace up and down, should edge away as they approach this silent power.

Wherever Christ appears in a picture it is noticeable that the artist cares less about showing the form and features of the man than the spirit. Always the people in the presence of Christ are held spell-bound by this radiating essence. Mary and Martha regard him with loving reverence; the disciples, carefully characterized, listen with wonder to his words, their natures strung to the highest tension. It is impossible not to realize that the speaker is no ordinary man, that his words are felt to be inspired, and prophetic, and it is also difficult to put a curb on one's enthusiasm for the artist. To the special natural qualifications that Mr. Tanner has brought to his work, he has added culture. All his abilities, mental and technical, seem to be well under control.

La Nouvelle Revue says, similarly:

We stand before a knowledge solid and sure of itself; the weighty strokes which, when seen from nearby, resemble a veneer of mahogany, evidently comes from a flowing and unctuous brush. Through the thick paint there plays a soft light which models the outline in chiaroscuro."

Throughout all his paintings Tanner shows a profound thoughtfulness, a penetrating psychology, and a nature truly poetic. The strength of his imaginative senses is perhaps best revealed by the following incident: While riding one night in a jiggling, ill-lighted omnibus, he was struck by the beauty of the color around him. Inside the omnibus the figures were dimly lighted by a soft cadmium; outside was the cool night with here and there a touch of moonlight. The colors fascinated him. But not wishing to use the interior of an omnibus, he conjured up the scene of "Judas Covenanting with the High Priest," and used the coloring in another setting.

The tendency in America is to undervalue Tanner's genius by regarding it racially. As *Current Literature* observes:

In America public recognition of Tanner's genius has been somewhat retarded by the fact that he is a Negro, and our publications have persistently spoken of him as the greatest Negro painter. But this classification of Tanner's work, while literally true, gives an erroneous impression. Although his paintings exhibit that full-blooded sense of rhythm which gives a peculiar charm to the art productions of his race, Tanner's work is above all racial distinctions. He should no longer be classed as the foremost Negro painter, but rather as one of the greatest artists America has produced.

In 1928 the French government, in recognition of Tanner's genius, made him a Chevalier of the Legion of Honor.

On his death in Paris, May 25, 1937, Paul Swann wrote of him:

A great soul has passed on to a higher plane. The artist in him has left many beautiful and really spiritual works for the delight and uplift of humanity. The man was as fine as his work. Modest, even timid, he concealed a very rich and mellow nature. More than others he has taught us that there is no barrier between races; that the love of beauty fuses and unifies all hearts. The subjects he chose to paint, in his style, which only a master could command, were his religious biography. He beheld all expressions as leading to the Source of Life. His God was a clear reality; an every day father who loved his children. Tanner surely was a favorite son! His passing once again reminds us that all salvation comes from the recesses of the inner man. His memory will, for those who knew him personally, be a beacon light! Especially for us worldly ones who have lost our way to peace. . . .

REFERENCES

Outlook, April 7, 1900.
Cosmopolitan, Vol. XXIX, p. 19, 1900.
World's Work, Vol. XVIII, 1909.
Current Literature, Vol. XLV, 1908.
Independent, December 31, 1908.
Who's Who in America, "Henry Tanner."

ADDITIONAL REFERENCES

Adams, Russell L., *Great Negroes: Past and Present*. Chicago, Afro-Am Publishing Company, 1963, 1964.

Brawley, Benjamin, *The Negro Genius*. New York, Dodd, 1940.

———, *The Negro in Literature and Art in the United States*, pp. 138–148. New York, Duffield and Company, 1929.

Cromwell, John Wesley, *The Negro in American History*, pp. 219–227. Washington, D.C., The American Negro Academy, 1914.

Fauset, Arthur H., *For Freedom*, pp. 162–165. Philadelphia, Franklin Publishing and Supply Company, 1927.

Locke, Alain Leroy, *The Negro in Art*, p. 134. Washington, D.C., Associates in Negro Folk Education, 1940.

Mathews, Marcia M., *Henry Ossawa Tanner, American Artist*. Chicago, University of Chicago Press, 1969.

Rollins, Charlemae Hill, *They Showed the Way*, pp. 121–125. New York, Thomas Y. Crowell Company, 1964.

Tanner, Henry Ossawa, *Illustrated Catalogue of Religious Paintings by the Distinguished American Artist, Mr. Henry O. Tanner*. New York, American Art Association, 1908.

George Washington Carver

AGRICULTURAL WIZARD OF TUSKEGEE
(1860–1943)

IF HE WHO MAKES two blades of grass grow where only one grew before is a benefactor of mankind, how shall we sufficiently appraise George Washington Carver, who made thousands more to do so? Carver revolutionized certain branches of agriculture in the southern United States, thereby benefiting millions of his fellow men in America and abroad. He was practically the founder of the $65,000,000 peanut industry of the Southern states.

Carver was in many ways one of the most remarkable men who even trod the earth. His life is one of the amazing romances of our times. Born in slavery at Diamond Grove, Missouri, he knew neither his father nor his mother. All three had been captured by night riders and taken into Arkansas. His master, Moses Carver, came in search of his property and succeeded in recovering the infant George by giving a broken-winded racehorse valued at $300 for him. Five years later, when freed, as millions of others by the Thirteenth Amendment, he was faced with all the disadvantages of poverty, race, and ignorance. With a born thirst for knowledge but with no school to go to, he borrowed an old spelling book and became his own teacher. Finding this too slow, he decided to leave the place of his birth and the unpleasant but certain care of his former master and ventured out into the world. He was then only ten.

His goal was the town of Neosho, a hundred or more miles away, where there was a free school for the ex-slaves. Begging rides and sleeping in barns and hayracks at night he reached this town and enrolled as a student. But only the teaching was free. There was the matter of food and shelter. He was homeless for weeks until he found work on a farm. As for the schoolhouse, it was a log hut, unheated and cold in winter, but the thought that he was getting what he desired most sustained him against all hardships.

When he had exhausted the possibilities of this school, he wandered on again. At Fort Scott, Kansas, he found a school that he liked and enrolled there. As a means of making a living, he went to work in a kitchen, washing pots and pans. This experience was to serve him well later: he learned cooking, which was to influence greatly the making of his many preparations. At night, after a hard day's work, he would prepare himself for college. But he was to leave Fort Scott in horror. A white mob took a Negro from the jail, beat out his brains, poured oil over the body, and set it on fire. Rackham Holt says, "The stench of burning human flesh rose in a noisome pall. It filled the boy's nostrils and seeped like a black cloud of terror into his brain. He shuddered through the night and before daylight could reveal the scene of man's ferocity he was away out of that place forever."

Wandering on to Minneapolis, Kansas, he entered high school, and supported himself by taking in laundry. On being graduated, he entered Simpson College, Iowa, and later Iowa State College, working his way through by doing odd jobs. In his department, that of agriculture, the other students were white and he was told that he could not eat at the table with them and would have to eat instead with the field hands in the basement. But his cheerfulness, good humor, and kindly manner soon won them over and he advanced rapidly. He won his bachelor of science and master of science; was elected a member of the faculty and appointed head of the bacterial laboratory in systematic botany. His students loved him. His wide knowledge of soils, rocks, birds, flowers, insects, and love of nature made study under him a pleasure. In the greenhouse he experimented with many kinds of plant-crossing and grafting, at all of which he was a master. He became known as "The Plant Doctor."

Alcorn College, Mississippi, hearing of him, wanted him as professor of agriculture, but while it was making up its mind, Booker T. Washington offered him the chair of chemical agriculture at Tuskegee Institute at a salary of $1000 a year and board. He hated to leave his friends at Iowa State College and they hated to see him go, but he felt that his "race" in the South needed him more and he accepted. This was in 1896.

Tuskegee Institue was then in its infantile beginnings and once more he had to start at the bottom. The Institute's farm of 2000 acres was in a most wretched condition. The soil, carelessly cultivated during the days of slavery and neglected for decades, was exhausted and riddled by wash-gulleys through which the topsoil had been carried off. As for the Institute's animals, their condition reflected the soil. Its thirty razorback hogs looked as though they had been "built for speed instead of for the table."

Carver started off in his usual systematic way. He made a careful study of the soil, plants, products, birds, insects, and the botanical conditions in general, then by the use of fertilizers and the rotation of crops produced such changed conditions that it seemed a miracle. From a plot that had once been abandoned he got 500 pounds of cotton and 80 bushels of sweet potatoes.

Looking still deeper into social conditions he saw that the great agricultural curse of the South was the reign of "King Cotton" under which the Southern oligarchs had grown fat. Since cotton could be easiest grown by ignorant slave labor, it was the principal crop and the forests were cut down to plant it. With the trees gone, the rains in time washed away the valuable topsoil, leaving in its place barren gulleys, thus making necessary the cutting down of more and yet more forests. Carver, looking about him, decided to challenge King Cotton on his throne. He brought the peanut on the scene.

His experiment was a success, thanks in some measure to the bollweevil, King Cotton's great enemy. Carver showed that the peanut could be used in undreamed-of ways. He developed more than 250 products from it including milk, flour, breakfast foods, oleomargarine, bisque for ice cream, peanut sauce, ink, vanishing cream, wood stains, and a separation effective in infantile paralysis. From the pecan nut he made more than sixty articles and from the sweet potato, seventy, including rubber, shoe blacking, and flour. From the native wild berries he produced tasty sweetmeats and from the different colored clays he extracted dyes. He solved the rural paint problems of the South by mixing these extracts from clays with discarded motor oil. In 1917 when war with Germany cut off the supply of aniline dyes, he extracted dyes of many colors from the neighboring clays, which, used on leather, cotton, wool, silk, and linen, remained fast against washing and sunlight. In short, he showed, as no one had ever done before, that almost everything about man could be pressed into his service. His exhibits displayed throughout the Deep South and to the Ways and Means Committee of the House of Representatives created amazement. Representative John N. Garner of Texas, later Vice President, called it "a most wonderful exhibition."

Carver did not confine his energies to Tuskegee. His great desire to be of service to humanity, regardless of color, led him into other parts of Alabama and then into other Southern states. He rode in filthy Jim Crow cars, spent nights in wretched cabins, and suffered insults in towns which bore the signs "Nigger, don't let the sun go down on you," "Nigger, read and run," and the like. Once in Montgomery, the capital of Alabama; when he went into the park to see the plants, after making sure there was no Jim Crow sign, he was driven out by the keeper, who said, "Niggers not allowed. Get out." In 1932, after being invited to speak to the Mississippi State College for Women, which was white, he was barred from speaking because of color, not without protest from many of the students.

In his travels he brought the farmers together, and after listening to their problems, taught them how to improve their crops and their livestock and how to keep out of debt. For the cotton growers he produced a cross that is officially known as "Carver's Hybrid," which prevented the destruction of the cotton boll by splashes of sand when it rained. At the annual State Fair of Alabama he was the principal attraction with his multitudinous exhibits.

Agricultural exporters throughout the nation sought his advice, and better-paid posts in less prejudiced environments came to him. Thomas Edison sent Hutcheson, his chief engineer, to Tuskegee to offer him a salary of six figures annually to take charge of one of his laboratories, but with his heart and soul ever in the advancement of his "race," he declined. Still later, he declined another such offer from his very good friend, Henry Ford. Joseph Stalin invited him in 1931 to come to superintend the cotton plantations of southern Russia and to make a tour of the U.S.S.R., but again he declined and sent one of his ablest students. His reason for not leaving Tuskegee, he would say, was "Mr. Washington placed me here nearly twenty-five years ago and told me to let my bucket down. I have always tried to do that and it has never failed to come up full and sparkling. Mr. Washington is not with us any more in person and I would not be true to my cause if I left."

Some of the greatest manufacturers in the country consulted him, among them Henry Ford, who named his school in Georgia after him. Ford called him "the greatest living scientist" and said, "I agree with him with everything he thinks and he thinks the same way I do." He visited Ford several times at Dearborn, Michigan, and when Carver became too ill to travel, Ford came to see him several times at Tuskegee. When the *Manufacturer's Record* offered a prize of $5,000 to the Southern state showing the greatest manufacturing possibilities, it went to Alabama, thanks to Carver. He advised Coffee County, Alabama, to shift from cotton to peanuts. It did and in 1934 held the world's record for peanut production.

Carver was regarded as taciturn by some and he was. This was no wonder as he met with considerable opposition even at Tuskegee and had to deal with so many stupid people; but when it came to his beloved work, he was electrified and electrifying where so many others in the scientific field were cold and dry.

Nowhere was this better exemplified than when he was called in 1921 before the Ways and Means Committee of the House of Representatives in a hearing for a proposed tariff on peanuts. Carver had come to the hearing in the old, baggy clothes he habitually wore, looking far more like a country "rube" than one of the world's greatest botanists. He was sitting in the back and came forward when his name was called. Two of the congressmen seeing the ill-kempt old man began to wisecrack. One said, "I suppose if you have plenty of peanuts and watermelons you're perfectly happy?" Another said, "What do you know about the tariff, old man?" Carver replied, "I don't know much but it's the thing that shuts the other fellow out." That had them laughing. He was then told that he had ten minutes to speak and no more. It would take him more than that to get out his exhibits but he began unpacking his bag of wonders and showing them what he had been able to do with the peanut, all the while making them laugh or making their mouths water with the delicacies he would pop into his mouth from time to time so that the delighted members kept extending his time until they forgot about time altogether. He finally stopped after an hour and forty-five minutes!

Carver possessed rare common sense too. He told his students and others:

Life requires thorough preparation. Veneer isn't worth anything; we must disabuse ourselves of the idea that there is a short cut to achievement; we must understand that education, after all, is nothing more than seeking and understanding relations of one thing to another. First you must get an idea about a given thing; then you must attempt to drift back to the cause; there is a life-study in the attempt to determine the first causes in any given thing. Ye shall know Science and Science shall make you free.

He said again, "We can never amount to much so long as our only possession is our own labor and that the very cheapest kind of labor." Again, "Stop talking so much. You never saw a heavy thinker with his mouth open." Ebony black himself, his advice about color is most appropriate: "If you have nothing but complexion to recommend you, you have no recommendation. If you know anything you recommend yourself." Again, "Creative genius is what makes people respect you. It isn't a color question, it's a question of whether you have what the world wants." He told his students, "When you can do the common things of life in an uncommon way you'll command the attention of the world."

Carver had a disregard, a disdain, for money that was phenomenal in a land where money counts for so much. In 1933, when the banks with his life savings of $40,000 failed, he said quietly,

"I heard about it. All I have is in those three. I guess somebody found a use for the money. I wasn't using it." And as was said, he declined Edison's offer, which could not have been less than $100,000 a year. As for what he earned afterwards, a total of $33,000, he gave it before his death to the establishment of the Carver Creative Research Laboratory at Tuskegee.

By many Carver was regarded as subservient—an "Uncle Tom." This is probably due to the fact that he was mild, soft spoken, innately modest, and lived strictly up to Christian teachings. "He is quite the most modest man I have ever met," said Booker T. Washington. And in addition to this natural timidity, he lived in a part of the United States where he was in perpetual danger of the lyncher's rope and torch. On July 4, 1923, a band of more than 100 Ku Klux Klanners rode onto the campus of Tuskegee Institute. Had the students exercised their right and tried to drive them off, there might have been a clash that would have washed the county in blood. But Carver could be determined when it was a question of his beloved work. He had many clashes with Booker T. Washington and more than once threatened to leave. Always he refused to do anything but what he considered right and best. When Booker T. felt that the sweet potato ought to have a home and arbitrarily decided that Macon County, Alabama, was its place of origin, Carver firmly refused to support him. When the congressional committee already referred to started to hear him and one of the members interrupted him for three minutes, he reminded the committee, which was composed largely of Southerners, of this. And when certain white societies wanted to borrow his exhibits but did not want him along with them, he refused. Finally, he had none of the incentives of an "Uncle Tom," namely, wealth and position, both of which he consistently refused. This man who started at the very bottom and was always subject to the scorn and abuse of the lowest Southern white had the world's recognition and praise showered on him. The Royal Society of London, England, first to honor him, elected him to membership. He was the winner of the Spingarn Medal; was one of the three winners of the Theodore Roosevelt Medal for distinguished service in 1939; was awarded the plaque of the International Federation of Architects, Engineers, Chemists and

Technicians; the annual award of the Catholic Conference of the South; the Humanitarian Award of the Variety Clubs of America for 1940 with a stipend of $1000; was on the Honor Roll on the Wall of Fame, World's Fair, 1939–1940; was named "Man of the Year" in 1942 by the Progressive Farmer's journal; given the Thomas A. Edison's Foundation Award for 1943; received honorary degrees from more than eleven universities, nine of them white; had his life story featured in a Metro-Goldwyn-Mayer motion picture before his death; and more than seventy schools, institutions, and societies were named after him.

For Mahatma Gandhi he devised a special vegetarian menu and received his warm thanks. In England a Member of Parliament, speaking of the great service he had rendered with his cheaply made camouflage paint and his recipes to the English people for using waste products, said, "Parliament, when the war is over, should give thanks to Dr. Carver." Sir Harry Johnson, famous colonial administrator and world traveler, mentioned him in two of his books. Sir Harry said of him in 1910, "No one I ever met in the New World taught me so much about plant distribution in North and South America." Again, Sir Harry wrote in his biography, "He is, as regards complexion and features, an absolute Negro; but in the cut of his clothes, the accent of his speech, the soundness of his science, he might be a professor of botany not at Tuskegee but at Oxford or Cambridge. Any European botanist of distinction, after ten minutes' conversation with the man, instinctively would deal with him *de puissance en puissance.*"

Efficiency Magazine of London said editorially, "If we were asked what living man had the worst start and the best finish, we would say, Dr. Carver. It is a great loss to us that we have no one like him in England."

At his death on January 5, 1943, the leading dailies of the United States eulogized him in columns of editorials and news space. The *New Orleans States* said:

Dr. George Washington Carver was one of the wonders of this age. His career astounds the student of eugenics. This Negro, born a slave, of parents who were slaves, whose parents or immediate forebears came fresh from the jungles, in Africa, became one of the foremost scientists of his time.

Those who believe and teach that a man's heritage determines his spiritual, mental and physical traits will be hard put to explain the source of Dr. Carver's amazing intellect. No other that we have ever heard of was more genuinely a self-made man. The slave boy had a yearning for books and an aptitude to absorb knowledge from them. A miracle in itself when, so far as is known, no person in his lineage had ever learned to read or write. His elemental schooling he won the hard way in his native Missouri. How hard that way would be for a friendless little human chattel needs no guessing. His higher schooling in the Iowa State College, paid for by his sturdy hands driven by a resolute will, won him a bachelor's degree in 1894 and a master's degree in 1896. . . .

Merely to catalogue his achievements would require much space. All peoples, races and creeds were the beneficiaries of the knowledge he gained in painstaking research—knowledge that made the soil more fruitful and created new products out of the earth's harvest. . . . His living has enriched humanity as his genius has enriched the soil.

President Franklin D. Roosevelt said:

The world of science has lost one of its most eminent figures and the race from which he sprang an outstanding member in the passing of Dr. Carver. The versatility of his genius and his achievements in diverse branches of the arts and sciences were truly amazing. All mankind is the beneficiary of his discoveries in the field of agricultural chemistry.

The things which he achieved in the face of early handicaps will for all time afford an inspiration of youth everywhere. I count it a great privilege to have met Dr. Carver and to have talked with him at Tuskegee on the occasion of my visit to the institute which was the scene of his long and distinguished labors.

The United States Congress named January 5 Carver Day.

REFERENCES

There are those who contend that Dr. Carver was not a scientist. In support they point out he was never listed in *American Men of Science*, which carried some eight of his Negro contemporaries. Others deny that he was even a chemurgist, that is, one who discovers ways of using products that would otherwise go to waste. But it seems here to be rather a matter of technical classification than of what was actually accomplished. Carver's forty-three published bulletins testify moreover to what he had done and recommended.

Perhaps what militated most against Carver's inclusion and what lowered him in the eyes of scientific men was his attributing his discoveries wholly to divine aid and entirely belittling his own personal efforts. However, in substance, this was nothing more nor less than what the nonreligious mind calls inspiration, that is, a state of mind which, beginning with a deep, inner desire to do certain things, when aided by long study and a very retentive memory, gives off at times illuminating flashes of how to solve a literary, musical, scientific, or other problem. The caveman undoubtedly was inspired when he accomplished his fine paintings of animals. In short, inspiration is a perfectly natural phenomenon with nothing supernatural about it. Carver was clearly unscientific in a technical sense when he called himself only an instrument of the diety.

But if he were not really a scientist, why did the scientific experts of the Bureau of Plant Industry of the United States Department of Agriculture appoint him a collaborator and often consult him? Were he not a scientist, how was he able to fool for nearly sixty years great universities, industrialists, inventors, and especially Edison, one of the greatest of all scientists? One fact is certain. Carver did open up a vast new world of by-products. He showed that things, as peanut hulls, which had been discarded for centuries, could be pressed into useful service, that almost all waste products could be profitably utilized. A favorite topic of his was one from Genesis, "Every herb that beareth seed, it shall be to you for meat." Another was, "The Earth is full of riches."

Carver, like all the truly great, was a man of vision. This writer recalls that in 1926 when Carver was showing him through his laboratory at Tuskegee, he saw synthetic rubber. Why, he asked himself, should one make synthetic rubber when there was so much of natural rubber? However, it was synthetic rubber that helped greatly in America's march to victory in World War II.

In addition to being a botanist, Carver had other gifts, the single pursuit of any one of which would have made him distinguished. An able painter, he had four of his paintings hung at the World's Columbian Exposition at Chicago in 1893, one of them, "Yucca," winning an honorable mention. Another was bought by the French government and hung in the Luxembourg, while thirty-six of these original paintings are now in the Carver Museum at Tuskegee Institute. He also wrote poetry, knew music, and had a good singing voice. As for his needlework, the Louisville *Courier-Journal* said, "Interesting and significant is the large display of Carver's needlework—fine crocheting, accurate craftsmanship in point and seam—which set beside his paintings bear another unique evidence of his knowledge, sharp and clear beyond the knowledge of most men, that these avenues are unending."

Carver used to guess the date of his birth as 1864, but Rackham Holt discovered from the census that it was 1860.

A facsimile of a letter in his own hand telling how he declined Edison's offer was reproduced in the Baltimore *Afro-American*, January 16, 1943. The sum has been variously fixed at from $100,000 to $175,000. Carver had been pledged not to say how much and he merely said it was an offer in six figures.

Carver had a rich vein of humor that won him many friends and made it possible for him to live and travel in the South. Once when a reporter from a national weekly called him "a toothless old man," he said, "This is nonsense. It's a great pity he didn't ask me, I would have told him. I am not toothless. Why, I had my teeth in my pocket all the time."

Merritt, Raleigh Howard, *From Captivity to Fame*. Boston, Meador Publishers, 1938.

Miller, B. G., *George Washington Carver, God's Ebony Scientist*. Grand Rapids, Mich., Zon Deruam Publishing House, 1943.

Holt, Rackham, *George Washington Carver*. Garden City, N.Y., Doubleday, Doran and Company, Inc., 1943.

Imes, G. L., *I Knew Carver*. 1943.

Graham, S., *Dr. George Washington Carver*. New York, J. Messier, 1944.

ADDITIONAL REFERENCES

Adams, Russell L., *Great Negroes: Past and Present*, pp. 56–57. Chicago, Afro-Am Publishing Company, 1963, 1964.

Brentano, Frances Isabella (Hyams), ed., *Nation Under God*, pp. 296–299. Great Neck, N.Y., Channel Press, 1964.

Carver, George Washington, . . . *The Pickling and Curing of Meat in Hot Weather*. Bulletin 24. Tuskegee Institute, Ala., Tuskegee Institute Press, June, 1925.

Clark, Glenn, *The Man Who Talks with the Flowers*. Saint Paul, Minn., Macalester Rank Publishing Company, 1939.

Elliott, Lawrence, *George Washington Carver: The Man Who Overcame*. Englewood Cliffs, N.J., Prentice-Hall, 1966.

Embree, Edwin R., *13 Against the Odds*, pp. 96–116. New York, The Viking Press, 1944.

Fauset, Arthur Hull, *For Freedom*, pp. 105–120. Philadelphia, Franklin Publishing and Supply Company, 1927.

Hagedorn, Herman, *Americans*, pp. 225–243. New York, The John Day Company, 1946.

Hughes, Langston, *Famous American Negroes*. New York, Dodd, Mead, 1954.

Lotz, Philip Henry, ed., . . . *Rising Above Color*, pp. 1–10. New York, Association Press, 1943.

Manber, David, *Wizard of Tuskegee*. New York, Crowell-Collier Press, 1967.

Ouington, Mary White, *Portraits in Color*. New York, The Viking Press, 1927.

Thomas, Henry, *50 Great Modern Lives*, pp. 319–328. Garden City, N.Y., Hanover, 1956.

Yost, Enda, *Modern Americans in Science and Invention*, pp. 147–162. New York, Frederick A. Stokes Company, 1941.

Jack Johnson

WORLD HEAVYWEIGHT CHAMPION AND DEMOLISHER OF
"THE WHITE HOPE"
(1878–1946)

WHEN STEVE BRODIE dived from the Brooklyn Bridge in 1886, his name reached into a wretched Negro cabin in Galveston, Texas, and so stirred a ragged Negro boy of twelve that he made up his mind to go to New York and meet Brodie in person. This flash of fancy, little as the black boy could have guessed it, was to lead him to the world's heavyweight championship, the most highly prized athletic honor since Onomastos won the belt at the thirteenth Olympic Games in 880 B.C.

The boy, John Arthur Johnson, L'il Arth'uh, as he was known to his companions, tried to stow away on a ship bound for New York, but was caught and put off. Finally, after several weeks he succeeded, but soon after the ship left, he was put off at Key West, where he found work as a sponge fisher in the shark-infested waters, and had a narrow escape from being eaten alive.

Boarding another ship, he was caught soon after it left port and handed over to the tender mercies of the cook, who worked him and beat him. Some kindhearted passengers rescued him and paid for his passage to New York, where he met Brodie, who befriended him for awhile.

He next found work in a stable in Boston, but while exercising a horse, it fell on him and broke his leg. While in the hospital he made friends who paid his passage back to Galveston, where

474

he went to work on the docks. Here he met rowdy youths and crap shooters with whom he had fist fights, in some of which he was beaten. Finally, he whipped the bully of the docks, who was bigger and older than himself, and thus became the "champion."

Leaving the docks, he went to work with a carriage painter, who was an amateur boxer and got him into fights whenever he could until he was the best boxer in the city, a reputation he was to retain in a fight with a grown man in a quarrel over dice. This man was so much bigger, stronger, and tougher than Johnson that his victory became the talk of the neighborhood and made him decide to become a professional boxer.

The next step in his career was his fight with a boxer who traveled with a show. This man, as a part of his performance, offered $25 to anyone who could stay four rounds with him. Johnson accepted the challenge and stayed four rounds but was so badly bruised that he had to stay in bed for two weeks.

Deciding now that he needed a larger field than Galveston, he planned to go to Springfield, Illinois, where he heard that boxers were being sought for a tournament. With no money, he boarded a fright train and arrived in Springfield, hungry and penniless on the very night of the fight. But tired as he was, he met and knocked out four of his opponents, leaving with a pocketful of cash and the plaudits of the crowd.

From Springfield he went to Chicago, where he was matched with an experienced boxer, older than himself, named Klondike. He was beaten but showed such fine form that he received greater applause than Klondike and was given more money than he had ever dreamed of having. But he lost it all the next day at the races and had to bum his way to Pittsburgh, where he had offers of a fight with a white opponent who was very tough. He won and left with his hat "brimming full of dollars."

After this he went to New York, but unable to get a fight there he returned to Galveston where he was matched with the famous Joe Choynski. But the police, stepping in, threw both fighters into jail.

Leaving Galveston after several fights there, he went to Hot Springs, Arkansas, and Memphis, winning little money but gaining much experience. Another fight at Galveston with Choynski was again stopped by the police and he was thrown into jail for three weeks. After several other fights he joined a big boxing show organized by Tom Sharkey and went to the wild mining town of Cripple Creek, Colorado, where he defeated Mexican Pete, a leading aspirant for world heavyweight honors. He was at this time only twenty.

In the next five years he fought fifty-six registered fights in which he lost only two, one to Choynski, and the other to Marvin Hart, later heavyweight champion. He also won the world's light-heavyweight championship from George Gardner at San Francisco, May 31, 1902.

By 1906 he had become the leading contender for the heavyweight title but his color was making it increasingly difficult to get matches with worthwhile opponents. Among those who took refuge behind the color line was James J. Jeffries, then the world champion. Johnson says:

It was not the fights but the fight to get those fights that proved the hardest part of the struggle. It was my color. They told me to get a "rep," but how was I to get a "rep" without meeting fighters in my class? But I made them fight me. I just kept plugging along, camping on their trails, and then taking what chances I could grab, until by and by the top-notchers saw that, sooner or later, they would have to take me on. As soon as I had shown what I could do, the fight public, most of the fans anyway, took sides with me and that helped a lot.

Finally, Jeffries retired and gave the title to Marvin Hart, who in 1905 had a decision over Johnson in a twenty-round bout at San Francisco. Hart, too, ducked Johnson until he lost his title to Tommy Burns, who also avoided Johnson as if he were the plague to the great disgust of true sportsmen the world over, including Edward VII of England, who called Burns a "Yankee Bluffer," and did all he could to bring the two together.

Johnson, eager for the match, made every possible concession to Burns in vain. For the next two years he pursued Burns around the world. "I virtually had to mow my way to Burns," he said. Finally, he caught up with him in Australia, where although Burns was taunted by the natives, he refused to fight.

Johnson, his money gone, was worrying how to get back to America when Lady Luck came his way in an extraordinary manner. He was at the races, and while greeting some friends, his bookie, taking a wave of his hand as a signal to place a bet on a horse on which Johnson had won the day before, did so. Result: Johnson won $15,000.

Back in America, he defeated Bob Fitzsimmons, former heavyweight champion, following it up with victories over the next three most prominent of his class: Kid Cutler, Sailor Burke, and Jim Flynn.

Johnson again began his pursuit of Burns, who under great pressure from fight fans the world over, finally agreed to meet him. But Burns' terms were the most extraordinary ever known in the history of boxing. He insisted, for instance, that his manager, McIntosh, should be referee. Of the $35,000 purse, he demanded $30,000.

The two met at Rushcutter's Bay, Sydney, Australia, December 26, 1906, in a twenty-round bout. When they met in the ring, it immediately was seen that it was not to be a battle of fists alone. Considerable ill-will had developed between the two over the years and it now exploded into a verbal battle. And this amused the spectators vastly. Burns was "the king of sharp-tongued pugilists" while Johnson was a master at good-natured joshing. In this wordy warfare Johnson had far the better of it and soon had most of those who favored Burns because he was white laughing.

From the first round of the fight with fists it became clear, too, that Burns hadn't the ghost of a show. Johnson simply played with him, hitting him at will, while entertaining the crowd with jokes. Pointing to a spot on Burns' anatomy, he would say, "Look, Tommy, I'm going to hit you right there." And he would.

Wishing to punish Burns and also to enjoy the laughter of the crowd, he allowed the fight to drag on until, in the fourteenth round, the police stopped the fight.

The plucky stowaway, roustabout, and longshoreman was champion at last!

What's more, he was really and truly a world champion. Since humanity is composed of many colors and since the earlier champions such as Sullivan, Corbett, and Jeffries had refused to fight other than white men, they had, in all logic, been champion of the whites only.

Johnson's victory was gall to a vast number of Americans to whom it seemed to symbolize the triumph of the so-called black race over the so-called white. Race feeling was much stronger then than now and in the Southern states, where such feeling had been long cultivated, the exploiters of Negro labor thought that as a consequence of the victory the blacks would become restless. Even in the highest social, religious, and educational circles the defeat was taken to heart by many.

On the other hand, the true American sportsmen, even those who had no relish for a black "idol," were resigned, feeling that the better man had won.

Johnson aggravated the former group by his actions. He seemed not to care what they thought. Lovable Peter Jackson would eventually have healed the wounded racial pride by his modesty but Johnson acted as if he loved to show up the whites after what he had experienced at their hands. He was an exhibitionist in public and obeyed Schopenhauer's counsel to great men, namely, not to be modest, to the letter. In the ring, with the bright lights and the gaze of the crowd on him, he loved to display himself and was as showy as a political spellbinder, a Billy Sunday, or a certain type of Southern congressman.

Johnson would emphasize his superiority over his opponents, most of whom were white, by putting their weakness into bold relief with feline stealth and care, and taunting them mercilessly to boot. In a white fighter this conduct would probably have been condoned, and even liked. But in a black man, who was expected to be respectful to white folks even when he was whipping one, it was unforgivable. Johnson had suffered all his life from color prejudice and it was almost too much to expect that one of his fighting nature was going to treat a white man whom he had as his mercy as "a bossman."

To make matters even worse, he became entangled with women—and white women at that. What difference did it make to his critics that these women had sought him out or had been introduced to him by white men? Had the women been black, however, he could have had as many affairs as Tommy Manville without enmeshing himself with stern American morality. In fact, such affairs then would only have made good humorous copy.

Also, if he had been a third-rater, he could have had white women as the lesser Negro fighters had, or as the white fighters had Negro women, and no one would have minded. But Johnson, the world's champion, as a winner of white women was too great an advertisement for so-called miscegenation. Other black men might be encouraged to take white wives and sweethearts, and black mistresses of white men might be encouraged to demand more than just loose relationships.

The result was that Johnson, in winning the championship, dragged with him into the limelight the whole race question with all its centuries of strife. After his second white marriage, anti-miscegenation laws were introduced into the legislature of almost every one of the states still without them, including enlightened Wisconsin and Minnesota.

Johnson was often in the courts, too, for speeding. Good-natured, calm, methodic, orderly in the ring, he compensated for the restraint of discipline there by stepping on the gas outside of it. The incidents in which he became involved were given nationwide publicity, always in an unfriendly way.

Most of Johnson's white friends deserted him, and many of his Negro friends, taking their cue from the former, dropped him too. Negro ministers imitated the lead of white ones in denouncing him from their pulpits. The question of the heavyweight championship became so involved with the color dispute that soon the two were indistinguishable.

The catchword of the day was "A White Hope," meaning a white man who could beat Johnson. A search was conducted by social leaders, ministers of the gospel, and college professors, as seriously as if so-called white civilization, its science, poetry, art, everything, depended upon a bruiser of one color beating a bruiser of another color. A reading of the newspapers of the time will show this is no exaggeration. Naturally the newspapers and prizefight promoters did much to inspire this persecution since they profited by it.

One after another the best fighters of the time were pitted against him, and one after another he slaughtered them, including Jack O'Brien and Al Kaufman.

There remained only one man, Jeffries, and a nationwide cry arose for him to restore "the supremacy of the white race." But Jeffries balked. Softened by years of retirement and indulgence, and probably afraid of Johnson from the first, Jeffries did not relish the prospect of meeting this fighting black demon. But public clamor grew so insistent that Jeffries was forced from behind the saloon bar and the color bar, and went off to the California mountains to train for the match.

Unpopular Johnson was now practically ignored as the current titleholder. Jeffries was dubbed "Undefeated Champion of the World." He had won twenty-two championship fights, and the white chauvinists, incited by the press, looked to him to save civilization from "black" domination as Christendom had looked to the Cid to save it from the black armies of Yusuf, the African, in Spain in 1088.

The two champions met at Reno, Nevada, on July 4, 1910, for a bout of forty-five rounds and a purse of $101,000, the largest then in the history of the ring.

Spectators came from all parts of the world—China, Japan, Australia, India, South Africa, South America. The racial angle of the bout had been played up until it seemed that racial supremacy in the world was at stake.

When the boxers entered the ring the reception given each was vastly different. Jeffries was given a tremendous ovation; Johnson, a roar of catcalls and boos. The crowd had come to see "the nigger get licked," and believing and hoping that Johnson was trembling at the sight of his formidable white opponent, yelled such epithets as "Cold Feet Johnson!" "Yellow!" "Now you'll get it, you big black coward!"

Jeffries was the favorite at 10 to 4, with plenty of money at 2 to 1. One oil man placed $35,000 on him. Johnson, calm, displayed his famous golden smile and bowed politely to the hostile crowd. *The New York Times* said of him, "Surrounded by a crowd among whom he had but few friends, he was as courteous as he was brave."

Both men were in splendid condition. Jeffries was taller than Johnson and outsized him in all save biceps and forearm measurements. He looked flawless. Every muscle was rugged and taut; legs sturdy; chest, vast and hairy—a veritable Hercules. As befitting his role, he wore American flags on his purple trunks.

Johnson weighed 218 pounds and was three years younger. His beautifully tapering body would have thrilled the most esthetic sculptor of ancient Greece or Rome.

Addressing the crowd, Jeffries announced, "This fellow has bothered me for a year and made me work like a dog. I'm going to give him the licking of his life."

To this Johnson jovially replied, "I'm going to tire Mr. Jeffries and then I'll get him."

The outcome was apparent in the very first round. Johnson strutted about good-naturedly, toying with Jeffries like a cat which lets a mouse get near its hole and then stops it just before it can reach it. At times, he deliberately offered his unguarded chin to Jeffries, meanwhile beaming at the audience, and joking with the reporters and telling them what to write over Jeffries' shoulders. In fact, the fight on which the world had hung so breathlessly for months was a farce. When, during one of the clinches, Jeffries hung onto him more desperately than ever, Johnson laughed, "Oh, Mr. Jeff, don't love me so."

In the eighth round Johnson announced, "I've got your measure, Mr. Jeff, and can put you down whenever I want to."

By this time Jeffries was a pitiable sight. What had been his right eye looked like a blue slit in a mess of puffed flesh; his left was swollen to almost twice its size. His nose was cracked, blood trickled down from his mouth, and he spat out gobs of blood. Johnson was almost untouched. The only blood on him came from his opponent.

Johnson permitted the fight to drag on, and Jeffries, with the blind instinct of a fighting animal, kept gamely on while the crowd pleaded with Johnson not to hit him anymore.

The end came in the fifteenth round. It was swift and terrible. Johnson, springing like a panther at Jeffries, rained blows on his battered face and Jeffries fell like a log. A vast roar of rage and disappointment went up from the crowd.

When Jeffries was brought to, Johnson went over to him. "Mr. Jeff," he said kindly, "you fought a square fight. I hope you have no hard feelings."

"No," said Jeffries, "but I ought to have got you." Then remembering how he had been dragged into this fight, he said to the reporters, "Save me from my friends." Later he declared that making the fight a racial issue had unnerved him from the start and that he had entered the ring unfit. Several experts held otherwise, however. They insisted that Johnson would have defeated Jeffries even at his best. William Muldoon, the celebrated trainer, said, "I believe he could have whipped Jeffries at any time during his professional career. The white man had plenty of strength up to the very finish. Therefore, I should say there is no excuse to be made. The best man won."

With the fall of the last of the "White Hopes," Johnson became more unpopular than ever. If white race pride had been indignant before, now it was infuriated. At Ogden, Utah, a gang of white toughs mobbed Johnson's private car. The hatred against Johnson was vented in attacks on Negroes over the nation. Riots broke out in New York, Washington, Chicago, and elsewhere. Scores of blacks and whites were killed, and thousands injured. The repercussions were felt in Africa and in every part of the world where ill-feeling existed between white and colored.

These disorders were followed by a long, bitter, wordy battle over the fight films. Censorship laws were passed by several states barring fight films and Jim Crow laws were tightened in the Southern states.

Johnson returned to Chicago, "bringing home the bacon"—$120,000—as he had promised his aged mother. The Negroes and a few white friends gave him a rousing welcome. For the next few days he was the most talked-of man on the globe.

With no other worlds to conquer, Johnson opened a café of sybaritic splendor in Chicago—Cabaret de Champion. On its walls hung a Rembrandt he had bought in Europe; a painting of himself and his white wife by Clarkson, one of America's leading artists; original oils representing biblical and historical scenes, one of them of Cleopatra. A feature of the establishment was a great silver cuspidor inlaid with gold.

The receipts were enormous. Whites and Negroes met there on friendly terms. But his enemies, who had planned to ruin him, fair or foul, denounced the place as a "miscegenation joint." At about this time, too, Johnson's white wife committed suicide, due, it is said, to Johnson's neglect of her for another white girl. This scandal was played up in its smallest details by the press.

To embarrass him further former white sweethearts of his began to reappear. He bought them off, but one of them, Belle Schreiber, daughter of a Milwaukee policeman, whom he had been taking around with him over the country, was hunted down by his enemies and induced to come and testify against him. Johnson had been paying her way across state lines and this was against the Mann Act, which had been passed to halt the bringing of women across state lines for purposes of prostitution. Johnson's affairs with her had taken place before the passage of the Mann Act, but to satisfy the desire for racial vengeance by the forces of law and order, which included the mob, the law was made retroactive and Johnson was sentenced to a year and a day in prison and $1000 fine. The offense had been purely a technical one. It is very common in the United States for men to pay the fare of their mistresses in streetcars, buses, ferries, etc., crossing state lines. Johnson was no more guilty than any one of the tens of thousands of these since he had not done it for gain like the white slavers.

Later this most unjust sentence was reversed by the appellate court but Johnson, while waiting for the decision, had fled the country. He said that he was so harassed by the shadowing of the federal agents and the way they were bothering his aged mother that bitter at his whole treatment in America he decided to leave it for good. He went to Canada, and from there took ship to Europe, forfeiting his $15,000 bail. Innocent before, he had now really broken the law. He was a fugitive from "justice."

When he arrived at Le Havre, France, and saw policemen lining the pier, he thought they were there to arrest him. But it was only to keep back the crowd, eager to see him.

Everywhere in Europe he was treated like an uncrowned king. As for his love affairs, the Europeans considered them indulgences permissible to a great man. Since when was a prizefighter expected to be a combination of Lord Chesterfield and St. Anthony? What if he went around with white women? Why, that showed his good taste in choosing a woman of their "race." In Paris, Brussels, Berlin, Vienna, Budapest, St. Petersburg, Madrid, Rome, the crowds stormed his automobile for handshakes and autographs. Even in prudish Britain he was mobbed by friendly crowds. Once during a royal procession his appearance diverted attention for awhile from George V.

He boxed a good deal in Europe and when war broke out in 1914 he went to Buenos Aires where he received a rousing welcome and gave several exhibition matches. He next went to Cuba, where a match was arranged for him with Jess Willard in Havana, and where preceding the fight it was hinted to him, he says, "in terms which I could not mistake, that if I permitted Willard to win, which would give him the title, much of the prejudice against me would be wiped out," and that it would be easier "to have the charges against me dropped."

Eager to see his mother again and on the chance that there would be no further prosecution of him, he agreed to lay down to Willard (who was a third-rater), in spite of his great reluctance to give up the title. Of this fight he says, "I could have disposed of him [Willard] long before the final round." The whole sordid story came out later. It is alleged that there was considerable dickering for the sum that Johnson was to receive for lying down and this was not agreed on finally until Johnson was being counted out. Near the count of ten he saw the signal, the wave of a handkerchief, that the sum demanded had been paid and he allowed the count to continue, it was said.

But when he made plans to return to America he found, as he said, that "such offers or hints of leniency as had been tendered to me were without substantial foundation" and that his chances of escaping prison were slight. Sending his wife home, he returned to London and then went to Spain where he gave boxing exhibitions. Then for lack of suitable fighters he took up bullfighting and succeeded so well that he had several offers to be a professional matador. At his first bullfight in Barcelona he killed three bulls.

After visiting other European countries he went back to Mexico where he opened a café at Tijuana, a racing center just across the American border, where business prospered especially from the patronage of Americans who came in numbers to see him. But the desire to see his mother and the fact that he was an exile away from his real friends finally decided him to return. He was given a year at hard labor at Leavenworth, where the warden of the prison turned out to be ex-Governor Dickerson of Nevada, who had made his fight with Jeffries possible. Dickerson, he said, had determined that he should have a fair chance in the fight with Jeffries and now proved to be his staunch friend and adviser. He was made physical director of the prison, had two bouts with the best fighters there, which he won, and was released at the end of eight months for his exemplary behavior.

Retiring from the ring, Johnson opened a boxing academy, but returned in 1926 to knock out Pat Lester, a white aspirant for the heavyweight championship. In October, 1931, at the age of fifty-three, he fought Jim Johnson, many years his junior and won the fight with a broken arm.

Johnson's fame increased with the years. An estimate of him, based on what the leading sports writers have said, credits him with the artistry of Peter Jackson, the scientific skill of Corbett, the rugged, hitting power of John L. Sullivan, the toughness of Fitzsimmons, and, when necessary, the ferocity of Jeffries.

In 1927 *The Ring*, a popular boxing magazine, nominated him "the greatest heavyweight boxer of all time." He defeated all the leading heavyweights and near heavyweights of his time, black and white, such as Langford, McVey, Jeannette, Monroe, Burns, Fitzsimmons, Jeffries, and Ketchel.

Tad, a veteran sportswriter, said:

Johnson's knowledge of boxing, along with his great strength and hitting power, made him almost invincible.

It was his easy-going manner in the ring that fooled many. He smiled and kidded in the clinches and many thought he was careless, but all the time he held his opponent safe, knew every move the other made and was at all times the boss of the job. Johnson was the greatest boxer of all times.

Damon Runyon, another noted sportswriter says:

Johnson could take fellows larger than himself and bounce them around the ring like pins at his own peculiar pleasure, chatting jovially with the crowd as he did so. He had a knack of catching punches as an outfielder catches the ball. He reached out and grabbed most of them before they got started.

Georges Carpentier, French heavyweight champion, said:

He was the shiftiest and in a defense game the cleverest, most cunning fighter I have ever seen. And he found it possible to do his fighting the while he chatted and prattled. He was conceited, but his conceit had at least some humor in it. With a weakness for the employment of words of an uncommon length, and as chief of the Malaprops, he always seemed to be most concerned in making some new and particularly vitriolic taunt.

Perhaps it would not be suspected, but it is nevertheless a fact, that when fighting had to be done he was the soul of good temper and playfulness, and yet there was much viciousness in him. When I sat at the ringside and watched Johnson against Moran I thought he was maddening in the casual way in which he caught a blow from Moran; I do believe that had he cared he could have prevented his opponent putting a glove on him: had it suited his purpose he could easily have ended the fight when he pleased. That it went twenty rounds was because it suited Johnson to make it last so long; he appeared to take a ghoulish pleasure in showing how severe were the limitations of Moran. (*My Fighting Life*)

No better proof of Johnson's skill can be cited than the fact that his face, ears, and skin, unlike those of most pugilists, bore no disfiguring marks.

Johnson's career was adventurous in other ways. During World War I he was nearly killed by a German shell at Boulogne; in Spain he narrowly escaped death when caught on the street between the fire of government troops and the revolutionists; he had several automobile accidents, and died in one.

Unlike most prizefighters, he was fairly well read and acquired considerable culture in his contact with leaders of art, science, politics, and industry. King Edward VII spent an hour chatting with him. Among other European rulers who invited him to their palaces were Franz Joseph II, Alphonso XIII, and Poincaré.

Johnson was fond of classical music and played the bass viol.

In October, 1936, he took the role of Rhadames, the Ethiopian general, in a Chicago Grand Opera Company production of *Aida*.

In no other country in the world are those who start at the bottom and reach the top more generally admired than in America. It is therefore quite impossible to exclude Johnson from America's galaxy of self-made men, for he was certainly one of the most brilliant examples. His rise from poverty to international fame had in it all those elements of romance and glitter that unfailingly delight mankind.

He tells the story in his own words:

Of course, I had the dreams and desires that are common to youth, but never in the wildest moments of my boyhood imagination did I vision myself the champion fighter of the world and the first man of my race ever to attain that distinction. Never did I imagine myself in the picturesque costume of a Spanish matador, or a victor in the bull-fighting arena, surrounded by cheering thousands in the gala attire of the festival in historic Barcelona. How incongruous to think that I, a little Galveston colored boy, should ever become an acquaintance of kings and rulers of the Old World, or that I should number among my friends some of the most notable persons of America and of the world.

REFERENCES

No account of Johnson's career would be complete without mention of his amatory adventures. They were his undoing. Mr. Dan Cupid staged a knockout against him almost every time. Never has Kipling's statement that the female is more deadly than the male been better proved. His first wife, a colored woman, deserted him; a colored sweetheart, whom he loved passionately, left him twice, taking his clothes and money. Later, when she was held in prison on a murder charge, he hired a lawyer for her, who secured her acquittal, after which Johnson set her up in business. While preparing for his fight with Ketchel, an old sweetheart appeared on the scene and he had to let himself down through a window to escape her.

His ill luck with Negro women made him decide, so he says, to foreswear colored women and to "make me determine that my lot henceforth would be cast only with white women."

But this was only dropping the low-powered female exploiter for a higher-powered one. The change brought him worse luck. His first white sweetheart, an Irish girl, turned out to be a heavy drinker and they soon parted; his first white wife, Etta Duryea, a member of an old New York family, killed herself; another Louise Cameron, whom he later married and divorced, brought him ruinous publicity before their marriage; a former sweetheart, Belle Schreiber, as was said, testified against him, ruined his career, and was largely instrumental in sending him to prison.

It is only fair to say that one or two of the white Delilahs were only pawns of the great Philistine "Color Prejudice," the same that kept Peter Jackson from the championship and Harry Wills from Jack Dempsey.

Ed W. Smith, noted white sports critic and referee, said:

"I know Jack to be possessed of one of the kindliest minds of any of the great athletes I ever came into contact with. Money never meant a great deal to this mighty man of brawn and ring brains. As far as the financial end of his dealings was concerned, Jack often displayed a childish simplicity. He wanted to do for others and always went the limit, sometimes, unfortunately for himself, beyond that. But many of Jack's predicaments came about as I happen to know, through a too-trusting faith in the white brother, be that to the everlasting discredit of the Caucasians with whom he dealt so confidently, almost implicitly."

J. B. Lewis, another white sportswriter, says similarly:

"When he successfully fought his way to the championship, instead of his success mitigating those racial prejudices and jealousies, they were intensified. And, more than that, there were many who called themselves good Americans and who considered themselves honorable, charitable and sportsmanlike, stubbornly refused to credit Jack with the same degree of consideration and respect that would have been given a white man even though that white man did far worse things in the world of morals than were ever done by Johnson, or rather which were often charged to him when, in fact, he had not done them.

"The scandals which have been woven about Jack are deplorable, and are responsible for placing him in a false and unjust light before the world. Jack makes no excuse for his conduct. He by no means pretends to be an angel, but one thing is certain—his conduct was by no means ever as bad as that of a great many men whom the world was kind enough to forget and to forgive. To Jack Johnson the world has not been kind, but Jack does not nurse bitterness because of this. He loves life and humanity."

With his fourth wife, Irene Pineau, of French ancestry, he found domestic peace and happiness at last.

This writer knew Johnson and lived a few doors from him in Chicago. He visited him in his home and talked with him but a few weeks before the automobile accident in which he died. Johnson was a very fine man but given to display, which, if a fault, is common to humanity, regardless of color or social status.

In this year, 1946, when America has become more tolerant racially, only those who lived around 1910 will believe possible the outcry against Johnson and the persecution of him. The white press, which has changed greatly since the First World War, was openly anti-Negro then. Most of the Chicago papers simply hounded him. All in all, this lovable and colorful figure, who did so much to make life less drab, was far more sinned against than sinning.

Johnson, Jack, *Jack Johnson In the Ring and Out.* 1927.

ADDITIONAL REFERENCES

Batchelor, Denzil, *Jack Johnson and His Times.* London, Phoenix Sports Books, 1956.

Farr, Finis, *Black Champion: The Life and Times of Jack Johnson.* New York, Scribner's, 1964.

Fleischer, Nathaniel S., *The Heavyweight Championship.* New York, G. P. Putnam's Sons, 1949.

Johnson, Jack, *Jack Johnson Is a Dandy: An Autobiography.* New York, Chelsea House Publishers, 1969.

Lardner, John, *White Hopes and Other Tigers.* Philadelphia, Lippincott, 1951.

Rice, Harold, *Within the Ropes*, pp. 108–115. New York, Stephen-Paul, 1946.

Van DenBergh, Tony, *The Jack Johnson.* London, Hamilton, 1956.

Matthew Alexander Henson

❦

FIRST MORTAL TO STAND ON THE TOP OF THE WORLD
(1866–1955)

MATTHEW HENSON belongs to that hardy race of adventurers which from man's earliest history paved the way for civilization by adding to it knowledge that was hitherto unattainable. While others stayed at home at ease, these courageous ones, often for sheer love of adventure, went across uncharted seas and burning deserts into unknown lands and primeval forests, risking their lives not only against the forces of nature but among the wild and savage peoples.

Henson's feat in reaching the North Pole holds a high place in the saga of these adventurers. He played a leading part in accomplishing what some of the finest and bravest men had been striving for for more than 2000 years.

The first known explorer to reach the Arctic regions was Pytheas, a Greek, in 325 B.C., who perished in the ice wastes. Since then the list of brave men who tried in vain is a long one—Frobisher, Perry, Rose, Rae, Inglefield, Kane, Greely, Nansen, and Amundsen, who later reached it by plane. Among those who lost their lives were gallant Sir John Franklin and his companions.

The greater part of the credit goes, of course, not to Henson, but to Robert E. Peary, one of the most courageous of all explorers. But Henson's role was so important that it seems safe to say that had there been no Henson, Peary's voyage to the Pole might have ended like all the others: in failure.

On Henson fell the duty of attending to details. These were so unusual and intricate that neglect of the least of them might have meant disaster and perhaps death for all.

As it was, the goal was reached only after twenty years of the most grueling labor.

Henson was born of poor parents in Charles County, Maryland. As a lad, he showed the stuff of which he was made by shipping as a cabin boy on a ship bound for China. On the next voyage, however, he sailed as an able seaman, a grade usually reached only after four years' apprenticeship.

At twenty-one he attracted the attention of Peary, then a naval lieutenant, who engaged him as his personal attendant. It was in this capacity that he went with Peary on an expedition to Nicaragua.

In 1891, when Peary started on his polar explorations, Henson went with him and had his first taste of the ice. It was not, however, until eighteen years later that the Pole was to be reached. Other expeditions tried to reach it during those years and also failed.

Polar exploration is accompanied by dangers and hardships almost impossible of comprehension by ordinary folks. Think of the discomfort of an unheated apartment in the winter and then try to imagine what it must be in the Arctic at 65 degrees below zero with no roof over one's head. The explorer must battle fields of ice and snow for months, run into raging blizzards, sleep in ice huts with ice for a flooring. As for food, there are no juicy steaks and sweetmeats but only pressed beef, hard as plug tobacco, stale bicuits, tough dog meat, or the sickening fat of seals.

Clothing is a great problem, for none has ever been devised that can keep one warm in the Arctic. The danger of frozen extremities is ever present. Freezing of the nose and the whole of the face is an ordinary experience, as not all of the face can be covered. If one tries to wrap up his face, his breath congeals on the covering and freezes to his face before he knows it; and when he tries to get it loose, he pulls off a patch of skin.

If one puts a mitten to his face during a blizzard he will find it covered with blood because the wind-driven granules of ice have been forced into the skin. The arctic wind is worse than any unskilled barber. Henson lost an eye from the flying ice.

If one stubs his toes against a block of ice he may not notice it then. But later when he pulls off his boot his toes may remain inside it, for when toes are frozen they become as brittle as icicles. Peary lost all of his toes but one in this way. As far as Arctic exploration is concerned, the comforts of civilization might as well not exist.

The explorer must rely completely on himself. All around him is the darkness of the polar day and night, which are for most of the year the same. The very silence is deadening to the nerves. It is interrupted only by the roar of a mountain of ice, splitting asunder. If the wind is high, masses of this ice will come hurtling through the air, with almost the force of a shell from a cannon. Nothing, nothing, except a white waste of utter desolation.

Every step is fraught with danger. Ice cracks as readily in extreme cold as when it is melting, and woe to the man or boat caught in a fissure because sometimes the fissure closes again, suddenly crushing everything caught between. If the ice is thin, one may suddenly find himself swept away forever from his companions on a floe with churning, icy waters all around him.

In the Arctic one is absolutely dependent on his dogs. They carry the supplies without which he would be lost. But they too are vulnerable. They are subject to a strange epidemic likely to kill the whole team. Sometimes, too, lack of food compels their masters to eat them. When this happens, death is not far away.

At home one longs for the end of winter. But in the Arctic it is almost always winter, with the job of building one's ice hut after the day's journey when nerves are exhausted. Yield to that desire to doze only for an instant and you may never wake again. For weeks, perhaps months at a time, you cannot take off your clothes. Bathing is impossible and the vermin breeding next to your skin make life a purgatory.

Under such conditions you plod on with accumulating weariness, and in constant peril, anxiety, and uncertainty. For what is your goal? A question mark.

Even today, when polar expeditions are undertaken by plane,

it is difficult. It still calls for stamina, courage, and determination. All in all, polar exploration is as dangerous as the battlefield and vastly more uncomfortable.

On that first voyage to the polar regions with Peary, Henson experienced every hardship and danger that have fallen to the lot of the Arctic explorer—except death. But in 1893 he was back with Peary, and again in 1895, 1897, 1899, and on every other of his expeditions until the Pole was finally reached.

Relating his experiences, Henson says:

The memory of the winter and summer of 1894 and 1895 will never leave me, the recollections of the long race with death across the 450 miles of the ice-cap of North Greenland in 1895 with Commander Peary and Hugh Lee, are still the most vivid."

On July 6, 1908, after eighteen months of preparation, Peary left on the voyage to the Pole that was to end in its discovery. The expedition, which sailed on the *Roosevelt*, was composed of specially picked men. They were all athletes. In the matter of physique, the white race had nothing finer to offer.

Among them were George Borup, athletic champion; Captain Bartlett, a polar veteran himself; and the scientists, Professors MacMillan and Marvin. Henson, the only Negro, was small in stature compared to the others, but he was as tough as rubber. He was forty-two at the time.

The greater part of the preparations was left to Henson, who was second in command. For instance, there was the making of the sledges, a matter of great importance. Henson designed a sledge which was superior to that of the Eskimos, who had been making them for centuries. The sledge made by Henson, which reached the North Pole, is now in the American Museum of Natural History in New York. As for the ship on which the expedition was to sail, Henson had every detail so well executed that Peary expressed perfect satisfaction with it.

The Arctic had no sooner been reached than some of the members of the expedition began to break down under the strain. The first to be sent back was Professor McMillan, a good-natured giant, whom his fellows called "the life of the funeral." Borup, the athlete, three Eskimos, and sixteen dogs followed him. Then went Dr. Goodsell, who was no longer fit to travel. Professor Marvin died.

The remainder continued, chopping their way through the ice, climbing over mountains, advancing, and retreating to advance. They were battling against the terrific forces of nature that had thus far held off every human invader. Each day brought physical punishment such as even a prizefighter is not called on to endure.

Finally, they reached a point 88 degrees north, the farthest then reached by man. From here it was 2 degrees to the pole—132 miles. Ahead lay the most difficult path to be traversed.

The temperature is 50 below zero. It is necessary to limit the number of men so that there will be fewer mouths to feed and more reserves in case of emergency. Six are to go on—Peary, Henson, and four of the fittest Eskimos. Peary has selected Henson not because of sentiment but because he is best qualified. "Primarily for his adaptability and fitness for the work," said Peary, "Secondly, because of his loyalty. . . . Henson can handle a sledge better than any man living except some of the best of the Eskimos."

A farewell party is given at which the principal dish is a stew made of a weak dog. Time has come to start. There are five sledges, eight dogs to each. Farewells are said by comrades who may never meet again.

"At last," says Henson, "the Captain [Bartlett] has gone, Commander Peary and I were alone (save for the four Eskimos), the same as we had been so often in the past years, and as we looked at each other, we realized our position and we knew without speaking that the time had come for us to demonstrate that we were the men who, it had been ordained, should unlock the door which held the mystery of the arctic. Without an instant's hesitation the order to push on was given."

The party traveled smoothly, thanks to the experience of twenty-three years of toil. Then Henson came very near to losing his life.

"It was during the march of the 3rd of April," he tells, "that I endured an instant of hideous horror." He was crossing a lane of moving ice when a block of ice he was using as a support slipped from under his feet and before he knew it he had fallen into the water.

Encumbered by his heavy clothing, he was sinking, his gloved hands unable to catch a hold on the ice, when one of Eskimos pulled him out.

"He had saved my life," says Henson, "but I did not tell him so, for such occurrences are taken as part of the day's work, and the sledge he had safeguarded was of much more importance for it held, as part of its load, the commander's sextant, the mercury, and the coils of pianowire that were the essential portion of the scientific part of the expedition." The same day Peary had a similar experience.

At last, on April 6, 1909, the party made camp. All felt sure from the distance they had covered that they had reached the Pole. Peary, completely worn out, went to sleep. Henson walked around outside to look things over. Later, when measurements were taken, it was discovered that Henson, during his walk, had been the first mortal to stand on the top of the world.

The simple truth is that when Peary actually had his fingers on the prize, he was too exhausted to take those last few steps to be first on the spot he had given so much to reach. Henson had pulled Peary much of that 132 miles. As was said, Peary had lost nine of his toes at various times.

"As I stood at the top of the world," says Henson, "and thought of the hundreds of men who had lost their lives in the effort to reach it, I felt profoundly grateful that I, as the personal attendant of the commander, had the honor of representing my race in the historic achievement."

Henson's story is supported by Commander MacMillan. Lowell Thomas, noted radio commentator, says:

Commander MacMillan has related elsewhere and told in public, that when Peary arrived at the Pole, he was too weak even to raise the American flag that he had brought with him especially for that purpose. According to MacMillan it was Henson who placed the Stars and Stripes at the top of the world while the leader sat exhausted on a sledge and feebly waved his hand.

The goal of the ages had been reached! Nothing was left now but to tell a waiting world. At least, so thought the heroes. But how poorly they were received is a well-known story. Frederick Cook, long a polar explorer himself, had returned a few weeks before, declaring that he had reached the Pole. As a result he had been awarded the honors.

Peary spent the next two years proving his claim, during which he had to answer many stupid questions from Congressmen, several of whom wanted to know why he had taken a Negro along when there were plenty of white men to pick from. Cook was discredited. The University of Copenhagen openly declared him a fraud and two of his fellow conspirators confessed their part in the deception. It was also discovered that Cook lied when he claimed he had ascended to the top of Mt. McKinley. (He was later sentenced to fourteen years in Atlanta penitentiary on an oil-stock swindle.)

Perry was finally given the Congressional Medal of Honor and promoted to the rank of admiral, which was, of course, a none too generous reward for one who had brought so much prestige to his country. England, which had been trying to reach the pole for 200 years, or before America had become a nation, was more generous. To encourage her polar explorers she had given them titles and sums of money ranging from $50,000 to $100,000.

And what of Henson, Peary's second in command? The government gave him nothing.

He had returned so weakened that he was forced to take a long rest. He had dropped in weight from 155 to 112 pounds. He was so haggard that his wife did not know him. Later he went on a lecture tour on which he received sometimes as much as $300 a week. A jazz dancer might have received a thousand.

When interest in the exploit faded—and it did not last for long —Henson was forced to take a porter's job at $16 a week. Later, through the efforts of friends in Congress, he was given a job in the U.S. Customs Service at $20 a week, which was later raised to $40.

He wrote a book, *A Negro Explorer at the North Pole*, which remained largely unsold. The white people were interested chiefly in Peary, while the Negroes, after a brief spasm of pride, promptly forgot about Henson. On one occasion some of his colored friends gave him a dinner and a gold watch.

Years later a group of white businessmen in the Bronx, New

York City, who heard of him for the first time, gave him a silver loving cup. This is the extent of the recognition he received.

In 1936 a bill to give him the Congressional Medal of Honor was introduced but nothing came of it. The same year, having reached seventy, he retired from the customs service on a small pension. In 1946, at the age of eighty, he was still strong and appeared at least fifteen years younger, contemplating, as Lowell Thomas said, "the luxury and comfort of modern Polar exploration."

REFERENCES

The common impression in America is that there is little or no use in polar exploration. People think of the polar regions as a blanket of ice and consider those who go up there on expeditions as fit subjects for a lunatic asylum.

If this is so, why have all the leading nations of the world been interested in reaching the North Pole? Were all the men who lost their lives trying to reach it fools?

Strange as it may seem, effort spent in reaching the arctic and antarctic regions may be worth as much as that spent in reaching elsewhere. The economic value of these regions is becoming more and more apparent. The Arctic Circle is rich in gold, oil, coal, fur, and fish. Its strategic importance in possible future wars is even greater. It is destined to be a great route for air traffic. In 1937 Russia established a meteorlogical station there for that purpose. Finally, in centuries to come the polar regions may be important centers of human population. Florida and New York were at one time in the frigid zone.

Some day Peary and Henson will be honored as we honor Columbus today. There is a foresight in nature that leads certain men to prepare the way for events that are to be—events the import of which they themselves but faintly glimpse. The world often calls such men fools, but life, wiser than all, knows what it is doing.

Hampton's Magazine, January, 1910.
Henson, M., *A Negro at the North Pole*. New York, 1912.
Liberty Magazine, July 17, 1926.
Thomas, Lowell, *This Week*, April 2, 1939.

ADDITIONAL REFERENCES

Adams, Russell L., *Great Negroes: Past and Present*, p. 55. Chicago, Afro-Am Publishing Company, 1963, 1964.

Brawley, Benjamin G., *Negro Builders and Heroes*, pp. 173–176. Chapel Hill, The University of North Carolina Press, 1937.

Fauset, Arthur Huff, *For Freedom*, pp. 121–128. Philadelphia, Franklin Publishing Company, 1927.

Henson, Matthew Alexander, *A Black Explorer at the North Pole*. New York, Walker, 1969.

Hughes, Langston, *Famous Negro Heroes of America*. New York, Dodd, Mead, 1958.

Mill, Floyd, *Ahdoolo! The Biography of Matthew A. Henson*. New York, Dutton, 1963.

Robinson, Bradley, *Dark Companion*. New York, R. M. McBride and Company, 1947.

Rollins, Charlemae Hill, *They Showed the Way*, pp. 83–87. New York, Thomas Y. Crowell Company, 1964.

Roland Hayes

ROLAND HAYES was the first Afro-American to rank with the great concert artists of his time. Before him there were other colored singers who won meritorious acclaim in Europe and America, but there was none who reached classic heights.

Few stories in fact or fiction rival that of the rise of Hayes. Born in an obscure village in Georgia where education and enlightenment were at their lowest civilized ebb, he began at the bottom of the ladder even there. His widowed mother, an ex-slave, eked out a meager living on a wretched farm for herself and her three children, suffering hunger and privation. Hayes said, "There were times when we desperately needed meat and flour and had no money in the house to pay for them." He started working at the age of nine. He and the other children took turns at going to the school, such as it was; the rest of the time was spent working on the farm and doing odd jobs for white people.

But young Hayes was cheerfulness itself. He sang as he worked, the natural beauty and sweetness of his tenor voice being such that even those who despised him because of the color of his skin were drawn to him. He began to take lessons. Later his greatest early inspiration was to come to him while scrubbing the floor of a white man's home. He heard a phonograph record of an operatic

Roland Hayes

selection. Ecstatic, he stopped to listen and a whole new
beauty opened itself to him. From the instrument was co
kind of beauty he felt within and meant to express.

When he was fourteen his mother, an ambitious woma
her family to Chattanooga, Tennessee, where there were
opportunities for schooling. They walked the long distance
and he found work in an iron foundry, he and his brother ta
turns at working and going to school. In this foundry he nea
lost his life. He was pulled into one of the machines and had
spend weeks in a plaster cast.

In his spare moments he studied singing, paying fifty cents a
lesson out of his meager earnings. Then one day a friend told
him of Fisk University, a Negro institution, and he went there
and was admitted after some difficulties. To earn his way, he
fired a furnace and later worked as a butler in the home of one
of his professors.

Later he went to Louisville, Kentucky, where he worked as a
waiter in one of the leading clubs. Years after, he sang as a guest
of honor at the same club. While working there he was asked by
Fisk University to sing with a choir at a missionary meeting. His
performance on that occasion was distinctive, and so warmly
praised that he decided to give himself wholly up to his art no
matter how great the sacrifice.

This was in 1911. His resolution was to demand all his courage, for the next ten years was to be a period of the most trying
self-denial and privation.

Having mastered the usual routine of studies, Hayes felt that
there was still something to be acquired that no one could teach
him, namely, a technique of his own with which he might express the finest and most beautiful feelings that stirred in his soul.

He toured the country with the Fisk Jubilee Singers, attracting
unusual attention. But he longed to be an individual artist.

Feeling himself competent to sing in the leading concert halls,
he tried hard to get engagements, but in these higher fields he
was refused. He lacked the glamor that came with publicity.
Moreover, he was black and no Negro had ever reached the
height to which he aspired. One white impresario told him, "You
know that I'm your friend. I want to advise you as sensibly as I

world of
501
ning the

, took
better
here
ing
rly
o

e got about as far as you can go in
public will never cotton to you."

ong his own people but his audiences
even one or two leaders in Negro musical
him as an upstart, and tried to handicap
ys. Sincere Negroes and unprejudiced whites,
d to predict a brilliant future for him. In 1915
ennsylvania Chatauqua Circuit singing Beethoven,
oinstein, and Polani. In the meantime, he studied
German.

his goals was to sing in Symphony Hall, Boston, but no
manager would even hear of it. He decided to be his
impresario, and with $400 of his savings, he rented the
for one night. When he asked the wife of the then Governor
Massachusetts to be one of his sponsors, she refused, saying
that she would not let her name be used in an affair that was
bound to be a failure. So hostile was the idea of having a Negro
sing in the sacred precincts of that hall that his paid advertise-
ments in the Boston dailies brought him "a storm of protest." The
concert, however, was a success. White and Negro friends filled
the hall to overflowing and applauded his classical and romantic
repertoire and his Negro spirituals.

There were other hard days to come but he had broken the ice.
He was now the leading Negro singer and with an extensive
"white" hearing. However, there was yet another handicap. He
was American, and as American singer, no matter how gifted
and accomplished, was considered inferior until he had Europe's
approval. Accordingly, with his entire savings of $1100, he left
for England, arriving there on April 23, 1920.

In London he was refused accommodation in several lodging
houses because of color. He found many who appreciated his
voice but his funds sank lower and lower. The concerts he gave
in order to make himself known ate deeper into them. "I practically lost my mind," he said. "I was hungry, my spirits were low,
the weather was stormy and cold, and I came down with pneumonia." However, his genius was making itself felt in the highest
musical circles in London. Then one day, a year after his arrival,
when life seemed darkest, came a turn that was to lift him to the

skies: He was summoned to give a command recital at Buckingham Palace—the highest honor that could come to an artist in
England.

He left his home in the royal carriage that had been sent for
him with his last shilling in his pocket; he returned famous with
his money worries over for life.

George V and Queen Mary were so delighted with his singing
of the spirituals and other American Negro songs, as well as some
European ones, that they asked for several encores and later detained him in conversation for more than an hour. The London
papers lauded him. The news electrified his friends in America
and had repercussions everywhere in musical circles. Those of his
own "race" who had hardly noticed him before became intensely
proud of him. Offers poured in on him by cable from America,
one of them from a leading concert manager to whom he had
once personally applied for an engagement, and who had turned
him down on account of his color.

Returning to America, he made his first appearance at Town
Hall in New York. Hundreds were turned away. At that concert
Hayes captivated his audience not only by the beauty of his voice
and the infinite ease of his singing, but also by his modest simplicity and the charm of his presence.

When, shortly afterwards, he gave a return engagement at
Carnegie Hall, one of the largest concert halls in America, the
house was completely sold out—stage seats, standing room, and
all—despite the rain and wind of a wretched winter day. Again
hundreds were turned away.

Later he sang for other royalty as the Queen-Mother of Spain
and the Queen of Greece. Prince Chigi-Saracini invited him to
sing in his salon to some of the most distinguished music lovers
of Europe in 1928. The praise given him on that occasion was
superlative.

He sang also in the most distinguished musical circles in
Europe and America and with the finest orchestras, among them
the Royal Philharmonic of Madrid; the Tivoli Symphony of
Copenhagen; the Concerts Colonne of Paris; Orchestra Mengel-
berg of Amsterdam, Vienna, and Berlin; with Russian orchestras
in Moscow; the Philadelphia, New York, and Detroit symphony

orchestras, with which he toured the United States, winning everywhere wide recognition for his interpretation of the classics and the Negro spirituals. In 1924 he was awarded the Spingarn Medal for excellence.

Hayes' career is an inspiration for all artists, regardless of so-called race or color. He deliberately chose the hardest path. He made his name as the leading Negro singer, but that was not enough for him. He decided to be known as a universal artist and to rise superior to race and nationality, since true art knows nothing of these limitations. He learned the classics of the white nations in their respective languages, absorbed the spirit in which the masters had written them, and then passing them through the alembic of his own fine, cultured personality, sang them with fresh and revealing interpretations. Once after he had sung for a German prince in Munich, the latter marveled that Hayes had been able to interpret a certain love song not only in the German spirit but in that of the prince's own class. The secret of his being able thus to appeal to all peoples was his worship of universal beauty and his deep human sympathy. Like Dunbar, he felt with all the world and because of this he had, like an organist, but to press certain keys and open certain stops to have his audience, no matter what its race or class, with him. In his own words, "I follow the guide that is within me—that part of God that is within me. Each I believe can achieve in his own calling, whatever it be, if he will follow that light."

He also said, "I am always reminding myself that it is not I, the individual, this is important but my work. When I appear on the stage I endeavor to maintain this ideal so that the audience will see my work rather than myself."

Had Hayes decided to confine his art to Negro spirituals, his climb to the heights would have been far easier, as then he would have stood without a peer.

At recitals he was asked to sing the spirituals oftener than his other songs. This is no doubt due to the beauty of the spirituals themselves and their deeper appeal as compared with love songs, because Hayes was without a rival in rendering the love songs of France, England, Germany, Italy, Russia, and other lands. His modest personality imparted to them a tenderness and a sweetness that aroused ecstasy in his hearers. Had he lived in the days of Louis XVI, he undoubtedly would have been idolized at Versailles by the court and its beautiful women, as was another famous Negro, Chevalier de St. Georges.

In physical appearance he seemed to be of unmixed African descent; he was somewhat under the average size and well proportioned. His tenor voice did not have the range of a Jan Peerce, and seemed more adapted for the salon than the concert hall; nevertheless, he compensated with lyric beauty for what he lacked in volume.

He was as delightful to meet off stage as on, being most considerate and cultured, with ideals as vigorous, as optimistic, and as unembittered by adversity as in his earliest days in the humble Georgia village.

He was profoundly interested in the advancement of his people. This is one reason he chose the harder path. He wished to show in his own way that Negroes are full-fledged human beings, and as such are capable of doing other than so-called purely Negro things. It is this desire to present his people in a better light that helped to spur him on. "My people," he once said, "come first to me, and I try to make every move count."

His fame and the magic of his voice remained undimmed for many years. He was one of the three or four singers of his time who would give three concerts a year at Carnegie Hall and still have a crowded house. The London *Times* said of one of his recitals, "His 'Pur Dicenti' shows both charm of voice and finish of style and nothing could have been better as an example of pure mezza-voice than 'Der Juengling an der Quelle'. . . . In the spirituals he brings the authentic note of sincerity and inspiration." The *Boston Globe* said, "Roland Hayes is not only an artiste—he is an institution and a name, the magic of which has spread his fame across oceans and continents."

The New York Times said of his recital at Carnegie Hall on November 2, 1946:

When the critic heard the Spiritual "Heaven" sung by Mr. Hayes with virtually all the beauty he gave it twenty years ago, the critic realized that the result was due to the perfection of rhythmic accent, the light, effective attack, the molding of each phrase, the amazing diction, the management of dynamic and color shading, all used in this case with a mezza voce which still has the beauty of texture of the full voice that once was as fine as they are now. These qualities were present throughout the expertly put together program, which did not end until the singer walked out still singing the last phrases of the last encore.

For instance, Julien Tiersot's "Le Tambourin" had a delicacy and a gnomish effect that perhaps would be impossible of achievement for anybody else in the world.

REFERENCES

Hayes' great dream is to build an institution of learning for Negroes with money earned by himself and thus make it easier for those who are in a similar position to his as a boy. For this purpose, he bought 600 acres of land at Curryville, Georgia, his birthplace, land on which his beloved mother had worked as a slave. Construction and other work on this farm were hindered by the war but it has been resumed, both colored and white laborers being employed.

Helm, McKinley, *Angel Mo' and Her Son: Roland Hayes*. Boston, Little Brown & Co., 1942.

ADDITIONAL REFERENCES

Adams, Russell L., *Great Negroes: Past and Present*, p. 150. Chicago, Afro-Am Publishing Company, 1963, 1964.

Bartlett, Robert Merrill, *They Dared to Live*, pp. 80–84. New York, Association Press, 1937.

Brawley, Benjamin G., *The Negro in Literature and Art in the United States*, pp. 177–182. New York, Dodd, Mead and Company, 1929.

Bullock, Ralph W., *In Spite of Handicaps*. New York, Association Press, 1927.

Fauset, Arthur Huff, *For Freedom*, pp. 135–150. Philadelphia, Franklin Publishing Company, 1927.

Harris, Charles Jacob, *Reminiscences of My Days with Roland Hayes*. Orangeburg, S.C., American Negro Authors, 1944.

Hayes, Roland, *My Songs: Aframerican Religious, Folk Songs*. Boston, Little, Brown, 1948.

Johnson, Charles Spurgeon, . . . *A Preface to Racial Understanding*, pp. 134–139. New York, Friendship Press, 1936.

Lotz, Philip Henry, ed., *Rising Above Color*, pp. 82–89. New York, Association Press; Fleming H. Revell Company, 1943.

Nordholt, T. W. Schulte, *The People That Walk in Darkness*, pp. 239–240, translated from *Het Volk Dat In Duisteruis Wandelt* (1956) © Van Loghum Slaterus. First published in English, London, Burke Publishing Company, Ltd., 1960.

"Roland Hayes: A Lifetime on the Concert Stage." *Ebony*, pp. 42–46 (September, 1946).

Carter G. Woodson

PIONEER IN NEGRO HISTORY AND EDUCATION
(1875–1950)

CARTER G. WOODSON, great pioneer in the popularizing of Negro history and the most voluminous writer and editor on that subject, won the outstanding position he now holds the hard way. Born in the remote town of New Canton, Virginia, his early schooling was so elementary and of such poor quality that he was justified in saying later that he "never went to school."

At seventeen he went to work in a coal mine at Huntington, West Virginia, but so great was his love of knowledge that despite the hard work he studied the Latin and English classics at night and otherwise prepared himself to enter the high school at Huntington. While working in the mines, a mass of loose slate fell on him, injuring his head.

After three years of self-tuition, he passed the high school examination with such high honors that he was given an advanced standing which permitted him to get his diploma only eighteen months after entrance. Years later he was to be principal of this school.

After his graduation from high school, his path led upwards. He got his A.B. and his master's degree at the University of Chicago. Harvard gave him his Ph.D., and at the Sorbonne, Paris, he was one of the most brilliant students in French language and literature of that year. In 1903 he went to the Philippines as a teacher and five months later was made a supervisor of education. Later he was principal of the Armstrong High School of Washington, D.C., then dean of the School of Liberal Arts of Howard University, and still later dean of the West Virginia Collegiate Institute.

Teaching was, however, not his chief love. He had been chafing for years at the misconceptions and falsities about Negroes, particularly in American textbooks, and now decided to throw the whole weight of his knowledge against them. It was not a popular move, not only with the editors of textbooks and the white public, but with the Negroes, who were apathetic. As he himself, writing in 1932, said:

When I arrived in Washington, D.C. in 1909 and began my researches, the people there laughed at me and especially at my "hayseed" clothes. At that time I did not have enough money to pay for a haircut. . . . When I, in my poverty had the "audacity" to write a book on the Negro the "scholarly" people of Washington laughed at it. When I started the Journal of Negro History in January 1916, a representative of this same group . . . made fun of me in public soon thereafter, saying, "I have known you as an author, and now I greet you as an editor; but you must remember that some magazines do not reach the second issue."

The *Journal of Negro History*, however, became firmly established as one of the most scholarly and authoritative journals in America, with many of its articles being widely quoted. Its contributors, who are both colored and white, are some of America's foremost scholars, while the magazine itself is to be found in some of the leading educational centers of Europe, Asia, Africa, Latin America, and the United States.

Woodson's outspokenness at the manner in which Negroes were being taught to despise themselves by their teachers brought him several powerful enemies among leading Negro educators; but undaunted, he attacked them fearlessly until they were forced to give their students a more self-respecting view of themselves. He once said at the annual meeting of the Georgia Teachers' and Educational Association at Atlanta:

I lament the teachers' ignorance of their rich racial heritage. Few of our college presidents could make more than ten percent on an examination in Negro history.

We spend millions yearly to straighten our hair and bleach our skins and some of us go so far as to have our noses lifted in the hope of looking like the white man. Monkeys too have straight hair and thin lips.

I advocate a more realistic and practical approach in education. It took me over thirty years to get over my Harvard education.

Dr. Woodson's most important work was the founding of the Association for the Study of Negro Life and History. With its center in Washington, the association has been a great distributor of books on the Negro, principally histories, some written by Woodson and some by others, which are used as textbooks in all grades of schools, from elementary to the university. So great has become the demand for these books that it now taxes the facilities of the publishing firm.

He was also the principal founder of Negro History Week which is by far the chief agency in popularizing Negro history and having it taught in schools over the nation. This week is in February of each year, and the governors of several states now announce it in a proclamation, calling on citizens to observe it. At the annual meeting held at this period recognized scholars of both "races" read papers, and prizes are given for the best works on Negro history during the year, while schools and colleges over the nation listen to lectures on Negro history and achievement. The effect of this in bettering the social and economic condition of the Negro and its beneficial effect on the ethics of white people over the past half-century are beyond any power to estimate.

Dr. Woodson wrote, compiled, and edited a goodly number of books, not to mention innumerable reviews and articles published in the *Journal of Negro History* and elsewhere. Among his published volumes are *A Century of Negro Education; History of the Negro Church; The Rural Negro; Education of the Negro Prior to 1861; Mis-Education of the Negro; African Backgrounds Outlined;* and *The Negro in Our History*. This last, published in 1922, is his most important work. Now in its eighteenth edition, it is in standard use in centers of education over the nation. In addition, Dr. Woodson collected a vast quantity of original documents on the Negro, which might otherwise have been lost, and deposited them in the Library of Congress.

Dr. Woodson was, all in all, tremendously effective in helping to improve the self-respect of Negroes, young and old, and giving them a brighter, more optimistic outlook. At the same time he was a force in helping white people view blacks with more appreciative eyes. While his contribution, due to its very nature, has not received the wide publicity of that of certain other noted Negroes, it is nonetheless deep and enduring.

ADDITIONAL REFERENCES

Adams, Russell L., *Great Negroes: Past and Present*, p. 114. Chicago, Afro-Am Publishing Company, 1963, 1964.

Franklin, John Hope, "The Place of Carter G. Woodson in American Historiography." *The Negro History Bulletin*, pp. 174–176 (May, 1950). Association for the Study of Negro Life and History, Washington, D.C.

Rollins, Charlemae Hill, *They Showed the Way*, pp. 153–156. New York, Thomas Y. Crowell Company, 1964.

Woodson, Carter Godwin, *The African Background Outlined; or, Handbook for the Study of the Negro*. Washington, D.C., Association for the Study of Negro Life and History, 1936.

———, and Wesley, Charles H., *The Negro in our History*. Washington, D.C., The Associated Publishers, 1962.

———, *The Mis-Education of the Negro*. Washington, D.C., The Associated Publishers, 1933.

———, *African Heroes and Heroines*. Washington, D.C., The Associated Publishers, 1944.

Paul Robeson

Paul Robeson

INTELLECTUAL, MUSICAL, AND HISTRIONIC PRODIGY
(1898–1976)

Paul Bustill Robeson was so remarkably gifted, physically and mentally, that development of any one of his talents would have been sufficient to bring him fame.

He was an athlete, orator, and linguist, as well as one of the world's foremost singers and actors. In America, England, Germany, Austria, France, and Russia his audiences filled the largest concert halls to overflowing.

Born at Princeton, New Jersey, the youngest son of a minister who had been a slave, Robeson showed unusual intellectual brilliance from his earliest years. At Rutgers College, a predominantly white institution, he was an honor man throughout his four years of study, his grades never averaging less than 95. Every year he received the highest prizes for oratory; and in his junior year the Phi Beta Kappa key, an exceptional distinction for a student.

On the athletic field he was equally capable. In the four major sports—football, baseball, track, and basketball—he excelled, being a four-letter man and winner of the coveted "R." He was also a member of the debating team and the glee club, and was the most sought-after singer in the college. These accomplishments, together with his exceptionally fine conduct and his good nature, made him the ideal student.

But his color was against him at first, and it was not without great difficulty that he proved his worth. When he entered Rutgers at the age of seventeen his great ambition was to play on the varsity football team. Accordingly, one September morning he appeared on the field with the scrub team against the varsity one, which was composed of giants fresh from six weeks' training in the pine woods. Those of the scrubs who showed greater possibilities than players on the varsity would be given the places of the latter, provided they survived the punishment they received from the varsity team, which fought not only to preserve its standing, but to keep the team intact.

Robeson, a young giant in height and build, was the only Negro among the scrubs. There had never been a black man on the Rutgers team, and the players on this occasion decided to maintain that tradition. In the game they apparently concentrated their efforts on Robeson, with the result that when the dust of battle cleared, he lay on the field with two broken ribs, a sprained arm, and a broken nose; then, whether accidentally or from spite, someone stepped on his hand with spiked shoes, gouging out a fingernail by the root.

Robeson felt the display of color prejudice even more than the physical injuries. It showed him clearly that he wasn't wanted because he was black. But undaunted, he decided that he would make them change their minds.

With his arm in a sling he watched the game day after day, studying every detail of it, then he volunteered again.

Seeing that his injuries were not yet healed, the coach advised him to wait, warning him that it would be his last chance. But Robeson was so determined that the coach told him to go out on the field.

In this second encounter Robeson showed them that he could be rough too. When the smoke of battle cleared this time six of the varsity eleven were carried off the field, thanks largely to Robeson's handling of them. Thereafter he became one of the most popular students on the team and in the college. Smiling, good-natured, courteous, he received numerous invitations to parties. At both formal and informal gatherings he was usually called on to sing Negro songs, which he cheerfully did.

As to the varsity team, those of its members who had objected to him at first were now wondering why they had done so. Later, in the last, crucial game of the season, it was his brilliant playing against Cupid Black's great eleven, with its seven All-Americans, that saved the day for Rutgers. Thereafter, he was picked for Walter Camp's All-America team, on which he played in 1917 and the following year. Camp called him "the greatest defensive end who ever trod a gridiron."

In recognition of his excellence in class and on campus, the president of the college, Dr. Demarest, chose him as commencement orator. Robeson selected as his title "Our New Idealism," and he set forth the potentialities of America's Negro citizens and predicted what would happen when America gave them unrestricted opportunity to contribute to the nation the wealth of their artistic gifts. His speech was a triumph—epochal, as it were, in the history of the college. At its close the professors and the students crowded around him to extend congratulations.

On leaving college he was faced with the predicament of choosing a profession because of his many gifts. With his 225 pounds of muscle, his six foot two and a half inches of stature and stamina, he was tempted to follow prizefighting. As an actor, singer, orator, he showed equal promise. Finally, he decided for the bar, and entering Columbia University, he took his LL.B. two years later.

While at Columbia his interest in the theatre increased. He played in *Simon the Cyrenian*, an amateur production, so creditably that he was offered the leading role in a professional production of *Taboo*, the theme of which was the race question. In this he appeared opposite Margaret Wycherly, and later in London with Mrs. Patrick Campbell, winning high praise from the press and public of New York and London.

In 1924, in New York, he took the leading role in Eugene O'Neill's *All God's Chillun Got Wings*. The opposition against this play, which dealt with the marriage of a Negro and a white woman, was nationwide. Determined efforts were made to stop its appearance. So-called law and order societies even appealed to the police. But although the play was rather poor and vague, Robeson's artistry won over even some of the newspapers that had opposed him most. The same year he had even greater success in O'Neill's *The Emperor Jones* in London.

It was not until April of the following year that he was to enter the field for which he later became best known. At the Provincetown Theatre in New York he gave, together with his accompanist, Lawrence Brown, what was said to be the first concert of all-Negro music by an individual singer on the white stage. Present were some of the leading music lovers, who realized for the first time, perhaps, the value of the spirituals. Robeson's voice, it was true, lacked training; nevertheless, his innate ability so compensated for this that his performance created a sensation in musical circles.

In 1928 his singing of "Ole Man River" in *Showboat* at the Drury Lane Theatre was one of the leading musical events of the year. When *Showboat* ended he was offered $5000 to appear in vaudeville, at the Palladium, which he refused.

The same year he appeared at the Albert Hall, the largest concert auditorium in the British Isles. Hundreds were unable to obtain seats. On his return to New York shortly afterward, he appeared at Carnegie Hall twice in two consecutive weeks to overflowing audiences.

Of his singing, James Douglas, musical critic of the *London Daily Express*, said:

> I have heard all the great singers of our time. No voice has moved me so profoundly with so many passions of thought and emotion. The marvel is that there is no monotony in the spiritual spell. It is effortless enchantment moving through fluctuant states of thought and feeling. . . .
>
> We laughed and wept. He broke our hearts with beauty. As he wiped the tears from his eyes, we wiped the tears from ours. He shook some of us into sobs. We applauded until we were weary, and we made him sing till he was weary. I have never seen a more unsated and unsatisfied audience.

His later concerts in the United States and his appearances at the Lewisohn Stadium and Robin Hood Dell were equally appreciated.

In 1930 he played Othello at the Savoy in London. Thanks to

his commanding appearance, his rich expressive voice, and his inner understanding of the racial theme, he was able to give new interpretations to the role, completely winning over even those newspaper critics who had objected to his appearing with a white woman, and even to his daring to portray Othello as a Negro at all. On the opening night he took twenty curtain calls.

Hannen Swaffer said in the *Daily Express*:

Paul Robeson destroyed last night the foolish idea accepted for many years that Iago is the better part in "Othello." He triumphed as a Moor, black, swarthy, muscular, a real man of deep color. A wonderful audience cheered Robeson's triumph. Colored people sat dotted about the house. Mrs. Paul Robeson sat in the third row of the stalls, next to Hugh Walpole. Famous players were there by the dozen. One editor walked out after the third act, saying that he did not like being near colored people, but otherwise there was no murmur that I heard.

Robeson's art conquered everything. Why should a black actor be allowed to kiss a white actress? I had heard a few people say beforehand.

There was no protest of that kind in the theatre. Five or six times before the last scene Robeson kissed Peggy Ashcroft full on the lips, and three times, when she was lying in bed, just before he "murdered" her.

It was in the part and that was that.

It was Paul Robeson's evening. Right at the end the company applauded him when he made a speech for all of them. "You do not know how proud I am to play this part in London," he said. Robeson has a right indeed, to be proud as he played it last night.

The *Daily Telegraph* said:

Great triumph for Robeson. Mr. Robeson's eagerly awaited "Othello" has justified expectation and is really a memorable performance.

Mr. Robeson comes of a race whose characteristic is to keep control of its passions only to a point and after that to throw controls to the winds. And so, when the madness of jealousy seizes this Othello under the subtle prickings of Iago's goad, we have no doubts concerning the genuineness of his passion. He is borne away helpless on the tide of that passion and the rest follows inevitably.

The London *Times*, which also carried a short biography of him, said:

Mr. Paul Robeson teaches us anew that Othello on the stage means something more to us than Macbeth, Hamlet or Lear. His history, as it shapes itself before our eyes, is more painfully exciting and terrible than theirs.

Undeniably, Mr. Robeson plays thrillingly upon the nerves and knocks at the heart. His performance is blemished here and there, but nowhere seriously flawed by an occasional dulling of his generally fine sense of the theatre, but we follow it with increasing pity and fear, sympathy, hope and dread. . . . Mr. Robeson is a Negro and thus revives the stage tradition that held down to the time of Edmund Kean of a coal-black Othello.

The *Chicago Tribune* (Paris edition) said, "Robeson made us feel that it was a tragedy of racial conflict, a tragedy of honor, rather than jealousy. Dignified, magnificent and black—Paul Robeson also made stage history."

His portrayal of Othello in America, 1934–44, was as enthusiastically praised and even more of a box-office success. In 1944–45 he made a tour of the United States with it. Burton Rascoe of the *New York World-Telegram* said of his performance in this play, "There has never been and never will be a finer rendition of this particular tragedy. It is unbelievably magnificent . . . there has simply been nothing on Broadway in years to earn our gratitude to the theatre more profoundly." And Howard Barnes said in the *Herald-Tribune*, "Othello is so illuminated and held in a taut and thrilling pattern that it becomes in many respects, something new and wonderful in the theatre."

Among his other stage-plays were *The Hairy Ape*, *Stevedore*, *Porgy*, and *Black Boy*. His *Toussaint L'Ouverture* lasted but three days in London, the theme of racial conflict with Negroes overcoming white people probably being too much for English audiences. As for his motion pictures, two or three of them, *The Emperor Jones*, *Showboat*, and *King Solomon's Mines*, received warm praise from the critics, while one, *Sanders of the River*, in which he played the role of Bosambo, an African chief, was voted the best foreign picture of 1935.

Robeson sang several times for George V at Buckingham Palace and was received and entertained in the homes of the elite of Berlin,

Paris, Vienna, Prague, Budapest, Bucharest, and elsewhere. It was in Russia, however, where he felt most at home and the freest. He said in 1935, "In Soviet Russia I breathe freely for the first time in my life. It is clear whether a Negro is politically a Communist or not, that of all the nations of the world, the modern Russians are our best friends."

In 1944 he received an award from the American Academy of Arts and Letters for excellent diction.

REFERENCES

Mention of Robeson would be incomplete without a word about his accompanist, Lawrence Brown, to whom Robeson attributed much of his success. Lawrence Brown is a distinguished pianist who has on several occasions played at Buckingham Palace, and is one of the three foremost arrangers of Negro spirituals, as well as one of the best read and most highly informed men of his time. He arranged most of the spirituals for Robeson, and joined him in the chorus of some of the songs. These great artists together were instrumental in revealing new beauties of the spirituals, their richness, tenderness, and humor. Largely through their efforts, Negro music has been raised to the same high level as Negro art.

In 1940 Robeson discovered a new sound control technique, which is described in *The New York Times,* December 8, of that year.

Robeson, E. G., *Paul Robeson, Negro.* London, V. Gollancz; New York, Harper and Brothers, 1930.
New Theatre, July, 1935.

ADDITIONAL REFERENCES

Adams, Russell L., *Great Negroes: Past and Present,* pp. 148–149. Chicago, Afro-Am Publishing Company, 1963, 1964.
Cruse, Harold Wright, *The Crisis of the Negro Intellectual,* pp. 285–301. New York, Morrow, 1967.
Embree, Edwin Rogers, *13 Against the Odds,* pp. 243–261. New York, The Viking Press, 1944.
Graham, Shirley, *Paul Robeson, Citizen of the World.* New York, J. Messner, Inc., 1946.
Hoyt, Edwin P., *The American Othello.* Cleveland and New York, The World Publishing Company, 1967.

Kempton, Murray, *Part of Our Time*, pp. 236–260. New York, Simon and Schuster, 1955.

Duington, Mary White, *Portraits in Color*. New York, The Viking Press, 1927.

Robeson, Paul, "Bonds of Brotherhood," in *Jewish Life Anthology 1946–1956*, pp. 196–199. New York, Jewish Currents, 1956.

Sergeant, Elizabeth Shepley, *Fire Under the Andes*, pp. 193–209. New York, Knopf, 1927.

Charles Clinton Spaulding

FINANCIAL GENIUS AND INSURANCE MAGNATE
(1874–1952)

CHARLES CLINTON SPAULDING, leading Negro financier and one of the most capable and successful insurance and banking executives of the United States, had a most inspiring career. Starting as a dishwasher, he became head of a business concern— The North Carolina Mutual Life Insurance Company—with assets of over $14 million.

Born in Columbus County, North Carlina, on a farm, and one of fourteen children, he started out under a great handicap, especially in the matter of education. Schooling for Negroes in the county was most elementary and crude. However, ambitious and eager to learn, he rapidly absorbed all that was available, supplementing it with other scanty reading matter.

With a vision of great things and with only the prospect of a wretched farming life before him, he decided to leave his native village and went to Durham, then a small town. Here he found work as a dishwasher, deciding to use that as a stepping-stone to better things. Cheerfulness and willingness in this humble post soon bore fruit and he was promoted to head bellboy and still later to waiter. Ever before him, however, were thoughts of a better education, and by saving his meager earnings and working afternoons and evenings, he was able to enter the public schools of the town.

On graduating in 1898, he was appointed head of a grocery company that had been newly formed by Negroes. Lack of interest among the original supporters of the business handicapped progress to the extent that Spaulding had to take over the business alone. Under this new arrangement the business did better but it remained small. However, this venture served to develop in him such qualities as foresight and business integrity, which were later to play so important a part in influencing his career and winning him friends and the respect of the community.

His reputation was to be his making. John Merrick, a progressive barber, and A. M. Moore, a practicing physician, of the town, conceived the idea of establishing a life insurance company to be owned and operated by Negroes. However, since both these men were already actively engaged, it was necessary to secure for their newly-founded business an individual whose time could be devoted exclusively to its promotion and whose general qualifications measured up to the exacting standards of proficiency necessary. Both had been observing the young groceryman and were so impressed with him that they offered him the post, which he accepted.

Thanks to Spaulding's resourcefulness, zeal, and business experience, the new company took definite form and began its uphill climb to prominence and stability. Later it was reorganized and he was made general manager; then secretary-treasurer; and finally, in 1923, on the death of Dr. Moore, he was made president, which position he held for many years.

The North Carolina Mutual Life Insurance Company demonstrated in a most striking way what Negroes can do to help themselves in business. It aided Southern progress in other ways: It taught Negroes thrift, improved their health with its health programs, and generally awakened their self-respect. Thanks to the company, the Negro community in Durham became one of the most progressive in America. Spaulding truly earned the gratefulness of the people of North Carolina, who named three high schools of the state for him.

In 1926 he was awarded the Harmon Foundation Gold Medal for distinguished achievement in business; Shaw University, Tuskegee Institute, and Atlanta University conferred honorary doctorates of law on him; and in 1942 the New York Chamber of Commerce, principally a white body, elected him to membership. Keenly interested in civic progress, he belonged to more than twenty organizations, such as the Colored Orphanage of Oxford, North Carolina, of which he was secretary-treasurer. He was also trustee, North Carolina College for Negroes; vice chairman, United Negro College Fund; trustee, Howard University; member, trustee board of the Southern Education Foundation, Inc.; and president emeritus of the National Negro Business League.

In the life of Charles Clinton Spaulding we find a man overcoming gloriously the very limited opportunity for progress in the rural South and fighting his way by sheer force of will and determination to a position of national prominence. Color alone prevented him from being one of the top bankers in the nation. He was a living example of his favorite motto: "Success is carved out by the chisel of efficiency, integrity, and hard work."

ADDITIONAL REFERENCES

Adams, Russell L., *Great Negroes: Past and Present*, p. 74. Chicago, Afro-Am Publishing Company, 1963, 1964.

Bardolph, Richard, *The Negro Vanguard*, pp. 260–264. New York, Vintage Books, 1961.

Bullock, Ralph W., *In Spite of Handicaps*. New York, Association Press, 1927.

Hughes, Langston, *Famous American Negroes*. New York, Dodd, Mead, 1954.

Spaulding, Charles Clinton, *Fifty Years of Progress in Business*, p. 7. Pittsburgh, Pittsburgh Courier, 1950.

Marian Anderson

"THE VOICE OF THE CENTURY"
(1908–1993)

MARIAN ANDERSON, the famous contralto, was born of poor parents in Philadelphia. Her father, a peddler of coal and ice, died when she was twelve and her mother, a former schoolteacher, took in washing to support the family.

Marian was born with a love of music and her gift as a singer appeared at an early age. At six she sang in a church concert and at eight was known as the baby contralto. To get money to buy a violin, she scrubbed her neighbors' steps. Soon her fame spread and many came to church especially to hear the child singer.

While in high school she gave little concerts at churches and centers to pay for her music lessons, getting as much as $20 at some of these. Then, as she progressed, it became necessary to find a superior teacher. This would cost more money and the people of her church, put their nickels and dimes together for a fund which they called "the Marian Anderson future." Under a new teacher, Guiseppe Boghetti, she rapidly developed into concert fitness and gave her first recital.

She was a success and showed such unusual talent that in 1925 she came out first in the auditions of New York Town Hall to select a soloist for the New York Philharmonic Society for their summer concerts in the Lewisohn Stadium. Of the 300 competitors, she was the best, and superlatively so. In the winter she became a soloist with the Philadelphia Symphony Orchestra.

Now launched as a concert artist, she gave recitals for the next four years, one of them at Carnegie Hall, New York. In 1930 she went to Europe and while there made several appearances, one of them in Berlin. She was highly praised by European musicologists as Roger Quilter, Sir Henry Wood, and Henry Newman, but the European audiences, more critical than Americans were not so enthusiastic about her. Since she had the natural ability, however, it was but a matter of her mastering the European lyrics as they were being interpreted in their native environment and in their own language. Kosti Vehanen of Finland, who was later to be her accompanist, relates how deeply he was affected when he heard her voice for the first time. He says:

It made me think of an exquisite flower that stands alone in a forest, where no human being has ever trod, the roots drinking the aged nectar from the soil, rich with every substance that sun, rain and fire can create. Such a flower blooms with superb loveliness, with a most delicate perfume, trembling with a tenderness never before felt. So the sound I heard swelled to majestic power, the flower opened its petals to full brilliance and I was enthralled by one of nature's rare wonders.

After a year's study she was prepared, and her later concert tours through Finland, Norway, Sweden, Denmark, France, Spain, Italy, Switzerland, Czechoslovakia, Poland, Austria, Hungary, Latvia, Estonia, the Soviet Union, and still later in Egypt and Palestine, were successes. At her appearance in Helsinki, Finland, tickets were sold out weeks in advance. Among those unable to get one was the conductor of the Finnish National Opera, who the next day begged to come over and turn the pages of her music while she practiced so that he could hear her.

In August, 1935, she was billed to sing at the Salzburg Musical Festival, in Germany, to which had flocked music lovers and famous maestros from many lands. At her concert the audience was comparatively small. Then an American woman living in that city, Mrs. Gertrude Moulton, feeling that Miss Anderson deserved to be better known, gave a private recital for her in her own home and invited the leading persons of the town, among them the archbishop, as well as the great maestros, including Arturo Toscanini. The members of that highly critical audience got the thrill of their lives. Toscanini, in an outburst of feeling, praised Miss Anderson to the skies. "What I heard today," he said, "one is privileged to hear only once in a hundred years."

Her return to America in the winter of that year was a re-sounding triumph for her in spite of a painful handicap she experienced a few days before her recital on December 30 at Town Hall. While coming over on the *Ile de France* she fractured a bone in her leg when her evening gown was caught in a steel staircase. When she appeared on the stage, her leg was in a plaster cast, but this was so carefully concealed that the audience knew of it only after the recital.

The leading music critics of New York poured out their praise on her while the music lovers thirsted for more. A month later she appeared at Carnegie Hall, which is several times larger than Town Hall, to an overflowing audience. Five weeks later she repeated her triumph in the same hall. America had found a new music idol. Over the radio she sang to millions.

In March, 1936, she returned to Europe, sweeping through like a triumphal queen. Everywhere she sang to capacity houses in the largest halls available. The Soviet Union was so captivated that the people there wished to keep her indefinitely and she had to extend her month's engagement to three months. In Paris she filled the Grand Opera, one of the largest auditoriums in the world, while hundreds of music lovers, unable to get in, surged in the Place de l'Opéra.

In the meantime, concert managers in South America were clamoring for her. In Brazil, Uruguay, Argentina, she was a "box-office avalanche." In Buenos Aires she gave twelve consecutive recitals with vociferous audiences pleading for more.

Probably no other artist of the first magnitude has given so many recitals as Miss Anderson. In the season of 1933–34 she gave 112 in Scandinavia alone. In 1938 she gave seventy in sixty cities of the United States, which was said to be the record up to that time—the longest, most intensive concert tour in history. But this record by no means marked the limit of her amazing vitality and the enduring strength of her voice. The following season she gave ninety-two concerts in seventy cities between November and

June. Five of these were in Carnegie Hall, which was a record for a single singer for that hall. The same year she went to Hawaii and in the summer sang at the Lewisohn Stadium and the Robin Hood Dell concerts. No auditorium in Europe or America is large enough to hold her audience. In 1945 she filled the great Hollywood Bowl to overflowing.

In 1946 she was on her twelfth consecutive tour of the United States, at no time able to fill the requests for appearances. She had traveled more than 300,000 miles, sung to more than 3,000,000 persons, not including her radio audiences and those of her recordings.

Other impressive tributes were bestowed upon Miss Anderson. In 1940 she was given the Bok Award of $10,000 for being Philadelphia's most distinguished citizen of that year. With this money she promptly established a fund, The Marian Anderson Award, for aiding talented young singers. Three American universities conferred Doctorates of Music on her; in 1938 she received the Spingarn Medal for international success as a concert artist; Liberia conferred on her the Order of African Redemption; France gave her the Prix de Chant for being the best voice on the records in Europe; the King and Queen of England invited her to sing at Buckingham Palace; she sang for Mr. and Mrs. Roosevelt at the White House; and Sibelius, composer of *Finlandia*, the national hymn of Finland, dedicated his *Solitude* to her.

The critics too were most unstinted in their praise of her. The *Philadelphia Inquirer* said, "More so than ever the only one who can equal or excel the great contralto is Marian Anderson, herself."

Howard Taubman of *The New York Times* said:

Today she is America's greatest contralto. She appears in more recitals each season than any other major artist and her fee is among the top five of the land. . . . There is a powerful appeal in Marian Anderson on the stage. Even before she sings a single song she has won her audience. She is tall and stately in figure and she takes her place before the piano with the simplicity and dignity of one who regards it a privilege to be permitted to sing. There is no ostentation, no sign of tension. She faces the audience calmly and confidently with never the slightest trace of a prima donna mannerism. . . . she wants the audience to forget Marian Anderson and become aware only of

Bach and Schubert and Brahms and the others who poured their innermost emotions into music. And when the applause and the cheers cascade through the theatre, she does not behave like a triumphant heroine; she is profoundly moved that her listeners are pleased.

The *Toronto Globe and Mail* said of one of her recitals in that city in 1946, "She has the richest, warmest contralto being heard today, and her range is spectacular. She is always the complete artist and never stoops to obvious tricks for effect."

In the worldwide welcome and appreciation of Miss Anderson there was but one sour note—a sort of anticlimax that was to increase her fame, if such a thing were possible. In 1939 the Daughters of the American Revolution refused to let her appear in Constitution Hall, Washington, D.C., because of her color. Even in Nazi Germany, where racial hate was believed to have reached its height, she had not been discriminated against. As a result, Mrs. Franklin D. Roosevelt resigned from that organization and an outdoor concert was arranged for Miss Anderson at the Lincoln Memorial. High officers of state, foreign ambassadors, leaders of society, and an audience of 75,000 came to hear her, and the concert was a devastating rebuke to the society that had barred her.

During the war she sang in army camps and on troop and hospital trains for the soldiers, cheering the well and the wounded with her favorite, Schuberts's "Ave Maria." At the Winter General Hospital she sang to 1500 and at Fort Knox to 7000.

Miss Anderson's principal charm was her perfectly natural and simple manner which remained unaffected by success, wealth, and the world's applause. When asked what was the greatest moment of her life she said that it was the day she could go home and tell her mother she need not work anymore. Truly it could be said of her, "She has conquered the world by the peaceful power of song."

REFERENCES

Vehanen, K., *Marian Anderson*. London, Whittlesey House; New York, McGraw-Hill Book Company, Inc., 1941.

Hurok, S., *Impresario*, pp. 237–261. New York, Random House, 1946.

ADDITIONAL REFERENCES

Adams, Russell L., *Great Negroes: Past and Present*, p. 154. Chicago, Afro-Am Publishing Company, 1963, 1964.

Anderson, Marian, *My Lord, What a Morning: An Autobiography*. New York, The Viking Press, 1956.

Bakeless, Katherine (Little), *In the Big Time*, pp. 91–109. Philadelphia, Lippincott, 1953.

Embree, Edwin Rogers, *Investment in People*, pp. 144–145. New York, Harper, 1949.

———, *13 Against the Odds*, pp. 139–152. New York, The Viking Press, 1944.

Ewen, David, *Men and Women Who Make Music*, pp. 80–89. New York, Merlin Press, 1949.

Gibbs, Margaret, *The DAR*, pp. 160–176. New York, Holt, Rinehart, and Winston, 1969.

Hughes, Langston, *Famous American Negroes*. New York, Dodd, Mead, 1954.

Lotz, Philip Henry, ed., *Rising Above Color*, pp. 11–17. New York, Association Press, 1943.

Stoddard, Ann (Glen), ed., *Top Flight: Famous American Women*, pp. 146–160. New York, Toronto, T. Nelson and Sons, 1946.

Thomas, Henry, *50 Great Modern Lives*, pp. 479–488. Garden City, N.Y., Hanover House, 1956.

Joe Louis

※ ※

THE SUPERMAN OF THE PRIZE RING
(1914–1981)

JOE LOUIS is phenomenal in the history of the prize ring. After he became a professional fighter he did not have an opponent against whom he really had to extend himself, as say, Corbett had to against Peter Jackson, Sullivan against Corbett, Dempsey against Firpo, or Tunney against Dempsey. Either the other champions were overrated and Joe Louis was superior to all of them; or the race of prizefighters had degenerated.

As *PM*, the New York daily, said, "Conn proved that a retreating fight against Louis won't do and Mauriello proved that an advancing one won't do either. Obviously the only way to fight Joe is by mail."

The fighter who came nearest to standing up against him was Tommy Farr, champion of the British Empire, who stayed the full fifteen rounds of the bout but suffered terrific punishment. As for Louis' defeat by Max Schmeling, it was later asserted after an investigation conducted by a Chicago daily that he was physically ill at the time.

Louis was born in Lexington, Alabama, and was taken as a child by his mother to Detroit. Like all the other Negro prizefighters, his background was poor and success came the hard way. At school, too, he was a failure, never being able to get further than the seventh grade. He did no better at trade school, where he was put to learn cabinet-making. His mother even tried to make a musician of him with no better results. But this did not mean he was mentally inferior. His skill had merely taken an athletic bent, as others are inclined to drawing or to music. It takes an exceptionally keen brain and lightning-like thinking to be a successful boxer.

On leaving trade school, he went to work in the Ford automobile plant at Detroit as a laborer. After the day's hard work he would go to a gymnasium, where he took lessons in boxing.

He engaged at this period in several amateur bouts; in three consecutive ones he was beaten, by Stanley Evans, Clinton Bridges, and Marek. Those knowledgeable in the game predicted that he would never make a first-class fighter because he was too phelgmatic and machine-like, and showed none of the flair and flash expected of a boxer. But Louis had an inner vision of his own capabilities and he persisted until in 1934 he became the national amateur 175-pound champion at St. Louis, Missouri. There was a man, one with a keen practiced eye, who saw great possibilities in him—Jack Blackburn, a Negro lightweight of the earlier days, and a past master at the art of training fighters. Blackburn took charge of him.

Louis now decided to become a professional. His best friends advised him strongly against that. Better, they said, his $25-a-week job at the Ford plant, which, at least, was certain. They reminded him of the great handicaps facing a Negro heavyweight; of the struggles of Peter Jackson and Jack Johnson; and of how Harry Wills, a first-class heavyweight, had been sidestepped by Jack Dempsey. Louis, however, decided to follow his star, and on July 4, 1934, fought his first professional bout with Jack Kracken, whom he knocked out in the first round.

His step was a very wise one. No other heavyweight in ring history has made such rapid progress or as much money in as short a time. In his first four years, 1934–1938, he earned $1,384,034. As for his opponents, three of whom were former champions, he beat every one of them between 1934 and 1946. During his career he had a total of seventy-one professional fights, fifty-four of which were won by knockouts, or technical knockouts and fourteen by decisions. Up to September 18, 1946, he fought twenty-three straight title defenses, or more than double the record of any other champion. Eight of these were in one year, 1941. Louis lost one fight by decision and two by knockout or technical knockout—once to Max Schmeling when Louis was on his way up and once (a technical knockout) to Rocky Marciano. Louis held the world's heavyweight championship from June 22, 1937, to March 1, 1949, when he retired undefeated.

Of his many fights, the three that created anything approaching the excitement of the old ring battles were: the fight with Primo Carnera, an Italian and former world champion, who stood six feet five and a quarter and weighed 254 pounds; his return bout with Max Schmeling, whom he knocked out in the first round with such force that Schmeling screamed in agony like a wounded animal; and the one with James J. Braddock, June 22, 1937, in which he won the championship by knocking out Braddock in the eighth round. His return engagement with Billy Conn in 1946, though looked forward to worldwide with expectation, was a tame affair, Conn proving too easy a foe.

In the year 1947 he stood alone, with no challenger in sight. Bill Corum, a sportswriter, said after his bout with Mauriello on June 18, 1946, "Louis is so far ahead of all the heavyweights in the world today that there is no second. . . . Fistically, the brown destroyer finds himself in the same position as Alexander the Great. There aren't any more worlds for him to conquer." And Arthur "Bugs" Baer said, "If there is anybody in the world left to fight Joe Louis I don't know his name. And if I did I wouldn't squeal."

Joe Louis was a great influence for good in prizefighting circles and in athletics, and a model of integrity for American youth. As a boy in school he got high marks for deportment and that would always be characteristic of him. Once when a cigar firm offered him a large sum for the use of his name he refused it saying that since he did not smoke he would not be able to speak of the merit of its cigars. On his release from the army in 1945, Major-General Kells, in presenting him the Legion of Merit, called him "a model soldier."

His utter lack of pose and thorough gentlemanliness made him a general favorite with the sportswriters. Arthur Daley of *The New York Times* said of him while he was waiting for Mauriello to be counted out:

In the opposite corner Louis stood as expressionless as Buddha. He was still champion of the world. When you look back on it, though, there was a definite expression that every spectator took away with him, the utter majesty of that regal figure, Joe Louis. Gosh, but he has class.

The Dark Destroyer has it in superabundance right down to his finger-tips. He has it in his kingly bearing and in his every motion in the ring, too. Being a champion isn't the easiest thing in the world but the Jolter wears his crown as gracefully and as naturally in his simple dignity as if he had been to the purple—or more so.

Joe Louis was sometimes referred to as "deadpan" because of his calm, unruffled manner and his apparent unconcern over things at which others get excited. But he was known to laugh boisterously. His humor was laconic and direct like his blows. When asked who had hit him the hardest in the prize ring, he said, "Uncle Sam, the tax man." When he was about to fight John Henry Lewis, a Negro, and it was suggested to him that he go easy with him because Lewis was his friend, he replied, "He's my pal, all right, so I'll put him away early—make it quick for him. That'll be easier." Quiet, good-natured, generous, Joe Louis was truly what Van Every said of him. "The finest example of coldly controlled fistic lightning" in ring history.

REFERENCES

Fleischer, N., *Black Dynamite*, Vol. II, pp. 1–11. 1938.

Van Every, E., *Joe Louis, Man and Super Fighter*. New York, Stores, 1936.

Miller, Margery, *Joe Louis, American*. New York, Current Booking, A. A. Wyn, 1945.

ADDITIONAL REFERENCES

Adams, Carswell, ed., *Great American Sports Stories*. New York, Stamford House, 1947.

Embree, Edwin Rogers, *13 Against the Odds*, pp. 231–241. New York, The Viking Press, 1944.

Fleischer, Nathaniel S., *The Heavyweight Championship*. New York, G. P. Putnam's Sons, 1949.

Johnston, Alexander, *Ten—and Out!* New York, Washburn, 1936.

Kessler, Gene, *Joe Louis, the Brown Bomber*. Racine, Wis., Whitman, 1936.

Louis, Joe, *My Life Story*. New York, Buell, Sloan and Pearce, 1947.

Rice, Grantland, *The Tumult and the Shouting*, pp. 247–254. New York, A. S. Barnes, 1954.

Rice, Harold, *Within the Ropes*, pp. 136–145. New York, Stephen-Paul, 1946.

Scott, Neil, *Joe Louis: A Picture Story of His Life*. New York, Greenberg, 1947.

Van Deusen, John George, *Brown Bomber*. Philadelphia, Borrevice and Company, 1940.

ADDITIONAL GREAT MEN
OF COLOR

Commentary

IN THIS SECTION Mr. Rogers has called attention to a selected number of great men of color that the world may have forgotten, and who are not recognized as men of color because of the European interpretation of African history that tried to prove, or at least imply, that everything of grandeur and greatness in Africa was brought in from the outside by white people, or at least people from Asia. Some of the personalities included here are Europeans who had some African blood, which was not generally known to their contemporaries. Others are great men of color whom some historians have arbitrarily classified as white. This section by itself, properly developed, would make another book, and a good one. It is included here in order to show the range of great African personalities and their impact on human history. When the complete story of some of the main personalities has been told the world will know that from the dawn of history African people have been players of importance in the unfolding human drama that, in essence, is the story of man.

J. H. C.

Great Men of Color in Brief

❧❧

EGYPT, ANCIENT AND MODERN

SETI THE GREAT was one of Egypt's mightiest rulers. He conquered the Hittites, Cushites, and many tribes of the Upper Nile. Rawlinson says, "Seti's face is thoroughly African, strong, fierce, prognathous, with depressed nose, thick lips, and a heavy chin." (*Story of Egypt*, p. 252. 1887. See portrait in *Sex and Race*, 2nd ed., Vol. I, p. 51.)

NEFERTARI AAHMES, an Egyptian queen, possessed great administrative ability and personal charm. Many monuments were erected to her and she was worshipped as the ancestress of the Eighteenth Dynasty. Aahmes, her husband, expelled the Shepherd Kings. Of him Rawlinson says, "He married a princess who took the name of Nefertari Aahmes, or 'the beautiful companion of Aahmes,' and who is represented on the monuments with pleasing features but a complexion of ebony blackness." (*History of Ancient Egypt*, Vol. II, pp. 209, 215, 216. 1880.)

SABACON, Ethiopian conqueror of Egypt and the founder of the twenty-fifth Dynasty, was a most humane ruler, according to Diodorus Siculus, who says that he went "beyond all his predecessors in worship of the gods and in kindness to his subjects." (*World History*, Book I, Chap. 5.)

TAHARKA (Tirhaqah of the Bible), was the son of Piankhy, Ethiopian conqueror of Egypt. While yet in his teens, he commanded an expedition sent by his uncle, Sabacon, against Sennacherib, King of Assyria. Seizing the throne, Taharka ruled Ethiopia, all of Egypt, and much of Assyria with wisdom. He put up many buildings and monuments while preparing for the struggle with Esarhaddon, successor of Sennacherib. (See sources and portraits in *Sex and Race*, Vol. I, pp. 43, 56. 2nd ed.)

MUSTAPHA EL NAHAS PASHA (1875–1965), successor to Zaglul Pasha, founder of the Wafd, or Home Rule Party, and former Egyptian Minister to the United States. In 1926, he was vice president of the Chamber of Deputies; in 1927, its president; and in 1928–30 and 1936–37, prime minister; in 1942–44, prime minister and minister of foreign affairs. In 1921–23 he was exiled by the British to the Seychelles Islands for his self-government activities. He received the highest decorations of his native land as well as others from Belgium, England, Chile and Greece. While Egyptian Minister to Germany he was attacked by three Nazi storm troopers who objected to his being with a German lady. Nahas Pasha, who was an athlete, routed all three. (See *International Who's Who*, 1945; see also "Who's Important in Government" in *Biographical Encyclopedia of the World*, p. 163, 1946.)

ARABIA AND EASTERN ISLAM

MOHAMMED, or Mohamet, born about A.D. 567, died June 7, 632, founder of Islam, the world's second most important religion and one of the greatest men of all times. Author of the Koran, he had a greater influence on Asia, North Africa, and parts of Europe than any individual before or since. Started life as a camel driver. He was a wise and capable administrator, an able reformer, and probably the world's greatest general of his time. Innumerable books have been written about him. (For source of his Negro ancestry see *Sex and Race,* 2nd ed., Vol. I, pp. 95, 96, 284.

ZAID BIN HARITH, Negro slave and third convert of Mohammed, was one of the Prophet's foremost generals. Mohammed adopted him as his son, made him governor of the proud Koreish, Mohammed's own tribe, and had him married into his own family, all of which were the highest honors possible. Zaid was killed in battle while leading his men against the Byzantines. (*Islamic Review*, Vol. XX, p. 226, June–July, 1932; Salik, S. A., *Early Heroes of Islam*, p. 49. Calcutta, 1926; Muir, W., *Life of Mohamet*, Vol. II, p. 48; Maulaua, M. A., *Muhammad the Prophet*. Lahore, 1924; *Encyclopedia of Islam*, see "Zaid".)

BARJAWAN, Negro eunuch, was virtual ruler of the Mohammedan Empire under his pupil, Hakem, the sixteenth caliph of the Fatimite Dynasty. Barjawan was assassinated at Cairo in 1000 by a palace clique which accused him of trying to imitate the tactics of another great Negro ruler of Egypt, Kafur. Barjawan was a multimillionaire. (*Ibn Khallikan*, trans. by Baron MacGuckin de Slane, *Biographical Dictionary*, Vol. I, p. 283; *Encyclopedia of Islam*, see "Barjawan.")

KARAKOOSH, Negro eunuch, was a famous architect and statesman. He built a fortress for Saladin, opponent of Richard I, Coeur de Lion, of England, in the wars of the Crusades. To get the stones he tore down two of the pyramids at Ghizeh. (Ebers, G., *Egypt*, Vol. I, pp. 234–236. 1886.)

MABED IBN OUBAD, son of a Negro slave, was Islam's greatest singer in the tenth century. His talents showed a superiority over all his rivals and he was called "the prince of singers." Alexander Christianowitsch says of him, "His intelligence, the beauty of his voice, the merit of his compositions, soon brought him fame and placed him above all the musicians of his age." (*Esquisse historique de la musique arabe*, pp. 18–20. 1863.) When he sang for the Caliph at Bagdad, the latter gave him 50,000 pieces of gold. Some of his compositions have survived.

HAFIZ BEHERAM, Grand Eunuch of Turkey, a Sudanese Negro, was the leading man in the empire after the sultan in 1877. Negro eunuchs from the first days of the Turkish empire enjoyed high power, and their chief was one of the three great dignitaries of that realm. (Millant, F., *L'Esclavage en Turquie*. Paris, 1912; Zambaco, D. A., *Les Eunuques*. Paris, 1911.)

According to the *New York Evening Telegram* of Feburary 8, 1933, the eunuchs, now a forlorn group, meet in a café in Constantinople regularly.

SAUDI ARABIA

SHEIKH HAFIZ WAHBA (1889–1969), envoy extraordinary and minister plenipotentiary for Saudi Arabia in England. Journalist, lawyer, minister of education, 1928–29, counsellor to King Ibn Saud. Member of the Saudi Arabian delegation to the United Nations Conference at San Francisco in 1945. Author of *The Arabian Peninsula* and works on Islamic philosophy. ("Who's Important in Government" in *Biographical Encyclopedia of the World*, p. 40, 1946.)

AFRICA

TARIK BIN ZAID, an ex-slave and the first Islamic conqueror of Spain, captured Mt. Calpe in A.D. 711, to which he gave his own name, Gibraltar, or Ghebel u Tarik (the Mountain of Tarik). The same year he defeated Roderick, King of the Goths, and ruler of Spain, at the Guadelete River. Against Roderick's army of 40,000, Tarik had only 12,000 men. Tarik's commander-in-chief and former owner, Musa, jealous of his ex-bondsman's success, struck him with a whip. When Tarik was received by the Caliph at Bagdad, he turned the tables on Musa, bringing about the latter's disgrace and imprisonment. (Makkari, *History of the Mohammedan Dynasties in Spain*, trans. by Pascual de Gayangos, Vol. I. London, 1843. For Tarik's Negro descent, see *Sex and Race*, Vol. I, 2nd ed., p. 286, for sources.)

JUDITH, Queen of the Falashas, or Black Jews, attacked Axum, sacred capital of Ethiopia, and captured it in A.D. 937. She killed nearly every member of the ancient family of Solomon and the Queen of Sheba. This warlike woman finally conquered all but a small portion of Ethiopia, and ruled it until her death in A.D. 977. (Morie, L. J., *Histoire d'Ethiopie*, Vol. II, Chap. 5. Paris, 1904; *African Soc. Jour.*, Vol. XXVIII, p. 60.)

PRESTER JOHN, Emperor of Ethiopia, who later became a legendary figure. The search for his kingdom and its alleged marvels ushered in an era of world exploration that resulted in the discovery of the New World. Tradition says that when he went to war, "thirteen crosses of gold were carried before him in wagons as his standard; his personal attendants were 10,000 knights and 100,000 footmen. There were no destitute in his kingdom, no thief, no liar, no robber, flatterer or miser. He had a marvelous mirror several stories high which permitted him to see all that was going on in his kingdom and detect all conspirators. He surpassed in riches all other potentates of the world and no less than sixty kings were his vassals. His power extended to India and included Babylon and the ancient tower of Babel." (Lobo, Jeronymo, *A Short Relation of the River Nile*. London, 1791; Ogilby, John, *Africa*, pp. 632–658. London, 1670.)

ABD-EL-MALIK, Emperor of Morocco, is an important figure in world history. His defeat of Don Sebastian, King of Portugal, at Alcassar-el-Kebir, August 4, 1578, brought about the downfall of Portugal as a world power. Abd-el-Malik had driven his brother, Mulai Mohammed, surnamed "The Negro" (his mother was a full-blooded Negro while his father was almost one), from the throne, and Mulai Mohammed allied himself with Don Sebastian. All three rulers mentioned were slain in this battle. (*Biographie Universelle*, Vol. XXIX, p. 521. *Larousse*, Vol. IX, p. 89. 1908.)

ALVAKI, King of the Congo. John Ogilby gives a full description of the pomp and the magnificence of this monarch, including his flock of sacred peacocks. The kings of the Congo sent ambassadors to the Holy See, one of whom, Don Antonio Emanuel, Marquis of Wunth, died at Rome and was buried there in 1608. The Pope himself gave this African nobleman the last benediction, while all the dignitaries of the church were present at his funeral. Pope Urban VIII commissioned Bernini to construct a mausoleum for him in the Cathedral of St. Marie-Major at Rome, and erected a monument in his honor in the Liberian Church. (*Intermédiare des Chercheurs et des Curieux*, Vol. LXII, p. 647. Paris. 1911; Ogilby, John, *Africa*. London, 1670.)

MULEY ARCHID (1631–1672), Emperor of Morocco and one of the world's most powerful rulers of his time. Noted for his conquests and the ruthless manner in which he suppressed banditry, thievery, and all wrongdoing in his kingdom. Brother of the renowned Mulai Ismael, who succeeded him. (*Biographie Universelle*, Vol. XXIX, p. 525. See also "Mulai Ismael" in *World's Great Men of Color*, Vol. I.)

DINGAAN, able and ferocious Zulu king, opposed the entry of the whites into what is now Natal and adjoining regions. He massacred the Boer leader Piet Retief and 60 whites, following this up with a massacre of 281 whites and 250 servants. For ten years he was a terror in that region until defeated on January 30, 1840, chiefly through the efforts of his half-brother Moanda, who wanted to rule. In commemoration of the massacre and his defeat, Dingaan's Day is celebrated in South Africa.

LOBENGUELA, King of Matabeleland, an immensely rich region of South Africa, fought off for years the mad rush of the British, Boers, and Portuguese for his gold and diamond lands. On November 1, 1891, his regiments, armed mostly with spears, dashed right up to the muzzles of the modern British machine guns with rare courage, but were defeated. A few days later, however, he wiped out a small British force. He resisted the invaders to the last, and died in January, 1894, of fever. His territory, seized by England, was called Rhodesia, in honor of Cecil Rhodes. Lobenguela is supposed to have hidden away a store of diamonds valued at millions of dollars, which have never been found. (Hole, H. M., *Passing of the Black Kings*. 1932; Wills, W. A., *Downfall of Lobenguela*. 1894; Cloete S., *Against These Three*. 1945; Chilvers, H. A., *Seven Lost Trails of Africa*, see chapter, "The Buried Millions of Lobenguela," pp. 101–116. 1930.)

MOHAMMED ABDULLAH, "The Mad Mullah," forced Great Britain to roll up the map of British Somaliland in 1910, after ten years of struggle. He defeated the British and Italians in many battles, and was an ally of Lidj Yassu, deposed ruler of Ethiopia. (Drake-Brockman, R. E., *The Mad Mullah*, pp. 175–189. London, 1912. *Illustrated London News*, January 13, 1894, p. 52, and June 23, 1894, p. 790.)

SIR APOLO KAGWA, Prime Minister of Uganda, was a brave and resourceful general. Converted to Christianity, he opposed the king, who was killing off the native Christians. He also successfully opposed the Europeans who were trying to seize his country, and held Uganda together despite disintegrating influences from within. At the coronation of King Edward VII, at which he represented his country, he was one of the most impressive figures because of his height and massive build. Sir Apolo emancipated the slaves, instituted industrial education, introduced the printing press, and generally promoted the advance of his country. He was knighted by Edward VII, and on his death in February, 1927, was eulogized by the English press. (Gollock, G. A., *Sons of Africa*. New York, 1928; Hattersley, C. W., *The Baganda at Home*. 1908.)

EL HADJ OMAR (1797–1864), great West African conqueror, organizer, and statesman. Conquered all of that region which was French Guinea, Senegal, and Timbuctoo, organizing it into the Empire of Sokoto, which flourished in commerce, learning, and industry. Defeated the French in many battles. (Hanotaux, G., *Les Colonies Françaises*, pp. 134–45.)

SIR SAMUEL LEWIS (1843–1903), was born at Freetown, Sierra Leone, of pure African stock. He became acting Chief Justice of Sierra Leone and was knighted by Queen Victoria in 1896. He did much to improve education and agriculture. He refused two chief justiceships. (Two other Negroes, born in the West Indies, served as chief justices, namely, Alexander Fitz-James of Trinidad, and John Carr. William Ferguson, a native African, was Captain-General and Governor-in-Chief of Sierra Leone; as was also Robert Dougan, a mulatto. Butt-Thompson, F. W., *Sierra Leone*, pp. 247–249. London, 1926.)

LEWANIKA, King of Barotseland, who died in 1916, was one of South Africa's greatest modern rulers. His country, which was nearly as large as France, was one of the wealthiest of that region and was well administered. He was the only ruling monarch present at the coronation of Edward VII, where his six feet four of height, athletic build, and natural dignity made him one of the most striking figures. His generosity further helped him to win the hearts of

the English people. (*Encyclopaedia Britannica*, see "Lewanika."
Hole, H. M., *Passing of the Black Kings.* 1932.)

KING NANA OFORI ATTA (1881–1943), King of Kings of the Gold
Coast, West Africa. Highly educated, he was one of Africa's greatest modern rulers. Very wealthy, he gave liberally to further education in West Africa. In 1928 he was knighted by George V at
Buckingham Palace.

HERBERT S. MACAULEY, C.E., F.R.G.S. (1864–1946), native of
Lagos, West Africa. Graduate of the British Institute of Architecture, civil engineer, architect, surveyor of crown lands, and founder
of the Nigerian National Democratic Party. Indomitable fighter for
the rights of his people. A skilled violinist, he was popular in elite
and royal circles while studying in England. Was member of the
London Architectural Association.

SIR ADEYMO ALAKIJA (1884–1952) of Nigeria. Distinguished
lawyer. Member of several important government committees.
Member Legislative Council, 1933–41. Appointed member of the
Legislative Council by the king in 1942. Awarded the Coronation
Medal and in 1945 was knighted by George VI at Buckingham
Palace for his services. Important in the business life of West
Africa, he was chairman of the board of directors of the Nigeria
Printing and Publishing Company; director of West African News-
papers, Ltd.; and held high positions in other businesses (*Biograph-
ical Encyclopedia of the World*, p. 1178. 1946.)

SIR ABDEL RAHMAN EL-MAHDI (1885–1959), religious leader of
the UMMA (or Independence Party of the Anglo-Egyptian Sudan).
One of the most influential men in modern Islam. Son of the great
Mahdi of Allah, he was a great force in the educational agricul-
tural, and social advancement of his people. He insisted on com-
plete severance of his people from both Egypt and England.
(*The New York Times*, November 14 and 20, 1946. See also
"Mohammed Ahmed—the Mahdi" in Vol. I.)

NNAMDI AZIKIWE (1904–   ), Africa's leading newspaper editor and journalist. Founder of four daily newspapers and other
periodicals, among them the militant *West African Pilot* of Lagos.

A fearless and outspoken opponent of imperialism and brilliant advocate for the rights of African peoples. Educated in American universities and was head of the Department of Sociology of Lincoln University. Was one of seven African editors invited to London by the British government in 1944. (Orizu, A. A. N., *Without Bitterness*, pp. 297–344. 1944; "Who's Important in Literature" in *Biographical Encyclopedia of the World*, p. 937. 1946.)

ANCIENT ROME

LUSIUS QUIETUS, died A.D. 117. One of Rome's greatest generals, and named by Emperor Trajan as his successor to the imperial purple. He probably came from the Sudan and brought with him Negro soldiers who helped Trajan conquer the Dacians. When the Jews revolted, Trajan sent him to suppress them, which he did with great severity. Milman says, "The insurrection was soon suppressed by Lusius Quietus, a man of Moorish race and considered the ablest soldier in the Roman army." (*History of the Jews*, Vol. II, p. 131. 1913.) For this Trajan named him Governor of Judea with unlimited powers. B. W. Henderson says of him, "He stands a grim figure with non-Roman facial features upon Trajan's Arch at Beneventum where suppliant Mesopotamia kneels holding out her hands in entreaty before the Emperor." (*Five Roman Emperors*, pp. 321–323. 1865; see also Dio Cassio, *Roman History*, trans. by Cary, Vol. VIII, pp. 419, 423; also Merivale, C. *History of the Romans*, Vol. VII, pp. 306, 310 *et seq.* 1865; Graetz, *History of the Jews*, Vol. II, pp. 397–401. 1898; *Jewish Encyclopedia*, "Lusius Quietus." For pictures of the Negro soldiers, their woolly hair tressed in regular Ethiopian style, who served under Quietus, see Froehner, W., *La Colonne de Trajane*, Vol. II, plate 88. Paris, 1872.)

MACRINUS (A.D. 164–218), Emperor of Rome. Dio Cassio (ca. A.D. 155–229) says of him, "Macrinus was a Moor by birth, from Caesarea, and the son of most obscure parents so that he was very appropriately likened to the ass that was led up to the palace by the spirit; in particular, one of his ears had been bored in accordance with the custom followed by the Moors. But his integrity threw even this drawback into the shade. As for his attitude towards law and precedent, his knowledge of them was not so accurate as his observance of them was faithful. He . . . was distinguished for his practical experience and comanded so many legions." He led the revolt against the tyrant Caracalla and had him assassinated, a fate that he himself later experienced, though he appears to have ruled with justice and mildness. (*Roman History*, trans. by Cary, Vol. IX, p. 361.) Caesarea is not in Morocco, but in Palestine. All Negroes, from no matter where, were then called Moors, or Ethiops. The fact that his ear was bored showed that he was a slave from the Sudan. (See "Kafur," in Vol. I of this work.)

EASTERN ROMAN EMPIRE

NICEPHORUS PHOCAS (ca. A.D. 912–969), greatest of the Byzantine rulers. Captured Crete from the Saracens and inflicted crushing defeats on them in Cilicia and Syria. Defeated the Bulgarians and Otto I of Germany and drove out the Negroes who had invaded southern Greece under their leader, Leo the African, and had occupied it. Leon Diacre and Liudprand, Bishop of Cremona, who went on a mission to Nicephorus, describes him as being very dark in color. Liudprand says that he was "black of skin as a Negro" and so extraordinarily ugly that "he would make one afraid to meet him at night." (Diehl, C., *Figures Byzantines*, Vol. I, p. 227. Paris, 1906; Schlumberger, L., Un Empéreus *Byzantin*. 1890; Leonis Diaconis, *De velitatione Bellica domini Nicephori Augusti*, in J. P. MIGNE, Vol. CXVII, pp. 926–1007. 1864; Joannis Zonare, *ibid*., CXXXV, pp. 177–230; Liuprand, *Works*, tans. by F. W. Wright, p. 236. 1930.)

SPAIN

LEO AFRICANUS (Athasan Ibn Mohammed), geographer and protégé of Pope Leo X, after whom he was renamed Leo, traveled extensively in Africa. His book, *Description of Africa*, was translated into many languages, and it was the leading reference on that continent for three centuries.

JUAN LATINO, professor of rhetoric, Greek, and Latin at the University of Granada in the sixteenth century. He was the author of the *Austriad*, a heroic poem in Latin dedicated to Don Juan of Austria, and was mentioned by Cervantes in *Don Quixote*. (Ocete, A. M., *El Negro, Juan Latino*. Granada, 1926; Spratlin, V. B., *Juan Latino*. 1938.)

SEBASTIAN GOMEZ, known as El Molato, disciple of Murillo. Some of his works are said to excel those of his master. His paintings are in the Cathedral of Seville, the Provincial Museum of Seville, the Church of the Venerables in Seville, El Prado at Madrid, and other galleries. (Another great Spanish Negro was Juan Pareja, born in 1606, whose paintings are in the Hispanic Museum of New York City. He was a former slave of Velásquez and studied under him. (O'Neil, A., *Dictionary of Spanish Painters*, Pt. I, p. 137, Pt. II, p. 40; *Emancipator and Free American*, trans. from the German [October 5, 1843]; Foa, E. R., "The Mulatto of Murillo", *Gems of Biography*, New York, 1877; Schomburg, A., "Pareja," *Opportunity Magazine* [March, 1928], Hispanic Society of America, New York, 1929.)

PORTUGAL

LUIS MOLINA (1535–1600), great religious reformer, held the chair of moral theology at the University of Evora, Portugal. His doctrines caused a great controversy in southern Europe. But he won after a hard struggle, and the Pope gave him the right to publish his books. Molina was one of the most illustrious of the Jesuit priests. The *Catholic Encyclopedia* devotes considerable space to him and his doctrines and says, "As a man, priest, and religious leader, Molina commanded the respect and esteem of his bitterest adversaries. During his whole life his virtues were a source of edification to all who knew him. To prompt obedience he joined true and sincere humility. His love for evangelical poverty was most remarkable; and in spite of bodily infirmity brought on by overwork, he never sought any mitigation in the matter of either clothing or food. He was a man of great mortification to the end of his life." (*Encyclopaedia Britannica*, 11th ed., "Molina"; for portrait, see *Sex and Race*, Vol. I, p. 160, 2nd ed.)

ITALY

ANNITA GARIBALDI (1821?–1894), native Brazilian woman and heroine of Italian independence, she was the wife of Garibaldi. An expert rider, she was a captain in her husband's legion and rode to battle beside him. She was described as a "woman of about twenty-eight, of a very dark complexion." She was ancestress of the present Garibaldi family. In 1932 a magnificent monument was dedicated to her in Rome by the King of Italy and Mussolini. (For a portrait of her, see *Sex and Race*, Vol. II, p. 58. For picture of her monument, see Boiteux, H., *Annita Garibaldi*, frontispiece. 1945; Leito de Castro, J. A., *Annita Garibaldi*. 1911; *Eloquenza*, Anno 22, Vol. I, pp. 185–189. Rome, 1932. Larg, D., *Garibaldi*, p. 166. 1934.)

RUSSIA

MIKHAIL M. EGYPTEOS (1861–1932), son of a Negro artist in the service of the Imperial Court and a Russian noblewoman. Major-General in the Russian Army under Czar Nicholas II. Graduated from the Emperor Nicholas I Academy with high honors in 1881. Graduated from Naval Construction Department of the Kronstadt Engineering College; also graduate of Naval College in naval architecture. In 1904 was Senior Naval Constructor of St. Petersburg Dockyard with rank of colonel. Promoted to major-general in 1911. Awarded several medals for his services, among them those of St. Anne, St. Vladimir, and Emperor Alexander III. On his retirement he became head of a private firm, the Nevskii Shipbuilding Yard. (*List of the Personnel of the Ships of the Navy, etc.*, published by the Statistical Section of the Principal Naval Staff, January 1, 1915, see Naval Constructors Corps: "Major-Generals." This information was kindly supplied by D. Fedetoff White, former officer of the Russian Navy and author of *Survival Through War and Revolution* and other books, who knew General Egypteos. The latter's daughter married a classmate of Mr. White's, Chief Engineer Michael Prestin, who now lives with her in Oslo, Norway. The couple have two children.)

ENGLAND: ROBERT BROWNING'S NEGRO ANCESTRY

ROBERT BROWNING (1812–1889) was one of England's greatest poets and dramatists. Frederick J. Furnivall, one of England's greatest scholars and head of the Browning Society of London, said that he was certain Robert Browning had a Negro strain. He says, "In colour, the poet's father was so dark that when, as a youth, he went to his creole mother's sugar plantation in St. Kit's, the beadle of the church ordered him to come away from the white folk among whom he was sitting and take his place among the colored people."

Browning's grandmother, Margaret Tittle, was a native of Jamaica, West Indies. Furnivall says further:

An old friend who has often sat in the house of the poet's father and knew the family well, says that they were all very dark and he believes in their dark blood. . . . That the white and the black blood occasionally mixed [in Jamaica] goes without saying, and the word "Creole" is often incorrectly used for Mulatto, Quadroon, or a person having a strain of Negro blood, a dash of the tar-brush. That Miss Tittle had this dash was understood by some of Robert III's second family [Browning's grandfather], and the eyes and color of Robert IV [Browning's father] confirmed it. . . . I hope, too, that the poet's American admirers in their dealings with the Negroes will not forget the possibility, to me, the certainty that Browning's grandmother had dark blood in her. (*Browning Society Papers*, February 28, 1890, pp. 31–36.)

Browning's biographers have been positively scandalized at this statement of Furnivall's. Mrs. Sutherland Orr (*Life and Letters of Robert Browning*, p. 7, 1908), for instance, denies it flatly. It is possible, however, that she did not have an open mind on the subject since she prefaces her objection with, "But many persons among us are very averse to the idea of such a cross; I believe its assertion, in the present case, to be entirely mistaken." On the other hand, Furnivall, who knew Browning well, must have seen signs of Negro ancestry to have been so positive. Thomas Carlyle also mentioned Browning's dark skin and said he believed it was due to his West Indian ancestry.

Professor Simmons of Harvard University seems to believe that Browning was of Negro ancestry. He says, "Unlike Browning or Dumas, Pushkin took his Negro ancestry very seriously." (*Pushkin*, p. 12.)

Finally, the whites of Jamaica were very much mixed. (See *Sex and Race*, Vol. II, pp. 122–133.) And since it was possible for Pushkin, who was so very much more removed from contact with masses of Negroes than Browning's ancestors, why should it seem so impossible in Browning's case? Furnivall thinks that one of the reasons why the Barretts, who were also from Jamaica, objected so strongly to the marriage of their daughter with him was because they knew he was of Negro ancestry. Browning's portrait does show in my opinion a Negro strain, especially the nose and the mouth. This Negroid aspect can easily be seen by covering the upper part of his face.

AUSTRIA

ANGELO SOLLIMAN (ca. 1721–1776), friend, favorite, and tutor of European royalty. Personal attendant of Prince Lobkowitz and later of Prince de Lichtenstein. Still later, companion of Joseph II of Austria, with the approval of his mother, Empress Maria Theresa, who felt that Angelo's influence on her son would help to make him a better king. Francis I, Emperor of the Holy Roman Empire, liked him so well that he invited him to enter his personal service. Abbé Gregoire (1750–1831), who wrote a sketch of him in his *Littérature des Nègres* (1808), spoke in highest terms of him. (Bauer, W. A., *Angelo Solliman, der Hochfürstliche Mohr*. Wien, 1922. For his portrait, see, *Sex and Race*, 2nd ed., Vol. I, p. 173.)

GERMANY

LUDWIG VAN BEETHOVEN (1770–1827). For Beethoven's Negro strain, see *Sex and Race*, Vol. III, pp. 306–309; Vol. I, 2nd ed., p. 8.

FRANCE

JOSEPH DAMINGUE ("Hercules"), born in Havana, Cuba, in 1761, was one of the most spectacular figures of the Napoleonic Wars. It is probably only his lack of education that prevented his being one of the great Napoleonic marshals. He was of gigantic build and was christened "Hercules" by Napoleon. Considered the prize of his regiment, he was reckless and a horseback fighter of great skill. He practically won the Battle of Arcole for Napoleon, who rewarded him with a captaincy and a gift of 5000 French pounds. This sum was five times as much as Napoleon gave to any of his generals in Italy save one, to whom he gave 2000 pounds. On one occasion Hercules, with a squad of only twelve men, charged two battalions of Croatians and prevented them from forming up. At the battles of the Pyramid and St. Jean d'Acre, he was one of the heroes of the day. When Napoleon upbraided him for being too reckless in one engagement, he replied that he had found the enemy too easy to beat. When Napoleon had one hundred swords made for the hundred bravest men in his armies, Hercules was one of the recipients. On his sword was engraved "For having beaten, with twenty-five guides, an Austrian column at the battle of Arcole." He was also one of the first to receive the Legion of Honor and the Golden Eagle. He was promoted to major, serving in the same regiment with Prince Eugène, Napoleon's stepson. But as he could neither read nor write, Napoleon shifted him to a regiment of Negro pioneers. This angered him; he felt that he ought to continue commanding white men, and leaving Napoleon, he retired to Italy. After Napoleon's downfall, he sided with Louis XVIII, was made aide-de-camp to General Fontanges, sent on a mission to Haiti, and retired with the rank of major-general. (Masson, F., *Cavaliers de Napoléon*, pp. 209–211. Paris, 1895.)

SEVERIANO DE HEREDIA, Cuban Negro, naturalized Frenchman, was born in 1826. He distinguished himself as a journalist and was elected to the Chamber of Deputies. In 1887 he entered the French cabinet as minister of public works. Inaugurated an era of better roads in France. His daughter became one of France's leading operatic singers. (*La Grande Encyclopédie*, Vol. XIX, p. 1165.)

FRANÇOIS FOURNIER DE PESCAY (1771–1833), one of France's greatest physicians of his time. Professor of pathology; surgeon-major of several French regiments; chief surgeon of the Paris police; and later private physician to Ferdinand VII, King of Spain. In 1814 he was appointed by Louis XVIII to be director of health and hygiene for the French Army. Wrote extensively on vaccination, tetanus, scrofula, and other maladies; compiled a medical dictionary, and was a biographer of note. (Michaud, *Biographie Universelle*, Vol. XIV, pp. 556–557.)

THEODORE CHASSERIAU, one of the world's most gifted painters, was born in Haiti in 1819 and was taken to France at an early age. An infant prodigy in music and drawing he was placed at the age of ten under Ingres, who when he saw Chasseriau at that tender age sketching from a live model exclaimed, "That child will be the Napoleon of painting." While still in his teens he became one of the leading painters of his times. At first he devoted himself to biblical subjects but later changed to North African and Shakespearean ones. Among his principal paintings are "Ali Ben Hamet, Caliph of Constantine," "The Tepidarium," "The Eunuch of the Queen of Ethiopia," and a suite of *Othello*. He died in 1856, at the age of thirty-seven. "One must compare him with a Raphael, a Mozart, and a de Musset," says Vaudoyer. (*La Grande Encyclopédie L'Art et les Artistes*, No. 40–44 (October, 1923–February, 1924), pp. 129–135; Bouvenne, A.; *L'Artiste*, Vol. II, pp. 161–178, 1887. For Chasseriau's portrait, see *Sex and Race*, Vol. II, p. 148.)

VICTOR SÉJOUR (1821–1874), born in New Orleans of Haitian parentage, was one of France's most prolific and popular playwrights. He had great influence at the French court, having served as secretary to Prince Napoleon, later Napoleon III. (Larousse, *Grand Dictionnaire Universel*, Vol. XIV, see "Séjour;" Tinker, E.

L., *Les Ecrits de Langue Française en Louisiane au 19 Siècle*, pp. 427–430. Paris, 1932; Davidson, J. W., "Living Writers of the South," in *Library of Southern Literature*, Vol. XV, p. 392; *Harper's New Monthly Magazine*, May, 1874, p. 247.)

LOUIS A. BRIÈRE DE L'ISLE, French general of engineers born in Martinique, June 4, 1827, and died June 17, 1896. He was Governor of Senegal, a post which he filled with ability and distinction. He commanded an expedition of 18,000 men in Indo-china, where he won several victories under great hardships, climatic and otherwise. He was inspector-general of Marines; Grand Officer of the Legion of Honor; and holder of the Médaille Militaire. (Petit, M., *Les Colonies Françaises*, Vol. II, p. 410; *La Grande Encyclopédie*, Vol. VIII, p. 17. See portrait in *Sex and Race*, Vol. II, p. 119.)

GRATIEN CANDACE, who was under-secretary of state in the Paul Boncour cabinet, is a native of Guadeloupe. A former professor of science, he left that post for the Assembly, of which he became a member in 1912. During his career he was secretary to Premier Viviani; rapporteur-general on war prisoners; editor of Premier Clemenceau's famous newspaper *Action*; vice-president of the Merchant Marine Committee; rapporteur on the State Railways. He served on important parliamentary committees dealing with colonial, maritime, and financial affairs. He was head of the budget for the French Navy and one of the most effective and polished speakers in the Chamber of Deputies. (See portrait, *Sex and Race*, Vol. II, p. 119.)

RENÉ MARAN, one of France's greatest living writers. Won France's foremost literary award, the De Goncourt Prize, in 1922, with his novel *Batoula*. Also a poet of distinction.

HAITI

GEORGES BIASSOU was the chief leader of black revolt in Haiti prior to Toussaint L'Ouverture. Coming directly from the slave hit, like other leaders of the period, Biassou displayed great military ability. Deserting to Spain, he served in the Spanish part of the island, and later attained the rank of field marshal.

J. B. BELLEY, an ex-slave, rose to be an adjutant-general in Napoleon's army, and was a delegate to the French Convention from Haiti. Belley's fiery speech before that assembly swept away the opposition of the slave interests and brought about a vote that ended slavery in Haiti. General Belley distinguished himself in an engagement at Savannah, Georgia. (Ardouin, *Etudes sur l'Histoire de Haiti*, Vol. II, pp. 168, 263; also Vol. V, p. 10.)

CHRISTOPHE (Henry I) was a forceful figure of the Haitian Revolution and builder of the mighty fortress of La Ferrière. He is the subject of J. W. Vandercook's *Black Majesty*. (See also "Toussaint L'Ouverture" and "Alexandre Pétion" in this volume.)

GENERAL JEAN P. BOYER (1775–1850), President of Haiti, was its ablest head of state since independence. Under him the whole island was united under a single government. Boyer overcame all warring factions struggling for power. After the deaths of Christophe and Pétion, Boyer brought about recognition of the republic by France, and carried out the reforms begun by his predecessor, Pétion. The twenty-five years of Boyer's administration are called "The Golden Age of Haiti." (See his portrait in *Sex and Race*, Vol. II, p. 101.)

DANTES BELLEGARDE (1877–1966), Haitian diplomat and author who has served as cabinet minister in his own land and as Minister to the United States, France, and the Vatican, as well as delegate to the League of Nations and a member of the Permanent Court of Arbitration of the Hague (1920–23). While at Geneva he was a member of a commission to investigate slavery and forced labor and was generally said to be the most brilliant orator at the League. Bellegarde contributed extensively to Haitian and French newspapers, and authored several books, one of which, *Morceaux Choisis d'Auteurs Haitians*, done in collaboration, was crowned by the French Academy. France has bestowed on him the Office of Public Instruction and the Legion of Honor of which he is a commander.

LORIMER DENIS (1905–   ), noted lawyer, educator, and ethnologist of Haiti. Chief of the Afro-Haitian Section, Bureau of Ethnology. Was associate member of the Eighth American Scientific Congress. Author of works on ethnology and numerous contributions to scientific journals of Haiti, France, and Canada. ("Who's Important in Science," in *Biographical Encyclopedia of the World*, p. 937. 1946.)

LOUIS VERGNIAUD PIERRE-NOEL (1910–1982), one of the greatest scientific artists. While in the United States, he was scientific draughtsman for Columbia University Department of Zoology; scientific artist at Harlem Hospital, and also for the American Museum of Natural History, Department of Ethnology (1935–38). He also did scientific drawings for Harvard University Medical School; Cranbrook Institute of Science; and Michigan Technical School. At one time artist and designer in the National Agricultural Production of Haiti and designer of postage stamps for the republic. His drawings, especially of insects, are of a rare, exquisite beauty. ("Who's Important in Art" in *Biographical Encyclopedia of the World*, p. 106. 1946.)

CANDELARIO CALOR MOTA (1898–1976), graduate of the Massachusetts Institute of Technology; studied also in Europe. Head of the Department of Civil Engineering, University of Puerto Rico. During the war was structural engineer attached to the United States Engineer Office of the War Department of Puerto Rico. Member, Boston Society of Bridge and Structural Engineers, American Association for the Advancement of Science, and other organizations. Author of numerous articles on technical subjects in engineering journals. ("Who's Important in Engineering" in *Biographical Encyclopedia of the World*, p. 1101. 1946.)

BRAZIL

MANUEL DEL SOCORRO RODRIQUEZ (1758–1818), a Cuban mulatto who started life as a carpenter and was self-educated, became one of Latin America's most brilliant literary and scientific figures and was in reality the founder of Latin American journalism. He was also a painter and a sculptor of ability. After an examination by experts he was appointed head librarian at Sante Fe de Bogota, Colombia. Founded first Latin American newspaper, *El Semanario* and *El Papel Periodico* in 1791. Gave lessons in cosmography and astronomy and his classes became the most notable center of learning in science and literature in Colombia. (*Enciclopedia Universal Ilustrada*, Vol. LI, p. 1268.)

PLACIDO (GABRIEL DE LA CONCEPCION (1809–1844), a Cuban mulatto. The most spontaneous poet in the entire literature of Spanish America. Opposed slavery so vigorously through his poems that he was sentenced to death and shot by the Spanish government. (*Enciclopedia Universal Ilustrada*, Vol. LXVI, p. 499, lists his poems. For his portrait, see *Sex and Race*, Vol. III, p. 221.)

JAO DO PATROCINIO (1854–1904), "The Abolition Tiger," led the fight against slavery in Brazil and brought about its abolition in 1888. Fiery orator, brilliant editor of the *Gazeta da Tarde*. (*Enciclopedia Universal Ilustrada*, Vol. XLII, p. 875. See his portrait in *Sex and Race*, Vol. II, p. 44.)

ANDRE REBOUCAS (1838–1898), one of the most famous engineers of his time. Great foe of slavery. (Reboucas, A. P., *Diario e notas autobiografias*. 1938; Verissimo, I. J., *Andre Reboucas*. 1939; Pierson, D., *Negroes in Brazil*, p. 168. 1942. For his portrait, see *Sex and Race*, Vol. III, p. 227.)

JOSEPH WHITE (1838–1918), Cuban, one of the world's greatest violinists. Entering the Conservatory of Paris at seventeen, he won first prize the same year against thirty-nine contestants and was named interim director. *Gazette Musical* (August 5, 1857) said of him, "In one year a conservatory candidate has climbed until he has won the highest praise of the greatest violinists in Europe." Gounod and Rossini lavished praise on him; the King of Spain, for whom he played in Madrid, gave him the Cross of Charles III; Emperor Napoleon III bestowed the Legion of Honor on him; Dom Pedro II of Brazil appointed him court violinist, gave him Paganini's famous violin (The Betts Strad, now valued at $100,-000), and later named him director of the Conservatory of Brazil.

White was an almost unmixed Negro. (Calegno, *Diccionario Biografico Cubano*. 1878. For his portrait, see *Sex and Race*, Vol. II, p. 44.)

H. E. NILO PECHANA (1857–1926), Cuban, one of Brazil's most eminent statesmen. In 1904 was President of the state of Rio de Janeiro; in 1906 elected Vice President of Brazil; and in 1910 became President. Played important role in bringing Brazil into the First World War. (Johnston, H. H., *Negro in the New World*, p. 106. 1910. See his portraits in *Sex and Race*, Vol. II, p. 47.)

MOREIRA, JULIANO, born in Bahia in 1872, was Brazil's leading neurologist and psychiatrist. He was superintendent of the Insane Asylum in Rio de Janeiro. Most warmly praised by visiting American physicians for his work. (See account in *Sex and Race*, Vol. II, pp. 43–44.) His works on psychiatry are among the best on that subject. (*Enciclopedia Universal Ilustrada*, Vol. XXXVI, p. 976; Pierson, D., *Negroes in Brazil*, pp. 169, 170. 1942.)

NICARAGUA

RUBEN DARIO (1867–1916), born at Metapa, Nicaragua, one of the greatest poets, and most important literary figures Latin America has produced and one of the great writers of the twentieth century. Noted for his universal grasp of life, and his varied and spontaneous style. Was editor of leading newspapers in Chile, Costa Rica, Salvador, and Guatemala and was also minister plenipotentiary of Nicargua to Spain. (*Enciclopedia Universal Ilustrada* devotes eight columns to him [Appendix 3, 1931]. For his portrait see *Sex and Race*, Vol. II, p. 148; for sources of his Negro ancestry, p. 70. Also Luis Alberto Sanchez calls him a "genial mulatto" in *Un Sudamericano en Norteamerica*, p. 44. Santiago de Chile, 1942.)

THE UNITED STATES

THOMAS BETHUNE, "Blind Tom" (1848–1908), perhaps the greatest untaught musician in the history of music. Born in slavery in Georgia, he became the leading musical wonder of his time. Almost blind, unable to read or write, and with no training whatever, he had a mastery of music and the piano that amazed the leading critics. Could repeat correctly any selection, however original, after hearing it once. Could play by heart over 5000 selections from Beethoven, Bach, Mozart, Rubinstein, and other masters. Earned a fortune for his master, Colonel Bethune, who took in $100,000 in one London season alone. Sixteen leading musicians once signed a statement about him which said in part, "Whether in his improvisations or performances of compositions by Gottschalk, Verdi and others; in fact, under every form of musical examination—and the experiments were too numerous to mention—he showed a capacity ranking him among the most wonderful in musical history." (*The Marvellous Musical Prodigy, Blind Tom.* Tower, Gildersleeve & Co., 1867; *Etude*, Vol. XXVI, No. 8, p. 532. 1908; *Pageant*, pp. 35–39. 1945.)

HENRY M. TURNER (1833–1915), Bishop of the African Methodist Episcopal Church. One of the most eloquent and determined of all fighters for the rights of the Negro. Born very poor, he educated himself with great difficulty and rose to be first Negro chaplain in the United States Army. Member of the Georgia legislature, 1868–72. Had served with distinction in the Civil War. Compiled a hymnbook and wrote a catechism and other works.

MARY CHURCH TERRELL (1863–1954), internationally known for her work on behalf of women, to which she has devoted herself since 1881. Was member of the Board of Education of Washington, D.C., for eleven years. Has written extensively for leading publications and is author of *A Colored Woman in a White World.*

R. NATHANIEL DETT (1882–1943), one of the most original of American composers. Famous especially for his "Listen to the Lambs." In 1920 he won two prizes at Harvard University, one for an essay on Negro music, and the other for his motet, "Don't Be Weary, Traveller." In 1930 conducted the Hampton Glee Club in a tour of seven European countries, receiving highest praise from press and public.

JOE GANS, "The Old Master" (1874–1909), generally said to be the greatest lightweight in ring history. A former oyster shucker of Baltimore, he won the championship from Frank Erne in one round in 1902. He was known for his deft, cat-like style and deadly precise punches. A life-size statue of him in bronze stands in the lobby of Madison Square Garden. Jim Tully wrote of him, "This superb lightweight had brains, poise and the soul of a dreamer." (Fleischer, N., *Black Dynamite*, Vol. IV. 1938–39.)

MARY M. TALBERT (1866–1923), internationally famous for her work among women. Organized Negro women to purchase the home of Frederick Douglass and make it a national shrine. Delegate to the International Council of Women held in Norway. In Holland she was the house guest of Queen Wilhelmina. Spingarn Gold Medallist.

LEWIS HOWARD LATIMER (1846–1928), one of the great pioneers in the development of electricity. Invented a carbon filament for the Maxim electric bulb and superintended the installation of electric lighting for the streets for New York, Philadelphia, London, and several other cities in 1881. Became associated with Thomas Edison in 1878 and also with Alexander Graham Bell, for whom he drew plans for the first telephone and assisted in preparing the patents. Later was chief draughtsman for General Electric and Westinghouse. Author of *Incandescent Lighting*. One of the twenty-eight Edison Pioneers (those who began with Edison), organized in 1918. (Obituary notice, *The New York Times*, on or about December 12, 1928; *Edison Pioneers: Addresses*, May 16, 1925.)

THOMAS WYATT TURNER (1877–1978), former professor of applied biology, Howard University; head of the department of biology, Hampton Institute. Expert on plant physiology and pathology; physiological effects of mineral nutriments on root growth in seed plants; physiological effects of nitrogen and of phosphorus on plants. (*American Men of Science*, p. 1816. 1944.)

THEODORE KENNETH LAWLESS, M.D. (1892–1971). Graduate of Harvard University with honors. Studied in hospitals of France, Germany, Austria, and Switzerland. One of America's leading dermatologists. Expert in bacteriology and syphilology. Headed medical laboratory of Northwestern University Medical School, Evanston, Illinois. Associate examiner of the National Board of

Examiners. Fellow of the American Medical Association and other scientific societies. (*American Men of Science*, p. 1036. 1944.)

WILLIAM A. HINTON, M.D. (1883–1959), syphilologist, bacteriologist. Expert on serology of syphilis and gonococcus infection in relation to public health. His test, which is named after him, is used by the Public Health Service of the United States as the best for determining the presence of syphilis, being extensively used in World War II by the army. Instructor of preventative medical hygiene, immunology, and bacteriology, Harvard Medical School. Pathologist and director of research, Boston Dispensary. Head of the Wasserman Laboratory, State Health Department of Massachusetts. (*American Men of Science*, p. 816. 1944.)

LLOYD A. HALL, PH.D. (1892–1971), chemist, inventor, and holder of more than fifty United States patents. Served as junior and senior chemist of Department of Health laboratories for city of Chicago; and as chief chemist for John Morrell and Company of Ottuma, Illinois. Assistant chief inspector of high explosives and research for United States government in World War I, and worked on secret war problems in World War II. Expert on meat product proteins; colloids and emulsions; fats, oils, yeast food; bakery materials; protein hydrosalates; flavoring and seasoning of foods and beverages; sterilization of foods, colloids, and enzymes; chemotherapeutic products; and food and biological chemistry. Consulting chemist for several large industrial firms. Member of several leading chemical societies and author of many articles on chemistry. (*American Men of Science*, p. 722. 1944; see portrait, *Sex and Race*, Vol. III, p. 722.)

A. PHILIP RANDOLPH (1889–1979), one of America's leading labor leaders and organizers. General organizer and one of the founders of the Brotherhood of Sleeping Car Porters, and its president. Worked long and vigorously for the equal treatment of Negroes, especially in labor. Able speaker and writer. His magazine, *The Messenger*, of which he was co-editor, fought so determinedly for the better treatment of Negroes in World War I that it was suppressed by the Department of Justice.

JAMES W. FORD (1893–1957), one of the ablest speakers in America. Veteran of World War I. Was engaged beginning in 1918 in organizing principally Negro labor. Traveled much in Europe studying labor conditions and addressing labor groups. Delegate to the Fourth World Congress of Labor Unions at Moscow, where he was elected to the Executive Committee. Studied Marxian economics, revolutionary theory and practice, history of the world labor movement, and allied subjects for eighteen months at Moscow. Founded and edited *The Negro Worker,* which he published in Hamburg, Germany, and which was extensively circulated in Europe and Africa. Communist candidate for vice presidency of the United States in 1936 and 1940.

WILLIAM GRANT STILL (1895–1978), one of the leading composers of America. Successfully orchestrated several successful Broadway shows, including the fifth *Earl Carroll's Vanities.* His works have been played by the leading symphony orchestras and at the Metropolitan Opera. In 1939 his theme song for the New York's World Fair was selected as the best in a nationwide competition.

RICHMOND BARTHÉ (1901–1989), sculptor of power and originality. His "Mother and Son" at New York World's Fair received high praise. Won $500 prize at Artists for Victory Exhibition, 1942. Executed Arthur Brisbane Memorial at Central Park, East, New York City. His works exhibited and purchased by some of the nation's leading art galleries, the Whitney Museum of American Art having three. His sculptures are sought by private collectors of Europe, Asia, and Latin America. (See *Who's Who in America.*)

WILLIAM S. TOWNSEND, dynamic labor leader. International President of United Transport Service Employees of America, CIO. Secretary of the CIO Committee to Abolish Racial Discrimination. Able speaker.

WILLIAM L. DAWSON (1899–1970), director of music, Tuskegee Institute. Band conductor, Century of Progress Exhibition at Chicago. Won John Wanamaker's music contests getting First Prize, Class I, in 1930 and First Prize, Class II, in 1931. Wrote several compositions which have been played by leading symphony orchestras, of which his *Scherzo* was premiered by the Philadelphia Symphony Orchestra led by Leopold Stokowski. ("Who's Who in Music" in *Biographical Encyclopedia of the World*, p. 999.)

CHARLES R. DREW, M.D., M.Sc. (1904–1950), world authority on blood plasma, serum, blood preservation, and blood substitutes. He was instrumental in saving an untold number of lives with his blood plasma project in the Second World War. In 1940 he was medical supervisor in charge of the collection of blood plasma for the British Army. Working through the Red Cross, he enlisted the support of hospitals and their staff of research experts, doctors, and nurses, and collected blood for transfusion, which, after being processed, was sent to the front. His work later served as a guide for doing the same in the American Army. In recognition of his services was awarded the Spingarn Medal in 1944. He was professor of surgery at Howard University, Washington, D.C. In 1942 won the E. S. Jones Award for medical research.

RUDOLPH DUNBAR (1907–   ), phenomenally brilliant clarinetist and symphony orchestra conductor. At nine, entered military band in British Guiana. Studied in New York, Paris, and Vienna. Studied conducting under Felix Weingartner and Philippe Gaubert and composition under Paul Vidal, director of composition, National Conservatory, Paris. Has conducted some of Europe's leading orchestras, as the Liverpool Symphony Orchestra, the Monte Carlo Symphony Orchestra, and Berlin Philharmonic, of which he was appointed conductor-in-chief in 1945. The same year he conducted the Concerts Colonne of Paris, Concerts Pasdéloup, Orchestre National de France, and the Concerts du Conservàtoire in a Festival of American Music in Paris for which he received superlative praise from the French press and leading conductors as Claude Delvincourt, director of the National Conservatory of Music, and Paul Parry. His *Treatise on Clarinet Playing* is a standard work, and now in its sixth edition. During the war he served as a war correspondent, writing of what he saw on the different fronts, for which he received high praise from the *Manchester Guardian*. (Marinette, *Festivals de Musique Américaine dirigés par Rudolph Dunbar*. Paris, 1945.)

REFERENCES

Since the number of sketches was limited to 200 (see introduction to Volume I), it was necessary to omit more than 100 persons who had been selected, some of whom, as St. Augustine, were great religious leaders, or like Major Taylor, Jesse Owens, El Ouafi of Marathon fame, and Silvio Cator of Haiti, had achieved world prominence as athletes. Furthermore, as regards living persons, the preference was generally given to those who, although remarkable, are not so much talked of. For instance, the *Biographical Encyclopedia of the World*, 1946, which is supposed to contain the names of the leading individuals of the world in certain fields such as literature, science, art, education, and religion, has the names of some forty or more Negroes of the United States, Latin America, and Africa who are not mentioned in this work. Hundreds of other Negroes, sketches of whom are in the *Britannica, Larousse, La Grande Encyclopédi, Enciclopedia Universal Ilustrada, International Who's Who,* the *British Who's Who, Who's Who in America, American Men of Science, Grande Encyclopedia Portuguesa e Brasileira, Dictionary of American Biography,* and other encyclopedias are left out also. Certain others are mentioned in the three volumes of *Sex and Race* as well as in the footnotes of this work. In short, the 200 persons mentioned in this work are not the 200 *greatest* Negroes, past and present, but among the greatest.